KT-294-207

Trans-Siberian Railway

Simon Richmond

Mark Elliott, Robert Reid, Mara Vorhees

ST PETERSBURG (p79)
Visit tsarist palaces, including the Hermitage, in Russia's most elegant and European city

MOSCOW (p98)
Savour the power, history and modern-day pleasures of Russia's awe-inspiring capital

TOBOLSK (p159)
Branch off to this historic town with a handsome kremlin

SUZDAL (p132)
Step back in time in the most photogenic and onion-dome-church-packed of the Golden Ring towns

TOMSK (p178)
Discover this old university town packed with charming wooden architecture

NIZHNY NOVGOROD (p134)
Cruise along the Volga River from Russia's 'third capital', a relaxed city with an impressive kremlin

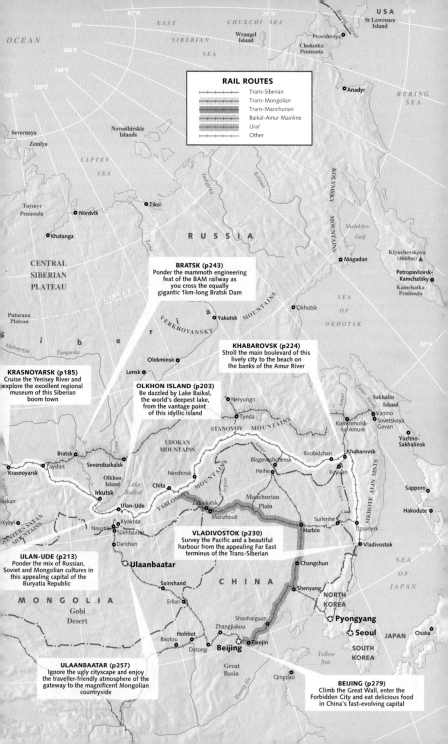

RAIL ROUTES

Trans-Siberian
Trans-Mongolian
Trans-Manchurian
Baikal-Amur Mainline
Ural
Other

BRATSK (p243)
Ponder the mammoth engineering feat of the BAM railway as you cross the equally gigantic 1km-long Bratsk Dam

KHABAROVSK (p224)
Stroll the main boulevard of this lively city to the beach on the banks of the Amur River

KRASNOYARSK (p185)
Cruise the Yenisey River and explore the excellent regional museum of this Siberian boom town

OLKHON ISLAND (p203)
Be dazzled by Lake Baikal, the world's deepest lake, from the vantage point of this idyllic island

VLADIVOSTOK (p230)
Survey the Pacific and a beautiful harbour from the appealing Far East terminus of the Trans-Siberian

ULAN-UDE (p213)
Ponder the mix of Russian, Soviet and Mongolian cultures in this appealing capital of the Buryatia Republic

ULAANBAATAR (p257)
Ignore the ugly cityscape and enjoy the traveller-friendly atmosphere of the gateway to the magnificent Mongolian countryside

BEIJING (p279)
Climb the Great Wall, enter the Forbidden City and eat delicious food in China's fast-evolving capital

Trans-Siberian Railway

There is nothing quite like the Trans-Siberian Railway. Survivor of the Communist Revolution, two world wars, famine, floods, freezing Siberian winters and sizzling summers, the route spanning seven time zones is the glue holding Russia's disparate regions together.

Imagine boarding a train in Moscow – Russia's awe-inspiring capital of Stalinist skyscrapers, the Kremlin, and oil billionaires and their entourages – and travelling seven straight days to the physically stunning port of Vladivostok on the edge of the Pacific, 9289km away. Or saying 'Ni hao' to Mao in Beijing's Tiananmen Sq and 'Privet' to Lenin in Red Sq, having traversed not only China and Russia but also the exhilarating open spaces of Mongolia. Or taking the far more off-the-beaten track route of the Baikal-Amur Mainline (Baikalo-Amurskaya Magistral, or BAM) through some of the most remote and beautiful parts of Siberia, with an essential pause at the sapphire dazzler Lake Baikal. All these places and much more lie on the Trans-Siberian rail routes covered in this guide.

With an average speed of around 60kph these Trans-Siberian services are not for travellers in a hurry. Nor are these working trains particularly glamourous. Nonetheless, a Trans-Siberian trip is never dull, not least because of the chance you'll have to interact with your fellow passengers over several days of travel. You'll discover that Russians are among the kindest people you could meet, ever ready to share their provisions and to engage in conversation. Whether you experience the Trans-Siberian route nonstop, savouring the slowly evolving landscapes, or – as we'd strongly advise – hop off and on the train at the host of fascinating places en route, one thing is for sure: this is the journey of a lifetime.

MARTIN

Cities

SIMON RICHMOND

Gaze at the spectacular mural overlooking the station in Kazan (p142)

Don't miss Tobolsk's St Sofia Cathedral (p160), Siberia's first stone kremlin

SIMON RICHMOND

OTHER HIGHLIGHTS

- Revel in the splendour of Catherine Palace (p96), St Petersburg.
- Feast on delicious Peking duck (p288) in Beijing.

PETER SOLNESS

Marvel at the grand St Basil's Cathedral (p109), Moscow

Be part of the rush-hour havoc in Beijing (p279)

NICHOLAS PAVLOFF

Cultures

MARK NEWMAN

Witness the eerie spectacle of traditional Siberian graves, as seen at Taltsy Museum of Wooden Architecture (p198)

OTHER HIGHLIGHTS

- Explore the white-stone Assumption Cathedral (p131) in the ancient city of Vladimir.

- Immerse yourself in the culture at *datsans* (buddhist temples) in Ulan-Ude (p215).

Spend the night in a traditional *ger* (felt yurt), Mongolia (p297)

SCOTT DARSNEY

View the traditional painted cottages in the town of Baikalskoe (p247)

SIMON RICHMO

Railway History

Take an interest in Russian history at this monument in Vladivostok (p230)

OTHER HIGHLIGHTS

- Learn about the history of the Trans-Siberian railway at museums in St Petersburg (p88) or Novosibirsk (p167).
- Visit intriguing historic train stations (p88) along the route.

Ride a train across the scenic 1km-long Yenisey River Bridge (p184), Krasnoyarsk

Witness a bit of railway history at this monument in Severobaikalsk (p244)

Festivals

OTHER HIGHLIGHTS

- Be amazed by elaborate ice sculptures during the Ice Lantern Festival (p276), Harbin.
- Catch fascinating arts events and performances at St Petersburg's White Nights Arts Festival (p90).
- Celebrate Easter (p305) like the locals by eating *kulichy* (dome-shaped cakes) and *paskha* (curd cakes).
- Join in the festivities of Chinese New Year (p305) in Beijing.

PAUL GREENWAY

Marvel at the opening parade of the Naadam Festival (p262), Ulaanbaatar

Join war veterans celebrating Victory Day (p88) on Palace Sq, St Petersburg

JONATHAN SM

С Днем
Победы!
1941-1945

Contents

Regional Map Contents

Central St Petersburg pp82-3

Central Moscow pp102-3

RUSSIA

Moscow to Yekaterinburg pp128-9

Yekaterinburg to Krasnoyarsk pp148-9

Tayshet to Sovetskaya Gavan via BAM pp240-1

Krasnoyarsk to Lake Baikal p184

Irkutsk to Vladivostok pp208-9

CHINA

Chita to Beijing pp270-1

MONGOLIA

Ulan-Ude to Beijing p254

Central Beijing p282

The Authors

SIMON RICHMOND
Coordinating Author, St Petersburg, Ulan-Ude to Beijing via Mongolia, Chita to Beijing via Manchuria, Beijing

Simon clocked up his first Trans-Siberian trip from Vladivostok in 1997, during which he was attacked by dogs, robbed on the train and got plastered on vodka at Lake Baikal. All this just whetted the award-winning travel writer's appetite and in 2001 he returned to Russia to coauthor the first edition of this book, hopping on and off the train from St Petersburg to the Pacific. The following year he was back in Russia and discovering the BAM as part of his research for *Russia & Belarus,* the new edition of which he has also coauthored. For this book, Simon scored the hat trick by travelling sections of the Trans-Siberian, Trans-Mongolian and Trans-Manchurian routes.

My Favourite Trip

I'll never forget the research trip I made for the first edition of this book, most likely because I got arrested, almost losing all my bags (including computer and notes) and money in the process. The day was saved by the wonderful Russian people who pulled together to reunite me with all my belongings. Either side of this pivotal event, I took time to further explore previously visited Russian cities such as St Petersburg (p79), Moscow (p98) and Irkutsk (p189), as well as discover gems such as Krasnoyarsk (p185), Tobolsk (p159) and Tomsk (p178). After 10 weeks on and

off the rails you'd have thought I'd have had enough, but what I remember most was the lump in my throat as I stepped on that final train from Khabarovsk (p224) to Vladivostok (p230).

MARK ELLIOTT
Yekaterinburg to Krasnoyarsk, Krasnoyarsk to Lake Baikal, Irkutsk to Vladivostok

Mark has been riding ex-Soviet trains for over a decade, having first crossed Central Asia in 1994 as a cheap way home from Japan. He's returned to the former USSR a dozen times since, fascinated to see the reality behind the misinformed Cold War propaganda that still influences many Western attitudes towards today's Russia. Beneath a gruff, deadpan exterior, it's the great humanity and warmth of the Russian soul that keeps drawing Mark back to Siberia. Mark has written a dozen guidebooks for diverse destinations from Azerbaijan to Greenland. He now lives in Belgium with the lovely Danielle, whom he met while jamming blues harmonica in a Turkmenistan club.

LONELY PLANET AUTHORS

Why is our travel information the best in the world? It's simple: our authors are independent, dedicated travellers. They don't research using just the Internet or phone, and they don't take freebies in exchange for positive coverage. They travel widely, to all the popular spots and off the beaten track. They personally visit thousands of hotels, restaurants, cafés, bars, galleries, palaces, museums and more – and they take pride in getting all the details right, and telling it how it is. For more, see the authors section on www.lonelyplanet.com.

ROBERT REID

Irkutsk to Vladivostok, Tayshet to Sovetskaya Gavan via BAM

Prompted by rebellion and the library's air-con on hot Oklahoma days, Robert picked up old copies of *Soviet Life* as a kid, then Dostoevsky paperbacks as a college kid. He studied Russian and spent his 'first summer of Russia' (1992) in St Petersburg and Moscow, where he also volunteered at Echo Moscow radio. He's travelled around Eastern Europe loads, updating the Bulgaria chapter for Lonely Planet's *Eastern Europe* guide. While updating sections of the Trans-Siberian route in Russia's Far East he counted 151 moustaches on Russian sidewalks, railways and boats. He lives barefaced in Brooklyn, New York.

MARA VORHEES

Moscow, Moscow to Yekaterinburg, Yekaterinburg to Krasnoyarsk

Mara has been travelling to Russia since the days of Cold Wars and communism. After the Soviet collapse, she lived for two years in Yekaterinburg, where she worked on a foreign aid project. In her adventures as a travel writer, she has spent two months riding the Trans-Siberian railroad, four weeks cruising the Volga River, two weeks circling the Golden Ring and seven seconds swimming in Lake Baikal. She is the author of Lonely Planet's guide to *Moscow* and coauthor of *Russia & Belarus*.

Getting Started

Given the number of options – which route to take, when to go, where to break the journey (if at all), whether to DIY or use the services of a tour operator – a Trans-Siberian trip requires some forethought. This chapter will help you sort your priorities, plan ahead and whet your appetite for the travelling pleasures to come.

WHEN TO GO

See Climate Charts (p300) for more information.

The main Trans-Siberian Railway tourist season runs from May to the end of September, with mid-July to early September being the busiest time for foreign visitors, as well as Russians coming and going on their annual holidays. Tickets for all trains during this time should be booked well ahead if at all possible, particularly for the Moscow–Beijing routes.

Although July and August are the warmest months in Siberia (with temperatures rising as high as 40ºC), they are often the dampest months in parts of European Russia, with as many as one rainy day in three. In these months the climate in Beijing can also be murder with soaring humidity – the total opposite to Mongolia, where clear skies make the sunlight intense. You may find May and June preferable or September and the first half of October, when autumn brings stunning colours as the leaves turn, particularly in Russia's Far East.

Winter nights are long and freezing, but if you're prepared for it this time of the year can also be fantastic. The theatres open, the furs and vodka come out, and the snow makes everything picturesque. In addition, Russian train tickets are sold at a discount in winter (particularly in November and most of December and January through April). The best winter month to visit is March, after the deep freeze of December to February.

Least liked everywhere are the first snows beginning in late October (but sometimes earlier) and the spring thaw (April), which turn everything to mud and slush.

See p305 for details on festivals and events, and p306 for details on holidays.

DON'T LEAVE HOME WITHOUT...

- Getting your visas – we'll guide you through the paperwork (p315).
- Very warm clothes and a long, windproof coat, if you're visiting during winter.
- Slip-on footwear, like thongs (flip-flops) or Chinese cloth sandals, and loose, comfortable clothes, such as a tracksuit for wearing on the train.
- Thick-soled, waterproof and comfortable walking shoes.
- Strong insect repellent for summer.
- A plug for a bathroom basin.
- Cards, phrasebooks, pocket dictionaries, and photos of family and your home for breaking the ice with your cabin mates.
- A stash of painkillers or other decent hangover cures.
- A sense of humour.

WHAT KIND OF TRIP?
Independent vs Group Tour

Independent travel in Russia, China and Mongolia can be a lot of fun, but don't expect it to be necessarily cheap or easy to organise. Away from the major cities your odds of meeting anyone who speaks English are slim; if you can speak and read some Russian and, on the Trans-Mongolian and Trans-Manchurian routes, Chinese and Mongolian, it will improve your trip no end. With limited language skills, everything you attempt will possibly be more costly and more difficult. However, it's far from impossible and if you really want to meet locals and have a flexible itinerary, this is the way to go.

To smooth the way somewhat, it's a good idea to consider using a specialist travel agency to arrange your visas, and make some of your train and accommodation bookings. Most will be happy to work on any itinerary to create your own individual package tour. It's also possible to arrange guides and transfers through an agency, and the prices can sometimes be better than you'd be able to negotiate yourself with or without language skills. Note, though, that if you use an agency *just* to book train tickets, you will certainly pay more (sometimes far more) than what you'd pay for the same tickets if you buy them yourself once in Russia, China or Mongolia. Outside of the busy June to August travel period and over a few key holidays, such as Easter, buying tickets yourself shouldn't be too much of a problem.

On group tours everything is taken care of and all you need do is pay and turn up. Tours can cater to special interests and range from backpacker basics to full-on tsarist luxury. You'll seldom be alone – which can be a curse as well as a blessing depending on the company. This will also cut down on your chances of interacting with locals: on some trips whole carriages of the train are filled with foreign tourists. Opportunities to head off the beaten track or alter the itinerary are also very limited, if not impossible.

Staying on the Train vs Getting On & Off

Aficionados of going nonstop from Moscow to Vladivostok or Beijing – both are journeys of seven days – often compare it to being on a sea voyage or having a beach holiday indoors. It's a chance to sleep and read, perhaps sharpen up your card-playing and chess skills with fellow passengers, while the landscape unreels in cinematic slow motion outside. Approached in this manner, the trip can be a relaxing, languorous experience, not to mention a chance to form some memorable relationships (see below).

IN PRAISE OF THE NONSTOP JOURNEY *Steve Noble*

After travelling the Trans-Siberian/Mongolian route several times, my favourite journey was nonstop from St Petersburg to Beijing (changing trains in Moscow). Boarding the train, I only spoke a few Russian words, but disembarked in Beijing fluent in vodka-speak Russian and able to communicate. During the eight-night journey, I met babushkas with offerings of tasty food, children who wanted to play, soldiers with copious amounts of vodka, students who taught me Russian and two sweetheart *provodnitsas* (carriage attendants), who helped me organise showers, among other things. Besides two Poles and three Romanians, I was the only foreigner onboard. With goodbye hugs and kisses at many stations en route, I had made many friends. Everyone wanted to know the foreigner. Russian curiosity and hospitality is truly amazing. If I could've stayed aboard that same train when it returned to Moscow that evening, I would've in a heartbeat.

TOP TENS

Best Railway Stations

Many of the historic stations along the Trans-Siberian route are worth visiting in their own right. From St Petersburg, the following stations are in order of appearance from west to east:

- Vitebsk (p88) – Style Moderne delight and starting point of Russia's first public railway to Tsarskoe Selo.
- Yaroslavl (p122) – fitting start or finish to the Trans-Siberian is this 1902 stylised reproduction of a traditional Russian fort.
- Novosibirsk (p165) – Siberia's largest station is a temple to the Trans-Siberian.
- Krasnoyarsk (p185) – big, grand and self-consciously spired, with a great mural of Lenin and comrades.
- Irkutsk (p189) – admire the well-proportioned classicism of this station.
- Severobaikalsk (p244) – Le Corbusier–style station on the BAM.
- Olovyannaya (p271) – a *stolovaya* (canteen) now occupies the pretty, if dishevelled original 1898 wooden station building.
- Tynda (p249) – futuristic Brezhnev meets *The Jetsons* structure, by far the city's most impressive architecture.
- Birobidzhan (p224) – the station's name is written in Hebrew; there's a star of David on the front of it, too, and a Jewish statue.
- Vladivostok (p230) – restored old beauty, with detailed ceiling murals.

Our Favourite Festivals & Events

Many travellers schedule their train journey to coincide with the events that take place throughout the year. There are plenty to choose from – peruse the following date-organised list:

- Ice Lantern Festival (Harbin), 5 January to 15 February (p276)
- Chinese New Year/Spring Festival (Beijing and Harbin), January/February (p305)
- Ice Festival (Khövsgöl Lake, Mongolia), 19 to 20 February (p305)
- Winteriada: International Baikal Nordic Games Festival (Irkutsk), February/March (p305)
- Easter (Russia), March/April (p305)
- Victory Day (Russia), 9 May
- White Nights Arts Festival (St Petersburg), June (p90)
- Roaring Hoofs International Live Music Festival (Ulaanbaatar), June/July (p305)
- Naadam (Ulaanbaatar), 11 and 12 July (p262)
- Mid-Autumn/Moon Festival (China), September/October (p306)

Tips for Blending in on the Train

Contributing author Robert Reid offers his sage, and sometimes satirical, advice on making like a local on the Trans-Siberian.

- Get yourself sporty – everyone dresses up as if they're headed to a parallel bars rally in Nikolaevsk-na-Amure! Think track pants, preferably striped. Adidas is a bonus.
- Men: clean-cut haircuts, please (something betwixt George Clooney and *Chariots of Fire*). If you're in a large group, ensure 10% to 20% of you have a moustache.
- Women: hair dye is happily received (bleaches, strawberries, root-beer cranberries for older gals, streaks of yellow) but NOT mandated.
- By all means wear coloured socks with your sandals!
- Drink beer on platforms at stops; drink vodka in wagons.
- Don't smile at strangers – only smile if something amuses you or you see someone you know.
- Loose cotton T-shirts are good to wear, nothing fancy, preferably labelled in English ('Russia', or my favourite: 'No Limits').
- Carry clear bags advertising your makeshift lunches: too many tomatoes, too many cucumbers and at least one full of *kolbasa* (sausage).
- Smoke – a lot (but not in the cabin; go between carriages for that).
- It'd help if you look Russian and speak the thing.

The aim, however, of this guide is to tempt you off the train and get you exploring the fascinating countries it passes through. At the very least we'd recommend breaking your journey once – the most obvious point being in Irkutsk (p189) to visit Lake Baikal. On the Trans-Mongolian route consider a stop in Ulaanbaatar (p257) en route to Beijing, while on the Trans-Manchurian route a pause in Harbin (p273) is a possibility. See p15, p21 and the highlights appearing at the start of individual destin ation chapters for other ideas of where to leave the train.

Bear in mind that there's no such thing as a hop-on, hop-off Trans-Siberian ticket – every time you disembark you'll have to buy a new onward ticket. This can all be arranged in advance with agents, and in the bigger cities along the route it's pretty simple to do it yourself; see each chapter for hints on where to buy tickets. Also consider the direction in which you might travel. If you want to meet Russians, starting at Vladivostok and heading west is recommended, since far fewer foreign travellers take this route than the popular eastbound services from Moscow or westbound from Beijing.

'The aim of this guide is to tempt you off the train and get you exploring the fascinating countries it passes through'

TRAIN BOOKINGS

For full details of the routes covered here see the route descriptions at the start of each of the destination chapters. For the first four days' travel from Moscow, the main Trans-Siberian, Trans-Manchurian and Trans-Mongolian services all follow the same route through the Urals and into western Siberia, over the Yenisey River and on to Irkutsk in eastern Siberia.

On the fifth day, after rounding the southern tip of Lake Baikal, the Trans-Mongolian train branches off, heading south for the Mongolian border 250km away. The Trans-Manchurian stays with the main line for 12 hours past Lake Baikal, before it also peels off, heading southeast for Zabaikalsk on the Chinese border, some 368km away.

For information on the types of trains and carriages travelling these routes, see p331.

Moscow to Vladivostok

The 1/2 *Rossiya* train is the top Moscow–Vladivostok service. If you're planning to stop off at Irkutsk, also consider using the 9/10 *Baikal,* reputed to be one of the best trains in Russia in terms of carriage standards and service.

Other good services that can be usefully included in a Moscow to Vladivostok itinerary include: the 15/16 *Ural* between Moscow and Yekaterinburg; 25/25 *Sibiryak* between Moscow and Novosibirsk; 7/8 *Sibir* between Novosibirsk and Vladivostok; 55/56 *Yenisey* between Moscow and Krasnoyarsk; and 5/6 *Okean* between Khabarovsk and Vladivostok.

If you're planning to frequently hop on and off trains and want to save some money along the way, it's a good idea to avoid the premium trains and go for the regular services, which will almost always be *platskart* (*platskartny*; open carriage; see p334). Most of these services are perfectly acceptable and take pretty much the same travelling time point to point as the premium trains.

Moscow to Ulaanbaatar & Beijing

The more popular of the two options running directly between Moscow and Beijing is the 3/4 Trans-Mongolian service, a Chinese train that travels via Ulaanbaatar and the only one to offer deluxe carriages (see p333) with showers.

If you're planning to stop off in Irkutsk, there's also the less fancy daily 264/263 service to/from Ulaanbaatar.

The weekly 19/20 Trans-Manchurian service is a Russian train and takes half a day longer to reach Beijing, but in doing so it avoids the need for a Mongolian visa.

COSTS & MONEY
Russia
Avoid the major cities and use the *platskart* carriages of overnight trains as an alternative to hotels and it's possible to live on US$30 per day. However, if you visit the main cities, eat Western-style meals in restaurants and travel on *kupe* (*kupeyny;* compartmentalised carriage) trains, US$80 per day is a more realistic figure. Prices drop away from the metropolises, but not significantly, and in remote areas, such as the Russian Far East, everything can cost considerably more.

Dual pricing is another issue. As a foreigner you'll find yourself paying more than a local pretty much always as far as admission to museums and tourist sites is concerned and sometimes at hotels, too (although not in Moscow or St Petersburg, where hotel prices are the same for everyone). It's not unusual for a foreigner to be charged 10 times the amount Russians are charged to enter museums – not entirely unfair given the vast disparity between average Western and Russian incomes. Remember your extra money is desperately needed to protect the very works of art and artefacts you've come to see. It's often fair game for taxi drivers and sometimes market sellers, who may think they can charge foreigners more – check with locals for prices, but don't expect that knowledge to be much use unless you can bargain in Russian. You'll rarely be short-changed by staff in restaurants, cafés and bars, though.

China
Costs in Beijing vary widely depending on the level of comfort expected. Once in Beijing, thrifty travellers can survive on as little as US$30 per

LONELY PLANET INDEX

Russia
Litre of petrol R15 to R20

Litre of bottled water R12

Bottle of local beer R70

Souvenir *matryoshka* doll R150 to R300

Take-away bliny R30

China
Litre of petrol Y3.5

Litre of bottled water Y4

Bottle of local beer Y3

Souvenir T-shirt Y25

Large lamb kebab Y2

Mongolia
Litre of petrol T780

Litre of bottled water T500

Bottle of local beer T1000

Souvenir T-shirt T15,000

Shashlyk T2500

TRAIN TICKET COSTS

In this book we typically quote *kupeyny* (*kupe*; compartmentalised carriage) fares. Expect SV (1st-class) fares to be double this amount and *platskartny* (*platskart*; open carriage) about 40% less. Children under five travel free if they share a berth with an adult, otherwise children under 10 pay half-fare for their own berth. On the Trans-Mongolian and Trans-Manchurian routes, kids under four travel free if they share a berth, while those under 12 pay around 75% of the full fare for their own berth.

Complicating matters is Russian Railways' policy of varying all fares according to seasons. In peak travelling seasons, for example early July to early August and around key holidays such as Easter and New Year, fares can be between 12% to 16% higher than the regular fare. The inverse happens at slack times of the year, such as early January to March, when there are discounts on fares. On *skory poezd* (fast trains) and *firmennye poezdy* (premium trains) it's also possible to have two grades of *kupe* fare: with or without meals.

Fares quoted in this book were collected at the time of writing and should be taken as a general guide only. The following table shows the cost for a *kupe* ticket:

	Irkutsk	Ulaanbaatar	Beijing	Vladivostok
Moscow to	R5400	R3800	R6413	R8000
Irkutsk to	–	R1600	–	R3840
Ulaanbaatar to	–	–	R6635	–

day by staying in youth hostels, travelling by bicycle or bus, and eating from street stalls and cafés. Less-austere travellers can expect to spend US$60 to US$80 per day for a decent hotel room, moderately priced meals and an occasional taxi ride. The range, of course, goes all the way up the scale to US$300 for a five-star luxury hotel and accompanying fancy meals.

In other major cities, such as Shanghai and Hong Kong, you can expect costs to be similar to Beijing, but in more rural parts of the country your budget will certainly go much further. Food costs remain reasonable throughout China, and the frugal can eat for as little as US$5 a day. Transport costs can be kept to a minimum by travelling by hard-seat on the train, or by bus.

Mongolia

Accommodation and food can cost as little as US$10 per day in Ulaanbaatar, but allow up to US$20 per day for better accommodation, some tastier, Western-style meals, and trips to the theatre and museums.

Elsewhere within Mongolia, travellers on organised tours spend around US$100 per day (more for extra luxuries). Independent travellers can see the same sights and stay in midrange accommodation for around US$80 per day. If you share the cost of a private jeep or minivan and camp rather than stay in more expensive *ger* (yurt) camps, you can bring this down to about US$25 to US$40 per day. If you're hitching and using public transport around the countryside, allow about US$10 to US$15 per day.

TRAVEL LITERATURE

Although you may think you have time on a Trans-Siberian journey to polish off *War and Peace* and several other Russian classics, the truth is that you may well be too busy getting to know your fellow passengers en route. Instead, read up before your trip on how the journey and cultures along the Trans-Siberian routes have been experienced in the past in the following, mainly nonfiction books.

The Trans-Siberian railway has been a rich source of inspiration for many writers. One of the best reads is Colin Thubron's *In Siberia,* where in addition to travelling along the railway, Thubron takes detours to places like the Entsy village of Potalovo near the Arctic Ocean and Magadan on the Sea of Okhotsk. Also appropriate reading for a Trans-Siberian journey are Thubron's earlier works *Among the Russians,* about travelling in European Russia during the 1970s, and *Behind the Wall,* describing his travels in China.

Eric Newby's classic *The Big Red Train Ride* is a hilarious account of hopping on and off the *Rossiya* between Moscow and Nakhodka – it's as much a snapshot of the Soviet era as it is of life on a train. Much more recently, the legendary Dervla Murphy hobbled through Siberia on a crook leg in *Through Siberia By Accident,* characteristically taking the less glamorous Baikal-Amur Mainline (Baikalo-Amurskaya Magistral; BAM) route to Tynda. Paul Theroux covers the journey, caustically as usual, in *The Great Railway Bazaar* and, a decade later, *Riding the Iron Rooster.*

In *Siberian Dawn: A Journey Across the New Russia,* Jeffrey Tayler paints an evocative but bleak picture of Siberia. The Russian-speaking author makes his way from the Russian Far East outpost of Magadan to Poland by bus and train, through some pretty hair-raising situations. More romantic (sometimes overly so) is Lesley Blanch's semiautobiographical *Journey Into the Mind's Eye,* which details the author's obsession with

HOW MUCH?

Russia
3-star double room
R3500 to R4000

1 hour of Internet access R50

2-course meal plus drink in a decent restaurant R600 to R1000

Short taxi ride R100

Metro ticket R10

China
3-star double room Y250

One hour of Internet access Y2

2-course meal plus drink in a decent restaurant Y50 to Y100

Short taxi ride Y10

Metro ticket Y6

Mongolia
Double room in budget guesthouse T14,000

One hour of Internet access T800

2-course meal in a decent restaurant T10,000

Short taxi ride T1000

Best seat at the Naadam opening T30,000

> **OTHER LONELY PLANET RESOURCES**
>
> Several other Lonely Planet books may be useful, especially for anybody spending a significant amount of time in areas away from the railway routes.
>
> For detailed information on each of the three countries covered by this guide see *Russia & Belarus, China* and *Mongolia*. The guides to Beijing, Moscow and St Petersburg are recommended for those staying in these cities for a while. The *Central Asia* guide is good for any travellers branching out along the Turk-Siberian route, while *Greenland & the Arctic* has the lowdown for those planning excursions in Russia's far, far north.
>
> Incredibly handy, especially if you're travelling independently and don't speak the languages of the countries, are Lonely Planet's *Mandarin Phrasebook, Mongolian Phrasebook* and *Russian Phrasebook*.

Russia and the Trans-Siberian railway. In *Wall to Wall: From Beijing to Berlin by Rail,* Mary Morris relates her personal experiences – which are not always positive – during a pre-Glasnost journey on the Trans-Mongolian route.

The best cycling-across-Siberia book is *Between the Hammer and the Sickle* by Simon Vickers, although you'll have to hunt around for it as it's out of print.

Fully fictional, but fine reading for its chapters on the Trans-Mongolian route and St Petersburg, is David Mitchell's dazzling debut *Ghostwritten*. James Meek's *The People's Act of Love* is also an imaginative fictional work set in Siberia in 1919, with its plot revolving around the Czech army legion which, in that tumultuous Civil War period, took control of the Trans-Siberian railway.

For more general books on Russia, start with Andrew Meier's acutely observed and elegiac *Black Earth: A Journey Through Russia After the Fall*. In dispatches from Chechnya, Norilsk, Sakhalin and St Petersburg, as well as Moscow, he sums up Russia's current situation superbly. Mark Taplin's *Open Lands – Travels through Russia's Once Forbidden Places* is an engrossing read, covering some of Russia's once off-limits cities, including Vladivostok and Nizhny Novgorod.

For an expat view of life in modern Beijing, dip into Rachel DeWoskin's *Foreign Babes in Beijing,* in which the author dishes the dirt on her life in the capital during the 1990s when she became a soap-opera star. For an insight into rural China, read Peter Hessler's *River Town: Two Years on the Yangtze,* full of poignant and telling episodes during the author's posting as an English teacher in the town of Fuling on the Yangzi River.

Lost Country: Mongolia Revealed, by Jasper Becker, is the strongest piece of contemporary travel writing about Mongolia, detailing what occurred during the darkest years of communism. *Wild East,* by Jill Lawless, is a tightly written, very funny account of the author's experience during the two years she spent editing the *UB Post*. Stanley Stewart's *In the Empire of Genghis Khan* is a mildly entertaining and brutally honest introduction to Mongolia by an Englishman who travelled 1000 miles by horseback across Central Asia and Mongolia.

INTERNET RESOURCES
Trans-Siberian Railway
Australian Broadcasting Company (http://abc.net.au/news/specials/transsiberia/default .htm) Slickly produced blog by the ABC's Russia correspondent Emma Griffiths about her 2005 Trans-Siberian journey.

Circumbaikal Railway (http://kbzd.irk.ru) Best website for background on the historic Circumbaikal railway.

Lonely Planet (www.lonelyplanet.com/journeys) Read blogs from the authors of this guide about their various Trans-Siberian journeys during 2005.

Man in Seat 61 (www.seat61.com) Mark Smith's amazingly comprehensive website is one of the travel information wonders of the Web. It has great up-to-date sections on the Trans-Siberian routes, plus practically any other rail service that you might need.

Trans-Siberia.com (www.trans-siberia.com) John Pannell's website has some good personal accounts of the journey, photos of his Trans-Siberian trips and links to other useful sources of information.

Trans-Siberian Railway Web Encyclopaedia (www.transsib.ru) The best Trans-Siberian website, regularly updated with tonnes of useful information and a huge photo library (there's also a German-language version at www.trans-sib.de).

Russia

CIA World Factbook (www.cia.gov/cia/publications/factbook/geos/rs.html) Read what the US Intelligence has on the Russkies.

Moscow Times (www.moscowtimes.ru) All the latest breaking national news, plus links to the sister paper *St Petersburg Times* and a good travel guide section.

Tourism Department of Russian Federation (www.russiatourism.ru/eng/) The official tourist website has a few useful bits of information.

Way to Russia (www.waytorussia.net) One of the most useful travel websites written and maintained by Russian backpackers. Lots of cool information, including details on arranging visas.

Your Train (www.poezda.net/en/) Invaluable website for planning train journeys to, from and inside Russia.

'Way to Russia (www.wayto russia.net) is written and maintained by Russian backpackers'

China

China Daily (www.chinadaily.com.cn) Get with the party line at the online mouthpiece of the Chinese Communist Party (CCP).

Human Rights in China (www.hrichina.org) Organisation set up in 1989 to promote human rights in China, with useful links.

Muzi China (http://china.muzi.com) General and travel information and news about China.

WildChina (www.wildchina.com) Far-flung treks around China, organised within China. Monthly email newsletter.

Zhongwen: Chinese Characters and Culture (www.zhongwen.com) Includes a pinyin chat room and an online dictionary of Chinese characters.

Mongolia

Mongolia National Tourism Centre (www.mongoliatourism.gov.mn) Includes lists of hotels, *ger* camps and travel agencies.

Mongolia Online (www.mol.mn) Has an arts calendar and covers news, currency-exchange rates, and weather in Ulaanbaatar.

Mongolia Today (www.mongoliatoday.com) A colourful online magazine covering all aspects of Mongolian culture.

Mongolia WWW Virtual Library (www.indiana.edu/~mongsoc) An excellent resource with lots of links.

UN in Mongolia (www.un-mongolia.mn) Offers lots of information, especially on the UN's Eastern Steppe Diversity project; check out the cultural magazine *Ger*.

Itineraries

CLASSIC ROUTES

THE TRANS-SIBERIAN ROUTE

One to Four Weeks /
Vladivostok to Moscow

Although this classic route can be done in either direction, we suggest going against the general flow by starting in **Vladivostok** (p230), at the far eastern end of Russia, so you can finish up with a grand party in either **Moscow** (p98) or, better yet, **St Petersburg** (p79).

Vladivostok, situated on a stunning natural harbour, merits a couple of days of your time, and it's also worth taking a break at **Khabarovsk** (p224), a lively city on the banks of the Amur River, an overnight hop to the west. Save a couple of days for **Ulan-Ude** (p213), a fascinating city where Russian and Buryat cultures mingle, and from where you can venture into the steppes to visit Russia's principal Buddhist monastery, **Ivolginsk Datsan** (p217). Just west of Ulan-Ude the railway hugs the southern shores of magnificent **Lake Baikal** (p198). Allow at least four days to see the lake, visit the equally lovely **Olkhon Island** (p203) and spend time in **Irkutsk** (p189), one of the Trans-Siberian's most important rail junctions.

Krasnoyarsk (p185), on the Yenisey River, affords the opportunity for scenic cruises along one of Siberia's most pleasant waterways. Crossing the Urals into European Russia, schedule a stop in **Yekaterinburg** (p150), a bustling historic city stocked with interesting museums and sites connected to the murder of the last tsar and his family. Also worth a break before Moscow and St Petersburg are the Golden Ring towns of **Vladimir** (p130) or **Suzdal** (p132), both packed with onion-domed churches, and a million miles away from the pace of the megacities to come.

This 9289km journey can be done nonstop in a week, but we recommend hopping on and off the train and making more of an adventure of it. Spend time seeing the sights in St Petersburg, Moscow and along the route, and you could easily stretch this trip to a month.

THE TRANS-MONGOLIAN ROUTE   One Week / Moscow to Beijing

This highly popular journey between **Moscow** (p98) and **Beijing** (p279) goes via the Mongolian capital of **Ulaanbaatar** (p257), allowing you to compare and contrast the three countries' cultures and people.

The 3/4 trains linking Moscow and Beijing run just once a week, taking just under seven days for the total 7865km journey. By hopping on and off other trains you can make up your own itinerary, and so fully explore the three countries this classic route passes through.

Get creative by breaking away from the regular Trans-Mongolian route. Take a boat from **Nizhny Novgorod** (p134) along the mighty Volga River to the fairy-tale-like **Makariyev Monastery** (p139). From Nizhny Novgorod you can reach **Yekaterinburg** (p150) either via the industrial hub of **Perm** (p139) – from where it's possible to take a trip to see the remains of a Gulag camp or an ice cave – or the old Tatar capital of **Kazan** (p142), with its World Heritage–listed kremlin.

Branch off from **Tyumen** (p156) to the atmospheric old Siberian town of **Tobolsk** (p159), then return by direct train to the appealing city of **Omsk** (p162). A direct train from here will allow you to bypass **Novosibirsk** (p165) and head straight to **Tomsk** (p178), a Siberian gem packed with gorgeous wooden architecture. **Krasnoyarsk** (p185) is the next logical overnight stop, from where you can push on to Irkutsk and Lake Baikal. Stop in either the southern lakeside town of **Port Baikal** (p202) or **Slyudyanka** (p204), from both of which you can make a trip along the **Circumbaikal Railway** (p205).

Crossing into Mongolia will seem to take forever. Reward yourself by alighting at Ulaanbaatar and taking time to explore the beautiful surrounding countryside, perhaps staying at a *ger* (yurt) camp in the **Gorkhi-Terelj National Park** (p268). Two more nights on the train and you'll finally be in Beijing with a fascinating city plus the whole of China waiting to be explored.

ROUTES LESS TRAVELLED

OFF THE BEATEN SIBERIAN TRACK

The 3400km Baikalo-Amurskaya Magistral (Baikal-Amur Mainline, or BAM) travels through some of the most rugged and unforgiving of Siberian landscapes. The line officially starts in the drab town of **Tayshet** (p242), but the closest big city, **Krasnoyarsk** (p185), has international flight connections if you wish to skip all points further west.

At **Bratsk** (p243) the train crosses a 1km-long dam. The town also has an excellent open-air ethnographic museum where you can see many of the traditional Siberian buildings rescued when the dam was built. Pleasant **Ust-Kut** (p244) can be used as a base for hydrofoil trips up and down the Lena River. If you're short on time, push on to **Severobaikalsk** (p244), beside Lake Baikal. This is the best base for exploring the relatively unvisited northern end of the lake and also has a small BAM museum.

The most technically difficult section of the BAM to construct comes en route to **Tynda** (p249), where the line climbs over and burrows through mountains, the longest tunnel being 15.34km at **Severomuysk** (p242). Home of the BAM construction company's headquarters, Tynda is a must-stop for its BAM museum and good *banya* (hot bath). From here you could detour along the unfinished Amuro-Yakutskaya Magistral (AYaM) railroad to its current terminus in **Neryungri** (p250), home to an enormous open-cut coal mine. Alternatively continue along the BAM route to **Komsomolsk-na-Amure** (p250), the largest city on the line and a great place to ponder the sacrifices and achievements made by hardy Soviet pioneers. Some 500km further east the BAM terminates at the naval base of **Sovetskaya Gavan** (p242), from where you can pick up a train that doubles back along the line before heading to **Vladivostok** (p230).

Rail enthusiasts and more adventurous travellers will not want to miss this alternative Trans-Siberian journey which, from Krasnoyarsk to Vladivostok, covers 5500km and takes at least six days without overnight stops. Begin in Moscow and you'll add on an extra 4098km and four straight days on the train.

THE BEIJING LOOP

You will want to schedule plenty of time in the fascinating city of **Beijing** (p279) either at the start or end of the trip. A day each is needed to tick off the Forbidden City and Tiananmen Sq, the Great Wall and the Summer Palace.

An excellent overnight service connects the capital with **Harbin** (p273), famous for its midwinter ice sculpture festival. Russians came here at the end of the 19th century to build the railway and handsome architectural evidence of their residence lies at the city's heart close to the Songhua River. Take a couple of days to enjoy Harbin's cosmopolitan atmosphere and visit the nearby **Siberian Tiger Park** (p275).

The Chinese-Russian border lies an overnight train ride away at **Manzhouli**; if you're not on one of the weekly Trans-Manchurian services through to Moscow, it's a simple process of hopping on a bus across to **Zabaikalsk** on the Russian side where you can reconnect with trains through to **Chita** (p219). That pleasant city is a great base for exploring a relatively unvisited area of Siberia where you'll discover a couple of beautiful Buddhist monasteries and a holy mountain at **Alkhanay** (p222). From **Ulan-Ude** (p213) you could branch down towards Mongolia, but since you've come this far it would be a great shame not to venture further west first to see **Lake Baikal**. Apart from Ulan-Ude possible bases for exploring the lake include **Slyudyanka** (p204), **Irkutsk** (p189), **Listvyanka** (p198) and **Olkhon Island** (p203).

Ulaanbaatar (p257) is certainly worth at least a couple of days. Its highlight is the lively and colourful Gandantegchinlen Khiid monastery. From Ulaanbaatar, it's two nights' journey back to Beijing through the Gobi Desert.

Arrange your Russian visa at home before starting out and also get a double-entry visa for China. The 6148km journey can be done in a minimum of a week, but you'll want to schedule around a month to get the most out of the trip.

Snapshot

RUSSIA

Coasting along on a wave of petrodollar profits, Russia is in far better economic shape than at any time in recent memory. Growth is running at over 7% per annum. Inflation is under control, with a consequent stabilisation of the rouble. Three-quarters of state enterprises have either fully or partly been privatised. In all the major cities you'll notice a burgeoning middle class with the commercial trappings that go with it.

Despite these improvements, Russia's economy still has a way to go before it can be said to have fully capitalised on its astonishing natural resources. The boom and bust period of the late 1990s, as well as the abandonment of the social safety net provided by communism, has left many people worse off. According to World Bank figures published in 2004, 20% of Russians live below the poverty line, defined as a monthly income of R1000 (less than €30, or US$38). At least 5.5 million people are unemployed, although many others considered 'employed' have jobs with little work and less pay. Corruption is practically endemic.

In the December 2003 elections the propresidential party United Russia took firm control of Russia's parliament, while in the subsequent presidential election Putin comfortably romped home for a second (and, unless he doesn't change the rules, final) term of office, but few people would say that either of these victories reflected Russians' true political opinions. A substantial part of the public's growing cynicism with the Kremlin owes to its increased control of media and local government, and the politicisation of the law enforcement system. In 2005 the US-based organisation Freedom House classified Russia as 'not free' for he first time since the demise of the Soviet Union in 1991. The KGB might be history, but ordinary Russians now look over their shoulders for Putin's shadowy force of *siloviki* (power people), an unholy alliance of authoritarian law enforcers and bureaucrats who many believe really run the country.

Putin has been accused of exploiting the recent wave of terrorist attacks, such as the 2004 hostage crisis in Beslan and bombing of Moscow's metro, to further curb civil liberties. Even so the international fight against terrorism has brought Russia well and truly out of the diplomatic cold. Relations with the US and both Trans-Siberian neighbours China and Mongolia might now be more cordial than in the past but Russia still has a way to go before it's fully trusted in the region again. Having seen popular revolutions recently sweep away the old guard in Ukraine and Kyrgyzstan, there is understandably a certain nervousness in the Kremlin that similar events could happen in Russia in the run-up to the 2008 presidential election.

CHINA

The Communist Party remains solidly entrenched and unchallenged in China. In 2003 a new president (Hu Jintao) and premier (Wen Jiabao) took charge, but any illusions that this would herald a move towards political liberalisation were dashed when the National People's Congress (NPC) denied Hong Kong the hope of choosing its next leader, flying in the face of the Chinese-British deal. State censorship of everything from Shakespeare to Rolling Stones lyrics continues and Internet access remains rigorously monitored, with a firewall 'protecting' China's citizens from BBC news in Chinese and other foreign pollutants.

FAST FACTS

Russia
Population: 143.4 million

Surface area:
17 million sq km

Life expectancy male/
female: 60.4/74 years

GDP per capita: US$9800

Extent of the Russian rail
network: 87,000km

State pension: about
R2000 per month

Net worth of the 27
richest Russians:
US$90.6 billion

Per capita consumption of
alcohol: 15.1L per year

Number of Nobel Prize
winners: 20

Time zones: 11

Livestock-to-person ratio:
13 to 1

Population below poverty
line: 36.1%

FAST FACTS

China

Population: 1.3 billion

Surface area:
9.5 million sq km

Life expectancy male/
female: 70.65/74.09 years

GDP per capita: US$5600

Extent of Chinese rail
network: 52,000km

Number of bicycles/cars
in Beijing: 10 million/
2 million

Literacy rate: 91%

Internet users: 94 million

Number of Chinese
characters: over 56,000

Length of the Great Wall:
7200km

In Beijing a heavy police presence saw the 15th anniversary of the 1989 Tiananmen massacre pass with little incident, apart from the arrest of at least 16 people in and around the square. Menaced into silence, Falun Gong (an outlawed spiritual movement) rarely makes it to the newspapers. The authorities may have successfully stamped out all dissent in the mainland, but they still have other problems to contend with. According to their own analysts, China has the largest disparity between urban rich and rural poor in the world. Considering the 750-million-strong peasantry perhaps it is no surprise that illegal Chinese immigrants still turn up on European shores. China's GDP may be growing at an annual rate of over 9%, but the banking system is teetering on the edge of crisis.

Nonetheless, big changes are afoot. The monks at the Shaolin Temple plan to register the Shaolin brand as a trademark in over 80 countries, while elite British private schools have decided that opening franchises in Communist China makes perfect sense. You can rocket from Shanghai's Pudong Airport into town at 430km/h on China's first Maglev train (although your hair can turn grey waiting for your rush hour bus to move on Beijing's congested streets). The authorities are aiming to transform the country into a top cricketing nation within two decades, while Manchester United signed Chinese striker Dong Fangzhuo in 2004. And let's not forget the upcoming 2008 Olympics – you certainly won't be able to while visiting Beijing!

MONGOLIA

In stark contrast to Russia and China, Mongolia has developed into a paragon of democracy since the end of communism in 1990. Free and fair elections have become the norm here, with voters overturning the ruling party three times in succession since 1996 – a fact that has made Mongolia a darling among international lenders and the donor community. In 2005 a 'grand coalition government', including ministers from both sides of the political divide, was in power (although political pundits felt sure it couldn't last). The country's president is former prime minister Nambaryn Enkhbayar.

FAST FACTS

Mongolia

Population: 2.8 million

Surface area:
1.56 million sq km

Life expectancy male/
female: 62.3/66.9 years

GDP per capita: US$1840

Extent of Mongolian rail
network: 1810km

Number of mobile phone
users: 404,400

Literacy rate: 98%

Inflation: about 6%

Livestock-to-person ratio:
13 to 1

Population below poverty
line: 36.1%

Mongolia's reversal of fortune is most evident on the streets of downtown Ulaanbaatar, where Korean taxis and Land Cruisers have all but erased the Russian Lada, and where fashion boutiques and elegant restaurants have made 'dollar shops' a distant memory. It's here that a burgeoning middle class is forging Mongolia's future, utilising the growing mining and tourism sectors.

Despite all this only half of Mongolians have access to clean drinking water and one-third still live under the poverty line. Infrastructure across the country is rudimentary and important economic sectors such as livestock husbandry have proven susceptible to natural disasters – some 11 million heads of livestock were killed between 1999 and 2002 in the wake of bad winter storms. The urban and rural poor grumble about ongoing corruption, and the environment suffers from new legislation that favours mining and business.

Increasingly Mongolia has turned to countries such as Japan, Korea, Germany, the US and the UK for assistance in redevelopment. Despite obvious challenges ahead there is hope that Mongolia can be a model for other developing countries. Its efforts to meet international expectations were rewarded in 2004 with admission to the 'Millennium Challenge Account', the US's multibillion-dollar foreign-aid programme designed to spur growth in low-income countries that display democracy and good governance.

History of the Railroad
Mara Vorhees & Simon Richmond

In the second half of the 19th century, the more advanced industrial states engaged in a worldwide contest for strategic advantage, economic fortune and imperial expansion. The competition took the form of continental conquest. Across Africa, Asia and the Americas, expeditions set off to explore hidden interiors, exploit material riches and tame 'uncivilised' natives. As industrial empires arose, railways became a means to, as well as a symbol of, great power and status. The number of miles of laid track and the production of more-powerful locomotives became indicators of industrial might, while the exquisite designs of railway stations and great halls became expressions of imperial pomp.

Russia's ambitions turned eastward towards the immense Siberian hinterland and distant Pacific coastline. Russia sought to consolidate existing holdings and to extend her influence in the region. At stake was Russia's claim over the still undeveloped and even undiscovered natural wealth of inner Eurasia. But these ambitions were checked by the Russian state's limited reach across these far-flung eastern territories. Until this time, the distance between St Petersburg and the Pacific was measured in an arduous overland trek or a hazardous sea voyage. The solution was found in the construction of the world's longest railroad, the Great Siberian Railway.

To the Great Ocean by Harmon Tupper is a lively take on the history of building the Trans-Siberian Railway. It's out of print, so look for it in libraries or order it from online booksellers.

AGE OF INDUSTRIAL EMPIRE

Russia was a latecomer to the industrial revolution. Russian society had long been dominated by a bloated autocratic state with close ties to an obsolete, land-owning aristocracy. With industrial entrepreneurs in short supply, the state was compelled to take the initiative in economic innovation, often by granting special concessions to foreign developers.

By the mid-19th century, Russia was slipping from the ranks of Europe's great powers. In 1857, Tsar Alexander II issued a Railway Decree, by which the state determined to reinvigorate the economy's preindustrial infrastructure with modern railway routes. Between 1860 and 1890, Russia constructed more kilometres of track than any other country except the USA. Railroads connected the central industrial region to the raw materials of the Urals and the agricultural products of the Black Earth region. Moscow became the hub of Russia's rail system, the terminus of nine different lines. This spurt of construction was mostly confined to European Russia. Fear of British encroachment from the Indian subcontinent prompted a Trans-Caspian line, which penetrated deep into Central Asia in the 1880s. Siberia, however, continued to remain a distant and undeveloped land.

In the 1840s, a geological expedition had discovered that the Chinese had left the Amur River region unsettled and unfortified. Shortly thereafter, the tsar appointed the ambitious and able Nikolai Muravyov as the governor general to Eastern Siberia. But unlike his predecessors,

For general histories of Russia, China and Mongolia flick through the following: Nicholas Riasanovsky's *A History of Russia*, Stephen Haw's *A Traveller's History of China* and Charles Bawden's *The Modern History of Mongolia*.

1833	1836
Russia's first steam locomotive invented by EA and ME Cherepanov	Russia's first passenger railway opens from St Petersburg to Tsarskoe Selo

RUSSIA'S EARLIEST RAILS

In 1833 EA Cherepanov and his son ME Cherepanov invented Russia's first steam railway loco-motive at Nizhny Tagil in the Urals (there's a model of it in Yekaterinburg, opposite the railway station – see p157). The locomotive and first Russian rail line, just 2km long, were built to sup-port the Urals' mining industry, although the Cherepanovs also sent one of their engines to Tsar Nicholas I in St Petersburg.

Here, in 1836, Russia's first public railway opened. Built by Austrian engineer Franz Anton von Gerstner and operating with British-built locomotives, it was a 24km line connecting the imperial capital to the Tsar's summer residence in Tsarskoe Selo. Nicholas I was so impressed with this new form of transport that plans were quickly made to roll out a rail network across European Russia.

Legend has it that when the tsar commanded the 650km route to be built in 1850 between Moscow and St Petersburg, he accidentally drew around his own finger on the ruler as he traced out a straight line between the cities. Engineers, too afraid to point out the error, duly incor-porated the kink into the plans, which became a 17km bend near the town of Novgorod.

The truth is somewhat more prosaic. The curve was actually built to circumvent a steep gra-dient that Russian steam locomotives of the time were not powerful enough to climb. In October 2001, the line was closed for 24 hours so that workers could finally straighten it out.

Muravyov was not content merely to reap the graft harvest that came with the office. He believed it was Russia's destiny to develop the Siber-ian Far East. With the tsar's approval, he collected some Cossacks and cruised the Amur, establishing towns for Russia and provoking fights with China. Preoccupied with foreign encroachment along the eastern seaboard, China was in no mood for hassles over Siberian forests. Thus, without bloodshed, Muravyov was able to re-draw the border with China along the Amur River in the north and the Ussuri River in the east in exchange for some cash and a promise of mutual security. At the tsar's request, Muravyov henceforth attached the sobriquet 'Amursky' to his name.

Muravyov-Amursky continued to pursue his vision of Siberian colon-isation. He became a leading advocate of a railway that would connect European Russia to the Far East. He attracted a long line of suitors from Russia, England and the USA, offering their own proposals for a railroad to the Pacific. But these petitions went unheeded in St Petersburg, where neither political support nor financial backing was forthcoming. In the last quarter of the 19th century, however, domestic and international events prompted a change in attitude in St Petersburg.

First, Russia's estate economy came under stress in the 1880s. Popula-tion growth and bad weather caused widespread famine and led to peas-ant unrest in the countryside. As a solution to the overcrowded villages and bread shortages, the government considered a policy of migration to the uncultivated lands of western and southern Siberia. The land-owning nobility were persuaded of the policy's merits as reports of pummelled foremen and torched manor houses became more frequent.

Second, in the late 19th century a regional intelligentsia began to write resentfully about Siberia's colonial status and admiringly about the American west. Regional elites tried to define a distinct Siberian

Before the Trans-Siberian Railway, it was quicker to travel from St Petersburg to Vladivostok by crossing the Atlantic, North America and the Pacific than by going overland.

1850	1857
Construction of railway between St Petersburg and Moscow begins	Tsar Alexander II issues Railway Decree to build a Russian rail network

cultural identity, which was rooted in the region's multiethnic frontier society. Their words fuelled fears that Siberia might go the same way as the Americas and seek political independence. In response, a consensus formed in Russia's ruling circles that Siberia's radicals and renegades needed to be reined in.

Third, the decline of the Chinese empire spurred the avaricious appetites of the great powers in the Far East. Russia's vulnerability in the Pacific was made very clear as early as the 1850s, when British and French warships launched assaults on the coastal town of Petropavlovsk-Kamchatsky on the Kamchatka peninsula during the Crimean War. The opening of the Suez Canal and the completion of the Canadian-Pacific Railway provided the British with easy access to the region. As a result, the 'Great Game', in which Russia and Great Britain vied for strategic leverage along the mountain passes of Central Asia, now spread to the coast of the Far East.

Finally, the most important event was a leadership change. In 1881 Tsar Alexander II was assassinated and succeeded by his son. Alexander II had earned a reputation as the 'Tsar Reformer', instituting sweeping internal changes meant to modernise and liberalise Russian society. Among his most notable reforms were the abolishment of serfdom and the introduction of local representative assemblies. By contrast, Alexander III was a political reactionary. He embraced the old regime's ideological pillars: autocracy, orthodoxy, empire. He aspired to rule through a strong centralised state. Much more so than his father, Alexander III embodied the nationalist spirit that infused the Age of Industrial Empire. He was anxious to join the competition for new territorial possessions and he swore to defend Russia's existing claims.

In 1886, Alexander III responded to a petition for support from the governor general of Irkutsk: 'How many reports from Siberian governors have I not read already, and I have to admit with shame and grief that until now the government has done nothing to satisfy the requirements of this rich but neglected region. It is time, high time.' In March 1891 the tsar officially proclaimed the undertaking of a Trans-Siberian railway, from the Urals to the Pacific, and dispatched his son and heir apparent, Nicholas, to lay the first stone at Vladivostok.

Victor Mote's *Siberia: Worlds Apart,* packed with pictures, graphs, maps and personal anecdotes, briefly covers the area's prehistory and then moves into the 20th century.

Starting in 1888 George Kennan produced 25 articles for *The Century* (later collected in *Siberia and the Exile System*) in which he attacked the tsarist government's policy of using Siberia as a prison camp.

TRAVELLING THE TRAKT

When the playwright Anton Chekhov set off in 1890 to investigate the notorious penal colony on the Russian Far East island of Sakhalin he travelled along the Trakt (Great Siberian Post Rd). It was much more a rough track than actual road; travellers could arrange transport at the posting stations spaced at about 40km intervals from each other. The mode of transport depended on the season with a sledge being used in winter and either a *kibitka* (covered cart) or a slightly more comfortable *tarantass* (carriage) available at other times. These were pulled by a *troika,* a group of three horses, driven by a *yamshchik* (driver) who was typically inebriated. Despite the undoubted discomfort and great length of the journey (it took Chekhov 2½ months to cross Siberia at what was considered a fast clip!) the American journalist George Kennan called transport along the route 'the most perfectly organised horse express service in the world'. Read Chekhov's impressions in *Journey to Sakhalin.*

1886	1891
Tsar Alexander III gives the thumbs-up to the idea of a Trans-Siberian railway	In Vladivostok Alexander III's son Nicholas lays first stone of Ussuri line to Khabarovsk

A STATE WITHIN A STATE

The task of building the Trans-Siberian Railway fell to one of imperial Russia's most industrious and talented statesmen, Sergei Witte. His rise to the highest levels of state service, given his modest pedigree, was testimony to his skills and shrewdness.

In *Road to Power: the Trans-Siberian Railroad and the Colonization of Asian Russia*, Steven Marks argues political concerns over competition with China and Korea contributed as much to the success of the railway as economic interests in developing Siberia.

Witte was entrusted by the tsar with overseeing the pedestrian details underlying the imperial vision. The Trans-Siberian Railway was no ordinary project and, thus, was not left to the ordinary process. The Siberian Railway Committee, a special panel with enhanced powers, was created to override the inevitable bureaucratic obstacles. At Witte's urging, the tsar named his son Nicholas to head the Committee. In so doing, Witte was able to exert influence on, and curry favour with, the 23-year-old tsarevitch.

As work progressed, the committee's scope expanded. It assumed responsibility for peasant resettlement to Siberia, diplomatic relations in the Far East and security forces along the route. In a jealous pique, the minister of foreign affairs remarked that Witte had built his own 'state within a state'.

For decades, proposals for a transcontinental railway had been quashed by frugal finance ministers. But that situation changed once the post was occupied by Witte, a devout Keynesian (even before Keynes!). After months of wooing the Rothschilds, they suddenly pulled out to protest Russian anti-Semitic legislation. Alexander, meanwhile, was swayed by the argument of economic nationalists, who warned against foreign participation in a project of such great strategic value. Witte was forced to raise money from a lean domestic economy.

Witte implemented a host of financial policies and manoeuvring to raise the necessary funds, including issuing bonds, raising taxes and taking out foreign loans. Finally, he set off a wave of inflation by printing extra roubles to cover the soaring construction costs. 'Better to lose money than prestige', he explained to the concurring tsar.

FROM TICKET SELLER TO EMPIRE BUILDER

The son of a colonial bureaucrat in the Caucasus and a graduate in mathematics, Sergei Witte (1849–1915) took a job selling train tickets in Odesa for the Southwest Railway Company just as Russia's railway boom got under way. He quickly mastered the logistics and finances of rail transport and was promoted to stationmaster, and then company director.

Witte's rare ability to turn a profit from the line and his efficient dispatch of troops during the first Balkans War earned him a post in the central railway administration in St Petersburg. His ascent continued with appointments as minister of transport and minister of finance, the latter probably the most powerful portfolio in the government.

Elite society considered Witte an outsider; his forceful personality and sudden appearance inside the tsar's court was much resented. But in Alexander III he had a most admiring patron. Moreover, Witte genuinely shared the tsar's vision of a Trans-Siberian Railway, describing it as 'one of the largest and most important undertakings of the 19th century, not only for the Motherland, but for all the world'. Truly a character of historic magnitude, Witte saw himself as Russia's Cecil Rhodes, an empire builder, and the Trans-Siberian Railway gave him the opportunity to realise this ambition.

1892	1893
Construction of Western Siberian line from Chelyabinsk to Ob River (Novosibirsk) starts	Construction of Central Siberian line from Ob River to Lake Baikal starts

The Trans-Siberian Railway also provided Witte with the opportunity to play diplomat, when he proposed to build a 560km short cut across Manchuria, rather than follow the northern bend in the Amur to Vladivostok. Already besieged with foreigners, the Chinese emperor rejected this indignity.

A determined Witte changed tactics. He bought the influence of senior Chinese statesmen, offered a generous loan to the close-to-bankrupt Chinese government and repackaged his proposal to look like a Chinese-Russian joint venture. The result was an 80-year lease agreement over a corridor of territory for the railway. The Manchurian diversion led to the formation of the East Chinese Railway Company and the Russo-Chinese Bank, which were both in fact fronts for the Russian Ministry of Finance.

In 1898, Witte negotiated further territorial concessions, allowing Russia to build a Southern Manchurian line to a warm-water outlet at Port Arthur (Dalian), located on the southern tip of the Liaodong Peninsula. The minister of finance, in effect, became the tsar's chief envoy to the Far East.

WORKING ON THE RAILROAD

Construction on the railway got under way almost immediately after the tsar's decree was issued in 1891. Beginning at Chelyabinsk, in the southern Urals, it was decided the line would run parallel to the old post road as far as Irkutsk. Then it would blaze an iron trail eastward through the untamed Baikal, Amur and Ussuri regions to Vladivostok, the eastern terminus on the Pacific.

This route was selected out of consideration for the south's warmer weather conditions and more arable lands, which would hopefully encourage new agricultural settlements. But it didn't please local industrialists and merchants, since it bypassed many larger mining colonies and river towns in the north. The line was later altered to accommodate these influential economic lobbies by including Perm, Yekaterinburg and Tyumen.

Building the world's longest railroad across a formidable landscape posed ongoing challenges of engineering, supply and labour. The railroad cut through thick forests, crossed countless rivers, scaled rocky mountains and traversed soggy quagmires. Work brigades were poorly outfitted. The heavy work was carried out using shovels and picks, while horses and humans did the hauling.

The builders had to keep the workers supplied with huge quantities of stone, timber and iron as well as with necessary food. Maintaining supply lines in Siberia's unsettled hinterland required the utmost resourcefulness.

No ready labour supply existed for this immense project. Workers were recruited, or conscripted, from all over the empire as well as from abroad. They toiled from dawn to dusk in the sweltering heat and freezing cold, and were preyed on by deadly diseases, forest bandits and hungry tigers.

The construction work was divided into seven territorial segments, starting simultaneously from the eastern and western terminus points.

The Russian railway system, covering 85,500km of track, is the second largest in the world after the USA's 228,464km of track.

1894	1895
Chinese agree to Russians building Manchurian line from Chita to Vladivostok	Construction of Trans-Baikal line from Lake Baikal to Sretensk starts

Western Siberian: 1892–96

From Chelyabinsk in the west (which is no longer part of the official Trans-Siberian route), it ran through Omsk and on to the Ob River, the site of present-day Novosibirsk. The western Siberian section was 1440km long and the easiest to build. For the engineers, the main challenge was attempting to span the many rivers that fed the Ob Basin. The crossings for the Irtysh and Ob Rivers both required the building of bridges that were almost 1km long. The region did not suffer from a shortage of materials or labour – the free peasants of western Siberia willingly enlisted in the work brigades, although many disappeared during the harvest season.

Central Siberian: 1893–98

The central Siberian section covered a distance of 1920km from the Ob through Krasnoyarsk and on to Irkutsk, west of Lake Baikal. The work of the engineers became more complicated on this leg, because of the mountainous terrain and the steep river valleys. The Yenisey River required a steel bridge nearly 1km in length. The earth – frozen until July and then swampy after the thaw – was less than ideal for digging. Water from the drained bogs collected in stagnant pools, which bred swarms of bloodthirsty mosquitoes around work sites.

Supply and labour now became chronic problems. Unlike on the plains, the line ran through forests with few settlements to tap for workers or provisions. The builders advertised throughout the empire, offering higher wages and bonuses to entice fresh forces. The shortage of skilled labour required for the stonework was especially acute.

'Water from the drained bogs collected in stagnant pools, which bred swarms of bloodthirsty mosquitoes around work sites'

Ussuri: 1891–97

Meanwhile, construction was under way in the east on the Ussuri section of the railway. Beginning in Vladivostok, the line ran northward through the Ussuri River Valley to Khabarovsk, a distance of about 800km. The forest terrain was more difficult for the engineers. Moreover, after the first tracks had been laid, it was discovered that the Amur rose as much as 10m during the spring, which meant redrawing the route and starting again. The builders faced severe labour shortages in this remote corner of the Far East. Despite initial misgivings, the construction brigades recruited over 8000 workers from the local Korean population and migrant Chinese labourers, over one-half of the total workforce for this section. They received lower wages than the Russian workers because, the foremen said, their work was inferior (though it may have been because they did not run tabs in the company canteen).

The builders of the Ussuri line introduced convict labour to the railroad, when 600 prisoners destined for incarceration on Sakhalin Island were instead ordered to start digging. Some prisoners escaped from their inexperienced handlers and went on a local crime spree. The project as a whole eventually employed nearly 15,000 convicts and exiles, with far better results. Many brigade foremen praised their contribution. Convicts, in turn, could work time off their sentences, and the living conditions were a small improvement over the tsar's prisons.

1898	1900
Chinese agree to Russians building Southern Manchurian line to Port Arthur (Dalian)	First Trans-Siberian services go into operation

Circumbaikal: 1901–04

Heading east from Irkutsk, the builders encountered their most formidable obstacle, Lake Baikal. No previous experience prepared the engineers for the frigid lake's steep rocky cliffs, which dominated the shoreline.

Engineers initially decided that construction of a railroad line around the lake would be impossibly expensive. Instead, the steamship *Baikal*, strong enough to smash through ice, was commissioned from a British firm. From April 1900 it transported train carriages between Port Baikal (p202) on the western shore and Mysovaya (now Babushkin), while passengers followed on the *Angara* – now salvaged and moored in Irkutsk. However, the ships proved less than efficient, being prey to severe storms and sometimes-impassable ice. This hindrance became a national security threat in 1904 – when Russia needed to transport troops and supplies to the front during the Russo-Japanese War temporary tracks were actually laid across the ice in an attempt to expedite the military movement. Tragically, the ice cracked under the very first train to attempt this crossing, and it sank into the Baikal's icy waters.

Despite earlier hesitation, the decision was made in 1901 to begin construction of a railway line that would skirt the southern edge of the lake, connecting Port Baikal and Mysovaya. The project was overseen by VA Savrimovich, a highly regarded engineer and surveyor. The cliffs around the lake made this the most challenging section of all to build. Tsar Alexander III brought in Armenian and Italian masons to design the elaborate portals and arched bridges. The pride of Mother Russia at the time, this section was nicknamed 'the Tsar's Jewelled Buckle'.

In the 1950s the Angara River was dammed, raising Lake Baikal by around 6m and submerging the railway line between Irkutsk and Port Baikal. A short-cut line bypassing this flooded section was built between Irkutsk and Slyudyanka – today's Trans-Siberian mainline. The remaining 94km of the Circumbaikal Railway became a somewhat neglected branch line. However, a few weekly minitrains still chug through its 39 completely unlit tunnels and over more than 200 bridges, much to the delight of tourists and train buffs; see p205 for details.

The Circumbaikal consumed four times as much stone as the entire Trans-Baikal section. Workers chiselled 39 tunnels into the lake's craggy capes and erected over 100 bridges and viaducts.

Trans-Baikal: 1895–1900

The Trans-Baikal section ran from the eastern shore of Lake Baikal past Ulan-Ude and Chita, then on to Sretensk on the Shilka River. For the engineers, this section of 1072km of dense forest was nearly as daunting as the Circumbaikal, and would prove more frustrating. The railroad had to scale the Yablonovy Mountains, rising 5630m above sea level. The rivers were not so wide, but they ran in torrents and cut steep valley walls. The tracks were laid on narrow beds along high mountain ledges. Dynamite was used to dig deeper into the permafrost to erect sturdier supports. Harsh weather, including summer droughts and heavy rains, exacerbated the difficulties. The great flood of 1897 washed away over 300km of laid track and 15 completed bridges.

Amur: 1907–16

The 2080km-long Amur section presented similar engineering, supply and labour challenges. The Amur required some of the longest and most

1901	1904
Construction of Circumbaikal line along southwestern shore of Lake Baikal starts	Japan attacks Port Arthur

complicated bridges, including a span of almost 2km across the Amur. The builders relied heavily on convict labour, supplemented by army units and Chinese migrants. Building materials, including iron rails, had to be imported from British and North American suppliers.

The Amur was the last section of the Trans-Siberian to be built, going into operation only in 1916. The railway's first travellers transferred into boats at Sretensk for a long river voyage down the Amur to Khabarovsk, where they could reboard the train. Later travellers bypassed the Amur, when the railway was diverted through northern China.

East Chinese: 1897–1901

In 1894 Russia secured the agreement from the weak Chinese empire that allowed for a Manchurian section of the Trans-Siberian Railway. From Chita, the 1440km-long East Chinese Railway turned southeast, crossing the Argun River and rolling through Harbin to Vladivostok. It sliced over 600km off the journey. Chinese officials had insisted on a narrow gauge to fit their existing rail system, but after a one-sided negotiation the Russian wide gauge was chosen. The terrain of flat steppe lands, wide mountain passes and fertile river valleys elated the exhausted builders.

However, other problems soon arose. In 1899, Chinese nationalism mobilised into a rancorous antiforeigner movement, the self-proclaimed 'Fists of Higher Justice'. Better known as the Boxer Rebellion, the movement quickly spread to Manchuria and the Russian-controlled railway. Stations and depots were set ablaze, 480km of track were torn up and besieged railroad workers took flight. The line was only able to return to service after the Russian military intervened.

For state leaders, time was of the essence, so the work brigades pressed on, driving a modern wedge into an ancient wilderness. Despite the many obstacles, construction proceeded apace. In August 1898, the first train rolled into the station at Irkutsk, two years ahead of schedule. In the same year, the line between Vladivostok and Khabarovsk went into operation. In 1900, service began on the Trans-Baikal section. At this point, a train journey across Siberia was possible, although supplemented in stages by water transport. The completion of the Amur line in 1916 represented the possibility of travelling exclusively by rail from St Petersburg in the west to the Pacific entirely within Russian territory.

RIDING THE RAILS

The Trans-Siberian Railway was introduced to the world at the Paris Exhibition in 1900. Visitors to the Russian pavilion were treated to visual images of Siberia's pristine rugged landscape and exotic native cultures. They were also impressed by the luxuriously decorated mock-up wagon displays. The 1st-class sleepers offered comfortable and commodious compartments. The dining car enticed visitors with caviar, sturgeon and other Russian delicacies. The exhibit featured a handsome smoking car, a music salon with piano, a well-stocked library, a fully equipped gymnasium and a marble and brass bath. The exhibit also boasted that the Trans-Siberian would shave off 10 days from the present travel time of five weeks from London to Shanghai. Here was elegance and efficiency, provided in high Russian style.

The price of a 1st-class ticket from Moscow to Vladivostok on the initial Trans-Siberian trains was R114.

1905	1907
Russia concedes Southern Manchuria to Japan but keeps control of East Chinese Railway	Construction of Amur line from Sretensk to Khabarovsk starts

The personal accounts of early travellers suggest that the actual journey did not live up to its advance billing. Although 1st-class accommodation was comfortable enough, most of the other promised indulgences were underwhelming, to say the least. East of Baikal the train routinely ran out of food and had to stop once a day at small stations en route. 'Today we did not eat until 3pm, and then it was vile,' wrote one cranky American traveller in 1902. 'There was one wretched little eating room filled with Russians. You may stand around and starve for all they care.'

In addition, the Trans-Siberian did not succeed in providing a more expeditious route to the Far East. The hastiness that went into construction was exposed in operation. Travellers experienced frequent delays, sometimes lasting days. The Trans-Siberian had the highest accident rate of any other line in the empire. Ties splintered, bridges buckled and rails warped. The locomotives chugged along at no more than 25km/h because of the risk of derailment at higher speed. One Beijing-bound passenger scribbled in resignation: 'A traveller in these far eastern lands gradually loses his impatience and finally ceases to care whether his train goes fast or slowly, or does not go at all. Certainly we have been two hours at this station for no apparent reason.' (This sentiment may ring true even for travellers today.)

A principal goal of the railway was to facilitate the resettlement of European Russia's rural inhabitants, in the hopes of easing social tensions and offering economic opportunities. In the 1800s the tsar had officially lifted restrictions on internal migration and opened up Siberia for colonisation. Between 1860 and 1890 less than 500,000 people moved to Siberia. But once the train came on line, the population's eastward drift turned into a raging torrent.

Between 1891 and 1914, over five million new immigrants settled in Siberia. Station halls were packed with hundreds of waiting peasants sleeping on the floor. Third-class fares were kept low so that ordinary subjects could ride the rails. One could travel for more than 3200km on the Trans-Siberian for less than R20. These wagons dispensed with any pretension of style or comfort. A 1st-class rider observed: 'The 3rd-class passengers are packed like sardines. Their cars hold nothing save wooden bunks, two tiers thereof, and each has four and sometimes six. One's health would certainly be jeopardised by a passage through them. I notice that our car is constantly guarded. I am not surprised, and do not object in the least.'

In *A Ribbon of Iron*, Annette Meakin, the first Englishwoman to circumnavigate the globe by rail in 1900, recounts her generally favourable impressions of the early Trans-Siberian train services.

RELIGION ON THE RAILS

The original pre-1917 Trans-Siberian trains included a Russian Orthodox church car, complete with icons, bells and a travelling priest. At stations along the route where a church had yet to be built the church car was used to hold services for the locals, railway workers and any interested passengers.

Jump forward a century to April 2005 and the Russian Orthodox Church has signed an agreement with Russian Railways to cooperate, among other things, on restoring chapels and mobile carriage chapels to the railway transport system station.

1916	**1917**
Completion of Amur line and Trans-Siberian route as it exists today	Bolshevik Revolution

WAR & REVOLUTION

Alexander III saw the Trans-Siberian Railway as the means by which the Russian empire would act as a great power in the Far East. Under his less able successor, Nicholas II, the construction of the railway instead provoked confrontations that exposed the manifold weaknesses of imperial Russia. The railway and railroad workers played prominent supporting roles in the tumultuous political events that subsequently toppled the tsarist autocracy and brought radical socialism to power in the early 20th century.

Robert Service is the writer of both a biography of Vladimir Ilych Lenin and the History of Twentieth Century Russia, *both excellent introductions to the dawn and progress of the Soviet era.*

The Russo-Japanese War

The East Chinese Railway involved Russia in the multilateral dismemberment of the Chinese empire. In the subsequent grab for territorial and commercial concessions in Manchuria, Russia came into direct conflict with imperial Japan. Witte was always inclined towards diplomacy in Russia's Far Eastern policy, but Nicholas fell under the sway of more adventurous advisors. 'What Russia really needs,' the minister of interior opined, 'is a small victorious war'.

The tsar's aggressive stance in the Far East provoked Japan to attack Port Arthur in February 1904. The overconfident Nicholas was dazed by the rapid string of defeats in the field. Japanese forces quickly seized the advantage over Russia's outnumbered troops, while the reinforcements remained stalled at Lake Baikal. The single-track, light-rail Trans-Siberian was simply overwhelmed by the demands of war. The tsar dispatched his prized Baltic fleet. In May 1905, the war concluded when – upon reaching the Tsushima Straits – the fleet was annihilated in just one afternoon. Nicholas summoned Witte to salvage Russia's dignity in the peace negotiations. Under the Treaty of Portsmouth, Russia agreed to vacate Southern Manchuria, but managed to hold on to the East Chinese Railway.

The 1905 Revolution

Russia's woeful performance in war unleashed a wave of anti-tsarist protest at home. The reactionary impulses of the regime were fully displayed in January 1905 when peaceful demonstrators, led by an Orthodox priest, were shot down in front of St Petersburg's Winter Palace. The 'Bloody Sunday' massacre did not quell the unrest, but instead incited more people to take to the streets. Among the most radical participants in the 1905 Revolution were the railroad workers.

At turns anecdotal and specific, A People's Tragedy: The Russian Revolution 1891–1924, *by erudite scholar Orlando Figes, paints a vivid picture of this tumultuous period in Russian history.*

Like most Russian workers, railroad employees laboured under harsh conditions, received scant wages and suffered tyrannical bosses. Unlike other sectors, however, the railroad workers could paralyse the economy by going on strike. The government maintained a special railway police force, 8000 strong, which spent its time intimidating labour organisers.

Railroad workers were quick to join the protest movement, as 27 different lines experienced strikes in the first two months of 1905. In April, they coordinated their efforts by forming an All-Russia Union of Railroad Workers. At first, they demanded economic concessions, such as higher wages and shorter hours, but soon their demands became more political, such as the rights to organise and strike.

1918	1920
Start of Russian Civil War; Czech army seizes control of western half of Trans-Siberian Railway	End of Russian Civil War

The government attempted to impose martial law over the railway system. The railway union responded by calling for a total shutdown of service. The strike started in Moscow, spread to every major railway line and sparked a nationwide general strike. The movement only subsided after the tsar issued the October Manifesto, which promised to reform the autocracy into a constitutional monarchy.

The Bolshevik Revolution

Radical railroad workers also played a crucial role in the Bolshevik Revolution of 1917. Exhausted by its involvement in WWI, the tsarist regime lost its ability to rule and fell to street demonstrators in February 1917. Nicholas' abdication created a power vacuum in the capital. The liberal provisional government hesitated to make decisions or end the war, which swung public sentiment towards the more radical political parties.

In an attempt to restore order, General Kornilov ordered his troops at the front to march on St Petersburg, with the intention of declaring martial law. Radicals and liberals alike took cover. But Kornilov's men never made it. Railroad workers went on strike, refusing to transport them, and the putsch petered out. Within weeks, Vladimir Ilych Lenin and the Bolsheviks staged a palace coup, deposed the provisional government and declared themselves rulers of Russia.

Geoffrey Elliot's *From Siberia with Love,* a family history of the author's Russian-exile grandfather, is fleshed out with almost manic attention to detail with much of the action occurring in Chita and Irkutsk.

The Russian Civil War

The Bolsheviks' claim on power was soon challenged. In the spring of 1918, as the war in Europe continued without Russia, a legion of Czech POWs tried to return home to rejoin the fighting. Unable to cross the front line in the west, they headed east. Along the way, they provoked a confrontation with the Bolsheviks. When the White Army, hostile to the Bolsheviks, came to support the Czechs, the Russian Civil War began.

The Czech legion seized control of the western half of the Trans-Siberian Railway; in the meantime, the Japanese, who had landed in Vladivostok, took control of the railway east of Baikal. A separatist Siberian Republic was formed in Omsk, that is, until tsarist naval officer Admiral Kolchak overthrew the Omsk government and declared himself supreme ruler of Siberia. Another former tsarist general reigned over the East Chinese Railway in Manchuria. Cossacks menaced the Trans-Baikal and Amur regions. Siberia had returned to the era of warlords.

It took the Bolsheviks more than three years to secure complete control over the Trans-Siberian and to establish Soviet power across Siberia. Kolchak was arrested, tried and shot for his less-than-sterling performance as supreme ruler.

Seventeen Moments in Soviet History (www .soviethistory.org) is a well-designed site that covers all the major events during the life of the USSR.

Development of Siberia

The construction of the Trans-Siberian Railway was intended to foster industrial development in Siberia. As such, an engineering and technical school was founded in the late 19th century in the city of Tomsk, to become Siberia's first university. Scores of factories, mills and mines sprung up along the route to feed the railroad's huge appetite for iron, bricks and lumber. However, Siberia's fledgling industries could not keep pace with the growing demand.

1929	1930s
Electrification of Trans-Siberian line begins	Construction of Baikal-Amur Mainline (BAM) starts

The project served as an economic stimulus for other regions. The mining and metal works in the Urals became the chief supplier of iron and steel. The sprawling manufacturing works around St Petersburg and Moscow were contracted to supply the rolling stock. By 1905 over 1500 locomotives and 30,000 wagons had rolled out of Russian factories. At the same time, the railway system as a whole employed over 750,000 workers involved with engines and rolling stock, traffic management, track maintenance and administration. Higher wages, as much as 50% above the norm, attracted railway employees to the Trans-Siberian line.

After coming to power, Russia's new Soviet rulers were committed to rapid industrial development. To meet this goal, they needed to gain wider access to Siberia's plentiful raw materials. Thus, they invested heavily in upgrading the Trans-Siberian Railway. A second track was built alongside the original single line. The light rails were replaced with heavier, more durable rails. Wooden bridges and supports were replaced with iron and steel. Working conditions on the railway did not improve much under the new socialist regime, but railway workers were now extolled for being in the vanguard of the industrial proletariat.

In the 1930s the Soviet regime launched a state-managed campaign of industrialisation, in which large-scale projects in Siberia figured prominently. The Kuznets Basin became a prodigious supplier of coal, coke, iron and steel.

At the same time, the paranoid and vengeful Soviet dictator, Josef Stalin, was engaged in a 'class war' against his own citizens and comrades. The victims of Stalin's terror who were not shot were sent to forced labour camps known as the Gulag (p138). Siberia's industrial revolution was built on the backs of millions of imaginary 'enemies of the people'.

In WWII, Nazi Germany's blitzkrieg invasion was an unintended impetus for Siberia, when the industrial stock of European Russia was hastily evacuated to safer interior locations. During the German occupation, the Trans-Siberian Railway served as a lifeline for Soviet survival. It furnished the front with the reinforcements and equipment that eventually wore down the formidable Nazis.

In the 1950s Siberian development was energised by the discovery of oil and gas. While these deposits were in the north, they promoted development in the cities along the railway, such as the oil refinery in Omsk and the chemical plant in Irkutsk.

Stalin's reform-minded successor, Nikita Khrushchev, denounced his former boss and liberated millions of labour-camp inmates. Meanwhile, incentive-laden offers lured new workers to the region, and the Siberian population became highly skilled. A uniquely planned academic community was created near Novosibirsk. Military industry flourished in secret cities, sheltering well-tended scientists and technicians. By 1970, 13 Siberian cities had populations of 250,000 or more.

During this time, Siberia's indigenous populations were increasingly assimilated into the lifestyle and culture of Soviet Russian society. In 1900, native peoples accounted for more than 15% of Siberia's total population but, by 1970, this number was less than 4%. Simultaneously, Siberia's development was having increasingly detrimental effects on the environment (see p62).

In 1911, Siberia recorded about nine million inhabitants; by 1959, the number had increased to nearly 23 million.

The Pulitzer Prize–winning *Gulag: A History* by Anne Applebaum is the definitive account of the forced labour camps of Russia's most desolate regions.

1931	1935
Opening of Turkestan-Siberian line from Novosibirsk to Central Asia	Russia sells East Chinese Railway in Manchuria to Japan

BRANCHING OUT

The Soviet regime intended to further develop overland access to the Eurasian continent so that travellers could reach ever more remote corners of the Far East. The construction and operation of branch lines throughout the Far East were entangled in the politics of the region for most of the 20th century.

The Trans-Manchurian

The Trans-Manchurian line connects Beijing to the Trans-Siberian at Chita, via the Russian-built East Chinese and South Manchurian Railways. The South Manchurian, however, fell to Japan as a spoil of war in 1905. At this time, American railroad baron EH Harriman made several generous bids to buy these routes from their respective operators. He saw a rare opportunity to realise his ambition of building a railroad line that circumnavigated the globe. Harriman's offers, however, were rebuffed.

In 1922 China persuaded Soviet Russia – which was weakened by war and revolution – to renegotiate the status of the East Chinese Railway between Vladivostok and Port Arthur. The Soviet government renounced its special economic privileges in Manchuria and agreed to joint custody of the railway. As Manchuria was the scene of an ongoing power struggle, the Russians had to continuously defend their (partial) claim to the railway line. During the 1920s the Russian managers were arrested by a Manchurian warlord and again by Chiang Kaishek (leader of the Kuomintang, the Chinese Nationalist Party), both of whom seized control of the railroad. In each case the aggressors were forced to relinquish their prizes and prisoners. In 1932 the Japanese took control of Manchuria, renaming it Manchukuo and installing the last Manchu emperor, Puyi, as a puppet ruler. Under pressure, Russia sold her interest in the East Chinese Railway to the new rulers in 1935.

This was not the end of the line, however. According to the secret protocols negotiated at Yalta, Winston Churchill and Franklin D Roosevelt conceded back to Stalin the East Chinese and South Manchurian rail lines, as part of the price of Soviet entry into the Pacific War. Russia's return to Manchuria was brief; the lines were given back to China in 1952 as a goodwill gesture to its new communist regime.

Ironically, geopolitics proved stronger than ideology. By the mid-1960s relations between China and Russia soured and the border was closed, thus stopping the Trans-Manchurian service. The low point was in 1969 when armed clashes occurred over Damansky Island in the Ussuri River, the border between the two communist neighbours. The so-called Sino-Soviet Split lasted until the early 1980s, and since this time Russian-Chinese relations have warmed considerably, allowing the Trans-Siberian to be reconnected to the Trans-Manchurian.

The Trans-Mongolian

The 2080km Trans-Mongolian line was built along the route travelled by the ancient tea caravans, from Beijing through Mongolia to Ulan-Ude. The line was built piecemeal, a direct result of fluctuations in the Russian-Chinese relationship.

Bernardo Bertolluci's *The Last Emperor* (1988) is a lavishly mounted, epic-scale story of Puyi, China's last imperial ruler.

In 2005 China and Russia settled a post-WWII dispute over 2% of their 4300km common border. For the first time, the whole border is legally defined.

1941	1952
Hitler invades Russia, bringing that country into WWII	China given control of Manchuria's East Chinese Railway

In the 1907 Peking–
Paris car rally, contestants
followed what would
become the Trans-
Mongolian rail route.
The winners were Italian
Prince Borghese and
journalist Luigi Barzini.

During the late 19th century, Mongolia was formally part of the Chinese Manchu empire. After centuries of neglect, China's officials became more interested in the region, much to the irritation of the Mongols. Plans were made to construct a railroad from Beijing to Örgöö (Ulaanbaatar). Instead, the Chinese empire collapsed in 1911.

Mongolia was very eager to be rid of its Chinese overlord but was too weak to fend for itself. Russia emerged conveniently as a protective patron of Mongolian independence. The Soviet Union consolidated its influence in 'independent' Mongolia through the signing of agreements on economic and military cooperation. In 1936 the announcement came of construction of a short rail route linking Mongolia to Soviet Buryatia, whose peoples shared close ethnic ties. This new line between Ulan-Ude and Naushki was completed in 1940, and in 1949, it was extended to the capital, Ulaanbaatar.

In the early 1950s, relations between the Soviet Union and communist China relaxed a bit, allowing the Chinese to finally begin work on the long-planned railroad connecting Beijing to Ulaanbaatar. Although train service began on this line in 1956, the Sino-Soviet Split in the 1960s closed the border. Like the Trans-Manchurian, the Trans-Mongolian line was reopened in the 1980s.

The Turkestan-Siberian

The Turkestan-Siberian (Turk-Sib) connects the Trans-Siberian to Central Asia. From Novosibirsk, the 1680km line heads south over the Altai Mountains and across the Kazakh steppe to Almaty. The line was first planned in the last years of the tsarist empire, when the initial segment of track was laid between Barnaul and Semipalatinsk. It was not completed, however, until the Soviet period, after Stalin made the Turk-Sib one of the more prominent construction projects of the first five-year plan.

The 1929 silent
documentary Turksib
about the Turk-Sib railway
is a classic example of
socialist-realist cinema
by Soviet film director
Viktor Turin.

The route was opened in 1931. The railway was built to facilitate the exchange of Central Asian cotton for western Siberian grain. This trade would keep the looms busy in the textile factories of the north, while the import of cheap food would free up more land for cotton cultivation in the south. The construction of the Turk-Sib was also meant to stimulate industrial development in the region, hence its nickname, 'the Forge of the Kazakh Proletariat'.

In 1996, newly independent Kazakhstan took over its section of the line for a state-managed railway firm. From the southern terminus at Lugovaya, the line extends to Chimknet in western Kazakhstan and to Bishkek in Kyrgyzstan.

The Baikal-Amur Mainline

The 4234km Baikalo-Amurskaya Magistral (Baikal-Amur Mainline, or BAM) begins west of Irkutsk and passes north of Lake Baikal on its way east to the Pacific coast; for details of travel along it see p239. The route was first considered as an option for the eastern end of the Trans-Siberian line in the 1880s, but it would not be until the 1930s that work actually started on its construction, the first phase being from Tayshet to Bratsk (p242).

1956	1974
Services start along Beijing to Ulaanbaatar line, but stop again in 1960s	Construction of BAM resumes

Although parts of the far eastern end of the line were built from 1944 partly using Japanese and German POWs as labour, the project was put on indefinite hold in 1953 after the death of Stalin. Its resumption, amid much propaganda fanfare, came in 1974, when Leonid Brezhnev hailed it the 'Hero Project of the Century'. The call went out to the youth of the Soviet Union to rally to the challenge of constructing the BAM. The response is evident from the names of towns along the line: Estbam, Latbam and Litbam, so called for the young workers from the Baltic states who built them.

The BAM was badly mismanaged. Instead of a construction chief, 16 different industrial ministries organised their own separate work teams with minimal coordination. By 1980, 50% of the managers had been replaced because of 'unsatisfactory work'. The project employed 100,000 workers, including 20,000 communist youth league 'volunteers'. Lacking housing and electricity, few workers re-enlisted and others simply deserted.

The BAM epitomised the best and worst of Soviet industrialisation. It blazed a trail through inhospitable climate and terrain, providing access to the region's mineral-rich basins. The BAM towns expanded with the new railway, which was being forced through virgin wilderness. Overcoming Siberia's swamps, its seven mountain ranges, its seemingly infinite number of rivers and, in particular, its vast swath of permafrost, pushed the cost of the project to a staggering US$25 billion (the original Trans-Siberian is estimated to have cost the equivalent of $500 million).

The BAM was officially opened in 1991, when it became possible to travel the whole length from Tayshet to Sovetskaya Gavan on the Pacific coast. However, the line's 15.34km Severomuysk tunnel, the longest in Russia, was only completed in 2003.

In 1984 a golden spike was used to connect the eastern and western ends of the BAM.

Go to www.eng.rzd.ru to read Russian Railway's PR version of the history of the BAM line.

The Trans-Korean

A new branch line is tentatively planned for the future. The Trans-Korean line, from Seoul in the south to Wonson in the north, would recreate the old Kyongwan Railway, from the early 20th century. The line would connect with the Trans-Siberian at Vladivostok, establishing an overland rail route between the Korean Peninsula and Central Asia and Europe.

A small but significant step forward was taken in September 2000, when North and South Korean leaders agreed to restore a short train service across the world's most heavily fortified border. To promote the project, North Korean leader Kim Jong Il made a much publicised junket

---

HIGH-SPEED TRAINS

It's unlikely that in the near future there will be high-speed trains, à la Japan's Shinkansen and France's TGVs, running along the entire Trans-Siberian route. However, Russian Railways is beginning to invest in high-speed rail infrastructure and locomotives. In March 2005 it signed an agreement with Germany's Siemens AG to manufacture 60 new generation high-speed electric trains – these will run along the Moscow–St Petersburg route as well as St Petersburg to Helsinki, Moscow to Minsk, and Moscow to major yet-to-be-specified Russian cities.

1980	1991
Trans-Mongolian and Trans-Manchurian lines reopen	Official opening of the BAM

on the Trans-Siberian in the summer of 2001. In Moscow, Kim met with Russia's President Vladimir Putin, and they announced that the Trans-Korean was 'entering the stage of active development'.

SIBERIA IN TRANSITION

After decades of overbearing central control, the fall of the communist regime in 1991 ignited a spontaneous diffusion of power across Russia's regions. This process was accelerated by Russia's President Boris Yeltsin, who urged regional leaders to 'take as much sovereignty as you can swallow'.

In Siberia, these dramatic events rekindled the separatist spirit. Siberian Accord, a confederation of regional political actors, was founded in Novosibirsk in 1991. Resentful of Moscow's grabbing hand, they were determined to wrest control of Siberia's natural resources away from central-government ministries. President Yeltsin, a former regional governor himself, defused the conflict through a negotiated compromise, by which Siberia's regions were granted greater political autonomy and a larger share of the region's wealth. His successor, Putin, however, has pursued a policy of gradual recentralisation.

In some ways, post-communist Siberia has come to resemble the 'Wild Wild East' of olden days. The privatisation of state property has given rise to a new breed of economic adventurer. Those who have succeeded in gaining control over Siberia's prized natural resources have reaped great fortunes. Siberia's regional governors openly defy the Kremlin's edicts and pillage the local economy for private gain.

Outlying towns and villages have been abandoned for lack of work and food. As a result, people are now leaving Siberia in droves. On a more positive note, the major cities along the railway, which were closed even to Soviet citizens, have been opened and integrated into the new post-Soviet Siberia. In foreign affairs, the improvement in Russian-Chinese relations has reopened the border in the Far East. The old Trans-Siberian link to Manchuria has been re-established and now supports a thriving business in cross-border trade and smuggling.

Some things, however, never change. For reasons of national security and public service, the Trans-Siberian Railway remains a state-managed monopoly. It continues to be one of the busiest railway lines in the world. Most importantly, the Trans-Siberian endures as the vital lifeline for the people of Siberia.

Electrification of the Trans-Siberian line, begun in 1929 and finally completed in 2002, allows a doubling of train weights, to 6000 tonnes.

In 2003 Russian Railways became a joint-stock company with the federal government, the sole owner of shares estimated at R1545.2 billion (more than US$50 billion).

The Cultures

A Trans-Siberian journey is a great opportunity to meet with Russians from all walks of life and to get to grips with Russia's culture. Those travelling the Trans-Mongolian and Trans-Manchurian routes can do likewise in both China and Mongolia. The following sections cover the basics, to help you start making some sense of these three countries.

Teach Yourself World Cultures: Russia, by Stephen and Tatyana Webber, is a decent layperson's stab at decoding all aspects of Russian culture.

RUSSIA
The National Psyche

Compared with the Chinese and Mongolians, Russians can initially come across as rather unfriendly. Although surly, uncommunicative Russians are still found in certain 'service' industries (things are, however, rapidly improving), the overwhelming Russian character trait is one of genuine humanity and hospitality. Once the ice has been broken on the train and in the towns you pass through, you'll typically find yourself being regaled with stories, drowned in vodka and stuffed full of food. This can be especially true outside the big cities, where you'll meet locals determined to share everything they have with you, however meagre their resources.

Unsmiling gloom and fatalistic melancholy remain archetypically Russian, but this is often used as a foil to a deadpan, sarcastic humour. You'll soon learn how deeply most Russians love their country. They will sing the praises of Mother Russia's great contributions to the arts and sciences, its long history and its abundant physical attributes, then just as loudly point out its many failures. The dark side of this patriotism is an unpleasant streak of racism. Don't let it put you off, and take heart in the knowledge that as much as foreigners may be perplexed about the true nature of the Russian soul, the locals themselves still don't have it figured out either! As the poet Fyodor Tyutchev said, 'You can't understand Russia with reason… you can only believe in her'.

Lifestyle

In the world's biggest country the way of life of a Nenets reindeer herder in Siberia is radically different from that of a marketing executive in Moscow or an Islamic factory worker in Kazan. Not only this, as Russia grows more prosperous, the gap between rich and poor – and the lives they lead – becomes larger.

THE RULES OF RUSSIAN HOSPITALITY

- If you're invited to a Russian home, always bring a gift, such as wine or a cake.
- Shaking hands across the threshold is considered unlucky. Wait until you're fully inside.
- If you give anyone flowers, makes sure there's an odd number as even numbers are for funerals.
- Remove your shoes and coat on entering a house.
- Once the festivities begin, refusing offered food or drink can cause grave offence.
- Vodka is for toasting, not for casual sipping. Wait for the cue.
- When you are in any setting with other people, even strangers such as those in a train compartment, it's polite to share anything you have to eat, drink or smoke.
- Traditional gentlemanly behaviour is not just appreciated but expected, as you will notice when you see women standing in front of closed doors waiting for something to happen.

A GUIDE TO BANYA ETIQUETTE *Steve Kokker*

After stripping down in the sex-segregated changing room, wishing '*Lyogkogo* (read as lyokh-kava) *para*' to their mates (meaning something like 'May your steam be easy!'), bathers head off into the *parilka* (steam room). After the birch-branch thrashing (best experienced lying down on a bench, with someone else administering the 'beating'), bathers run outside and, depending on their nerve, plunge into the *basseyn* (ice-cold pool).

With eyelids draped back over their skull, they stagger back into the changing room to their mates' wishes of '*Slyogkim parom*' (Hope your steam was easy!). Finally, bathers drape themselves in sheets, sip restorative cups of tea or beer and discuss world issues before repeating the process. Most *banya* experts go through the motions about five to 10 times over a two-hour period.

This said, there are common features to life across Russia. For the vast majority of urban Russians, home is within a drab, ugly housing complex of Soviet vintage. Although quite cosy and prettily decorated on the inside, these apartments are typically cramped and come with no attached garden. Instead, a large percentage of Russian families have a dacha, a small country house. Often little more than a bare-bones hut (but sometimes quite luxurious) these retreats offer Russians refuge from city life and as such figure prominently in the national psyche. On half-warm weekends, places such as Moscow begin to empty out early on Friday as people head to the country. Around Siberian cities, such as Irkutsk and Chita, the small wooden dwellings you see close to the train tracks will be dacha, too.

One of the most important aspects of dacha life is gardening. Families grow all manner of vegetables and fruits to eat over the winter. Flowers also play an important part in creating the proper dacha ambience, and even among people who have no need to grow food the contact with the soil provides an important balm for the Russian soul. It's also quite likely that a dacha will have a traditional *banya* (hot bath) attached to it.

Go to www.unpo.org and www.eki.ee/books /redbook for profiles of over 80 ethnic groups in lands currently or once ruled by Russia.

For centuries, travellers to Russia have commented on the particular (in many people's eyes, peculiar) traditions of the *banya*. To this day, Russians make it an important part of their week and you can't say you've really been to Russia unless you've visited a *banya*. The main element of the *banya* is the *parilka* (steam room). Here, rocks are heated by a furnace, with water poured onto them using a long-handled ladle. Often, a few drops of eucalyptus or pine oils (sometimes even beer) are added to the water, creating a scent in the burst of scalding steam that's released into the room. After this some people stand up, grab hold of a *venik* (a tied bundle of birch branches) and beat themselves or each other with it. Though it can be painful, the effect can also be pleasant and cleansing: apparently, the birch leaves (sometimes oak or, agonisingly, juniper branches) and their secretions help rid the skin of toxins.

Many city *banya* are run-down and unappealing (a classy exception is Moscow's splendid Sanduny Baths, p111). Grab any chance to try a traditional countryside *banya:* nearly all the guesthouses on Olkhon Island in Lake Baikal (see p203) have them.

Population

Close on three-quarters of Russia's 143.5 million people live in cities and towns. Rural communities are withering: in the 2002 census, of Russia's 155,000 villages, 13,000 had been deserted and 35,000 had populations of less than 10 people.

Russia is also facing an alarming natural decline in its population – around 0.45% per year. In the last decade alone the population has plummeted by some six million people. The average life expectancy for a Russian man is 60 years, for a woman 74. At current rates the population will decline to 123 million by 2030. Much of this is due to the population's staggering health problems related to a diet high in alcohol and fat. Accidental deaths due to drunkenness are frequent.

About 81.5% of Russia's people are ethnic Russians. The next largest ethnic groups are Tatars with 3.8% (the capital of Tatarstan is Kazan), followed by Ukrainians (3%), Chuvash (1.2%), Bashkirs (0.9%), Belarusians (0.8%) and Moldavians (0.7%). The remaining 8.1% belong to dozens of smaller ethnic groups, all with their own languages and cultural traditions (in varying degrees of usage), and practising different religions.

Over 30 original indigenous Siberian and Russian Far East peoples now make up less than 5% of the region's total population. Along the Trans-Siberian routes, the main ethnic groups you'll encounter are Mongol Buryats in and around Ulan-Ude (see p212) and Lake Baikal; and the Nanai in the lower Amur River basin near Khabarovsk.

Anna Reid's *The Shaman's Coat* is both a fascinating history of the major native peoples of Siberia and the Russian Far East and a lively travelogue of her journeys through the region.

Media

Genuine freedom of speech has migrated from TV to the newspapers, the best of which offer editorial opinions largely independent of their owners' or the government's views. The leading paper, and one of the most respected, is *Kommersant,* owned by the anti-Putin Boris Berezovsky, closely followed by *Izvestiya* (bought in 2005 by Gazprom, the state-owned gas monopoly). *Novaya Gazeta* is a staunchly anti-Putin tabloid. Other tabloid-type (but not necessarily format) papers are *Komsomolskaya Pravda;* the Putin-friendly *Argumenty i Fakty;* and *Moskovsky Komsomolets,* which varies with the political wind.

He who controls the TV in Russia, rules the country – and no-one else understands this better than President Vladimir Putin who has waded in with all the might of the state against channels such as NTV that once dared to criticize his administration. Not that Russian TV is managed by some sort of Soviet-styled spooks. In fact the heads of the main state channels – Channel 1 and Rossiya – were among those young journalists who gave Russian audiences a taste of editorial freedom in the 1990s. Many faces on the screen remain the same, but news and analysis are increasingly uncontroversial.

Russian TV provides a wide choice of programmes, some modelled on Western formats, some unique to Russia. Documentaries have been

---

RUSSIA'S RAILWAY GAZETTE

Although those in charge at the old Soviet mouthpiece *Izvestiya* may challenge it, *Gudok* claims to be the longest consistently published daily newspaper in Russia. *Gudok* – which means signal and also denotes the whistle sound of trains – has been in business since December 1917. The importance of a newspaper for the railway workers was instantly recognised by Vladimir Ilych Lenin and the Bolsheviks who knew the only way they could gain a grip on such a huge country would be to control the railways.

Still partly owned by Russian Railways and the trade union of railway workers, the broadsheet had writers of the calibre of Mikhail Bugakov (author of *The Master and Margarita*) working for it in the 1920s and 1930s. In today's competitive media market, *Gudok* takes a populist approach to news coverage. You should be able to find it – only available in Cyrillic – on sale at stations across the country.

especially good in the last years, and the national channel Kultura, dedicated entirely to arts and culture, is always worth a look. RenTV, a channel owned by the state power grid, has news coverage with a bit more bite.

See also p296.

Religion

The English website of the Russian Orthodox Church, containing details of its history and current practices, can be found at www.mospat.ru.

Since the end of the atheist Soviet Union, religion has made an incredible comeback in Russia, and in particular the Russian Orthodox Church (Russkaya Pravoslavnaya Tserkov). Since 1997 the Russian Orthodox Church has been legally recognised as the leading faith, but the Russian constitution enshrines religious freedom so the Church respects Islam (the country's second-largest religion with up to 20 million practitioners), Judaism, Buddhism and the nation's myriad animist religions.

Along the Trans-Siberian route you'll have chances to encounter many of these religions in buildings ranging from St Petersburg's **Grand Choral Synagogue** (☎ 713 8186; Lermontovsky pr 2; ⏰ 11am-3pm Mon-Wed, 11am-2pm Thu & Fri, services 10am Sat; Ⓜ Sadovaya or Sennaya Ploshchad) to Kazan's Kul Sharif Mosque (p144) and the Buddhist *datsans* (temples) near Ulan-Ude (p217) and Chita (p222) in Siberia. Most often, though, it will be the Russian Orthodox Churches, many with soaring onion-dome cupolas, that will leave the most vivid impression.

Russian Orthodoxy is highly traditional, and the atmosphere inside a church is formal and solemn. Churches have no seats, no music (only melodic chanting) and many icons (see p48), before which people will often be seen praying, lighting candles and even kissing the ground.

The Virgin Mary (*Bogomater;* Mother of God) is greatly honoured. The language of the liturgy is 'Church Slavonic', the old Bulgarian dialect into which the Bible was first translated for Slavs. Paskha (Easter) is the focus of the Church year, with festive midnight services launching Easter Day.

In most churches, Divine Liturgy (Bozhestvennaya Liturgia), lasting about two hours, is held at 8am, 9am or 10am Monday to Saturday, and usually at 7am and 10am on Sunday and festival days. Most churches also hold services at 5pm or 6pm daily.

Arts

Much of Russia's enormous contribution to world culture in most domains of the arts has been since the 19th century.

MUSIC, BALLET & OPERA

Many visitors will want to see a Russian ballet or opera performance at either Moscow's famous Bolshoi (p118), or St Petersburg's Mariinsky (p92), home of the Kirov Ballet. Ballet and opera are generally performed at the same venues, which are often architectural masterpieces in them-

---

CHURCH-GOING DOS & DON'TS

As a rule, working churches are open to one and all, but as a visitor take care not to disturb any devotions or to offend sensibilities. On entering a church men bare their heads, while women usually cover their heads. Women visitors can often get away without covering their heads, but miniskirts are unwelcome and even trousers on women sometimes attract disapproval. Hands in pockets, or crossed arms or legs, may attract frowns. Photography at services is generally not welcome; if in doubt, you should ask permission first.

selves. The ballerinas in Novosibirsk may not be as fleet-footed, and the operas in Ulan-Ude may be in Buryat, but tickets can be remarkably good value compared with what you'll pay in Moscow or St Petersburg.

The roots of Russian music lie in folk song and dance and Orthodox Church chants. Mikhail Glinka (1804–57), in operas like *A Life for the Tsar* and *Ruslan and Lyudmila,* was the first to merge these with Western forms. Modest Mussorgsky (1839–81), Nikolai Rimsky-Korsakov (1844–1908) and Alexander Borodin (1833–87) continued to explore and develop Slav roots.

Pyotr Tchaikovsky (1840–93) also used folk motifs but was closer to the Western tradition. His *1812 Overture,* his ballets *Swan Lake* and *The Nutcracker,* and his opera *Eugene Onegin* are still among the world's most popular works. Sergei Rachmaninov (1873–1943), Igor Stravinsky (1882–1971) and Dmitry Shostakovich (1906–75) are other influential composers of the 20th century.

Russian music is not all about classical composers. Ever since the Beatles broke through the Iron Curtain of the 1960s, Russians both young and old have been keen to sign up for the pop revolution. By the 1970s and 1980s punk and heavy metal were influencing local groups such as Akvarium, DDT and Nautilus Pompilius. The god of Russian rock, though, was Viktor Tsoy, lead singer of the group Kino. His early death in a 1990 car crash ensured his legendary status; his grave, at the Bogoslovskogo Cemetery in St Petersburg, has been turned into a shrine, much like Jim Morrison's in Paris. There's also the 'Tsoy Wall' on ul Arbat in Moscow, covered with Tsoy-related graffiti. Russia's doyenne of pop is Alla Pugacheva who's still belting the hits out in her 50s. Among current artists to listen out for are Leningrad, an entertaining group of rockers from St Petersburg, as well as the singer Zemfira, and progressive rock group Mumiy Troll.

LITERATURE
Russia's equivalent of Shakespeare is Alexander Pushkin (1799–1837); he's revered as the father of Russian literature and you'll find many Russians who can recite some of his verses, usually from his most famous work, *Yevgeny Onegin.* Mikhail Lermontov (1814–41) is another major figure, who like Pushkin died young in a duel.

Nikolai Gogol (1809–52) was a master of romantic realism; his classics include the mordantly satiric *Dead Souls* and *The Inspector General.* Fyodor Dostoevsky (1821–81) is internationally known for the St Petersburg–based *Crime and Punishment, The Idiot* and *The Brothers Karamazov.* His four years of hard labour in a camp near Omsk formed the basis of *The House of the Dead.* Other giants of literature include Leo Tolstoy (1828–1910; *War and Peace* and *Anna Karenina*) and the playwright Anton Chekhov (1860–1904). Boris Pasternak (1890–1960) wrote *Dr Zhivago,* which was filmed on an epic scale by David Lean, and possibly did more than any work to influence Western perceptions of Siberia. It's a richly philosophical, epic novel offering personal insights into the revolution and Russian civil war. Pasternak had to smuggle it into Britain in 1958 to get it published.

Russian publishing is currently booming with the traditional Russian love of books as strong as ever. One of the most popular novelists is Boris Akunin whose series of historical detective novels featuring the foppish Russian Sherlock Holmes, Erast Fandorin, include *The Winter Queen,* and *Turkish Gambit,* made into a recent hit Russian movie. The award-winning novels of Andrei Makine, born in the Russian Far East but long

Natasha's Dance: A Cultural History of Russia by Orlando Figes is a fascinating book that offers plenty of colourful anecdotes about great Russian writers, artists, composers and architects.

based in France where he has won the country's top two literary awards, are also worth discovering, especially *A Hero's Daughter,* which charts the impact of the Soviet Union on a family from WWII to the 1990s. His *Once Upon the River of Love* is about life in a small village near the Trans-Siberian Railway.

VISUAL ARTS

Up until the 17th century religious icons were Russia's key art form, though clearly they were conceived as religious artefacts and only in the 20th century did they really come to be seen as 'works of art'.

In the 18th century, Peter the Great encouraged Western trends in Russian art, which led to the Peredvizhniki (Wanderers) movement in the following century. The movement gained its name from the touring exhibitions with which it widened its audience, and its leading figures included Vasily Surikov, infamous for painting vivid Russian historical scenes; Nikolai Ghe, who depicted biblical and historical scenes; and Ilya Repin, perhaps the best-loved of all Russian artists. The best places to view works by these artists are St Petersburg's Russian Museum (p85) and Moscow's Tretyakov Gallery (p110).

At the start of the 20th century, Russian artists dabbled in impressionism, Art Nouveau and symbolism as well as a home-grown avant-garde futurist movement, which in turn helped Western art go head over heels. Notable artists of this period include Natalia Goncharova, Vasily Kandinsky and Kasimir Malevich. Socialist realism was the driving force during the early and mid-Soviet periods when art had to serve the state's political purposes.

Artists are now freer than they ever were to depict all aspects of Russian life. Although many contemporary painters of note have left Russia for the riches of the West, the country is still churning out promising young artists; for a review of some of the most interesting go to www.waytorussia.net/whatisrussia/art.html. The **Moscow Biennale of Contemporary Art** (http://moscowbiennale.ru/en), a month-long festival organised and partly funded by Russia's Ministry of Culture, aims to establish the capital as an international centre for contemporary art.

CINEMA

From Sergei Eisenstein's *Battleship Potemkin* (1925) right through to Alexey German's *My Friend Ivan Lapshin* (1982), Soviet cinema ex-

> An excellent website devoted to Russian architecture is http://archi.ru/english/, which has an index of the country's key buildings.

ARCHITECTURE IN SIBERIA

Although you'll find traditional Russian wooden architecture across European Russia, Siberia has the best examples. Many villages, relatively accessible around Lake Baikal and in the Barguzin Valley, retain whole streets of *izba* (log houses) whose main decorative features are carved, brightly painted window frames. This construction style was taken further in Siberian city town houses, where the carvings of eaves and window frames became so intricate that they're now known as 'wooden lace'. The classic place to see this is Tomsk (p179), although some great individual examples have survived in Krasnoyarsk, Irkutsk (p194), Tobolsk (p160) and Tyumen (p156).

Before the Russians colonised Siberia, native Siberians were mostly nomadic. Their traditional dwellings fall into three main types: tepee-style cones of poles covered with skins or strips of bark (the Evenki *chum*); hexagonal or cylindrical frameworks of poles covered with brush and earth (the Altai *ail*, or similar western Buryatian equivalents); and round, felt-covered tent houses (the yurts of nomadic Tuvan and Kazakh herders). Examples of all these dwellings can be found in open-air museums, including near Bratsk (p243), Listvyanka and Ulan-Ude (p215).

celled in producing classic movies. Eisenstein's *Alexander Nevsky* (1938) contains one of cinema's great battle scenes. Mikhail Kalatozov's *The Cranes are Flying* (1957) – a love story set during WWII – was awarded the Palme d'Or at Cannes in 1958. Of later Soviet directors, the dominant figure was Andrei Tarkovsky, whose films include *Andrei Rublyov* (1966) and *Solaris* (1972), the Russian answer to *2001: A Space Odyssey*.

Nikita Mikhalkov's *Burnt by the Sun* won the Oscar for Best Foreign Film in 1994 but, at that time, Russian film production was suffering as state funding dried up and audiences stayed away from cinemas. By the end of the decade the local industry was back on track with hits such as Alexey Balabanov's gangster drama *Brother* (1997), Alexander Sokurov's *Molokh* (1999) and the ambitious *Russian Ark* (2002) set in the Hermitage, and Andrei Zvyagintsev's moody thriller *The Return* (2003). A recent success is Timur Bekmambetov's sci-fi fantasy thriller *Night Watch* (2004).

CHINA
The National Psyche
Despite having experienced tremendous social upheaval over the past century, and having to cope with current political and economic uncertainties, the Chinese remain an energetic and optimistic people, excited about the rapid modernisation taking place in their country. With the 2008 Olympic bandwagon in full swing, the Chinese are eager to introduce their long-standing cultural traditions to the world and be accepted as a modern, progressive nation.

The concept of 'face' is important: it means not behaving in a way that would embarrass someone and cause them to lose status in front of their peers. One sure way for foreigners to make someone lose face in China is to lose their temper in public. Not only will the person targeted lose face, the foreigner loses face as well for being weak and unable to control their emotions. The Chinese pride themselves on self-control and when flustered or embarrassed will often giggle or give an evasive response, rather than deal with the situation directly.

Despite language barriers, you'll regularly meet locals who are eager to strike up a conversation and, for many, practise their English. In some rural areas, foreigners remain an exotic curiosity and will be greeted with stares, giggles and a chorus of 'hellos' that can irritate even the most thick-skinned of travellers. Getting angry doesn't help – it's likely your Chinese audience will have no idea why you are getting angry and fits of temper will inevitably create more excitement and draw larger crowds.

The lack of privacy is perhaps one of the most disconcerting aspects of a visit to China. Most Chinese grow up in small apartments in crowded conditions and are not accustomed to Western standards of privacy. This applies to trains, buses, tourist sites and even toilets.

The website http://chineseculture.about.com is a good resource on culture and society in China with links to a variety of topics including food, holidays and martial arts.

Lifestyle
Chinese culture is traditionally centred on the family. In past Chinese society, the family provided support for every family member, including livelihood and long-term security. Extended family remains exceedingly important, with grandparents commonly acting as caretakers for grandchildren and with adult children working and financially supporting their ageing parents.

The end of cradle-to-grave welfare (the 'iron rice bowl') has brought increasing pressure on families who struggle to meet the rising costs of health care and education. Economic pressures have had an impact on

---

CHINESE ETIQUETTE DOS & DON'TS

- When beckoning to someone, wave them over to you with your palm down, motioning to yourself.

- If someone gives a gift, put it aside to open later to avoid appearing greedy.

- Always take off your shoes when entering a Chinese home.

- When meeting a Chinese family, greet the eldest person first, as a sign of respect.

- Always present things to people with both hands, showing that what you are offering is the fullest extent of yourself.

---

many young Chinese who are putting off marriage or having children until they've acquired enough money to ensure their financial security. It's estimated that today 14% of Chinese urban households consist of a single adult, or a childless couple who both work.

The rapid development of the 1990s has raised the standard of living for many Chinese, who now face a dazzling array of consumer choice and experience a lifestyle very different from earlier generations. Unfortunately, recent educational and economic opportunities are only available to a small segment of the population. The majority of Chinese live in the countryside, shut off from the benefits of China's economic reforms.

The growing gap between China's rich and poor is one of the worst in the world. The rural communities in inland China are the most poverty stricken, but those on the investment-laden east coast fare better. Farmers who can least afford it are expected to pay for their own health care and the education of their children. Many rural families have been forced to move to the cities, where they often find low-paying jobs in unsafe conditions. The government has promised to address these devastating trends, but few incentives have been put in place.

Red Azalea by Anchee Min is a moving story of a young woman caught up in the horrors of the Cultural Revolution.

While all of this sounds pretty bleak, development has also had some positive effects. With an increasingly open society, and with more exposure to the outside world, the Chinese are finding new forms of self-expression that were previously frowned upon by the communist authorities. Artists and writers are freeing themselves from earlier political restraints, contributing to a burgeoning literary and art scene that has been stifled for many years. Censorship is still common, though what defines something as 'taboo' or 'off limits' can be arbitrary.

Population

China is home to 56 ethnic groups, with Han Chinese making up 92% of the population. China's other ethnic groups are usually referred to as 'national minorities'. One of the largest minority groups is Mongolian, found in the Inner Mongolia region in the north of the country, bordering Mongolia proper.

China faces enormous population pressures, despite comprehensive programs to curb its growth. Over 40.5% of China's population live in urban centres, putting great pressure on land and water resources. It's estimated that China's total population will continue to grow at a rate of eight to 10 million each year and even with population programs such as the one-child policy, experts claim that China needs at least 30 more years to achieve zero population growth. The unbalanced gender ratio (117 boys to every 100 girls) and a rapidly ageing population are serious problems that the authorities are trying to address.

Media

All media is strictly controlled and censored. China's largest-circulation Chinese-language daily is the *People's Daily*. It has an English-language edition on www.english.peopledaily.com.cn.

Chinese Central TV (CCTV) has an English-language channel, CCTV9. CCTV4 also has some English programmes. Your hotel may have ESPN, Star Sports, CNN or BBC News 24. See also p296.

Religion

Chinese religion has been influenced by three streams of human thought: Taoism, Confucianism and Buddhism. All three have been inextricably entwined in popular Chinese religion along with ancient animist beliefs. The founders of Taoism, Confucianism and Buddhism have been deified. The Chinese worship them and their disciples as fervently as they worship their own ancestors and a pantheon of gods and spirits.

The Chinese communist government professes atheism. It considers religion to be base superstition, a remnant of old China used by the ruling classes to keep power. Nevertheless, in an effort to improve relations with the Muslim, Buddhist and Lamaist minorities, in 1982 the Chinese government amended its constitution to allow freedom of religion. However, only atheists are permitted to be members of the Chinese Communist Party (CCP). Since almost all of China's 55 minority groups adhere to one religion or another, this rule precludes most of them from becoming party members.

Muslims are believed to be the largest identifiable religious group still active in China today, numbering perhaps 2% to 3% of the nation's population. The government has not published official figures of the number of Buddhists – hardly surprising given the ideological battle it has been waging with Tibetan Buddhists, who have been fighting for decades to preserve their culture if not their country. There are around three million Catholics and four million Protestants. It's impossible to determine the number of Taoists, but the number of Taoist priests is very small.

'The Chinese communist government professes atheism'

Traditional Chinese religious beliefs took a battering during the Cultural Revolution when monasteries were disbanded, temples were destroyed and the monks were sometimes killed or sent to the fields to labour. Since Mao's death, the Chinese government allowed many temples (sometimes with their own contingent of monks and novices) to reopen as active places of worship. All religious activity is firmly under state control and many of the monks are caretakers within renovated shells of monasteries, which serve principally as tourist attractions and are pale shadows of their former selves.

Arts

With its long, unbroken history and culture, China has made one of the greatest artistic contributions to humankind. Sadly, much of China's ancient art treasures have been destroyed in times of civil war or dispersed by invasion or natural calamity. Many of China's remaining great paintings, ceramics, jade and other works of art were rescued by exile beyond the mainland – in Taiwan, Singapore, Hong Kong and elsewhere. Fortunately since the early 1970s a great deal of work has been done to restore what was destroyed in the Cultural Revolution.

China today has a flourishing contemporary art scene, with private galleries competing with government-run museums and exhibition halls. Chinese artists are increasingly catching the attention of the international art world and joint exhibitions with European or American artists are now

---

CHINESE OPERA

Chinese opera has been in existence formally since the northern Song dynasty (AD 960), developing out of China's long balladic tradition. Performances were put on by travelling entertainers, often families, in teahouses frequented by China's working classes. Performances were drawn from popular legends and folklore. Over 300 different types of opera developed throughout the country, with Beijing opera being officially recognised in 1790, when performances were staged for the imperial family.

Chinese opera is fascinating for its use of make-up, acrobatics and elaborate costumes. Face painting derives from the early use of masks worn by players and each colour suggests the personality and attributes that define a character. Chinese audiences can tell instantly the personality of characters by their painted faces. In addition, the status of a character is suggested by the size of headdress worn – the more elaborate, the more significant the character. The four major roles in Chinese opera are the female role, the male role, the 'painted-face' role (for gods and warriors) and the clown.

---

common. The second **Beijing Biennale** (www.bjbiennale.com.cn) held in September 2005 included 500 works from over 60 different countries. In the capital you'll also have the chance to see the traditional performance art of Chinese Opera (see above).

Along the Trans-Manchurian route the architecture stands out from the rest of China, primarily as a result of foreign influences in the region. At the turn of the 20th century, much of Manchuria was occupied – either economically or militarily – by Russia, Japan and various European powers, all of whom left their mark on the cities in this region. The best example is Tianjin, which contains quarters once dominated by Austro-Hungarians, Belgians, Germans, Italians and Japanese. In Daoliqu (p275), the oldest part of Harbin, onion domes and ornamental façades reveal the city's Russian roots.

MONGOLIA
The National Psyche
The nomadic life of the people, the timelessness of the land and the delicate relationship with the earth and its resources have all had a profound effect on the Mongolian character. These factors have made Mongolians humble, adaptable, unfettered by stringent protocol, good-humoured and uncannily stoic. You may well wonder if these are the same people that for centuries were vilified in the West as the 'scourge of God'. Indeed, compared with Russians and Chinese you're likely to find Mongolians the most easily approachable in terms of attitudes.

The great emptiness of their landscape has seemingly kindled a strong curiosity of outsiders. But, more significantly, it has also made hospitality a matter of sheer necessity rather than a chore or social obligation. Hospitality is something that is, quite simply, crucial to survival. In effect, every home on the steppes serves as a hotel, restaurant, pub, repair shop and information centre. This hospitality extends readily to strangers and it is usually given without fanfare or excitement.

The Mongolian *ger* (traditional, circular felt tent) plays a vital role in shaping both the Mongolian character and family life. Its small confines compels families to interact with one another, to share everything and to work together, tightening relationships between relatives. It promotes patience, makes inhibitions fade away and prevents privacy. It also hardens the sensibilities: *ger* dwellers must fetch their own water and fuel, difficult tasks especially in the dead of winter.

Lifestyle

Half the population of Mongolia lives permanently in urban areas, while the other half are either truly nomadic, or seminomadic, living in villages in the winter and grazing their animals on the steppes during the rest of the year. Urban Mongolians typically live in Russian-style apartment blocks while the nomads live in the one-room, felt *ger*.

Usually equipped with traditional furnishings that are painted bright orange with fanciful designs, *gers* are set out in a like manner with three beds around the perimeter, a chest covered with Buddhist relics at the back wall and a low table for dining. Everything revolves around a central hearth, with the women's side to the right and the men's to the left. The head of the household sits at the northern end of the *ger* with the most honoured guest to the right. The area near the door is the place of lowest rank and the domain of children.

Ovoos (large piles of rocks on Mongolian mountain passes) are repositories of offerings for local spirits. Walk around an *ovoo* clockwise three times, toss an offering onto the pile (another rock should suffice) and make a wish.

Although one-third of Mongolians live well below the poverty line (less than US$30 per month), this does not necessarily mean that people are going hungry. The reason is the strong family network. One family member with a decent job has the responsibility to support their family and distribute their wealth among siblings. Approximately 100,000 Mongolians live and work abroad, about 8% of the workforce, and many send money home to their families. In Ulaanbaatar, an average salary is US$100 per month and steadily climbing.

Since the late 1990s there has been a major shift to urban areas, especially Ulaanbaatar, which is bursting at the seams. With the exception of a handful of places benefiting by either mining or tourism, rural areas languish in neglect.

Population

The great majority (about 86%) of Mongolians are Khalkh Mongolians (*khalkh* means 'shield'). The other sizable ethnic group, the Kazakhs, make up about 6% (110,000) of the population and live in western Mongolia. The remaining 8% of the population are ethnic minority groups, including some 47,500 ethnic Buryats who live along the border with Russia. Population growth is at an all-time low, having fallen from 2.4% to 1.4% over the past 15 years. The government is planning subsidies for newlyweds and newborns.

MONGOLIAN ETIQUETTE DOS & DON'TS

When meeting Mongolians or visiting a *ger* (yurt), note the following customs and habits:

- Avoid walking in front of an older person, or turning your back to the altar or religious objects (except when leaving).
- If someone offers you their snuff bottle, accept it with your right hand. If you don't take the snuff, at least sniff the top part of the bottle.
- Try to keep *ger* visits to less than two hours to avoid interrupting the family's work.
- Don't point a knife in any way at anyone; when passing a knife to someone ensure that the handle is facing the recipient; and use the knife to cut towards you, not away.
- Don't point your feet at the hearth, at the altar or at another person. Sleep with your feet pointing towards the door.
- If you have stepped on anyone, or kicked their feet, immediately shake their hand.
- Don't stand on, or lean over, the threshold, or lean against a support column.
- Don't touch another person's hat.

THE GREAT MONGOLIAN HERO

Although generally reviled as a bloodthirsty barbarian in the West, Chinggis (Genghis) Khaan (c AD 1167–1227) is a national hero in Mongolia. His legacy is very much a modern-day rallying point for Mongolians who are proud of what their fearless ancestor achieved. Chinggis' face adorns money, stamps, even vodka, and an Ulaanbaatar hotel, rock band and brewery are named after him.

Having been voted 'Man of the Millennium' by *Time* magazine, the tide of opinion on the great Khaan is changing. Adding weight to the argument that he was as much a skilful diplomat as brutal warrior are books such as *Genghis Khan and the Making of the Modern World* by Jack Weatherford. Trans-Mongolian travellers might also want to ponder how he practically pioneered travel from China to the eastern edge of Europe way back in the 13th century.

Media

Mongolia's media is pretty free to express antigovernment opinions compared with that in Russia and certainly China. Major daily newspapers in Mongolia include *Ardiin Erkh* (People's Right), *Zunny Medee* (Century News), *Odriin Sonin* (Daily News) and *Önöödör* (Today).

All the TV stations have political allies; Channel 25 favours the democrats, Channel 9 prefers the Mongolian People's Revolutionary Party (MPRP) and the others go with whomever is in power. MNTV has a 10-minute news bulletin in English at 10pm on Monday, Wednesday and Friday. Local TV stations don't start broadcasting until the afternoon and switch off around 11pm.

See also p296.

Religion

Around 80% of Mongolians claim to be Buddhist of the Mahayana school, as practised in Tibet. Some 5%, mainly Kazakhs living in the west of the country, follow Islam. Approximately 5% claim to be Christians, Mongolia's fastest-growing religion, and around 10% are atheist (the creed of the former communist state). In northern Mongolia Buddhism is mixed with elements of shamanism. Freedom of religion has only opened up again since the fall of communism in 1990 and there is growing competition between Buddhism and Christianity in both urban and rural areas.

Developed by the Arts Council of Mongolia, the website www.mongol-art.mn has extensive information on dance, music, film, theatre and art.

Arts

From prehistoric oral epics to the latest movie from MongolKino film studios in Ulaanbaatar, the many arts of Mongolia convey the flavour of nomadic life and the spirit of the land. Traditional Mongolian music, which can be heard at concerts in Ulaanbaatar, is usually played on a *morin khuur* (horsehead fiddle), a two-stringed vertical violin and a lute. These instruments are also used by some of Mongolia's popular rock bands, including Hurd and Chinggis Khaan.

There are also several unique traditional singing styles. The enigmatic *khöömii* – throat singing – has the remarkable effect of producing two notes simultaneously – one low growl and the other an ethereal whistling. Translated as 'long songs', *urtyn-duu* use long trills to relate traditional stories about love and the countryside.

Mongolia's best-known modern poet and playwright is Dashdorjiin Natsagdorj (1906–37), regarded as the founder of Mongolian literature. His dramatic nationalist poems and plays are still performed in Mongolian theatres today. There's also been a recent revival in Mongolian cinema with the brightest star being Byambasuren Davaa, who together with Luigi Falomi directed *The Weeping Camel* (2003), a moving documentary about a camel that rejects its offspring, and how the family that owns it attempts to reconcile their differences.

Much of Mongolia's visual arts is religious in nature. Religious scroll paintings, depicting deities and their enlightened qualities, can be found on family altars in many homes. Another traditional style of painting is *zurag* – landscape storytelling. These landscapes include intricate sketches depicting every aspect of Mongolian life. Balduugiyn Sharav (1869–1939) is Mongolia's best-known painter in this style. The sculptor Zanabazar (1635–1723) is one of Mongolia's most revered artists, as well as religious and political leaders. He is known primarily for his bronze cast statues, which are now on display in monasteries and museums around Ulaanbaatar.

Environment

Part of the Trans-Siberian Railway's attraction for travellers with even the slightest interest in natural history is the variety of terrain along the route and the abundance of wildlife it holds. Much of the region's wildlife is naturally shy, hidden from view or too distant to be observed well. Nevertheless, it's still possible to see interesting wildlife and vegetation from the train compartment, sometimes very close to the track. There are also frequent opportunities to get off and explore the countryside at leisure and in more detail, the most popular stop being World Heritage–listed Lake Baikal.

The Wild Russia website (www.wild-russia.org) belongs to the US-based Center for Russian Nature Conservation, which assists and promotes nature conservation across Russia.

THE LAND

Russia, China and Mongolia – the three nations linked by the Trans-Siberian routes – cover over a quarter of the globe in total, with Russia being the world's largest country, China the fourth biggest and Mongolia the eighteenth biggest. The bulk of the railway traverses the geographical entity known as Inner Eurasia, an immense territory bounded by Europe in the west, the Middle East and India in the south, and China in the east. Its physical environment has shaped its social evolution from prehistoric times to the present day. Most notably, the region remained only sparsely populated for centuries (and it's hardly overpopulated these days!).

Inner Eurasia's remote interior location, far away from the oceans and moisture-bearing winds, fosters a climate of harsh extremes. When global warming forced back the great ice sheets that covered the continent more than 10,000 years ago, it resulted in four distinct ecological zones in inner Eurasia: tundra, taiga, steppe and desert. The tundra includes the upper reaches of Siberia, extending to the Arctic coast. Under snow for nearly two-thirds of the year, the ground remains in a frozen condition of permafrost, even in summer. The tundra supports little vegetation and fauna, though the wintry northern coast is home to sea mammals.

The Russian taiga is a major carbon sink, removing an estimated 500 million tonnes of carbon from the atmosphere each year.

South of the tundra, the taiga comprises a dense forest belt that runs from Scandinavia across Siberia to the Pacific coast. The taiga's soil is poor for farming, but its woods and rivers were rich in fauna until relatively recently. Below the taiga lies the steppe, which spans the continent from the plains north of the Black Sea across Central Asia through Mongolia to the western edge of China. This gently rolling, semiarid grassland is unsuitable for cultivation, but it provides sufficient vegetation to support large herds of grazing animals. To the south, the steppe becomes arid and gives way to the deserts of central and eastern Asia. The Gobi Desert in Mongolia and China retains a thin grass cover that sustains some of the hardier herbivores.

Six of the world's 20 longest rivers are in Russia. Forming the China-Russia border the east-flowing Amur (4416km) is nominally the longest, along with the Lena (4400km), Yenisey (4090km), Irtysh (4245km) and Ob (3680km), all of which flow north across Siberia ending up in the Arctic Ocean. In fact, if one was to take the longest stretch, including tributaries (as is frequently done with the Mississippi-Missouri River System in North America), the Ob-Irtysh would clock up 5410km and the Angara-Yenisey a phenomenal 5550km. The latter might, in fact, be the world's longest river if you were to include Lake Baikal and the Selenga River (992km), which directly feed into it.

Beautiful Lake Baikal itself is the world's deepest lake, holding nearly one-fifth of all the world's unfrozen fresh water. Europe's longest river, the Volga (3690km), rises northwest of Moscow and flows via Kazan and Astrakhan into the Caspian Sea, the world's largest lake (371,800 sq km). Lake Onega (9600 sq km) and Lake Ladoga (18,390 sq km), both northeast of St Petersburg, are the biggest lakes in Europe.

WILDLIFE

The extent and variety of habitat in Russia, China and Mongolia support a huge range of species; so many, in fact, that we can only sketch an outline of the rich fauna and flora here.

Animals

The wild animals living in the area bordering the railway are amazingly varied, recalling what Western Europe was like before civilisation took its toll. What follows is a selection of the most characteristic (if not always the most easily observable) species.

BIRDS

Birds are numerous and seen more often than other animal species on the journey. However, many birds are shy and secretive, have restricted habitat preferences or are absent in winter. Following is a representative selection of those that might be encountered or are typical of the area.

Geese you can spot include the greylag goose *(Anser anser)*, the largest of the 'grey' geese and familiar as the ancestor of the domestic farmyard goose; and the bean goose *(A. fabalis)*, smaller and darker than the greylag. Breeds of duck include the common mallard *(Anas platyrhynchos)*, the less common Baikal teal *(A. Formosa)* and the falcated teal *(A. falcate)*.

Coots *(Fulica atra)* prefer the more open areas of lakes, so are easily visible. The common or mew gull *(Larus canus)* is widespread throughout the region, particularly on the larger lakes and rivers, as is the black-beaded gull *(L. ridibundus)*. The little gull *(L. minutus)*, the world's smallest at only 26cm long, is usually seen gliding and dipping over lakes picking mosquitoes off the surface in summer.

The common tern *(Sterna hirundo)* may be seen hovering over lakes and wide rivers before plunging in to catch fish. Not as common, despite its name, is the common crane *(Grus grus)*. In autumn, large flocks set off on migration with loud bugling calls, returning the following spring to breed.

The grey heron *(Ardea cinerea)* is the only waterbird likely to be seen near the train line. Tall and grey, with a long shaggy crest, it will be seen wading cautiously through shallow water or standing hunched on the shores of lakes and rivers. The lapwing *(Vanellus vanellus)* is a widespread, attractive wading bird, easily identified by its wispy crest and, in flight, very rounded wings. The little ringed plover *(Charadrius dubius)*, a member of the same wader family, is much smaller, sandy brown above, white below with a black collar. The dainty yellow wagtail *(Motacilla flava)* is a summer visitor to marshes, water meadows and lake edges throughout the region. The male is mainly yellowish, the female more buffish.

The magnificent white-tailed eagle *(Haliaeetus albicilla)* is easily identified by its huge size, broad wings and short wedge-shaped tail. The equally impressive golden eagle *(Aquila chrysaetos)* is slightly smaller, with a longer tail and, in the adults, a golden brown head and hind neck.

Mongolia's Wild Heritage by Christopher Finch, written in collaboration with the Mongolian Ministry of Nature & Environment, is an outstanding book on Mongolia's fragile ecology, along with excellent photos.

China Birding (www.cn birds.com) can fill you in on overwinter sites, migration routes and the geographical distribution of your feathered friends in China.

The common buzzard *(Buteo buteo)* is one of the most numerous and often-seen raptors. The general shape is not dissimilar to an eagle, but a buzzard is considerably smaller, with a less protruding head. With more angled and longer wings than a buzzard, the black kite *(Milvus migrans)* is another soaring raptor. Its most distinctive feature is its long, shallowly forked tail.

The peregrine *(Falco peregrinus)* rises above its intended victim – a flying duck or pigeon perhaps – and with lightning speed (over 150km/h) strikes a deadly blow with its outstretched talons. Like all falcons, the peregrine has rather pointed wings in comparison with those of eagles, buzzards and hawks.

The goshawk *(Accipiter gentiles)* is the largest of the hawks. Capable of catching prey up to the size of a goose (hence its name), surprise is the key to its hunting success; it glides low to the ground, swerving in and out of the trees, hoping to catch its victim unawares. A smaller and more common version of the goshawk is the sparrowhawk *(A. nisus)*.

Useful books for bird spotters are *A Field Guide to the Birds of Russia* by VE Flint et al and the Collins Field Guide *Birds of Russia* by Algirdas Knystautas.

CANINE FAMILY

Although largely hunted to extinction in Europe, wolves *(Canis lupus)* remain a significant and important part of the ecosystem in Siberia and Mongolia. You're much more likely to hear the unmistakable distant howling than see them, though. (The howl, incidentally, is a contact call to assemble or keep the pack together.) Resembling an Alsatian dog, the wolf is typically greyer with a broader head, smaller ears and pale yellow eyes.

In wolf society there is a strong sense of responsibility, obedience, cooperation and sharing. The species also performs a useful function in keeping populations of other animals under control and should only be destroyed when its activities are in direct conflict with raising domestic animals.

A member of the same family as the wolf, the fox *(Vulpes vulpes)* is much more familiar and easily observed. Apart from being a useful scavenger, an efficient predator of rats and mice, and an aesthetically attractive animal in its own right, the fox is also faithful to the same mate for life.

CERVINE FAMILY

Among the largest and most easily spotted of animals along the route are deer. The roe deer *(Capreolus capreolus)* is the one you'll most likely see out at the edge of the forest and in the fields. Its small size and antlers also enable it to move quickly through dense undergrowth or conceal itself.

The website www.wwf china.org has details of the WWF's projects for endangered and protected animals in China.

The impressive moose or elk *(Alces alces)*, the largest of the deer family, are common, particularly in the wetter and more open parts of the forest. The males sport antlers up to 2m wide and can stand over 2m high at the shoulders. It's unlikely that you'll see the timid red or maral deer *(Cervus elaphus)*. The sturdy stag carries impressive antlers, shed annually in early spring. In the late summer he sheds the velvety skin that covers the new antlers.

Even rarer is the musk deer *(Moschus moschiferus)*, long hunted for the pungent secretion produced in their abdominal glands and widely used in expensive perfumes. The males don't grow antlers; instead, both sexes have tusks (actually extended upper canines) protruding about 6cm in males, less in females. These are used with deadly effect in the rutting season in December and January.

FELINE FAMILY

The lynx *(Felis lynx)* is rarely seen, but easily identified by the tufted ears and short black-ringed tail. This solitary, nocturnal animal's much-prized coat of fur is reddish or greyish in background colour, more or less covered with indistinct dark spots.

The Siberian tiger *(Panthera tigris altaica)*, also known as the Amur or Manchurian tiger, used to occur throughout the region's vast forests, but its valuable fur and taste for domestic animals and humans has led to its demise over virtually all of its former territory. See p275 for more details on these magnificent animals and how you can get an up-close look at them in Harbin's Siberian Tiger Park.

Heavy on photographs, *Baikal, Sacred Sea of Siberia* is a pictorial tribute to the great lake with text by travel writer and novelist Peter Matthiessen.

MUSTELID FAMILY

Mustelids include otters *(Lutra lutra)*, stoats and weasels, all of which occur widely in the Trans-Siberian region. Otters, being nocturnal hunters, are best spotted in early morning or dusk on land, where they always eat their fish (or other prey). Well adapted to the bitterly cold conditions of the Siberian winter otters have no need to hibernate or migrate, so are active and visible year-round.

THE ECOLOGY OF LAKE BAIKAL

Lake Baikal's wildlife is unique. Thanks to warm water entering from vents in the bottom of the lake, and the filtering action of countless millions of minute crustaceans called epishura, the water is exceptionally clear and pure – although unfortunately less so now than formerly (see p63).

Over 1000 species of plants and animals live in the lake (nearly all endemic), including over 200 of shrimp and 80 of flatworm; one of the latter is the world's largest and eats fish! Uniquely for a deep lake, life exists right down to the bottom.

The many kinds of fish include the endemic *omul*, Baikal's main commercial fish. A remarkable species, the *omul* is reputed to emit a shrill cry when caught. It spawns in the Selenga River, but its main food source is the endemic Baikal alga, *melosira*, which has declined drastically because of pollution.

The *golomyanka* – a pink, translucent oilfish with large pectoral fins – is endemic to Baikal. It's unusual in having no scales and being viviparous, giving birth to live young, about 2000 at a time. It is the lake's most common fish, although its numbers have been depleted by pollution. By day it lives in the deep, dark depths, rising at night to near the surface.

Golomyanka is the preferred food of the Baikal seal, or *nerpa (Phoca siberica)*, the world's only freshwater seal, with no relatives nearer than the ringed seal of the Arctic. *Nerpas* are attractive, gentle creatures with unusually large eyes set in round flat faces, enabling them to hunt down to at least 1500m below the surface – even at night. Despite their size (less than 1.5m, making them the world's smallest seal), they have particularly strong claws for forcing their way through winter ice and keeping their breathing holes open. Pups are born in late winter. At the top of the food chain, Baikal seals have been greatly affected by pollution and are still harvested by local people. However, their population hovers around the 50,000 mark.

There is plenty of other wildlife around the lake. The huge delta, nearly 40km wide, formed by the sediment brought down to the lake by the Selenga River, is a great attraction to wild fowl and wading birds. In summer such beautiful and rare species as the Asiatic dowitcher and white-winged black tern nest there, while in autumn vast numbers of waterfowl from the north use the mudflats and marshes to rest and feed on their migration south – a sort of international bird airport – while many overwinter there, too.

Vast numbers of caddis flies and other insects hatch and swarm on the lake in summer, providing a rich and vital food source for all kinds of wildlife, from fish to birds. Despite their lack of visual impact for the Trans-Siberian traveller, these tiny insects, along with the microscopic plant and animal organisms, form the base of the pyramid of wildlife that graces this unique area.

The largest of the mustelids, the wolverine *(Gulo gulo)* somewhat resembles a long brown badger in shape, but its fur is brown, with lighter patches on its head and flanks. Immensely strong, it can rip the head off its prey. Decapitated heads of animals as large as reindeer have been found high up in conifer trees! Like all fur-bearing animals it has suffered at the hands of trappers. However, this species has got its own back to some extent, as it is well known (and unpopular) for robbing traps.

The sable *(Martes zibellina)* is almost exclusively a Siberian animal. It is virtually confined to the vast stretches of forest east of the Yenisey River and notably in the forests around Lake Baikal. The sable's luxurious dark brown fur almost brought it to the brink of extinction as a result of relentless trapping. Now there are perhaps several thousand in the wild, counting those inside and outside national park areas around Baikal. Though still obtained by trapping and shooting wild animals, most sable furs now come from farmed animals.

Glutton is the old name for the wolverine, which has an insatiable appetite. It will literally eat anything from minute plants, berries and insects to carrion and the largest species of deer, which it stalks and ambushes.

RODENT FAMILY

The beaver *(castor fiber)* is the largest rodent in the northern hemisphere, growing up to a grand 1.3m in length and weighing up to 40kg. Exclusively vegetarian, its favourite food is the bark and branches of waterside trees. It stores branches and other vegetation for the winter in underwater chambers inside its lodge, where the young are also born. These lodges are wonderful feats of engineering, with an elaborate system of interconnected chambers and tunnels for different purposes, with ventilation shafts incorporated.

Though beavers are not frequently seen by the casual observer (nowadays they are rarer because they are being hunted for fur), their conspicuous dams and lodges are clear evidence of their presence along the stretches of river where they occur.

Other rodents, including muskrats, squirrels, chipmunks, rats, voles and mice, form an integral part of the ecosystem. On a massive scale, they replenish the soil through their regular burrowing and eating routines, and provide an indispensable food source for creatures higher up the food chain.

URSINE FAMILY

In Russian the brown bear *(Ursus arctos)* is called *medved,* reflecting the animal's love of *med* (honey). Unfortunately, bears are not usually held in high esteem by Russian hunters, who kill them even in winter, when specially trained dogs are used to scent out the lairs in which they hibernate. Despite this, and also the high mortality of the cubs who are dependent on their mothers for two or three years, brown bears still occur widely, if sparsely, in Siberia, with several distinguishable subgroups. It is easily the heaviest animal of the area, with males weighing up to 350kg and females up to 250kg. If you see one in the wild, you should stay well clear as they are highly dangerous.

Among Lake's Baikal's unique species of sponge is one that has been traditionally used to polish silverware.

Plants

The taiga is the habitat through which much of the railway passes in Siberia. In some places it is dominated by conifers, particularly Siberian pine *(Pinus sibirica),* in others by mixed conifer and deciduous trees, and in yet other places it's all deciduous. Silver firs, spruce, larch and birch often mingle with maple and aspen, while by the innumerable lakes, ponds and rivers willows and poplars dominate – in June and July the poplars' white fluffy seeds float everywhere like snow.

A particularly beautiful species of birch *(Betula dahurica)* with an unusual dark bark grows near Lake Baikal, while at the far eastern end of the journey, in Ussuriland, you will see the impressively tall white-barked elms *(Ulmus propingua)* and Manchurian firs *(Abies holophylla)* – the latter with pink, purple or orange-buff bark – as well as the more familiar cork, walnut and acacia trees. The almost subtropical climate here is quite different from the harsher conditions further west in Siberia, allowing a lush profusion of exotic flowers.

The leaf litter at the base of trees swarms with invertebrate life, which not only transforms dead vegetation into fertile humus, but also provides food for animals and birds. On the forest floor mosses, lichens, ferns and fungi thrive, including the colourful but deadly fly agaric *(Amanita muscaria)*. The dense leaf canopy above inhibits the growth of flowering plants and shrubs, but in more open areas and clearings it is a different picture; in such places flamboyant rhododendrons, azaleas, ryabina, spiraea, asters, daisies, gentians and vetches delight the eye in summer.

Though still extensive, much of the forest has been cleared for agricultural purposes or to sell for timber, so large tracts of cultivated fields and eroded scrubland where trees once stood are a common sight. There are also extensive but natural open treeless steppes. Of the many kinds of grass that grow wild here the most attractive are the aptly named feather grasses, which rise and ripple in the wind like the surface of the sea.

China is one of the Earth's main centres of origin for plants. It claims more than 17,300 species of endemic seed plants.

NATIONAL PARKS & NATURE RESERVES
Russia

Russia has 100 official *zapovedniki* (nature reserves) and 35 national parks. Along or close by the Trans-Siberian route you'll find several, including Russia's oldest protected reserve, the Barguzin National Reserve (p219) within the 269-sq-km Zabaikalsky National Park. These are areas set aside to protect fauna and flora, often habitats of endangered or unique species. Some reserves are open to visitors and, unlike in the old days when your ramblings were strictly controlled, today you can sometimes hire the staff to show you around.

Apart from the parks around Lake Baikal, also see p238 for details of the Sikhote-Alin Nature Reserve near Vladivostok and p187 for information on Krasnoyarsk's Stolby Nature Reserve. Also check out www.baikal .eastsib.ru/gbt/index_en.html or www.earthisland.org/project for details of volunteer programmes in the three national parks and four nature reserves surrounding Lake Baikal.

China

China has an incredibly diverse range of natural escapes scattered across the country. Since the first nature reserve was established in 1956, around 2000 more parks have joined the ranks, protecting about 14% of China's land area, and offering the traveller a wonderful variety of landscapes and diversity of wildlife. Many of the parks are intended for the preservation of endangered animals, while others protect sacred mountains.

But before you pack your hiking gear and binoculars, be prepared to share many of the more popular reserves with expanding commercial development. Tourism is generally welcomed into these reserves with open arms, meaning pricey hotels, more roads, gondolas, hawkers and busloads of tourists. With a little effort, you can often find a less beaten path to escape down, but don't expect utter tranquillity.

Along the Trans-Manchurian route bird-watchers should consider a visit to the Zhalong Nature Reserve (p278).

Mongolia

The 54 protected areas in Mongolia constitute a very impressive 13.5% of the country. The Ministry of Nature & Environment (MNE) in Mongolia classifies protected areas into four distinct categories. In order of importance:

National Parks Places of historical and educational interest; fishing and grazing by nomadic people is allowed and parts of the park are developed for ecotourism.

Natural & Historical Monuments Important places of historical and cultural interest; development is allowed within guidelines.

Natural Reserves Less important regions protecting rare species of flora and fauna, and archaeological sites; some development is allowed within certain guidelines.

Strictly Protected Areas Very fragile areas of great importance; hunting, logging and development are strictly prohibited, and there is no established human influence.

The strictly protected areas of Bogdkhan Uul, Great Gobi and Uvs Nuur Basin are biosphere reserves included in Unesco's **Man and Biosphere Programme** (www.unesco.org/mab).

To visit these parks – especially the strictly protected areas, national parks and some national monuments – you will need to obtain a permit. These are provided by the local Protected Areas Bureau (PAB) office, or from rangers at the entrances to the parks. The permits are little more than an entrance fee, but they are an important source of revenue for the maintenance of the parks. Entrance fees are set at T3000 per foreigner and T300 per Mongolian (although guides and drivers are often excluded).

Close to Ulaanbaatar, you'll find the Gorkhi-Terelj National Park (p268) and the Bogdkhan Uul Strictly Protected Area containing the temple Manzushir Khiid (p267). You'll also find the holy mountain Tsetseegun Uul (p268).

Russia has the world's largest natural gas reserves, the second-largest coal reserves and the eighth-largest oil reserves – just as well, since it's the world's third-largest energy consumer.

ENVIRONMENTAL ISSUES

Russia

Russia may have ratified the Kyoto Protocol in 2004, but the fact is that care for the environment has long been a very low priority in the eyes of the nation's rulers. Sadly, the Soviet Union's enthusiasm for rapid

---

RESPONSIBLE TRAVEL

As closely as some Russians, Chinese and Mongolians live with nature, they don't always respect it: littering and poaching are everyday pastimes. Responsible travellers will be appalled by the mess left in parts of the countryside and at how easily rubbish is thrown out of train windows. Accept that you're not going to change how people live, but that you might be able to make a small impression by your own thoughtful behaviour. To help preserve the natural environment consider the following tips while travelling:

▪ Don't litter and minimise waste by using minimal packaging.

▪ Refill your water bottle from the train's samovar and consider using purification tablets or iodine in tap water rather than relying on bottled water.

▪ Avoid buying items made from endangered species (eg exotic furs, caviar that isn't from legal sources).

▪ Support local enterprises, environmental groups and charities trying to improve these countries' environmental scorecard, such as the **Great Baikal Trail project** (www.earthisland .org/project) to construct a hiking trail around Lake Baikal, or **Ger to Ger** (www.gertoger.com), a project working with nomadic families to help preserve Mongolia's environment.

LAKE BAIKAL'S ENVIRONMENTAL ISSUES

Home to an estimated 60,000 *nerpa* seals, Lake Baikal is beautiful, pristine and drinkably pure in most areas. As it holds an astonishing 80% of Russia's fresh water, environmentalists are keen to keep things that way. In the 1960s, despite the repression of the Soviet system, it was the building of Baikal's first (and only) lakeside industrial plant that galvanised Russia's initial major green movement. That plant, the Baikalsk paper-pulp factory, is still monitored today while the owners argue over a costly clean-up plan assisted by the World Bank.

These days some two-thirds of Baikal's shoreline falls within parks or reserves, so similar factories would not be allowed. But the ecosystem extends beyond the lake itself. Another challenge includes polluted inflows from the Selenga River, which carries much of Mongolia's untreated waste into the lake. The most contentious of recent worries is the US$16 billion Eastern Siberia oil pipeline from Tayshet to the Pacific coast. The route deliberately loops north avoiding the lakeshore itself. Nonetheless, when finished, some 80 million tonnes of oil a year will flow across the lake's northern water catchment area, an area highly prone to seismic activity. Environmentalists fear that a quake-cracked pipeline could spill vast amounts of oil into the Baikal feedwaters. Ironically, the government decree allowing the project to proceed was signed in December 2004, just days after a huge earthquake caused the disastrous Southeast Asian tsunami.

For much more information, click to the websites of regional eco-groups **Baikal Wave** (www .baikalwave.eu.org/eng.html) and **Baikal Watch** (www.earthisland.org/baikal/), as well as the wonderful **Baikal Web World** (www.bww.irk.ru), which has a lot of information about the wildlife, history and legends of the lake.

---

industrialisation has been matched only by its wilful ignorance of the often devastating environmental side effects, which are still very evident today.

Obsessed with fulfilling production plans, Siberian managers during the Soviet years showed little regard for the harmful practices of their factories. As a result, the major industrial areas in the Kuznets Basin, Irkutsk and Krasnoyarsk have since been declared environmental catastrophes, with irreparably damaged soil and water. Lake Baikal served as a receptacle for raw waste, discharged from a paper mill and towns along its shore.

See www.eia.doe.gov /emeu/cabs/russenv.html for a good overview of current environmental issues in Russia.

Environmental awareness in Russia is rising, but the booming economy is having its own detrimental effect. Higher standards of living have put more cars on the roads and substantially increased solid waste generation. The government is trying to improve its act and has passed sound environmental protection laws; enforcing these laws is another thing entirely.

China

See http://china.org.cn, a Chinese government site with a link to a page covering environmental issues.

As a developing country experiencing rapid industrialisation, it's not surprising that China has some hefty environmental issues to contend with. Unfortunately, China's huge population makes its environmental plights infinitely bigger than those of other nations. Air pollution, deforestation, endangered species, and rural and industrial waste are all taking their toll. Seven of the world's 10 most polluted cities are in China, with most of the country's major cities lying smothered under great canopies of smog.

The biggest source of this pollution is coal. It provides some 70% of China's energy needs and around 900 million tonnes of it go up in smoke yearly. The result is immense damage to air and water quality, agriculture and human health, with acid rain falling on about 30% of the country.

THE GREEN WALL OF CHINA

If you visit Beijing in spring and experience the sand storms that send residents rushing around with plastic bags over their heads, you may not be so surprised to hear that the city may one day be swallowed up by the Gobi Desert. Only 150km away, the winds are blowing the sands towards the capital at a rate of 2km a year, with 30m dunes closing in. In their wake, these massive dust storms have left entire towns abandoned and environmental refugees numbering in the millions. They've also brought about bizarre weather effects, like 'black winds' and 'mud rains'. Experts blame the problem on overgrazing and deforestation; every month 200 sq km of arable land in China becomes a desert.

In a rather late attempt to fend off the desert, China's government has pledged US$6.8 billion to build a green wall between Beijing and the sands; at 5700km long, it will be longer than the Great Wall of China. Unfortunately, the work so far doesn't appear to be doing the trick. Few of the millions of planted trees are surviving, while overirrigation, air pollution, erosion and corruption – all of which are playing a role in the desertification – remain unaddressed. As researchers, bureaucrats and villagers try to hammer out a solution, the sands are beginning to find their way across the Pacific, dropping grit on Vancouver and bringing unreal sunsets to San Francisco.

With the Olympics on their way and its entry into the World Trade Organization (WTO), China seems to have changed its policy of 'industrial catch-up first, environmental clean-up later' to one of tidying up its environmental act now. Nevertheless, analysts continue to point to an impending environmental catastrophe, fearing that the efforts could well be too little, too late.

In *The River Runs Black*, Elizabeth Economy gives a fascinating account of China's environmental crisis. Her perspective is neither melodramatic nor dull, and very readable.

The impact of China's environmental problems unfortunately doesn't stop at the country's borders (see above). Across the north of China, rampaging natural fires are believed to consume more than 200 million tonnes of coal each year, further exacerbating China's contribution to global warming.

Mongolia

The natural environment of Mongolia remains in good condition compared with that of many Western countries. The country's small population and nomadic subsistence economy have been its environmental salvation.

However, it does have its share of problems. Communist-era production quotas put pressure on grasslands to yield more crops and support more livestock than was sustainable. The rise in the number of herders and livestock through the 1990s has wreaked havoc on the grasslands; some 70% of pastureland is degraded and around 80% of plant species near village centres have disappeared.

Forest fires, nearly all of which are caused by careless human activity, are common during the windy spring season. In 1996 alone around 80,000 sq km of land was scorched, causing up to US$1.9 billion in damages.

Other threats to the land include mining (there are over 300 mines), which has polluted 28 river basins. The huge Oyu Tolgoi mine in Ömnögov will require the use of 360L of water *per second*, which environmentalists say might not be sustainable. Neighbouring China's insatiable appetite for minerals and gas is prompting Mongolia to open up new mines, but the bigger threat is China's hunt for the furs, meat and body parts of endangered animals. Chinese demand results in the killing each year of 2000 musk deer and well over 200,000 marmots.

Urban sprawl, along with a demand for wood to build homes and to use as heating and cooking fuel, is slowly reducing the forests. This destruction of the forests has also lowered river levels, especially the Tuul Gol near Ulaanbaatar. In recent years the Tuul Gol has actually gone dry in the spring months due to land mismanagement and improper water use.

Large-scale infrastructure projects are further cause for concern. Conservationists are worried about the 'Millennium Rd', which is being built before the finalisation of environmental impact studies. Its completion is sure to increase mining and commerce inside fragile ecosystems. The eastern grasslands, one of the last great open spaces in Asia, will come under particular threat.

Air pollution is becoming a serious problem, especially in Ulaanbaatar. At the top of the Zaisan Memorial in the capital, a depressing layer of dust and smoke from the city's three thermal power stations can be seen hovering over the city. This layer is often appalling in winter, when all homes are continuously burning fuel and the power stations are working overtime. Ulaanbaatar has also suffered from acid rain, and pollution is killing fish in the nearby Tuul Gol in central Mongolia.

Mongolians consider eating wolf meat and lungs good for respiratory ailments, while consuming the intestines can aid digestion. Powdered wolf rectum is used for haemorrhoids. Hanging a wolf's tongue around one's neck cures gland and thyroid ailments.

Food & Drink

Travellers on the Trans-Siberian route will have ample opportunities to sample the very best (and sometimes the worst) of Russia's kitchens. Those heading into or out of China will have a mind-boggling array of regional delicacies to explore, while those travelling the Trans-Mongolian route can add in hearty nomadic-inspired Mongolian dishes. One thing's for sure: you won't go hungry!

In most Russian cities the three-course set-menu *biznes* lunch, generally served noon to 4pm Monday to Friday, is a great bargain, costing as little as R100 to R150 (up to R250 in Moscow and St Petersburg).

STAPLES & SPECIALITIES
Russia

Russia has a great culinary heritage enriched by influences from the Baltic to the Far East. The country's rich black soil provides an abundance of grains and vegetables used in the wonderful range of breads, salads and appetisers of its cuisine, and for the base in the distinctive soups that are the highlight of any Russian meal. Russia's rivers, lakes and seas yield up a unique range of fish and, as with any cold climate country, there's a great love of fat-loaded dishes – Russia is no place to go on a diet!

Get into the Russian way of starting a meal with a few *zakuski* (hors d'oeuvres), which are often the most interesting items on the menu and usually a good choice for vegetarians. Soups, such as borsch, made with beetroot, *lapsha* (chicken noodle) and *solyanka* (a thick broth with meat, fish and a host of vegetables) can be a meal in themselves, served with piles of bread and a thick dollop of sour cream. Main dishes often come with a salad garnish, but you'll usually have to order rice or potatoes as side dishes.

During summer outdoor pizza and *shashlyk* (kebab) stalls pop up all over the place. Other standard snacks you'll find are *pirozhki* (pies) and bliny (pancakes served with a range of fillings). Useful for nibbling on long journeys is *kolbasa*, a salami-like sausage, which is made in a wide

---

TRAVEL YOUR TASTEBUDS

You'll discover a variety of regional food specialities along the rail routes. Here are a few of our favourites:

- *Omul* (a cousin of salmon and trout) is endemic to Lake Baikal and considered a great delicacy.
- *Oblyoma*, a dried, salty fish found in the Volga, is eaten most often as a snack food with beer.
- *Kalmary* (calamari), *kraby* (crab) and *grebeshki* (scallops) are all standard items on Vladivostok menus.
- *Manti* (steamed, palm-sized dumplings), known as *pozy* or *buuzy* in Buryatiya and *pyan-se* (a peppery version) in the Russian Far East.
- *Húntun* (wontons), filled with leeks and minced pork, served in northern China.
- Noodles topped with *lûròu huáng miàn* (sliced donkey meat) or hearty *kăo yángròu* (roasted mutton) are also popular in northeastern China.
- *Öröm* (sometimes called *üürag*) – a rich, sweet-tasting Mongolian cream made by warming fresh cow's milk in a pot and then letting it sit under a cover for one day.
- Mongolian blueberry jam, a summer speciality.

variety of styles and can go down pretty well with bread, tomato and raw onion.

China

Although it's possible to dine on the many different regional styles of Chinese food across the country, Trans-Mongolian and Trans-Manchurian travellers will most commonly be served northern Chinese cuisine, where the *fàn* (grain) in the meal is usually wheat or millet, rather than rice. Its most common incarnations are as *jiǎozi* (steamed dumplings) or *chūnjuǎn* (spring rolls). The most famous northern dish, Peking duck (or Beijing duck as it is called today), is also served with typical ingredients: wheat pancakes, spring onions and fermented bean paste. The range of *cài* (vegetable or other accompanying dishes) is limited in the north. The cuisine relies heavily on freshwater fish, chicken and, most of all, cabbage.

The influence of the Mongols is evident in northern Chinese cuisine. Mongolian hotpot and Mongolian barbecue are adaptations from Mongol field kitchens. Animals that were hunted on horseback could be cooked in primitive barbecues made from soldiers' iron shields on top of hot coals. Alternatively, a soldier could use his helmet as a pot, filling it with water, meat and condiments. Mutton is now the main ingredient in Mongolian hotpot.

The most common method of cooking in Beijing is 'explode-frying', or deep-frying in peanut oil. Although northern Chinese cuisine has a reputation for being bland and unsophisticated, it has the advantage of being filling and therefore well suited to the cold climate.

In Beijing, of course, every region of China and most regions of the world are represented in the splendid restaurant scene. The options range from the street stalls at Donghuamen Night Market to chic (and pricey) fusion restaurants where East meets West. Eating out in this cosmopolitan city is an adventure that should be seized with both chopsticks!

Mongolia

The culinary masters of Mongolia's barren steppes have always put more stock in survival than taste. Mongolian food is therefore a hearty, if somewhat bland, array of meat and dairy products. Out in the countryside, potatoes are often considered exotic, leavened bread a treat and spices a cause for concern.

The streamlined diet reflects Mongolia's nomadic lifestyle. Nomads cannot reasonably transport an oven, and so are prevented from producing baked goods. Nor can nomads plant, tend to or harvest fruits, vegetables, spices or grains. Nomads can, however, eat the food that their livestock produces.

Dairy products – known as 'white foods' – are the staple for herdsmen in the summer. Camel's milk, thick cream, dried milk curds and fermented cheese are just a few of the delicacies you may sample (most of which taste like sour, plain yoghurt). During winter the vast majority of Mongolians survive on boiled mutton and flour.

DRINKS
Russia

Vodka can be bought everywhere. Better Russian brands include Flagman, Gzhelka and Russky Standart (Russian Standard). Today beer is overtaking vodka in popularity and for good reason – the quality is

---

In *A Year of Russian Feasts* Catherine Cheremeteff-Jones recounts how Russia's finest dishes have been preserved and passed down through the feast days of the Russian Orthodox Church.

The following three websites will teach you more about Russian, Chinese and Mongolian cuisine, respectively: www.ruscuisine.com, http://chinesefood.about .com and www.9v.com /crystal/kerij-e/docs /cooking.htm.

excellent and it's cheap at around R30 for a 500mL bottle. The market leader is Baltika, making a range of 12 different brews; No 3, the most common, is a very quaffable lager.

Many locals prefer their wine *polusladkoe* (semisweet) or *sladkoe* (sweet). The latter is often little short of diluted alcoholic sugar. *Bryut* (very dry and only for sparkling wine), *sukhoe* (dry) and *polusukhoe* (semi-dry) reds can be found, though getting a good dry white can be quite tough. Locally produced sparkling wine Shampanskoye is remarkably cheap (around R300 a bottle) and popular, and rarely anything like champagne.

Russian brandy is called *konyak*. The finest comes from the Caucasus. Standards vary enormously, but local five-star brandies are generally a very pleasant surprise. *Kvas* is fermented rye bread water, and is often dispensed on the street from big, wheeled tanks. It is mildly alcoholic, tastes not unlike ginger beer, and is a wonderfully cool and refreshing drink in summer.

Tap water is suspect in some cities and should definitely be avoided in St Petersburg. Many people stick to bottled water, which is ubiquitous and cheap.

Russians are world-class tea drinkers: the traditional brewing method is to make an extremely strong pot, pour small shots of it into glasses and fill the glasses with hot water from the kettle. Putting jam, instead of sugar, in tea is quite common.

Coffee comes in small cups, and unless you buy it at kiosks or stand-up eateries, it's usually quite good. There's been an explosion of Starbucks-style cafés all across Russia's bigger cities – cappuccino, espresso, latte and mocha are now as much a part of the average Russian lexicon as elsewhere.

Other drinks, apart from the ubiquitous canned soft drinks, include *sok* (juice) and *kefir* (yoghurtlike sour milk).

China

Legend has it that tea was first cultivated in China about 4000 years ago in the modern-day province of Sichuan. Today tea is a fundamental ele-

---

DRINKING ETIQUETTE IN RUSSIA & MONGOLIA

At bars, restaurants and on trains, it's odds-on if you get talking with Russians they'll press you to drink with them. Even people from distant tables, spotting foreigners, may be seized with hospitable urges.

If it's vodka being drunk, they'll want a man to down the shot in one, neat of course; women are usually excused. This can be fun as you toast international friendship and so on, but vodka has a knack of creeping up on you from behind and the consequences can be appalling. It's traditional (and good sense) to eat a little something after each shot.

Refusing a drink can be very difficult, and Russians will probably continue to insist until they win you over. If you can't stand firm, drink in small gulps with copious thanks, while saying how you'd love to indulge but you have to be up early in the morning (or something similar). If you're really not in the mood, one sure-fire method of warding off all offers (as well as making people feel quite awful) is to say '*Ya alkogolik*' (*Ya alkogolichka* for women): 'I'm an alcoholic.'

Mongolians are not quite so pushy when it comes to drinking alcohol, but it's worth noting at least one local vodka drinking tradition. Before the first sip, honour the sky gods and the four directions by dipping your left ring finger into the glass and flicking drops into the air four times as well as touching the finger to your forehead.

ment of Chinese life, with green tea the most popular beverage throughout the country. Other local beverages include sugary soft drinks and fresh, sweet yoghurt, available from street stalls and shops across the country. The latter is typically sold in small milk bottles and consumed through a straw.

Beer is also very popular, the best known Chinese brew being Tsingtao, produced in the formerly German town of Qingdao (the Chinese inherited the brewery). A notable Beijing brand is Yanjing. Note that Chinese 'wines' are actually spirits, many used primarily for cooking or medicinal purposes. Chinese red and white wines tend to unanimously get the thumbs down from Westerners.

Imported beverages, such as soda, beer and coffee, are available at many shops and restaurants. And yes, Starbucks has opened its doors in Beijing, inspiring many local cafés to follow suit.

> The question '*Nǐ chī fànle ma?*' (Have you eaten yet?) is a common greeting among Chinese people and is taken to show the significance of food in Chinese culture.

Mongolia

Mongolians commence every meal with a cup of weak tea to aid digestion. In the countryside, many people drink *süütei tsai* (salty tea), which is a taste that is hard to acquire.

The most famous Mongolian alcoholic drink is *airag* (sometimes called *koumiss*), fermented mare's milk. Herders make it at home with an alcohol content of about 3%. If further distilled, it becomes the more potent *shimiin arkhi,* a clear spirit with 12% alcohol content. Mongolians have inherited a penchant for vodka from their former Russian patrons; they used to export vodka to Russia, but now consume much of it themselves. Several pubs in Ulaanbaatar brew their own light and dark beers (see p265).

> Mongolia has about 175 distilleries and 27 breweries. Drink with caution, as some 11% of these places regularly fail health quality inspections.

WHERE TO EAT & DRINK
On the Trains

At times a trip on the Trans-Siberian Railway can seem like an endless picnic, with all manner of foods being picked over and shared among fellow passengers in the compartments. The dining cars on Russian trains are private operations: the food served in them can vary enormously in quality, and they are best favoured more for their makeshift role as a social centre than for any gastronomic qualities. The dining cars are the place to meet fellow travellers, drink beer and play cards, and generally hang out.

The dining cars are changed at each country's border, so en route to Beijing you will get Russian, Chinese and possibly Mongolian menus (although it's unlikely there'll be a car attached between the Russian border and Ulaanbaatar). A meal with accompanying drink will rarely cost above US$10 paid in local currency. Dining cars are open from approximately 9am to 9pm local time, although this is by no means certain and with the time-zone differences knowing when to turn up can be a constant guessing game.

Also, during the peak summer season on the more popular Trans-Siberian services, such as the *Rossiya* and *Baikal,* the dining car can be booked out at certain times by tour groups. On both these trains and a few others it's possible to buy a ticket that includes all meals – probably not the best of ideas given the variable nature of what's on offer, and only worth considering if you have a total aversion to shopping en route.

In the dining car you will often find a table of pot noodles, chocolate, alcohol, juice and the like being peddled by the staff. They sometimes make the rounds of the carriages, too, with a trolley fileed with various snacks and drinks. The *provodnitsas* (carriage attendants) also offer their own drinks and nibbles. Prices are cheap but overinflated compared to what you would pay at the kiosks or to the babushkas at the station halts.

Off the Trains

Many of the recipes in *Imperial Mongolian Cooking: Recipes from the Kingdoms of Ghengis Khan,* by Marc Cramer, are from the author's grandfather, who worked as a chef in Siberia.

Shopping for supplies at most Russian stations is all part of the fun of a journey on the Trans-Siberian Railway (note that this is not the case, though, in Mongolia and China, where you will find very little food available on the platforms). The choice of items can be excellent, with fresh milk, ice cream, grilled chicken, boiled potatoes, home cooking such as *pelmeni* (dumplings) or *pirozhki* (savoury pies), buckets of forest berries and smoked fish all on offer. It's a good idea to have plenty of small change on hand, but you'll rarely have to worry about being overcharged.

Today in most Trans-Siberian cities there's plenty of choices when it comes to places to eat. Meals in the best new restaurants (where you'd typically pay between R500 and R1000 for a meal) can be fine renditions of Russian classics with fresh and tasty ingredients. In contrast, a *stolovaya* is a cafeteria-style place often found outside train stations, and in office blocks and government institutions, where a meal rarely tops R100.

Ulaanbaatar has a fine range of restaurants, but if you leave the capital be prepared for gastronomic purgatory. In cheap restaurants throughout Mongolia, mutton is the special of the day, every day: mutton with rice, mutton in goulash etc. A *guanz* is a canteen that often offers little but mutton and noodles. In the countryside, the *guanz* is often housed in a *ger* (yurt) and may be a traveller's only eating option apart from self-catering.

Fortunately, many places in Ulaanbaatar – as well as *ger* camps that cater to foreigners – have expanded their menus. A few restaurants serve Mongolian hotpot and Mongolian barbecue, but these are really Chinese adaptations of ancient Mongolian cooking techniques. You are more likely to sustain yourself on *buuz* (steamed dumplings) and *khuushuur* (fried pancakes with mutton).

It's hard to go hungry in China as just about everywhere you go there will be a myriad of food options to suit most budgets. The word *fàngdiàn* usually refers to a large-scale restaurant that may or may not offer lodging. A *cānguǎn* is generally a smaller restaurant that specialises in one particular type of food. The most informal type of restaurant is the *cāntīng,* which has low-end prices, though the quality of the food can be quite high.

Tourist-friendly restaurants can be found around tourist sights and often have English signs and menus. Sometimes food can be quite overpriced and geared towards foreign tastes. It's easy to find restaurants that cater to Chinese clientele – just look for noisy, crowded places; the noisier the better.

VEGETARIANS & VEGANS

Russia is pretty tough on vegetarians, although some restaurants have thankfully caught on, particularly in Moscow, St Petersburg and the other large cities. Russian main dishes are heavy on meat and poultry, and vegetables are often boiled to near death – even the tasty vegetable and fish soups are usually made using meat stock. If you're a vegetarian,

---

DINING ON THE RAILS   *Simon Richmond*

The bespectacled chef on the Harbin to Manzhouli train, with cigarette dangling from mouth, hands caressing his ample belly protruding from liberally stained overalls, did not inspire confidence. However, when he came to take my order he kindly helped me to decipher the handwritten Chinese menu. Together we arrived at a meal choice of duck with carrots and onions, stir-fried peppers and carrots, rice and soup, all washed down with some Harbin beer. Almost in an instant the freshly cooked, perfectly palatable food was laid before me, amazingly all for less than US$5.

My next restaurant car meal was in Russia on the train from Chita to Irkutsk. Even though this service originated in Chita, I was faced with the common situation of Russian restaurant cars: that many items on the menu were not available. Uncommonly, the smiling waitress was pleasantly disposed to our group, and eventually we managed to settle on the old stand-by of *solyanka*, a spicy Korean carrot salad, and mushrooms baked in sour cream – all totally delicious. Several vodka toasts followed.

No food was available on the train from Sükhbaatar to Ulaanbaatar, nor was there a buffet car attached to the service I caught out of the Mongolian capital towards the Chinese city of Hohhot. However, my ticket for the latter train did include a food voucher for which I received a not completely inedible meal of vacuum-packed sliced beef, a bread roll, a dry biscuit, bottled water and some instant coffee powder. The *provodnitsa* (carriage attendant) also brought around some cups of tea for dinner and breakfast, although later she wanted to be paid for this service.

---

say so, early and often. You'll see a lot of cucumber and tomato salads, and – if so inclined – you will develop an eagle eye for *baklazhan* (eggplant), plus the rare good fish (if you eat fish) and dairy dishes. *Zakuski* include quite a lot of meatless ingredients, such as eggs and mushrooms. If you're travelling during Lent, you'll find that many restaurants have special nonmeat menus.

Despite vegetarianism having a 1000-year history in China, eating meat is a status symbol, symbolic of health and wealth. Many Chinese remember all too well the famines of the 1950s and 1960s, when having anything to eat at all was a luxury. Even vegetables are often fried in animal-based oils, and soups are most commonly made with chicken or beef stock. In Beijing vegetarianism is slowly catching on, and there are new chic vegetarian eateries appearing in fashionable restaurant districts. These are often pricey establishments and you pay for ambience as well as the food.

A traditional Chinese vegetarian menu will often consist of a variety of 'mock meat' dishes made from tofu, wheat gluten and vegetables. Some of the dishes in China are quite fantastic to look at, with vegetarian ingredients expertly sculpted to look like spare ribs or fried chicken. Sometimes the chefs will even go to great lengths to create 'bones' from carrots and lotus roots. Some of the more famous vegetarian dishes include vegetarian 'ham', braised vegetarian 'shrimp' and sweet and sour 'fish'.

Mongolia is a difficult, but not impossible, place for vegetarians. If you don't eat meat, you can get by in Ulaanbaatar, but in the countryside you will need to take your own supplements and preferably a petrol stove. Vegetables other than potatoes, carrots and onions are rare, relatively expensive and usually pickled in jars, so the best way for vegetarians to get protein is from the wide range of dairy products. Vegans will either have to be completely self-sufficient, or be prepared to modify their lifestyle for a while.

EAT YOUR WORDS

This glossary is a brief guide to some basics. The italics in the transliterations indicate where the stress in the word falls; see p342 for further tips on pronunciation.

Useful Phrases

RUSSIA

Do you have a table ...?

yest′ sva·*bod*·ni *sto*·lik ...

У вас есть свободный столик ...?

for two	na dva·*ikh*	на двоих
for three	na tra·*ikh*	на троих

Do you have an English menu?

an·*gli*·ski men·*yu mozh*·na

У вас есть английское меню можно?

Please bring (a/an/the) ...

pri·ne·*si*·te pa·*zhal*·sta ...

Принесите, пожалуйста ...

ashtray	*pye*·pel′·ni·tsu	пепельницу
bill	shyot	счёт
fork	*vil*·ku	вилку
knife	nozh	нож
plate	ta·*ryel*·ku	тарелку
glass of water	sta·*kan vo*·di	стакан воды
with/without ice	s l′·*dom*/byez l′·*da*	со льдом/без льда

I'm a vegetarian.

ya ve·ge·ta·ri·*a*·nets/ya ve·ge·ta·ri·*an*·ka (m/f)

Я вегетарианец/Я вегетарианка.

I don't eat meat.

ya nye yem myas·*no*·va

Я не ем мясного.

I can't eat dairy products.

ya nye yem ma·*loch*·na·va

Я не ем молочного.

Do you have any vegetarian dishes?

u vas yest′ ve·ge·ta·ri·*an*·ski·e *blyu*·da

У вас есть вегетарианские блюда?

Does this dish have meat?

e·ta *blyu*·da myas·*no*·e

Это блюдо мясное?

Does it contain eggs?

v e·tam *blyu*·de yest′ *yay*·tsa

В этом блюде есть яйца?

I'm allergic to nuts.

u me·*nya* a·ler·*gi*·ya na a·*ra*·khi

У меня аллергия на орехи.

CHINA

I don't want MSG.	*Wǒ bú yào wèijīng.*	我不要味精
I'm vegetarian.	*Wǒ chī sù.*	我吃素
not too spicy	*bù yào tài là*	不要太辣
menu	*càidān*	菜单
bill (cheque)	*mǎidān/jiézhàng*	买单/结帐
set meal (no menu)	*tàocān*	套餐
let's eat	*chī fàn*	吃饭
cheers!	*gānbēi*	干杯
chopsticks	*kuàizi*	筷子
knife	*dàozi*	刀子
fork	*chāzi*	叉子
spoon	*tiáogēng/tāngchí*	调羹/汤匙
hot	*rède*	热的
ice cold	*bīngde*	冰的

MONGOLIA
I can't eat meat.
　bi makh i-dej cha-dakh-gui   Би мах идэж чадахгүй.
Can I have a menu please?
　bi khool-nii tses avch bo-lokh uu   Би хоолны цэс авч болох уу?
How much is it?
　e-ne ya-mar ü-ne-tei ve   Энэ ямар үнэтэй вэ?
What food do you have today?
　ö-nöö-dör ya-mar khool-toi ve   Өнөөдөр ямар хоолтой вэ?
When will the food be ready?
　khool khe-zee be-len bo-lokh ve   Хоол хэзээ бэлэн болох вэ?

Food Glossary
RUSSIA
Breakfast

bli·*ny*	блины	leavened buckwheat pancakes; also eaten as an appetiser or dessert
blin·chi·ki	блинчики	bliny rolled around meat or cheese and browned
ka·sha	каша	Russian-style buckwheat porridge
kye·fir	кефир	buttermilk, served as a drink
am·*lyet*	омлет	omelette
tva·*rog*	творог	cottage cheese
yay·*tso*	яйцо	egg
ya·*ich*·ni·tsa	яичница	fried egg

Lunch & Dinner

za·*ku*·ski	закуски	hors d'oeuvres
pyer·vi·e *blyu*·da	первые блюда	first courses (usually soups)
vto·*ri*·e *blyu*·da	вторые блюда	second courses or 'main' dishes
gar·*ya*·chi·e *blyu*·da	горячие блюда	hot courses or 'main' dishes
de·*syer*·ti	десерты	sweet courses or desserts

Methods of Preparation

va·*ryo*·ni	вареный	boiled
zhar·ni	жареный	roasted or fried
at·var·*noy*	отварной	poached or boiled
pe·*chyo*·ni	печёный	baked
fri	фри	fried

Appetisers

ik·*ra*	икра	black (sturgeon) caviar
ik·*ra kras*·na·ya	икра красная	red (salmon) caviar
gri·*bi* v sme·*ta*·ne	грибы в сметане	mushrooms baked in sour cream
zhul'·*yen* iz gri·*bov*	жульен из грибов	another name for mushrooms baked in sour cream
sa·*lat* iz pa·mi·*do*·rav	салат	tomato salad
sa·*lat* sta·*lich*·ni	салат столичный	salad of vegetable, beef, potato and egg in sour cream and mayonnaise

Soup

borsch	борщ	beetroot soup with vegetables and sometimes meat
lap·*sha*	лапша	noodle soup

ak·*rosh*·ka	окрошка	cold or hot soup made from cucumbers, sour cream, potatoes, eggs, meat and *kvas*
sal·*yan*·ka	солянка	thick meat or fish soup
u·*kha*	уха	fish soup with potatoes and vegetables
khar·*cho*	харчо	traditional Georgian soup of lamb, rice and spices
shchi	щи	cabbage or sauerkraut soup

Fish

ri·ba	рыба	fish
a·set·*ri*·na	осетрина	sturgeon
syom·ga	сёмга	salmon
su·*dak*	судак	pike, perch
fa·*ryel'*	форель	trout

Poultry & Meat Dishes

mya·sa	мясо	meat
an·tre·*kot*	антрекот	entrecôte – boned sirloin steak
ba·*ra*·ni·na	баранина	lamb or mutton
bif·stra·ga·*nov*	бифстроганов	beef stroganov – beef slices in a rich cream sauce
bif·*shteks*	бифштекс	'steak', usually a glorified hamburger
gav·*ya*·di·na	говядина	beef
ga·lub·*tsi*	голубцы	cabbage rolls stuffed with meat
zhar·*ko*·e pa da·*mash*·ne·mu	жаркое по-домашнему	meat stewed in a clay pot 'home-style', with mushrooms, potatoes and vegetables
pti·tsa	птица	chicken or poultry
kat·*lye*·ta	котлета	usually a croquette of ground meat
kat·*lye*·ta pa *ki*·ev·ski	котлета по-киевски	chicken Kiev; fried chicken breast stuffed with garlic butter
kat·*lye*·ta po- *zhar*·skaya	котлета по-жарски	croquette of minced chicken
kal·ba·*sa*	колбаса	a type of sausage
mya·sa pa ma·nas·*tir*·ski	мясо по-монастирски	meat topped with cheese and sour cream
pel'·*mye*·ni	пельмени	small meat dumplings
plov	плов	pilaf – fried rice with lamb and carrots
po·zi	пози	large meat dumplings
svi·*ni*·na	свинина	pork
shash·*lyk*	шашлык	skewered and grilled mutton or other meat
tef·te·li	тефтели	meat-and-rice balls

Vegetables

o·va·shchi	овощи	vegetables
gar·*ni*·ri	гарниры	any vegetable garnish
bak·la·*zhan*	баклажан	eggplant/aubergine
ches·*nok*	чеснок	garlic
ga·*rokh*	горох	peas
gri·*bi*	грибы	mushrooms

ka·*pus*·ta	капуста	cabbage
kar·*tosh*·ka/kar·*to*·fel′	картошка/картофель	potato
mar·*kov*′	морковь	carrots
zye·len′	зелень	greens
a·gur·*yets*	огурец	cucumber
pa·mi·*dor*	помидор	tomato

Fruit

fruk·ti	фрукты	fruit
ab·ri·*kos*	абрикос	apricot
a·pel′·*sin*	апельсин	orange
vish·nya	вишня	cherry
ba·*nan*	банан	banana
vi·na·*grad*	виноград	grapes
gru·sha	груша	pear
ya·bla·ka	яблоко	apple

Other Foods

mas·la	масло	butter
pye·rets	перец	pepper
ris	рис	rice
sa·khar	сахар	sugar
sol′	соль	salt
sir	сыр	cheese
khlyeb	хлеб	bread

Desserts

ma·*ro*·zhe·na·e	мороженое	ice cream
ki·syel′	кисель	fruit jelly/jello
kam·*pot*	компот	fruit in syrup
pi·*rozh*·na·e	пирожное	pastries

CHINA
Methods of Preparation

chǎo	炒	fry
hóngshāo	红烧	red-cooked (stewed in soy sauce)
kǎo	烤	roast
yóujiān	油煎	deep-fry
zhēng	蒸	steam
zhǔ	煮	boil

Rice Dishes

jīchǎofàn	鸡炒饭	fried rice with chicken
jīdàn chǎofàn	鸡蛋炒饭	fried rice with egg
mǐfàn	米饭	steamed white rice
shūcài chǎofàn	蔬菜炒饭	fried rice with vegetables
xīfàn; zhōu	稀饭；粥	watery rice porridge *(congee)*

Noodle Dishes

húntun miàn	馄饨面	wontons and noodles
jīsī chǎomiàn	鸡丝炒面	fried noodles with chicken
jīsī tāngmiàn	鸡丝汤面	soupy noodles with chicken
májiàng miàn	麻酱面	sesame paste noodles
niúròu chǎomiàn	牛肉炒面	fried noodles with beef
niúròu miàn	牛肉汤面	soupy beef noodles

ròusī chǎomiàn	肉丝炒面	fried noodles with pork
shūcài chǎomiàn	蔬菜炒面	fried noodles with vegetables
tāngmiàn	汤面	noodles in soup
xiārén chǎomiàn	虾仁炒面	fried noodles with shrimp
zhájiàng miàn	炸酱面	bean and meat noodles

Bread, Buns & Dumplings

cōngyóu bǐng	葱油饼	spring onion pancakes
guōtiē	锅贴	pot stickers/pan-grilled dumplings
mántóu	馒头	steamed buns
ròu bāozǐ	肉包子	steamed meat buns
shāo bǐng	烧饼	clay-oven rolls
shǔijiān bāo	水煎包	pan-grilled buns
shuǐjiǎo	水饺	boiled dumplings
sùcài bāozi	素菜包子	steamed vegetable buns

Soup

húntun tāng	馄饨汤	wonton soup
sān xiān tāng	三鲜汤	three kinds of seafood soup
suānlà tāng	酸辣汤	hot and sour soup

Beef Dishes

gānbiān niúròu sī	干煸牛肉丝	stir-fried beef and chilli
háoyóu niúròu	蚝油牛肉	beef with oyster sauce
hóngshāo niúròu	红烧牛肉	beef braised in soy sauce
niúròu fàn	牛肉饭	beef with rice
tiěbǎn niúròu	铁板牛肉	sizzling beef platter

Chicken & Duck Dishes

háoyóu jīkuài	蚝油鸡块	diced chicken in oyster sauce
hóngshāo jīkuài	红烧鸡块	chicken braised in soy sauce
jītuǐ fàn	鸡腿饭	chicken leg with rice
níngméng jī	柠檬鸡	lemon chicken
tángcù jīdīng	糖醋鸡丁	sweet and sour chicken
yāoguǒ jīdīng	腰果鸡丁	chicken and cashews
yāròu fàn	鸭肉饭	duck with rice

Pork Dishes

biǎndòu ròusī	扁豆肉丝	shredded pork and green beans
gūlǔ ròu	咕噜肉	sweet and sour pork
guōbā ròupiàn	锅巴肉片	pork and sizzling rice crust
háoyóu ròusī	耗油肉丝	pork with oyster sauce
jiàngbào ròudīng	酱爆肉丁	diced pork with soy sauce
jīngjiàng ròusī	京酱肉丝	pork cooked with soy sauce
mùèr ròu	木耳肉	wood-ear mushrooms and pork
páigǔ fàn	排骨饭	pork chop with rice
qīngjiāo ròupiàn	青椒肉片	pork and green peppers
yángcōng chǎo ròupiàn	洋葱炒肉片	pork and fried onions

Seafood Dishes

gélí	蛤蜊	clams
gōngbào xiārén	宫爆虾仁	diced shrimp with peanuts
háo	蚝	oysters
hóngshāo yú	红烧鱼	fish braised in soy sauce
lóngxiā	龙虾	lobster

pángxiè	螃蟹	crab
yóuyú	鱿鱼	squid
zhāngyú	章鱼	octopus

Vegetable & Bean Curd Dishes

báicài xiān shuānggū	白菜鲜双菇	bok choy and mushrooms
cuìpí dòufu	脆皮豆腐	crispy skin bean curd
hēimù'ěr mèn dòufu	黑木耳焖豆腐	bean curd with wood-ear mushrooms
hóngshāo qiézi	红烧茄子	red cooked aubergine
jiācháng dòufu	家常豆腐	'home-style' tofu
jiāngzhí qīngdòu	姜汁青豆	string beans with ginger
lúshuǐ dòufu	卤水豆腐	smoked bean curd
shāguō dòufu	砂锅豆腐	clay pot bean curd
sùchǎo biǎndòu	素炒扁豆	garlic beans
sùchǎo sùcài	素炒素菜	fried vegetables
tángcù ǒubǐng	糖醋藕饼	sweet and sour lotus root cakes
yúxiāng qiézi	鱼香茄子	'fish-resembling' aubergine

Fruit

bālè	芭乐	guava
bōluó	菠萝	pineapple
gānzhè	甘蔗	sugar cane
lí	梨	pear
lìzhī	荔枝	lychee
lóngyǎn	龙眼	'dragon eyes'
mángguǒ	芒果	mango
píngguǒ	苹果	apple
pútáo	葡萄	grape
xiāngjiāo	香蕉	banana
xīguā	西瓜	watermelon

MONGOLIA

shöl	шөл	soup
ban-shtai shöl	банштай шөл	dumpling soup
gu-ril-tai shöl	гурилтай шөл	handmade noodle soup
goi-mon-tai shöl	гоймонтой шөл	noodle soup
no-goon zuush	ногоон зууш	vegetable salad
bai-tsaan zuush	байцаан зууш	cabbage salad
luu-van-giin zuush	луувангийн зууш	carrot salad
niis-lel zuush	нийслэл зууш	potato salad
khuu-rag	хуурга	fried food
khuu-shuur	хуушуур	fried meat pancake
buuz	бууз	steamed mutton dumplings
tsui-van	цуйван	fried slices of dough with meat
bif-shteks	бифштекс	patty
makh	мах	meat
kho-ni-ny makh	хонины мах	mutton
shni-tsel	шницель	schnitzel
khuur-ga	хуурга	fried meat and flour in sauce
khor-khog	хорхог	meat roasted from the inside with hot stones
shar-san ön-dög	шарсан өндөг	fried egg
talkh	талх	bread
shar-san ta-khia	шарсан тахиа	fried chicken

zai-das/so-sisk	зайдас/сосиск	sausage
za-gas	загас	fish
bu-daa-tai	будаатай	rice
no-goo-toi	ногоотой	vegetables
tom-stei	төмстэй	potato
tsö-tsgii	цөггий	sour cream

DRINKS
Russia

va-*da*	вода	water
mi-ne-*ral*-na-ya va-*da*	минеральная вода	mineral water
ko-fe	кофе	coffee
chay	чай	tea
ma-la-*ko*	молоко	milk
sok	сок	juice
bez-al-ka-*gol'*-ni na-*pi*-tak	безалкогольный напиток	soft drink
vod-ka	водка	vodka
ig-*ris*-ta-e vi-*no*/sham-*pan*-ska-e	игристое вино/шампанское	sparkling wine/champagne
kras-na-e vi-*no*	красное вино	red wine
bye-la-e vi-*no*	белое вино	white wine
kan-*yak*	коньяк	brandy
pi-*vo*	пиво	beer
kvas	квас	fermented bread drink

China

bái pútáo jiǔ	白葡萄酒	white wine
báijiǔ	白酒	Chinese spirits
chá	茶	tea
dòujiāng	豆浆	soya bean milk
hóng pútáo jiǔ	红葡萄酒	red wine
kāfēi	咖啡	coffee
kāi shuǐ	开水	water (boiled)
kěkǒu kělè	可口可乐	Coca-Cola
kuàngquán shuǐ	矿泉水	mineral water
mǐjiǔ	米酒	rice wine
nǎijīng	奶精	coffee creamer
niúnǎi	牛奶	milk
píjiǔ	啤酒	beer
qìshuǐ	汽水	soft drink (soda)
suānnǎi	酸奶	yoghurt
yézi zhī	椰子汁	coconut juice

Mongolia

tsai	цай	tea
ban-shtai tsai	банштай цай	dumplings in tea
süü-tei tsai	сүүтэй цай	Mongolian milk tea
ra-shaan us	рашаан ус	mineral water
shar ai-rag	шар айраг	beer
air-ag	айраг	fermented mare's milk

St Petersburg
Санкт Петербург

The birthplace of Russia's passenger railways, St Petersburg makes a fine start or finish to any Trans-Siberian journey. The locals call the city, simply, Piter. In its time – some 300 action-packed years and counting – it has been known by several other names all resonant of and appropriate to its pivotal place in Russian history. But whatever it's called there's no denying that St Petersburg is one of the most glorious cities in Russia, if not the world.

Look up from the banks of the Neva River and the canals that meander through the heart of the city and you'll gaze upon a seamless showcase of 18th- and 19th-century architecture. Enter these palaces and mansions and you'll discover a mind-boggling collection of museums covering practically everything from anthropology to zoology, and culminating in the truly breathtaking artistic collection belonging to the Hermitage.

It's small wonder that such an environment has nurtured some of Russia's greatest artists and cultural movements. Creativity continues to throb through the city's veins manifesting itself in a hedonistic and experimental nightclub and performing arts scene, as well as a delicious crop of restaurants.

Not everything is perfect: St Petersburg's splendour goes hand in hand with corruption, crime, decay, squalor and pollution. If anything, though, this gritty reality makes the city's dazzling façades and lightness of spirit seem even more magical. St Petersburg's beauty is one with a human face and all the more appealing for that.

HIGHLIGHTS

- Lose yourself amid the artistic treasures and imperial interiors of the **Hermitage** (p85)
- Cruise the **canals** (p90) for a boatman's perspective on the city's architecture and pretty bridges
- Enjoy a world-class opera or ballet performance at the beautiful **Mariinsky Theatre** (p92)
- Admire the Grand Cascade's symphony of fountains at **Petrodvorets** (p95)
- Feel your jaw hit the parquet floor as you take in the gilded splendour of **Catherine Palace** (p96)

- TELEPHONE CODE: 812
- POPULATION: 4.4 MILLION

HISTORY

St Petersburg was born when Peter the Great founded the Peter & Paul Fortress on the marshy estuary of the Neva River in 1703. A city built to grand design by mainly European architects swiftly followed. By the early 19th century St Petersburg had firmly established itself as the cultural centre of Russia. But at the same time as writers, artists and musicians, such as Pushkin, Turgenev and, later, Tchaikovsky and Dostoevsky, lived in and were inspired by the city, political and social problems were on the rise.

Industrialisation brought a flood of poor workers and associated urban squalor to St Petersburg. Revolution against the monarchy was first attempted in the short-lived coup of 14 December 1825. The leaders (who included members of the aristocracy and who became known as the Decembrists) were banished to the outer edges of the empire (see p194).

The next revolution was in 1905, sparked by the 'Bloody Sunday' of 9 January when more than a hundred people were killed and hundreds more were injured after troops fired on a crowd petitioning the tsar outside the Winter Palace. The tsar's government limped on, until Vladimir Lenin and his Bolshevik followers took advantage of Russia's disastrous involvement in WWI to instigate the third successful revolution in 1917. Again, St Petersburg (renamed a more Russian-sounding Petrograd in 1914) was at the forefront of the action.

To break with the tsarist past, the seat of government was moved back to Moscow, and St Petersburg was renamed Leningrad after the first communist leader's death in 1924. The city – by virtue of its location, three million–plus population and industry – remained one of Russia's most important, thus putting it on the frontline during WWII. For 872 days Leningrad was besieged by the Germans, and one million perished in horrendous conditions.

After the war Leningrad was almost entirely reconstructed. As the Soviet Union came tumbling down, the city renamed itself St Petersburg in 1991. Millions of roubles were spent on restoration for the city's tricentenary celebrations and St Petersburg looks better now probably than at any other time in its history – a source of great pride to local boy made good President Vladimir Putin, who often returns to his birthplace to show it off to official visitors.

ORIENTATION

St Petersburg sprawls across and around the delta of the Neva River, at the end of the easternmost arm of the Baltic Sea, the Gulf of Finland. Entering St Petersburg at its southeastern corner, the Neva first flows north and then west across the middle of the city, dividing there into several branches and forming the islands making up the delta. The two biggest branches, which diverge where the Winter Palace stands on the south bank, are the Bolshaya (Big) Neva and Malaya (Small) Neva; they flow into the sea either side of Vasilyevsky Island.

If you arrive by train from Moscow, your entry point will be Moskovsky vokzal (Moscow Station) at the eastern end of Nevsky pr, St Petersburg's main thoroughfare, which heads west for about 3km through the heart

---

ST PETERSBURG IN...

One Day
Take a tour of the **Hermitage** (p85). Enjoy an afternoon stroll in the nearby **Summer Garden** (p87) and a peek inside the beautifully restored **Sheremetyev Palace** (p87) along the Fontanka Canal. Hop on a boat for an early evening **cruise** (p90). If you're quick, you could also squeeze in a visit to **St Isaac's Cathedral** (p87), climbing its colonnade for a bird's-eye view of the city.

Two Days
On day two explore the splendid **Russian Museum** (p85). Move on to the polychromatic **Church of the Saviour on Spilled Blood** (p87). After lunch head across the Neva River to explore the **Peter & Paul Fortress** (p89). If you have time, continue around to the **Strelka** (p88) to see the museums there, or to enjoy the view.

Four Days
Following on from the previous two days, spend a day each exploring the imperial parks and palaces at **Petrodvorets** (p95) and **Tsarskoe Selo** (p96). Cap off your trip with a performance at the **Mariinsky Theatre** (p92).

of the city towards the south bank of the Neva and the Winter Palace. All trains from the Baltic countries and Eastern Europe arrive at Vitebsky vokzal (Vitebsk Station), 2km southwest of Moscow Station. Trains from Helsinki end up at Ladozhsky vokzal (Ladoga Station) across the Neva in the eastern area known as the Vyborg Side.

The other main areas north of the Neva are Vasilyevsky Island, on the westernmost side of the city – at its eastern end is the Strelka (Tongue of Land), where many of the city's early buildings stand; and the Petrograd Side, a cluster of delta islands marked by the Peter & Paul Fortress.

Maps

Dom Knigi (below) has the best map selection, including maps of transport routes and several street directories.

INFORMATION
Bookshops

Anglia (Map p86; ☎ 279 8284; nab reki Fontanki 40; ☽ 10am-7pm; Ⓜ Gostiny Dvor) St Petersburg's only English-language bookshop.

Dom Knigi (Map p86; ☎ 325 6696; Nevsky pr 62; ☽ 8am-11pm Mon-Sat, 9am-10pm Sun; Ⓜ Gostiny Dvor) Good selection of guidebooks and maps at St Petersburg's largest bookshop.

Emergency

The following numbers have Russian-speaking operators. If you need to make a police report and don't speak Russian, first contact the City Tourist Information Centre (p84). For serious matters contact your embassy or consulate (p304).

Ambulance (☎ 03)
Fire (☎ 01)
Gas leak (☎ 04)
Police (☎ 02)

Internet Access

Internet cafés are common in St Petersburg. Wi-fi hot spots are also scattered across the city, including at City Bar (p92) and Zoom Café (p91).

Café Max (Map p86; ☎ 273 6655; Nevsky pr 90/92; per hr R40; ☽ 24hr; Ⓜ Mayakovskaya) Wi-fi available. Also has a branch in the Hermitage (p85).

FM Club (Map p86; ☎ 764 3674; ul Dostoevskogo 6A; per hr R60; ☽ 10am-8am; Ⓜ Vladimirskaya)

Quo Vadis? (Map p86; ☎ 571 8011; Nevsky pr 24; per hr R80; ☽ 24hr; Ⓜ Gostiny Dvor) Wi-fi available.

Internet Resources

http://enlight.ru/camera/index_e.htm The excellent Wandering Camera website includes some 300 photo albums of the city.

http://spb.yell.ru/eng/default.asp?site=spb Yellow Pages for St Petersburg.

www.eng.gov.spb.ru Official site of the St Petersburg government.

www.saint-petersburg.com Has information on sights, current events and listings, a virtual city tour, online hotel booking and an up-to-date traveller's message board.

Laundry

Stirka (Map p86; ☎ 314 5371; Kazanskaya ul 26; ☽ 9am-11pm Mon-Fri, 10am-1am Sat & Sun; Ⓜ Nevsky Prospekt) Combines a café-bar with a laundrette – what a good idea! A 5kg wash costs R100 with espresso included. The dryer is R30 per 20 minutes.

Left Luggage

All the major train stations have luggage lockers and/or left-luggage services.

Media

The following English-language publications are available free at many hotels, hostels, restaurants and bars across the city:

In Your Pocket (www.inyourpocket.com/russia /st_petersburg/en) Monthly listings booklet with useful up-to-date information and short features.

Pulse (www.pulse.ru) Slick colour monthly with fun features and reviews.

St Petersburg Times (http://sptimesrussia.com) Published every Tuesday and Friday, this newspaper is the best source of information. It has an indispensable listings and arts review section.

Medical Services

The following clinics are open 24 hours and have English-speaking staff:

American Medical Clinic (Map p86; ☎ 740 2090; www.amclinic.ru; nab reki Moyki 78; Ⓜ Sadovaya)

British-American Family Practice (Map p86; ☎ 327 6030, 999 0949; Grafsky per 7; Ⓜ Dostoevskaya)

International Clinic (Map p86; ☎ 320 3870; www .icspb.com; ul Dostoevskogo 19/21; Ⓜ Ligovsky Prospekt)

Look for the sign *apteka*, or the usual green cross, to find a pharmacy. The following are two central pharmacies that are open 24 hours:

Apteka (Map p86; ☎ 277 5962; Nevsky pr 83; Ⓜ Ploshchad Vosstaniya)

Apteka Petrofarm (Map p86; ☎ 314 5401; Nevsky pr 22; Ⓜ Nevsky Prospekt)

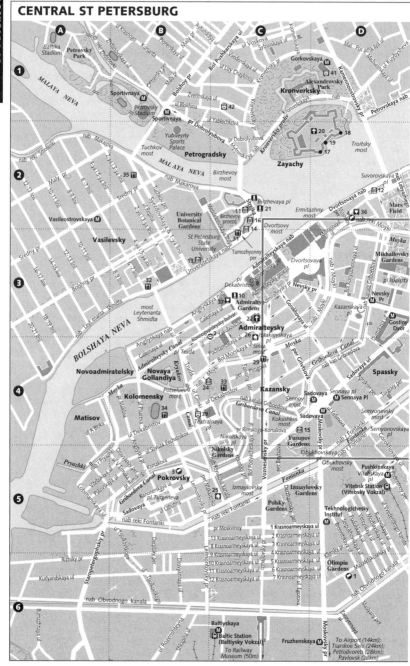

CENTRAL ST PETERSBURG

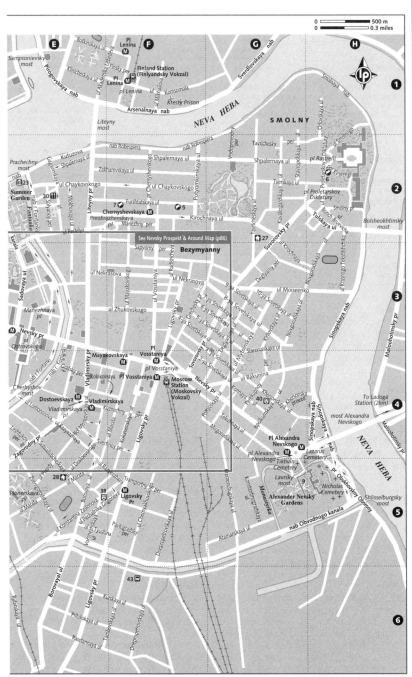

Money

There are currency-exchange offices all along Nevsky pr. ATMs are located inside every metro station, in hotels and department stores, main post offices and along major streets.

Post

Post office branches are scattered throughout the city. All the major air-courier services are available in St Petersburg.
Central Post Office (Map pp82-3; ☎ 312 8302; www.spbpost.ru; Konnogvardeysky Bul 4; ☺ 9am-8pm Mon-Sat, 10am-6pm Sun; Ⓜ Sadovaya) The express mail service EMS Garantpost is available here.

Telephone

Calling from a private phone is the simplest, though not necessarily cheapest, option – except for local calls, which are free.

See p312 for details of mobile-phone service providers. You can buy a local SIM card at any mobile-phone shop from as little as R300 – there's a handy phone shop inside the Quo Vadis? Internet café (see p81).

Local phonecards are available from shops, kiosks and metro stations, and can be used to make local, national and international calls from any phone. Better value for international calls are call centres – look for the sign Mezhdunarodny Telefon.

The most convenient is the **Central Telephone Office** (Map p86; Bolshaya Morskaya ul 28; ☺ 24hr; Ⓜ Nevsky Prospekt).

Toilets

Portakabin-type toilets (R10) outside metros and the major sights are common. Shopping centres and chain cafés, such as Idealnaya Chashka and Chainaya Lozhka, are the best places to look for a clean, odour-free loo.

Tourist Information

City Tourist Information Centre Sadovaya ul (Map p86; ☎ 310 8262; www.ctic.spb.ru; Sadovaya ul 14/52; ☺ 10am-7pm Mon-Sat; Ⓜ Gostiny Dvor); Dvortsovaya pl (Map p86; Dvortsovaya pl 12; ☺ 10am-7pm Mon-Sat, 10am-4pm Sun; Ⓜ Nevsky Prospekt) The city tourist office's website is a paltry affair in Russian only. The English-speaking staff are vague about most things but will do their best to help, particularly if you are a crime victim (as we can personally attest). The Dvortsovaya pl branch is in a glass booth outside the Hermitage.

Travel Agencies

The English-speaking staff at the following agencies can issue visa invitations and assist in getting a visa registered once you've arrived.
Ost-West Kontaktservice (Map p86; ☎ 327 3416; www.ostwest.com; Nevsky pr 105; ☺ 10am-6pm Mon-Fri; Ⓜ Ploshchad Vosstaniya) Offering apartment rentals,

organised tours and tickets – heck, staff will even sell you a Lomo (it's the city's official distributor of that nifty little Russian camera).

Sindbad Travel (Map p86; ☎ 332 2020; www.sindbad .ru; 2-ya Sovetskaya ul 12; ☺ 9am-10pm Mon-Fri, 10am-6pm Sat & Sun; ⓜ Ploshchad Vosstaniya) This is the main office of the agency owned by the HI St Petersburg International Hostel (p90); it also has a branch inside the hostel itself. It's a Western-style discount air-ticket office, staffed by friendly, knowledgeable people. It also sells ISIC/ITIC/IYTC cards and can book youth hostel accommodation through the IBN system.

DANGERS & ANNOYANCES

Watch out for pickpockets, particularly along Nevsky pr around Griboedova Canal and in crowded places such as theatres and cinemas. Non-Caucasians should be aware that St Petersburg is notorious for race-related violent attacks. Avoid wandering around alone late at night or venturing out to the suburbs solo at any time.

Every year in early spring and during winter thaws, several people die when hit by giant icicles falling from rooftops and balconies; take care to make sure one of these monsters is not dangling above your head. From May to September mosquitoes are another nightmare.

Never drink unboiled tap water in St Petersburg as it could contain harmful bacteria, such as *Giardia Lamblia,* a parasite that causes stomach cramps, nausea, bloated stomach, diarrhoea and frequent gas.

SIGHTS

In a few days you'll only be able to scratch the surface of what St Petersburg has to offer, particularly if you include a day trip to one of the country palaces. The following are the major sights; for more information, see Lonely Planet's *Russia & Belarus* or *St Petersburg* city guide.

The Hermitage & Dvortsovaya Ploshchad

Mainly set in the magnificent Winter Palace, the **Hermitage** (Map p86; ☎ 571 3465; www .hermitagemuseum.org; Dvortsovaya nab 34; adult R350, ISIC cardholders & under 17 free, use of camera/camcorder R100/350; ☺ 10.30am-6pm Tue-Sat, 10.30am-5pm Sun) fully lives up to its sterling reputation. You can be absorbed by its treasures for days and still come out wishing for more. Enter via Dvortsovaya pl.

The museum's main entrance is from **Dvortsovaya ploshchad** (Palace Sq), one of the most impressive and historic spaces in the city. Stand back to admire the palace and the central 47.5m **Alexander Column**, named after Alexander I and commemorating the 1812 victory over Napoleon. Enclosing the square's south side is the **General Staff Building** (Map p86; ☎ 314 8260; Dvortsovaya pl 6-8; adult/student R200/free; ☺ 10am-6pm Tue-Sun), two great classical blocks joined by arches and topped by a chariot of victory. Inside is a branch of the Hermitage.

Queues to enter the Winter Palace, particularly from May to September, can be horrendous. Avoid them by booking your ticket online through the Hermitage's website: US$16 gains you entrance plus use of camera or camcorder to the main Hermitage buildings; US$24 is for the two-day ticket to all the Hermitage's collections in the city. You'll be issued with a voucher that allows you to go straight to the ticket booth.

Joining a tour is another way to avoid queuing. These whiz round the main sections in about 1½ hours and provide an introduction to the place in English. It's easy to 'lose' the group and stay on until closing time. To book a tour call the museum's **excursions office** (☎ 571 8446; ☺ 11am-1pm & 2-4pm); staff will tell you when they are running tours in English, German or French and when to turn up. Tours cost R1500 for up to 25 people.

Russian Museum

Facing onto the elegant pl Iskusstv (Art's Sq) is the former Mikhailovsky Palace, now the **Russian Museum** (Map p86; ☎ 595 4248; www.rus museum.ru; Inzhenernaya ul 4; adult/student R300/150; ☺ 10am-5pm Mon, 10am-6pm Wed-Sun), housing one of the country's finest collections of Russian art. After the Hermitage you may feel you have had your fill of art, but try your utmost to make some time for this gem of a museum.

The museum owns three other city palaces, all worth visiting if you have time, where permanent and temporary exhibitions are held: the **Marble Palace** (Map pp82-3; ☎ 312 9196; Millionnaya ul 5; adult/student R300/150; ☺ 10am-5pm Wed-Mon); the **Mikhailovsky Castle** (Engineers' Castle; Map p86; ☎ 313 4173; Sadovaya ul 2; adult/student R300/150; ☺ 10am-5pm Mon, 10am-6pm Wed-Sun); and the **Stroganov Palace** (Map p86;

NEVSKY PROSPEKT & AROUND

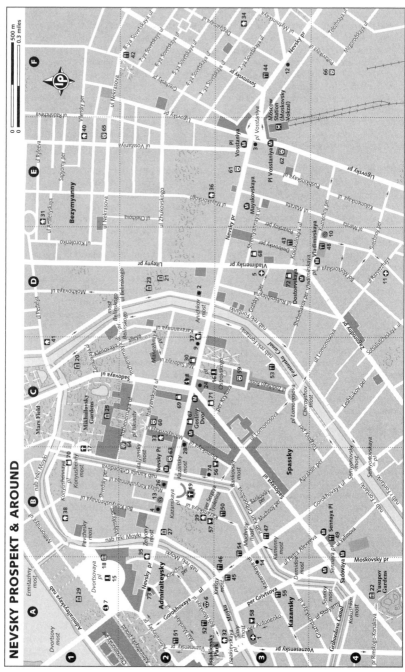

☎ 219 1608; Nevsky pr 17; adult/student R300/150; ☺ 10am-5pm Tue-Sun). A ticket for R600, available at each palace, covers entry to all of them within a 24-hour period.

Church of the Saviour on Spilled Blood

This multidomed dazzler of a **church** (Map p86; ☎ 315 1636; eng.cathedral.ru; Konyushennaya pl; adult/student R270/150; ☺ 11-7pm Thu-Tue Oct-Apr, 10am-8pm Thu-Tue May-Sep), partly modelled on St Basil's in Moscow, was built between 1883 and 1907 on the spot where Alexander II was assassinated in 1881 (hence its gruesome name). The interior's 7000 sq metres of mosaics fully justify the entrance fee.

St Isaac's Cathedral

The golden dome of this **cathedral** (Map pp82-3; ☎ 315 9732; eng.cathedral.ru; Isaakievskaya pl; adult/student R270/150; ☺ 10am-8pm Thu-Mon, closed last Mon of the month) dominates the city skyline. Its lavish interior is open as a museum, but many visitors just buy the separate ticket to climb

the 262 steps up to the **colonnade** (adult/student R120/70; ☺ 10am-7pm Thu-Mon, closed last Mon of the month) around the dome's drum; the views make the climb worthwhile.

Summer Garden

Perhaps St Petersburg's loveliest park, the **Summer Garden** (Map pp82-3; ☺ 10am-10pm May-Sep, 10am-8pm Oct–mid-Apr) is a great place to relax. In its northeast corner is the modest, two-storey **Summer Palace** (☎ 314 0456; adult/student R300/150; ☺ 10am-5pm Wed-Mon early May-early Nov) built for Peter from 1710 to 1714. Inside it's stocked with early-18th-century furnishings of limited appeal.

Sheremetyev Palace

Facing the Fontanka Canal, the splendid **Sheremetyev Palace** (1750–55) houses two lovely museums. The **Museum of Theatrical & Musical Arts** (Map p86; ☎ 272 4441; www.theatremuseum.ru/eng; nab reki Fontanki 34; adult/student R150/75; ☺ noon-6pm Wed-Sun; Ⓜ Gostiny Dvor) contains a lovely collection of beautifully decorated instruments. Upstairs the palace rooms have been wonderfully restored; you get a great sense of how cultured life must have been here.

In a separate wing of the palace, reached from Liteyny pr, is the charming **Museum of Anna Akhmatova in the Fountain House** (Map p86; ☎ 272 2211; www.akhmatova.spb.ru/en; Liteyny pr 53; adult/student R120/80; ☉ 10am-5.30pm Tue-Sun, closed last Wed of month; Ⓜ Mayakovskaya), filled with mementos of the poet and her family, all persecuted during Soviet times.

Yusupov Palace

Best known as the place where Rasputin met his untimely end, the **Yusupov Palace** (Map pp82-3; ☎ 314 9883; nab reki Moyki 94; adult/student R350/250; ☉ 11am-5pm; Ⓜ Sadovaya or Sennaya Ploshchad) sports a series of sumptuously decorated rooms culminating in a gilded jewel box of a theatre, where performances are still held. Admission includes an audio tour in English or several other languages. Places are limited to 20 daily for the Murder of Rasputin tour (adult/student extra R150/120) on each of the two English-language tours.

Railway Museums

Every child's dream will be realised at the **Museum of Railway Transport** (Map p86; ☎ 315 1476; www.railroad.ru/cmrt in Russian; Sadovaya ul 50; adult/student R100/50; ☉ 11am-5pm Wed-Sun, closed last Thu of month; Ⓜ Sadovaya or Sennaya Ploshchad), which holds a fascinating collection of scale locomotives and model railway bridges often made by the engineers who built the real ones. As the oldest such collection in the world (the museum was established in 1809, 28 years before Russia had its first working train!), it includes models of Krasnoyarsk's *Yenisey Bridge*, the ship that once carried passengers and trains across Lake Baikal. It also has a sumptuous 1903 Trans-Siberian wagon complete with a piano salon and a bathtub.

Train spotters should also hasten to view the impressive collection of full-sized locomotives at the **Railway Museum** (☎ 768 2063; nab Obvodnogo Kanala; adult/student R100/50; ☉ 10am-6pm; Ⓜ Baltiyskaya), behind the old Warsaw Station: some 75 nicely painted and buffed engines and carriages are on display, including one dating from 1897.

HISTORIC TRAIN STATIONS

As the birthplace of Russia's railway system, it's not surprising that St Petersburg has some grand train stations. The oldest and most elegant is **Vitebsk Station** (Map pp82-3; Ⓜ Pushkinskaya), originally built in 1837 for the line to Tsarskoe Selo. The current building dates from 1904 and is partly graced with gorgeous Style Moderne (Russian Art Nouveau) interior decoration.

While at **Moscow Station** (Map p86; Ⓜ Ploshchad Vosstaniya), look up at the expansive ceiling mural in the main entrance hall. There's a striking bust of Peter the Great in the hall leading to the platforms.

Finland Station (Map pp82-3; Ⓜ Ploshchad Lenina), rebuilt after WWII, is famous as the place where, in April 1917, Lenin arrived from exile and gave his legendary speech atop an armoured car in the square. Lenin's statue, pointing across the Neva, stands outside the station.

For more historic train stations along the Trans-Siberian Route, see p15.

Vasilyevsky Island

Some of the best views of St Petersburg can be had from Vasilyevsky Island's eastern 'nose' known as the **Strelka**. The two **Rostral Columns** on the point, studded with ships' prows, were oil-fired navigation beacons in the 1800s; on some holidays, such as **Victory Day**, gas torches are still lit on them.

The best of many museums gathered on Vasilyevsky Island is the riverside **Menshikov Palace** (Map pp82-3; ☎ 332 1112; www.hermitage museum.com/html_En/03/hm3_9.html; Universitetskaya nab 15; adult/student R200/100; ☉ 10.30am-4.30pm Tue-Sun), built in 1707 for Peter the Great's confidant Alexander Menshikov. Now a branch of the Hermitage (p85), the palace's impressively restored interiors are filled with period art and furniture.

The **Museum of Anthropology & Ethnography** (Map pp82-3; ☎ 328 1412; www.kunstkamera.ru/english; entrance on Tamozhyonny per; adult/student R100/50; ☉ 10.30am-6pm Tue-Sat, 10.30am-5pm Sun), also known as the Kunstkamera, was established in 1714 by Peter the Great, who used it to display his ghoulish collection of monstrosities, notably preserved freaks, two-headed mutant foetuses and odd body parts: they still draw the crowds today.

Housed in what was once the Stock Exchange, the **Central Naval Museum** (Map pp82-3; ☎ 328 2502; www.museum.navy.ru/index_e.htm; Birzhevaya pl 4; adult/student R100/15; ☼ 11am-6pm Wed-Sun, closed last Thu of the month), is a must for naval enthusiasts. Next door, the **Museum of Zoology** (Map pp82-3; ☎ 328 0112; www.zin.ru/mus_e.htm; Universitetskaya nab 1/3; adult/child R60/30, free Thu; ☼ 11am-6pm Sat-Thu) has some amazing exhibits, including a complete woolly mammoth, thawed out of the Siberian ice in 1902, and a live insect zoo!

Peter & Paul Fortress

Set aside some time to explore the **fortress** (Map pp82-3; ☎ 238 4550; Petropavlovskaya krepost, Kronverkskaya nab; free entry to grounds, admission to all buildings adult/student R120/60; ☼ 11am-6pm Thu-Mon, 11am-5pm Tue May-Sep, Cathedral & Bastion 11am-6pm daily; Ⓜ Gorkovskaya), as there's plenty to do and see here. Dating from 1703, this is the oldest building in St Petersburg, planned by Peter the Great as a defence against the Swedes. It never saw action and its main use up to 1917 was as a political prison.

To get a sense of the scale of the place, and for river views, walk the **Nevskaya Panorama** (adult/student R50/30; ☼ 10am-8pm) along part of the battlements, then enter the **SS Peter & Paul Cathedral**, whose 122m-tall, needle-thin gilded spire is one of the city's defining landmarks. Its magnificent baroque interior is the last resting place of all of Russia's prerevolutionary rulers from Peter the Great onward, except Peter II and Ivan VI.

At noon every day a cannon is fired from **Naryshkin Bastion**. In the south wall is **Nevsky Gate**, where prisoners were loaded onto boats for execution. Notice the plaques showing water levels of famous floods.

WALKING TOUR

Walking Nevsky Pr – Russia's most famous street – is an essential St Petersburg experience. Starting at Dvortsovaya pl, notice the gilded spire of the **Admiralty** (Map pp82–3) to your right as you head southeast down Nevsky towards the Moyka River. Across the Moyka, Rastrelli's baroque **Stroganov Palace** (Map p86), containing a branch of the Russian Museum (p85), is looking grand after restoration for the 2003 tricentenary.

A block beyond the Moyka, on the southern side of Nevsky pr, see the great arms of the **Kazan Cathedral** (Map p86; ☎ 318 4528; www.kazansky.ru in Russian; Kazanskaya pl 2; admission free; ☼ 10am-7pm) reach out towards the avenue. It's a working cathedral, so please show some respect for the local customs if you enter. Services are held at 10am and 6pm.

Opposite the cathedral is the **Singer Building** (Map p86), a Style Moderne beauty recently restored to all its splendour when it was the headquarters of the sewing machine company. A short walk south of the cathedral, along Griboedova Canal, sits one of St Petersburg's loveliest bridges, the **Bankovsky most** (Map p86). The cables of this 25.2m-long bridge are supported by four cast-iron gryphons with golden wings.

View the lavish **Grand Hotel Europe** (p90), built between 1873 and 1875, redone in Style Moderne in the 1910s and completely renovated in the early 1990s. Across Nevsky pr, the fashionable arcades of **Gostiny Dvor** (Map p86) department store face the clock tower of the former **Town Duma** (Map p86), seat of the prerevolutionary city government. One of the world's first indoor shopping malls, Gostiny Dvor dates from 1757–85.

The arcade at 48 Nevsky pr, the **Passazh** (Map p86) department store, is also beautiful (notice the glass ceilings), while on the corner of Sadovaya ul is the Style Moderne beauty **Yeliseyevsky** (Map p86; Nevsky pr 56; ☼ 9am-9pm Mon-Fri, 11am-9pm Sat & Sun), the most sumptuous 'grocery store' you may have ever seen.

An enormous statue of **Catherine the Great** stands at the centre of **Ploshchad Ostrovskogo** (Map p86), commonly referred to as the Catherine Gardens. The square's western side is taken up by the lavish **National Library of Russia** (Map p86), St Petersburg's biggest with some 31 million items; at the southern end is **Aleksandrinksy Theatre** (Map p86), also known as the Pushkin Theatre, where Chekhov's *The Seagull* premiered in 1896.

Nevsky pr crosses the Fontanka Canal on the **Anichkov most** (Map p86), with its famous 1840s statues (sculpted by the German Pyotr Klodt) of rearing horses at its four corners.

WALK FACTS

Start Ploshchad Dvortsovaya
Finish Anichkov most
Distance 2km
Duration Around one hour

ST PETERSBURG

TOURS

The best tour guides to help show you St
Petersburg are with **Peter's Tours** (www.peters
walk.com). Its standard walking tour (R400)
departs from the HI St Petersburg International Hostel (right) at 10.30am daily. It
also offers lots of cool themed tours,
with customised tours kicking off at R800
an hour for up to four people from May to
November.

Viewing St Petersburg from a boat is an
idyllic way to tour the city, and during the
main tourist season (May to October) there
are no shortage of opportunities to do this.
There are four regular fixed-route hop-on,
hop-off cruises on large **water buses** (tickets
R200; ☼ 11am-7pm), which run from several
landing stages around St Petersburg's centre. At the same places you'll find many
private operators of smaller cruise boats
(from around R150 for 40 minutes), as well
as small boats that can be hired as private
water taxis. You'll have to haggle over rates:
expect to pay around R1500 an hour for a
small group.

FESTIVALS & EVENTS

The city's biggest event is the **White Nights
Arts Festival**, which includes numerous events
ranging from folk to ballet. The official festival dates are the last 10 days of the month
but all kinds of arts events and performances take place across the city throughout
June and often into July, with the Mariinsky
Theatre taking the lead.

SLEEPING

Unless otherwise mentioned, the accommodation rates in St Petersburg are for high
season and include breakfast.

The following agencies can arrange homestays (from US$30 per night) and apart-
ment rentals (from US$60 per night) across
the city:

City Realty (Map pp82-3; ☎ 312 7842; www.city
realtyrussia.com; Bolshaya Morskaya ul 35; Ⓜ Nevsky
Prospekt)

Host Families Association (HOFA; Map pp82-3;
☎ /fax 275 1992; http://webcenter.ru/~hofa; ul Tav-
richeskaya 5/25; Ⓜ Ploshchad Vosstaniya) Homestays
start with basic B&B rooms (single/double from US$25/40).

Ost-West Kontaktservice (Map p86; ☎ 327 3416;
www.ostwest.com; Nevsky pr 105; ☼ 10am-6pm Mon-Fri;
Ⓜ Ploshchad Vosstaniya) For details about its services,
see p84.

Budget

Nord Hostel (Map p86; ☎ 571 0342; www.nordhostel
.com; Bolshaya Morskaya ul 10; dm/d €24/48; Ⓜ Nevsky
Prospekt; Ⓛ) The Nord Hostel lies in an un-
beatable location, and has spacious dorms
in an elegant old building, newish Ikea fit-
tings, free Internet access and international
calls. Booking in advance via the Web is
advised.

Russian Room (Map p86; ☎ 900 9928; www.russian
room.org; Apt 32, Vilensky per 5; dm/d €15/35; Ⓜ Ploshchad Vosstaniya; Ⓛ) This is the main of the
two locations for Russian Room (the other,
open during summer only, is at ul Pestelya
13/15; Map p86), which gives travellers a
chance to stay in a cosy Russian apartment.
Advance booking is essential; it can also
arrange visa invitations for €22 and registration for €10.

Hotel California (Map pp82-3; ☎ 901 301 6061;
www.hotelcalifornia.ru; Apt 36, 67/17 ul Marata; dm from €16;
Ⓜ Vladimirskaya; Ⓛ) The entrance to this well-
equipped, comfortable new hostel is through
the courtyard on Sotsialistcheskaya ul. Run
by some rock musicians, it promises to be a
lively place to stay.

HI St Petersburg International Hostel (Map p86;
☎ 329 8018; www.ryh.ru; 3-ya Sovetskaya ul 28; dm/d
US$23/56; Ⓜ Ploshchad Vosstaniya; Ⓛ) St Peters-
burg's oldest hostel remains popular among
travellers. It has several clean, simply furnished dorms and one double room; all
rates are slightly cheaper from November to
March and for ISIC and HI cardholders.
There's also a kitchen for self-catering and
a video room.

Midrange & Top End

Rachmaninow Antique-Hotel (Map p86; ☎ 327 7466; 3rd fl, Kazanskaya ul 5; s & d from US$170; Ⓜ Nevsky Prospekt; ⊠ 🖵) At this stylish mini-hotel the minimalist décor is offset by antiques, and contemporary photography and paintings throughout the premises.

Pushka Inn (Map p86; ☎ 312 0913; www.pushka inn.ru; nab reki Moyki 14; s/d/apt from €100/160/200; Ⓜ Nevsky Prospekt; ⊠ 🖵) Offers modern furnished rooms and apartments, some overlooking one of the city's prettiest stretches of canal. The spacious, well-equipped apartments are a great deal.

Polikoff Hotel (Map p86; ☎ 314 7925; www.poli koff.ru; Nevsky pr 64/11; s/d from €80/100; Ⓜ Gostiny Dvor; ⊠ 🖵) Tricky to find (the entrance is through the brown door on Karavannaya ul, where you'll need to punch in 26 for reception), the Polikoff has rooms brimming with contemporary cool décor, a central location and pleasant service.

Arbat Nord Hotel (Map p86; ☎ 703 1899; www.ar bat-nord.ru; ul Artilleriyskaya 4; s/d €185/195; Ⓜ Chernyshevskaya; ⊠ 🖵) This sleek new hotel offers comfortable rooms, a good restaurant and friendly English-speaking staff.

Alexander House (Map pp82-3; ☎ 259 6877; www .a-house.ru; nab Kryukova kanala 27; s/d from R4995/5735, prices quoted in units; Ⓜ Sadovaya or Sennaya Ploshchad; ⊠ 🖵) This boutique hotel's 14 spacious rooms are each named and tastefully styled after the world's top cities. There's a comfortable lounge area with an attached kitchen for guests' use, and even a separate library and restaurant.

Grand Hotel Europe (Map p86; ☎ 329 6000; www .grand-hotel-europe.com; Mikhailovskaya ul 1/7; s/d/ste from US$470/510/690; Ⓜ Nevsky Prospekt; ✕ ⊠ 🖵) The height of luxury. Deservedly popular are the 17 terrace rooms with spectacular views across the city's rooftops. The beautiful Style Moderne décor of some of its bars and restaurants is worth a look in its own right. Rates are for a room only.

EATING
Restaurants

Zov Ilyicha (Map p86; ☎ 717 8641; Kazanskaya ul 34; mains R300-400; ⏰ 1pm-2am; Ⓜ Sadovaya) 'Lenin's Mating Call' is hands-down the city's ultimate Soviet kitsch restaurant. Even better, the Russian food is extremely good. Screenings of racy videos mean no under-18s are admitted.

Restoran (Map pp82-3; ☎ 327 8979; Tamoz henny per 2; meals R400-500; Ⓜ Vasileostrovskaya) Chic minimalist décor provides an ideal setting for a range of traditional Russian dishes. There's a good table of appetisers and salads, and home-made, flavoured vodkas.

Yerevan (Map p86; ☎ 703 3820; nab reki Fontanki 51; mains R400-500; Ⓜ Nevsky Prospekt) This classy Armenian restaurant has appealing ethnic design touches and equally impressive traditional food made with ingredients from 'ecologically pure' regions of Armenia.

Tandoori Nights (Map p86; ☎ 312 8782; Voznesensky pr 4; mains R300-400, prices in units; Ⓜ Nevsky Prospekt) The city's most stylish Indian restaurant also serves great food, a mix of traditional and modern recipes road-tested by a top London Indian chef.

Taverna Oliva (Map p86; ☎ 314 6563; Bolshaya Morskaya ul 31; mains R200; Ⓜ Nevsky Prospekt) There's nothing taverna-like about this cavernous place decorated in an array of Greek styles. The menu is traditional, and the food is both excellent value and extremely good – especially the salad bar.

Sukawati (Map p86; ☎ 312 0540; Kazanskaya ul 8; mains R160; ⏰ noon-5am; Ⓜ Nevsky Prospekt) Russia's first Indonesian restaurant offers stylish décor and delicious reasonably authentic food, with many dishes for vegetarians.

Russky Kitsch (Map pp82-3; ☎ 325 1122; Universitetskaya nab 25; meals R300; ⏰ noon-4am; Ⓜ Vasileostrovskaya) The self-proclaimed 'period of perestroika café' raises bad taste to an ironic art. Come for a drink and a gawp.

Cafés & Quick Eats

Zoom Café (Map p86; Gorokhovaya ul 22; mains R140; Ⓜ Nevsky Prospekt; ✕) This relaxed café offers tasty European and Russian food (with 20% off all prices till 4pm), wi-fi access and also a no-smoking zone.

THE AUTHOR'S CHOICE

Fasol (Map p86; ☎ 571 0907; Gorokhovaya ul 17; mains R150; Ⓜ Nevsky Prospekt) A few of the modern Russian-style dishes at this popular minimalist-design café include the namesake *fasol* (beans), but we really love its *forsh-mak* (chopped herring salad) with freshly fried potato pancakes. The atmosphere is relaxed, making it a wonderful place just to hang out.

Chaynaya Lozhka (Map p86; Nevsky pr 44; mains R100; ☼ 9am-10pm; Ⓜ Gostiny Dvor) Piter is blanketed with these brightly decorated cafés serving excellent bliny and salads, and a wide range of loose leaf teas and infusions.

Kilikia (Map p86; ☎ 327 2208; Gorokhovaya ul 26/40; mains R200-300; ☼ noon-3am; Ⓜ Nevsky Prospekt) Served here are excellent-value Armenian and Russian dishes, and there's usually live music most evenings.

Herzen Institute Canteen (Map p86; Herzen Institute courtyard, nab reki Moyki 48; mains R50-100; ☼ noon-6pm Mon-Sat; Ⓜ Nevsky Prospekt) Though it shares the kitchen of Chinese restaurant Kharbin (☎ 311 1732; nab reki Moyki 48), this bargain outlet caters to Herzen Institute students, who come in droves at lunch.

Bliny Domik (Map p86; ☎ 315 9915; Kolokolnaya ul; meals R100-200; ☼ 8am-11pm; Ⓜ Vladimirskaya) Try breakfast or a late lunch at this long-running favourite to avoid the crowds. It's set up like a country home, but isn't too kitsch like other places.

Baltic Bread (Map p86; www.baltic-bread.ru/eng; Vladimirsky pr 19; sandwiches R40; ☼ 10am-9pm) This outstanding bakery/café has a new ritzy branch in the Vladimirsky Passazh shopping mall serving some 80 different types of baked goods; come here for an espresso (R50), cake (R30) or sandwich. Also check out its original branch (Map p86; Grechesky pr 25).

Olyushka & Russky Bliny (Map pp82-3; Gagarinskaya ul 13; mains R55-75; ☼ 11am-6pm Mon-Fri; Ⓜ Chernyshevskaya) Students at the nearby university swear by these authentic canteens that hark back to the simplicity of Soviet times. Olyushka serves only handmade *pelmeni* (dumplings), while Russky Bliny does a fine line in melt-in-the-mouth pancakes.

Stolle (Map pp82-3; pies R50; ☼ 8am-10pm) Dekabristov 33 (ul Dekabristov 33; Ⓜ Sadovaya or Sennaya Ploshchad); Dekabristov 33 (ul Dekabristov 19; Ⓜ Sadovaya or Sennaya Ploshchad); Vasilyevsky Island (Syezdovskaya and 1-ya linii 50; Ⓜ Vasileostrovskaya) Its savoury and sweet pies are so yummy we guarantee you'll be back for more. Either Dekabristov branch is close to the Mariinsky Theatre, although 33 is the more appealing.

Café Idiot (Map pp82-3; ☎ 315 1675; nab reki Moyki 82; meals R300; ☼ 11am-1am; Ⓜ Sennaya Ploshchad; ✗) An ideal place to visit for a nightcap or supper after attending the Mariinsky (since its kitchen stays open late) is this eternally popular vegetarian café/bar.

Self-Catering

Kuznechny Market (Map p86; Kuznechny per; ☼ 8am-8pm; Ⓜ Vladimirskaya) The best fresh-produce market in town.

Recommended supermarkets:

Lend (Map pp82-3; Vladimirsky Passazh, Vladimirsky pr 19; ☼ 24hr; Ⓜ Dostoevskaya)

Passazh (Map p86; Nevsky pr 48; ☼ 10am-10pm; Ⓜ Gostiny Dvor)

Perekrestok (Map p86; PIK, Sennaya pl 2; ☼ 24hr; Ⓜ Sennaya Ploshchad)

DRINKING

Dacha (Map p86; Dumskaya ul 9; ☼ 6pm-6am; Ⓜ Nevsky Prospekt) One of the few places in St Petersburg where you will find a truly mixed ethnic crowd of fun, interesting people. Dacha is an amazingly popular DJ bar, with cheap drinks and fabulous music that has everyone up and dancing.

Tsinik (Cynic; Map p86; ☎ 312 8779; per Antonenko 4; ☼ 11am-3am Sun-Thu, 11am-6am Fri & Sat; Ⓜ Sadovaya or Sennaya Ploshchad) Laid-back, no-frills cellar bar with a cool, student-slacker/arty crowd. It also has the only men's toilets in the world with the walls entirely covered with Pushkin's poem *Eugene Onegin*.

Red Lion (Map pp82-3; ☎ 571 4526; pl Dekabristov 1; ☼ 24hr; Ⓜ Sadovaya or Sennaya Ploshchad) Cavernous bar that pounds with atmosphere, offering a wide range of beers, big-screen TVs, a dance floor and standard British pub grub.

City Bar (Map pp82-3; ☎ 314 1037; Millionnaya ul 10; ☼ 11am-last client; Ⓜ Nevsky Prospekt) This popular expat bar also offers wi-fi, and a free book, DVD and video lending library.

Tinkoff (Map p86; ☎ 718 5566; www.tinkoff.ru; Kazanskaya ul 7; ☼ noon-2am; Ⓜ Nevsky Prospekt) Come to this gigantic contemporary brewery to sample one of eight fresh microbrewed beers. There's also good food, including a sushi bar.

ENTERTAINMENT

Check Friday's *St Petersburg Times* for up-to-date listings.

Classical Music, Ballet & Opera

The main season is September to the end of June. In summer many companies are away on tour, but plenty of performances are still staged. Tickets cost R300 to R4000.

Mariinsky Theatre (Map pp82-3; ☎ 326 4141; www.mariinsky.ru/en; Teatralnaya pl 1; ☼ box office 11am-7pm; Ⓜ Sadovaya or Sennaya Ploshchad) Home to the world-famous Kirov Ballet and Opera company. A a visit here is a must, if only to wallow in the sparkling glory of the interior. Book and pay in advance on the website.

Mussorgsky Opera & Ballet Theatre (Map p86; ☎ 585 4305; www.mikhailovsky.ru; pl Iskusstv 1; Ⓜ Nevsky Prospekt) It's generally cheaper and easier to get tickets to the performances staged here.

The grand **Bolshoy Zal** (Big Hall; Map p86; ☎ 710 4257; www.philharmonia.spb.ru/eng/indexi.html; Mikhaylovskaya ul 2; Ⓜ Gostiny Dvor) is one of the two concert halls of the Philharmonica's Symphony Orchestra, the other being the **Maly Zal imeni Glinki** (Small Philharmonia; Map p86; ☎ 571 8333; Nevsky pr 30; Ⓜ Nevsky Prospekt).

Live Music

Check the Russian-language websites of the following venues for details on current gigs.

Platforma (Map p86; ☎ 719 6123; www.platforma club.ru; ul Nekrasova 40; cover R100-200; ⏲ 24hr; Ⓜ Ploshchad Vosstaniya) Some of St Petersburg's most interesting bands and coolest DJs play at this convivial space. It's also a fine place to eat, or for a drink earlier in the evening when you can browse its bookstore.

Red Club (Map p86; ☎ 277 1366; www.clubred.ru; Poltavskaya ul 7; cover R100-400; ⏲ 7pm-6am; Ⓜ Ploshchad Vosstaniya) Behind Moscow Station, this great warehouse venue is a mainstay for local groups.

Moloko (Map pp82-3; ☎ 274 9467; www.moloko club.ru; Perekupnoy per 12; cover R50-100; ⏲ 7pm-midnight Wed-Sun; Ⓜ Ploshchad Vosstaniya) Great bands running the gamut of genres play here.

Fish Fabrique (Map p86; ☎ 764 4857; www.fish fabrique.spb.ru; Pushkinskaya ul 10, entrance through arch at Ligovsky pr 53; cover R70-150; ⏲ 3pm-late; Ⓜ Ploshchad Vosstaniya) Legendary bar set in the building that's the focus of the avant-garde art scene. Live bands kick up a storm at 10pm.

Nightclubs

Griboedov (Map pp82-3; ☎ 764 4355; www.griboe dovclub.ru; Voronezhskaya ul 2A; cover R200, free 5-8pm; ⏲ 5pm-6am; Ⓜ Ligovsky Prospekt) Managed by the same people behind Hotel California, this hip club, in an artfully converted bomb shelter, is a guaranteed fun night out.

Tunnel (Map p86; ☎ 233 4015; www.tunnel club.ru; cnr Lyubansky per & Zverinskaya ul; cover R250-350; ⏲ midnight-6am Fri & Sat; Ⓜ Gorkovskaya) The original 'underground' club, quite literally since it occupies a bomb shelter. Come here for hardcore electronic dance music.

Par.spb (Map pp82-3; ☎ 233 3374; www.par.spb .ru; Aleksandrovsky Park 5B; cover R400; ⏲ 11am-6am Fri-Sun) This stripped-back, arty club, with two dance spaces and a chill-out area, offers different music each night and a strict door policy.

SHOPPING

Souvenir Market (Map p86; Konyushennaya pl; ⏲ 10am-dusk; Ⓜ Nevsky Prospekt) This very well-stocked souvenir market is diagonally across the canal from the Church of the Saviour on Spilled Blood (p87).

Tovar dlya Voennikh (Map p86; Sadovaya ul 26; ⏲ 10am-7pm Mon-Sat; Ⓜ Gostiny Dvor) The best place to buy cool Russian military clothes and memorabilia. Look out for the circular green and gold sign with Military Shop written in English; the entrance is inside the courtyard.

La Russe (Map p86; ☎ 572 2043; www.larusse.ru; Stremyannaya ul 3; ⏲ 11am-8pm; Ⓜ Mayakovskaya) Lots of rustic old whatnots and genuine antiques are for sale at this quirky, arty store.

GETTING THERE & AWAY
Air

Pulkovo-1 (☎ 704 3822; http://eng.pulkovo.ru) is the domestic terminal that serves St Petersburg, and **Pulkovo-2** (☎ 704 3444; http://eng.pulkovo.ru) is the international.

St Petersburg has direct air links with most major European capitals and cities across Russia. Tickets for all airlines can be purchased from travel agencies and from the **Central Airline Ticket Office** (Map p86; ☎ 315 0072; Nevsky pr 7; ⏲ 8am-8pm Mon-Fri, 8am-6pm Sat & Sun; Ⓜ Nevsky Prospekt), which also has counters for train and international bus tickets.

Bus

St Petersburg's main bus station, **Avtovokzal No 2** (Map pp82-3; ☎ 766 5777; nab Obvodnogo kanala 36; Ⓜ Ligovsky Prospekt) – there isn't a

BUSES FROM ST PETERSBURG			
destination	buses per day	duration (hr)	one-way fare (R)
Helsinki	2	8	1700
Moscow	1	12	480
Riga	2	11	500
Tallinn	7	7½	550-650

No 1 – has both international and European Russia services.

Tickets can be purchased here and at the Central Airline Ticket Office (p93).

Train

The three major long-distance train stations in St Petersburg are: **Ladoga** (☎ 768 5304; Zhanevsky pr 73; Ⓜ Ladozhskaya), for services to/from Helsinki and the far north of Russia; **Moscow** (Map p86; ☎ 768 4597; pl Vosstaniya; Ⓜ Ploshchad Vosstaniya), for Moscow, the Urals

and Siberia; and **Vitebsk** (Map pp82-3; ☎ 768 5807; Zagorodny pr 52; Ⓜ Pushkinskaya), for the Baltic states and Eastern Europe.

Tickets can be purchased at the train stations, the **Central Train Ticket Office** (Map p86; ☎ 762 33 44; nab kanala Griboedova 24; ☼ 8am-8pm Mon-Sat, 8am-4pm Sun; Ⓜ Nevsky Prospekt) and the Central Airline Ticket Office (p93).

DOMESTIC SERVICES

There are 12 to 14 daily trains to Moscow, all departing from Moscow Station:

RAIL ROUTES FROM ST PETERSBURG

Trains from St Petersburg to Moscow

Train no & name	Departure	Duration (hr)	Fare (R)
1 *Krasnya Strela*	11.55pm	8	1700
3 *Ekspress*	11.59pm	8	1700
5 *Nikolaevsk Ekspress*	11.35pm	8	1700
23 *Yunost*	1.10pm	8	1300
159 *Avrora*	4.00pm	5½	1300
163 *ER200*	6.30pm	4½	1700
165 *Nevsky Ekspress*	6.30pm*	4½	1700

Notes: *Mon, Thu & Fri only

Domestic Trains from St Petersburg

Destination	Train no	Departure	Duration (hr)	Fare (R)
Kazan	103	4.36pm MS†	27½	1482
Nizhny Novgorod (Gorky)	59	5.24pm MS	15½r	1600
Omsk	13	8.40pm MS†	53½	3037

Notes: MS – Moscow Station   †odd days

International Trains from St Petersburg

Destination	Train no & name	Departure	Duration (hr)	Fare (R)
Brest	49	3.01pm VS	19	932
The Brest train No 49 has carriages that are detached there and go on to Budapest and Prague:				
Budapest	49	3.01pm VS*	45	5330
Prague	49	3.01pm VS‖	40½	3790
Helsinki	034 *Repin*	7.28am LS	6	1856
Helsinki	036 *Sibelius*	4.28pm LS	6	1856
Kaliningrad	079	6.16pm VS	27½	1247
Kyiv	053	9.11pm VS	24	961/1102‡
Minsk	051	7.03pm VS	15	1166
Odesa	19	11.40pm VS	35	1260
The Odesa train has carriages that are detached along the way and go on to Berlin and Warsaw:				
Berlin	19	11.40pm VS§	31	4670
Warsaw	19	11.40pm VS§	29	2240
Riga	037	9.46pm	13	1812
Vilnius	391	8.28pm†	15¼	1387/1499#

Notes: LS – Ladoga Station   VS – Vitebsk Station   *Tues & Sun   ‖Mon, Wed, Thu, Sun   †odd days   §daily except Thu
‡Russian/Ukrainian train   #Russian/Lithuanian train

the table opposite lists the best services. If you want to save money, four services (the 19, 27, 29 and 55) have *platskart* (*platskartny*; open carriage) tickets for R350.

INTERNATIONAL SERVICES

Two daily trains run between St Petersburg and Helsinki: the Russian-operated *Repin*, and the *Sibelius* run by **Finnish Railways** (www.vr.fi). For details on services going to Helsinki see the table 'International Trains from St Petersburg' (opposite).

Services to Berlin, Budapest, Kaliningrad, Kyiv, Prague and Warsaw pass through Belarus; for these journeys you must hold a transit visa. Note that border guards have been known to force people off trains and back to where they came from if they don't have a visa.

GETTING AROUND

St Petersburg's excellent public transport system makes getting around the city simple and inexpensive. Pack a sturdy pair of walking shoes, because the city centre is best seen on foot.

To/From the Airport

About 17km south of the city centre, the airport is easily and (very) cheaply accessed by both metro and bus. From Moskovskaya metro, bus 39 runs to Pulkovo-1, the domestic terminal, and bus 13 runs to Pulkovo-2, the international terminal. There are also plenty of *marshrutky* (fixed route minibuses). The trip takes about 15 minutes and costs just R15 (R20 for a metro/bus combination), or you can take the buses and *marshrutka* K3 all the way from the airport to Sennaya Ploshchad in the city centre or K39 to Ploshchad Vosstaniya. All buses stop directly outside each of the terminals.

Taxis should charge around R600 to get to the city (R400 is the price from the city to the airport). Expect that most taxi drivers will request more once they realise you're a foreigner and be prepared to haggle or take the bus.

Public Transport

The **metro** (☼ 5.30am-midnight) is usually the quickest way around the city and you'll rarely wait more than three minutes for a train. *Zhetony* (tokens; R10) can be bought

from booths in the stations. More convenient and better value are *karta* (magnetic-strip, multiride cards) valid for seven, 15 or 30 days, with various multiples of rides. All stations have card-reading turnstiles – place your card in the slot and when it comes back out you'll see a green light to proceed if there's sufficient credit left on the card.

AROUND ST PETERSBURG

PETRODVORETS ПЕТРОДВОРЕЦ

On the Gulf of Finland, **Petrodvorets** (☎ 427 7425; www.peterhof.org; ul Razvodnaya 2), just 29km west of St Petersburg, is arguably the most impressive of St Petersburg's suburban palaces. It's largely a reconstruction, having been pretty much demolished during WWII, but it is still mightily impressive – even when it's swarming with tourists, as it very frequently is.

The centrepiece of the palace is the **Grand Cascade & Water Avenue**, a symphony of over 140 fountains and canals. To see them you are required to pay to enter the **Lower Park** (adult/student R300/150; ☼ 9am-8pm Mon-Fri, 9am-9pm Sat & Sun). They only work from mid-May to early October (from 11am to 5pm Monday to Friday and 11am to 6pm Saturday and Sunday), but the wonderful gilded ensemble still looks marvellous at any time of the year.

Between the cascade and the **Upper Garden** (admission free) is the **Grand Palace** (adult/student R430/215; ☼ 10.30am-6pm Tue-Sun, closed last Tue of month). Amid all the eye-boggling interiors, many find the finest room is the simplest – Peter's study, apparently the only one to survive the Germans. The estate features several other buildings of interest – all with their own admission charges and separate opening hours – which can easily take up a day to tour fully.

Getting There & Away

To get to Petrodvorets, hop on the K404 bus that arrives and departs from outside the Baltic Station (R30, 40 minutes) and get off at the main entrance to the Upper Garden, which is on Sankt Peterburgsky pr. There's also a reasonably frequent suburban train (R20, 30 minutes) from the Baltic Station to Novy Petrodvorets, from where you'll have to take any bus but 357 to the fifth stop,

---

THE LENINGRAD BLOCKADE

The Leningrad Blockade was the city's defining event of the 20th century. Around one million people died from shelling, starvation and disease in what's called the '900 Days' (actually 872). By comparison, the USA and UK suffered about 700,000 dead between them in all of WWII.

After the war began on 22 June 1941, with the Germans fast approaching, many residents fled. Art treasures and precious documents from the Hermitage and other museums were moved out by the train-load; factories were evacuated and relocated to Siberia; historical sculptures were buried or covered with sandbags. Yet no-one could have predicted the suffering to come.

The Nazi plan, as indicated in a secret directive, was to 'wipe the city of Petersburg from the face of the earth'. A fragile 'Road of Life' across frozen Lake Ladoga was the only (albeit heavily bombed) lifeline the city had for provisions and evacuations.

Food was practically nonexistent, and at one point rations were limited to 175g of sawdust-laden bread a day. People ate their pets, even rats and birds disappeared from the city. The paste behind wallpaper was scraped off and eaten, leather belts were cooked until chewable. Cannibalism started in the shelters for refugees from the neighbouring towns; without ration cards, they were among the first to die. The exhausted and starved literally fell over dead on the streets. There were periods when over 30,000 people per day died of hunger.

More than 150,000 shells and bombs were dropped on the city during the blockade, the effects of which are still visible on some buildings (notably on the west wall of St Isaac's Cathedral and the northwest corner of the Anichkov most). Still, life went on. Concerts and plays were performed in candlelit halls, lectures given, poetry written, orphanages opened, brigades formed to clean up the city. Most famous was the 9 August 1942 concert of Shostakovich's 7th Symphony by the Leningrad Philharmonic, broadcast nationally by radio from the besieged city.

According to survivors, random acts of kindness outnumbered incidents of robbery and vandalism, and lessons learned about the human spirit would be remembered for a lifetime. From a poem by Olga Berggolts, written after the blockade was lifted: 'In mud, in darkness, hunger, and sorrow, where death, like a shadow, trod on our heels, we were so happy at times, breathed such turbulent freedom, that our grandchildren would envy us.'

For a detailed, harrowing description of the blockade, read Harrison Salisbury's *900 Days: the Siege of Leningrad*.

---

another 10 minutes. Alternatively there are *marshrutky* to Petrodvorets from outside metro Avtovo.

Another option from May to September is the *Meteor* hydrofoil (one-way/return R250/450, about 30 minutes), which runs from the jetty in front of St Petersburg's Hermitage every 20 to 30 minutes from 9.30am to at least 7pm.

TSARSKOE SELO & PAVLOVSK
ЦАРСКОЕ СЕЛО И ПАВЛОВСК

The popular and impressive imperial estate of **Tsarskoe Selo** (Tsar's Village; ☎ 465 2281; http://eng.tzar.ru; Sadovaya ul 7) is located in Pushkin, 25km south of St Petersburg. The big draw here is the baroque, Rastrelli-designed **Catherine Palace** (Yekaterininsky dvorets; adult/student R500/250; ☺ 10am-6pm Wed-Mon, closed last Mon of the month), built between 1752 and

1756, but almost destroyed in WWII. The exterior and 20-odd rooms have been expertly restored; the Great Hall and the Amber Room are particularly dazzling.

Wandering around **Catherine Park** (Yekaterininsky Park; adult/student R100/50; ☺ 6am-11pm) surrounding the palace is a pleasure. In the outer section of the park is the **Great Pond**, fringed by an intriguing array of structures, including a Chinese Pavilion, purposely Ruined Tower and Pyramid where Catherine the Great buried her dogs.

To escape the masses head 4km further south to **Pavlovsk** (adult/student R80/40; ☺ 9am-9pm), the park and palace designed by Charles Cameron between 1781 and 1786, and one of the most exquisite in Russia. Pavlovsk's **Great Palace** (☎ 470 2155; www.pavlovskart.spb.ru; ul Revolutsii; adult/student R370/185; ☺ 10am-6pm Sat-Thu, closed Fri & last Mon of the month), burnt down in WWII, was fully restored by 1970. The sprawling park itself is a delight to explore.

Getting There & Away

Marshrutky (R25, 30 minutes) regularly shuttle to both Pushkin and Pavlovsk from outside metro Moskovskaya.

Infrequent trains run from St Petersburg's Vitebsk Station. For Tsarskoe Selo, get off at Detskoe Selo Station (R21), and for Pavlovsk (R28) at Pavlovsk Station. It's about half an hour by foot to either place.

From the Detskoe Selo Station frequent *marshrutky* (R10, 5 minutes) go to Tsarskoe Selo; many continue on to Pavlovsk Station (for entry to the park) and to the front of Pavlovsk's palace. Walking at least one way across Pavlovsk's park is recommended.

Moscow Москва

Sunlight glinting off gold-domed churches. Scantily clad women emerging from sleek, black cars. Uniformed military marching across the vast expanse of Red Sq. This is Moscow – the political, economic and cultural capital that defines this massive nation.

Russia's medieval roots are here: the Kremlin still shows off the splendour of Muscovy's grand princes; St Basil's Cathedral recounts the defeat of the Tatars. Yet this place also recalls Russia's more recent history, still fresh in our memories. On Red Sq, the founder of the Soviet state lies embalmed. And only a few kilometres away, his heir, Boris Yeltsin, heroically defied the army – leading to the demise of that same state.

Moscow has always been known for the diversity of its population and the richness of its culture. Today, more than ever, visitors and residents alike can enjoy events ranging from the classic to the progressive. Whether a Tchaikovsky opera or an Ostrovsky drama, classical performing arts in Moscow are among the best – and cheapest – in the Western world. The Tretyakov Gallery and Pushkin Museum of Fine Arts house internationally famous collections of Russian and impressionist art.

Of course, New Russia comes with new forms of art and entertainment. The bohemian side of Moscow – be it a beatnik band at an underground club, or an avant-garde exhibit at the Central House of Artists – provides a glimpse of Russia's future. Sometimes intellectual and inspiring, sometimes debauched and depraved, it is *always* eye-opening.

HIGHLIGHTS

- Be awestruck by the endless array of jewels and weapons at the **Kremlin Armoury** (p107)
- Marvel at the artistry of the **Moscow metro** (p122)
- Sip a cappuccino at the **Café Pushkin** (p116)
- Bargain for trash and treasure at **Izmaylovo market** (p119)
- Pay your respects at **Novodevichy Cemetery** (p111)

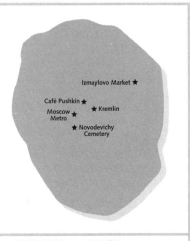

Izmaylovo Market ★

Café Pushkin ★
Moscow ★ ★ Kremlin
Metro
★ Novodevichy
Cemetery

■ TELEPHONE CODE: 495 | ■ POPULATION: 10.4 MILLION

HISTORY

Moscow's recorded history dates to the mid-12th century, when Yury Dolgoruky constructed the first Kremlin at a strategic spot atop the Borovitsky Hill. Moscow blossomed into an economic centre.

In the 13th century, the Mongols burned the city to the ground. The Golden Horde was interested in tribute, and Moscow was conveniently situated to monitor the river trade and road traffic. Moscow's Prince Ivan acted as tax collector, earning himself the moniker 'Moneybags' (Kalita), and Moscow developed into a regional capital.

Towards the end of the 15th century, the once diminutive duchy emerged as an expanding state under the reign of Grand Prince Ivan III (the Great). To celebrate his successes, he imported a team of Italian artisans for a complete renovation of the Kremlin. The city developed in concentric rings outward from this centre. Under Ivan IV (the Terrible), the city earned the nickname of 'Gold-Domed Moscow' because of its multitude of monastery fortresses and magnificent churches.

In 1712 Peter the Great startled the country by announcing the relocation of the capital to St Petersburg. In the early 1800s, Moscow suffered further at the hands of Napoleon Bonaparte. But after the Napoleonic Wars, Moscow was feverishly rebuilt and industry prospered.

When the Bolsheviks gained control of Russia in 1917, the capital returned to Moscow. Stalin devised an urban plan for the city: historic cathedrals and monuments were demolished; in their place appeared the marble-bedecked metro and neo-Gothic skyscrapers. In the following decades, Moscow expanded at an exponential rate.

Moscow was the scene of the most dramatic events of the early 1990s' political transition. Boris Yeltsin led crowds protesting the attempted coup in 1991; and two years later, he ordered the army to blast the parliament into submission. Within the Moscow city government, the election of Mayor Yury Luzhkov in 1992 set the stage for the creation of a big-city boss: his interests range from the media to manufacturing and from five-star hotels to shopping malls. While the rest of Russia struggled to survive the collapse of communism, Moscow emerged as an enclave of affluence.

MOSCOW IN...

Two Days

Spend one day seeing what makes Moscow famous: **St Basil's Cathedral** (p109), **Lenin's Tomb** (p108) and the **Kremlin** (p104). Allow a few hours in the afternoon to gawk at the gold and gems in the **Armoury** (p107). Art lovers should spend their second day at either the **Pushkin Museum of Fine Arts** (p109) or the **Tretyakov Gallery** (p110), both world-class art museums. Afterwards, spend some time exploring the surrounding neighbourhoods.

Four Days

Take in all of the activities suggested in the two-day itinerary. On the third day, visit **Novodevichy Convent** (p111), where so many scenes from Russian history have been played out. Finally, hit the money machine and head to **Izmaylovo market** (p119) for some serious souvenir shopping.

One Week

Take in all of the activities suggested in the four-day itinerary. Then, plan an excursion to the Golden Ring, visiting **Rostov-Veliky** (p124) and **Sergiev Posad** (p123).

ORIENTATION

Picture Moscow as five ring roads that spread out from the centre: the Inner Ring Road, about 500m north of the Kremlin; the dual-carriageway Boulevard Ring (Bulvarnoe Koltso), about 1km from the Kremlin; the busy Garden Ring (Sadovoe Koltso), 2km out; the high-speed, eight-lane Third Ring (Tretoe Koltso), about 4.5km from the Kremlin; and the Outer Ring Road, also called MKAD, a highway that forms the city limits about 15km from the Kremlin.

Radial roads spoke out across the rings, and the Moscow River meanders across everything from northwest to southeast. The Kremlin, a north-pointing triangle with 750m sides, is at Moscow's heart in every way. Red Sq lies along its eastern side while the Moscow River flows to the south.

About 2.8km northeast of the Kremlin is Komsomolskaya pl, Moscow's transportation hub. Three bustling train stations dominate this square, including Yaroslavsky vokzal (Yaroslavl Station), the most important of Moscow's nine train stations for Trans-Siberian travellers. Next door is Leningradsky vokzal (Leningrad Station), for services to and from St Petersburg, while across the road is Kazansky vokzal (Kazan Station), the terminus for some trains from the Urals including the main service from Yekaterinburg.

If you're arriving in Moscow on trains from Western and Eastern Europe your likely entry points will be Belorussky vokzal (Belarus Station), 2.8km northwest of the Kremlin, or Kievsky vokzal (Kyiv Station), 2.4km to the west.

Maps
An excellent map store, **Atlas** (Map pp102-3; ☎ 928 6109; Kuznetsky most 9; ⏱ 9am-8pm Mon-Fri, 10am-6pm Sat, 11am-5pm Sun; Ⓜ Kuznetsky Most) stocks city and regional maps covering the whole country.

INFORMATION
Bookshops
Biblio-Globus (Map pp102-3; ☎ 928 3567; Myasnitskaya ul 6; ⏱ 9am-9pm Mon-Fri, 10am-9pm Sat, 10am-8pm Sun; Ⓜ Lubyanka) A huge store with lots of reference and souvenir books on language, art and history, and a good selection of maps and travel guides.
Bookberry (Map pp102-3; ☎ 291 8303; Nikitsky bul 17; ⏱ 10am-11pm; Ⓜ Arbatskaya) A slick new chain that offers the city's best selection of guidebooks and maps.
House of Foreign Books (Map pp102-3; ☎ 928 2021; ul Kuznetsky most 18/7; ⏱ 10am-8pm Mon-Sat, 11am-7pm Sun; Ⓜ Kuznetsky Most) A small shop specialising in foreign titles, including a decent selection of guidebooks.

Emergency
Ambulance (☎ 03)
Crisis hotline (☎ 244 3449, in English 937 9999)
Fire (☎ 01)
Police (☎ 02)

Internet Access
Besides the plethora of Internet cafés, wireless access is also becoming more common around Moscow. Take advantage of free wireless access at several upscale hotels, as well as NetLand or Time Online. A more complete listing of clubs and cafés with wireless access is found at http://wifi.yandex.ru.
Internet Club (Map pp102-3; ☎ 292 5670; Kuznetsky most 12; per hr R60; ⏱ 9am-8pm Mon-Fri, 10am-midnight Sat & Sun; Ⓜ Kuznetsky Most) Small, simple and very central.

NetCity Kamergersky per (Map pp102-3; ☎ 292 0111; Kamergersky per 6; per hr R60; ⏱ 10am-11pm; Ⓜ Teatralnaya); Paveletskaya pl (☎ 969 2125; Paveletskaya pl 2/1; per hr R60; ⏱ 9.30am-midnight; Ⓜ Paveletskaya) Work stations offer form more than function, but are sufficient to surf the Net.
NetLand (Map pp102-3; ☎ 781 0923; Teatralny pro 5; per hr R40-60; ⏱ 24hr; Ⓜ Kuznetsky most or Lubyanka) A loud, dark club that fills up with kids playing games.
Phlegmatic Dog (Map p106; ☎ 995 9545; Okhotny Ryad, ground level; Internet access free; ⏱ 10am-1am; Ⓜ Okhotny Ryad) Recently voted 'most stylish' Internet café in the world by Yahoo! Mail. Free Internet access with the purchase of food or drink.
Time Online Okhotny Ryad (Map p106; ☎ 363 0060; per hr R65-75; ⏱ 24hr; Ⓜ Okhotny Ryad); Belorusskaya (Map pp102-3; ☎ 363 0060; Bolshaya Kondratevsky per 7; per hr R65-75; ⏱ 24hr; Ⓜ Belorusskaya) Offers copy and photo services, as well as over 200 zippy computers or free wi-fi access.

Internet Resources
http://eng.menu.ru A comprehensive list of Moscow restaurants, including location details and menus.
www.expat.ru Run by and for English-speaking expats living in Russia. Provides useful information about real estate, children in Moscow, social groups and more.
www.maps-moscow.com An energetic group of international journalists raising awareness of architectural preservation issues in Moscow.
www.moscowout.ru A full calendar of events in the capital, with links to restaurant and movie reviews, nightlife, and activities for kids.
www.moscow-taxi.com Viktor the virtual taxi driver provides extensive descriptions of sites inside and outside Moscow, as well as hotel booking and other tourist services.

Media
element (www.elementmoscow.ru) This oversized newsprint magazine comes out weekly with restaurant reviews, concert listings and art exhibits.
Go (www.go-magazine.ru) The *Moscow Times'* monthly entertainment guide.
Moscow Times (www.moscowtimes.ru) The undisputed king of the hill in locally published English-language news is this first-rate daily, which covers Russian and international issues, as well as sports and entertainment. The Friday edition is a great source for what's happening at the weekend.

Medical Services
36.6 Pharmacy Kitay-Gorod (Map pp102-3; ul Pokrovka 1; Ⓜ Kitay-Gorod); Kuznetsky most (Map pp102-3; Kuznetsky most 18; Ⓜ Kuznetsky Most); Novy Arbat (Map pp102-3; ul Novy Arbat 15; Ⓜ Smolenskaya or Arbatskaya); Tverskaya

(Map pp102-3; ul Tverskaya 25; Ⓜ Tverskaya or Mayakov-skaya) A chain of 24-hour pharmacies.

American Medical Center (Map pp102-3; ☎ 933 7700; www.amcenters.com; Grokholsky per 1; ☻ 24hr; Ⓜ Prospekt Mira) Offers 24-hour emergency service, consultations and a full range of specialists, including paediatricians and dentists. Has an on-site pharmacy with English-speaking staff.

Botkin Hospital (Map pp102-3; ☎ 237 8338, 945 7533; 2-y Botkinsky pro 5; Ⓜ Begovaya) The best Russian facility.

European Medical Center (Map pp102-3; ☎ 933 6655; www.emcmos.ru; Spirdonevsky per 5; ☻ 24hr; Ⓜ Mayakovskaya or Tverskaya) Includes medical and dental facilities, which are open around the clock for emergencies. The staff speaks 10 different languages.

Money

Banks, exchange counters and ATMs are ubiquitous in Moscow. Credit cards, especially Visa and MasterCard, are widely accepted in upscale hotels, restaurants and stores.

Alfa-Bank (☻ 8.30am-8pm Mon-Sat) Arbat (Map pp102-3; ul Arbat 4/1; Ⓜ Arbatskaya); Kuznetsky most (Map pp102-3; Kuznetsky most 7; Ⓜ Kuznetsky Most); Marriott Grand Hotel (Map pp102-3; ul Tverskaya 26; Ⓜ Mayakovskaya) Usually changes travellers cheques. ATMs at the branches listed dispense either roubles or US dollars.

American Express (☎ 933 6636; fax 933 6635; ul Usachyova 33; ☻ 9am-5pm; Ⓜ Sportivnaya) The most reliable place to cash American Express travellers cheques. It also offers ATM, mail holding and travel services for AmEx cardholders.

Western Union (☎ 797 2197) For wire transfers.

Post, Telephone & Fax

Moscow pay phones operate with cards that are widely available in shops, kiosks and metro stations. The cards come in a range of units. The phones are fairly user-friendly, and most of them have an option for directions in English. Make sure you press the button with the speaker symbol when your party answers the phone.

For international calls, it is often easier to place your call from the Central Telegraph, where you prepay for your call.

Central Telegraph (Map pp102-3; Tverskaya ul 7; ☻ post 8am-10pm, telephone 24hr; Ⓜ Okhotny Ryad) Offers telephone, fax and Internet services.

FedEx (☎ 234 3400) Air courier services. Call for information on drop-off locations and to arrange pick-ups.

Main post office (Map pp102-3; Myasnitskaya ul 26; ☻ 8am-8pm Mon-Fri, 9am-7pm Sat & Sun; Ⓜ Chistye Prudy)

Tourist Information

Moscow has no tourist information centre, but plenty of information is available at hostels and upscale hotels, as well as through travel agencies.

Travel Agencies

G&R International (☎ 378 0001; www.hostels.ru; ul Zelenodolskaya 3/2, 5th fl; ☻ 24hr; Ⓜ Ryazansky Prospekt) Organises itineraries, providing visa support and selling transport tickets.

Infinity Travel (☎ 234 6555; www.infinity.ru; Komsomolsky pr 13; ☻ 9am-9pm Mon-Fri, 11am-3pm Sat & noon-4pm Sun; Ⓜ Park Kultury) Affiliated with the Travellers Guest House, this on-the-ball travel company offers rail and air tickets, visa support and trans-Siberian and Central Asian packages.

DANGERS & ANNOYANCES

Unfortunately, street crime targeting tourists has increased in recent years, although Moscow is not as dangerous as paranoid locals may have you think. As in any big city, be on your guard against pickpockets and muggers. Be particularly careful at or around metro stations at Kursky vokzal (Kursky Station) and Partizanskaya, where readers have reported specific incidents.

Some police officers can be bothersome, especially to dark-skinned or otherwise foreign-looking people. Practical advice from a Moscow synagogue is 'cover your kippa'. Other members of the police force target tourists. Reports of tourists being hassled about their documents and registration have declined. However, it's still wise to carry a photocopy of your passport, visa and registration stamp. If stopped by a member of the police force, don;t hand over your passport! It is perfectly acceptable to show a photocopy instead.

Scams

Beware of well-dressed people dropping wads of money on the streets of Moscow. A common scam in Moscow involves a respectable-looking person who 'accidentally' drops some money on the pavement as he passes by an unsuspecting foreigner – that's you. Being an honest person, you pick up the money to return it to the careless person, who is hurrying away. A second guy sees what is happening and tries to stop you from returning it, proposing that you split the money and, well, split.

MOSCOW

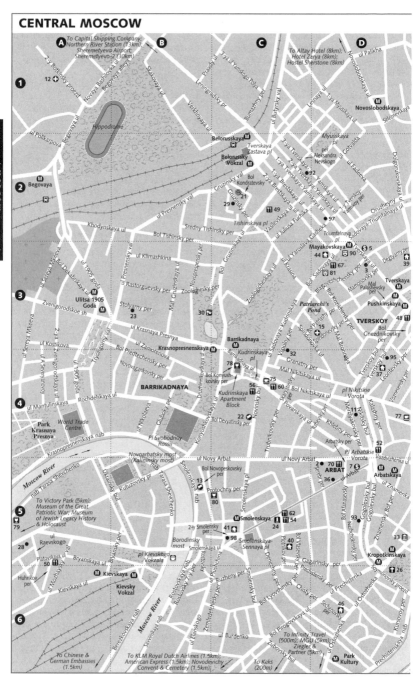

CENTRAL MOSCOW

MOSCOW

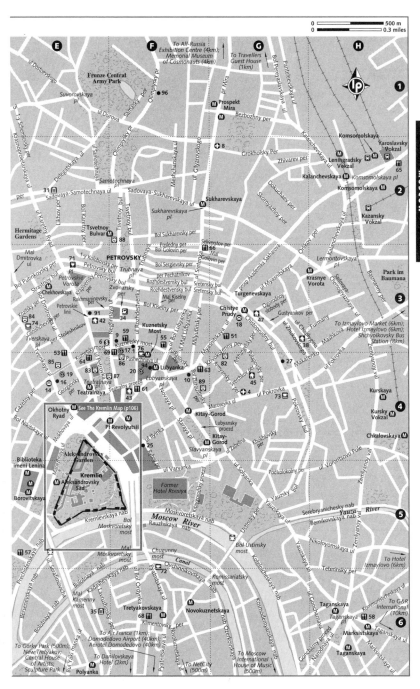

This is a no-win situation. These guys are in cahoots. While you are negotiating about how to split the money – or arguing about returning it – the first guy realises he is missing his cash so returns to the scene of the crime. But lo and behold, the cash you give him is not enough: some is missing and you are culpable. This leads to a shakedown or any number of unpleasantries.

The moral of the story is that the streets of Moscow are not paved with money. Re-sist the temptation to pick up money that's lying on the pavement.

SIGHTS
Kremlin
The apex of Russian political power and once the centre of the Orthodox Church, the **Kremlin** (Map p106; ☎ 202 3776; www.kremlin.museum.ru; adult/student R300/150, photography permit R50; ⊙ 9.30am-4pm Fri-Wed; Ⓜ Aleksandrovsky Sad, Borovitskaya or Biblioteka im Lenina) is not only the

kernel of Moscow but of the whole country. It's from here that autocratic tsars, communist dictators and democratic presidents have done their best – and worst – for Russia.

Occupying a roughly triangular plot of land covering little Borovitsky Hill on the north bank of the Moscow River, the Kremlin is enclosed by high walls 2.25km long with Red Sq outside the east wall. The best views of the complex are from Sofiyskaya nab across the river.

The main ticket office is in Aleksandrovsky Garden, just off Manezhnaya pl. The ticket covers entry to all buildings except the Armoury and Diamond Fund Exhibition; it also does not include the special exhibits that are sometimes held inside Patriarch's Palace or inside the Ivan the Great Bell Tower. In any case, you can and should buy tickets for the Armoury here, to avoid queuing up once inside. Arrive early before tickets sell out. Before entering the Kremlin, deposit bags at the nearby **left luggage office** (per bag R60; 🕙 9am-6.30pm), beneath the Kutafya Tower.

There's also an entrance at the southern Borovitskaya Gate, mainly used by those heading straight to the Armoury or the Diamond Fund Exhibition.

Inside the Kremlin, police will keep you from straying into the out-of-bounds areas. Visitors wearing shorts will be refused entry.

Numerous freelance guides tout their services near the Kutafya Tower, with prices ranging from R300 to R600 per hour, and the quality varying widely. Capital Tours (see p113) offers standard daily tours of the Kremlin and Armoury, while Patriarshy Dom Tours (see p113) offers more in-depth tours of the Kremlin cathedrals, sometimes including a visit to the otherwise off-limits palaces.

GOVERNMENT BUILDINGS

The **Kutafya Tower** (Map p106), which forms the main visitors' entrance today, stands away from the Kremlin's west wall, at the end of a ramp over the Aleksandrovsky Garden leading up to the **Trinity Gate Tower** (Map p106). On the way to central Sobornaya pl you'll pass a series of buildings that are closed to visitors. On the right is the 17th-century **Poteshny Palace** (Map p106), where Stalin lived, and the bombastic marble, glass and concrete **State Kremlin Palace** (Map p106), formerly the Palace of Congresses, built from 1960 to 1961 for Communist Party congresses and now used by both the Bolshoi and Kremlin Ballet companies (see p119). On the left is the **Arsenal** (Map p106), home to the Kremlin guard and ringed by 800 captured Napoleonic cannons, and the yellow, triangular former **Senate** (Map p106) building, now the ultimate seat of power in the modern Kremlin, the offices of the president of Russia. Next to the Senate is the 1930s **Supreme Soviet** (Map p106) building.

PATRIARCH'S PALACE

The palace contains an exhibit of 17th-century household items, including jewellery, hunting equipment and furniture. From here you can access the five-domed **Church of the Twelve Apostles** (Map p106), which

---

HISTORY OF THE KREMLIN

A 'kremlin' is a town's fortified stronghold. The first wooden wall around Moscow was built in the 1150s, and the Kremlin grew with the importance of Moscow's princes, becoming in the 1320s the headquarters of the Russian Church, which had shifted from Vladimir. The 'White Stone Kremlin' – with limestone walls – was built in the 1360s, with almost the same boundaries as today.

At the end of the 15th century, Ivan the Great brought master builders from Pskov and Italy to supervise new walls and towers (most of which still stand), as well as the Kremlin's three cathedrals. Although Peter the Great shifted the capital to St Petersburg, tsars continued to show up here for coronations and other celebrations.

Over the years, the biggest threat to the Kremlin was Napoleon, who blew up parts of it before his retreat in 1812. Fortunately, the arrival of Russian troops prevented total destruction. The citadel wouldn't be breached again until the Bolsheviks stormed it in November 1917.

The Kremlin remained closed to the public until 1955. It was Stalin who, in 1935, had the imperial double-headed eagles removed from the wall's five tallest towers, replacing them with the distinctive red-glass stars still there today.

MOSCOW

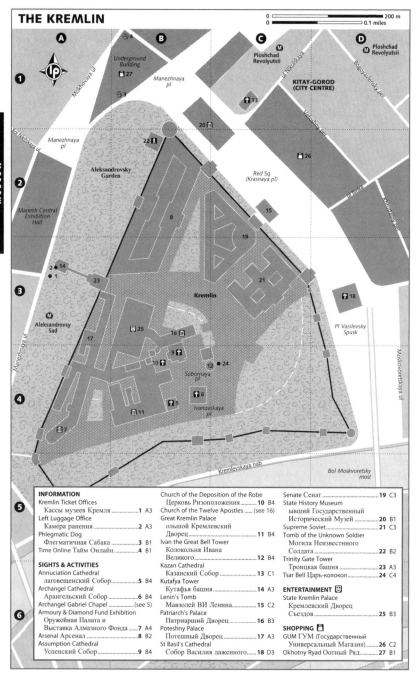

THE KREMLIN

has a gilded, wooden iconostasis and a collection of icons by leading 17th-century icon painters.

The Patriarch's Palace often holds **special exhibits** (adult/student R300/150), which require an additional ticket and reservation time.

ASSUMPTION CATHEDRAL

On the northern side of Sobornaya pl, with five golden helmet domes and four semicircular gables facing the square, is this cathedral (Map p106), built between 1475 and 1479. As the focal church of prerevolutionary Russia, it's the burial place of most heads of the Russian Orthodox Church from the 1320s to 1700. The tombs are against the north, west and south walls.

The iconostasis dates from 1652 but its lowest level contains some older icons, including the *Virgin of Vladimir* (Vladimirskaya Bogomater), an early-15th-century Rublyov-school copy of Russia's most revered image, the *Vladimir Icon of the Mother of God* (Ikona Vladimirskoy Bogomateri). The 12th-century original, now in the Tretyakov Gallery (see p110), stood in the Assumption Cathedral from the 1480s to 1930.

The delicate little single-domed church beside the west door of the Assumption Cathedral is the **Church of the Deposition of the Robe** (Map p106), built between 1484 and 1486 by masons from Pskov.

IVAN THE GREAT BELL TOWER

With its two golden domes rising above the eastern side of Sobornaya pl, the 16th-century Ivan the Great Bell Tower is the Kremlin's tallest structure, visible from 30km away. Exhibitions from the Kremlin collections are shown on the ground level of the **bell tower** (Map p106; adult/student R100/50).

Beside the bell tower (not inside it) stands the **Tsar Bell**, which is the world's biggest bell. Sadly, this 202-tonne monster never rang. North of the bell tower is the **Tsar Cannon**, cast in 1586 for Fyodor I, whose portrait is on the barrel. Shot has never sullied its 89cm bore – and certainly not the cannonballs beside it, which are too big even for this elephantine firearm.

ARCHANGEL CATHEDRAL

Back on Sobornaya pl, this 1508 **cathedral** (Map p106) at the square's southeastern corner was for centuries the coronation, wed-

ding and burial church of tsars. The tombs of all of Moscow's rulers from the 1320s to the 1690s (except Boris Godunov, who is buried at Sergiev Posad – see p123) are here. Tsarevich Dmitry (Ivan the Terrible's son, who died mysteriously in 1591) lies beneath a painted stone canopy. Ivan's own tomb is out of sight behind the iconostasis, along with those of his other sons.

ANNUNCIATION CATHEDRAL

At the southwest corner of Sobornaya pl, this cathedral (Map p106), built by Pskov masters in 1489, was the royal family's private chapel. Ivan the Terrible's first marriage disqualified him under Orthodox law from entering the church proper, so he had the southern arm of the gallery converted into the **Archangel Gabriel Chapel**, from which he could view services through a grille.

The cathedral contains the celebrated icons of master painter Theophanes the Greek. Theophanes probably painted most of the six icons at the right-hand end of the diesis row, the biggest of the six tiers of the iconostasis. *Archangel Michael* (the third icon from the left on the largest of the six tiers of the iconostasis) is ascribed to Andrei Rublyov, who may also have painted the adjacent *St Peter*.

The basement – which remains from the previous 14th-century cathedral on this site – contains a fascinating exhibit on the **Archaeology of the Kremlin**. The artefacts date from the 12th to 14th centuries, showing the growth of Moscow during this period.

ARMOURY

The 700-room State Kremlin Palace is used for official visits and receptions, but isn't open to the public. In the Kremlin's southwestern corner is the **Armoury** (Map p106; adult/student R300/175; 🕐 10am, noon, 2.30pm & 4.30pm), a numbingly opulent collection of treasures accumulated over time by the Russian State and Church. Tickets specify entry times.

Of the Armoury's nine rooms, Rooms 6 and 7 are the most fascinating, containing royal regalia such as the joint coronation throne of boy tsars Peter (the Great) and his half-brother Ivan V (with a secret compartment from which Regent Sofia would prompt them), the 800-diamond throne of Tsar Alexey Mikhailovich, and the coronation dresses of 18th-century empresses.

MOSCOW

If the Armoury doesn't sate your diamond lust, there are more in the separate **Diamond Fund Exhibition** (☎ 229 2036; adult/student R350/175; ☺ 10am-noon & 2-5pm Fri-Wed), which is in the same building as the Armoury. The lavish collection shows off the precious stones and jewellery garnered by tsars and empresses over the centuries, including the largest sapphire in the world.

ALEKSANDROVSKY GARDEN

A good place to relax is the pleasant garden (Map p106) along the Kremlin's western wall. At the garden's northern end is the **Tomb of the Unknown Soldier**, containing the remains of a soldier who died in December 1941 at km41 of Leningradskoe sh – the nearest the Nazis came to Moscow. The changing of the guard happens every hour from 10am to 7pm in summer, and to 3pm during winter. Opposite the gardens is Manezhnaya pl and the underground Okhotny Ryad shopping mall (p119), a popular meeting spot for young Muscovites.

Red Square .

Immediately outside the Kremlin's northeastern wall is the infamous **Red Sq** (Kras-

naya ploshchad; Map p106). It was once a market square adjoining the merchants' area in Kitay-Gorod. Red Sq has always been a place where occupants of the Kremlin chose to congregate, celebrate and castigate for all the people to see.

Incidentally, the name 'Krasnaya ploshchad' has nothing to do with communism or the blood that flowed here: *krasny* in old Russian meant 'beautiful' and only in the 20th century did it come to mean 'red', too.

LENIN'S TOMB

The granite **tomb** (Map p106; ☎ 923 5527; admission free; ☺ 10am-1pm Tue-Thu, Sat & Sun; Ⓜ Ploshchad Revolyutsii), standing at the foot of the Kremlin wall, is one of Red Sq's must-see sights, especially if the former leader is eventually buried beside his mum in St Petersburg. Before joining the queue at the northwestern corner of Red Sq, drop your camera at the left-luggage office in the State History Museum (see opposite), as you will not be allowed to take it with you. Humourless guards ensure that visitors remain respectful during the visit. After trooping past the embalmed, oddly waxy figure, emerge from his red and black stone tomb and inspect

---

LENIN UNDER GLASS

Red Sq is home to the world's most famous mummy, that of Vladimir Ilych Lenin. When he died of a stroke (on 22 January 1924, aged 53), a long line of mourners patiently gathered in winter for weeks to glimpse the body as it lay in state. Inspired by the spectacle, Stalin proposed that the father of Soviet communism should continue to serve the cause as a holy relic. So the decision was made to preserve Lenin's corpse for perpetuity, against the vehement protests of his widow, as well as his own expressed desire to be buried next to his mother in St Petersburg.

Boris Zbarsky, a biochemist, and Vladimir Vorobyov, an anatomist, were issued a political order to put a stop to the natural decomposition of the body. The pair worked frantically in a secret laboratory in search of a long-term chemical solution. In the meantime, the body's dark spots were bleached, and lips and eyes sewn tight. The brain was removed and taken to another secret laboratory, to be sliced and diced by scientists for the next 40 years in the hope of uncovering its hidden genius.

In July 1924, the scientists hit upon a formula to successfully arrest the decaying process, a closely guarded state secret. This necrotic craft was passed on to Zbarsky's son, who ran the Kremlin's covert embalming lab for decades. After the fall of communism, Zbarsky came clean: the body is wiped down every few days, and then, every 18 months, thoroughly examined and submerged in a tub of chemicals, including paraffin wax. The institute has now gone commercial, offering its services and secrets to wannabe immortals for a mere million dollars.

In the early 1990s, Boris Yeltsin expressed his intention to heed Lenin's request and bury him in St Petersburg, setting off a furore from the political left as well as more-muted objections from Moscow tour operators. It seems that the mausoleum, the most sacred shrine of Soviet communism, and the mummy, the literal embodiment of the Russian Revolution, will remain in place for at least several more years.

where Stalin, Leonid Brezhnev and many of communism's other heavy hitters are buried along the Kremlin wall.

ST BASIL'S CATHEDRAL

No building says 'Russia' more than **Pokrovsky Cathedral** (St Basil's Cathedral, Sobor Vasiliya Blazhennogo; Map p106; ☎ 298 3304; Krasnaya pl 2; admission US$3; ☺ 11am-5pm Wed-Mon; Ⓜ Ploshchad Revolutsii), commonly known as St Basil's. Rising from the slope at Red Sq's southern end, this crazy confusion of colours and shapes was created between 1555 and 1561, replacing an existing church, to celebrate Ivan the Terrible's taking of the Tatar stronghold of Kazan. Its design is the culmination of a wholly Russian style that had been developed for building wooden churches.

The misnomer St Basil's actually refers only to the northeastern chapel, which was added later. It was built over the grave of the barefoot holy fool Vasily (Basil) the Blessed, who predicted Ivan's damnation and added correctly, as the army left for Kazan, that Ivan would murder a son. Vasily, who died while Kazan was under siege, was buried beside the church that St Basil's soon replaced. He was later canonised.

STATE HISTORY MUSEUM

At the northern end of the square, this **museum** (Map p106; ☎ 292 4019; www.shm.ru; adult/student R150/75; ☺ 11am-7pm Wed-Mon; Ⓜ Ploshchad Revolyutsii) has an enormous collection covering the Russian empire from the Stone Age onwards. The building, dating from the late 19th century, is itself an attraction – each room is in the style of a different period or region, some with highly decorated walls echoing old Russian churches. A **joint ticket** (adult/student R230/115) allowing access to the State History Museum and St Basil's Cathedral is available at either spot.

Tiny **Kazan Cathedral** (Map p106; ul Nikolskaya 3; admission free; ☺ 8am-7pm, evening service Mon 8pm; Ⓜ Ploshchad Revolyutsii) is opposite the museum entrance. It's a replica of the original, which was founded in 1636 and demolished on Stalin's orders in 1936, allegedly because it impeded the flow of parades through Red Sq.

Arbat District

Bound by the Moscow River in the southeast, this district includes the area south of ul Novy Arbat (or ul Vozdvizhenka) and in-side the Garden Ring. It includes ul Arbat, the 1.25km pedestrian mall stretching from Arbatskaya pl on the Boulevard Ring to Smolenskaya pl on the Garden Ring.

ULITSA ARBAT

The Arbat – Moscow's most famous street – is something of an art market, complete with instant portrait painters, soapbox poets, jugglers and buskers (and some pickpockets). It is an interesting walk, dotted with old pastel-coloured merchant houses and tourist-oriented shops and cafés. Near ul Arbat's eastern end, the **Wall of Peace** (Map pp102–3) is composed of hundreds of individually painted tiles on a theme of international friendship. The statue at the corner of Plotnikov per is of **Bulat Okudzhava** (Map pp102–3), the 1960s cult poet, singer and songwriter who lived at No 43 (see p110).

PUSHKIN MUSEUM OF FINE ARTS

Moscow's premier foreign-art museum is the **Pushkin Museum of Fine Arts** (Map pp102-3; ☎ 203 7998; www.museum.ru/gmii; ul Volkhonka 12; adult/student R300/150, audio guide R250; ☺ 10am-6pm Tue-Sun; Ⓜ Kropotkinskaya). It is famous for its impressionist and postimpressionist paintings, but also has a broad selection of European works from the Renaissance onwards, mostly appropriated from private collections after the revolution. There is also an amazing array of statues through the ages.

CATHEDRAL OF CHRIST THE SAVIOUR

Dominating the skyline along the Moscow River is the gargantuan **Cathedral of Christ the Saviour** (Map pp102-3; ☎ 201 2847; www.xxc.ru; admission free; ☺ 10am-5pm; Ⓜ Kropotkinskaya). It sits on the site of an earlier and similar church of the same name, built from 1839 to 1883 to commemorate Russia's victory over Napoleon. The original was destroyed during Stalin's orgy of explosive secularism. Stalin planned to replace the church with a 315m-high 'Palace of Soviets' (including a 100m statue of Lenin) but the project never got off the ground – literally. Instead, for 50 years the site served an important purpose as the world's largest swimming pool.

Zamoskvorechie

Zamoskvorechie (Beyond-Moscow-River) stretches south from opposite the Kremlin, inside a big river loop.

ARBAT, MY ARBAT

Arbat, my Arbat, you are my calling
You are my happiness and my misfortune.

Bulat Okudzhava

For Moscow's beloved bard Bulat Okudzhava, the Arbat was not only his home, it was his inspiration. Although he spent his university years in Georgia dabbling in harmless verse, it was only upon his return to Moscow – and to his cherished Arbat – that his poetry adopted the freethinking character for which it is known.

He gradually made the transition from poet to songwriter, stating that, 'Once I had the desire to accompany one of my satirical verses with music. I only knew three chords; now, 27 years later, I know seven chords, then I knew three.' While Bulat and his friends enjoyed his songs, other composers, singers and guitarists did not. The ill feeling subsided when a well-known poet announced that '...these are not songs. This is just another way of presenting poetry.'

And so a new form of art was born. The 1960s were heady times – in Moscow as elsewhere – and Okudzhava inspired a whole movement of liberal-thinking poets to take their ideas to the streets. Vladimir Vysotsky and others – some political, some not – followed in Okudzhava's footsteps, their iconoclastic lyrics and simple melodies drawing enthusiastic crowds all around Moscow.

The Arbat today – crowded with tacky souvenir stands and overpriced cafés – bears little resemblance to the hallowed haunt of Okudzhava's youth. But its memory lives on in the bards and buskers, painters and poets who still perform for strolling crowds on summer evenings.

STATE TRETYAKOV GALLERY

Nothing short of spectacular, the **State Tretyakov Gallery** (Map pp102-3; ☎ 951 1362, 953 5223; www.tretyakov.ru; Lavrushinsky per 10; adult/student R225/130, audio tour R120; ☯ 10am-6pm Tue-Sun; Ⓜ Tretyakovskaya) holds the world's best collection of Russian icons and an outstanding collection of other prerevolutionary Russian art, particularly the 19th-century Peredvizhniki (see p48). Within the museum grounds, the **Church of St Nicholas in Tolmachi** is the church where Pavel Tretyakov (one of the museum's founders) regularly attended services. The centrepiece is the revered 12th-century *Vladimir Icon of the Mother of God*, protector of all of Russia.

NEW TRETYAKOV

The premier venue for 20th-century Russian art is the new building of the State Tretyakov Gallery on Krymsky val, better known as the **New Tretyakov** (Novaya Tretyakovskaya Galereya; ☎ 238 1378; adult/student R225/130; ☯ 10am-6.30pm Tue-Sun; Ⓜ Park Kultury). Besides the plethora of socialist realism, the exhibits showcase avant-garde artists like Kasimir Malevich, Vasily Kandinsky, Marc Chagall, Natalia Goncharova and Lyubov Popova.

In the same building as the New Tretyakov, the **Central House of Artists** (Tsentralny Dom Khudozh-nikov; ☎ 238 9634; adult/student R50/20; ☯ 11am-7pm Tue-Sun; Ⓜ Park Kultury) is a huge exhibit space used for contemporary art shows.

Behind the complex is a wonderful, moody **Sculpture Park** (Park Skulptur; ☎ 290 0667; Krimsky val 10; admission R50; ☯ 9am-9pm; Ⓜ Park Kultury). Formerly called the Park of the Fallen Heroes, it started as a collection of Soviet statues (Stalin, Felix Dzerzhinsky, a selection of Lenins and Brezhnevs) put out to pasture when they were ripped from their pedestals in the post-1991 wave of anti-Soviet feeling. These discredited icons have now been joined by contemporary work.

GORKY PARK

Part ornamental park, part funfair, Gorky Park is one of Moscow's most festive places to escape the hubbub of the city. Officially the **Park of Culture** (Park Kultury; ☎ 237 1266; Krymsky val; adult/child R50/15; ☯ 10am-10pm; Ⓜ Park Kultury), it's named after Maxim Gorky, and stretches almost 3km along the river upstream of Krymsky most. You can't miss the showy entrance, marked by colourful flags waving in the wind and the happy sounds of an old-fashioned carousel. Inside, Gorky Park has a small Western amusement park with two roller coasters and a dozen other terror-inducing attractions.

Outer Moscow
NOVODEVICHY CONVENT & CEMETERY
A cluster of sparkling domes behind tur-
reted walls on the Moscow River, **Novodevichy Convent** (Novodevichy Monastir; ☎ 246 8526;
adult/student R150/75, photo permit R60; ☼ grounds
daily 8am-8pm, museums Wed-Mon 10am-5pm; Ⓜ Sportivnaya) is rich with history and treasures.
Founded in 1524 to celebrate the retaking
of Smolensk from Lithuania, the convent is
notorious as the place where Peter the Great
imprisoned his half-sister Sofia for her part
in the Streltsy rebellion.

Adjacent to the convent, **Novodevichy
Cemetery** (Novodevichy Kladbishche; admission R30;
☼ 9am-6pm; Ⓜ Sportivnaya) is among Moscow's
most prestigious resting places – a veritable
'who's who' of Russian politics and culture.
You will find the tombs of Anton Chekhov,
Nikolai Gogol, Vladimir Mayakovsky, Konstantin Stanislavsky, Sergei Prokofiev, Sergei Eisenstein, Andrei Gromyko, and many
other Russian and Soviet notables.

ALL-RUSSIA EXHIBITION CENTRE
Nowhere sums up the rise and fall of the
Soviet dream like this **exhibition centre** (Vseros-
sissky Vystavochny Tsentr, VVTs; ☎ 544 3400; www.vvc
entre.ru; pr Mira; ☼ pavilions 10am-6pm, grounds 9am-
7pm; Ⓜ VDNKh). The old initials by which it's
still commonly known, VDNKh, tell half the
story – they stand for Vystavka Dostizheny
Narodnogo Khozyaystva SSSR (USSR Economic Achievements Exhibition).

Originally created in the 1930s, VDNKh
was expanded in the 1950s and '60s to im-
press upon one and all the success of the
Soviet economic system. Two kilometres
long and 1km wide, it is composed of wide
pedestrian avenues and grandiose pavilions,
glorifying every aspect of socialist construction from education and health to agriculture, technology and science. The pavilions
represent a huge variety of architectural
styles, symbolic of the contributions from
diverse ethnic and artistic movements to
the common goal. Here you will find the
kitschest socialist realism, the most inspiring of socialist optimism and, now, the
tackiest of capitalist consumerism.

The soaring 100m titanium obelisk is a
monument to Soviet space flight. In its base
is the **Memorial Museum of Cosmonauts** (Muzey
Kosmonavtov; ☎ 283 8197; adult/child R40/20, English
audio guide R100; ☼ 10am-7pm Tue-Sun; Ⓜ VDNKh),

a high-concept series of displays from the
glory days of the Soviet space programme.

VICTORY PARK & AROUND
This huge memorial complex celebrates
the Great Patriotic War. The park includes
endless fountains and monuments, as well
as the memorial **Church of St George**. The **Museum of the Great Patriotic War** (☎ 142 4185; ul
Bratiev Fonchenko 10; admission R30; ☼ 10am-5pm Tue-
Sun; Ⓜ Park Pobedy), within the park, has a diorama of every major WWII battle. Exhibits
highlight the many heroes of the Soviet
Union, and show weapons, photographs,
documentary films, letters and much other
authentic wartime memorabilia.

Make arrangements in advance to visit the
Museum of Jewish Legacy History and Holocaust
(☎ 148 1907; Minskaya ul; admission free; ☼ 10am-6pm
Tue-Thu, noon-7pm Sun; Ⓜ Park Pobedy).

ACTIVITIES
What better way to cope with Moscow than
to have it steamed, washed and beaten out
of you? There are traditional *bani* (hot
baths) all over town. If you aren't shy, general admission to shared facilities is cheaper
than renting a private bath. See also p44, for
a guide to *banya* etiquette.

Banya on Presnya (Map pp102-3; ☎ men 255 5306,
women 253 8690; Stolyarny per 7; per hr R300; ☼ 8am-
10pm Mon-Sat, 2-10pm Sun; Ⓜ Ulitsa 1905 Goda) lacks
the old-fashioned decadent atmosphere of
Sanduny. Nonetheless, this new, clean place
provides a first-rate *banya* experience.

Sanduny Baths (Map pp102-3; ☎ private 925 4631,
general 925 4633; www.sanduny.ru; Neglinnaya ul 14; private
room per hr from R1200, general admission per hr R500-700;
☼ 8am-10pm) is the oldest and most luxuri-
ous *banya* in the city. A work of art in itself,
the Gothic Room has rich wood carving
and the main shower room has an almost
aristocratic Roman feel to it.

There's no shortage of winter in Moscow,
so take advantage of it. You can rent ice
skates and see where all those great Russian figure skaters come from at **Gorky Park**
(opposite) or **Chistye Prudy** (Map pp102–3).
Bring your passport to rent skates.

WALKING TOUR
This walking tour winds its way through
Kitay-Gorod, which – settled in the 13th
century – is one of the oldest parts of Moscow. Kitay-Gorod translates as 'Chinatown',

MOSCOW

but the name actually derives from *kita*, meaning 'wattle'. It refers to the palisades that reinforced the earthen ramp erected around this early Kremlin suburb.

Start at the Hotel Metropol and walk east down Teatralny pro to the gated walkway. This historical complex is **Old Fields (1)**, and includes excavations of the 16th-century fortified wall that used to surround Kitay-Gorod and the foundations of the 1493 Trinity Church, as well as the memorial statue of Ivan Fyodorov, the 16th-century printer responsible for Russia's first book.

Walk down Tretyakovsky pro to Nikolskaya ul, Kitay-Gorod's busiest street. Turn right to head west on Nikolskaya ul, which used to be the main road to Vladimir.

The green and white building, with the lion and unicorn above its entrance at No 15, is the **Synod Printing House (2)**, where Ivan Fyodorov reputedly produced Russia's first printed book in 1563. Up until the early 19th century, Kitay-Gorod was something of a printing centre, home to 26 out of Moscow's then 31 bookshops. The **Zaikonospassky Monastery (3)** at Nos 7 to 9 refers to the busy icon trade that also took place here.

WALK FACTS

Start Teatralnaya pl (Ⓜ Teatralnaya)
Finish Staraya pl (Ⓜ Kitay-Gorod)
Distance 1.5km
Duration Two hours

Turn left on Bogoyavlensky per and head south, looking for the Moscow Baroque Epiphany Cathedral on the right-hand side. The church was built in the 1690s, but the **Monastery of the Epiphany (4)** dates to the 13th century.

Continue to ul Ilyinka, which was Moscow's financial heart in the 18th and 19th centuries. The old **Stock Exchange (5)** is on the corner at No 6. Built in the 1870s, it now houses the Chamber of Commerce and Industry.

Turn left and walk down Khrustalny per. The Old Merchants' Court – **Gostinny Dvor (6)** – occupies the block between uls Ilyinka and Varvarka. It is now completely renovated and filled with shops, including some excellent stops for souvenir hunters.

Take another left and head east on ul Varvarka, which is crowded with tiny churches, old homes and what remains of the giant Hotel Rossiya. The pink and white **St Barbara's Church (7)**, now government offices, dates from 1795 to 1804. The reconstructed 16th-century **Old English House (8)**, white with peaked wooden roofs, was the residence of England's first emissaries to Russia.

Built in 1698, the **Church of St Maxim the Blessed (9)** at No 4 is now a folk-art exhibition hall. Next along is the pointed bell tower of the 17th-century **Monastery of the Sign (10)**, incorporating the monks' building and a golden-domed cathedral.

Tucked in between the street and the former Hotel Rossiya is the small but rather interesting **Romanov Chambers in Zaryadie Museum (11**; ☎ 924 4529; ul Varvarka 10; admission R150; ⌚ 10am-5pm Thu-Mon, 11am-6pm Wed), which is devoted to the lives of these high-ranking nobles. The colourful **St George's Church (12)** at No 12 dates from 1658.

Cross ul Varvarka and walk up Ipatyevsky per. The enchanting 1630s **Church of the Trinity in Nikitniki (13)** is an exquisite example of Russian baroque hidden amid the overbearing façades of the surrounding buildings.

Head east on Ipatyevsky per out to Staraya pl. At the southern end of Staraya Pl, **All Saints Cathedral on the Kulishka (14)** was built in 1687. In 1380, Dmitry Donskoy built the original wooden church on this site to commemorate those who died in the battle of Kulikovo. Some remains of the old city wall can be seen in the underground passage at the corner of ul Varvarka and Staraya pl.

COURSES

Cooking

Russian cooking classes are hard to come by, but Patriarshy Dom Tours (see right) does offer an occasional half-day course. Learn to whip up some bliny, then eat them for lunch.

Language

Check the *Moscow Times* for advertisements for Russian tutors and short-term courses.

Liden & Denz Language Centre (☎ 254 4991; www .lidenz.ru; Gruzinsky per 3-181, ground fl; 16hr course R4480; Ⓜ Belorusskaya) More-expensive courses service the business and diplomatic community with less-intensive, evening courses.

Ziegler & Partner (☎ /fax 939 0980; www.study russian.com; Moscow State University, cnr ul Akademika Khokhlova & pr Vernadkogo; 2-wk, 40hr course US$860; Ⓜ Universitet) A Swiss group offering individually designed courses, from standard conversation to specialised lessons in business, law, literature etc.

MOSCOW FOR CHILDREN

Kids may not appreciate an age-old icon or a Soviet hero but Moscow has plenty to offer the little ones.

For starters, the city is filled with parks, such as **Aleksandrovsky Garden** (p108), which has a playground and plenty of room to run around. Or take them to **Gorky Park** (p110) – thrilling rides in summer and ice skating in winter make it the ultimate Russian experience for children. For a more post-Soviet experience, the **All-Russia Exhibition Centre** (p111) also has amusement park rides and video games.

Russia excels at the circus, and crazy clowns and daring acrobatics are all the rage at the atmospheric **Nikulin Circus** (p119). Another Russian favourite is the puppet theatre. **Obraztsov Puppet Theatre and Museum** (Map pp102-3; ☎ 299 3310, 299 5563; Sadovaya Samotechnaya ul 3; Ⓜ Tsvetnoy Bulvar) runs colourful Russian folk tales and adapted classical plays; kids can get up close and personal with the incredible puppets at the museum.

What better entertainment for kiddies than performing kitties? At the **Kuklachev Cat Theatre** (Map pp102-3; ☎ 249 2907; Kutuzovsky pr 25), Yuri Kuklachev's acrobatic cats do all kinds of stunts to the audience's delight. Kuklachev says, 'We do not use the word *train* here because it implies forcing an animal to do something; and you cannot force cats to do anything they don't want to. We *play* with the cats.' Bigger cats are the highlight of the **Moscow Zoo** (Map pp102-3; ☎ 255 6367; www.zoo.ru/moscow; cnr Barrikadnaya & Bolshaya Gruzinskaya uls; admission R80; ⓨ 10am-8pm Tue-Sun May-Sep, 10am-5pm Tue-Sun Oct-Apr; Ⓜ Barrikadnaya), an obvious destination for children.

TOURS

For new perspectives on Moscow neighbourhoods, fine views of the Kremlin, or just good old-fashioned transportation, a boat ride (adult/child R200/100, end to end 1½ hours, departing every 20 minutes) on the Moscow River is one of the city's highlights. The main route runs between Kievsky vokzal (Map pp102–3) and the Novospassky most near Novospassky Monastery. There are six intermediate stops, including one at Gorky Park and another at Ustinsky Most near Red Sq (Map pp102–3).

The boats seat about 200 people (most Muscovites are actually going somewhere, not just out to enjoy the ride) and are operated by the **Capital Shipping Company** (☎ 458 9624; www.cck-ship.ru; Rechnoy Vokzal, Leningradsky sh 51; Ⓜ Rechnoy Vokzal). Boats run from mid-April to mid-October.

Other useful tour companies:

Capital Tours (Map pp102-3; ☎ 232 2442; www .capitaltours.ru; Gostiny Dvor, ul Ilyinka 4; Ⓜ Kitay-Gorod) This spin-off of Patriarshy Dom offers a twice-daily Kremlin/Armoury tour (US$37/20, 10.30am and 3pm Friday and Wednesday) and Moscow city tour (US$20/10 per adult/child, 11am and 2.30pm). Tours departs from Gostiny Dvor.

Patriarshy Dom Tours (Map pp102-3; ☎ /fax 795 0927; http://russiatravel-pdtours.netfirms.com; Vspolny per 6, Moscow school No 1239; Ⓜ Barrikadnaya) Provides unique English-language tours on just about any specialised subject; some provide access to otherwise closed museums. Day tours range from US$16 to US$40 per person. Look for the monthly schedule at Western hotels and restaurants or online.

FESTIVALS & EVENTS

See p305 for a list of Russian spectaculars. While Mayor Luzhkov is a keen proponent of bread and circuses for the masses, the festivals are an ever-changing lot from year to year; consult the Moscow newspapers for what's on.

Standout seasons to visit are late spring (May or June) and early autumn (September or October), when the city's parks are filled with flowering trees or colourful leaves. The city is spruced for the May holidays and City Day, both festive times in the capital.

Winter Festival An outdoor funfest during early January for those with antifreeze in their veins (though plenty of people use vodka for this purpose). Teams compete to build elaborate ice sculptures in front of the Pushkin Museum of Fine Arts and on Red Sq.

Golden Mask Festival (☎ 755 8335; www.golden mask.ru) Two weeks of performances by Russia's premier drama, opera, dance and musical performers, culminating in a prestigious awards ceremony. Brightens up otherwise dreary March and April.

Moscow Forum (☎ 290 5181; www.ccmm.ru) A contemporary music festival held every year in April at the Tchaikovsky Conservatory.

Interfest (☎ 917 2486; www.miff.ru) Short for the Moscow International Film Festival, which takes place in June.

City Day (Den Goroda) Celebrates the city's birthday every year on the first weekend in September. The day kicks off with a festive parade, followed by live music on Red Sq and plenty of food, fireworks and fun.

December Nights Festival Held at the main performance halls, theatres and museums from mid-December to early January. Classical music at its best, performed in classy surroundings by the best Russian and foreign talent.

SLEEPING

The optimal area to stay is within the Garden Ring, which guarantees easy access to major sights and plenty of dining and entertainment options. Tverskoy and Arbat Districts are particularly lively. If you do find yourself far from the centre, look for easy access to the metro.

Budget

Galina's Flat (Map pp102–3; ☎ 921 6038; galinas flat@mtu-net.ru; ul Chaplygina 8, No 35; dm/s/d R300/

540/750; Ⓜ Chistye Prudy; 🖳) It's just that – a private, Soviet-era flat with a few extra rooms that Galina rents out. Staying at Galina's feels like staying in your friend's crowded apartment – cosy, comfortable and convivial. She has six beds, as well as kitchen and laundry facilities, but she doesn't provide visa support. Galina can help you find a spot at her neighbours' or in other apartments if her place is full.

Travellers Guest House (☎ 631 4059; www.tgh.ru; Bolshaya Pereyaslavskaya ul 50, fl 10; dm R690, s/d with shared bathroom R1350/1650, d with private bathroom R1800; Ⓜ Rizhskaya; 🖳) Calls itself Moscow's 'first and only' budget accommodation. Perhaps the first but no longer the only, this place is still one of the better options for budget travellers. Despite its location on the 10th floor of a drab hotel, it manages to maintain a vibrant, hostel-like atmosphere, thanks to the travellers hanging out in the common lounge and the services available through the affiliated Infinity Travel (p101). From Rizhskaya metro, walk away from pr Mira and turn right under the highway bridge. Walk along Bolshaya Pereyaslavskaya ul until you see the tall, unnamed hotel on the left side of the road.

Hotel Izmaylovo (Gamma Delta; ☎ 737 7187, 737 7104; www.izmailovo.ru; Izmaylovskoe sh 71; s/d from R1440/1540; Ⓜ Partizanskaya; 🖳) Built for the 1980 Olympics, this hotel has 8000 beds, apparently making it Europe's biggest hotel. Four of the five buildings are budget accommodation, but Gamma-Delta is the snazziest and most service-oriented. If you need to escape the frenetic atmosphere that surrounds Izmaylovo market, it's just a few steps to lovely Izmaylovsky Park.

Hostel Sherstone (☎ 711 2613; www.sherstone .ru; Gostinichny pro 8/1, fl 3; dm/s/d R600/1200/1550;

THE AUTHOR'S CHOICE

Golden Apple (Map pp102–3; ☎ 980 7000; www.goldenapple.ru; ul Malaya Dmitrovka 11; r from R9000; Ⓜ Pushkinskaya or Chekhovskaya; ✄ 🐾 🖳) Calling itself Moscow's first boutique hotel, this smallish, slick hotel is indeed a novelty. The location is prime – in the heart of Moscow's shopping district and steps from the serenity of Hermitage Gardens. A classical edifice fronts the street, but the interior is sleek and sophisticated. The rooms are decorated in a modern, minimalist style – subdued whites and greys punctuated by contrasting coloured drapes and funky light fixtures. But comfort is also paramount, with no skimping on luxuries like heated bathroom floors and down-filled duvets. Even if you can't afford to spend the night, it's worth dropping in to have a drink in the lounge – walls splashed with colour – or to dine at the relatively subdued but highly acclaimed restaurant. This is the best of New Russia: contemporary, creative and classy.

FIND A FLAT

Hotels in Moscow can easily break your bank. In response to the shortage of affordable accommodation, some entrepreneurial Muscovites have begun renting out flats on a short-term basis. Flats are equipped with kitchens, and sometimes with other useful amenities, like Internet access. Often, a good-sized flat is available for the price of a hotel room or less. It is an ideal solution for travellers in a group, who can split the cost.

Several websites provide information about apartments for rent. The apartments vary widely, but many have photos available online. Apartments are around US$80 to US$120 per night, with prices decreasing for longer stays. Expect to pay more for fully renovated, Western-style apartments.

- www.apartmentres.com – bills itself as gay-friendly lodging. Most flats include free airport transfers and international phone calls.
- www.enjoymoscow.com – Rick's apartments are off the Garden Ring between Sukharevskaya and Tsvetnoy Bulvar metro stations.
- www.flatmates.ru/eng – a site for travellers looking for somebody to share short- or long-term accommodation in Russia.
- www.hofa.ru – has apartments from €40 per night and homestays from €20 per night.
- www.rentline.ru – offers online reservations for a variety of centrally located flats, starting from US$80 per night.
- www.unclepasha.com – Uncle Pasha is an unbelievable grouch, but his flat – at US$75 per night – is a great deal. He also maintains an extensive list of other budget accommodation options and will help you locate one.

M Vladykino) The tree-lined streets west of the Botanical Gardens comprise something of a hotel district (thus, the name of the street, which means 'Hotel Way'). This friendly YHA hostel occupies one floor of a hotel by the same name. Its main advantage is the English-speaking staff, but rooms and services are also satisfactory. From Vladykino metro, cross busy Botanicheskaya ul and continue west on Gostinichny pro.

Hotel Zarya (☎ /fax 788 7277; Gostinichnaya ul 4/9; s/d from R1350/1500; M Vladykino) A complex of short brick buildings, also near the Botanical Gardens, about 1km south of Hostel Sherstone. Renovation of the rooms is ongoing, so the cheapest ones are pretty plain. But the reception is welcoming and the atmosphere is cosy. Upgraded rooms with new furniture and bathrooms are R2100/2700.

Midrange

East-West Hotel (Map pp102–3; ☎ 290 0404; www .eastwesthotel.ru; Tverskoy bul 14/4; s/d R4800/6500; M Pushkinskaya; ⊠ 🖵) Located on the loveliest stretch of the Boulevard Ring, this small hotel evokes the atmosphere of the 19th-century mansion it once was. It is a kitsch but charming place with 26 individually decorated rooms and a lovely fountain-filled courtyard. Prices include breakfast.

Hotel Budapest (Map pp102–3; ☎ 923 1060; www .hotel-budapest.ru; Petrovskie linii 2/18; s/d with breakfast R3850/5450; M Kuznetsky Most; ⊠ 🖵) This 19th-century neoclassical edifice makes a perfect retreat after strolling in the swanky shopping district that surrounds it. The grandeur does not extend to the rooms unless you dish out some extra cash for a suite (from R5775), but the hotel is excellent value.

Danilovskaya Hotel (☎ 954 0503; hotdanil@cityline .ru; s/d with breakfast from R3300/3900; M Tulskaya; ⊠ 🖵 🕿) Moscow's holiest hotel is on the grounds of the 12th-century monastery of the same name; nearly all the rooms have a view of the beautiful grounds. The rooms themselves are simple but clean, and breakfast is modest: no greed, gluttony or sloth to be found here.

Hotel Sverchkov (Map pp102–3; ☎ 925 4978; Sverchkov per 8; s/d with breakfast from R2600/3000; M Chistye Prudy) On a quiet residential lane, this is a tiny 11-room hotel in a graceful 18th-century building. Though the rooms are nothing special, this place is a rarity for its intimacy and hominess.

MOSCOW

Hotel Peking (Map pp102-3; ☎ 209 2215; www .hotelpekin.ringnet.ru; Bolshaya Sadovaya ul 5/1; d from R2500; Ⓜ Mayakovskaya) With ongoing renovation, this Stalinesque building boasts a prime location towering over Triumfalnaya pl. It's hard to see past the flashing lights of the casino, but this place is blessed with high ceilings, parquet floors and the marble staircase. The upgraded rooms (singles/ doubles R3500/4200) – elegantly decorated in jewel tones – are worth the investment.

Hotel Arbat (Map pp102-3; ☎ 244 7628; fax 244 0093; Plotnikov per 12; s/d with breakfast from R4320/5130; Ⓜ Smolenskaya) One of the few hotels that manages to preserve some appealing Soviet camp, from the greenery-filled lobby to the mirrors behind the bar. The whole place has an anachronistic charm. Its location is also very charming – on a quiet residential street, just steps from the Arbat.

Hotel Belgrad (Map pp102-3; ☎ 248 1643; www .hotel-belgrad.ru; Smolenskaya ul 8; s/d R2560/2880; Ⓜ Smolenskaya) The big block has no sign and a stark lobby, giving it a ghost-town aura. Rooms are similar – poky but functional, unless you pay for upgraded 'tourist' or 'business-class' accommodation (R4160 to R5280). The advantage is the location, which can be noisy but is convenient to ul Arbat.

Kazakh Embassy Hotel (Map pp102-3; ☎ 208 0994; Chistoprudny bul 3; s/d with breakfast R2700/3000; Ⓜ Chistye Prudy) Caters – as you may guess – to guests and workers of the nearby Kazakh embassy. But anyone can stay in this grand, modern building that fronts the prestigious Boulevard Ring.

Altay Hotel (☎ 482 5703; altayhotel@comail.ru; Botanicheskaya ul 41; s/d with breakfast R2200/2890; Ⓜ Vladykino; ⓧ ⓛ) The classiest place to stay in the hotel district near the Botanical Gardens. The place has been completely revamped, from the elegant lobby to the tastefully decorated guest rooms. Only a few old-school rooms remain (singles/doubles R800/1250). Convenient to the metro.

Recommended for transit travellers who need to crash between flights:

Sheremetyevo-2 (☎ 578 5753/4; fax 739 4464; Sheremetyevo-2 airport; r from R3450) More affordable than the nearby Novotel. You can walk here from the airport, or use the Novotel's free shuttle.

Aerotel Domodedovo (☎ 795 3868; fax 795 3569; Domodedovo airport; s & d from R3500; ⓧ ⓧ ⓛ ⓛ) A brand-new hotel within walking distance of its namesake airport. Excellent value.

Top End

Hotel Metropol (Map pp102-3; ☎ 927 6000; www .metropol-moscow.ru; Teatralny pro 1/4; s/d from R9000/ 10,500; Ⓜ Teatralnaya; ⓧ ⓧ ⓛ ⓛ) Nothing short of an Art Nouveau masterpiece, the historic Metropol brings an artistic touch to every nook and cranny, from the spectacular exterior to the grand lobby to the individually decorated rooms. The overall effect is breathtaking, but the charm lies in the details, like stained-glass windows, Oriental rugs and early-20th-century furnishings. Located opposite the Bolshoi; it's worth stopping in just to check out the exquisite stained-glass ceiling in the restaurant.

Hotel Tiflis (Map pp102-3; ☎ 733 9070; www.hotel tiflis.com; ul Ostozhenka 32; s/d incl breakfast from R7100/ 9200; Ⓜ Park Kultury or Kropotkinskaya; ⓧ ⓧ ⓛ ⓛ) Georgians know hospitality; the proof is in the fine restaurants, like the landmark Tiflis (opposite), and now this hotel by the same name. With only 30 rooms, this refined four-star offers an intimate atmosphere and personalised service. Ask for a room with a balcony overlooking the fountain-filled patio.

EATING

In Soviet days, eating out meant either a cheap meal at the local cafeteria, or for special occasions, nearly identical food at a cheesy hotel restaurant. These days, theme restaurants are all the rage. From the Uzbek restaurant with a live camel out front, to the French restaurant with a Gothic cathedral interior, restaurateurs are going all out to ensure their patrons' dining experiences are at least interesting.

Restaurants

Correa's (Map pp102-3; ☎ 933 4684; Bolshaya Gruzinskaya ul 32; sandwiches R200-300, brunch R400-600, meals R600-1000; ⓨ 8am-midnight; Ⓜ Belorusskaya or Belorussky Vokzal) It's hard to characterise a place that's so simple. It is a tiny space of only seven tables. Large windows and an open kitchen guarantee that it does not feel cramped, just cosy. The menu – sandwiches, pizzas and grills – features nothing too fancy, but everything is prepared with the freshest ingredients and the utmost care.

Café Pushkin (Map pp102-3; ☎ 229 5590; Tverskoy bul 26a; business lunches R525, meals R1500-2000; ⓨ 24hr; Ⓜ Pushkinskaya) The queen mother of *haute russe* dining, with an exquisite blend

---

THE AUTHOR'S CHOICE

Tiflis (Map pp102-3; ☎ 290 2897; ul Ostozhenka 32; meals R1000-1500; Ⓜ Kropotkinskaya or Park Kultury) Moscow is the best place outside the Caucasus to sample the rich, spicy cuisine of the former Soviet republic of Georgia. And Tiflis is the best place in Moscow. The name comes from the Russian word for the Georgian capital, Tblisi, and when you enter this restaurant, you may think you are there. Its airy balconies and interior courtyards recall a 19th-century Georgian mansion – a romantic and atmospheric setting. Tiflis takes Caucasian cuisine upscale. The *kharcho* (beef soup) is thick and rich, while the *basturma* (grilled lamb) is spicy and cooked to perfection. The dishes are particularly delectable when accompanied by the Tiflis wine, produced by the restaurateur's winery in Georgia. According to Moscow foodies, Tiflis counts among its regular customers the Russian Minister of Foreign Affairs, Igor Ivanov, who happens to be of Georgian descent.

---

of Russian and French cuisines; service and food are done to perfection. The lovely 19th-century building has a different atmosphere on each floor, including a richly decorated library and a pleasant rooftop café.

Simple Pleasures (Map pp102-3; ☎ 207 4043; ul Sretenka 22; meals R800-1000; ☺ noon-midnight Mon-Fri, 2pm-midnight Sat & Sun; Ⓜ Sukharevskaya) The chef is American, but the menu is wide-ranging, including his favourite dishes from Italy, Spain and the American South. The common denominator is fresh ingredients and simple cooking techniques, an ideal match for this comfortable, uncluttered space.

GlavPivTorg (Map pp102-3; ☎ 928 2591; ul Bolshaya Lubyanka 5; business lunches R125-195, meals R600-1000; Ⓜ Lubyanka) At the 'central beer restaurant No 5', every effort is made to re-create an upscale apparatchik dining experience. The Soviet fare is authentic, but not too authentic. So you may get a side of peas, but they will be fresh and sweet. Add three varieties of tasty beer brewed on-site, and you've got a restaurant to suit any ideology.

Eastern Quarter (Map pp102-3; ☎ 241 3803; ul Arbat 45/24; meals R400-600) Uzbeks cooking in the open kitchen and more Uzbeks filling up the dining room are the sign that this Central Asian eatery is serving some of Moscow's best national cuisine. The speciality: tasty, filling rice *plov* (pilaf rice with diced mutton and vegetables).

Yolki-Palki (Map pp102-3; meals R200-400; ☺ 11am-midnight) Tverskoy District (☎ 928 5525; Neglinnaya ul 8/10; Ⓜ Kuznetsky Most); Arbat District (☎ 291 6888; ul Novy Arbat 11; Ⓜ Arbatskaya); Zamoskvorechie (☎ 953 9130; Klimentovsky per 14; Ⓜ Tretyakovskaya) This excellent Russian chain is beloved for its country cottage décor and its well-stocked salad bar. Outlets all over the city specialise in traditional dishes and cheap beer.

Starlite Diner (Map pp102-3; ☎ 290 9638; ul Bolshaya Sadovaya 16; meals R500-700; ☺ 24hr; Ⓜ Mayakovskaya) Outdoor seating and classic diner décor make this a longtime favourite of expats in Moscow. The extensive brunch menu includes all kinds of omelettes, French toast and freshly squeezed juice. Otherwise, you can't go wrong with burgers and milkshakes, any time of day or night.

Jagannath (Map pp102-3; ☎ 928 3580; Kuznetsky most 11; meals R300-500; ☺ 10am-11pm; Ⓜ Kuznetsky Most) If you are in need of vitamins, come to this funky vegetarian café, restaurant and store. Service is slow but the sublime food is worth the wait.

Il Patio (Map pp102-3; business lunches R190-280, meals R400-500) Arbat District (☎ 201 5626; ul Volkhonka 13a; Ⓜ Kropotkinskaya); Barrikadnaya (☎ 785 6553; Novinsky bul 31; Ⓜ Barrikadnaya); Taganskaya (☎ 230 6662; Taganskaya ul 1/2; ☺ 8am-11pm; Ⓜ Taganskaya) Patio Pizza has gone upscale, with a more Italian name and a more stylish look. Wood-oven pizzas and fresh salad bars are the highlights of the menu.

Karetny Dvor (Map pp102-3; ☎ 291 6376; Povarskaya ul 52; meals R600-800; ☺ 24hr; Ⓜ Barrikadnaya) Moscow's most popular Caucasian place has a simple, relaxed interior and a green, leafy courtyard. Go for classic Azeri fare like dolmas in grape leaves, and lamb kebabs.

Cafés

Coffee Bean (Map pp102-3; ✗) Tverskoy District (☎ 788 6357; Tverskaya ul 10; ☺ 8am-11pm; Ⓜ Pushkinskaya); Zamoskvorechie (☎ 953 6726; Pyatnitskaya ul 5; ☺ 8am-10pm; Ⓜ Tretyakovskaya); Chistye Prudy (☎ 923 9793; ul Pokrovka 18; ☺ 8am-10pm; ☺ Chistye Prudy) One could claim that Coffee Bean started the coffee thing in Moscow – the original outlet on Tverskaya has been around for years. It's still the coolest café in the city, with high ceilings, fantastic architectural details and large windows looking out onto the main drag. Coffee runs around R100; it's that rare place that does not allow smoking.

Coffee Mania (Map pp102-3) Kuznetsky Most (☎ 924 0075; Pushechnaya ul; 🕑 8am-11pm; Ⓜ Kuznetsky Most); Barrikadnaya (☎ 290 0141; Kudrinskaya pl 46/54; 🕑 8am-midnight; Ⓜ Barrikadnaya); Bolshaya Nikitskaya (☎ 775 4310; Bolshaya Nikitskaya ul 13, Moscow Conservatory; 🕑 8am-1am; Ⓜ Aleksandrovsky Sad) This is a popular spot to grab a cup o' joe or a light lunch. The Bolshaya Nikitskaya branch has a delightful outdoor seating area in front of the conservatory.

Loft Cafe (Map pp102-3; ☎ 933 7713; Nikolskaya ul 25; meals R800-1000; 🕑 9am-midnight; Ⓜ Lubyanka) On the top floor of the Nautilus shopping centre, you'll find this tiny, trendy café with a fantastic view of Lubyanka sq. Innovative, modern dishes fuse the best of Russian cuisine with Western and Asian influences.

Quick Eats

Moo-Moo (Map pp102-3; meals R100-200; 🕑 9am-11pm) Arbat District (☎ 241 1364; ul Arbat 45/23; Ⓜ Smolenskaya); Lubyanka (☎ 923 4503; Myasnitskaya 14; Ⓜ Lubyanka) You will recognise this place by its black-and-white Holstein-print décor. It offers you an easy approach to all the Russian favourites.

Drova (Map pp102-3; meals R200-400, all-you-can-eat buffet R350; 🕑 24hr) Chistye Prudy (☎ 925 2725; Myasnitskaya ul 24; Ⓜ Chistye Prudy); Arbat District (☎ 202 7570; Nikitsky bul 8a; Ⓜ Arbatskaya); Tverskoy District (☎ 229 3227; ul Bolshaya Dmitrovka 7; Ⓜ Teatralnaya) The self-serve buffet ranges from *solyanka* (soup from pickled vegetables and potato) to sushi and sweet-and-sour pork. It's not the best place to sample any of these items, but the price is right.

Pelmeshka (Map pp102-3; ☎ 292 8392; ul Kuznetsky most 4/3; breakfast R60, lunch R125, meals R150-200; 🕑 11am-midnight; Ⓜ Teatralnaya) Serves many different kinds of *pelmeni* (Russian-style ravioli stuffed with meat), the most filling of Russian favourites. It's packed at lunchtime, a sign that it is tasty as well as cheap.

Self-Catering

Ramstore (Map pp102-3; ☎ 207 3165; www.ramstore .ru; Komsomolskaya pl 6, Moskovsky Univermag; 🕑 24hr; Ⓜ Komsomolskaya) The Turkish-owned supermarket – just opposite Yaroslavsky vokzal – is an ultraconvenient place to stock up for your Trans-Siberian journey.

Dorogomilovsky market (Map pp102-3; Mozhaysky val 10; Ⓜ Kievskaya) Moscow's *rynky* (food markets) are bustling places full of activity and colour. Even if you are not buying, it's fun to see what's for sale: tables piled high with fresh produce; golden honey in jars that are as big as basketballs; vibrantly coloured spices pouring out of plastic bags; and silver fish posing on beds of ice.

DRINKING

Bar 30/7 (Map pp102-3; ☎ 209 5951; ul Petrovka 30/7; 🕑 24hr; Ⓜ Chekhovskaya) This slick new bar on the Boulevard Ring is the latest place to see and be seen in Moscow. If you can snag a seat in the attached 'sun room' seating area, you will enjoy a lovely view of the boulevard promenade. Good luck, as the place gets packed on weekends.

Real McCoy (Map pp102-3; ☎ 255 4144; Kudrinskaya pl 1; business lunches R180, meals R500-1000; 🕑 24hr; Ⓜ Barrikadnaya) The main features of this 'bootlegger's bar' are walls plastered in old newspapers and a dining room crowded with expats. The menu includes barbecue ribs, seafood curry and everything in between. This is a popular spot for drinking, especially during the two-for-one happy hour specials (5pm to 8pm daily).

Red Bar (Map pp102-3; ☎ 730 0808; 22-24 Kutuzovsky pro; beers R175, meals R1400-1750; 🕑 noon-3am; Ⓜ Kievskaya) On the 27th floor of a skyscraper overlooking the Moscow River, Red features funky décor and a fabulous view. The name refers to its colour, not its politics: the place is draped in swanky red, except the glistening white piano.

Tinkoff (Map pp102-3; ☎ 777 3300; Protochny per 11; 500mL beer R120, meals R600-800; 🕑 noon-2am; Ⓜ Smolenskaya) Moscow's branch of this nationwide microbrewery features sports on the big screen, lagers and pilsners on draught, and a metre-long sausage on the menu.

ENTERTAINMENT

Moscow can easily keep you entertained for months. To find out what's on see the weekly magazine *element* and the weekly entertainment section in Friday's *Moscow Times*. For a laugh, try the *Exile*.

Classical Music, Opera & Ballet

Bolshoi (Map pp102-3; ☎ 250 7317; www.bolshoi.ru; Teatralnaya pl 1; tickets R200-2000; Ⓜ Teatralnaya) A night at the Bolshoi is still one of Moscow's most romantic options. Ballet and opera companies perform a range of Russian and foreign works in the glittering auditorium. At the time of research, the Bolshoi was preparing to close its main stage for renovations, expecting to reopen in 2008. The smaller Novaya Stena (new stage) will remain open.

State Kremlin Palace (Map p106; ☎ 928 5232; www .kremlin-gkd.ru; ul Vozdvizhenka 1; Ⓜ Aleksandrovsky Sad) The Bolshoi does not have a monopoly on ballet and opera in Moscow. Leading dancers also appear with the Kremlin Ballet and the Moscow Classical Ballet Theatre, both of which perform here.

Moscow International House of Music (☎ 730 1011; www.mmdm.ru; Kosmodamianskaya nab 52/8; tickets R60-600; Ⓜ Paveletskaya) This graceful, modern building opened in 2003. It has three halls, including Svetlanov Hall, which holds the largest organ in Russia. Needless to say, organ concerts held here are impressive.

Tchaikovsky Concert Hall (Map pp102-3; ☎ 299 3957; www.philharmonia.ru; Triumfalnaya pl 4/31; Ⓜ Mayakovskaya) Home to the famous State Symphony Orchestra.

Theatre & Circus

Chekhov Moscow Art Theatre (Map pp102-3; ☎ 632 4105; http://art.theatre.ru; Kamergersky per 3; Ⓜ Okhotny Ryad) Also known as MKhT, this is where method acting was founded over 100 years ago. Watch for English-language versions of Russian classics performed by the **American Studio** (☎ 292 0941).

Nikulin Circus (Old Circus at Tsvetnoy Boulevard; Map pp102-3; ☎ 200 0668; www.circusnikulin.ru; Tsvetnoy bul 13; tickets R50-500; Ⓨ Thu & Fri 7pm, 2.30pm & 6pm Sat & Sun; Ⓜ Tsvetnoy Bulvar) The show here usually mixes dance, cabaret and rock music with the animals and acrobats. Performance schedules are subject to change.

Maly Theatre (Map pp102-3; ☎ 923 2621; Teatralnaya pl 1/6; Ⓜ Teatralnaya) A lovely theatre founded in 1824, performing mainly 19th-century works.

Nightclubs

Karma Bar (Map pp102-3; ☎ 924 5633; Pushechnaya ul 3; cover R100-200; Ⓨ 7pm-6am Thu-Sat, 11pm-6am Sun; Ⓜ Kuznetsky Most) A worldly mix of Asian food, Latin music and Russian fun. Thursday nights usually feature live music, while the other nights are for DJs and dancing (free lessons from 9pm to 11pm Friday to Saturday). Add to the mix happy hours and

hookah pipes and you've got one of Moscow's top expat clubs.

Keks (☎ 246 0864; ul Timura Frunze 11; meals R200-300; Ⓨ 11am-late; Ⓜ Park Kultury) Finally, a trendy place that won't bust the budget. Converted from a textile factory, this place now features black and white photos, deep, comfy armchairs, and a balcony ideal for watching the dance floor. And the dance floor is worth watching on Friday and Saturday nights, when DJs spin cool music and young folks turn out in droves.

Propaganda (Map pp102-3; ☎ 924 5732; Bol Zlatoustinsky per 7; meals R300-400; Ⓨ noon-7am; Ⓜ Lubyanka) This longtime favourite place is a café by day, but at night they clear the dance floor and let the DJ do his stuff. This is a gay-friendly place, especially on Sunday nights.

bilingua (Map pp102-3; ☎ 923 6683; Krivokolenny per 10/5; meals R200-500; Ⓨ 24hr; Ⓜ Chistye Prudy) Crowded with grungy, artsy student types, this café also sells books and funky clothing. If you can stand the smoke, it's a cool place to grab a bite to eat and listen to live music (nightly).

Both **Bunker** (Map pp102-3; ☎ 200 1506; ul Tverskaya 12; Ⓨ 10pm-7am; Ⓜ Mayakovskaya) and its sister club **B-2** (Map pp102-3; ☎ 209 9918; ul Bolshaya Sadovaya 8; Ⓜ Pushkinskaya) have cheap food and drinks, and live music almost every night.

SHOPPING

Artists set up their stalls on ul Krymsky val, opposite the entrance to Gorky Park (p110), and in the underground walkway. There are also galleries within the Central House of Artists (p110) in the Arbat District.

Izmaylovo market (admission R15; Ⓨ 9am-6pm Sat & Sun; Ⓜ Partizanskaya) This sprawling area is packed with art, handmade crafts, antiques, Soviet paraphernalia and just about anything you might want for a souvenir.

GUM (Map p106; ☎ 921 5763; Krasnaya pl 3; Ⓨ 10am-10pm; Ⓜ Ploshchad Revolyutsii) On the eastern side of Red Sq, this 19th-century building is a sight in itself. It houses a huge collection of pricey shops.

Okhotny Ryad (Map p106; ☎ 737 8449; Manezhnaya pl; Ⓨ 11am-10pm; Ⓜ Okhotny Ryad) Built in the 1990s, this mall was originally filled with expensive boutiques and no people, but times have changed. Now the stores cater to all income levels and are usually packed. There is a big, crowded food court on the ground floor.

MOSCOW

GETTING THERE & AWAY

Air

Of Moscow's five airports, two of them service most international flights and most flights to destinations along the Trans-Siberian railroad. Moscow's main international airport is **Sheremetyevo-2** (☎ 956 4666; www.sheremetyevo-airport.ru), 30km northwest of the city centre. Across the runways (and accessible by shuttle bus), **Sheremetyevo-1** services many domestic flights, especially to/from St Petersburg and northern European Russia.

Domodedovo (☎ 933 6666; www.domodedovo.ru), 40km south of the city centre, has undergone extensive upgrades in recent years in order to service more international flights. Most notably, all British Airway flights now fly in and out of Domodedovo.

You can buy airline tickets at most travel agencies (see p101). Airline offices in Moscow include:

Aeroflot (Map pp102-3; ☎ 753 5555; www.aeroflot.ru; ul Petrovka 20/1; Ⓜ Chekhovskaya)

Air France (☎ 937 3839; www.airfrance.ru; ul Korovy Val 7; Ⓜ Oktyabrskaya)

British Airways (Map pp102-3; ☎ 363 2525; Business Centre Parus, 1-ya Tverskaya Yamskaya ul 23; Ⓜ Belorusskaya)

Delta Air Lines (Map pp102-3; ☎ 937 9090; www.delta.com; Gogolevsky bul 11; Ⓜ Kropotkinskaya)

KLM Royal Dutch Airlines (☎ 258 3600; www.klm.com; ul Usachyova 33/2; Ⓜ Sportivnaya)

Lufthansa (Map pp102-3; ☎ 737 6400; www.lufthansa.com; Renaissance Moscow Hotel, Olimpiysky pr 18; Ⓜ Prospekt Mira)

SAS (Map pp102-3; ☎ 775 4747; www.sas.ru; 1-ya Tverskaya Yamskaya ul 5; Ⓜ Mayakovskaya)

Transaero (Map pp102-3; ☎ 241 4800; Smolensky 2-y per 3; Ⓜ Smolenskaya)

Boat

In summer, passenger boats from Moscow ply the rivers and canals of Russia all the way north to St Petersburg, and south to Astrakhan or Rostov-on-Don. The navigation season is generally May to September, although it depends on the route. The Moscow terminus for these sailings is the **Severny Rechnoy Vokzal** (Northern River Station; ☎ 457 4050; Leningradskoe sh 51; Ⓜ Rechnoy Vokzal). Take the metro to Rechnoy vokzal, then walk 15 minutes due west, passing under Leningradskoe sh and through a nice park.

Capital Shipping Company (☎ 458 9624; www.cck-ship.ru; Rechnoy Vokzal, Leningradskoe sh 51; Ⓜ Rechnoy Vokzal) Operates transit boats departing regularly from Moscow's Severny Rechnoy Vokzal.

Cruise Marketing International (☎ 800-578 7742; www.cruiserussia.com; 3401 Investment Blvd, Ste 3, Hayward CA USA) Offers a series of 11- and 15-day cruises between Moscow and St Petersburg, with stops in little villages and Golden Ring towns.

Bus

Buses run to a number of towns and cities within 700km of Moscow. Bus fares are similar to *kupe* (*kupeyny;* compartmentalised carriage) train fares. Buses tend to be crowded, but they are usually faster than the *prigorodny* (suburban) trains. To book a seat go to the long-distance bus terminal, the **Shchyolkovsky bus station** (Ⓜ Shchyolkovskaya), 8km east of the city centre. Queues can be bad, so it's advisable to book ahead, especially for travel on Friday or weekends.

Train

Moscow has nine main stations. Multiple stations may service the same destination, so confirm the arrival/departure station.

Belorussky vokzal (Belarus Station; Map pp102-3; ☎ 251 6093; Tverskaya Zastava pl; Ⓜ Belorusskaya) Serves trains to/from Smolensk, Kaliningrad, Minsk, Warsaw, Vilnius, Berlin; some trains to/from the Czech Republic; and suburban trains to/from the west.

SAMPLE DOMESTIC FLIGHTS FROM MOSCOW

Destination	Flights per day	Duration (hr)	One-way fare (R)
Chita	5 weekly	6	10,000
Irkutsk	2	5½	8500-9000
Kazan	2	1	2500-2900
Khabarovsk	3	8	11,980
Krasnoyarsk	1	4½	6950
Nizhny Novgorod	2	1	1800-2300
Novosibirsk	6	4	3600-6800
Omsk	2	3	3500-4800
Perm	2	2	5000-5150
St Petersburg	20	50min	2800-3500
Tomsk	1	3	6800
Tyumen	6	2½	4400-5700
Ulan-Ude	1	5½	9500
Vladivostok	3-4	8½	12,500-13,800
Yekaterinburg	11	2½	5300-5400

Kazansky vokzal (Kazan Station; Map pp102-3; ☎ 264 6556; Komsomolskaya pl; Ⓜ Komsomolskaya) Serves trains to/from Kazan, Izhevsk, Ufa, Ryazan, Ulyanovsk, Samara, Novorossiysk, Central Asia; some to/from Vladimir, Nizhny Novgorod, the Ural Mountains, Siberia; the Volga; and suburban trains to/from the southeast, including Bykovo airport.

Kursky vokzal (Kursk Station; Map pp102-3; ☎ 916 2003; pl Kurskogo Vokzala; Ⓜ Kurskaya) Serves trains heading south and east, including to the Caucasus, eastern Ukraine, Crimea, Georgia, Azerbaijan. It also has some trains to/from Vladimir, Nizhny Novgorod and Perm.

MOSCOW

TRAINS DEPARTING FROM MOSCOW

Trains from Moscow to St Petersburg

Train no & name	Departure time	Station	Duration (hr)	Fare (R)
2 *Krasnaya Strela*	11.55pm	–	8	1700
4 *Ekspress*	11.59pm	–	8	1700
6 *Nikolaevsky Ekspress*	11.30pm	–	8	1700
24 *Yunost*	12.30pm	–	8	1300 (seat)
160 *Avrora*	4.30pm	–	5½	1300 (seat)
164 *ER200*	6.28pm	–	4½	1700 (seat)

International Trains from Moscow

Destination & train no	Departure time	Station	Duration (hr)	Fare (R)
Almaty 008	10.25pm*	Kazansky	78	4100
Beijing 004	9.51pm	Yaroslavl	132	6413
Kaliningrad 029	2.06pm	Belarus	22	3650
Kharkhiv 019	9.25pm	Kursk	13	700
Kyiv 001	11.23pm*	Kievsky	14	1033
Minsk 001	10.25pm	Belorussky	10	1200
Riga 001	7.11pm	Rizhsky	16	2030
Tallinn 034	6.15pm	Leningradsky	15	1560
Ulaanbaatar 006	9.30pm	Yaroslavl	101	3800
Vilnius 005	7.01pm	Belorussky	15	1588
Warsaw 011	22.15pm	Belarus	20	2200

Trans-Siberian Train Fares from Moscow

Destination & train no	Departure time	Station	Duration (hr)	Fare (R)
Chita 002	9.20pm*	Yaroslavl	94	8000
Irkutsk 010	11.30pm*	Yaroslavl	77	5400
Kazan 028	7.28pm	Kazan	11	1150
Khabarovsk 002	9.20pm*	Yaroslavl	135	9060
Krasnoyarsk 056	4.35pm	Yaroslavl	59	6400
Nizhny Novgorod 062	4.55pm	Kursk	4½	300 (seat)
Novosibirsk 026	4.35pm†	Yaroslavl	46	5300
Omsk 048	8.16pm†	Kazan	41	3550
Perm 018	9.40pm	Yaroslavl	20½	2300
Tomsk 038	10.45pm*	Yaroslavl	55	5600
Tyumen 060	5.40pm†	Kazan	35	2800
Ulan-Ude 002	9.20pm*	Yaroslavl	85	6600
Vladivostok 002	9.20pm*	Yaroslavl	149	8000
Vladimir 816	6.04pm	Kursk	2½	208
Yekaterinburg 016	4.08pm	Kazan	26	2350

note: * odd days   † even days

Kievsky vokzal (Kyiv Station; Map pp102-3; ☎ 240 1115; pl Kievskogo Vokzala; Ⓜ Kievskaya) Serves Kyiv and Prague, as well as suburban trains to/from the southwest.

Leningradsky vokzal (Leningrad Station; Map pp102-3; ☎ 262 9143; Komsomolskaya pl; Ⓜ Komsomolskaya) Serves Tver, Novgorod, Pskov, St Petersburg, Vyborg, Murmansk, Tallinn, Helsinki.

Paveletsky vokzal (Pavelets Station; ☎ 235 0522; Paveletskaya pl; Ⓜ Paveletskaya) Serves trains heading south, including the express train to Domodedovo airport.

Rizhsky vokzal (Riga Station; ☎ 631 1588; Rizhskaya pl; Ⓜ Rizhskaya) Serves Latvia, as well as suburban trains to/from the northwest.

Savyolovsky vokzal (Savyolov Station; ☎ 285 9005; pl Savyolovskogo Vokzala; Ⓜ Savyolovskaya) Serves suburban trains to/from the north.

Yaroslavl vokzal (Yaroslavl Station; ☎ 921 5914; Komsomolskaya pl; Ⓜ Komsomolskaya) Serves most trains to Siberia, the Far East, China and Mongolia.

For long-distance trains it's best to buy your tickets in advance. Tickets on some trains may be available on the day of departure, but this is less likely in summer. Always take your passport along when buying a ticket.

Tickets are sold at the train stations, but it is much easier to buy tickets from a travel agent (see p101) or *kassa zheleznoy dorogi* (railway ticket office). These are often conveniently found in hotel lobbies. Most local agencies charge a small service fee, but be careful of international travel agencies that may charge considerable mark-ups.

One agency selling airplane and train tickets with many outlets around town: **GlavAgenstvo** (Map pp102-3) Lubyanka (☎ 924 8728; Teatralny pro 5/1; Ⓜ Lubyanka); Tverskoy (☎ 290 2771; Tverskoy bul 14/5; Ⓜ Pushkinskaya) Additional outlets are in Sheremetyevo-1 airport, as well as Belorussky and Leningradsky vokzaly.

GETTING AROUND
To/From the Airport

An express train from Savyolovsky vokzal to Sheremetyevo airport is expected by the end of 2007. In the meantime, there is no convenient way to reach the main international airport. Minibuses travel between Rechnoy vokzal and Sheremetyevo-1, with Sheremetyevo-2 as the middle stop in either direction. They make the journey as soon as they are full, which is about every 30 minutes or less. City bus 551 also follows this route, but takes much longer.

A taxi arranged on the spot between Sheremetyevo airport and the city centre takes about 45 minutes (with no traffic) and should not cost more than R800. It's better to arrange one in advance (see below).

An express train leaves **Pavelets vokzal** (Ⓜ Paveletskaya) every half-hour for Domodedovo airport (R100, 45 minutes). This route is particularly convenient, as you can check into your flight at the train station. Alternatively, a taxi fare to/from the city centre is R700 to R800, with the trip taking one to 1½ hours, depending on traffic.

Bus, Trolleybus & Tram

Buses, trolleybuses and trams are useful along a few radial or cross-town routes that the metro misses, and for reaching sights away from the city centre. Tickets (R10) are usually sold on the vehicle.

Metro

The metro is the easiest, quickest and cheapest way of getting around Moscow. Many of the stations are marble-faced, frescoed, gilded works of art. The trains are generally reliable: you will rarely wait on the platform for more than two minutes. Nonetheless, they get packed during rush hour. Up to nine million people a day ride the metro, more than the London and New York City systems combined.

The 150-plus stations are marked outside by 'M' signs. Magnetic tickets (R13) are sold at ticket booths. It's useful to buy a multiple-ride ticket (10 rides for R120, 20 for R195), which saves you the hassle of queuing every time.

Taxi

Almost any car in Moscow could be a taxi if the price is right. Expect to pay R100 to R150 for a ride around the city centre.

Official taxis – recognisable by the chequerboard logo on the side and/or a small green light in the windscreen – charge about the same. No driver uses a meter (even if the cab has one), and few will admit to having any change. Don't hesitate to wave on a car if you don't like the look of its occupants. It's best to avoid riding in cars that already contain more than one person.

To book a taxi in advance, call the **Central Taxi Reservation Office** (Tsentralnoe Byuro Zakazov Taxi; ☎ 927 0000; www.cbz-taxi.ru).

AROUND MOSCOW

Ancient Rus grew up northeast of Moscow in the clutch of towns that is now known as the Golden Ring. In many cases, the whitewashed walls of these once-fortified cities still stand; the golden spires and onion domes of their monasteries still mark the horizon. Bells ring out from towering belfries; robed holy men scurry through church doors; historical tales recall mysterious, magical times.

The Golden Ring – so called for its wealth of architectural and artistic riches – is one of Russia's most delightful destinations. The towns covered here are accessible from Moscow by day trip. Additionally, the old capital of ancient Rus and the Orthodox Church, Vladimir (p130), is a stop along the train route heading east into the Urals. Trans-Siberian travellers should certainly take this route and stop off at Suzdal (p132), the most enchanting Golden Ring destination.

SERGIEV POSAD СЕРГИЕВ ПОСАД

☎ 254 from Moscow, ☎ 49654 from other cities / pop 100,000 / ⊗ Moscow

According to old Russian wisdom, 'there is no settlement without a just man; there is no town without a saint'. And so the town of Sergiev Posad tributes St Sergius of Radonezh, founder of the local Trinity Monastery and patron saint of all of Russia. The

MOSCOW

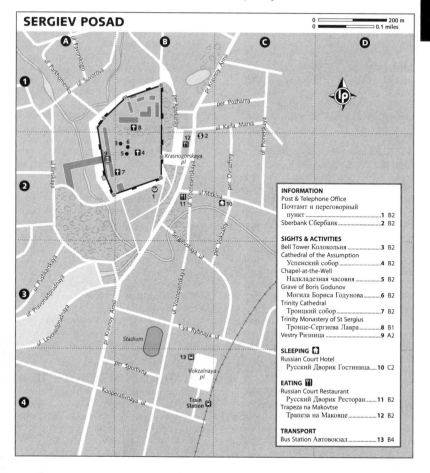

SERGIEV POSAD

0 _____ 200 m
0 _____ 0.1 miles

MOSCOW

monastery – today among the most important and active in Russia – exudes Orthodoxy. Bearded priests bustle about; babushkas fill bottles of holy water; crowds of believers light candles to St Sergius, Keeper of Russia. This mystical place is a window into the age-old belief system that has provided Russia with centuries of spiritual sustenance.

Often called by its Soviet name of Zagorsk, Sergiev Posad is 60km from the edge of Moscow on the Yaroslavl road. It is an easy day trip from Moscow – a rewarding option for travellers who don't have time to venture further around the Golden Ring.

Pr Krasnoy Armii is the main street, running north–south through the town centre. The train and bus stations are on opposite corners of a wide square to the east of pr Krasnoy Armii. The monastery is about 400m north of here.

Information

Post & telephone office (pr Krasnoy Armii 127A) Outside the southeastern wall of the monastery.
Sberbank (pr Krasnoy Armii; ☺ 9am-4pm Mon-Fri) Exchange facilities available, but no ATM.

Sights

The **Trinity Monastery of St Sergius** (Troitse-Sergieva Lavra; ☎ 45 356, 45 350; admission free, guided tour R600, photos R150; ☺ 10am-6pm) is an active religious centre with a visible population of monks in residence; visitors should refrain from photographing them. Female visitors should wear headscarves, and men are required to remove hats in the churches.

Built in the 1420s, the squat, dark **Trinity Cathedral** is the heart of the Trinity Monastery. The tomb of St Sergius stands in the southeastern corner, where a memorial service goes on all day, every day. The icon-festooned interior, lit by oil lamps, is largely the work of the great medieval painter Andrei Rublyov and his students.

The star-spangled **Cathedral of the Assumption** was modelled on the cathedral of the same name in the Moscow Kremlin. It is closed to the general public but included as a part of guided tours. Outside the west door is the **grave** of the tsar Boris Godunov.

Nearby, the resplendent **Chapel-at-the-Well** was built over a spring that is said to have appeared during the Polish siege. The five-tier baroque **bell tower** took 30 years to build

in the 18th century, and once had 42 bells, the largest of which weighed 65 tonnes.

The **vestry** (admission R160; ☺ 10am-5.30pm Wed-Sun), behind the Trinity Cathedral, displays the monastery's extraordinarily rich treasury, bulging with 600 years of donations by the rich and powerful – tapestries, jewel-encrusted vestments, solid-gold chalices and more.

Sleeping & Eating

Russian Court Hotel (☎ 75 392; www.zolotoe-koltso.ru; ul Mitkina 14/2; s/d with breakfast Mon-Fri from R1500/1900, Sat & Sun R1700/2100; P 🐾) Some of the rooms at this delightful hotel boast views of the onion domes peeking out above white-washed walls. The place is quite modern, despite the rustic style.

Russian Court Restaurant (☎ 45 114; pr Krasnoy Armii 134; meals R500-800; ☺ 10am-9pm) Not to be confused with the hotel by the same name, this restaurant is decorated like a Russian dacha. Appropriately enough, it features wait staff in peasant dress and hearty country cuisine. The place is popular with tour groups in summer.

Trapeza na Makovtse (☎ 41 101; pr Krasnoy Armii 131; meals R500-800; ☺ 10am-9pm) Location, location, location. The highlight of this 'refectory' is alfresco dining in the shadow of the spires and cupolas. Dining is also pleasant inside, where live music plays nightly.

Getting There & Away

The fastest transportation option is the daily express train from Moscow's Yaroslavsky vokzal to Rostov (one hour from Moscow).

Suburban trains also run every half-hour (R55, 1½ hours); take any train bound for Sergiev Posad or Aleksandrov. To go north to Rostov-Veliky (3½ hours) or Yaroslavl (five hours), you may have to change at Aleksandrov.

Bus services to Sergiev Posad from Moscow's VDNKh metro station depart every half-hour from 8.30am to 7.30pm (R50, 70 minutes).

ROSTOV-VELIKY РОСТОВ-ВЕЛИКИЙ
☎ 48536 / pop 40,000 / ☺ Moscow

For a place called Rostov-Veliky, or 'Rostov the Great', this town gives the impression of a sleepy village. Perhaps for this reason, the magnificent Rostov kremlin catches visitors off guard when its silver domes and whitewashed stone walls appear amid the dusty streets. Rostov is one of the prettiest of Golden Ring towns, idyllically sited on shimmering Lake Nero. It is also one of the oldest, first chronicled in 862.

Rostov is about 220km northeast of Moscow. The train and bus stations are together in the drab modern part of Rostov, 1.5km north of the kremlin.

Sights

Rostov's main attraction is its unashamedly photogenic **kremlin** (☎ 61 717; admission grounds R5, exhibits each R15-25; ⏰ 10am-5pm). Although founded in the 12th century, nearly all the buildings here date from the 1670s and 1680s.

With its five magnificent domes, the **Assumption Cathedral** dominates the kremlin, although it is just outside the north wall. Beyond service hours, you can get into the cathedral through the door in the church shop on ul Karla Marksa. The cathedral was here a century before the kremlin, while the belfry was added in the 1680s. Each of 15 bells in the belfry has its own name; the largest, weighing 32 tonnes, is called Sysoi. The monks play magnificent bell concerts, which can be arranged through the excursions office, in the west gate, for R250.

The west gate (the main entrance) and the north gate are straddled by the **Gate-Church of St John the Divine** and the **Gate-Church of the Resurrection**, both of which are richly

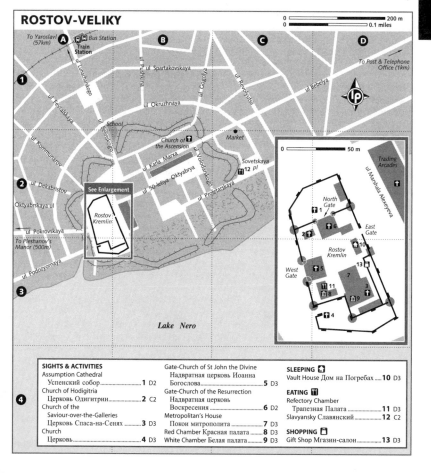

ROSTOV-VELIKY

decorated with 17th-century frescoes. Enter these churches from the monastery walls, which you can access from the stairs next to the north gate. Like several other buildings within the complex, these are only open from May to September. Between the gate-churches, the **Church of Hodigitria** houses an exhibition of Orthodox Church vestments and paraphernalia.

The metropolitan's private chapel, the **Church of the Saviour-over-the-Galleries**, has the most beautiful interior of all, covered in colourful frescoes. These rooms are filled with exhibits: the **White Chamber** displays religious antiquities, while the **Red Chamber** shows off *finift* (enamelware), a Rostov artistic speciality.

Although the ticket office is in the west gate, you can also enter the kremlin through the north gate. Don't leave without stopping at the gift shop behind **Metropolitan's House** to shop for *finift* souvenirs and to sample the home-brewed *medovukha* (honey ale).

Sleeping & Eating

Pleshanov's Manor (Usadba Pleshanova; ☎ 76 440; www.hotel.v-rostove.ru; ul Pokrovskaya 34; r Mon-Fri R1200; Sat & Sun R1500; 💻 🐾) This 19th-century manor house – once the residence of a merchant and philanthropist family – is now a welcoming inn with a nice restaurant, cosy library and wood sauna. The charm of the common areas does not extend to the rooms, which are modern and fresh, but bland. Prices, which include breakfast, decrease between October and April.

Vault House (☎ 31 244; s/d with shared bathroom R350/600, d with private bathroom R1400-1600) Right inside the kremlin, and near the east gate, this place has clean, wood-panelled rooms that vary in size and view.

Refectory Chamber (☎ 62 871; meals R200-400; 🕙 9am-5pm, later in summer) The attraction of the refectory is also its atmospheric location inside the kremlin, near Metropolitan's House. The grand dining room is often crowded with tour groups supping on traditional Russian fare.

Slavyansky (☎ 62 228; Sovetskaya pl 8) About 100m east of the kremlin, the semiswanky Slavyansky gets many a recommendation from the locals. Come here if you're looking for traditional Russian fare in a romantic setting.

Getting There & Around

The express service from Yaroslavsky vokzal (R180, three hours) is the fastest train from Moscow. Otherwise, some long-distance trains stop at Rostov-Veliky en route to Yaroslavl. You can also catch a suburban train, which requires changing at Aleksandrov.

Bus 6 runs between the train station and the town centre.

Moscow to Yekaterinburg

The leg of the Trans-Siberian railroad that traverses European Russia is well travelled. All of the major destinations are serviced by their own dedicated trains from Moscow, as well as by the *Rossiya* and the *Vostok* and other longer-distance trains, which stop at these destinations before continuing east to Siberia and beyond. As a result, finding transportation and obtaining tickets is a relatively easy task for travellers who wish to stop and explore the destinations along the route between Moscow and Yekaterinburg.

And they are worth exploring. Vladimir and Nizhny Novgorod are one of the oldest towns in Russia, with magnificent churches and ancient kremlins showing off their medieval roots. A short road trip from Vladimir, the storybook setting of Suzdal is a highlight of the 'Golden Ring' of historic towns around Moscow. Along the mighty Volga River, the Tatar capital of Kazan recently celebrated 1000 years since its founding as a stronghold of the marauding nomads from the east. And while Perm suffers from its reputation as a provincial outpost, it is a convenient and comfortable base for some fascinating trips in the Urals.

Trains crossing European Russian follow two different paths. The *Rossiya*, *Vostok* and most other trains continuing east take a northern route, which travels through Vladimir, Nizhny Novgorod and Perm, before crossing the Europe–Asia border and reaching Yekaterinburg. Other train services – such as the Moscow–Yekaterinburg direct train 16, *Ural* – follow a more southerly route via Kazan. If you can't bear to miss any of these enticing destinations, it is also possible to jump between the northern and southern routes, reaching Kazan directly from Nizhny Novgorod or on a slower train from Perm.

HIGHLIGHTS

- Recall medieval Rus in the ancient capital of **Vladimir** (p130)
- Sip honey-sweet mead on the steps of the trading arcades at **Suzdal** (p134)
- Admire the view over the Volga from Nizhny Novgorod's **kremlin** (p135)
- Visit the Tatar mosques and markets in **Kazan** (p144)
- Shiver in the darkness of a cell at **Perm-36** (p142)

■ ROUTE DISTANCE: 1814km	■ DURATION: 26 HOURS

MOSCOW TO YEKATERINBURG

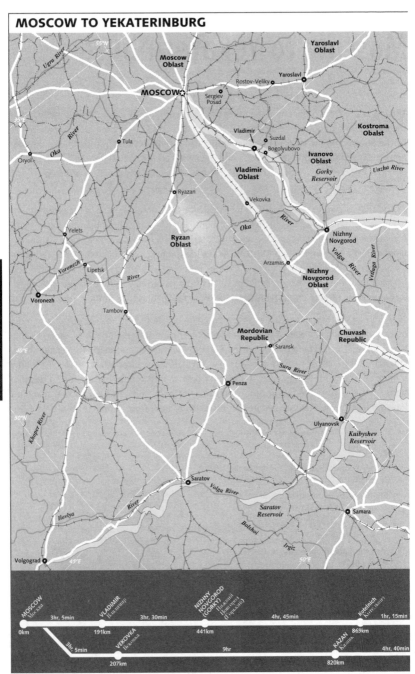

MOSCOW TO YEKATERINBURG

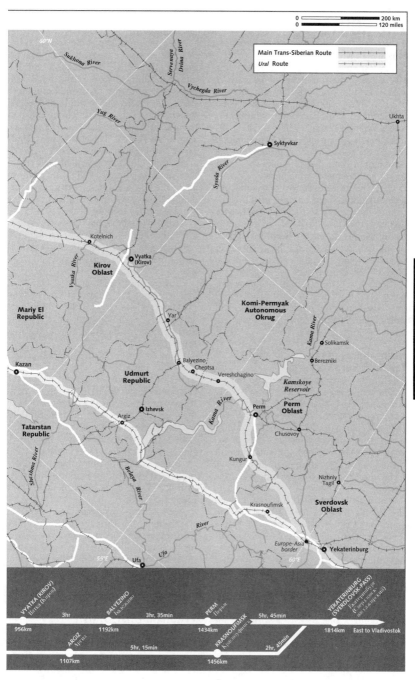

THE ROUTE

Moscow to Nizhny Novgorod

In the 21st century, all Trans-Siberian trains take a new eastern route out of Yaroslavsky vokzal (Yaroslavl Station). They head through Moscow's grey suburbs and sylvan satellite communities of dacha (country houses) towards **Vladimir** (191km), where there's a 20-minute stop. As you approach Vladimir look out for the golden spires and domes of the Assumption Cathedral (see opposite), high on the embankment to the north.

Cast your gaze northward as you pull out from Vladimir for a glimpse of the 12th-century monastery complex at **Bogolyubovo** (200km), then do a quick turn to the south-facing window to see the beautiful Church of the Intercession on the Nerl, sitting in splendid isolation at the confluence of the Nerl and Klyazma Rivers.

There is a 12-minute stop at **Nizhny Novgorod** (441km), Russia's third-most populous city, where the modern station is still called by the Nizhny Novgorod's Soviet-era name of Gorky.

Nizhny Novgorod to Yekaterinburg via Perm

The *Rossiya* and other services to Siberia and beyond all head northeast from Nizhny Novgorod, crossing over the mighty Volga River about 1km outside the station. You'll then chug along past the farmland and taiga of Nizhny Novgorod Oblast (region) towards **Kotelnich** (869km), the junction with the old Trans-Siberian route from Yaroslavl. Here, the time is Moscow time plus one hour.

Just outside Kotelnich the train crosses the Vyatka River, a meandering 1367km waterway that gives its name to **Vyatka** (956km), often called by its old Soviet moniker of Kirov. There's a 15-minute stop here, but little reason to get out and explore other than to stretch your legs or search the kiosks for supplies.

Yar (1126km) is the first town you'll pass through in the Udmurt Republic, home to the Udmurts, one of Russia's four major groups of Finno-Ugric people. Around here the countryside becomes wonderfully picturesque with plenty of pretty painted log cabins to be spotted. At **Balyezino** (1192km)

there's a change of locomotive during the 19-minute halt.

After crossing Cheptsa River at 1221km, the train enters the town of the same name. **Cheptsa** (1223km) is the junction with line that runs between Perm and Kazan. About 40km further east, you'll cross into Perm *oblast* and the foothills of the **Ural Mountains**, which stretch about 2000km from Kazakhstan to the Arctic Kara Sea. The mineral-rich, densely wooded Urals rarely break 500m above sea level in this area, so it's difficult to actually tell you're in a mountain range. Still, with glimpses above the pine and birch forests across verdant rolling landscapes, this is one of the more attractive sections of the route.

Around **Vereshchagino** (1314km), named after the late-19th-century painter VV Vereshchagin, turn forward your watch as local time becomes Moscow time plus two hours.

Crossing the broad Kama River (1432km) you will spot the industrial city of **Perm** (1434km), where trains make a 15-minute stop. Check out the steam locomotive on the northern side of the train as you pull into the station.

From **Kungur** (1535km) the railway follows the Sylva River. The crucial thing to keep an eye out for beyond here is the **Europe-Asia Border Obelisk** (1777km), a large white monument on the southern side of the train. One of several monuments marking this continental divide, it is understated, at best. Eric Newby also wasn't impressed. In *The Big Red Train Ride* he wrote, 'We were in Asia, at last – but… there was nothing to see except a lot of deciduous trees in leaf…' For a more monumental border marker see p156.

Approaching Yekaterinburg, the train travels along the Usovaya River, affording picturesque views of a small lakes district on the south side. The first major station in Asian Russia – but still 260km short of the official beginning of Siberia – is **Yekaterinburg** (1814km), which merits a 15- to 30-minute stop.

VLADIMIR ВЛАДИМИР

☎ 49222 / pop 360,000 / ⌚ Moscow

High up on Vladimir's slope above the Klyazma River sits the solemnly majestic Assumption Cathedral, built to announce

MOSCOW TO YEKATERINBURG VIA KAZAN

As well as the main Trans-Siberian route from Moscow to Yekaterinburg outlined in this chapter there is also a more southerly route that travels via the Tatar capital of Kazan. The flagship train 16, known as *Ural*, follows this route, as do many other trains travelling from Nizhny Novgorod to Kazan.

The first major stop east of Moscow is **Vekovka** (207km), home to a glassware factory. Along the platform the food and drink hawkers are vastly outnumbered by factory workers flogging off sets of cut-glass tumblers, giant brandy glasses, vases, chandeliers and the like.

Arzamas-II (562km) is the junction for trains running from Nizhny Novgorod to Kazan and further south along the Volga. From here, the train traverses the Chuvash Republic. The Chuvash people are descended from the Bulgars (as are the Tatars), although most of them do not live within the territorial boundaries of this artificially drawn region.

The train stops for 16 minutes in **Kazan** (820km), capital of the autonomous republic of Tatarstan. The original 19th-century train station has been handsomely restored and now houses a waiting room. See p142 for more information.

Continuing east there's a 10-minute stop at **Argiz-1** (1107km), where you may spot old steam locomotives still in use for shunting. At 1150km the *Ural* crosses the Kama River, which flows northeast to Perm.

At **Krasnoufimsk** (1456km) the local time is two hours ahead of Moscow time. This small country station is often a good place to buy berries and other forest fruits, sold by locals on the platform. From here, you will pass through the Urals' rolling mountain scenery, with lake views to the south as you near the terminus at **Yekaterinburg** (1814km).

Vladimir's claim as capital of Rus. These days, Vladimir – 178km east of Moscow – feels more like a modern, provincial town than an ancient capital. Nonetheless, the grandeur of medieval Vladimir shines through the commotion of this busy, industrial town. The exquisite examples of Russia's most formative architecture, along with some wonderfully entertaining museums, make Vladimir one of the jewels in the Golden Ring.

Orientation

Vladimir's main street is called Bolshaya Moskovskaya ul, although it sometimes goes by its former name, ul III Internatsionala. This is where you'll find the main attractions such as the Golden Gate and the Cathedrals of the Assumption and St Dmitry. The train and bus stations are on Vokzalnaya ul at the bottom of the slope and 500m east.

Information

Internet@Salon (cnr uls Gagarina & Bolshaya Moskovskaya; per hr R30; 9am-9pm)

Post & telephone office (ul Podbelskogo; 8am-8pm Mon-Fri)

Sberbank (Bolshaya Moskovskaya ul 27; 9am-7pm Mon-Fri, 9am-5pm Sat) Exchange facilities and an ATM.

Sights

Begun in 1158, the **Assumption Cathedral** (☎ 325 201; admission R100; 1.30-4.30pm Tue-Sun) is a white-stone version of Kyiv's brick Byzantine churches. The cathedral used to house the *Vladimir Icon of the Mother of God*, brought from Kyiv by Andrei Bogolyubsky. A national protector bestowing supreme status to its city of residence, the icon was moved to Moscow in 1390 and can now be found in the Tretyakov Gallery (p110).

Inside the working church, a few restored 12th-century murals of peacocks and prophets holding scrolls can be deciphered about halfway up the inner wall of the outer north aisle. The real treasures are the *Last Judgment* frescoes by Andrei Rublyov and Daniil Chyorny, painted in 1408 in the central nave and inner south aisle, under the choir gallery towards the west end.

Just east of the Assumption Cathedral you'll find the smaller **Cathedral of St Dmitry** (1193–97), where the Vladimir-Suzdal art of stone carving reached its pinnacle. The church is permanently closed, but the attraction here is its exterior walls, which are covered in an amazing profusion of images.

The grand building between the cathedrals is known as the **Chambers** (☎ 323 320; Bolshaya Moskovskaya ul 58; admission R150; ☒ 10am-5pm Tue-Sun), containing a children's museum, art gallery and historical exhibit.

Across the small street, the **History Museum** (☎ 322 284; Bolshaya Moskovskaya ul 64; admission R50; ☒ 10am-4pm Tue-Sun) displays many remains and reproductions of the ornamentation from the Cathedrals of the Assumption and St Dmitry.

Vladimir's Golden Gate – part defensive tower, part triumphal arch – was modelled on the very similar structure in Kyiv. Originally built by Andrei Bogolyubsky to guard the main, western entrance to his city, it was later restored under Catherine the Great. Now you can climb the narrow stone staircase to check out the **Military Museum** (☎ 322 559; admission R50; ☒ 10am-4pm Fri-Wed) inside. It is a small exhibit, the centrepiece of which is a diorama of old Vladimir being ravaged by nomadic raiders. Across the street to the south you can see a remnant of the old wall that protected the city.

Sleeping & Eating

Golden Gate Hotel (☎ 323 116; www.golden-gate.ru; Bolshaya Moskovskaya ul 17; s/d with breakfast R1800/2300) The 14 rooms at the shiny new Golden Gate Hotel are spacious and comfortable, with large windows overlooking the activity on the main street – or a central courtyard, if you prefer. The attached restaurant is one of the town's best, and is popular with tour groups.

Hotel Vladimir (☎ 323 042; tour@gtk.elcom.ru; Bolshaya Moskovskaya ul 74; s/d with bathroom from R950/1300, r without bathroom per person R350-500) This conveniently located option has acceptable rooms for all price ranges (upgraded singles/doubles cost R1150/1600). It is a friendly place with lots of services, including restaurant, bar and parking.

Getting There & Away

The daily express train between Moscow's Kursky vokzal (Kursk Station; R208, 2½ hours) and Nizhny Novgorod (R290, 2½ hours) stops in Vladimir, as do many slower trains. Privately run buses (R100, three hours) also leave regularly from Kursky vokzal and Kazansky vokzal (Kazan Station) to Vladimir. They do not run on a timetable, but leave as they fill up.

There are scheduled buses to/from Moscow's Shchyolkovsky station, as well as Suzdal (R20, one hour, half-hourly) and Nizhny Novgorod (R180, five hours, six daily).

SUZDAL СУЗДАЛЬ
☎ 49231 / pop 12,000 / ☒ Moscow

Flower-drenched meadows, the winding Kamenka River and the dome-spotted skyline make this medieval capital the perfect fairy-tale setting. Suzdal, 35km north of Vladimir, has earned a federally protected status, which has limited development in the area. As a result, its main features are an abundance of ancient architectural gems and a decidedly rural atmosphere. Judging from the spires and cupolas, Suzdal may have as many churches as people.

Orientation & Information

The main street, ul Lenina, runs from north to south through Suzdal. The bus station is 2km east along Vasilievskaya ul.

Post & telephone office (Krasnaya pl; ☒ 8am-8pm) Open 24 hours for phone calls.

Sberbank (ul Lenina; ☒ 8am-4.30pm Mon-Fri) Exchange office.

Vneshtorgbank (Kremlyovskaya ul; ☒ 10am-5pm Tue-Fri, 10am-3.30pm Sat & Sun) A central bank which has an ATM.

Sights

KREMLIN
The 1.4km-long earth rampart of Suzdal's kremlin, founded in the 11th century, today encloses a few streets of houses and a handful of churches, as well as the main cathedral group on Kremlyovskaya ul.

The **Nativity of the Virgin Cathedral**, its blue domes spangled with gold, was founded in the 1220s. Only its richly carved lower section is the original white stone, the rest being 16th-century brick. The inside is sumptuous with 13th- and 17th-century frescoes and 13th-century damascene west and south doors. At the time of research, the cathedral was under restoration and was closed indefinitely.

The **Archbishop's Chambers** house the **Suzdal History Exhibition** (☎ 21 624; admission R30; ☒ 10am-5pm Wed-Mon). The exhibition includes the original 13th-century door from the cathedral, photos of its interior and a visit to the 18th-century **Cross Hall** (Krestovaya palata), which was used for receptions. The tent-roofed 1635 bell tower on the east side of the yard contains additional exhibits.

SAVIOUR MONASTERY OF ST EUTHYMIUS
Founded in the 14th century to protect the town's northern entrance, Suzdal's biggest **monastery** (☎ 20 746; admission to each exhibit R40-50, all-inclusive R280; ☼ 10am-6pm Tue-Sun) grew mighty in the 16th and 17th centuries after Vasily III, Ivan the Terrible and the noble Pozharsky family funded impressive new stone buildings and big land and property acquisitions. It was girded with its great brick walls and towers in the 17th century.

Inside, the **Annunciation Gate-Church** houses an interesting exhibit on Dmitry Pozharsky

(1578–1642), leader of the Russian army that drove the Polish invaders from Moscow in 1612.

A tall 16th- to 17th-century bell tower stands before the seven-domed **Cathedral of the Transfiguration of the Saviour**. Every 90 minutes from 10.30am to 4.30pm, a short concert of chimes is given on the bell tower's bells. The cathedral was built in the 1590s in 12th- to 13th-century Vladimir-Suzdal style. Inside, restoration has uncovered some bright 1689 frescoes by the school of Gury Nikitin from Kostroma. On summer weekends a short but heavenly a cappella concert takes place once an hour. The **tomb of Prince Dmitry Pozharsky** is by the cathedral's east wall.

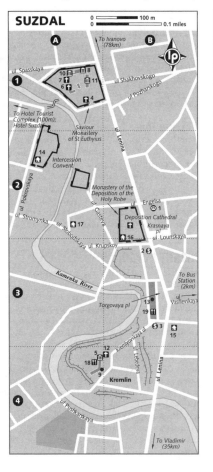

SUZDAL

MOSCOW TO YEKATERINBURG

The 1525 **Assumption Church** facing the bell tower adjoins the old Father Superior's chambers, which house a display of Russian icons. The **monks' quarters** across the compound contain a museum of artistic history.

At the northern end of the complex is the old **monastery prison**, set up in 1764 for religious dissidents. It now houses a fascinating exhibit on the monastery's military history and prison life, including displays of some of the better-known prisoners who stayed here. The combined **hospital** and **St Nicholas' Church** (1669) contains a rich museum of 12th- to 20th-century Russian applied art, much of it from Suzdal itself.

Activities

The rolling hills and picturesque countryside around Suzdal are ideal for outdoor adventures, such as horse riding and mountain biking. The **Hotel Tourist Complex** (Gostinichny Turistsky Kompleks, GTK; ☎ 23 390; ul Korovniki 45; ⊙ 10am-6pm) rents out bicycles, snowmobiles and skis, and also offers horse-riding tours.

Sleeping

Likhoninsky Dom (☎ 21 901; aksenova-museum@rnt .vladimir.ru; Slobodskaya ul 34; s/d with breakfast R1500/1800) Suzdal's most charming place to stay is on a quiet street near the town centre. The 17th-century merchant's house has five rooms and a pretty garden. It feels like home, thanks to the kindly ladies who run it.

Hotel Falcon (☎ 20 088, 20987; www.hotel-sokol.ru; Torgovaya pl 2A; s/d with breakfast from R1300/2200) This attractive new hotel is ideally located opposite the trading arcades. Its 40 rooms are all simply decorated and fully equipped with new wooden furniture and modern bathrooms. The elegant restaurant is also recommended. Prices decrease significantly between October and April.

Hotel Rizopolozhenskaya (☎ 24 314; ul Lenina; s/d with breakfast R620/1000) Housed in the decrepit Monastery of the Deposition, this hotel is Suzdal's cheapest place to stay. Some rooms have been renovated but they vary widely, so it's wise to ask for a preview before you commit.

Hotel Suzdal (☎ 21 530; www.suzdaltour.ru; s/d with breakfast from R1580/1800; ✕ ▯ ▨) One of three hotels within the Hotel Tourist Complex (see left). This place is low on charm but high on facilities: the complex includes a fitness centre, a bowling alley, several restaurants and a cheaper 'motel' (single/double R1120/1340). GTK also rents the cosy cabins at Pokrovskaya Hotel (single/double with breakfast R1820/2400), on the grounds of the Intercession Convent.

Eating & Drinking

Kremlin Refectory (☎ 21 763; meals R300-500; ⊙ 11am-11pm) The main attraction here is the atmospheric location inside the Archbishop's Chambers. This place has been serving tasty, filling Russian favourites for 300 years.

Mead Tasting Hall (☎ 20 803; tasting menu R120-150; ⊙ 10am-5pm Mon-Fri, 10am-8pm Sat & Sun) Hidden in the back part of the trading arcades, this hall is done up like a church interior – floor-to-ceiling frescoes, arched ceilings and stained-glass windows. The menu features different varieties of *medovukha*, a mildly alcoholic honey ale that was drunk by the princes of old. A few other places to eat are in the trading arcades.

Getting There & Away

The bus station is 2km east of the centre on Vasilievskaya ul. Some long-distance buses continue past the station into the centre; otherwise, a *marshrutka* (fixed-route minibus) will take you there. Buses run every half-hour to/from Vladimir (R20, one hour). One daily bus goes directly to/from Moscow's Shchyolkovsky bus station (R145, 4½ hours).

NIZHNY NOVGOROD
НИЖНИЙ НОВГОРОД

☎ 8312 / pop 1.31 million / ⊙ Moscow

Often called Russia's 'third capital', Nizhny Novgorod is markedly less cosmopolitan than Moscow and St Petersburg. But its ancient kremlin on the banks of the Volga and its pleasant pedestrian promenade make it an appealing place to spend a few days.

During Soviet times the city was named Gorky, after the writer Maxim Gorky, who was born here in 1868. Literature connoisseurs will find several museums in his memory. Everyone else will find one of Russia's most dynamic provincial capitals, replete with eating and entertainment opportunities.

History

Founded in 1221, Nizhny Novgorod has long been an important trading centre. Barges used to dock on the river and exchange goods; this floating market later became a huge trade fair, the Yarmarka, a tradition that continues to this day. In the 19th century it was said, 'St Petersburg is Russia's head; Moscow its heart; and Nizhny Novgorod, its wallet'.

The presence of many industries connected with the military (submarine construction, for example) meant that Nizhny Novgorod was closed to foreigners for many decades; this is one reason why the late Andrei Sakharov, physicist, dissident and Nobel laureate, was exiled here in the 1980s (see right).

Orientation

Nizhny Novgorod, lying on the southern bank of the Volga River, is split by the Oka River. The train and bus stations are side by side on the western side of the Oka. The kremlin sits on the high eastern bank overlooking the Volga. Outside its southern wall, the city's main streets spoke out from pl Minina i Pozharskogo. From here the pleasant, pedestrian ul Bolshaya Pokrovskaya heads south to pl Gorkogo.

MAPS
Dom Knigi (☎ 442 273; pl Lenina; ☺ 10am-7pm Mon-Fri, 10am-6pm Sat, 11am-4pm Sun) carries maps with local transport routes, and also has some English-language books.

Information
Central post office (pl Gorkogo; ☺ 24hr)
Pauteen.ru (Sergievskaya ul 1; per hr R40; ☺ 11am-5am) Internet café.
Post office (ul Bolshaya Pokrovskaya 7; ☺ 8am-7pm Mon-Sat, 8am-3pm Sun) Near the kremlin.
Sberbank (ul Bolshaya Pokrovskaya 3; ☺ 8am-6pm Mon-Fri, 9am-2pm Sun) ATM and currency exchange services.
Volga Telecom (☎ 301 270; pl Gorkogo; per hr R40; ☺ 24hr) A convenient Internet facility with plenty of computers.

Sights
KREMLIN
The mighty walls of the kremlin and its 11 towers date from the 16th century. Sometimes the ramparts are open, providing a sweeping view of the kremlin grounds and

beyond; climb up through the restaurant in the Kladovaya Bashnya gate.

Inside, most of the buildings are government offices. The small, 17th-century **Cathedral of the Archangel Michael** (☺ 9am-2pm) is a functioning church. Behind it, an eternal flame burns near a striking **monument** to the heroes of WWII.

At the northeast end of the grounds, the former governor's house is now home to the **Nizhegorodsky State Art Museum** (☎ 391 373; admission R30; ☺ 10am-5pm Wed-Mon). Exhibits here range from 14th-century icons to 20th-century paintings by artists such as Syatoslav Rerikh and Vasily Surikov.

SAKHAROV MUSEUM
A reminder of more-repressive times, the **Sakharov museum** (☎ 668 623; pr Gagarina 214; admission R30; ☺ 10am-5pm) provides visitiors with a sobering but fascinating view of Andrei Sakharov's life.

Sakharov was a nuclear physicist who was involved in developing the Soviet Union's first hydrogen bomb. Over the years, he became one of the main figures opposing the Soviet regime from within. In 1975 Sakharov was awarded the Nobel Peace Prize but never dared to go to pick it up.

Sakharov was exiled to Gorky in 1980, and his wife Elena Bonner joined him in 1984. Located in the flat where they lived, the museum documents their lives before and after their exile. You can see the telephone that was installed in 1986, expressly so that Mikhail Gorbachev could call to inform Sakharov of his pending release. To get here catch minibus 104 or 4 from pl Minina i Pozharskogo.

GORKY MUSEUMS
Fans of Maxim Gorky can visit the historic wooden houses where the writer lived and worked. The best is the **Gorky Museum** (☎ 361 651; ul Semashko 19; ☺ 9am-5pm Tue, Wed & Fri-Sun), where he lived during his 30s. For a more in-depth look at the events and personalities that influenced Gorky's work, visit the **Gorky Literary Museum** (☎ 338 589; ul Minina 26; ☺ 9am-5pm Wed-Sun).

LOWER VOLGA ARCHITECTURE MUSEUM
This open-air **museum** (☎ 651 598; Gorbatovskaya ul 39; admission R50; ☺ 10am-4pm Sat-Thu) has a pleasant woodland site and a collection

MOSCOW TO YEKATERINBURG

NIZHNY NOVGOROD

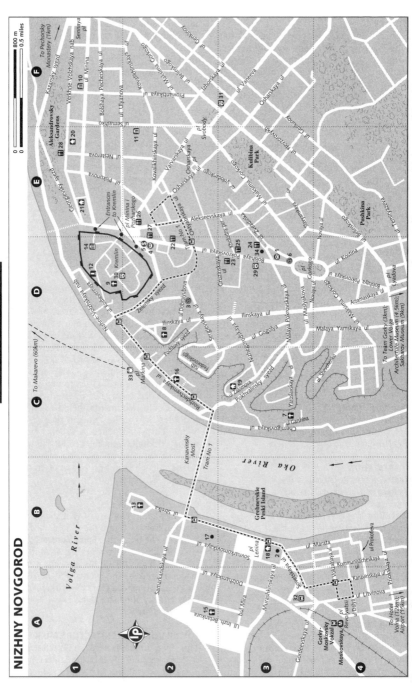

INFORMATION		
Central Post Office		
Центральный почтампт	**1**	D3
Dom Knigi Дом Книги	**2**	B3
Pauteen.ru	**3**	D2
Post Office Почтампт	**4**	D2
Sberbank Сбербанк	**5**	D2
Volga Telecom		
Волга Телеком	**6**	D3
SIGHTS & ACTIVITIES		
Annunciation Monastery		
Благовещенский монастырь	**7**	C3
Assumption Church		
Успенская церковь	**8**	D2
Cathedral of the		
Archangel Michael Собор Михаила		
Архангела	**9**	D1
Gorky Literary Museum		
Литературный		
Музей Горького	**10**	F1
Gorky Museum		
Музей Горького	**11**	E2
Monument to Heroes of WWII		
Памятник Отечественной		
войны	**12**	D1
Nevsky Cathedral		
Невский собор	**13**	B2
Nizhegorodsky State Art Museum		
Художественный музей	**14**	D1
Saviour Old Market Cathedral		
Спасский староярмарочный		
собор	**15**	A2
Stroganov Church		
Строгановская церковь	**16**	C2
Yarmarka Ярмарка	**17**	B2
SLEEPING		
Central Hotel		
Гостиница Центральная	**18**	B3
Nizhegorodsky Hotel Complex		
Нижегородский		
Гостиничный Комплекс	**19**	C3
October Hotel		
Гастиница Октябрьская	**20**	E1
Volga Slope Hotel		
Гостиница Волжский		
Откос	**21**	E1
EATING		
Bar Bochka Бар Бочка	**22**	D2
Broadway Pizza		
Бродвей пицца	**23**	D3
English Embassy		
Английское Посольство	**24**	D3
Gorod Gorky		
Город Горький	**25**	D3
Mexican Studies		
Мексиканские Этюды	**26**	E2
Michelle Мишель	**27**	E2
Potato Papa		
Картофельный Папа	**28**	E1
ENTERTAINMENT		
Jam Prestige		
Джем Престиж джаз клуб	**29**	D3
Kremlin Concert Hall		
Кремлевский		
Концертный Зал	**30**	D1
Pushkin Theatre of		
Opera & Ballet		
Театр оперы и балета	**31**	F3
TRANSPORT		
Bus Station		
Автостанция	**32**	A3
River Station		
Речной вокзал	**33**	C2
Turbyuro Турбюро	**34**	D3

of traditional wooden buildings, some of which are open for visitors. The highlight is the **Pokrovskaya church**, a beautiful wooden church dating from 1731.

CHURCHES & MONASTERIES

The proliferation of onion domes and golden spires in Nizhny Novgorod is a ubiquitous reminder of the city's rich history.

The 13th-century **Annunciation Monastery**, located above Chernigovskaya ul, is the oldest church in town, but it's not open to the public. The 17th-century stone **Assumption Church** is unique in that its design was normally exclusive to wooden churches. The baroque **Stroganov**, otherwise known as **Nativity Church**, has retained its magnificent stone carvings.

On the west bank of the Oka River is the eye-catching **Nevsky Cathedral**. The **Saviour Old Market Cathedral** sits behind the **Yarmarka**, the handsomely restored exhibition hall on pl Lenina.

Tours

Team Gorky (☎ 651 999; www.teamgorky.ru; ul 40 let Oktyabrya 1a) organises adventure tours in the Volga region and beyond, including several three-day trips in the region (per person from €85) and a 10-day bike tour of the Golden Ring (per person €560).

Sleeping

October Hotel (☎ 320 670; www.oktyabrskaya.ru; Verkhne-Volzhskaya nab 9A; s/d with breakfast from R2900/ 4500; ☐) This business hotel has a prime location overlooking the Volga. All of the rooms are renovated with new furniture, modern bathrooms and a hint of post-Soviet kitsch.

Volga Slope Hotel (☎ 390 530; fax 194 894; Verkhne-Volzhskaya nab 2A; r from R800) This Soviet relic has friendly staff and decent rooms for the excellent price. Nicer, renovated rooms overlooking the Volga run at around R2500, while budget travellers may appreciate the cheapies (from R300) with shared facilities.

Nizhegorodsky Hotel Complex (☎ 305 387; www .hotel.r52.ru; ul Zalomova 2; s/d with breakfast from R900/1200) A 15-minute walk from Nizhny's main drag, this old-style place is good value. The facility is not the most attractive, but rooms are adequate and service is friendly.

Hotel Volna (☎ 961 900; www.volnahotel.ru; ul Lenina 98; s/d from R4480/6700; ☒ ☒ ☐ ☒) Nizhny Novgorod's top hotel offers all the facilities you'd expect, including tastefully decorated rooms, an impressive breakfast spread, a well-equipped gym and a couple of upscale restaurants. The location, 9km south of the station (but near the end of the metro), is not in its favour.

Central Hotel (☎ 775 500; www.hotel-central.ru; Sovetskaya ul 12; s/d from R1100/1700) The location of this hotel near the station is convenient, but the flip-side is that it attracts a rough and tumble crowd (as does the casino in the lobby). Nonetheless, service and security are satisfactory. Upgraded rooms cost R1700/2200 with breakfast, but the difference in comfort level is negligible.

Eating & Drinking

English Embassy (☎ 336 165; ul Zvezdinka 12; business lunches R150, meals R300-500; ☺ 8am-midnight Sun-Thu, 8am-2am Fri & Sat) This convivial British pub offers all your favourites, from steak and eggs for breakfast, to roast beef and pudding for dinner, to fish and chips for the late-night munchies. A good selection of draught beers is available from the wood and brass bar.

Gorod Gorky (☎ 332 017; Bolshaya Pokrovskaya ul 30; meals R150-400; ☺ 11am-midnight) Of several Soviet nostalgia places, this quietly upmarket choice is the most entertaining. Enter through the archway to Dom Ofitserov (look for the 'Muzey CCCP' sign). Walk through a waxwork Leonid Brezhnev's office into the dining room, littered with Soviet memorabilia and Beatles photos. The food is surprisingly good, and you can compare how much it costs today with how little it cost in 1974.

Michelle (☎ 192 914; Bolshaya Pokrovskaya ul 6; meals R150-300; ☺ 10am-11pm) This place is – first and foremost – a coffee bar, offering several varieties of aromatic brew in a simple café setting. The menu also features soups and sandwiches and dishes with French nuances – innovative fare for the price.

Bar Bochka (☎ 335 561; Bolshaya Pokrovskaya ul 14; meals R200-400; ☺ noon-midnight) An old-school Georgian place. The dark, basement location has a bar-like atmosphere, live crooners and shashlyk (meat kebab) for every palate.

Mexican Studies (☎ 391 460; pl Minina i Pozharskogo 2; meals R300-600; ☺ noon-midnight) This place takes Mexican food seriously. See if you can pass the test by finishing off plates piled high with rice and beans, burritos, fajitas and empanadas. Conveniently located opposite the kremlin, it is the place to go for something spicy.

Recommended for cheap eats:

Broadway Pizza (☎ 917 916; Bolshaya Pokrovskaya ul 31; pizza from R45; ☺ 8am-4am) A great stop for a late-night snack.

Potato Papa (☎ 194 101; Verkhne-Volzhskaya nab; meals R60-100; ☺ 11am-9pm) A cafeteria with lovely river views.

Entertainment

Jam-Prestige (☎ 333 246; ul Bolshaya Pokrovskaya 49A; admission R50-200; ☺ shows 8-9pm) For jazz, blues

---

THE GULAG

The Siberian exile system was abolished at the turn of the 20th century, but Stalin brought it back with a vengeance, expanding it into a full-blown, home-grown slave trade. It was during his rule that Siberia became synonymous with death. He established a vast bureaucracy of resettlement programs, labour colonies, concentration camps and special psychiatric hospitals, commonly known as the Gulag.

The Gulag's inmates – some of whose only 'offence' was to was to joke about Stalin or steal two spikelets of wheat from a *kolkhoz* (collective farm) field – cut trees, dug canals, laid railway tracks and worked in factories in remote areas, especially Siberia and the Russian Far East. A huge slice of the northeast was set aside exclusively for labour camps, and whole cities were developed as Gulag centres.

The Gulag population grew from 30,000 in 1928 to eight million in 1938. Prisoners were underfed, mistreated and literally worked to death; the average life expectancy was about two years, and 90% of inmates didn't come out alive. The Gulag system continued well after WWII: Boris Yeltsin announced the release of Russia's 'last 10' political prisoners from a camp near Perm in 1992.

Anne Applebaum, author of the definitive *Gulag: A History,* believes that at least 18 million people passed through the camp system. Many more suffered, though. Nadezhda Mandelstam, whose husband Osip Mandelstam, a highly regarded poet, was exiled to Siberia in 1934, wrote that a wife considered herself a widow from the very moment of her husband's arrest. She was almost right – Osip lasted four years before dying at the Vtoraya Rechka transit camp in Vladivostok.

and rock and roll, this small basement dive is a great venue. The place also hosts swing dancing on Monday and Saturday, so bring along your dancing shoes.

Kremlin Concert Hall (☎ 391 187; ☿ shows 6pm) The concert hall at the west end of the kremlin is home to the philharmonic, playing a full schedule of classical concerts throughout the year.

Pushkin Theatre of Opera & Ballet (☎ 351 640; ul Belinskogo 59) This beautifully renovated theatre is also recommended for Russian classics.

Getting There & Away

AIR
Several flights daily make the journey to Moscow (R1000 to R3000, one hour). **Lufthansa** (☎ 759 085) flies directly to and from Frankfurt three times a week. Airline tickets are available at agencies around the city, including the **Turbyuro** (☎ 104 503; ul Zvezdinka 10; ☿ 10am-7pm Mon-Sat).

BOAT
The **Rechnoy vokzal** (River Station; ☎ 303 666) is on Nizhne-Volzhskaya nab, below the kremlin. Apart from short trips along the Volga (see right), this is where you can find out about the summer cruises linking Nizhny Novgorod with St Petersburg, Moscow and cities further down the Volga.

BUS
Buses go to/from Moscow's Shchyolkovsky bus station (R300, nine hours, five daily) and to/from Vladimir (R180, 4½ hours, four daily).

TRAIN
The Nizhny Novgorod train station still goes by its old name of Gorky-Moskovsky vokzal (so 'Gorky' appears on most timetables). It is located on the western bank of the Oka River, at pl Revolyutsii. Several trains go to Moscow (seven hours), including one fast train (R300, 4½ hours), which departs every morning at 6.30am. All of these services stop at Vladimir (R240, two to three hours). One train also continues all the way to St Petersburg (R1500, 16 hours).

Heading east, trains stop at all major points along the Trans-Siberian route – the next stop being Perm (R1700, 14 hours).

Trains also depart to Kazan (R640, nine hours, daily).

The **service centre** (☎ 483 470) at the train station is helpful for buying tickets, and also offers other services such as Internet access.

Getting Around
Tram 1 is very convenient, starting from the train station, crossing the Kanavinsky most (bridge) and climbing the hill to the kremlin. There are plans to extend the metro across the river but that's unlikely to happen during the life of this book. Currently you might use it only to get to Hotel Volna.

AROUND NIZHNY NOVGOROD
Makarevo Макарево
☎ 249 / pop 180 / ☿ Moscow
The sleepy village of Makarevo is around 60km east of Nizhny Novgorod along the Volga. The fortified stone walls and church domes of its **Makariev Monastery** (☎ 26 967; admission R150; ☿ 9am-5pm) look magnificent on the approach from the river.

The monastery and surrounding village, founded in 1453, thrived on vibrant river trade through the 19th century. The monastery was closed during the Soviet period, but a few nuns returned in 1991 to help restore the churches. Today four churches are working, but only 20 nuns live here. The village of 180 people is made up of rustic wooden cottages, as well as a small museum in the old school house. Most locals come here for a day of sunbathing by the river; bring a picnic as there are only a few small shops.

From Nizhny Novgorod, boats to Makarevo (3½ hours) depart in the morning from near the river station and return in the evening.

PERM ПЕРМЬ
☎ 3422 / pop 1 million / ☿ Moscow + 2hr
Dominated by heavily trafficked avenues and concrete blocks, Perm is a modern, industrial city that most travellers could bear to miss. Its chequered history, however, draws them in – to bear witness to the thousands of years that were lost by prisoners at the notorious labour camp Perm-36; and to discover what has become of the once-secret city of Molotov (named during

the Soviet period for the foreign minister who was also the namesake of the explosive cocktail).

Today, Perm is not so menacing, but its reputation as a bland, provincial capital persists (Chekhov used Perm as inspiration for the city that his *Three Sisters* were so desperate to leave). This is quite unfortunate, as the city boasts its fair share of cultural attractions, from a championship basketball team to a one-of-a-kind art collection.

Economically, the city is thriving. Evidence of its military history is everywhere, but so are signs of ongoing economic development, from shiny new bank buildings to sushi bars.

Orientation & Information

Perm sprawls along the south bank of the Kama River. The city centre is at the intersection of ul Lenina and Komsomolsky pr, and Perm II train station is about 2.5km southwest of here.

Internet Centre (☎ 373 605; Kommunisticheskaya ul 77; per hr R30; ⏲ 24hr) Often crowded with young boys playing video games, but the large, dark hall contains plenty of computers.

Main post office (ul Lenina 29; per hr R30; ⏲ 24hr) Also offers Internet access.

Permtourist (☎ 906 237; www.permtourist.ru; ul Lenina 58) Arranges local excursions as well as cruises along the Kama River and further to the Volga.

Sberbank (ul Lenina 31; ⏲ 10am-8pm Mon-Sat) Cashes travellers cheques and gives credit card advances.

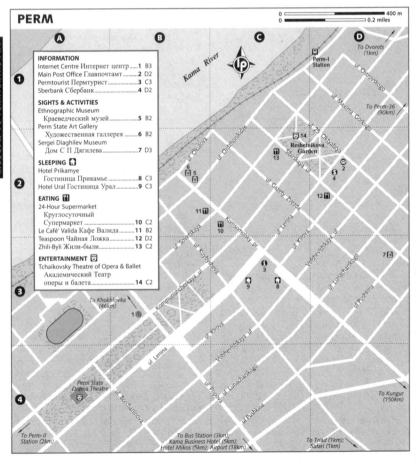

PERM

INFORMATION
Internet Centre Интернет центр......**1** B3
Main Post Office Главпочтамт.........**2** D2
Permtourist Пермтурист.................**3** C3
Sberbank Сбербанк.........................**4** D2

SIGHTS & ACTIVITIES
Ethnographic Museum
   Краеведческий музей...............**5** B2
Perm State Art Gallery
   Художественная галлерея........**6** B2
Sergei Diaghilev Museum
   Дом С П Дягилева....................**7** D3

SLEEPING
Hotel Prikamye
   Гостиница Прикамье................**8** C3
Hotel Ural Гостиница Урал...........**9** C3

EATING
24-Hour Supermarket
   Круглосуточный
   Супермаркет.........................**10** C2
Le Café' Valida Кафе Валида......**11** B2
Teaspoon Чайная Ложка...........**12** D2
Zhili-Byli Жили-были.................**13** C2

ENTERTAINMENT
Tchaikovsky Theatre of Opera & Ballet
   Академический Театр
   оперы и балета.....................**14** C2

Sights

Housed in the grand Cathedral of Christ Transfiguration on the banks of the Kama, the **Perm State Art Gallery** (☎ 129 524, 122 395; www.sculpture.permonline.ru; Komsomolsky pr 4; admission R30; ☺ 10am-6pm Tue-Fri, 11am-7pm Sat, noon-6pm Sun) is renowned for its collection of Prikamye wooden sculpture. Dating back to the 17th century, the religious figures are examples of a primitive style that is unique to the Perm region. The museum also contains a large collection of icons, some works by the Peredvizhniki (Wanderers) of the 19th century, and some temporary exhibits by contemporary artists.

Next door, the **Ethnographic Museum** (☎ 122 456; Komsomolsky pr 6; admission R10; ☺ 10am-6pm Sat-Thu) mainly features stuffed animals with some exhibits on local history.

The **Sergei Diaghilev Museum** (☎ 120 610; Sibirskaya ul 33; admission free; ☺ 9am-6pm Mon-Fri) is a small, lovingly curated exhibition on world-famous ballet and opera impresario Diaghilev (1872–1929), whose family came from the Perm region.

Sleeping

Hotel Ural (☎ 906 030; ural-hotel@permtourist.ru; ul Lenina 58; s/d from R720/1000) Average distance from front desk to drab room: about 1km. This monolith has the charm of an apparatchik, but the location is convenient. For R1500/1800 you'll get a slightly upgraded single/double with a telephone, a TV and breakfast. Another decent and affordable option, Hotel Prikamye, is right next door.

Two small, upscale hotels are about 5km from the city centre on the way to the airport. **Kama Business Hotel** (☎ 280 248; www.kama-hotel.ru; ul Baumana 25b; s with breakfast from R2900; 🍴🖳) and **Hotel Mikos** (☎ 241 999; www.micos.perm.ru; Stakhanovskaya ul 10a; s/d from R2400/2900; 🍴🖳) are both popular with business travellers and require advanced booking.

Eating

The terrace overlooking the Kama River just outside the Perm State Art Gallery (above) is a good place for beer and shashlyk from a *letny kafe* (summer café).

Le Café Valida (☎ 103 393; Komsomolsky pr 7; meals R500-800; ☺ 8am-2am) 'Coffee…like Art' reads the menu. Coffee is not the only thing that is artistic at this trendy place: a DJ works the wax in the midst of a funky, modern décor, and Perm's fashionable set nibble on creative salads and snacks while checking each other out.

Zhili-Byli (☎ 125 771; Sibirskaya ul 9; meals R150-200; ☺ 11am-2am) A chain with outlets around the region, this *traktir* (tavern) is a popular spot for affordable Russian favourites. You can fill up at the salad bar, which is a godsend for vegetarians.

Teaspoon (☎ 126 048; Sibirskaya ul 19a; meals R30-60; ☺ 9am-10pm) Serving tea (R12), coffee and bliny (pancakes; R18), this little café is a perfect stop for breakfast or for a light lunch. Service is cafeteria-style, but the setting is light and clean, attracting lots of students and young people.

To stock up for your train ride, visit the central **supermarket** (cnr Komsomolsky pr & ul Sovetskaya; ☺ 24hr).

Entertainment

Triad (☎ 347 256; ul Kuybysheva 66; ☺ noon-6pm Mon-Fri, 10am-6am Sat & Sun) Check out this neon-lit entertainment complex for bowling (R300 to R600) or billiards (R100 to R200), but skip the overpriced bar. The Safari nightclub is tucked into the parking lot behind the complex.

Tchaikovsky Theatre of Opera & Ballet (☎ 123 087; Kommunisticheskaya ul 25) If your cultural inclinations lean towards the classical, take in a performance at the beautiful baroque theatre that dominates Reshetnikova Garden. It is home to one of Russia's top schools of performing arts.

Getting There & Away

Perm II, the city's major train station, is on the Trans-Siberian route. Many trains travel the route from Moscow, including the *firmeny* (a nicer, long-distance train) called the *Kama* (R1950, 20 hours). Heading east, the next major stop is Yekaterinburg (R650, six hours). Trains also travel every second day to Kazan (16 hours, R706) – more frequently in summer. Note that some trains to Kazan depart from the *gorny trakt* (mountain track) on the north side of Perm II, as opposed to the *glavny trakt* (main track).

The **ticket office** (☺ 9am-8pm) in the lobby of Hotel Ural is useful for airline and train tickets. The smaller Perm-Station, northeast of the centre, is used for suburban trains only.

MOSCOW TO YEKATERINBURG

There are three daily Aeroflot flights to/from Moscow Domodedovo (R3500), with additional flights to Yekaterinburg (R2500, four weekly) and St Petersburg (R5100, two weekly). **Lufthansa** (☎ 284 442) flies to/from Frankfurt twice a week.

Plans for a new bus station near Perm-II train station will probably not be realised until 2007. In the meantime, use the old station at the southern end of ul Popova for buses to Khokhlovka (below) and Chusovoy, for Perm-36 (below).

Getting Around

Buses 110, 119 and 120 serve the airport (35 minutes), or take a taxi for about R250. Take tram 7 or any bus or trolleybus between Perm II Station and Hotel Ural.

AROUND PERM

Khokhlovka ХОХЛОВКА

☎ 3422 / ⊙ Moscow + 2hr

The **Architecture-Ethnography Museum** (☎ 997 182; admission R35; ⊙ 9am-6pm Mon-Sun late-May–mid-Oct) is set in the rolling countryside near the village of Khokhlovka, about 45km north of Perm. Its impressive collection of wooden buildings includes two churches · dating back to the turn of the 18th century. Most of the structures are from the 19th or early 20th centuries, including an old firehouse, a salt production facility and a Khanty *izba* (log house). A few buses a day serve Khokhlovka from Perm (R50, one hour).

Perm-36 Пермь-36

Once an ominous island in the Gulag Archipelago, **Perm-36** (☎ 120 030; www.perm36.ru; admission R60, guided tour R600; ⊙ by appointment) is now a fascinating museum and moving memorial to the victims of political repression.

For most of its history since 1946 Perm-36 was a labour camp for political prisoners – in other words, dissidents. Countless artists, scientists and intellectuals spent years in the cold, damp cells, many in solitary confinement. They worked at mundane tasks like assembling fasteners, and survived on measly portions of bread and gruel.

Much of the evidence of this history was destroyed when the camp was closed in 1988, but museum staff are dedicated to re-creating the camp as it was. Windowless cells and barbed wire are eerie reminders that this history is not so distant. The exhibits make the reality of prison life all too clear.

The memorial centre is about 10km from the town of Chusovoy, which is 100km east of Perm. A new road makes the museum accessible by bus from Perm. Alternatively, museum staff can make arrangements for a taxi for about R3000. Museum management plans to build a small on-site hotel and conference facility, expected to open in 2007.

Kungur Кунгур

☎ 34271 / pop 76,600 / ⊙ Moscow + 2hr

Founded in 1663, the town of Kungur was a copper-smelting centre during the 17th and 18th centuries. Many notable (though dilapidated) buildings remain from its heyday, including the **All Saints Church**, a 17th-century **governor's house** and a 19th-century arcade, **Gostiny Dvor**. Get the full story at the **Regional Local Studies Museum** (ul Gogolya 36; admission R20; ⊙ 11am-5pm).

Kungur was long a popular destination for potential spelunkers investigating the **Kungur Ice Cave** (Ledyanaya peshchera; admission R350; ⊙ 10am-5pm), about 5km out of town. The extensive network of caves stretches for more than 5km, although only about 1.5km are open for explorers. The grottoes are adorned with unique ice formations, frozen waterfalls and underground lakes. In Perm, **Permtourist** (☎ 906 237; www.permtourist.ru; ul Lenina 58) arranges tours here, as well as accommodation in the adjacent **Stalagmit Hotel** (☎ /fax 39 723; r R600, upgraded r from R1200).

Trains from Perm (R60, 2½ hours, eight daily) arrive at the station on ul Bachurina in Kungur. A day trip is possible if you start early, but check the train schedule in advance.

KAZAN КАЗАНЬ

☎ 8432 / pop 1.1 million / ⊙ Moscow

Kazan is the capital of the Tatarstan Republic, home to the descendants of the nomadic Turkic tribe that wreaked particular havoc in ancient Rus. The atmosphere of this intriguing autonomous republic is redolent of Central Asia. The spires of many mosques dot the skyline – including the grand Kul Sharif Mosque inside the historic kremlin.

Nationalism is strong here, as evidenced by the bilingual signposts and the ubiquitous green, white and red of the Tatar flag. Ethnic pride was particularly passionate in 2005, when the city of Kazan celebrated 1000 years since its founding. Many parks and buildings received a massive makeover in anticipation of the celebration, so the city centre is looking better than ever.

History

Kazan, one of Russia's oldest Tatar cities, dates back to 1005. Capital of the Kazan khanate in the 15th and 16th centuries, it was famously ravaged in 1552 by Ivan the Terrible, who forced the Muslim khan to become Christian. St Basil's Cathedral

in Moscow was built to celebrate Kazan's downfall. The city later flourished as a gateway to Siberia.

During Soviet times, Kazan became the capital of the Tatar Autonomous Republic. In autumn 1990, this oil-rich region (now renamed Tatarstan) declared its autonomy from the rest of Russia, launching several years of political warfare with Moscow. But full independence remains unlikely given that 43% of the population is Russian.

Orientation

Kazan's city centre is flanked in the north by the Kazanka River and in the west by the Volga; the train station is on the east bank of the Volga. The main drag, ul Baumana,

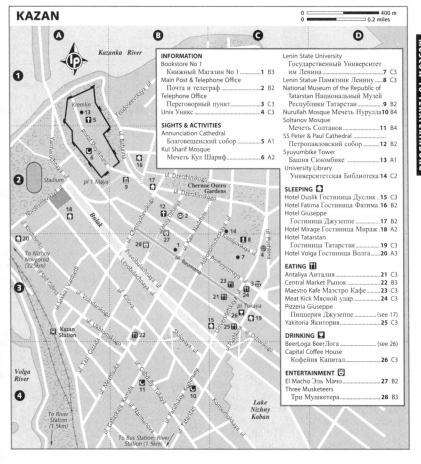

KAZAN

0   400 m
0   0.2 miles

INFORMATION
Bookstore No 1
  Книжный Магазин No 1 ....**1** B3
Main Post & Telephone Office
  Почта и телеграф **2** B2
Telephone Office
  Переговорный пункт................**3** C3
Unix Уникс **4** C3

SIGHTS & ACTIVITIES
Annunciation Cathedral
  Благовещенский собор **5** A1
Kul Sharif Mosque
  Мечеть Кул Шариф **6** A2

Lenin State University
  Государственный Университет
  им Ленина **7** C3
Lenin Statue Памятник Ленину **8** C3
National Museum of the Republic of
  Tatarstan Национальный Музей
  Республики Татарстан **9** B2
Nurullah Mosque Мечеть Нурулла**10** B4
Soltanov Mosque
  Мечеть Солтанов **11** B4
SS Peter & Paul Cathedral
  Петропавловский собор **12** B2
Syuyumbike Tower
  Башня Сююмбике **13** A1
University Library
  Университетская Библиотека **14** C2

SLEEPING
Hotel Duslik Гостиница Дуслик ..**15** C3
Hotel Fatima Гостиница Фатима.**16** B2
Hotel Giuseppe
  Гостиница Джузеппе................**17** C3
Hotel Mirage Гостиница Мираж.**18** A2
Hotel Tatarstan
  Гостиница Татарстан **19** C3
Hotel Volga Гостиница Волга......**20** A3

EATING
Antaliya Анталия **21** C3
Central Market Рынок **22** B3
Maestro Kafe Маэстро Кафе.......**23** C3
Meat Kick Мясной удар...............**24** C3
Pizzeria Giuseppe
  Пиццерия Джузеппе ....(see 17)
Yakitoria Якитория.......................**25** C3

DRINKING
BeerLoga BeerЛога ....(see 26)
Capital Coffee House
  Кофейня Капитал....................**26** C3

ENTERTAINMENT
El Macho Эль Мачо **27** B2
Three Musketeers
  Три Мушкетера **28** B3

Kazanka River

Kremlin

Stadium

pl 1 Maya

Chernoe Ozero Gardens

ul Dzerzhinskogo

ul Baumana

To Nizhny Novgorod (325km)

Kazan Station

pl Tukaya

Volga River

To River Station (1.5km)

To Bus Station; River Station (1.5km)

Lake Nizhny Kaban

is about 500m east of the train station, running from the kremlin in the northwest down to busy ul Tatarstan, which goes to the bus station and river station.

Information

Bookstore No 1 (☎ 924 510; ul Baumana 19; 9am-6pm) A central bookstore with a good selection of maps and books about Tatar history and culture.

Main post & telephone office (Kremlyovskaya ul 8; per hr R30; 8am-7pm Mon-Fri, 9am-6pm Sat & Sun) Has Internet facilities.

Telephone office (cnr uls Pushkina & Profsoyuznaya; per hr R30; 8am-9pm Mon-Fri, 10.30am-6pm Sat & Sun) Has Internet facilities.

Unix (Kremlyovskaya ul, 2nd fl; per hr R40; Mon-Sat) A student computer centre that is open to the public for Internet services.

Sights

KREMLIN

Declared a Unesco World Heritage site in 2000, Kazan's striking kremlin is the focal point of the city's historic centre. It is home to government offices, pleasant parks and a few religious buildings that should be open and operating. Some of the white limestone walls date from the 16th and 17th centuries.

Completely renovated for the 2005 celebrations, Kazan's **Annunciation Cathedral** was originally designed by the same architect responsible for St Basil's Cathedral in Moscow. The new iconostasis – designed in the Pskov style – is similar to that of the Assumption Cathedral inside the Moscow Kremlin.

Nearby, the slightly leaning 59m-high **Syuyumbike Tower** is named after a long-suffering princess who was married to three successive khans. According to legend, Ivan the Terrible launched his siege of Kazan as a result of Syuyumbike's refusal to marry him. To save her city, the princess agreed to marry the tsar, but only if he could build a tower higher than any other mosque in Kazan in a week. Unfortunately for Syuyumbike, the tower was completed, driving her to jump to her death from its upper terrace shortly thereafter.

Today, the tower competes with a rival landmark inside the kremlin. The enormous **Kul Sharif mosque** was constructed on the site of a mosque by the same name, which was burnt and destroyed after Ivan the Terrible captured the city in 1552.

NATIONAL MUSEUM OF THE REPUBLIC OF TATARSTAN

Opposite the kremlin's main entrance, the **museum** (☎ 928 984; Kremlyovskaya ul 2; exhibit admission R15-100; 10am-5pm Tue-Sun) is in an ornate building dating from 1770. It contains a wide range of exhibits, including Tatar history, water and wildlife, and local artists. The Gallery of Zarif is a unique exhibit by a local artist-philosopher.

SS PETER & PAUL CATHEDRAL

Among Kazan's several Russian Orthodox churches, the most attractive is the **SS Peter & Paul Cathedral** (ul Musy Dzhalilya 21; 1-3pm). Built between 1723 and 1726, this baroque cathedral, with its heavily decorated façade and soaring iconostasis, commemorates the visit of Tsar Peter I to the city in 1722.

LENIN STATE UNIVERSITY

At the foot of Kremlyovskaya ul, you can't miss the overbearing classical façade of the main building of **Lenin State University**, where Vladimir Ilych himself was a student. Across the street, the **statue** of a young Lenin looks like he's on his way to class. However, the plaques don't tell us that he was actually expelled from the university for revolutionary activity and questionable ties. The **university library** (cnr Astronomicheskaya & Kremlyovskaya uls) has an exquisitely decorated exterior.

MOSQUES

Many of the mosques in Kazan are clustered around the rather dumpy southwestern corner of town. Near the central market is the **Soltanov Mosque** (ul Gabdully Tukaya 14), dating from 1867, and the **Nurullah Mosque** (ul Kirova 74), which has been rebuilt several times since 1849.

Sleeping

Visa registration is a tricky business in Tatarstan, and cheaper hotels may be hesitant to accept foreign guests staying more than two nights.

Hotel Fatima (☎ 924 636; ul Karla Marksa 2; s/tw R600/900) Within spitting distance of the Kremlin walls, this brand-new hotel is a great bargain. Bathrooms are shared, but the whole place is modern and clean. You can't beat it, for the price.

Hotel Volga (☎ 316 349; fax 921 469; ul Said-Galieva 1A; s/d with bathroom from R900/1500, without bathroom R500/820) Convenient to the train station, this nicely revamped hotel has rooms for every budget (although the mid-range rooms get booked early). Rooms facing the street can be noisy, but the place is clean and welcoming. Prices include a buffet breakfast.

Hotel Giuseppe (☎ 926 934; hotelgiuseppe@mi.ru; Kremlyovskaya ul 15/25; s/d with breakfast from R3040/5700; ☒) Hidden inside the restaurant of the same name (see below), this friendly place has rooms that are spacious and comfortable – even plush by Kazan standards. On weekdays they are often booked by business travellers, so reserve in advance if possible. Cash only.

Hotel Mirage (☎ 780 505; www.summithotels.com; ul Kirova 1A; r from R6000; ☒ ☒ ▣ ☒) This new, international-standard hotel is ideally located between the train station and the kremlin. With a plush, modern décor, it somehow seems out of place in this ancient city, but it is still a very welcome addition for business travellers and luxury-minded guests.

Hotel Tatarstan (☎ 388 379; fax 316 704; ul Pushkina 4; s/d from R1400/1600) Location is the primary advantage of this concrete slab of a hotel. Rooms are Soviet-standard – not exactly stylish nor particularly comfortable, but clean and functional.

Hotel Duslik (☎ /fax 923 320; Pravobulachnaya ul 49; s/d R1200/1800) Despite Hotel Duslik's stark lobby, this place has simple but nicely renovated rooms that are good value for the price. Unfortunately, the quality of the service – and the consistency of the room prices – does not match the quality of the rooms.

Eating & Drinking

Pizzeria Giuseppe (☎ 326 934; Kremlyovskaya ul 15; pizza R50-100) A lively place for pizza, pasta and cappuccino. The place is not big on atmosphere, but it still attracts young couples and families, who fill up on tasty, inexpensive Italian treats.

BeerLoga (☎ 922 436; ul Pushkina 5; meals R300-500; ☽ noon-2am) Ten beers on tap and a whole range of spicy sausages are the features of this Bavarian beer bar. The rustic décor and convenient location make this a popular spot.

Capital Coffee House (☎ 926 390; ul Pushkina 5; breakfast R50; ☽ 8am-midnight Mon-Fri, noon-midnight Sat & Sun) Next door to Kazan's trendiest brewpub is the city's trendiest coffee house. Come for the wide range of coffee drinks or for free wi-fi access.

Yakitoria (☎ 922 713; ul Pushkina 3; sushi R40-60, meals R200-400; ☽ 11am-6am) Moscow's favourite sushi bar has gone national, with this very popular outlet on Kazan's main square. Service is pleasant and efficient, quickly turning over tables at this busy, bustling place.

Meat Kick (☎ 929 332; ul Profsoyuznaya 9; meals R400-600) Besides the highly sought-after salad bar, this place offers Western-style steakhouse fare. For a sample of the Volga's riches, try the upscale seafood restaurant in the same building.

Central market (ul Mezhlauka) This colourful, sprawling place is good for stocking up on snacks or just for browsing.

Also recommended:

Maestro Kafe (☎ 921 338; ul Baumana 47; breakfast R50; ☽ 24hr) Specialises in bliny and coffees; a great place for breakfast or a late-night snack.

Antaliya (☎ 383 803; ul Baumana 74; mains R100-150; ☽ 10am-10pm) Popular for Turkish treats, including shawarma (sandwich made of spicy grilled lamb or chicken on flat bread) and Efes beer.

Entertainment

El Macho (☎ 925 883; ul Musy Dzhalilya; cover R50-150; ☽ noon-5am) Mexican food and Latin music are the attractions of this popular club. It varies from day to day, but live music and free salsa lessons are often on the programme.

Three Musketeers (☎ 923 711; ul Baumana 42/9; cover R100; ☽ noon-5am) This stylish basement club has wide range of entertainment options, including pool tables, dance floor, live music and – for better or for worse – male and female striptease.

Getting There & Away

The beautifully restored original train station on ul Said Galieva serves only as a waiting room these days. Long-distance tickets can be purchased in the sleek new building that is north of the tatty, suburban train station. On the 2nd floor you'll find a service centre that is useful if the ticket counters on the ground-floor are overly crowded.

Yekaterinburg to Krasnoyarsk

Crossing Siberia along the old post road, Anton Chekhov wrote 'You'll be bored from the Urals to the Yenisey'. It's true that the scenery for most of this stretch isn't going to blow you away, but the lack of window gawping is by no means a bad thing. In fact, the clever way to cover this sector is in a series of overnight hops. Siberia's most interesting larger cities seem to have been deliberately placed to make this easy, and good timetabling means that handy night trains cover the very sections you're most likely to need. Happily these tickets rarely need to be booked more than a day or two ahead.

With fascinating historical context, Yekaterinburg offers one of the most popular stops along the Trans-Siberian route, though some travellers find it visually disappointing. An overnight train from Yekaterinburg takes you on to Tobolsk with its fine kremlin and lovable unkempt old-town area. The next sensible hop is to Omsk, whose modestly appealing old core is worth a day between overnight connections. Many Trans-Sibbers head next for gigantic Novosibirsk with its train museums and a plethora of international bars and restaurants. However, much more interesting is to get off instead in appealing Tomsk, which has a delightful blend of Siberian wooden architecture and a lively student atmosphere. From either Tomsk or Novosibirsk, branch line trains can whisk you south towards the glorious mountains of the Altai for rafting, hiking or simply relaxing on the picturesque banks of Teletskoye Ozera, a lesser-known alternative to Baikal.

Vibrant Krasnoyarsk has an attractive setting and offers some intriguing alternatives to the Trans-Siberian mainline if you're continuing east.

HIGHLIGHTS

- Stroll through the intriguing, kremlin-crowned old city of **Tobolsk** (p160)

- Enjoy the youthful energy and wooden architecture of **Tomsk** (p178)

- Follow the pilgrims to the Romanovs' execution site in **Yekaterinburg** (p152)

- Hike, raft or just relax in the beautiful, fascinating **Altai Mountains** (p178)

- Discover Trans-Siberian history at Novosibirsk's **railway museums (p167** and p177)

YEKATERINBURG TO KRASNOYARSK

■ ROUTE DISTANCE: 2287KM | ■ DURATION: ONE DAY, EIGHT HOURS

THE ROUTE

Yekaterinburg to Omsk

Major trains halt at **Yekaterinburg** for 15 to 30 minutes. The cultural and economic capital of the Urals, it's famous as the birthplace of Boris Yeltsin and the death-place of Tsar Nicholas II. Wander across the street for a look at the old train station, which now houses a Railway Museum (see p152).

Siberia officially begins at 2102km. Trains stop for 15 minutes in **Tyumen** (2138km), Siberia's oldest Russian settlement, now a dynamic oil-rich city.

From Tyumen our route detours 221km northeast off the official Trans-Siberian line to the old Siberian capital of **Tobolsk**. Near the 212km marker, east-facing windows have fine if distant views of Tobolsk's kremlin.

Back on the main Trans-Siberian route east, the next major stop is for 15 minutes at **Ishim** (2428km), which was famous for its 19th-century Nikolskaya trade fairs (revived since 1991). It retains a striking, white-washed 1793 cathedral. At 2497km, local time becomes Moscow time plus three hours. Swampy land provides opportunities for bird-spotters.

There's another 15-minute halt at agro-processing town **Nazyvaevskaya** (2562km); if you're riding straight from Moscow you'll now be into day three of your journey. After the six-span Irtysh River bridge, trains pause

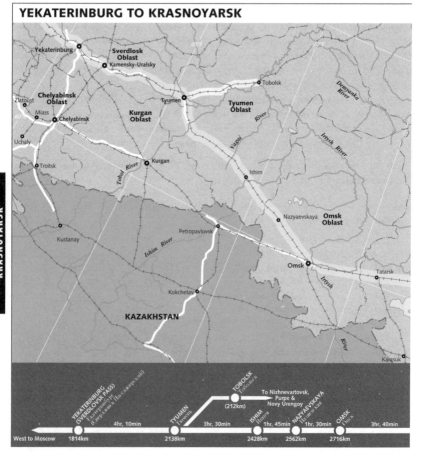

YEKATERINBURG TO KRASNOYARSK

for 25 minutes in **Omsk** (2716km) where Fyodor Dostoevsky was exiled in 1849.

Omsk to Krasnoyarsk

If you notice an increase in passing trains after Omsk, blame it on coal from the Kuzbas Basin east of Novosibirsk going to the smelting works of the Urals. In freight terms this is the world's busiest section of railway.

Barabinsk (3035km), a 17-minute stop, was once a place of exile for Polish Jews. The surrounding Barabinsk Steppe is a boggy expanse of grassland and lakes that was formerly the homeland of the Kirghiz people.

At around 3330km get ready for the seven-span, 870m-long bridge across the Ob, one of the world's longest rivers. During the 20-minute stop at **Novosibirsk** (3343km), inspect the grand station interior, a real temple of the Trans-Siberian.

At 3479km, time shifts to make it Moscow time plus four hours. The 25-minute halt at **Taiga** (3565km) provides plenty of time to wish you were heading 79km north up the branch line to **Tomsk**. This is not a Womble (as Brits of a certain age may expect, from the kids' TV program) but a charming old Siberian city.

Spot an engine repair yard to the south as you approach **Mariinsk** station (3713km), a 20-minute stop. Originally named Kiysk, the town grew wealthy as the focus of a Siberian gold rush. It was renamed in 1857 to honour Tsar Alexander II's wife Maria.

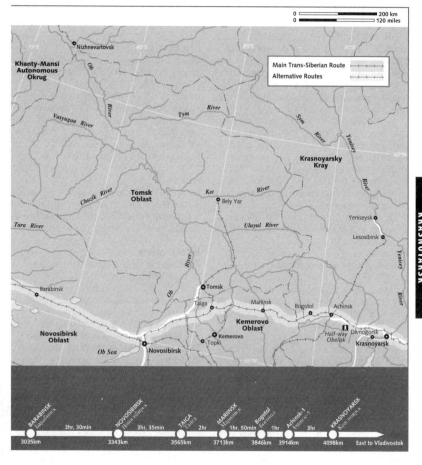

At 3820km the line enters Krasnoyarsky Kray, a vast territory of enormous mineral and forest wealth. It covers 2.5 million sq km stretching all the way to the Arctic coast.

After brief stops at **Bogotol** (3846km) and **Achinsk-1** (3914km) the railway starts twisting through woodlands and over hills with cinematic landscapes to enjoy.

A small, easily missed white obelisk south of the train line at 3932km marks the halfway point between Moscow and Beijing (via Ulaanbaatar).

Major services stop for 20 minutes at **Krasnoyarsk** (4098km, p185). That's just long enough to nip out and see a fine communist-era mural in red mosaics decorating a wall on the station square outside.

YEKATERINBURG ЕКАТЕРИНБУРГ

☎ 343 / pop 1.29 million / ⏱ Moscow + 2hr

From the execution of Tsar Nicholas II and his family in 1918 to the high-profile Mafia killings in the 1990s, Yekaterinburg is notorious for its bloody history. Contemporary Yekaterinburg remembers these events, attracting pilgrims and tourists alike to the sites associated with the Romanov deaths.

As the economic and cultural capital of the Urals region, the city offers visitors more than a dramatic history. The Urals' mineral wealth is on display in the city's many museums, while the ongoing economic boom is evident in the crowded cafés and clubs around the centre. Yekaterinburg also has the accommodation options and facilities to serve as a convenient base for adventure activities and winter sports in the Urals.

History

Yekaterinburg was founded as a factory-fort in 1723 as part of Peter the Great's push to exploit the Ural region's mineral riches. The city was named after two Yekaterinas: Peter's wife (later Empress Catherine I), and the Russian patron saint of mining.

Yekaterinburg is most famous as the place where the Bolsheviks murdered Tsar Nicholas II and his family in July 1918. Six years later, the town was renamed Sverdlovsk, after Yakov Sverdlov, a leading Bolshevik who was Vladimir Ilych Lenin's right-hand man until he died in the flu epidemic of 1919.

WWII turned Sverdlovsk into a major industrial centre, as hundreds of factories were transferred here from vulnerable areas west of the Urals. The city was closed to foreigners until 1990 because of its many defence plants. Remnants of this era still litter the city, with fighter planes proudly displayed in schoolyards and missiles arranged outside the city's Military History Museum.

It was one such missile that in 1960 brought down the US pilot Gary Powers and his U2 spy plane in this area. Powers was exchanged for a Soviet spy in 1962.

During the late 1970s a civil engineering graduate of the local university, Boris Yeltsin, began to make his political mark, rising to become regional Communist Party boss before being promoted to Moscow in 1985.

In 1991 the town reassumed its original name. After suffering economic depression and Mafia lawlessness in the early 1990s, business has been on the upswing for the past decade.

Orientation

The train station is 2km north of the city centre, which is roughly bordered by pr Lenina in the north, ul Malysheva in the south, pl 1905 Goda in the west and ul Lunacharskogo in the east. Ul Sverdlova runs south from the station, changing its name to ul Karla Libknekhta closer to the centre. Pr Lenina crosses the dammed Iset River three blocks west of ul Karla Libknekhta.

MAPS

Karta (☎ 375 6290; Pervomayskaya ul 74; ⏱ 9am-1pm & 2-6pm Mon-Fri, 9am-2pm Sat) offers an extensive selection of maps of Yekaterinburg and Sverdlovsk, as well as other cities and regions.

Information

Alfa-Bank (☎ 371 4226; ul Malysheva 33A) Has a 24-hour ATM that dispenses roubles or US dollars.

Coffee.IN (☎ 277 6873; ul 8 Marta 8; per hr R50; ⏱ 24hr) Internet café located in the shopping centre Mytny Dvor. Enter from the back.

Dom Knigi (☎ 358 1898; ul Antona Valeka 12; ⏱ 9am-7pm) Best for foreign-language and local-interest books.

Ekaterinburg Guide Center (☎ 268 1604; www.ekaterinburg-guide.com; ul Krasnoarmeyskaya 1, Bolshoy Ural Hotel, side entrance) An enthusiastic group that organises English-language tours of the city and trips into the countryside. Popular excursions include rafting, hiking and biking trips in the Urals (€40 to €52 per person), as well as Ganina Yama (p156) and the Europe–Asia border (see p156). Also arranges discounted accommodation and homestays.

YEKATERINBURG

0 —— 600 m
0 —— 0.4 miles

INFORMATION
Alfa-Bank Альфабанк **1** A5
Coffee.IN..**2** A5
Ekaterinburg Guide Center
　Екатеринбургский центр
　гидов ....(see 23)
Gutabank Гутабанк **3** A5
Karta Карта магазин **4** D4
Main Post Office Почтамт **5** B5
US & UK Consulates General
　Генеральные консульства
　Великобритании и США **6** B6

SIGHTS & ACTIVITIES
Afghanistan War Monument
　Памятник Афганской Войны.....**7** C5
Ascension Church
　Вознесенская церковь...............**8** B4
Chapel of the Revered Martyr Grand
　Princess Yelisaveta Fyodororna...(see 17)
Chapel of St Catherine
　Часовня Святой Екатерины **9** B5
Church of the Blood
　Церковь на Крови....................**10** B4
Geological Alley
　Геологическая аллея **11** B5
Museum of Architecture & Industry
　Музей истории архитектуры города

и промышленной
　техники Урала **12** B5
Museum of Fine Arts Музей
　изобразительных искусств....**13** B5
Order of Lenin Орден Ленина......**14** B5
Railway Museum
　Железнодорожный музей......**15** B3
Rastorguev-Kharitonov Mansion
　Усадьба Расторгуев-
　Харитонова **16** B4
Romanov Death Site
　Место убийства Романовых....**17** B4
Tatishchev & de Gennin Statue
　Памятник Татищеву и
　дэ Геннин **18** B5
Ural Geology Museum
　Уральский геологический
　музей.....................................**19** A6
Urals Mineralogical Museum
　Уральский музей
　минералогии.......................(see 23)
Water Tower
　Водонапорная башня **20** B5

SLEEPING
Academy of Geology Hotel
　Гостиница Академии
　геологии **21** C5

Atrium Palace Hotel
　Атриум палас-отель **22** B6
Bolshoy Ural Hotel
　Гостиница Большой Урал.........**23** C5
Country Inn ....(see 23)
Hotel Iset Гостиница Исеть.........**24** C5
Hotel Magister
　Гостиница Магистр..................**25** A6
Hotel Premier
　Гостиница Премьер.................**26** C6
Hotel Sverdlovsk
　Гостиница Свердловск **27** B3

EATING
Dacha Дача **28** A5
Em Sam Ем сам **29** A5
Georgian Kitchen
　Грузинская кухня **30** B6
Grand Buffet Гранд-буфет **31** A6
Kupets Купец..............................**32** A6
Mak Pik Мак Пик **33** A5
Nigora Нигора............................**34** A6
Port Stanley Порт Стенли **35** B6
Uspensky Shopping Center
　(Food Court) Успенский
　торговый центр **36** A5

DRINKING
Coffee Shop No 7 Кофейня No 7 ..**37** A5
Gordon's Гордонс.......................**38** B5
Old Dublin Старый Дублин **39** B5
Rosy Jane Рози Джейн **40** B5
Tinkoff Тинкофф **41** B6

ENTERTAINMENT
Opera & Ballet Theatre
　Театр оперы и балета **42** B5
Philharmonic Филармония **43** B4
Vodoley Водолей........................**44** B4
Zebra Зебра **45** A6

SHOPPING
Artists' Market
　Рынок Художников **46** A5

TRANSPORT
Northern Bus Station Автовокзал.**47** B3
Railway & Air Kassa
　Железнодорожные и
　Авиа кассы ....(see 1)
Transaero City Centre Трансаэро ..**48** C5

Gutabank (☎ 359 2621; pr Lenina 27; ☼ 9am-4.30pm Mon-Fri) One of the few places in the city that accepts travellers cheques.

Main post office (pr Lenina 39; ☼ 10am-7pm Mon-Fri) Offers Internet and international telephone connections.

Ural Expeditions & Tours (☎ 376 2800; http://welcome-ural.ru; 23 Posadsakaya ul) This group of geologists from the Sverdlovsk Mining Institute has found a unique way to market its skills and knowledge – leading trekking, rafting and horse-riding trips to all parts of the Urals. English-speaking guides.

Sights

ROMANOV DEATH SITE

On the night of 16 July 1918, Tsar Nicholas II, his wife and children were murdered in the basement of a local merchant's house, known as Dom Ipateva (named for its owner Nikolai Ipatev). During the Soviet period the building housed a local museum of atheism, but it was demolished in 1977 by then-governor Boris Yeltsin, who feared it would attract monarchist sympathisers.

Today, the site, on ul Karla Libknekhta, is marked by an iron cross dating from 1991, and a second marble cross from 1998 when the Romanovs' remains were sent to St Petersburg for burial in the family vault.

The Byzantine-style **Church of the Blood** (☎ 371 6168; ul Tolmachyova 34) now dominates this site. While many believe the funds could have been better spent, this church was built to honour the Romanov family, now elevated to the status of saints. Rumour has it that the controversial church contains the most expensive icon in all of Russia.

Nearby, the pretty wooden **Chapel of the Revered Martyr Grand Princess Yelisaveta Fyodorovna** (☼ 9am-5.30pm) honours the royal family's great-aunt and faithful friend. After her relatives' murders, this pious nun met an even worse end, when she was thrown down a mineshaft, poisoned with gas and buried. You can visit this spot, where a monastery has recently been built, on a trip to Nizhnyaya Sinyachikha (p156).

Across the street from the Church of the Blood are the ostentatious **Rastorguev-Kharitonov mansion** and the restored **Ascension Church** (ul Karla Tsetkin 11). Behind them, a pretty park climbs up the hill known locally as the Yekaterinburg Acropolis.

Just east of here, pl Sovetskoy Armii is dominated by the powerful **Afghanistan War Monument**, known as the Black Rose. The giant soldier with downcast head primarily commemorates losses in Russia's Afghanistan War (1979–89), but plaques around the statue also note those lost in other conflicts during the Cold War years.

ISTORICHESKY SKVER

This area, better known as the *plotinka* (little dam), was where Yekaterinburg began back in 1723. Water from the dam (reconstructed twice since that date) powered an iron forge, a mint and a stone-cutting works. Now you'll find a clutch of tiny museums housed in the historic buildings where the city grew up. Peek into the **water tower**, one of the city's oldest structures. Then head over to the old mining-equipment factory and mint buildings. These contain the **Museum of Architecture & Industry** (☎ 371 4045; ul Gorkogo 4 & 5; ☼ 11am-6pm Tue-Sat), which displays the machinery used in the mining industry from the 18th and 19th centuries up through WWII.

East on pr Lenina, the founders of Yekaterinburg – Tatishchev and de Gennin – proudly hold the tsar's decree. This **statue** to the founders of the city was unveiled on the city's 275th anniversary in 1998. The nearby **Chapel of St Catherine** was erected in the same year on the site of a former cathedral honouring the patron saint of mining.

The bridge on ul Lenina holds the red sculpted **Order of Lenin** given to the city for honourable service during WWII. On the west side of the *plotinka* is **Geological Alley**, a small park dotted with rocks from the Ural region. The star exhibit of the **Museum of Fine Arts** (☎ 371 0626; ul Voevodina 5; admission R50; ☼ 11am-6pm Wed-Sun) is the Kasli Iron Pavilion that won prizes in the 1900 Paris Expo.

RAILWAY MUSEUM

The newest addition to Yekaterinburg's many museums is the long-awaited **railway museum** (☎ 358 4222; ul Chelyuskintsev; ☼ noon-6pm Tue-Sat). Housed in the old train station, dating from 1881, its exhibits highlight the history of the railroad in the Urals area, and include a re-creation of the office of the Stalin-era railway director.

OTHER MUSEUMS

For a stunning introduction to Urals semi-precious stones, visit Vladimir Pelepenko's private collection, also known as the **Urals**

Mineralogical Museum (☎ 350 6019; ul Krasnoarmey-skaya 1A; admission R50; ☺ 10am-7pm Mon-Fri, 10am-5pm Sat & Sun), in Bolshoy Ural Hotel. This impressive collection contains thousands of examples of minerals, stones and crystals from the region, many crafted into mosaics, jewellery and other artistic pieces.

More-serious geologists will appreciate the **Ural Geology Museum** (☎ 251 4938; ul Kuybysheva 39; admission R50; ☺ 11am-5pm Mon-Sat), which has over 500 carefully catalogued Ural region minerals and a collection of meteorites.

Activities
Winter in the Urals lasts a long time, making this a terrific place for winter sports. The rolling hills that surround Yekaterinburg are breathtaking when covered with a fresh layer of snow.

Ural Expeditions & Tours (p150) can arrange dog-sledding excursions (per person €65), as well as winter hikes and snowmobile trips.

If there's no time to leave the city, head to **Mayakovsky Park**, 5km south of town, for cross-country skiing. Take tram 3 from the train station or 29 from ul Lenina. Equipment is available to rent.

Tours
The Ekaterinburg Guide Center (p150) offers a wide variety of guided tours, the most basic being the two-hour 'brief look' (€48). Prices include transportation, museum entry and the services of an excellent, English-speaking guide. Another option is the 'Romanov Execution' tour (€77), which takes three to four hours and includes a trip to Ganina Yama (p156).

Sleeping
BUDGET
Ekaterinburg Guide Center (☎ 268 1604; www.eka terinburg-guide.com; ul Krasnoarmeyskaya 1, Bolshoy Ural Hotel, side entrance; 1-/2-/3-person homestays €22/36/52) Experience real Russian living by staying with a local family. Prices include breakfast. The agency also rents apartments for €40 to €50 per night – a bargain if you are travelling in a group.

Bolshoy Ural Hotel (☎ 350 6695; fax 355 0583; ul Krasnoarmeyskaya 1; s with/without bathroom R1450/500) This place lives up to its name: if nothing else, it is indeed *bolshoy* (large), occupying an entire city block. The somewhat seedy

atmosphere is buffered by the prime location – steps from the Opera Theatre and the all-important Gordon's Scottish pub.

Academy of Geology Hotel (☎ 350 0508, 350 0510; pr Lenina 54, Bldg 6; r with breakfast R1200) This decent budget option offers attentive service and four smart, spacious rooms. Located in a quiet complex off the main road, it is difficult to find. Enter the courtyard from ul Bazhova and look for the marble entryway with the unmarked metal door. Unfortunately, this place does not register visas, so it is not a good option for visitors staying more than a day or two.

MIDRANGE
Hotel Iset (☎ 350 0128; hotel_resr@etel.ru; pr Lenina 69; s/d with breakfast from R2900/3600) If the Iset looks funky from the street, that's because it is shaped like a hammer and sickle when seen from the sky. All the rooms at this retro Soviet-style hotel have been upgraded, featuring hardwood floors, new bathrooms and odd furniture ensembles. It's all part of the charm.

Hotel Sverdlovsk (☎ 353 6574; fax 353 6248; ul Chelyuskintsev 106; s/d from R1200/1500) Gives a choice between cheap and dilapidated rooms or upgraded and overpriced. In its favour is its location, opposite the station.

Country Inn (ul Malysheva) Under construction at the time of research, this hotel is expected to be a Western-managed three-star tourist hotel, filling a void of midrange accommodation options. It is supposed to open in 2006; contact the Ekaterinburg Guide Center (p150) for information.

TOP END
Hotel Premier (☎ 355 3882; www.premier-hotel.ru; ul Krasnoarmeyskaya 23; s/d with breakfast R4000/5300; ☒ ☐) A small and personable European-style hotel offering comfortable rooms. Rooms can be a bit stuffy in winter when air-con is not working, but otherwise they are spacious and stylish. The location offers the best of both worlds: a quiet residential street just a few steps from the main drag.

Hotel Magister (☎ 229 7044, 257 4206; magister1@ etel.ru; ul 8 Marta 50; s/d with breakfast R4100/4600; ☒ ☐) Quaint, comfortable rooms and accommodating staff make the Magister a long-standing favourite with visitors to Yekaterinburg. Brand-new windows block out the noise from the busy street below.

This small, private hotel is 'home' for many long-term business travellers, so book well in advance.

Atrium Palace Hotel (☎ 3596000; www.atriumhotel .ru; ul Kuybysheva 44; s/d €210/260; ✗ ⌨ ▣ ▣) Atrium Palace once claimed to be the only five-star hotel east of Moscow. This snazzy place has several pricey restaurants, a popular bar and nightclub, plus a fitness centre and sauna. Rack rates are quoted, but discounts are usually available, especially if you make your reservation through the Ekaterinburg Guide Center (p150).

Eating

RESTAURANTS

Dacha (☎ 379 3569; pr Lenina 20A; meals R200-300; ⌚ noon-midnight) Each room in this restaurant is decorated as a room in a Russian country house, from the casual garden to the more formal dining room. It's a great place to enjoy unbeatable Russian cuisine and hospitality.

Port Stanley (☎ 355 1955; ul Gorkogo 10; meals R600-1000; ⌚ noon-midnight) The sunny terrace on the banks of the Iset makes this a top spot for dining in summer, while the modern interior is also pleasant. The menu is seafood – not from the Iset, we hope. Sample Russian favourites like grilled sturgeon or herring salad, or more-exotic fare like sea bass or lobster.

Nigora (☎ 376 3941; ul Malysheva 19; meals R200-300; ⌚ noon-midnight) This restaurant offers spicy, filling Uzbek food – soup and *plov* (meat and rice) to fill the belly and warm the soul. Heavy wooden tables and a low, painted ceiling add to the cosy, welcoming atmosphere.

Georgian Kitchen (☎ 350 0541; ul Belinskogo 20; meals with wine R300-500; ⌚ 24hr) This is a classic Georgian place, complete with kitschy artwork and Christmas lights. But the shashlyk, *kharcho* (rice with beef or lamb and soup) and *khachapuri* (Georgian cheese bread) are spicy and delicious. And the keyboardist-crooner belting out the ballads never fails to inspire some dancing (or perhaps that's the Georgian wine).

Grand Buffet (☎ 359 8366; ul Malysheva 36; meals R250-350; ⌚ noon-midnight) All-you-can-eat buffet featuring Russian fare. You'll find nearly anything you are craving, as the basement saloon serves Tex-Mex and there's also an Italian place next door.

Em Sam (☎ 376 6066; ul Malysheva 27; meals R150-300; ⌚ 11am-midnight) Sushi is all the rage across Russia, and Yekaterinburg is no exception. Lunch specials and a convenient location make this place popular. There is another outlet in Bolshoy Ural Hotel.

QUICK EATS & SELF-CATERING

Uspensky food court (☎ 371 6744; ul Vaynera 10; meals R30-100; ⌚ 10am-8pm) On the top floor of the Uspensky shopping centre, this food court offers burgers, pizza, sandwiches, sushi and more. Floor-to-ceiling windows provide a sweeping view of the city centre and a new perspective on the activity below.

Mak Pik (☎ 371 6898; pr Lenina 24/8; meals R100; ⌚ 9am-10pm) Now located in several spots around the city, Yekaterinburg's original fast-food restaurant specialises in burgers like the 'Big Mak Pik'; it also serves pizza, *pelmeni* (Russian-style ravioli stuffed with meat) and, of all things, sushi.

Kupets (ul 8 Marta 48; ⌚ 24hr) If you're looking for a large, Western-style supermarket with a wide selection of Russian and imported food items, head here.

Drinking

Coffee Shop No 7 (☎ 378 9370; ul Voevodina 4; breakfast R100-200; ⌚ 8am-midnight) A pleasant location on the *plotinka*, smooth jazz and frothy cappuccinos. What more can you ask from your local coffee shop?

Old Dublin (☎ 376 5173; ul Khokhryakova 23; meals R400-600, 500mL Guinness R140; ⌚ noon-2am) A favourite with expats in Yekaterinburg, this pub is actually owned – partially – by an Irish bloke.

Gordon's (☎ 355 4535; Krasnoarmeyskaya ul 1; business lunches R180, meals R400-600; ⌚ noon-2am) The aforementioned Irish bloke opened this Scottish pub in 2005, and it promises to be a popular spot, thanks to the excellent food and 12 beers on tap. Bartenders in kilts don't hurt, either.

Rosy Jane (☎ 371 0607; ul Lenina 34; ⌚ 24hr) An English pub – not to be confused with the Scottish pub down the street and the Irish pub around the corner. The dark wood bar features seven draught beers and more than 150 kinds of whisky.

Tinkoff (☎ 378 4008; Krasnoarmeyskaya 64; 500mL beers R120; ⌚ noon-2am) This microbrewery features seven home-grown brews as well as some seasonal specialities, plus a menu of sausages, sandwiches and other tasty snacks. You will recognise the restaurant's open layout and industrial décor if you have been to Tinkoff outlets in other cities.

Entertainment

Vodoley (☎ 377 7277; ul Shevchenko 9; ☺ 1pm-6am) There is something for everyone at this entertainment complex – from bowling to billiards to dining to dancing. There is strict face control at the door, so be sure to dress the part.

Zebra (☎ 377 6891; ul Malysheva 44; ☺ 10pm-10am) If you are serious about dancing, this is the place to strut your stuff. Progressive, house and techno music plays all night long.

Philharmonic (☎ 371 4682; www.filarmonia.e-burg.ru; ul Karla Libknekhta 38) Yekaterinburg's top venue for the classical performing arts often hosts visiting directors and soloists, as well as the regular performances of the acclaimed Urals academic orchestra.

Opera & Ballet Theatre (☎ 350 8057; pr Lenina 45A; tickets from R100) The level of professionalism is not quite on par with the Philharmonic, but the ornate baroque theatre is still a lovely place to see the Russian classics.

Shopping

Dominated by the Stalinesque town hall and the looming statue of Lenin, the main city square, pl 1905 Goda, is about 200m west of Istorichesky Skver (square). It is flanked by two department stores and the new Uspensky shopping centre (opposite). Further west, artists sell their wares along the tree-lined strip in the centre of pr Lenina.

Getting There & Away

AIR

The main airport is **Koltsovo** (☎ 226 8909, 264 4202), 15km southeast of the city centre. Flights go three times a day to/from Moscow (R6000, 2½ hours).

Flights depart almost daily to Irkutsk (R7500, four hours), Novosibirsk (R5200, two hours), Samara (R4000, two hours), St Petersburg (R6000, 2½ hours) and Vladivostok (R13,000, 11 hours).

Some of these flights are operated by Urals Airlines, which has a poor record for safety violations (including seven emergency landings in 2004!). A US consulate advisory warns against flying on any Urals Airlines flights until this record improves.

Several airlines operate flights directly to Europe, two or three times a week: **Lufthansa** (☎ 264 7771) operates flights to Frankfurt (€400 return); **British Airways** (☎ 264 4216) flies to London (€500 return); and **Czech Airlines** (☎ 264 4214) flies directly to Prague (€550). **Transaero City Centre** (☎ 365 9165; pr Lenina 50) handles bookings for all airlines.

TRAIN

Yekaterinburg – often still 'Sverdlovsk' on timetables – is a major rail junction with connections to all stops on the Trans-Siberian route. Trains to/from Moscow go frequently, but the most comfortable one is the *Ural* (R2050, 26 hours, daily). Depending on the route, the next major destination heading west is either Perm (R650, seven hours) or Kazan (R1275, 15 hours). Trains also run to Tyumen (seat R230, 4½ hours) and Tobolsk (R630, nine hours). Heading east, the next major stops are Omsk (R1200, 12 hours) and Novosibirsk (R1280, 21 hours).

You can buy tickets at the main train station (level three in the west wing) or at outlets throughout the city, including the convenient **Railway and Air Kassa** (☎ 371 0400; ul Malysheva 31; ☺ 7am-9pm). Buying a ticket from Yekaterinburg to Moscow is rarely a problem; however, securing one eastward to Irkutsk and beyond can be tricky. If you're on a tight schedule, it's advisable to make an advance booking through a travel agency, such as Ekaterinburg Guide Center (p150).

Getting Around

Bus 1 will take you from the train station to Koltsovo airport (45 minutes) from 5.30am to 11pm.

Many trolleybuses (pay on board) run up and down ul Sverdlova/ul Karla Libknekhta between the train station and pr Lenina. Trams 4, 13, 15 and 18 and bus 28 cover long stretches of pr Lenina, with bus 4 continuing to the southern bus station. The smaller northern bus station, primarily serving regional destinations, is near the train station.

A single metro line runs between the northeastern suburbs and the city centre, with stops at the train station (Uralskaya), pl 1905 Goda and ul Kuybysheva near Hotel Magister (Geologicheskaya).

STRADDLING THE CONTINENTS

If you wish to have one foot in Europe and one in Asia, you can head 40km west of Yekaterinburg on the Moskovsky Trakt to the **Europe-Asia border**. Erected in 1837 at a 413m high point in the local Ural Mountains, the marker here is a popular spot for wedding parties to visit on their postnuptial video and photo jaunts. Hire a taxi from Yekaterinburg for R150 per hour or make arrangements for this excursion through Ekaterinburg Guide Center (p150) for €20 to €27 per person.

In an attempt to make this geographic landmark more accessible to intracontinental travellers, city officials are in the process of erecting a new, more prominent marker at another spot along the border, conveniently just 17km from Yekaterinburg. The city has grand plans for monuments, museums, parks and gift shops, as well as European and Asian restaurants on their respective sides of the border.

Sceptics should be assured that this is more than a symbolic meeting of east and west. The site – on the watershed of the Iset and Chusovaya Rivers – was confirmed by scientists who examined geological records and studied the patterns of water flow. This clash of continents is the real deal.

AROUND YEKATERINBURG
Ganina Yama Ганина Яма
After the Romanov family was shot in the cellar of Dom Ipateva, their bodies were discarded in the depths of the forests of Ganina Yama, 16km northeast of Yekaterinburg. In their honour, the Orthodox Church has built the exquisite **Monastery of the Holy Martyrs** (☎ 343-217 9146; admission free) at this pilgrimage site. Set deep in the peaceful birch forest, the wooden buildings were constructed using ancient methods, which preclude the use of nails. An observation platform overlooks the mine shaft where the remains were deposited and burned. According to the Orthodox Church, this is the final resting place of the Romanov family and therefore sacred ground.

To reach Ganina Yama by public transport, take the *elektrichka* (suburban train) to Shuvakish. Be sure to check the return train schedule in advance. If you hire a taxi from Yekaterinburg, take the road to Nizhny Tagil and look for the wooden signpost in the median 16km out of the city. Follow the signs to the monastery.

Alternatively, Ekaterinburg Guide Center (p150) offers a three-hour tour for €20 to €27 per person that goes to Ganina Yama.

Nizhnyaya Sinyachikha & Around
Нижняя Синячиха
☎ 243 / ◔ Moscow + 2hr
The pretty village of Nizhnyaya Sinyachikha, about 150km northeast of Yekaterinburg and 12km north of the town of Alapaevsk,

is home to an open-air **Architecture Museum** (☎ 246-75118; admission R20, guided tour R50; ◔ 10am-4pm). Here there are 15 traditional Siberian log buildings featuring displays of period furniture, tools and domestic articles. The stone cathedral houses a collection of Ural region folk art. This impressive collection of art and architecture was gathered from around the Urals and recompiled by the single-handed efforts of Ivan Samoylov, an enthusiastic local historian.

About 2km west of Nizhnyaya Sinyachikha is a monastery dedicated to Grand Princess Yelisaveta, on the spot where she died (see p152). Three buses a day go to Alapaevsk (R110, 3½ hours).

TYUMEN ТЮМЕНЬ
☎ 3452 / pop 507,000 / ◔ Moscow + 2hr
Founded in 1586, Tyumen was the first Russian fort in Siberia. Today the city exudes a sense of growing prosperity as the booming capital of a vast, oil-rich *oblast* (region) that stretches to the Arctic Circle. The city has a businesslike drive and youthful bustle best experienced on weekend evenings by strolling in the fairground of City Park. Pleasant and liveable, Tyumen has tree-lined streets and a fair few older buildings amid all the new construction, but if you have limited time you're better stopping in Tobolsk.

Orientation
The train station lies at the end of ul Pervomayskaya, 1.5km south of the main commercial artery, ul Respubliki, which runs

some 5km from the fine Trinity Monastery to well beyond the bus station.

City maps are sold at **Magazin Knizhny** (ul Privokzalnaya 28A, Polyklinka Bldg; ☺ 8.30am-6pm Mon-Sat, 9am-4pm Sun), hidden away near the train station.

Information
Internet Salon (ul Respubliki 12; per hr R28.80; ☺ 11am-8pm)
Main post office (ul Respubliki 56; ☺ 8am-8pm Mon-Sat, 9am-6pm Sun)
Telephone office (ul Respubliki 51; ☺ 24hr) Has prepay Internet.
Trikita (Megafon Shop, ul Melnikayte 100; Internet per hr R30; ☺ 24hr) Slow but handy for Hotel Vostok.
Web Khauz (ul Respubliki 61; Internet per hr R28; ☺ 11am-8pm) Entry from ul Profsoyuznaya, up two flights of stairs then along a balcony.

Sights
Behind a kremlinesque wall on the Tura riverside, the picturesque 1727 **Trinity Monastery** (Cvyato Troitsky; ul Kommunisticheskaya 10) is Tyumen's finest sight. But there are plenty more fine churches, notably the voluptuously curved baroque **Znamensky Cathedral** (ul Semakova 13) dating from 1786 and the similar **Saviour's Church** (ul Lenina).

The **Fine Arts Museum** (Muzey Izobrazitelnykh Iskusstv; ☎ 469 115; ul Ordzhonikidze 47; admission R40; ☺ 10am-5pm Tue-Sun) has an impressive and eclectic collection including an original by Vasily Kandinsky. Close to the large **Lenin Statue** (Tsentralnaya pl) several remnant older buildings have been turned into museums, notably the wooden **Marsharov House Museum** (☎ 461 310; ul Lenina 24; admission US$2; ☺ 9.30am-12.30pm & 1.30-4.30pm Wed-Sun) and sweet little **First House Museum** (Istoriya Adnovo Dma; ☎ 464 963; ul Respubliki 18; admission US$1; ☺ 9.30am-4.30pm Wed-Sun).

Further east, the **Geological Museum** (☎ 751 138; ul Respubliki 142) is one of the best of its type, and there's a modern **war memorial** nearby shaped like a gigantic metal candle.

Towards the train station, notice the **FD Class steam locomotive** (ul Pervomayskaya) hidden in the trees.

Sleeping
BUDGET
Hotel GUBD (☎ 247 434; ul Sovetskaya 124; s/tw R250/400) A great-value central cheapie. Some better rooms (single or twin R500) have private bathrooms.

Hotel Vostok (☎ 205 350; fax 206 124; ul Respubliki 159; s/tw from R580/740) East of the city centre but very accessible on bus 25 from the train station, this vast Soviet monster offers repainted but tired rooms with private bathrooms. A few well-renovated singles are available for R1158.

Resting rooms (komnaty otdykha; Tyumen train station; dm/tw R170/800) The clean 8th-floor dormitories share somewhat unexciting seatless toilets but have panoramic views of the endless railway activity below. Exit the station via the main doorway and re-enter by a separate door on your left.

MIDRANGE
Hotel Neftyanik (☎ 461 687; www.neftyanik.ru; ul Chelyuskintsev 12; s/tw/d R1200/1400/2040) This hotel is handy for the older parts of town, thoroughly renovated and reasonable value for money, though some staff members are less than helpful.

Hotel Prometey (☎ 250 021; fax 251 423; ul Sovetskaya 61, 5th fl; s/tw/d R1250/1700/1700) Rebuilt rooms with pleasant new furniture, although bathrooms don't quite reach the same standards. In twin rooms the beds are barely wide enough for stick insects.

Hotel Tura (☎ /fax 282 209; ul Melnikayte 103A; s/d R1370/2160) Small well-kept hotel near the Vostok with pleasantly subdued décor and new shower-booth bathrooms.

TOP END
Hotel Tyumen (Kvoliti Otel; ☎ 494 040; www.hotel tyumen.ru/en; ul Ordzhonikidze 46; s/d R3500/4400, ste R6000-7700) This is a typical international-standard business hotel complete with muzak and pinging elevators. The ground-floor Vienna Cafe has a wide-ranging English-language menu.

TO KAZAKHSTAN BY ACCIDENT
Constructed from 1892 to 1895, the original West Siberian Railway linked Chelyabinsk (252km south of Yekaterinburg) with proto-Novosibirsk via Petropavlovsk and Omsk. Between Yekaterinburg and Omsk, some trains still use this line. However, as Petropavlovsk is now in northern Kazakhstan, the route is a visa nightmare. It simply isn't worth the hassle – take a train routed via Tyumen instead.

TYUMEN

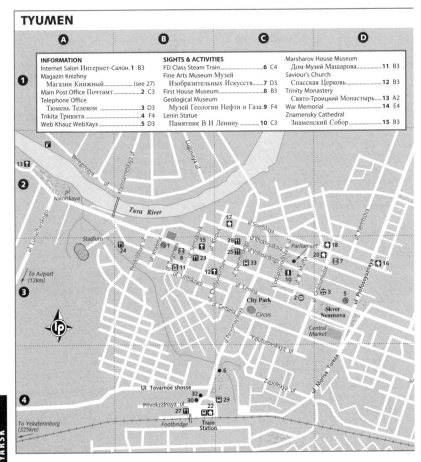

Eating & Drinking

Korolevskaya Trapeza (☎ 451 248; ul Lenina 4; business lunches R200, meals R250-650, cover after 8pm R60; ☾ noon-midnight Mon-Sat) Here you'll find imaginative and subtle Russo-European cuisine dished up in a pseudo-medieval atmosphere of high-vaulted ceilings with crusader murals. Enter from behind Osminog Casino and Italika Pizzeria.

Kofeynya (☎ 466 083; ul Semakova 19; espresso R40; ☾ 8am-11pm) Tyumen's top coffee house with an astonishing range of special grinds and *mate* (South American) teas served in authentic wooden bulbs that look like opium pipes.

Pinta Taverna (☎ 250 220; ul Dzerzhinskogo 38; meals R200-400, beers R60-100; ☾ 11am-2am) Cosy farmyard-styled cellar with waitresses in peasant costumes watched by a stunted model cow.

Pivnoy Klub (☎ 283 669; ul Melnikayte 103; meals R65-140, beers from R40; ☾ 10am-11pm) This low-key bierkeller pub has heavy wooden seats and serves perfectly cooked chicken *ragu* using wonderfully crunchy fresh vegetables. Next door is the popular Fridays fast-food joint.

Stolovaya (ul Privokzalnaya 28A, Polyclinic Bldg; meals R30-50; ☾ 7.45am-3pm & 4-10pm) Fill up for less than the cost of a coffee elsewhere in this unrepentantly Soviet-era cafeteria beside the station.

Trian Supermarket (ul Volodarskogo 23; ☾ 24hr) All-hours supermarket with hot, spit-roast chicken.

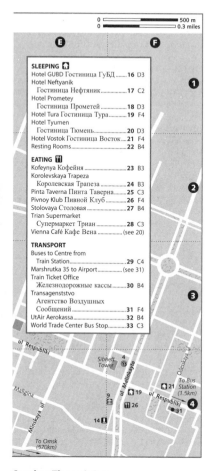

Getting There & Away

Trains depart to all Trans-Siberian destinations. Useful overnight connections include Omsk (R700, 8 hours, departs 8.47pm) and Kazan (R1100, 22 hours, departs 4pm). At least three trains daily run to Tobolsk for R180 *platskart* (*platskartny;* open carriage), taking 4½ hours, or take the bus (R260, five hours, seven daily). While the ugly train station undergoes its long-term reconstruction, rail tickets are sold across the square at ul Pervomayskaya 62. Alternatively buy them at **Transagenststvo** (ul Respubliki 156; ☼ 8am-8pm) near Hotel Vostok. It also sells air tickets. **UtAir** (☎ 453 131; ul Pervomayskaya 58A; ☼ 8am-8pm) flies to Moscow (from R5000) and various regional and Central Asian cities.

Getting Around

From the train station bus 25 serves Hotel Vostok and passes near the bus station (hop off at the 'Neptun/Stroitel' stop then walk a block east, crossing the big clover-leaf junction of uls Permyakova and Respubliki). Bus 13 from the train station loops around to the Hotel Neftyanik; switch to frequent bus 30 or 14 in front of the World Trade Center building to reach the Trinity Monastery. The route follows ul Respubliki westbound, but returns through the centre on ul Lenina. From outside Transagenststvo, *marshrutka* (fixed-route minibus) 35 (R18 plus R8 per bag, 40 minutes) runs to the airport regularly until 8.40pm.

TOBOLSK ТОБОЛЬСК

☎ 34511 / pop 98,000 / ☼ Moscow + 2hr
Star attractions of Tobolsk, Siberia's former capital, are its handsome kremlin and a charmingly decrepit old town, full of collapsing old wooden houses and churches. The city is 247km northeast of Tyumen and makes an easy alternative stopping point on your journey. Although it's off the Trans-Siberian mainline, direct overnight trains arrive from Yekaterinburg and Omsk.

An early visitor to the city was Yermak Timofeevich, whose band of Cossack mercenaries sacked the nearby Tatar stronghold of Sibir in 1582. Tobolsk's original fort was built five years later.

Although the locals were Muslim Tatars, Tobolsk became the seat of Siberia's first bishopric in 1620 as Christianity tried to stamp out incest, wife-renting and spouse-stealing by sexually frustrated Cossacks.

From 1708 the city became the region's politico-military hub but its strategic importance started to wane in the 1760s when it was bypassed by the new Great Siberian Trakt. Involuntary guests included many Decembrists (see p194) in the 1830s, Dostoevsky (en route to exile in Omsk) and Tsar Nicholas II who spent several doomed months here with his family in 1917.

The city's remarkably hospitable population remains 30% Tatar.

Orientation

The train station is 10km northeast of the modern city centre. That's an area of ugly Soviet-era concrete blocks around Hotel Slavyanskaya. Don't lose hope! Some 3km further south the delightful kremlin overlooks the intriguing old town that lies on the Irtysh flood plain below.

Information

Gazprombank (ul Oktyabrskaya; ☺ 9am-1pm & 2-4pm Mon-Thu, 9am-3pm Fri) Changes money.

Post office (Komsomolsky pr, M/R 42; ☺ 8am-6pm) Has an attached telephone office.

Servis Tsentr (per hr R28.80; ☺ 8am-10pm) An Internet service behind the post and telephone offices.

Sights

KREMLIN

Within the tower-studded 18th-century walls of the **kremlin** (☺ grounds 8am-8pm) are the intriguing but disused **Trading Arches** (Gostiny Dvor) and the glorious 1686 **St Sofia Cathedral** whose central dome has recently been gilded. Less eye-catching from outside, but containing splendid arched ceiling-murals, is the 1746 **Intercession Cathedral** (Pokrovsky Sobor). Between the two, the 1799 **bell tower** was built for the Uglich bell (below), a copy of which is in the **Museum of the Spiritual Cultures of Western Siberia** (☎ 23 715; admission R20; ☺ 10am-4pm Wed-Sun). This museum is housed within the elegant **Arkhereisky mansion**. The upper storey has a stylishly re-created 19th-century drawing room as well as plenty of stuffed animals. The middle floor has a *chum* (tepee-style cone of poles covered with skins or strips of bark) amid some interesting ethnographic items. The museum shop sells detailed but hard-to-read city maps. The eerie 1855 **Tyuremny Zamok** (Krasnaya pl 5; admission R20; ☺ 10am-4pm

---

THE FIRST SIBERIAN EXILE

Russian history is surreal. The first famous exile to Siberia was not human but a 300kg bell. In 1581 this **Uglich bell** had been used to call an insurrection on the murder of Tsar Boris Godunov's heir Tsarevich Dmitry. Astonishingly, Godunov's wrath turned upon the inanimate bell: he ordered it to be publicly flogged, had its tongue ripped out and then ordered it to be dragged to Tobolsk by banished citizens. Did the flogger smirk? Sadly, there's no record. The bell later regained its metallic voice in a specially built tower in Tobolsk's kremlin but it has long since sneaked home to Uglich.

Wed-Sun) was once a holding-prison where tsarist exiles were temporarily incarcerated awaiting their final rural banishment.

OUTSIDE THE KREMLIN

Built in 1887 for Tobolsk's 300th anniversary, the delightful little **Fine Art Museum** (ul Oktyabrskaya; admission R35, video cameras R100; ☺ 10am-5pm Wed-Sun) contains a collection of WWI-era Russian avant-garde canvases. Arguably more interesting are the fine local bone-carvings. Some are by Minsalim Timergazeev, a spiritual Tatar eccentric with wild-flowing grey hair who has his own workshop in the art shop next door, **Minsalim Folk Trade** (☎ 22 650; dimini@zmail.ru; ul Oktyabrskaya 2; admission free; ☺ 9am-5pm). For many travellers, meeting Minsalim is one of the highlights of a trip to Siberia. He'll happily demonstrate how to turn antler fragments into shaman-shapes using Heath Robinson–esque elastic-band technology. His son speaks English.

OLD TOWN

Wooden stairs lead down beneath the kremlin's **Pryamskoi Vzvoz** (gateway) to the wonderful old town, full of weather-beaten, partly ruined churches and angled wooden homes sinking into the soggy marshland.

Near the 1918 **Victory Chapel**, uls Mira and Kirova converge at a small square. Here the **Tobolsk Rayon Administration Building** (ul Mira 10) was the exile home of the last tsar before his journey to execution in Yekaterinburg. The **Tsar Nicolas II Office-Museum** (Kabinet-Muzey Imperatora Nikolaya II; ☎ 22 776; admission R15), upstairs beyond a security check, is one small room restored close to its 1917 appearance.

The **Archangel Mikhail Church** (ul Lenina 24) two blocks east has a colourfully restored interior. The character of Tatianna Larina in Alexander Pushkin's *Eugene Onegin* is said to have been modelled on Natalia Fonvizina, a Decembrist wife who prayed here when not cultivating pineapples in her hothouse. More photogenic is the semiderelict 1759 **Zachary and Elisabeth Church** (ul Bazarnaya ploschad) with soaring black-tipped spires. Beyond the main red-brick **mosque** (☎ 22 748; ul Pushkina 27), weave through the muddy lanes of Tatar cottages to reach the splendid baroque shell of the **Krestovozdvizhenskaya Church**.

The modest **Siberian-Tatar Cultural Centre** (Tsentr Sibirsko-Tatarskoi Kultur; ☎ 22 713; ul Yershova 30)

has a minor museum (admission R10; ⏱9am to noon and 1pm to 5pm Monday to Friday), exhibitions and occasional Tatar musical shows.

Sleeping & Eating

Hotel Sibir (☎ 22 390; pl Remezova 1; with breakfast s R490-650, tw/ste R1300/1330) Perfectly situated

for the kremlin, this good-value hotel has flashes of style, most notably in some of its full-facility suites. Unremarkable standard single rooms have share-pair bathrooms for R490 and private ones for R650. Breakfast is served in its inviting restaurant.

Hotel Slavyanskaya (☎ 99 101; www.hotel.tob.ru in Russian; 9th Mikrorayon, ul Mendeleeva; s/tw R2000/3500;

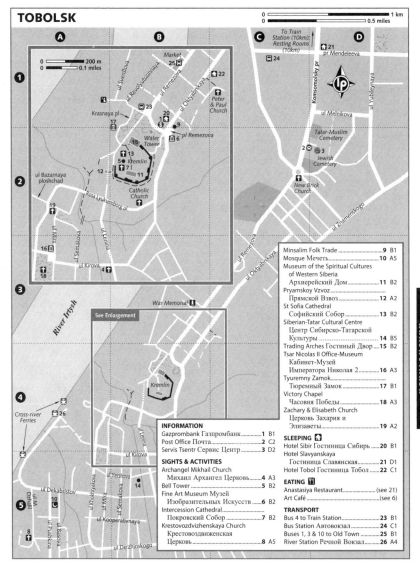

TOBOLSK

0 ——— 1 km
0 ——— 0.5 miles

Minsalim Folk Trade	**9** B1
Mosque Мечеть	**10** A5
Museum of the Spiritual Cultures	
of Western Siberia	
Архиерейский Дом	**11** B2
Pryamskoy Vzvoz	
Прямской Взвоз	**12** A2
St Sofia Cathedral	
Софийский Собор	**13** B2
Siberian-Tatar Cultural Centre	
Центр Сибирско-Татарской	
Культуры	**14** B5
Trading Arches Гостиный Двор	**15** B2
Tsar Nicolas II Office-Museum	
Кабинет-Музей	
Императора Николая 2	**16** A3
Tyuremny Zamok	
Тюремный Замок	**17** B1
Victory Chapel	
Часовня Победы	**18** A3
Zachary & Elisabeth Church	
Церковь Захария и	
Элизаветы	**19** A2

SLEEPING 🛏
Hotel Sibir Гостиница Сибирь ... **20** B1
Hotel Slavyanskaya
   Гостиница Славянская ... **21** D1
Hotel Tobol Гостиница Тобол ... **22** C1

EATING 🍴
Anastasiya Restaurant ... (see 21)
Art Café ... (see 6)

TRANSPORT
Bus 4 to Train Station ... **23** B1
Bus Station Автовокзал ... **24** C1
Buses 1, 3 & 10 to Old Town ... **25** B1
River Station Речной Вокзал ... **26** A4

INFORMATION
Gazprombank Газпромбанк ... **1** B1
Post Office Почта ... **2** C2
Servis Tsentr Сервис Центр ... **3** D2

SIGHTS & ACTIVITIES
Archangel Mikhail Church
   Михаил Архангел Церковь ... **4** A3
Bell Tower ... **5** B2
Fine Art Museum Музей
   Изобразительных Искусств ... **6** B2
Intercession Cathedral
   Покровский Собор ... **7** B2
Krestovozdvizhenskaya Church
   Крестовоздвиженская
   Церковь ... **8** A5

YURI GAGARIN LIVES! *M Guppy, Worthing, UK*

The train ride's alcoholic theme had been set that morning when a kindly couple with two be-mused toddlers treated me to breakfast. Thoughtful. But challenging. Vodka and *sala* (salted pork fat) aren't really my thing. Especially not before 10am. Then that evening I met Yuri Gagarin. No, not THE Yuri Gagarin, of course. The great cosmonaut has long since mutated from living human to heroic icon. This fresh-faced young Yuri, nonetheless, had some pretty astonishing talents of his own when it came to 'rocket fuel'. In a single evening, while wowing many impressionable young ladies with his ID card, he managed to consume almost 10L of beer. Predictably the toilet stayed busy all night.

P)) This unusually luxurious Western-standard hotel suffers somewhat from its un-exciting new-town position. Some discounts are available.

Resting rooms (komnaty otdykha; ☎ 95 222; train station; dm R178) Clean and friendly, the po-sition's utterly impractical for visiting the city but ideal if you're arriving blurry-eyed off the Omsk train or awaiting the 5.23am service to Tyumen. Showers cost R35 extra.

Hotel Tobol (☎ 46 614; ul Oktyabrskaya 20; s/d/tw R420/780/960) Dingy last resort.

Art Café (☎ 24 347; ul Oktyabrskaya; coffee R40, meals R350) Anglo-Iranian owner Jacob can cook up British, Russian or international meals to order, bakes fat-free cakes and tells improbable but true yarns of his former hair-pulling antics. It's in the Fine Art Mu-seum (see p160) basement.

Anastasiya Restaurant (☎ 40 138; meals R200-450; 7am-11pm) Seek out the great downstairs pub at Hotel Slavyanskaya, and eat at its unexpectedly good-value restaurant.

Getting There & Away

Tobolsk is a stop on the line to Nizhnevar-tovsk, Purpe and Novy Urengoy. Connec-tions to Trans-Siberian stations include overnighters from Yekaterinburg (R850, 12 hours) and Omsk (R890, 12 hours), though the latter arrives at 5am northbound. For Tyumen, trains (R167 *platskart*, 4¾ hours) are supplemented by seven daily buses (R260, five hours). Buses run several times daily to Tyumen (R260, five hours).

From the **river station** (☎ 96 617) ex-tremely slow river ferries travel south to Omsk (third/first class R612/1674, three per month in summer), taking over two days. Heading north allow almost five days to reach the Arctic-Circle city of Salekhard (R740/2411).

Getting Around

Bus 4 and *marshrutka* 20 link the train sta-tion, new town and kremlin. Buses 1, 3 and 10 travel past the kremlin and loop around the old town. Bus 1 passes the mosque.

OMSK ОМСК

☎ 3812 / pop 1.3 million / Moscow + 3hr

Don't be put off by your first impressions of Omsk, 568km east of Tyumen. Crossing the Irtysh River you'll see a line of giant cranes like skeletal giraffes and the usual rows of drab apartment blocks. But the old city centre, where the Om River joins the Irtysh, has parks, quirky public sculptures and a stretch of stately 19th-century build-ings along ul Lenina, the main shopping drag. There's also decent-value budget ac-commodation and great dining, but the main incentive to stop in Omsk is that it neatly breaks the journey from Tobolsk (or Yekaterinburg) to Tomsk (or Novosibirsk) into two painless overnight rides.

History

Starting as a 1716 Cossack outpost, by 1824 Omsk had replaced Tobolsk as the seat of the governor general of Siberia. It became a major dumping ground for exiles. These included Dostoevsky, whose *Buried Alive in Siberia* describes the writer's wretched Omsk imprisonment (1849–53) during which he nearly died from a flogging. During the Civil War, Admiral Alexander Kolchak briefly made Omsk the seat of his anti-Bolshevik government until fleeing to Irkutsk where he was executed in 1919. Today Omsk is an-other city doing quite nicely on the proceeds of Russia's oil boom.

Orientation

From the train station, 4km south of the city centre, jump straight onto trolleybus

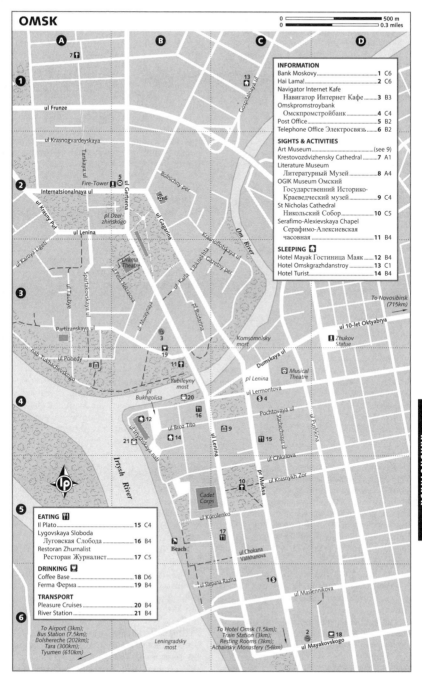

OMSK

0 ——————————— 500 m
0 ——————————— 0.3 miles

INFORMATION
Bank Moskovy..................................**1** C6
Hai Lama!..**2** C6
Navigator Internet Kafe
    Навигатор Интернет Кафе **3** B3
Omskpromstroybank
    Омскпромстройбанк.................**4** C4
Post Office......................................**5** B2
Telephone Office Электросвязь...**6** B2

SIGHTS & ACTIVITIES
Art Museum..............................(see 9)
Krestovozdvizhensky Cathedral **7** A1
Literature Museum
    Литературный Музей.................**8** A4
OGIK Museum Омский
    Государственний Историко-
    Краеведческий музей.................**9** C4
St Nicholas Cathedral
    Никольский Собор......................**10** C5
Serafimo-Alexievskaya Chapel
    Серафимо-Алексиевская
    часовная **11** B4

SLEEPING
Hotel Mayak Гостиница Маяк **12** B4
Hotel Omskgrazhdanstroy **13** C1
Hotel Turist....................................**14** B4

EATING
Il Plato...**15** C4
Lygovskaya Sloboda
    Луговская Слобода **16** B4
Restoran Zhurnalist
    Ресторан Журналист..................**17** C5

DRINKING
Coffee Base **18** D6
Ferma Ферма **19** B4

TRANSPORT
Pleasure Cruises **20** B4
River Station **21** B4

ul Frunze

ul Krasnogvardeyskaya

Tarskaya ul

Fire-Tower

Internatsionalnaya ul

ul Krasny Put

ul Lenina

ul Karola Ligeti

pl Dzer-
zhinskogo

ul Gagarina

ul Gertsena

Bolnichny per

Krasnoflotskaya ul

Om River

Gospitalnaya ul

Lizknekhta

Gazety per

Drama
Theatre

ul Taube

Spartakovskaya ul

ul Pavl Nikitina

ul Karla

Lizknekhta

pl Buddina

To Novosibirsk
(715km)

ul 10-let Oktyabrya

Partizanskaya ul

nab Tukhachevskogo

ul Pobedy

Komsomolsky
most

Zhukov
Statue

Dumskaya ul

Musical
Theatre

Yubileyny
most

pl
Bukhgolisa

pl Lenina

ul Lermontova

Pochtovaya ul

ul Pushkina

Stachechnaya ul

Stachechnaya ul

ul Broz Tito

ul Lenina

ul Chkalova

Irtysh River

ul Irtyshskaya nab

Cadet
Corps

pr Marksa

ul Krasnykh Zor

ul Korolenko

Beach

ul Chokana
Valikhanova

ul Stepana Razina

ul Maslennikova

To Airport (3km);
Bus Station (7.5km);
Bolshereche (202km);
Tara (300km);
Tyumen (610km)

Leningradsky
most

To Hotel Omsk (1.5km);
Train Station (3km);
Resting Rooms (3km);
Achairsky Monastery (54km)

ul Mayakovskogo

4 up pr Marksa, a major commercial thoroughfare with stolidly Soviet architecture. Get off at central pl Lenina, dominated by a hideous musical theatre with a roof like a giant ski jump. From near here the city's attractive old core stretches north along ul Lenina across the little Om River.

Information

Bank Moskovy (pr Marksa 10; ☑ 10am-1pm & 1.45-4pm Mon-Fri, 10am-3pm Sat) Good euro rates and 24-hour ATM.

Hai Lama! (☎ 287 866; ul Mayakovskogo 15; per hr R25 plus per MB R3; ☑ 24hr) Fast Internet.

Navigator Internet Kafe (ul Lenina 14/1; per hr R25-35 plus per MB R3, beers R30-60; ☑ 9am-10pm) Nightshift R90 to R120 plus R2 per MB.

Omskpromstroybank (ul Lermontova 20; ☑ 10am-2pm & 3-6pm Tue-Fri, 9am-2pm Sat) Good dollar rates.

Post office (ul Gertsena 1; ☑ 8am-7pm Mon-Sat, 10am-5pm Sun)

Telephone office (ul Gagarina 34; ☑ 24hr)

Sights

Pseudo-Napoleonic flourishes make the **Drama Theatre** Omsk's most ornate historical building, though other fine century-old buildings can be found down ul Lenina to the pointy little 1908 **Serafimo-Alexievskaya Chapel**. Across Yubileyny most (Yubileyny bridge) the **OGIK Museum** (Omsky Gosudarstvenny Istoriko-Krayevadchesky muzey; ☎ 314 747; ul Lenina 23A; admission R25; ☑ 10am-6.30pm Tue-Sun) has a strong historical and ethnographic collection and an historic framed map of the original Trans-Sib line running from Chelyabinsk to Vladivostok. The next-door **Art Museum** (Omsky Muzey Iskusstv; ☎ 313 677; admission R100; ☑ 10am-6pm Tue-Sun) has a lot of fussy pottery but the rectilinear 1862 building is a curiosity in itself. It was built as the Siberian governor's mansion, hosted passing tsars (an original throne survives) and housed the government of the counterrevolutionary Whites during Kolchak's brief reign (1918–19).

Further south, the stately 19th-century **St Nicholas Cathedral** (Svyato-Nikolsky Sobor; ul Lenina 27A) was used as a cinema during Soviet times.

The limited attractions of the **Literature Museum** (☎ 242 965; ul Dostoevskogo 1; admission R40; ☑ 10am-6pm Tue-Sun) include interesting old city photos and some Dostoevsky doodles from his unhappy Omsk years.

Activities

Fancy a **river trip**? Various pleasure boats depart regularly from just west of Yubileyny most. Scenery is nothing special but for a relaxing afternoon you could float 55km to **Achairsky Monastery** (R160, 4½ hours return). The complex has been totally rebuilt since 1992, having been used as an infamous Gulag in earlier decades. Highlights are the impressive five-storey bell tower and a holy spring that flows out beneath a cute wooden chapel in the birch woods nearby.

Sleeping

BUDGET

Hotel Omskgrazhdanstroy (☎ 251 247; ul Gospitalnaya 19; dm/s/tw R210/350/660) Rooms are not sexy but they are clean, large and remarkably good value. All have private bathrooms. The area isn't attractive but it's within walking distance of the historic centre.

Resting rooms (komnaty otdykha; ☎ 442 347; dm/tw R250/700) Rebuilt, clean and unusually appealing, they're in a separate building: exit the main station, turn left and find the door before the baggage *kassa* (ticket office).

Hotel Omsk (☎ 310 721; fax 315 222; ul Irtyshskaya Naberezhnaya 30; dm R350, s R650-1200, tw R1200-1600) This tall, drab concrete block is very rarely full. Somewhat shabby, typically Soviet rooms are survivable and some have views. It's halfway between the train station and the centre: take any bus along pr Marksa to the circus then walk five minutes through Pobedy Park to the riverside.

MIDRANGE

Hotel Mayak (☎ /fax 315 431; www.hotel-mayak.ru; ul Lermontova 2; s/tw R1920/2640) Within the rounded end of the vaguely ship-shaped Art Deco river station, the small, stylish rooms have artistic lines. Reception is friendly and rates are half if you stay under 12 hours.

Hotel Turist (☎ 316 419; www.tourist-omsk.ru; ul Broz Tito 2; s R1330-2100, tw R1640-2350) The best rooms are splendidly rebuilt and well worth the price. However, economy versions are looking pretty worn. Some English is spoken at the smart new reception.

Eating & Drinking

Restoran Zhurnalist (☎ 511 313; ul Lenina 34; lunches R90-160, dinners R270-600; ☑ noon-1am) This reliable restaurant has tasty, good-value Russian food and an atmospheric interior of framed cameras, ticking old clocks and newspaper ceilings.

Ferma (☎ 247 827; ul Partizanskaya 2; beers R45-60, snacks R80-200; ☽ noon-midnight) Communist iconography is delightfully mocked in this amusing cellar bar-café beneath a splendid old-Omsk building. Original 1960s posters need no commentary as they hilariously explain how to deal with bacteriological attack (ie cockroaches) and how to slice the ideologically perfect cheese-and-salami sandwich.

Lygovskaya Sloboda (☎ 311 540; ul Lenina 20; meals R350-1000; ☽ noon-1am) This appealingly traditional, upmarket Russian restaurant has a handy bakers' window (☽ 10am to 8pm) in the side selling tempting pastries and croissants.

Il Plato (☎ 310 315; ul Marksa 5; salad-bar lunches R150-215, dinners to R600; ☽ 9am-midnight Mon-Sat, noon-midnight Sun) Handily situated and much nicer than you'd guess from the ugly exterior, this chain pizzeria does R90 omelette-and-toast breakfasts with bottomless coffee. In the same building are a roast chicken joint and a Czech-retro pub-restaurant.

Coffee Base (ul Mayakovskogo 17; coffee R29-100; ☽ 10am-11pm) Caffeine heaven.

Getting There & Away

Westbound trains on the main Trans-Siberian line travel regularly to Moscow (42 hours). Train 67 is best for Yekaterinburg (R1200, 13 hours) via Tyumen (R700, 7½ hours). For Tobolsk (R410 *platskart*, 13¾ hours, departs 4pm), train 395 gets in bright and early. Eastbound, train 88 is best for Novosibirsk (R420 *platskart*, 9½ hours) but there's also a direct train to much more interesting Tomsk (trains 38 or 272; R620 *platskart*, 14 hours). Although train tickets are sold conveniently from the **rechnoy vokzal** (river station; ☎ 398 563; pl Bukhgoltsa; ☽ 9am-7pm), commission can be a whopping R150. Here you can also buy air tickets or catch very leisurely Rechflot ferries to Tobolsk (R612/1674 third/first class, 62 hours) three times monthly in summer.

Omsk's **airport** (☎ 517 570; ul Inzhenernaya 1) is on the western bank of the Irtysh River. Useful domestic destinations include Moscow (R5500, several daily), St Petersburg (R5510, twice weekly) and Irkutsk (R6050, three times weekly).

Getting Around

From the train station, trolleybus 4 and *marshrutka* 335 run along pr Marksa to pl Lenina, past the main post office and on for miles up Krasny Put. No 60 serves the airport.

NOVOSIBIRSK НОВОСИБИРСК

☎ 383 / pop 1.5 million / ☽ Moscow + 3hr

This city wouldn't exist if it wasn't for the Trans-Siberian Railway. Train enthusiasts may wish to see Siberia's biggest station, a new railway museum and a locomotive collection at nearby Seyatel. And those seeking Irish bars will be delighted by the choice. However, for atmosphere and sightseeing consider stopping in Tomsk instead. Either Novosibirsk or Tomsk make possible starting points for visiting the beautiful Altai Mountains (see p178).

History

Founded in 1893, the city grew around the Ob River bridge that was then being built for the Trans-Siberian Railway. Named Novo-Nikolayevsk until 1925 for the last tsar, it grew rapidly into Siberia's biggest metropolis, a key industrial and transport centre exploiting coalfields to the east and mineral deposits in the Urals. In the 1930s the construction of the Turkestan-Siberian (Turk-Sib) railway south from Novosibirsk to Almaty in Kazakhstan made the city a crucial transport link between Russia and Central Asia.

Orientation

Despite its daunting scale, Siberia's biggest city has a relaxed and manageable centre. Vokzalnaya magistral runs 1.5km from the train station, meeting the main commercial axis, Krasny pr, at central pl Lenina. Some 30km south of the centre near the great Ob Sea (reservoir), Akademgorodok is Siberia's biggest and best known 'science suburb'.

MAPS

Dom Knigi (Krasny pr 51; ☽ 10am-8pm Mon-Sat, 10am-7pm Sun) bookshop has a good range of maps including detailed Altai topographics, if you're heading for the hills.

Information

Paying for a night at Hotel Sibir is the only 100% certain way to get tourist visas registered. Hotel Novosibirsk might also oblige.

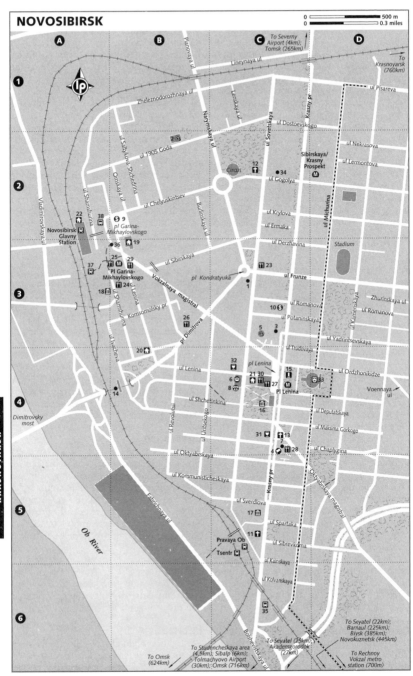

NOVOSIBIRSK

0   500 m
0   0.3 miles

To Severny
Airport (4km);
Tomsk (265km)

To
Krasnoyarsk
(760km)

ul Pisareva

Lineynaya ul

Panovaya ul

Zheleznodorozhnaya ul

ul Dostoevskogo

Lenskaya ul

Narymskaya ul

ul 1905 Goda

2 @

ul Saltykova-Shchedrina

Omskaya ul

ul Chelyuskintsev

Circus

12

● 34

ul Gogolya

Sibirskaya/
Krasny
Prospekt
Ⓜ

ul Nekrasova

ul Lermontova

ul Krylova

ul Ermaka

ul Shamshurina

Novosibirsk
Glavny
Station

22

38

● 9
pl Garina-
Mikhaylovskogo

● 36

19

ul Derzhavina

ul Michurina

Stadium

25   29
pl Garina-
Mikhaylovskogo
37   Ⓜ
24

ul Sibirskaya

Vokzalnaya magistral

23

ul Frunze

18   ul Lenina

Komsomolsky pr

pl Kondratyuka

1

10 ●

ul Romanova

ul Kamenskaya

Zhurinskaya ul

ul Romanova

ul Shamshurina

ul Nacheva

26

pr Dimitrova

ul Potaninskaya

5
@

3
●

ul Yadrintsevskaya

20

ul Trudovaya

ul Lenina

32

pl Lenina

21 30

15

Ⓜ

33

ul Ordzhonikidze

Voennaya
ul

ul Revolutsii

ul Uritskogo

6 ⊗
8

27
Pl Lenina

14

ul Shchetinkina

16

ul Deputatskaya

ul Maksima Gorkogo

31

13

ul Chaplygina

4

28

ul Oktyabrskaya

Krasny pr

Oktyabrskaya magistral

ul Kommunisticheskaya

Fabrichnaya ul

Ob River

ul Sverdlova

17

ul Spartaka

11

Pravaya Ob
Tsentr

ul Sibrevkoma

ul Kainskaya

ul Kolyvanskaya

35

Bolshevistskaya ul

To Seyatel (22km);
Barnaul (225km);
Biysk (385km);
Novokuznetsk (445km)

To Seyatel (25km);
Akademgorodok
(27km)

To Studencheskaya area
(4.5km); Sibalp (6km);
Tolmachyovo Airport
(30km); Omsk (716km)

To Omsk
(624km)

To Rechnoy
Vokzal metro
station (700m)

Dimitrovsky
most

INTERNET ACCESS

Computer Klub Arena (☎ 220 3939; ul 1905 Goda 41; per hr R15 plus per MB R3; ☺ 8am-9pm) Fun, submarine décor interior accessed downstairs through the courtyard of a school. Nightshift R110 from 10pm, booking required.

Internet Tsentr (☎ 291 8841; ul Trudovaya 1; per 30min R30; ☺ 9am-10pm) Beneath an apartment block down the first alley off Vokzalnaya magistral walking from pl Lenina. Nightshift R110.

MONEY

TransKreditBank (ul Lenina 86; ☺ 9.30am-1pm & 2-5pm Mon-Fri) Handy for the train station. The ATM works 24 hours.

Vneshtorgbank (Krasny pr 35; ☺ 9am-5pm Mon-Sat) Decent euro rates.

POST

Main post office (ul Lenina 5; ☺ 8am-9pm Mon-Fri, 8am-7pm Sat & Sun)

TELEPHONE

Telephone office (ul Sovetskaya 33; ☺ 24hr)

TRAVEL AGENCIES

Altair (☎ 212 5115; www.altairtour.ru; ul Sovetskaya 65, office 15) Helpful, with English spoken.

Sibalp (☎ 346 3191; http://sibalp.unpo.ru) Specialists for tailor-made small-group Altai exploration trips. English-speaking homestays and city tours arranged. Will meet travellers at their hotel.

STA-Novosibirsk (☎ 223 9534; www.sibtravel.com/eng; ul Oktyabrskaya 45A; ☺ 7am-1pm & 2-6pm) Can book you into 'closed' hotels for just R100 over normal costs.

Sights

Novosibirsk's pl Lenina is dominated by the huge, silver-domed **Opera & Ballet Theatre** (Krasny pr 36; ☺ season Oct-Jun). Bigger than Moscow's Bolshoi, its grand interior alone makes performances one of the city's highlights (see p177). In front, wearing a flapping coat, the dashing **Lenin statue** is flanked by waving partisans vainly trying to direct the chaotic traffic.

Close to the train station, the brand-new **West Siberian Railway Museum** (☎ 345 7359; ul Shamshurina; admission free; ☺ 8am-5pm Mon-Fri) should be open by the time you read this. There's also a somewhat tatty **FD21 Steam Locomotive** where pr Dimitrova tunnels under the tracks.

In an elegant mansion, the **Local Studies Museum** (Kraevedchesky muzey; ☎ 218 1773; Krasny pr 23; admission R150; ☺ 10am-5.30pm Tue-Sun) has Altai shaman coats, cutaway pioneer houses and some splendid religious artefacts. The **State Art Museum** (Khudozhestvenny muzey; ☎ 223 3516; http://gallery.nsc.ru; Krasny pr 5; adult/student R150/80; ☺ 10am-5.20pm Tue-Fri, 11am-5.20pm Sat & Sun) has an extensive collection including icons and distinctive mountainscapes by celebrated Russian painter Nikolai Rerikh.

The pretty little **Chapel of St Nicholas** (Chasovnya Svyatitelya Nikolaya; pr Krasny) was said to mark the geographical centre of Russia when built in 1915. Demolished in the 1930s, it was rebuilt in 1993 for Novosibirsk's centenary. The gold-domed 1914 **Cathedral of the**

Ascension (Voznesensky sobor; ul Sovetskaya 91) has a wonderful, colourful interior with a soaring central space that's unexpected from its fairly squat exterior appearance. The 1898 **Alexander Nevsky Cathedral** (sobor Alexandra Nevskogo; Krasny pr 1A) is a red-brick Byzantine-style building with gilded domes and bright new murals.

Sleeping

Novosibirsk hotels are poor value by Siberian standards. Currently only those that we list here accept foreigners, though some others will if booked through a travel agency (p167).

Hotel Sibir (☎ 223 1215; centre@gk-sibir.sibnet.ru; ul Lenina 21; s/d with breakfast from R2100/2600; 🖳) Proudly considering itself 'international', the Sibir has English-speaking receptionists, money exchange, tour and ticketing booths and a lounge bar in its unrepentantly 1970s lobby. King bedded 'studios' (double R5400 with air-con) are splendid. However, in the styleless standard rooms the parquet floors are worn and some of the furniture is ageing.

Station Hotel (☎ 229 2376; Novosibirsk Glavny train station, 2nd fl; dm/tw/tr R500/1200/1500, s/tw with bathroom R2800/3500) Only for those with onward rail tickets. Half-price for 12-hour stays. It's frequently full.

Hotel Tsentralnaya (☎ 222 3638; fax 227 660; Lenina 3; s/tw R700/1000, with bathroom R1500/2200) Perfectly central. The no-frills basic rooms here have shared, survivable bathrooms and dodgy lifts. While it's hardly exciting, this is Novosibirsk's best available budget option. However, sometimes foreigners are randomly refused.

Hotel Novosibirsk (☎ 220 1120; fax 216 517; Vokzalnaya magistral 1; s/tw with breakfast from R1100/1700) Opposite Novosibirsk Glavny train station, this glum 23-storey Soviet-era tower has mediocre, overpriced Soviet-era rooms. The cheapest share a toilet and washbasin between pairs of rooms and lack showers altogether. You'll pay over R1800 for a private bathroom. Breakfast is lacklustre.

Homestays (s R700-1000, tw R1100-1500) are organised through **Uyut Kvartirnoe Byuro** (☎ 202 009; www.risp.ru/~hotel in Russian; Novosibirsk Glavny train station). Rates are half-price for 12 hours. For similar rates, tour agency **Sibalp** (☎ 346 3191; http://sibalp.unpo.ru) can arrange English-speaking hosts.

Eating

The choice is endless within a block or two of pl Lenina – just stroll down ul Lenina, Krasny pr or Vokzalnaya magistral where the Irish pubs and Wild West bars also do good, if pricey, food. Marginally cheaper eateries huddle near metro Studencheskaya.

Zhili Byli (ul Lenina 1; meals R130-450; 🕑 11am-11pm) Prices are reasonable in this central, Disney-esque 'Siberian village'. There's an English menu, and stuffed bliny for R45 to R90. It's above GrillMaster (burgers R39 to R54) and Pizza-Pasta (slices R36 to R42).

Lanch Kafe (☎ 270 581; meals R200-350) At the rear of the Zhili Byli building, entered from the park, is this popular place, above which are a great Italian restaurant and a chilled-out, cushion-floored DJ-bar serving sushi.

Mexico Kafe (☎ 210 3420; Oktyabrskaya magistral 49; meals R350-800; 🕑 noon-1am) Great Mexican food served within an atmospheric basement decorated with Aztec icons.

Ne Goryuy (☎ 217 5636; meals R300-900; 🕑 noon-1am) Down the next stairway from Mexico Kafe is this ultramodern, mood-lit basement for classy Georgian cuisine.

Balkan Grill (☎ 217 2288; ul Frunze 3; meals R500-1300, beers R190; 🕑 11am-11pm) Whitewashed brickwork and vines give a Mediterranean feel. The menu is in English and the portions are enormous. Credit cards accepted.

Blues Kafe (☎ 346 1931; ul Geodezicheskaya 1; beers R50-70, lunch R95-125 before 5pm) This cosy place is near Studencheskaya metro, one block west through the market. *Chiziki* (cheese balls; R60) are better than the BB King salad.

QUICK EATS & SELF-CATERING

Kuzhina (☎ 229 4119; pr Dimitrova 1A; meals R140-250; 🕑 11am-10pm) This is a relatively upmarket point-and-pick cafeteria chain. Amid giant vegetables, the décor has an olde-Russia feel despite the angular new glass architecture.

Blinnaya (ul Vokzalnaya 2; snacks R20-45; 🕑 9am-10pm; 🉑) A neat, unpretentious little place handy for a pancake, or an R9 Nescafé or R38 beer while awaiting a train.

Kaskad (ul Vokzalnaya 2; 🕑 7.30am-10pm) Multi-roomed grocery store with a takeaway, pay-by-weight salad bar and a basic sit-down *pelmenaya* (place serving dumplings).

Supermarket Khoroshy (Vokzalnaya magistral 4; 🕑 24hr) Sells groceries at any time.

(Continued on page 177)

St Isaac's Cathedral (p87), St Petersburg

Rostral Column (p88), the Strelka,
Vasilyevsky Island, St Petersburg

Statues, Grand Cascade & Water Avenue
(p95), Petrodvorets, St Petersburg

Marble Palace (p85), St Petersburg

Kremlin (p104), Moscow

Guitarist, Moscow (p118)

Wall of Peace (p109), Ulitsa Arbat, Moscow

Lenin's Tomb (p108), Red Sq, Mocsow

Statue and Kremlin (p144), Kazan

SIMON RICHMOND

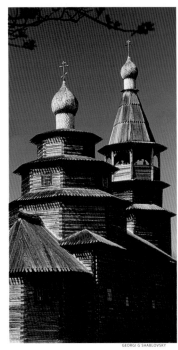
GEORGI G SHABLOVSKY
Wooden churches, Nizhny Novgorod (p134)

Muslim men at mosque (p144), Kazan
PETER SOLNESS

Lenin mural, Krasnoyarsk station, Krasnoyarsk (p185)

Russian women, Novosibirsk (p165)

Mosque, Tobolsk (p159)

Olkhon Island (p203), Lake Baikal

Vladivostok station, Vladivostok (p230)

Pedestrians, Chita (p219)

Horses of the Buryat people (p212), Ulan-Ude

174

PETER SOLNESS

Track workers, Khabarovsk (p224)

Selling *airag* (fermented mare's milk; p69) to passengers at train station, Sainshand (p257)

PATRICK HORTON

Train cook at station, Novosibirsk (p165)

PETER SO

Zaisan Memorial (p261), Ulaanbaatar

Milk being filtered to make *airag* (p69)

Locals playing draughts and chess,
Ulaanbaatar (p257)

Horse race, Naadam Festival (p262)

Forbidden City (p281), Beijing

Martial arts, Beijing (p279)

Hutong (narrow alleyways; p286), Beijing

Gate of Heavenly Peace (p284), Tiananmen Square, Beijing

(Continued from page 168)

Drinking

People's Bar & Grill (☎ 275 5000; Krasny pr; beers from R48, espressos R39; ☺ noon-2am) This top people-watching spot has a hip modern vibe and an Anglo-American retro theme. Enter down stairs opposite St Nicholas chapel.

Saint Patrick's (☎ 222 2296; ul Lenina 8; ☺ noon-2am) Downstairs through this could-be-anywhere Irish bar, the Tserp I Molot (Hammer & Sickle) karaoke bar is amusingly decked with tongue-in-cheek Soviet iconography.

Entertainment

Novosibirsk is a lively place with dozens of nightclubs, bowling alleys, concert halls and theatres fully listed in Russian on www .novosibout.ru.

Opera & Ballet Theatre (☎ 227 1537; www.opera -novosibirsk.ru; Krasny pr 36; admission R35-200; ☺ Sep-Jun) Don't miss a night at this gigantic venue.

Rock City (☎ 227 0108; www.rockcity.ru in Russian; Krasny pr 37, 3rd fl; typical admission R200; ☺ variable) For more-contemporary music from Latin dancing to heavy rock concerts, head to Rock City, above the Old Irish pub.

Getting There & Away

AIR

There are two airports but most major airlines use big **Tolmachyovo airport** (☎ 216 9230; http://tolmachevoeng.faktura.ru), 30km west of Novosibirsk off the Omsk road. The website gives approximate timetables. **Siberia Airlines** (☎ toll-free 8-800 200 0007; www.s7.ru), the biggest regional carrier, has flights to Germany and several east-Asian cities plus a comprehensive domestic network. Regular connections include Moscow (R6300, R8600 return), St Petersburg (R7080 booked six days ahead) and Irkutsk (R5490 to R6100, 2¾ hours). The central **Aviakassa** (ul Gogolya 3; ☺ 8.30am-8pm) is one of dozens of places at which you can purchase air tickets.

BUS

From the **bus station** (Krasny pr 4) around 20 daily buses serve Tomsk (R170, five hours). Shared taxis shave an hour or more off the journey for roughly double the price.

TRAIN

The main train station, **Novosibirsk Glavny** (ul Shamshurina 43), has daily long-distance trains.

For Moscow (48 to 55 hours via Omsk, Tyumen and Yekaterinburg), comfortable train 25 (even days) is easy to book. However, the cheaper 339 (1.30am, odd days) takes one night longer, saving on hotel accommodation as well as the fare. Of a dozen possible trains to Omsk the handiest overnighter is train 87 (R420 *platskart*, nine hours, daily). For Krasnoyarsk (R541 *platskart,* 12 to 14 hours), train 84 (13¾ hours overnight, even days) is well timed and rarely full.

For Altai, the 601 runs overnight to Biysk (R280 *platskart*, 10¾ hours, daily) via Barnaul (5½ hours). For Khakassia and Tuva you can go to Abakan direct (train 68, 23 hours, daily) or in two overnight hops via Novokuznetsk (train 605, R690, 9½ hours). Trains to Almaty, Kazakhstan (R1500, 32 to 37 hours) run daily at 5pm.

If queues are horrendous at the station's main ticket desks, you can buy them relatively swiftly from the upstairs **service centre** (☺ 4.30am-2am; commission R100) – no English spoken – or in Hotel Sibir.

Getting Around

Garina-Mikhaylovskogo, the metro stop for the main train station, is on a three-stop cross line. At Sibirskaya/Krasny pr this intersects with the main north–south line running across the river to Studencheskaya and pl Karla Marksa. For the city centre, *marshrutky* are generally handier. From outside Novosibirsk Glavny train station take trolleybus 2 to Severny airport, *marshrutka* 1122 to Tolmachyovo airport, Akademgorodok-bound 1015 for Seyatel and Studencheskaya-bound 1212 for the city centre (pl Lenina) and bus station.

AROUND NOVOSIBIRSK

Seyatel Сеятель
☎ 383

Beside the Akademgorodok highway, 24km south of central Novosibirsk, the **Locomotive Collection** (☎ 292 033; admission R50; ☺ 11am-5pm Sat-Thu) is a star attraction for train enthusiasts. It features 69 brightly painted and lovingly maintained trains and carriages dating from 1891 including one supposedly used by the last tsar. Directly across the tracks is Seyatel suburban train station from which it's 10 minutes' walk to the **Sun Museum** (Muzey Solntsa; ☎ 339 9126, mobile ☺ 913-943 9835; sun-museum@yandex.ru; ul Ivanova 11A, 2nd fl;

adult/child R30/20; ☺ call ahead). Keep asking for directions! Small but spiritually uplifting, this place examines sun-symbolism across cultures. Artist-sculptor curator Valery Lipenkov speaks basic English and plays resonant *bila* (flat bells) for interested guests.

To reach Seyatel take the roughly hourly suburban trains (R18) that use a small open platform somewhat south of the main Novosibirsk Glavny station (R28) or use *marshrutka* 1015 from outside. Returning it's often easier to use bus 622 (1015 fills up in Akademgorodok) but you'll have to change onto tram or metro at Rechnoy vokzal south of Novosibirsk's central area.

Akademgorodok Академгородок
☎ 383

Akademgorodok suburbs were elite Soviet academic townships full of research institutes. Attached to most Siberian cities, they attracted scientists by offering special perks and relatively spacious apartments in peaceful surroundings. Nearly 3km south

of Seyatel, Novosibirsk's Akademgorodok is Siberia's biggest, nestled in taiga close to the beaches of the Ob Sea. The Akademgorodok idea is interesting, but the reality is frustrating for tourists. Although most institutes have 'museums', these mostly open only for invited academics. Package tourists get channelled to the unspectacular **Geological Museum** (☎ 332 837; ul Koptyuga; admission R150; ☺ by arrangement) where spotting purple Yakutian charoite is less memorable than witnessing the unreconstructed Sovietness of the guides delivering their mesmerising monotone monologues. Is it self-parody?

Bus 7 from Akademgorodok runs towards Seyatel station and the Sun Museum.

TOMSK ТОМСК
☎ 3822 / pop 473,000 / ☎ Moscow + 4hr

Siberia's most likable city, Tomsk is an underappreciated gem, 270km northeast of Novosibirsk. Home to some of Siberia's best traditional wooden architecture, it's also a lively university city where there's even a

---

ADVENTURES IN THE ALTAI

Declared a Unesco World Heritage site in 1998, the glorious lake-dotted mountains of the Respublika Altay (Altai Republic) are an adventure playground for Russia's outdoor types, while its riverside lodges and camps are a very popular summer getaway for city dwellers.

Siberia's highest peak, 4506m Mt Belukha, stands on the Kazakhstan border and can be climbed from the tiny village of Tyungur where **Lenalp** (www.russia-climbing.com) has a well set-up hiking and rafting base. For something much more relaxing, **Teletskoye Ozera** is Altai's equivalent of Lake Baikal and arguably even more picturesque. Do-nothing lakeside hotels and camps in **Artybash** make it a most congenial place to unwind. There are more lodges along the banks of the Katun River, notably in **Chemal** and **Souzga** south of Gorno-Altaisk, the Altai Republic's capital. Nearby, **rafting** is a common pursuit for local tourists, ranging from quick fun-splashes to multiday sporting adventures. Five-day adventures can cost from a mere US$150 per person but you'll generally get what you pay for; better but much pricier tours include tastier food, wetsuits and more safety boats. Dozens of local agencies in Barnaul, Novosibirsk (p167) and beyond can help, but unless you use a specialist agency don't expect anyone to speak English.

Access starts with overnight train rides from Tomsk or Novosibirsk to Biysk via Barnaul. From across Biysk's station square, buses continue (two hours, eight daily) to Gorno-Altaisk (450km southeast of Novosibirsk). Stop here to get a special Altai visa registration (you'll need a letter from your visa's sponsor stating your destinations). Once registered, buses or shared taxis then whisk you to Chemal, Artybash, Tyungur or down the beautiful Chuysky Trakt. That's the main road to Olgii in Mongolia, passing ancient standing stones, burial mounds, petroglyphs, canyons and passes before emerging in a mountain-ringed steppe-land sprinkled with nomad yurts. For great maps try Dom Knigi (p165) in Novosibirsk.

Be aware that advance preparation is wise. Very few foreigners come this way, and even local tourists rarely venture much beyond Chemal. Much of the region's better accommodation and hiking guides (essential for trekking) are booked solid in July and August while from May to early July, you'll need to be very careful of ticks (which carry potentially fatal encephalitis).

For much more-detailed information, see Lonely Planet's *Russia & Belarus*.

hope of finding English-speakers in pubs and restaurants. Although 80km off the Trans-Sib mainline, it's not really a diversion as there are handy overnight through trains from both Omsk and Krasnoyarsk.

Founded in 1604, Tomsk was an important administrative and commercial town on the Great Siberian Trakt at its Tom River crossing. When the city was bypassed by the Trans-Siberian Railway its commercial importance declined, but its renowned academic institutions and the surrounding *oblast*'s oil wealth are today bringing Tomsk a renewed economic dynamism. Its much-celebrated 400th anniversary brought a further face-lift in 2004.

Orientation

The train station and next-door bus station are about 2.5km southeast of pr Lenina, Tomsk's appealing main commercial street.

Accurate bus-route maps are sold at news kiosks in the stations.

Information

Left-luggage at the train station is easy to miss; it's downstairs from within the *prigorodny kassa* (suburban train ticket office; entered by a separate door at the northern end of the main station building).

Internet Salon Plazma (☎ 529 446; ul Kuznetsova 15; per hr R16-28; ⏰ 9am-10pm)

Main post office (pr Lenina 95; Internet per hr R20; ⏰ 9am-7.30pm Mon-Fri, 8am-5pm Sat, 9am-5pm Sun)

Netcafé (☎ 281 441; pr Lenina 32; per 30min R16 plus per MB R2.5; ⏰ 9am-11pm)

SberBank (pl Lenina 12; ⏰ 9am-7pm Mon-Fri, 9-5pm Sat) Changes travellers cheques.

SibakademBank (☎ 527 489; ul Belinskogo 15A; ⏰ 9am-7pm Mon-Fri, 9am-5pm Sat) Great rates for US dollars.

Tomskturist (☎ 528 179; pr Lenina 59; ⏰ 9am-7pm Mon-Fri, 11am-4pm Sat) City tours.

Sights

Tomsk is famous for 'wooden lace' architecture – carved windows and tracery on old log and timber houses. Great examples include the restored **Shishkov House** (ul Shishkova 10), the spired **Russian-German House** (1906; ul Krasnoarmeyskaya 71), the **Dragon House** (ul Krasnoarmeyskaya 68) and the fan-gabled **Peacock House** (ul Krasnoarmeyskaya 67A). Many more line **ul Tatarskaya**, which is several blocks west of ul Krasnoarmeyskaya.

Tomsk's original fortress site on **Resurrection Hill** features the recently rebuilt 'Golden Gate' **wooden tower** and the **Tomsk History Museum** (admission R15; ⏰ 11am-5pm Tue-Sun), which is mainly interesting for the view from its lookout turret (R10). From the top you can see seven historic churches, but not the Dracula-gothic **Voznesenskaya Church** for which you'll need to stroll on up cobbled ul Bakunin.

Cafés, theatres and century-old architecture make for delightful strolling along pr Lenina. Start on formless pl Lenina, which mixes ugly Soviet monstrosities with the splendid 1784 **Epiphany Cathedral**, the former **trading arches** and the small but revered **Iverskaya Chapel** (Iverskaya Chasoviya; ⏰ 10am-6pm). The wonderful **1000 Melochey Shop** (pl Lenina; ⏰ 10am-7pm Mon-Sat, 10am-6pm Sun) features griffins and 1906 Art Nouveau ironwork flourishes.

Tomsk's appealing commercial district is most bustling south of per Nakhanovicha where you'll find the well-stocked if somewhat stuffy **Tomsk Art Gallery** (☎ 514 106; per Nakhanovicha 5; adult R50; ⏰ 10am-5.30pm Tue-Sun). Other small museums include two rooms within the **Atashev Palace & Regional Museum** (http://museum.trecom.tomsk.ru in Russian; pr Lenina 75; admission R20 & R11; ⏰ 10am-6pm Wed-Sun), which was once a church. Across the road, the eerie prison-dungeon of the cruel NKVD (later the KGB) is now a memorable **Oppression Museum** (☎ 516 133; pr Lenina 44, rear entrance; admission R18; ⏰ 2-6pm Mon-Fri). Tours are recommended, but are only available in Russian.

Further south in resplendently leafy grounds, the classically colonnaded **university buildings** explain Tomsk's popular title of 'the Oxford of Siberia'. Pr Lenina finally ends 600m beyond at the powerful mother-and-son **WWII Memorial** in the Lagerny Gardens, behind which are views of the meandering River Tom and the taiga beyond.

Sleeping

BUDGET

TGU Hotel (☎ 528 386; pr Lenina 49, 5th fl; dm R250, s R500-600, d R700) Brilliant-value newly renovated rooms with private bathrooms (except in the dorms). Reservations are usually essential, with a R100 booking fee. Enter from the rear; no lift.

YEKATERINBURG TO KRASNOYARSK

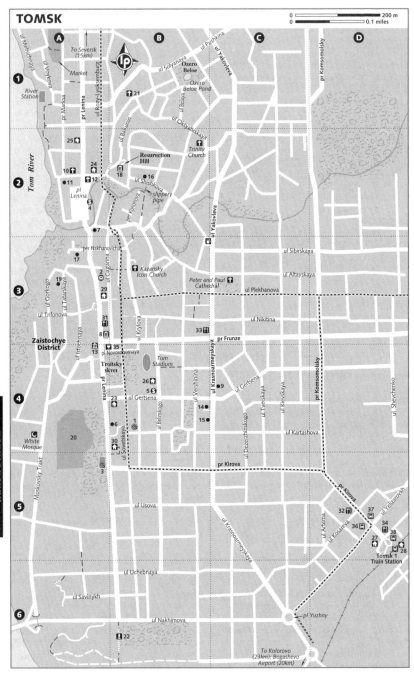

TOMSK

Hotel Sputnik (☎ 526 660; www.sputnik.tomsk turist.ru; ul Belinskogo 15; s/d/tw/tr R550/750/900/960) Smartened-up Soviet rooms share refitted new bathrooms.

Resting rooms (komnaty otdykha; Tomsk 1 train station; dm/tw R200/700) Perfectly clean, new rooms with sparkling shared toilets and shower. No rail ticket required. Curfew 1am to 5am.

Hotel Severnaya (☎ 512 324; pr Lenina 86; dm/tw/d R300/900/1300) Despite the smart new façade, rooms are sad and share communal squat toilets.

MIDRANGE & TOP END

Hotel Magistrat (☎ 511 111; www.magistrathotel.com; pr Lenina 15; d/tw/ste R2800/3850/4500; ✗ ▯) Luxurious brand-new rooms behind a palatial 1802 façade. English is spoken and the restaurant is lavish. Only the suites are air-conditioned.

BonApart (☎ 534 650; bon_apart@mail.ru; ul Gertsena 1A; s/tw/d/ste R1550/1850/1850/2400) New, full-comfort midrange hotel, lacking only a lift.

Sibir Forum (☎ 530 280; pr Lenina 91; s/tw/d/ste 1700/1900/2100/2800) Appealingly bright, fully renovated rooms on two floors of the otherwise unreconstructed Hotel Siberia.

Hotel Tomsk (☎ 524 115; pr Kirova 65; s/tw R1800/ 1900) This well-upgraded Soviet tower is handy for the stations but rather overpriced given the very small bathrooms. Tatty older rooms cost only R1500.

Eating & Drinking

Wonderful cafés, restaurants and cheap 'bistro' cafeterias abound on pr Lenina.

FoodMaster (pr Lenina 83; meals R100-450; ⏱ 11am-1am) This place is great value, has splendid

olde-worlde décor and a menu in English that ranges from Chinese to Mexican to Italian.

Sibirsky Pub (☎ 530 047; www.siberian-pub.ru in Russian; ul Novosobornaya 2; mains R10 0-200, Guinness per pint R140; ⏱ noon-3am) This is Tomsk's British pub with English spoken, a filling R144 lunch deal and live bands at weekends.

Pizza Rio (ul Krasnoarmeyskaya 31; slices R41; ⏱ 24hr) Both better, and better value, than Trattoria.

People's Bar & Grill (☎ 443 315; ul Krasnoarmeyskaya 31; beers from R60, meals R250-600; ⏱ noon-2am) Below Pizza Rio, and very hip.

Gastronom (pr Kirova 59; ☺ 24hr) Close to the station, this is a handy grocery.

Trattoria (per Nakhimova 2) An inviting and modern pizzeria-cafeteria, although prices are relatively high.

Getting There & Away

From Tomsk I (main) station there are daily services to Moscow's Yaroslavsky vokzal (Yaroslavl Station; 56½ hours). Train 37 leaves around 10am and is handy for Tyumen (22½ hours). For Omsk summer-only train 437 (R850 *platskart*, 15 hours, even days) is more convenient. *Platskart* carriages run to Irkutsk (34 hours) via Krasnoyarsk (R420, 14½ hours) daily in summer, even days in winter. For Altai take trains to Barnaul (R442, 14¾ hours, even days) then switch to bus for Biysk or Gorno-Altaisk.

From the bus station next door, shared taxis (R500, 3½ hours) are a much option faster than buses (R260, 5½ hours, 20 daily) for Novosibirsk.

Tomsk has some flight connections available to Moscow and the northern oil cities but there is always much more choice from Novosibirsk.

Getting Around

From just near the train station, bus 4 travels west and then runs north along the length of pr Lenina from pr Kirova, approximately paralleled by tram 2. Handy *marshrutka* 7 starts at pl Yuzhny (where *marshrutky* back from Kolorovo might leave you – see p181), passes the train station, heads west along pr Frunze, then travels up pr Lenina.

Krasnoyarsk to Lake Baikal

By Trans-Siberian standards this route is just a short hop. But it offers several intriguing possible variants. Krasnoyarsk, whose grand new, spired station looks vaguely like a Prussian Helmet, is the most sensible point to switch onto the wild Baikal-Amur Mainline (Baikalo-Amurskaya Magistral; BAM) for northern Lake Baikal and beyond. It's also where trains head south towards the fascinating Tuva Republic for throat singing or encounters with real-life shamans. You could even take one of the regular summer ferries up the 4102km Yenisey River: these steam all the way to the Arctic Circle and beyond, though without Norilsk permits you'd have to return to Krasnoyarsk again. Vastly easier river excursions whisk visitors an hour south to Divnogorsk by hydrofoil to observe one of Russia's biggest dams.

For many travellers, magical Baikal, the world's deepest lake, is the highlight of a Trans-Siberian odyssey. The tracks actually pass right along the southern shore, offering great views, especially between Slyudyanka and Baikalsk. With a little spoken Russian and a sense of adventure, lakeside Slyudyanka actually makes a feasible hop-off point, as it's the starting point for visiting the enticing mountain spa of Arshan and for taking the beautiful Circumbaikal Railway. However, the vast majority of foreign visitors get off instead at Irkutsk, a much bigger and more attractive city, where you can find English-speaking assistance. As Irkutsk is actually 70km from the lake, use buses or tours to see the glorious waters whether at convenient, tourist-orientated Listvyanka or meditational Olkhon Island, which is increasingly Baikal's favoured getaway. To visit eastern Baikal (p218), continue to Ulan-Ude (p213).

HIGHLIGHTS

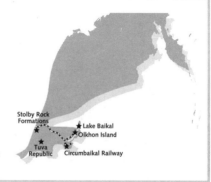

- Beat the crowds to meditatively beautiful **Olkhon Island** (p203)

- Ride the slow but scenic **Circumbaikal Railway** (p205) hugging Baikal's lakeshore cliffs

- Contemplate the weird **Stolby rock formations** (p187) near Krasnoyarsk

- Take a fascinating cultural and scenic side trip to the wild **Tuva Republic** (p190)

- Cross **Lake Baikal** (p198) on the winter ice or by summer hydrofoil

ROUTE DISTANCE: 1088KM	DURATION: ONE DAY, 17½ TO 20 HOURS

THE ROUTE

Heading east out of Krasnoyarsk (4098km), trains cross a 1km-long **Yenisey River bridge**, whose 1898 original won a gold medal at the 1900 Paris Expo. The *Rossiya* makes short stops at **Zaozernaya** (4265km), from where a line runs north to the off-limits space centre of Krasnoyarsk-45, and at **Kansk-Yeniseysky** (4344km). Historic Kansk, founded in 1640, boasts a scattering of century-old buildings, a renovated Trinity Cathedral and a cinematographic museum.

Ilanskaya (Ilansky; 4377km) has a small **museum** (10am-5pm Mon-Fri) in the 100-year-old, red-brick locomotive depot at the west-ern end of the station, and an old locomotive and water tower behind the wooden station building. You'll have 20 minutes, but we really recommend that you *don't* take photographs. Getting arrested can mess up all your plans.

At **4474km**, the train passes into Irkutsk *oblast* (region); local time becomes Moscow time plus five hours.

The *Rossiya* stops five minutes at **Tayshet** (4515km), the Trans-Siberian's westernmost junction with the BAM and once an infamous transit point for Gulag prisoners.

If riding straight through from Moscow, you're now on day four and already halfway to the Pacific. As the railway skirts the foothills of the **Sayan Mountains**, endless taiga

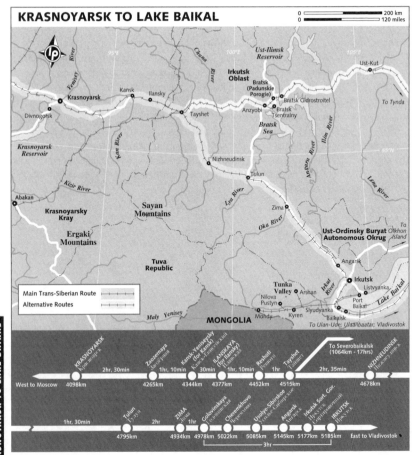

KRASNOYARSK TO LAKE BAIKAL

forests and a real sense of wilderness set in. However, at around **4560km** the line rises above the taiga and sweeps around bends for many kilometres offering good photo opportunities.

There's a 15-minute stop at **Nizhneudinsk** (4678km), where Cossacks first built a fortress in 1649. Today the molybdenum mines and a 'Mice Factory' (sic), which the town lists inscrutably as 'attractions', are unlikely to appeal. Further east the landscape becomes flatter and the forests have been extensively logged. At **Tulun** (4795km) a road heads 225km north to Bratsk (p243). Trains pause for two minutes.

After a 20-minute stop in the former exile-town **Zima** (4934km), which translates ominously as 'winter', the train heads southeast, shadowing the Angara River. There are several inconsequential short stops, including at **Angarsk** (5145km), whose oil and petrochemical industries are economically important if hardly attractive. There's a clock museum if you really want to get off.

Around the **5171km** marker, look north through the trees; 50m beyond the tracks behind two barbed wire fences are neat rows of decommissioned old tanks and rocket-launcher trucks (without rockets) rusting away thinking of their Cold War heyday.

The train crosses the Irkut River 3km before **Irkutsk** (5185km) station. Once nicknamed the 'Paris of Siberia', Irkutsk is the most popular Siberian stop for most transcontinental travellers, notably as a launching point to reach Lake Baikal, 70km further southeast.

KRASNOYARSK КРАСНОЯРСК

☎ 3912 / **pop 871,000** / ◷ Moscow + 4hr

Backed by attractive spikes of jagged, forested foothills, Krasnoyarsk has a much more appealing setting than most typically flat Siberian cities. While architecture isn't a particular strength, amid the predominantly unaesthetic concrete of post-WWII industrialisation are a few outstandingly well-embellished timber mansions and a sprinkling of Art Nouveau curves. Pleasant river trips and the nearby Stolby Nature Reserve, as well as the region's best concert halls, theatres and museums, make Krasnoyarsk a most agreeable place to break a Trans-Siberian journey between Lake Baikal and Tomsk (or Novosibirsk).

Orientation

The city's ferro-concrete central square is near the Yenisey River's north bank, where pedestrianised ul Uritskogo is gashed by ul Veynbauma. The Stolby Nature Reserve is around 20km away, south of the Yenisey.

MAPS

Extremely useful Krasnoyarsk transport maps (R38) are sold within the bus, train and river stations, at the Regional Museum (below) and from bookshops, such as **Russkoye Slovo** (ul Lenina 28; ◷ 10am-2pm & 3-7pm Mon-Fri, 10am-3pm Sat).

Information

Inpexbank (pr Mira 5; ◷ 10am-8pm Mon-Sat, 10am-1pm & 2-5pm Sun) Long hours and good rates for Euros. For dollars use ROSBank.

Internet Klub (ul Lenina 153; per hr R35; ◷ 9am-10pm) Beneath Mister Dzhin.

Internet Termen (☎ 653 290; ul Parizhskoy Kommuny 33; per hr R40; ◷ 9am-10pm Mon-Fri, 11am-10pm Sat & Sun)

KBPE (Krasnoyarskoye Byuro Putishestvy i Ekskursy; ☎ 271 626; alftur@hotelkrs.ru; Ground fl, Hotel Krasnoyarsk; ◷ 10am-6pm Mon-Fri, 10am-3pm Sat) Commercial tour agency.

Paradoks (☎ 239 795; pr Mira 96; per hr for up to 3MB R25; ◷ 24hr) The best, central Internet access. Entered from an inner courtyard facing sign to the Alazani Georgian restaurant.

Post office (ul Lenina 62; ◷ 8am-7pm Mon-Sat)

ROSBank (pr Mira 7; ◷ 9am-7pm Mon-Fri, 10am-5pm Sat) Gives good rates for US dollars cash and changes travellers cheques.

Sberbank (ul Ablakhovykh 2; ◷ 9.30am-7pm Mon-Sat) Exchange services; fairly handy for the train station.

Telephone office (pr Mira 102; ◷ 7am-2pm & 3pm-midnight)

Sights

MUSEUMS & CHURCHES

The **Regional Museum** (Kraevedchesky muzey; ☎ 226 511; ul Dubrovinskogo 84; admission R30; ◷ 11am-7pm Tue-Sun) is one of Siberia's best. It's housed in a marvellously incongruous building that looks more suited to Luxor – the architect was obsessed with Egypt. Exhibits include a full-scale replica of a boat used by the Cossack explorers and a fine ethnographic section on indigenous shamanic peoples. The appealing gift shop sells old coins, medals, postcards and excellent maps.

The lovely **Surikov Museum-Estate** (Muzey-usadba V I Surikova; ☎ 231 507; ul Lenina 98; admission R30;

☑ 11am-6pm Tue-Sat) preserves the house, sheds and vegetable patch of 19th-century painter Vasiliy Surikov (1848–1916). The heavy-gated garden forms a refreshing oasis of rural Siberia right in the city centre. More of Surikov's work is on show at the cute **Surikov Art Museum** (☎ 272 558; ul Parizhskoy Kommuny 20; ☑ 11am-6pm Tue-Sun).

Permanently docked below an ugly Exhibition Centre, the **SV Nikolay** (admission $0.20; ☑ 10am-6pm Tue-Sun) was a boat on which Lenin was transported to exile in 1897. It houses some intriguing exhibits, but was being restored at the time of research.

For great city views climb Karaulnaya Hill to the **Chasovnya Chapel**, which features

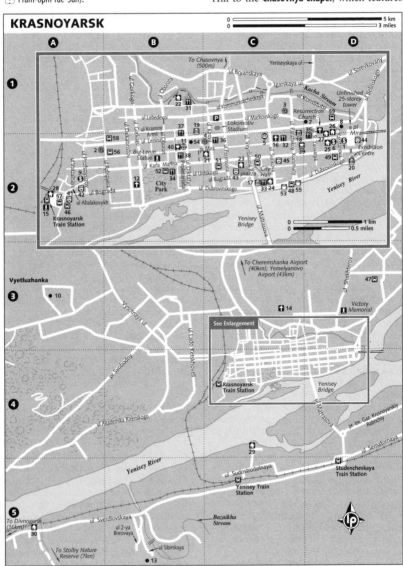

on the Russian R10 banknote. At noon there's a deafening one-gun salute here. Attractive old churches include the fancy 1795 **Intercession Cathedral** (Pokrovsky sobor; ul Surikova) and the top-heavy but elegant 1804–22 **Blagoveshchensky Church** (ul 9 Janvarya), whose icon-filled interior billows with incense.

STOLBY NATURE RESERVE

Arguably Krasnoyarsk's greatest attractions are the spiky volcanic rock pillars called Stolby. These litter the woods in the 17,000-hectare Stolby Nature Reserve (Zapovednik Stolby) south of the Yenisey River, around 20km from the city centre. The main concentration is reached by walking 7km down a track from near Turbaza Yenisey, itself over 10km southwest of the city centre by bus 50a from the station. Much easier access is via a **chair lift** from beside **Kafe Bobrovy log** (ul Sibirskaya). This usually runs year-round on request, but was closed throughout 2005 during a massive ski-slope redevelopment. From the top of the chair lift, walk two minutes to a great viewpoint or around 40 minutes to reach the impressive **Takmak Stolby**.

Tours are available, personalised in English with **SibTourGuide** (☎ 512 654; www.sibtour guide.com) – priced according to itinerary – or all in Russian through KBPE (p185; six-hour tours per person for groups of many/three/two/one R500/700/1000/1500). Remember that encephalitis-infected ticks are dangerous between May and July.

DIVNOGORSK

The scenic Yenisey River gorge is popularly viewed from Krasnoyarsk to Divnogorsk hydrofoil rides. A 5km taxi-hop beyond Divnogorsk jetty is the impressive 1km-long **hydroelectric dam** (GES). Visiting the turbine rooms isn't allowed, but from a distance you can observe the remarkable moving basin that allows ships to cross the dam. Boat rentals are available on the reservoir beyond. Hydrofoils (R70, 45 minutes) sail between Krasnoyarsk and Divnogorsk every two hours from May to late September. Pay on board. The trip is also pleasant by road allowing a stop in semi-quaint Ovsyanka village, with its cute wooden **St Innokenty Chapel** (ul Shchetinkina) and two interesting **House Museums** (ul Shchetinkina 26 & 35; admission R30; ⓨ 10am-6pm Tue-Sun) related to celebrated writer Victor Astafyev (1924–2001).

INFORMATION		
Inpexbank Инпексбанк	1	D2
Internet Klub Интернет Клуб	2	A2
Internet Termen		
Интернет Термен	3	C1
KBPE	(see 23)	
Paradoks Парадокс	4	C2
Post office	5	C2
ROSBank	6	D2
Russkoye Slovo Русское Слово	7	D1
Sayan Ring Travel	8	D1
Sberbank	9	A2
SibTourGuide	10	A3
Telephone office		
Междугородный телефон	11	B2

SIGHTS & ACTIVITIES		
Catholic Church (Organ Hall)	12	B2
Chair Lift Фуникюльор	13	B5
Chasovnya Chapel Часовня	14	C3
Communist Era Mosaic	15	A2
Intercession Cathedral		
Покровский Собор	16	C2
Regional Museum		
Краеведческий музей	17	C2
Surikov Art Museum		
Художественный музей		
имени В И Сурикова	18	C2
Surikov Museum-Estate	19	B1
SV Nikolay Св Николай	20	D2

SLEEPING		
Hotel Gostiny Dvor		
Гостиница Гостиный Двор	21	C2

Hotel Kolos		
Гостиница Колос	22	B1
Hotel Krasnoyarsk		
Гостиница Красноярск	23	C2
Hotel Ogni Yeniseyya		
Гостиница Огни Енисея	24	C2
Hotel Oktyabrskaya		
Гостиница Октябрьская	25	D2
Krasnoyarskstroystrategiya		
Гостиница		
Красноярскстройстратегия	26	D1
Metelitsa Guest House		
Метелица	27	D2
Resting Rooms		
Комнаты Отдыха	28	A2
Siberian Safari Club		
Сибирский Сафари Клуб	29	C4
Turbaza Yenisey		
Турбаза Енисей	30	A5

EATING		
Central Market		
Центральный Рынок	31	B1
Gastronom Krasnyyar	32	C2
Kofeynya Кофейня	33	C2
Luch Луч	34	B2
Mama Roma	35	D2
Nevskoe Kafe		
Невское Кафе	36	C2
Subito Субито	37	B1
Telega Телега	38	B2
Terrasa Kafe		
ЛучюТерасса Кафе	(see 34)	

DRINKING		
Kafe Retro Кафе Ретро	39	C2
Kantri Кантри	40	B2

ENTERTAINMENT		
Che Guevara Че Гувара	41	A2
Havana Club Гавана Клуб	42	A2
Opera-Ballet Theatre		
Театр оперы и балета	43	C2
Philharmonia Филармония	44	D2
Rock-Jazz Kafe		
Рок-Джаз Кафе	45	C2

TRANSPORT		
Bus 50a to Zoo	46	A2
Bus Station Автовокзал	47	D3
Buses to Divnogorsk	48	C2
Eastbound Trolleybus 7	49	D2
Eastbound Trolleybus 7	50	C2
Eastbound Trolleybus 7,		
Bus 50a to Zoo	51	C2
Eastbound Trolleybus 7,		
Bus 50a to Zoo	52	B2
Hydrofoils to Divnogorsk	53	C2
KrasAir	54	B2
River Station Речной вокзал	55	C2
Trolleybus 5 from		
Train Station	56	B2
Trolleybus 7 to Centre	57	A2
Trolleybus 7 to Train Station &		
Bus 91 to Vyetluzhanka	58	B2
Westbound Trolleybus 7,		
Bus 50 to Zoo	59	D1

Tours

Youthful university teacher Anatoliy Brewhanov offers thoughtfully personalised English-speaking tour services aimed at independent travellers with **SibTourGuide** (☎ 512 654; www.sibtourguide.com). It has a useful website, and can recommend congenial homestays and offers imaginative trips.

Sleeping

For English-speaking homestays try **Sib-TourGuide** (☎ 512 654; www.sibtourguide.com; s/d US$25/40). Rates include breakfast and pick-up from the train station. Most are in Vyetluzhanka (bus 91).

BUDGET

Hotel Gostiny Dvor (☎ 232 857; pr Mira 81; dm R300-550, s R700-850, tw R600-1100) Superb central position, lovely façade and, despite the ropey reception area, rooms are fully renovated sharing new toilets and showers between two or three rooms. Kettles in some rooms.

Krasnoyarskstroystrategiya (☎ 276 612; pr Mira 12; s R280-530, tw R650-910) Good value if utterly unpronounceable. Rooms are very pleasant by ex-Soviet standards; bathrooms are shared between pairs of rooms. Enter from ul Karatanova.

Turbaza Yenisey (☎ 698 110; ul Sverdlovskaya 140/7; d/tw R400/400; ✗ P) Good-value neatly renovated rooms share sparkling clean showers. The location is ideal for Stolby hikes, but way out of the city centre. No café.

Resting Rooms (☎ 586 086; Krasnoyarsk train station; dm for 12hr from R180) Excellent brand-new dorms at the train station.

Hotel Ogni Yeniseyya (☎ 275 262; ul Dubrovinskogo 80; s R590-820, tw R1380-1500) Miserable rooms off bile-green corridors but there are private bathrooms and visa registration is possible.

MIDRANGE

Rates include breakfast.

Siberian Safari Club (☎ 613 335; http://tlcom.krs.ru/safari; ul Sudostroitelnaya 117a; s/d 2500/3000) This intimate, peaceful 20-room hotel is arguably Krasnoyarsk's most appealing if you don't mind the awkward location on the southern river bank. Attentive staff speak English, and there's a classy terrace restaurant (meals R300 to R800). Booking is advisable (25% fee). Three smaller single rooms cost R1300. Bus 36 stops a 10-minute walk away.

Hotel Oktyabrskaya (☎ 273 780; www.tlcom.krs.ru/october; pr Mira 15; s/d/tw R2300/2600/2900) Comfortable and professionally run, with rooms approximating chintzy Western standards albeit without air-conditioning. Satellite TV includes CNN in English. There's a trendy lobby area arranged around a very stylish juice bar.

Hotel Krasnoyarsk (☎ 273 754; www.hotelkrs.ru; ul Uritskogo 94; s/tw/ste from R1440/1900/2660; ✷) This sprawling eight-storey concrete slab dominates Krasnoyarsk's central square. It retains the Soviet vintage *dezhurnaya* (floor lady) system, but is well kept with bright corridors, totally rebuilt full-service rooms and English-speaking receptionists. Only the suites have air-conditioning.

Metelitsa Guest House (☎ 625 298; pr Mira 14A; s R1895-2295, d R2295-2895; P) Small, central and reasonably comfy, but aimed mainly at Russian *biznesmen*.

Eating

In summer, shashlyk (meat kebab) stands overlook the waterfront near the river station and the fountain-filled central square comes alive with open-air cafés. There are dozens of restaurants, coffee houses and pizzerias along pr Mira and ul Lenina.

Telega (☎ 595 987; pr Mira 91; business lunch R120; ◷ noon-2am) All-you-can-eat deals at the extensive buffet (R250) are great for avoiding linguistic problems.

Luch (☎ 662 064; www.kinoluch.ru; ul Karla Marksa 149) This modernistic complex contains a cinema, nightclub and several eateries from fast food to fine Russian cuisine. Try the great glassed-in **Terrasa Kafe** (top fl; meals R100-350, coffee R50 to R80; ◷ noon-6am), with fine views, a wide-ranging menu and a remarkably filling R100 lunch deal daily.

Kofeynya (☎ 232 696; ul Dubrovinskogo 82; coffees R60-150, meals R200-900; ◷ 8am-midnight) This coffeehouse and Goldilocks-style cellar restaurant is overpriced, but handy for set breakfasts (R180), and English menus.

Mama Roma (☎ 661 072; www.mamaroma.ru; pr Mira 50a; pizza R192-480, pasta R144-256; ◷ 11am-1am) Krasnoyarsk's top pizzeria, but for quick slices **Subito** (ul Lenina 110; pizza slices R38; ◷ 10am-10pm) is ideal.

Nevskoye Kafe (☎ 272 793; ul Lenina 91; meals R70-120, tea R4.50; ◷ 9am-11pm) Not lovely but unspectacularly presentable, a step above what you'd expect from such cheap dining.

For self-catering there's a bustling **Central Market** (8am-6pm), and **Gastronom Krasnyyar** (pr Mira 50A; 24hr) has a good range of food-stuffs.

Drinking

Kantri (☎ 230 246; pr Mira 102a; business lunch R150, small beers R50-110) Atmospherically under-lit Wild West–saloon pub beneath a rather twee, upmarket coffee house.

Kafe Retro (☎ 277 203; pr Mira; coffees R30-70, beers R40-70; noon-midnight) Good style to price ratio for real coffee.

Entertainment

Rock-Jazz Kafe (☎ 523 305; ul Perensona 20; admission R80, beers R30; noon-midnight) A venue for live bands (from 6pm weekends) featuring an up-turned motorcycle centrepiece. Enter through a small bar beside the Dublin Irish Pub.

Che Guevara (☎ 595 857; ul Profsoyuzov 3; admission after 7pm R300-500, cocktails R100-190; noon-1am Sun-Wed, noon-5am Thu-Sat) A fun saloon-club with 1950s pin-ups and a Commy-Cuba theme. For entertainment, there's dancing or a live-music programme.

Havana Club (☎ 216 416; ul Abalakovikh 134; admission R30-180) Almost next door to Che Guevara, the big Havana Club is best on Thursday Latin night. Opening hours vary.

Opera-Ballet Theatre (☎ 278 697; ul Perensona 2; tickets from R60) Up to five early evening shows per week from October to June.

Philharmonia (☎ 274 930; pl Mira 2b) The Philharmonia has three concert halls showcasing folk, pop and classical music.

Getting There & Away
AIR

From Krasnoyarsk's Yemelyanovo airport, 46km northwest of the city, you can fly to Germany plus almost anywhere in Russia, including Moscow (R8700, three daily) and Kyzyl in Tuva (R3210, four weekly), mostly using **KrasAir** (☎ 236 366; www.krasair.ru).

BOAT

Every few days in summer passenger boats from Krasnoyarsk's spired **river station** (rechnoy vokzal; ☎ 274 446; 8am-7pm) ply the Yenisey to Dudinka (1989km, 4½ to five days). Permit regulations mean foreigners may not proceed beyond Igarka, though that's above the Arctic circle. The four-day journey (R1800 to R4278) is meditational if not especially scenic. Igarka has an interesting permafrost museum, but no roads to anywhere else, so you'll have to return by boat or plane to Krasnoyarsk. For more details see Lonely Planet's *Greenland & the Arctic* guide.

TRAIN

All major Trans-Siberian and China-bound trains stop at Krasnoyarsk. Train 055 is the best sleeper choice for Novosibirsk (12½ hours) – a *platskart* (*platskartny*; open carriage) ticket costs R541 to Yekaterinburg (33 hours) and Moscow (60 hours), while very handy train 609 runs overnight to Tomsk (R420 *platskart*, 14 hours). Six or more trains daily take around 19 hours to Irkutsk (R505 *platskart*). Train 092 along the BAM takes 30 hours to Severobaikalsk continuing alternate days to Tynda.

Start a trip towards Tuva (p190) with overnight train 124 (11 hours) to Abakan, the fastest of three overnight options. *Kupe* (*kupeyny*; compartmentalised carriage) tickets cost R630.

There are railway **booking offices** (9am-6pm) in the river and bus stations.

Getting Around

From assorted points near the train station, trolleybus 7 and several buses run via the city centre towards Hotel Oktyabrskaya. Some follow ul Karla Marksa, others pr Mira but most return via ul Lenina. Bus 50a crosses the river and passes ul Sibirskaya (1.5km walk from the chair lift) and the Turbaza Yenisey (for Stolby access). Trolleybus 2 runs along pr Mira to the *avtovokzal* (intercity bus station), from where bus 135 takes about 50 minutes to Yemelyanovo airport.

Both buses and hydrofoils to Divnogorsk depart from behind Krasnoyarsk's river station.

IRKUTSK ИРКУТСК
☎ 3952 / pop 591,000 / Moscow + 5hr

Though still 70km from its shores, Irkutsk is the nearest big city to glorious Lake Baikal and the easiest place from which to organise Baikal adventures if your Russian isn't up to much. With some fancifully re-built churches and patches of grand 19th-century architecture the city is well worth a day or two, though the streets can feel somewhat seedy at night. Beware that in summer accommodation can be stretched and relatively expensive by Siberian standards. Book ahead.

History

Founded in 1651 as a Cossack garrison to control the indigenous Buryats, Irkutsk was the springboard for 18th-century expeditions to the far north and east. This included Alaska, then known as 'Irkutsk's American district'.

As eastern Siberia's trading and administrative centre, Irkutsk dispatched Siberian furs to Mongolia, Tibet and China in exchange for silk and tea. Its most illustrious 19th-century residents were Decembrists (see p194) and Polish rebels who formed a rough-hewn aristocracy valuing education, the arts and political awareness.

Three-quarters of the city burnt down in the disastrous fire of 1879. However, the Lena Basin gold rush of the 1880s quickly

KHAKASSIA & TUVA

Around 200,000 Tuvans make up 64% of the population of the **Tuva Republic** (capital: Kyzyl), an other-worldly region where the mesmerising grassland hills are ringed by beautiful forested mountains. Tuvans are an ethnically Mongol people, whose Tibetan Buddhist faith retains strong elements of shamanism. Today Tuva's active shamans and its gamut of Mongolian-style cultural pursuits, including sumo-style khuresh wrestling, are part of its attraction. But a special draw is Tuva's extraordinary khöömei throat singing. Hearing some is easy on the soundtrack of Oscar-nominated film Genghis Blues or by downloading tracks from www.tarbagan.com. But witnessing the extraordinary sounds coming live from a Tuvan throat is one of Siberia's most surreal experiences.

Tuva was part of the Chinese Empire in the 18th and 19th centuries before becoming nominally independent as Tannu Tuva from 1921 to 1944. Tannu Tuva is best remembered for its fanciful triangular postage stamps, and for inspiring the classic travel book Tuva or Bust by Ralph Leighton and Richard Feynman. Traditionally, Tuvans were hunters or herders of reindeer, horses, sheep and yak. Today a few seminomadic Tuvan herders still live in summer yurt tents, though these are a vastly less common sight than the similar ger (felt) tents you will see across the nearby Mongolian border.

En route to Tuva you'll likely transit the **Khakassia Republic** (capital: Abakan). The ethnically Turkic Khakass people are the local remnants of the 'Yenisey Kyrgyz' empire that stretched from Kazakhstan to Lake Baikal from the 6th to the 13th century. The Khakass were once shamanistic nomadic herders, but widespread Christianisation accompanied heavy Russian colonisation, and they now represent just over 10% of the republic's population. Nonetheless, their long history has left the vast flat grasslands pocked with some remarkable standing stones and kurgan (grave mounds). In the far south Khakassia and Southern Krasnoyarsk Kray meet Tuva in the spectacularly spiky Ergaki Mountain range. See Lonely Planet's Russia & Belarus guide for more details.

Visiting Khakassia & Tuva

Khakassia's dull but pleasantly green capital Abakan is an easy overnight train hop from Krasnoyarsk. Shared taxis meet arriving trains and continue across a wonderfully scenic road to Kyzyl in Tuva (R800, 5½ hours), where charming professional translator **Aylana Irguit** (☎ 39422-13 796 home, 39422-34 790 work; www.tyvantranslator.com; per hr US$15-40) can help you meet throat singers and **EcoTuva** (☎ 39422-10 527 or 14 579; www.ecotuva.ru) offers imaginative excursions.

Krasnoyarsk-based agency **Sayan Ring Travel** (☎ /fax 3912-522 481; www.gotosiberia.ru; office 545, Metropol Bldg, pr Mira 10, Krasnoyarsk; ☿ 10am-7pm Mon-Fri) runs regular full-comfort tours of the region that include accommodation in tourist yurt camps, cultural shows and excursions to Shushenskoye, where Lenin was exiled. Similar but tailor-made trips are well-priced from Abakan-based agent **Abakan Tours** (☎ 39022-23 284; parkhotel@inbox.ru, attention: Sergei Mechtanov; Hotel Park-Otel, Abakan; ☿ 9am-noon & 1-5pm Mon-Fri). While in Abakan, train buffs should take half an hour to visit the new **Railway Museum** (Muzey Zheleznoy Dorogi; Abakan station concourse; admission R30; ☿ 11am-7pm Wed-Mon). It's diagonally across the station forecourt and exhibits engineers' uniforms through the ages, 22 types of historical rail-couplings and a model of Abakan station in 1925.

restored its grand brick mansions and public buildings, many of which still stand today.

Irkutsk did not welcome news of the October Revolution. The city's well-to-do merchants only succumbed to the Red tide in 1920, with the capture and execution of white army commander Admiral Kolchak, whose statue has recently been re-erected. Soviet-era planning saw Irkutsk develop as a sprawling industrial and scientific centre, which it remains today.

Orientation

The bustling train station is directly across the Angara River from the city centre. Grand ul Karla Marksa is the historic commercial centre. From the administrative centre (pl Kirova), ul Lenina parallels the river to the Raising-of-the-Cross Church, where it becomes ul Sedova. Nearly 6km further south this road's continuation reaches the Angara Dam (GES). Many hotels, souvenir stalls and bookshops sell various city maps. Shop around as prices vary drastically.

Information

INTERNET ACCESS

Epitsentr (ul Sukhe-Batora 18; per hr R45-60; ☿ 24hr) Best Internet connection in town.

Kofeynya Karta (ul Marata 38; per hr R45; ☿ 9am-11pm) An inviting cellar Internet coffee shop serving real espresso (R33).

Web-Ugol (ul Lenina 13; per hr R45; ☿ 10am-10pm) Downstairs, easy to miss.

INTERNET RESOURCES

Baikal.ru (www.baikal.ru) Partly translated with old-postcard portraits of various Irkutsk streets.

ICC (www.irkutsk.com) History, maps and tourist information.

IrkutskOut (www.irkutskout.ru in Russian) Café and restaurant listings.

MONEY

Bank Soyuz Booth (Hotel Baikal, bul Gagarina 44) Changes money, including Chinese yuan, 22 hours a day.

Guta Bank (ul Dzerzhinskogo) foyer booth (☿ 11am-3pm & 4-6.45pm Mon-Fri); Valyutnaya Kassa No 1 (☿ 9am-2pm & 3-5pm Mon-Fri) Good US dollar rate from the foyer booth. Travellers cheques cashed from inside Valyutnaya Kassa No 1.

PHOTOGRAPHY

Yustas Photo-Salon (ul Sukhe-Batora; ☿ 10am-6pm) Passport photos for those Mongolian visas.

POST & TELEPHONE

Main telephone office (ul Proletarskaya 12) Has 24-hour ATMs.

Post office (ul Stepana Razina 23; ☿ 8am-8pm Mon-Fri, 9am-8pm Sat & Sun) Bigger branches are at per Bogdanov 8 and ul Karla Marksa 28.

TOURIST INFORMATION

Visitor Information Office (☎ 406 706; http://baikal info.ru; ul Karla Marksa 26B; ☿ 9am-8pm Mon-Fri, 9am-4pm Sat & Sun) Useful and very unusual for Russia, but not always very imaginative beyond the tours that it sells.

TRAVEL AGENCIES

Local tour operators can organise excursions, book hotels and get train tickets, but most have only one or two overstretched English speakers. Patience pays.

BaikalComplex (☎ 389 205; www.baikalcomplex.irk.ru) Busy, well-organised operation, offering homestays and tailored trips for Western travellers. Call to arrange a meeting.

Baikaler (☎ 336 240; www.baikaler.com) Imaginative Jack Sheremetoff speaks good English and is well tuned to budget travellers' needs. Imaginative tours and a great central hostel.

Green Express (☎ 563 400; www.greenexpress.ru; 7th fl, ul Baikalskaya 291; ☿ 9am-6pm Mon-Fri) Big, professional outfit, with a hotel in Listvyanka, yurts on Olkhon Island, and many mountain-biking, horse-riding and other tour options.

Sights

DECEMBRIST HOUSES

After completing their terms of labour near Chita, many Decembrists settled in Irkutsk with their families, who had earlier followed them into exile (see p194). Two of the homes (those of Prince Sergei Trubetskoy and Count Sergei Volkonsky) are now touching museums, complete with furnishings and pictures of family and friends.

The grey **Volkonsky House Museum** (☎ 207 532; per Volkonskogo 10; admission R50; ☿ 10am-6pm Tue-Sun) is through big heavy gates, just a short walk behind the pretty pink Preobrazheniya Gospodnya Church. The mansion is set in a courtyard with stables, a barn and servant quarters (beware of the dog). Downstairs is an (over-) renovated piano room; upstairs is a photo exhibition. Labels are in Russian only, but a R70 pamphlet tells the stories.

When Volkonsky House is closed on Monday try the smaller **Trubetskoy House Museum** (☎ 275 773; ul Dzerzhinskogo 64; admission R40; ☿ 10am-6pm Thu-Mon).

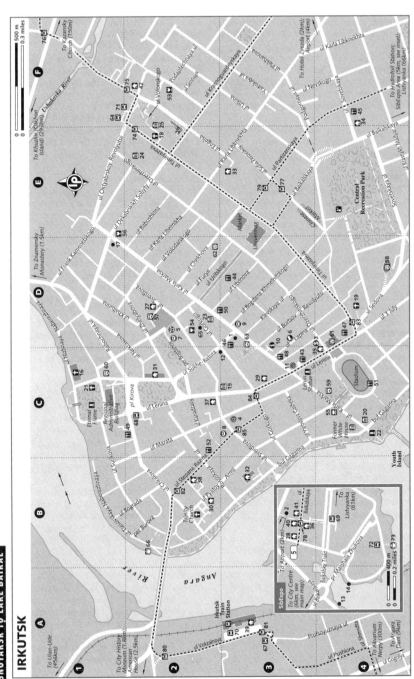

OTHER MUSEUMS & GALLERIES

Irkutsk's pleasant if fairly standard **Regional Museum** (Kraevedchesky muzey; ☎ 333 449; ul Karla Marksa 2; foreigner R100; ☼ 10am-6pm Tue-Sun) is within a fancy 1870s brick building that formerly housed the Siberian Geographical Society, a club of Victorian gentlemen-explorers. Equivalent museums in Chita and Krasnoyarsk are more impressive, though exhibits on the BAM and Trans-Sib railways are passingly interesting. The gift shop is great for birch-bark boxes (from R80) and jewellery made from chaorite, a unique purple Siberian mineral. Across the road, a bushy-bearded **statue of Tsar Alexander III**

on the riverfront promenade has replaced the Trans-Siberian Obelisk that formerly stood here.

The grand old **Art Gallery** (ul Lenina 5; foreigner R50; ☼ 10am-6pm Wed-Mon) has a valuable if poorly lit collection ranging from Mongolian *thangka* (Buddhist iconographic painting) to Russian-impressionist canvasses. Behind a photogenic 1909 façade, its **sub-gallery** (ul Karla Marksa 23; admission R60; ☼ 10am-6pm Tue-Sun) is strong on Siberian landscapes and petroglyph rubbings, and has some superb 17th-century icons.

A collection of Soviet tanks and missile launchers guard the **Dom Ofitserov** (ul Karla

---

THE DECEMBRIST MOVEMENT

Across Siberia, notably in Irkutsk, Chita and Novoselenginsk, interesting museums commemorate the 'Decembrist' gentlemen-rebels. This group of aristocratic, liberal-leaning army officers had occupied Senate Sq in St Petersburg in an ill-conceived coup against Tsar Nicholas I. The date was 26 December 1825, hence their soubriquet.

The mutineers were poorly organised and outnumbered, but Nicholas I was loathe to mark the start of his reign with a full-blown domestic massacre. After a stand-off, which lasted most of the day, troops fired several canister shots into the square killing about 60 people. The rebellion crumbled and five leaders were executed. Another 121 organisers were sentenced to hard labour, prison and exile in Siberia where they became romantic heroes of a sort. But the real heroes were their womenfolk, many of whom abandoned their lives of comfort and sophistication to follow their husbands or lovers into exile. The first was the faithful Yekaterina Trubetskaya. The story goes that having travelled 6000km by coach to Nerchinsk, she immediately descended into the silver mines to find her husband.

Others had to wait for months in Irkutsk or Chita for permission to see their men, meanwhile setting up small social circles that encouraged 'Western civilisation' in these hitherto wild-east backwaters. Over two decades the exiled families opened schools, formed scientific societies and edited newspapers. Maria Volkonskaya, popularly known as the 'Princess of Siberia', founded a local hospital and opened a concert theatre, in addition to hosting musical and cultural soirees in her home.

The Decembrists were granted amnesty when Nicholas I died in 1855. Although many of them, including Maria Volkonskaya, returned to St Petersburg, their legacy lived on for decades.

Marksa 47), which has a sporadically open museum and occasional concerts of patriotic songs.

CHURCHES

The formerly magnificent Annunciation Cathedral, which once dominated pl Kirova, was extensively damaged in the Russian Civil War and demolished to make way for a hulking Party headquarters, now the regional administration building. The cathedral is still visible in photos exhibited in the belfry-museum of the 18th-century **Saviour's Church** (Spasskaya Tserkov; ul Sukhe-Batora; admission R100; 10am-6pm Tue-Sun), whose exhibits are less exciting than the views from the top (if you're allowed up).

Much more eye-catching is the fairy-tale ensemble of the **Bogoyavlensky Cathedral** (ul Nizhnaya Naberezhnaya; 8.30am-5pm) whose ongoing restoration continues to add a colourful dazzle to the otherwise rather grimy riverfront.

Set in a leafy garden the 1762 **Znamensky Monastery** is 1.5km beyond, behind a noisy traffic circle. Echoing with mellifluous plainsong, the interior has splendidly muralled vaulting, a towering iconostasis and a gold sarcophagus holding the miraculous relics of Siberian missionary St Innokent.

Celebrity graves outside include those of Decembrist darling Yekaterina Trubetskaya (see above) and of explorer Grigory Shelekhov, who claimed Alaska for Russia. Out the front is a 2004 **statue** of Arctic explorer turned White-Russian commander Admiral Kolchak, who was executed nearby by Bolshevik troops in 1919. Some still see him as a traitor for fighting against Lenin's men, hence the exaggeratedly high plinth to reduce vandalism.

Built in 1758, the baroque **Raising of the Cross Church** (Krestovozdvizhenskaya Tserkov; ul Sedova) is one of the few churches that remained open to worshippers during the Soviet era. It dominates the skyline of Irkutsk seen from the Trans-Siberian Railway.

OTHER HISTORIC STRUCTURES

A few charming **wooden houses** with lacy, carved decoration can still be found in Irkutsk's older neighbourhoods, especially on ul Dekabriskikh Sobyty east of ul Timiryazeva. The grandest brick architecture is along ul Karla Marksa, which hosts various minor museums. Opposite the Regional Museum is the former **White House** (Bely dom; ul Karla Marksa), built in 1804 as the residence of the governors general of Eastern Siberia. It's now a university science library.

NERPA SEALS

Nessie and Tito, two much-loved *nerpa* (Baikal freshwater seals), perform 'shows' every half-hour at **Akvarium Nerpy** (☎ 435 047; ul 2-Zheleznodorozhnaya 66; admission R70; 🕑 11am-6.30pm Wed-Sun). Feats include 'singing' (nasal flatulence?!), break-dancing, ball-tossing and even basic mathematics! Take *marshrutka* (fixed route minibus) 3.

ANGARA DAM & SIBEXPO AREA

Some 6km southeast of the city centre, the 1956 **Angara Dam** is 44m high and 2km long. Its construction raised Lake Baikal by up to 6m causing various human and environmental problems. The dam itself is hardly an attraction, but moored nearby is the **Angara steamship**. This icebreaker ferry was originally imported in kit form from England to carry Trans-Siberian Railway passengers across Lake Baikal. The trains went on her bigger sister-ship *Baikal,* which sank years ago. Officially closed to visitors, the Angara is currently used as a drinks store for a nearby summer café, but the impressive engines still work, as you might see should the café owner decide to befriend you.

Sleeping

Tourist agencies can arrange homestays in Irkutsk and the villages around Lake Baikal. Prices start at around R500 per bed, though R800 is more common. Check the location you're offered: the cheapest places can be 10km or more from the city centre. Finding accommodation in Irkutsk can be tricky in summer and phone reservations aren't always honoured, so consider faxing a confirmation (there'll be a charge). Hostels accept email bookings without a fee.

Irkutsk has three new if tiny private youth hostels. All have good, shared toilets, shower and kitchen. All are ideal for finding English-speaking assistance and meeting fellow travellers.

BUDGET

Baikaler Hostel (☎ 336 240; www.baikaler.com; Apt 11, ul Lenina 9; dm R500; 🔀) Super central, beds are limited at this wonderful homestay-hostel. No drop-ins without prior reservation.

Irkutsk Downtown Hostel (☎ 334 597; www.downtownhostel.irkutsk.ru; Apt 12, ul Stepana Razina 12; dm/d R400/1080) Cosy, 10-bed apartment-hostel above the Yantar grocery. Enter from rear

door spray-graffitied 'Hostel'. Phone ahead for the door entry code. Though central, this area is slightly dubious at night.

Baikalhostel (☎ 525 742 or 527 798; www.baikalhostels.com; Apt 1, ul Lermontova 136; dm €9-10) German-owned hostel with rave reviews from travellers despite the inconvenient and insalubrious location, several kilometres south of the train station: take *marshrutka* 12 to Mikrochirurgia Glaza stop.

Hotel Gornyak (☎ 243 754; ul Lenina 24, enter from ul Dzerzhinskogo; s R900-1200, tw R1800) Friendly, central and small, the Gornyak has reasonably presentable rooms with private shower and toilet, some affected by road noise. Per hour rates available.

Uzory (☎ 209 239; ul Oktyabrskoy Revolyutsi 17; s/tw/tr R550/800/1200) Clean, unpretentious rooms with leopard-skin patterned blankets. The communal toilets and shower are being re-built. Apocryphal backpacker folklore claims that impecunious travellers can get discounts for sleeping on the billiard table.

Hotel Profsoyuznaya (Obshchezhitiye Gostinichogo Tipa Profsoyuznaya; ☎ 357 963; fax 357 855 for bookings; ul Baikalskaya 263; dm R295, tw R590-708, tr R826) Simple but well-kept Soviet-era rooms, albeit far from the city centre in the distant Sib-Expo area. Tram 5 stops outside.

Arena Obshchezhitiye (☎ 334 663; ul Sverdlova 39; s/tw/tr/q R300/600/900/1200) Staff are grumpy and rooms are ragged, but no worse than you'd expect for the price. Entered through a warren of prison-like brown-metal doors, it's very central and often full.

Hotel Agat (☎ 242 320; ul Piyatoy Armii 12; tw R1000) Uninspired but with clean communal toilet and shower. Plenty of peeling paint.

Resting Rooms (Irkutsk train station; r per hr R18, plus sheets R40) There are also rooms available at the train station.

MIDRANGE & TOP END

Hotel Zvezda (☎ 540 000; www.zvezdahotel.ru; ul Yadrintseva 1zh; s/d R2900/3300, ste R5500-9000; P 🔀 🖵) Inviting Swiss chalet–style hotel, with modern rooms, attentive service and English-speaking staff. On the way to the airport down a side street off ul Sovetskaya.

Sun Hotel (☎ 255 910; www.xemi.com/sunhotel; ul Baikalskaya 295B; s €100-115, d €120-135; P 🔀 🖵) Unusually stylish with dark-wood furnishings and impressive bathrooms, though inconveniently located. Reception staff speak English, but the lobby lacks facilities.

Solnyshonok (3rd fl, ul Baikalskaya 259; s/d €50/65) Next-door sister hotel to the Sun Hotel, Solnyshonok is cheaper, but lacks a lift.

Hotel Gloria (☎ 540 326; www.gloriahotel.ru; ul Sovetskaya 58; s/tw/d R3200/3600/3600, ste R5000-5500; 🖭) New pastel-beige tower with nine international-class rooms and two bigger suites, which have bath as well as shower. English is spoken and the minibars overflow with alcoholic choice.

Hotel Delta (☎ 217 876; www.grandbaikal.ru; ul Karla Libknekhta 58; s/d R2000/3000) Motel-standard rooms with little panache, but good value for its relatively central position. It's vastly preferable to the old Soviet hotels.

Hotel Rus (☎ 242 715; http://rus.baikal.ru; ul Sverdlova 19; s R1457-1603, d R1845, ste R2710-2981) Cosy by Soviet standards, but redecoration of the rooms is skin-deep. There's a great village-style restaurant here, too.

Hotel Baikal (Hotel Intourist, Hotel Irkutsk; ☎ 250 167; www.baikal-hotel.ru; bul Gagarina 44; s R1500, tw R2370-3200) This presentable Soviet-era concrete slab has upgraded rooms, some with good river views. Only the most expensive doubles come close to Western standards.

Other possibilities:

Baikal Business Centre (☎ 259120; www.bbc.ru; Baikalskaya ul; s/tw R3400/4200; Ⓟ 🖭) Functionally upper-market business hotel.

Hotel Angara (☎ 255 105; www.angarahotel.ru; ul Sukhe-Batora 7; s/d from R1400/2100) Central but outrageously overpriced. Room quality varies.

Eating

The modern but lively **Central Market** (ul Chekhova) overflows with fresh produce, while cafés and restaurants abound, especially along ul Karla Marksa.

Pervach (☎ 202 288; ul Chkalova 33; meals R240-350) Pervach offers imaginative Baikal-based menus in a vaulted stone and brick basement, heated by real fires in winter. Some English is spoken.

Kafe 16 (☎ 242 682; ul Sukhe-Batora 16; coffees R40-80, meals R270-500; 🕒 10am-11pm) Enticing brown and beige tones purring with jazz beckon you through a unique Art-Deco clamshell archway. Hard-hitting espressos (R40), French wines (R80 per glass) and great garlic-edged fried cheese starters.

Arbatsky Dvorik (☎ 200 633; ul Uritskogo; meals R450-800; 🕒 11am-midnight) An upmarket restaurant with an English menu, and a remarkable interior of imitation house-fronts, doorways

and lanterns. Access is incongruously by walking through congenial, ever-popular **Fiesta** (snacks R45-120; 🕒 noon-11pm), a fast-food eatery.

Snezhinka (☎ 344 862; opp ul Karla Marksa 25; meals R220-330; 🕒 11am-midnight) Warm, cosy belle-époque café-restaurant, with attentive service and consistently good food.

U Dzhuzeppe (☎ 258 348; Stadium arches; meals R70-170; 🕒 11am-11pm) Almost-elegant décor and sensible prices, with menu items like fruity eggplant (R90) and stuffed squid (R110). Menu in English.

Figaro Pizza (☎ 270 607; ul Sovetskaya 58; pizza R100-270, beers from R50; 🕒 10am-midnight) The most authentic pizzeria in town.

CAFÉS

Wiener Café (Venskoye Kafe; ☎ 202 116; ul Stepana Razina 19; coffees R40-70, meals R180-300; 🕒 10am-11pm) Marble-top tables, Parisian bar-chairs and sepia photos with a separate window for takeaway pastries.

Kino Kafe (ul Karla Marksa 22; tea R3, beers R20, snacks R10-40; 🕒 11am-10pm) Within the architecturally delightful Khudozhestveny Cinema is a basic, supercheap café and handy toilet. Enter from ul Krasnoarmeyskaya and walk past the ticket windows and art exhibits.

QUICK EATS

Domino (ul Lenina 13A; meals R70-140; 🕒 24hr) Popular for all-night fast food.

Blinnaya (ul Sukhe-Batora; meals R40-90; 🕒 10am-6pm Mon-Fri, 10am-4pm Sat) A cheap yet neat mini cafeteria-café.

Kafe Temp (ul Lenina 25; meals R40-70; 🕒 10am-8pm) Archetypal 1970s décor would make this perfect for a Soviet nostalgia movie. Food is approximately edible.

Russkaya Chaynaya (☎ 201 678; ul Karla Marksa 3; coffees R40-100, meals R200-350; 🕒 10am-11pm) Splendid fin-de-siècle interior and summer beer garden.

Drinking

Liverpool (☎ 202 512; ul Sverdlova 28; imported beers R50-100; 🕒 noon-late) It's a superbly idiosyncratic Beatles theme-pub. Newcastle Brown Ale in Irkutsk – whatever next?

U Shveyka (☎ 242 687; ul Karla Marksa 34; beers R50-55, meals R170-400; 🕒 noon-midnight; 🖭) This atmospheric cavern with staring elk-head and yin-yang condiments also has a good summer beer terrace.

KRASNOYARSK TO LAKE BAIKAL

Cheshskaya Pivovarnaya (☎ 538 482; Krasnogvardeyskaya ul 29; beers R47-53, meals R180-300; ☺ noon-midnight) This unpretentious microbrewery-pub creates its own Czech-style pilsner.

Peshchera (☎ 243 414; Circus Bldg, ul Zhelyabova; beers R35; ☺ 11am-11pm) It's the liveliest of four smoky, semicheap bars set into the sides of the circus building.

Entertainment

On summer evenings romantic couples and jolly groups of locals stroll the Angara promenade and grassy areas behind the fine **Okhloplov Drama Theatre** (☎ 333 361; ul Karla Marksa 14).

Circus (☎ 336 139; ul Zhelyabova; seats R100-250) Puts on eye-boggling Cirque du Soleil–style performances. Avoid the cheapest front seats where you'll get poor views and a regular splashing.

Philharmonic Hall (☎ 245 076; ul Dzerzhinskogo 2) This historic building stages regular children's shows and musical programmes from pop to classical.

Musical Theatre (☎ 342 131; ul Sedova; seats R60-300; ☺ ticket office 11am-6.30pm Tue-Sun) Pantomimes, costumed musical-comedy shows and ballets take place here in a big concrete auditorium.

Organ Hall (pl Kirova) Organ concerts are held in the 1881 Polish Catholic church.

Stratosphera Night Club (www.strata-club.ru; ul Karla Marksa 15; admission from R100; ☺ 6pm-6am Fri-Sun) Irkutsk's late-night hot spot has a bowling alley, two-storey disco and three-storey drink prices.

Poznaya Disko-bar (ul Chekhova 17; admission R50; beers R45; ☺ 9pm-late) This tobacco-fugged dive is popular with student drinkers on modest budgets, but it can be rough.

Getting There & Away

AIR

Irkutsk's antiquated little 'international' airport is near the city centre. Foreign destinations include Shenyang (US$170) and Tianjin (US$330), both twice weekly. **MIAT** (☎ 203 458; www.miat.com; ul Lapina 11), based at the Mongolian consulate, flies to Ulaanbaatar (US$210) twice or thrice weekly; prices discounted to as little as US$64 in winter.

Dozens of domestic destinations include Moscow (from R6650, daily), St Petersburg (from R7500, three per week), Yekaterinburg (R7680, eight weekly), Vladivostok (10

weekly) and Khabarovsk (R5450 to 6200, six per week).

Handy regional hops available include Kyzyl (R3940, Saturday) in Tuva and Nizhneangarsk (R2160) for Severobaikalsk (twice weekly).

Tickets are sold by a convenient **Central Air Agency** (☎ 201 517; ul Gorkogo 29; ☺ 8am-7pm).

BOAT

In July and August hydrofoils buzz right up Lake Baikal to Severobaikalsk and Nizhneangarsk (R1400, 11½ hours) stopping en route in Port Baikal (change of boats possible) and Olkhon Island (R1100). Departures from Irkutsk are timetabled at 8.50am on Tuesday and Friday, returning next day, but changes and cancellations are fairly frequent. An extra Irkutsk–Olkhon–Irkutsk service runs on some Thursdays. There's an airline-style baggage limit.

Between once and four times daily, June to September, hydrofoils also serve Listvyanka (R130, 1¼ hours) and Bolshie Koty (R180, 1¾ hours).

All of the above depart from the 'Raketa' hydrofoil station beyond the Angara dam in Solnechny mikrorayon, two minutes' walk from bus 16 stop 'Raketa'.

From a different jetty beside Kafe Iveriya, **VSRP** (☎ 287 467) hydrofoils run to Bratsk (R460, 12½ hours) on Tuesday, Saturday and certain Thursdays from June to late September.

BUS

The Visitor Information Office organises minibuses to Olkhon Island. From the **bus station** (☎ 209 115; ☺ 6am-7pm) book tickets ahead for Arshan (R220, 8am) and Khuzhir on Olkhon Island (R370, 9am). For Listvyanka, buses (R30, 1¼ hours, five daily) are supplemented by fairly regular *marshrutky* (R60, 50 minutes) leaving when full from outside. For Bratsk, comfortable private express buses have special ticket booths opposite the bus station.

TRAIN

The elegant old train station has numbered sections. No 1 has advance domestic ticketing. No 2 sells same-day domestic tickets. Upstairs in area No 3 is the **Servis Tsentr** (☎ 636 501) for **international tickets** (☺ 8am-7pm) and the resting rooms, while downstairs is left-luggage. A fourth area beyond sells *elektrichka* (suburban train) tickets to local destinations, including Slyudyanka (R38.20) via Tyomnaya Pad, and is the access route to platforms.

Though expensive, the best train to/from Moscow is the 9/10 *Baikal* (R4150 *kupe*, 77 hours). *Platskart* berths on slower trains, such as train 240/250 (87 hours), cost only R1820 via Krasnoyarsk (R505, 19 hours).

There are several alternate-day trains for Vladivostok, including trains 2 (R3840 *kupe*, 72 hours) and 230 (R3400 *kupe*, 75 hours) via Khabarovsk (58 to 60 hours).

Trains for Beijing (R3800) pass through Irkutsk on Tuesday at 9am or via Mongolia on Saturday at 6am. Trains to Ulaanbaatar cost R1600: fast train 6 (Friday and Saturday) is a full 10 hours quicker than the daily 364 (35 hours).

In any case, heading east consider stopping in Ulan-Ude. That's eight hours away, but worth travelling by day to enjoy the views of Lake Baikal en route.

Train tickets are also sold at the Central Air Agency (commission R80), Hotel Baikal (commission R100 domestic, R300 international) and upstairs in the airport (commission R70).

Getting Around

From the train station, *marshrutka* 20 runs through the city centre to the airport, trams 1 and 2 run to uls Lenina and Timiryazeva, while bus 7 crosses to pl Kirova, then loops round the city centre and out past the Znamenskaya Monastery. Bus 16 continues down ul Lenina, past the Raising of the Cross Church and (eventually) the dam looping back past the hydrofoil station to the Angara steamship. Slow tram 5 from Hotel Profsoyuznaya trundles to the Central Market, from where tram 4 goes past the bus station. Trolleybus 4 (R5) links the city centre to the airport via Hotel Gloria.

Within the central area, walking is usually the best idea.

WESTERN LAKE BAIKAL

Lake Baikal, the 'Pearl of Siberia', is a crystal-clear body of the bluest water. It's drinkably pure, surrounded by rocky, tree-covered cliffs and so vast that one can sail for hours without the mountain backdrops becoming appreciably closer.

Shaped like a banana, Lake Baikal – 636km from north to south, but only 60km wide – was formed by rifting tectonic plates. Though nearly 8km of the rift is filled with sediment, it is gradually getting deeper as the plates separate. It will eventually become the earth's fifth ocean, splitting Asian continent. In the meantime it's the world's deepest lake: 1637m near the western shore. As such, it contains nearly one-fifth of the world's fresh, unfrozen water – more than North America's five Great Lakes combined.

Swimmers brave enough to face Baikal's icy waters (never warmer than about 15°C) risk vertigo, as it is possible to see down as far as 40m. In February and March one can drive right across on the 1m-thick ice, though this is safest in the north and most practical between Severobaikalsk (p244) and Ust-Barguzin (accessed from Ulan-Ude, p213).

The lake itself is a living museum of flora and fauna, 80% of which is found nowhere else on the planet, most famously the loveable black-eyed *nerpa* (freshwater seals) and salmon-like *omul* fish which are delicious smoked. For more details on Baikal, see p59 and p63.

Taltsy Museum of Wooden Architecture
Музей Деревянного Зодчества Тальцы

About 47km east of Irkutsk, 23km before Listvyanka, **Taltsy** (foreigner/local R80/20 plus camera fees; ☒ 10am-6pm summer, 10am-4pm winter) is an impressive outdoor collection of old Siberian buildings set in a delightful riverside forest. Amid the renovated farmsteads are two chapels, a church, a watermill, some Tungusi graves and the eye-catching 17th-century Iliminsk Ostrog watchtower. Listvyanka–Irkutsk buses stop on request at Taltsy's apparently deserted entrance access road. Don't worry. The ticket booth is only a minute's walk through the forest.

Listvyanka Листвянка
☎ 3952 / pop 2500 / ☒ Moscow + 5hr

The nearest Lake Baikal village to Irkutsk, Listvyanka offers winter dog-sledding, summer boat and horse rides and is ideal for watching the Siberian nouveau riche at play. Without doubt it's Baikal's most visited tourist spot. Yet outside busy weekends, the village is still reasonably quiet, with inspiring views towards the distant snowcapped Kamar Daban Mountains.

Hugging the Baikal banks, ul Gorkogo is the main road from Irkutsk, though it doubles as a strolling promenade. It links three disconnected valleys of old wooden cottages. Two of these, ul Gudina (east) and ul Chapaeva (west) are either side of the port area where hydrofoils arrive and buses terminate at a little market. The wider Krestovka valley (uls Ostrovskogo, Kulikova and Gornaya) is 15 minutes' walk west towards Irkutsk. Another 2km west at Rogatka is the Limnological Institute and the ferry jetty for Port Baikal. Central Nikola is centred 4km beyond that.

Basic maps are available on www.irkutsk .org/fed/maps/listmap.jpg and sold from a small, helpful tourist information booth, which opens sporadically at the port/bus stand.

SIGHTS

Having glimpsed Lake Baikal and eaten fresh-smoked *omul* fish at the port, many visitors are left vaguely wondering what to do next. Fishing-boat rides (charters from R800 per hour) or gentle strolls are a common time-filler with old log cottages to photograph up uls Gudina and Chapaeva, though ongoing gentrification is starting to impinge on their architectural integrity. About 2km west in **Krestovka**, the pretty if unremarkable **Svyato-Nikolskaya Church** was named for an apparition of St Nicholas, which supposedly saved its sponsor from a Baikal shipwreck.

Another 2km towards Irkutsk at **Rogatka**, tour groups are herded into the **Limnological Institute** (☎ 250 551; ul Akademicheskaya 1; foreigner/local R180/80; ☼ 9am-7pm Jun-Sep, 9am-5pm rest of year), where gruesomely discoloured fish samples and seal embryos in formaldehyde are now supplemented with tanks containing a sad, living *nerpa* seal and various Baikal fish that you'd otherwise encounter on restaurant menus.

Walking up the hill behind the Soviet-era Baikal Hotel leads to some attractive viewpoints from a short ski-run.

ACTIVITIES

From December to March, **Baikal Dog Sledding Centre** (☎ 112 829 or 112 799; ole-tbaikaledog@mail .ru; ul Gornaya 17, Krestovka) offers thrilling dog-

sledding on forest tracks. The shortest 3km run with three dogs costs R600, but whole multiday cross-Baikal expeditions are possible with bigger dog teams. The owners' sons speak English.

On the warmer winter weekends snow-mobiles and even horses can be informally hired on the ice near the Proshly Vek restaurant, while hovercraft rides are available from the main port area. On the beach-front, locals photograph each other in front of weirdly shaped frozen waves.

SLEEPING

There is a vast choice of accommodation. However, with minimal public transport, no taxi service and no left-luggage office, finding a room without reservations in summer can take some tiresome trekking around. Leave heavy bags in Irkutsk. Any accommodation under R500 is likely to be very basic with an outside squat toilet, dorm-style beds or both. Virtually every Irkutsk tour agent has its own guesthouse or homestay in Listvyanka, and the tourist office at the port can make suggestions when it opens.

There are a few handy but predominantly unexotic homestays on lakefront ul Gorkogo.

Along uls Gudina and Chapaeva, two ribbons of attractive wooden cottages, very basic homestays are available at ul Chapaeva 6, 44 and 64 and ul Gudina 77. If you want indoor toilets try ul Gudina 13a or 71, or ul Chapaeva 24, 65 or 69.

Slightly less convenient than the port area for public transport, Krestovka is nonetheless more of a 'real' village and offers an ever-expanding choice.

Several resorts are tucked invisibly away off the Listvyanka to Irkutsk road in Nikola, including around Nikola village which stretches 3km towards the Rogatka ferry-jetty. Often comfortable, but somewhat inconvenient if you lack your own transport.

Budget

Galina Vasilyevna's Homestay (☎ 112 798; ul Kulikova 44, Krestovka; dm/tr R300/900) Cheap, saggy dorm beds in a delightfully genuine old home with large traditional stove-heater, but minimal facilities. Ask for keys at the Darya grocery shop. An indoor toilet functions in summer.

KRASNOYARSK TO LAKE BAIKAL

BAIKAL

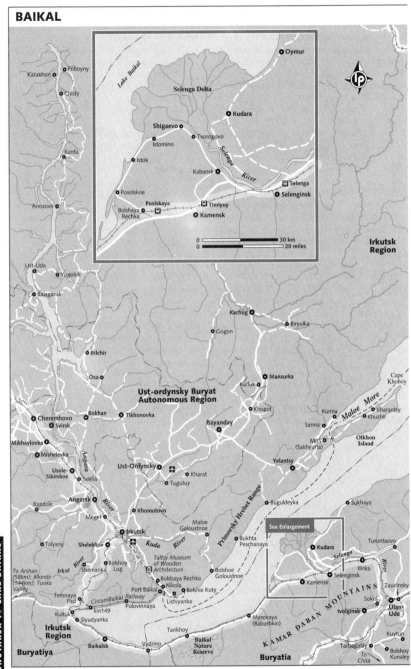

Enlargement (top inset):

Oymur

Lake Baikal

Selenga Delta

Kudara

Shigaevo
Tvorogovo
Istomino

Istok

Kabansk
Selenga River
Selenga
Selenginsk

Posolskoe

Poslskaya
Bolshaya
Rechka
Timlyuy
Kamensk

Irkutsk Region

0   30 km
0   20 miles

Main map:

Karakhun
Priboyny
Chisty

Karda

Anosovo

Ust-Uda
Yugolok
Balagansk

Kachug
Biryulka
Gogon

Bilchir

Osa
Manzurka
Cape Khoboy

Ust-ordynsky Buryat Autonomous Region

Karluk
Khogot
Kurma
Kharantsy
Khuzhir

Cheremhovo
Svirsk
Bokhan
Tikhonovka
Bayanday
Sarma
MRS (Sakhyurta)
Olkhon Island
Maloe More

Mikhaylovka
Mishelevka

Usole-Sibirskoe
Telma

Ust-Ordynsky
Kharat
Tugutuy
Yelantsy

Razdole
Khomutovo
Maloe Goloustnoe
Buguldeyka
Sukhaya

Angarsk
Meget

Talyany
Shelekhov
Irkutsk
Kuda River
Bukhta Peschanaya

See Enlargement

To Arshan
(58km); Mondy
(144km); Tunka
Valley
Irkut River
Shamanka
Bolshoy Lug
Taltsy Museum of Wooden Architecture
Bolshaya Rechka
Nikola
Bolshoe Goloustnoe
Kudara
Turuntaevo

Temnaya Pad
CircumBaikal Railway
Port Baikal
Bolshie Koty
Listvyanka
Selenginsk
Ilinka
Selenga River
Zaudinsky

Kultuk
km149
Polovinnaya
Kamensk
Sokol

Slyudyanka
Ivolginsk
Ulan-Ude

Irkutsk Region
Baikalsk
Mysovaya (Babushkin)
Kuytun

Buryatiya
Vydrino
Tankhoy
Baikal Nature Reserve
Tarbagatay
Bolshoy Kunaley

Buryatia
KAMAR DABAN MOUNTAINS
To Chita

Primorsky Hrebet Range

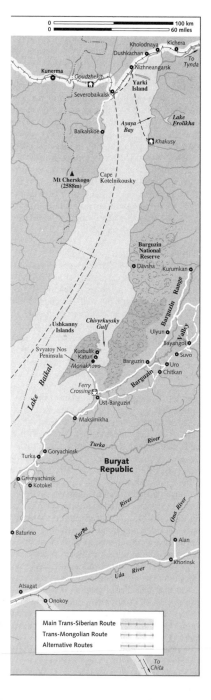

Priboy (☎ 112 839; upper fl, ul Gorkogo 101; dm/tw R250/1200) Cheap but unappealing dorms right at the lakeside. Keys are available from the Askat shop (open 8am to 8pm) or the restaurant (open noon to 11pm) downstairs.

National Park Hostel (☎ 112 520; ul Gorkogo 39; dm R400) Three bare-bones three-bed dorms and a communal kitchen within the Pribaikalsky National Park information centre. The toilet doesn't work in winter.

Midrange

Derevenka (☎ 250 459; www.village2002.narod.ru; ul Gornaya 1, Krestovka; s/d R1300/1400, midsummer R1400/1700) On a ridge behind the Baikal-front road, this place offers lovely little wooden huts with stove-heaters, private toilets and hot water (but not showers). It's run by a friendly family, who can organise snowmobile, sled and boat rentals. *Banya* (hot bath, like a sauna) costs R200.

Baikalskiye Terema (☎ 112 599; info@greenexpress .ru; ul Gornaya 16, Krestovka; s/d R2500/2700) For Western comforts this fully equipped pine-furnished hotel remains Listvyanka's snazziest option. Half-price room rates are available for 12-hour stays. There's a sports-activities centre, but compare prices.

U Ozera (☎ 250 444; Irkutsk highway km3; d winter/summer R1800/2500) New, reasonably comfortable if cramped motel overlooking the lake, between Krestovka and Rogatka.

Ersi (☎ 112 546; www.ersi.baikal.ru; ul Chapaeva 65; tw R1000-1289) Cheaper than sleeping inside, take a R480 bed in the Mongolian *ger*-yurt tent. Nikolai speaks English, and can arrange boat and bicycle excursions when in residence.

Briz (☎ 250 468; www.baikal-briz.ru; ul Gudina 71; standard s/tw summer R1500/1700, winter R1200/1400) A good price-quality balance with in-room toilets and distant Baikal views from the nicer rooms. In summer there are more basic hut beds at R750.

Top End

Anastasia Resort (☎ 112 191; www.baikalhotel.ru; ul Angarskaya 8, Nikola; s R4500, d R5500-6000, ste R10,000-24,000; ℗) Splendid, comfortable new 18-room hotel complex sits right on the Angara waterside in central Nikola, with pretty views from many rooms. It's walking distance from an Irkutsk–Listvyanka bus stop, but about 7km from Listvyanka port.

EATING

Near the port are numerous vendors pedalling delicious smoked *omul* fish and cafés.

Shury Mury (☎ 250 452; sandwiches R25-60, meals R150-350; ⊗ 10am-11pm) Has a lakeside summer terrace.

Proshly Vek (☎ 112 554; ul Lazlo 1; meals R200-470) The most atmospheric eatery, 2.5km west of the port between U Ozera and Krestovka.

GETTING THERE & AWAY

Five daily buses (R30, 1¼ hours) and roughly hourly *marshrutky* run from Listvyanka port to Irkutsk passing the Limnological Institute, Nikola and Taltsy museum. Taxis from Irkutsk want at least R1000.

Mid-May to late September, hydrofoils stop at Listvyanka port between Irkutsk (R180) and Bolshie Koty (R80) at least daily, more frequently on weekends.

Year-round a tiny, battered car-ferry lumbers across the Angara to Port Baikal from Rogatka. It supposedly departs at 8.15am, 4.15pm and 6.15pm but times are by no means guaranteed.

Various short trips by yachts, fishing boat or even hovercraft are available at the main port depending on the season. For longer cruises inquire well ahead through Irkutsk agencies. In winter **Baikaler** (www.baikaler.com) runs a one-day excursion from Irkutsk to Listvyanka, Bolshie Koty and across the ice to a tunnel on the Circumbaikal Railway for R1200 per person.

Port Baikal Порт Байкал
☎ 3952

From 1900 to 1904 the Trans-Siberian Railway tracks led here from Irkutsk. They continued on Lake Baikal's far eastern shore at Mysovaya (Babushkin). The rail-less gap was plugged by ice-breaking steamships, including the *Angara*, now restored in Irkutsk (p195). Later the tracks were extended south and around the lake. This Circumbaikal Railway (p205) required so many impressive tunnels and bridges that it earned the nickname 'The Tsar's Jewelled Buckle'. With the damming of the Angara River in the 1950s, the original Irkutsk to Port Baikal railway section was submerged and replaced with an Irkutsk–Kultuk short cut (today's Trans-Siberian Railway). That left poor little Port Baikal to wither away at the dead end of a rarely used branch line.

Seen from Listvyanka across the unbridged mouth of the Angara River, Port Baikal looks like a rusty semi-industrial eyesore. But the view is misleading. A kilometre southwest of Stanitsa (the port area), Port Baikal's **Baranchiki** area is a ramshackle 'real' village, with lots of unkempt but authentic Siberian cottages and a handy selection of accommodation options. The village rises steeply, making for good short walks, with excellent Baikal viewpoints easily accessible. Awkward ferry connections mean that Port Baikal remains largely uncommercialised, lacking Listvyanka's 'attractions' but also its crowds. Thus it's popular with meditative painters and hikers. But its main draw is the Circumbaikal train ride from Slyudyanka (see p205).

SLEEPING & EATING

Yakhont (☎ 250 496 or 622 977; www.yahont.irk.ru; ul Naberezhnaya 3, Baranchiki; dm/tw R800/2400) This traditionally designed log house is decorated with eclectic good taste by well-travelled, English-speaking owners. Guests congregate in the stylish communal kitchen-diningroom, above which rooms have perfect Western bathrooms. For those on tighter budgets a cute but waterless cliff-front cottage offers an appealing dormitory option. Advance bookings are essential; major expansion is planned. See opposite for transport options.

B&B Baikal (☎ 250 463; www.baikal.tk; ul Baikalskaya 12, Baranchiki; bed/half-board R500/800) Set 400m back from the lakeside in a house with a conspicuous, wood-framed new picture window, various newly decorated but unpretentious rooms share two Western style toilets and a shower.

Anastasia Shishlonova's Homestay (ul Naberezhnaya 12-1, Baranchiki; bed/half-board R150/300) The delightful Shishlonova family offer rooms in their wonderfully positioned Baikal-facing home and a cute if minuscule hut-room in the yard. There's fresh milk from the cow, who greets you on the walk to the challenging pit-toilet. No running water.

Lyudmila Masalitina's Homestay (ul Vokzalnaya 7/2, Stanitsa; dm/q R150/600) In the unattractive Stanitsa area, this friendly homestay is great value and very handy for the Listvyanka ferry. The toilet is a scary outhouse.

As yet Port Baikal has no café, but there are three grocery kiosks at Baranchiki and two in Stanitsa.

GETTING THERE & AWAY

The ferry to Listvyanka (20 minutes) runs year-round, supposedly three times daily at 7.10am, 3.50pm and 5.15pm, but times can change at whim. There are direct hydrofoils to Irkutsk (50 minutes) in summer. Rare trains come via the very slow Circumbaikal Railway. For guests, the Yakhont offers speed-boat charters (R2000 per hour) and R300 pick-ups to/from Listvyanka.

Bolshie Koty Болшие Коты

pop 350

Founded by 19th-century gold miners, roadless Bolshiye Koty makes an easy day trip by boat or ice-drive from Listvyanka or a picturesque if somewhat hair-raising hike. The little **museum** opposite the jetty has a few pickled crustaceans and stuffed rodents. Otherwise, the village is simply a pleasant place to stroll, snooze and watch fish dry. A few basic homestays include ul Baikalskaya 55, with a lovely lakeside position, and neater, inland ul Zarechnaya 11b. Great fresh-smoked *omul* are sold at the port when boats arrive.

Hydrofoils originating in Irkutsk (R180) depart from Listvyanka (R80, 25 minutes) at least daily in summer, staying nearly two hours before returning. That's plenty for most visitors.

Olkhon Island Остров Ольхон

pop 1500 / ⏲ Moscow + 5hr

Halfway up Baikal's western shore and reached by a short ferry journey from Sakhyurta (aka MRS), the serenely beautiful Olkhon Island is a wonderful place from which to view the lake and relax during a tour of Siberia.

Considered one of five global poles of shamanic energy by the Buryat people, the 72km-long island's main settlement is **Khuzhir**, which has seen something of a tourist boom over the last few years thanks mainly to the inspiring efforts of Nikita's Guest House, which also runs the **tourist information office** (⏲ 9am-9pm) outside the guesthouse. For a good map of the island go to www.baikalex.com, or get printed maps from the tourist information office.

Although high season is July and August, also consider visiting here during the quiet winter months when you can drive across the ice to the island until early April.

Olkhon was reconnected to the electricity grid in 2005 and mobile phones now work in Khuzhir, but as yet there are no landlines.

SIGHTS & ACTIVITIES

There are unparalleled views of Baikal from sheer cliffs that rise at the island's northern end, culminating at dramatic **Cape Khoboy**. Day-long jeep trips, including lunch, cost (R350) and can be arranged through Nikita's Guest House and other guesthouses in Khuzhir.

Khuzhir's small **museum** (ul Pervomayskaya 24; admission free; ⏲ 10am-6pm), next to the village school, is worth a look. Consider dropping by **Nikita's Guest House** even if you aren't staying there to admire the inventive kid's playground and general atmosphere of the place. A short walk north of Nikita's, the unmistakable **Shaman Rocks** are neither huge nor spectacular, but they make a perfect meditational focus for the ever-changing cloudscapes across the picturesque Maloe ·More (Little Sea). East of the rocks is a long strip of sandy beach.

The island's southern end is rolling grassland – great for off-road mountain biking or gentle hiking, and if Baikal proves too cold for a dip you can cool off in the small **Shara-Nur Lake**.

SLEEPING & EATING

The large complex of upmarket-looking wooden cabins under construction at the time of research on the north edge of town will be the latest in an ever-growing range of places to stay in Khuzhir.

Irkutsk travel agents (p191) offer a choice of basic cottage homestays in Khuzhir for around R600 (full board). If you just show up there's a fair chance of finding a similar place from R450. Toilets are always outside the rooms and the *banya* will cost extra.

The village is small enough that it won't take you long to find the following recommended places.

Nikita's Guest House (http://olkhon.info; ul Kirpichnaya 8, Khuzhir; full board per person R530) Run by a former Russian table-tennis champ and his wife, Siberia's premier hang-out for travellers is a wonderful place to stay and eco-friendly to boot. If it's full (as it often is in high season), they'll find you a place to stay elsewhere in the village. The basic rooms on-site are attractively decorated. Scrub up in an authentic *banya* and pig out on delicious home-cooked meals. There's a packed schedule of excursions and activities.

Solnechnaya (☎ 3952-389 103; www.web-olkhon.com; ul Solnechnaya 14; full board R510-570) Not quite as happening a scene as Nikita's, but still a pleasant place to stay offering a good range of activities. Accommodation is in two-storey cabins; cooler 1st-floor rooms being the more expensive.

Ventsak (ul Baikalskaya 42; full board per person R480) The most appealing of Khuzhir's smaller guesthouses has a handful of cabins in a quiet spot just off the village's main street. The shower and *banya* block is in good condition, and there's a comfortable communal lounge area.

Yurt Camp Harmony (www.greenexpress.ru; full board per person sharing 4-bed yurt R800) Several kilometres north of Khuzhir near the tiny hamlet of Kharansti, Green Express (p191) runs this camp site, with some 20 large circular felt tents shaded by trees on a lakeside. It's used for the company's tours but independent travellers can stay if there's room. Dog-cart rides are available in summer.

GETTING THERE & AWAY
From June to August there are at least two and usually three daily buses between Khuzhir (R370, seven hours) and Irkutsk, with an additional minibus leaving from Nikita's Guest House daily at 8.30am (R300). Frequency drops off drastically outside the high season. With a little warning, agencies or hostels can usually find you a ride in a private car to Irkutsk (R700/2500 seat/car, 5½ hours). Prices include the short ferry ride to MRS. Mid-January to March an ice-road replaces the ferry. When the ice is partly formed or partly melted, the island is completely cut off for a few weeks.

In summer a hydrofoil service operates three times weekly from Irkutsk to Olkhon (R1100, seven hours), dropping passengers near the ferry terminal, from where it's possible to hitch a lift into Khuzhir. Two of the hyrdofoils continue to Severobaikalsk.

Maloe More Малое Море
☎ 3952
The relatively warm, shallow waters of the **Maloe More** (Little Sea) offer a primary donothing holiday attraction for Siberians. Main attractions are swimming, hiking to

mini waterfalls, and drinking. Dozens of camps, huts and resorts are scattered amid attractive multiple bays backed by alternating woodland and rolling grassland scenery. Since each widely spaced 'resort' is frequently prebooked and hard to access without private transport, you'd be wise to first visit Irkutsk travel agents and leaf through their considerable catalogues. Booking something not too far from MRS makes it easier to continue later to Olkhon Island. Arguably the most appealing bay is **Bukhta Kurkutskaya**, where the Baza Otdykha Naratey has showers and bio-toilets. Several new resorts offer weekly transfers from Irkutsk for guests (around R400), such as **Baikal-Dar** (☎ 266 336; www.dar.irk.ru; d/tr full board R1600/2400). The further, Olkhon-facing **Khadarta Bay** between Sarma and Kurma is becoming ever more popular.

From June to late August minibuses run to Kurma (R380, 5½ hours) at 9am via Sarma (R320) from the courtyard of Irkutsk's Visitor Information Office. They return at 2pm the same day. Public buses from Irkutsk serve MRS.

SLYUDYANKA СЛЮДЯНКА
☎ 39544 / pop 18,800 / ◷ Moscow + 5hr
Lacking any architectural charm, Slyudyanka rarely tempts Westerners off the train. Yet the drab, functional town has a great lakeside setting, is backed by mountains and is the best place to start Circumbaikal train rides (opposite). It's also an ideal launching point for reaching the splendid, peak-backed Tunka Valley and its popular spa-village Arshan (opposite).

Slyudyanka 1, the famously all-stone **train station**, is a mere five minutes' walk from Lake Baikal's shore. Walking there you'll pass a photogenic little **church** in multi-coloured, Scooby Doo style. The in-Russian **museum** (Kraevedchesky muzey; ☎ 2351; ul Zhelezno-dorozhnaya 22; admission R30; ◷ 11am-5pm Sun-Thu) across the tracks has some intriguing archaeological finds, but specialises in railway history. There's an old Circumbaikal Railway switching box and a very useful identification guide to 47 locomotive types from various eras.

With shared showers and seatless toilets, the simple, friendly **hotel** (☎ 23 071; ul Frunze 4, M/R Perival; dm/s/tw R300/400/800) charges half-price for 12-hour stays. To get there from

Slyudyanka 1 train station, cross the long footbridge and walk two blocks further: a little to your left you'll find a small **bus station** (ul Lenina), from where the hotel is 4km west by very frequent *marshrutka* 1 (last at 11pm). A taxi costs R40. Lugubriously UV-lit **Kafe Germez** (☎ 51 089; ul Lenina 54; meals R50-70) is halfway.

For better accommodation head 35km east to the smelly, lakeside ski-resort of **Baikalsk**, where the **Hotel Uyut** (☎ 37 312; www .baikaltur.ru; Stroitelnaya 13; d low/mid season R800/1000, high season R1200-1600) is well equipped.

Trains from Irkutsk take approximately 3¼ hours (*elektrichka*) or 2½ hours (express) to Slyudyanka 1. Two cheap, slow, but incredibly scenic *elektrichka* trains run daily to Baikalsk (R18, 1½ hours), where Baikalsk Passazhirsky halt is much nearer the Uyut than Baikalsk mainline station.

Minibuses from outside Slyudyanka station depart to Arshan at the ungodly time of 4.45am (this can be even earlier depending when train 125 arrives from Ulan-Ude). An additional bus to Arshan (R75, two hours) leaves at 2pm from the bus station, from where bus 103 runs six times daily to Baikalsk.

ARSHAN АРШАН

☎ 30156 / pop 900-3800 (seasonal) / ⊙ Moscow + 5hr
Sawtooth Sayan peaks rise spectacularly above the cute Buddhist villages of the wide, rural Tunka Valley. This area attracts wilderness hiker-climbers, but it's main draw is undoubtedly the little spa village of Arshan. It's nestled right at the foot of soaring forested mountains offering relaxing short walks to a series of rapids between sulphur-scented sips. There are plenty of longer, more challenging treks and climbs here, too. More detailed information is available at http://tunki.baikal.ru (in Russian).

CIRCUMBAIKAL RAILWAY

The historic Circumbaikal route (p33) from Slyudyanka to Port Baikal is one of Baikal's most popular tourist jaunts. Excruciatingly slow or a great social event? Opinions are mixed as the train chugs scenically along cliff ledges above the limpid lake waters on this lake-hugging branch line. You'll need to juggle sunglasses, a fan and a torch as the carriages are unventilated and unlit.

The most picturesque route sections are around **Polovinnaya** (approximately halfway) and the bridge area at **km149** (one hour from Slyudyanka), where there's also a small **Rerikh museum**. Views are best if you can persuade the driver to let you ride on the front of the locomotive – possible on certain tour packages. Note that *from* Port Baikal most trains travel by night, so are useless for sightseeing.

The Circumbaikal's old stone tunnels, stolby-cliff cuttings and bridges are an attraction even if you don't ride the train: in winter it's possible to drive alongside certain route-sections on ice-roads from Kultuk. Hiking sections of the peaceful track is also popular. Walking from Port Baikal leads to some pleasant if litter-marred beaches. Or get off an Irkutsk–Slyudyanka *elektrichka* train at Temnaya Pad and hike down the stream valley for about an hour. You should emerge at km149 on the Circumbaikal track. Continue by train to Port Baikal if you've timed things carefully.

Travelling the Circumbaikal

From a side platform at Slyudyanka I station, *matanya* (short, wooden-seated trains) currently depart at 1pm, two to four times weekly (R32, six hours) – check the timetables carefully. To get a seat you'll need to join the scrum to board around half an hour before departure. Get off at Baranchiki, the penultimate halt, for Port Baikal's best accommodation. In summer an additional tourist train direct from Irkutsk departs at around 7am on Saturdays. A wonderfully detailed website (http://kbzd.irk.ru) has regularly updated timetables, plus photographs of virtually every inch of the route.

There are roughly a dozen isolated *turbazy* (holiday camps) of varying quality along the route. Perhaps the most usefully positioned is the rambling, very basic **Baza Alpinistov** (☎ 902-178 3502; dm R100) at km149. Bring your own food. Alternatively, several Irkutsk travel agents run organised Circumbaikal tours (see p191). BaikalComplex includes a charter-ferry to get you to Listvyanka avoiding a forced overnight in Port Baikal.

Arshan's main street, ul Traktovaya, is patchily attractive where lined in places with old-fashioned log cottages. From the big, six-storey Sayan Sanatorium, this street heads 2km straight towards the mountains passing the post office, **Internet Zal** (ul Traktovaya 32; per hr R50; ⏰ 11am-1pm & 2-6pm Mon-Fri, 12.30-6pm Sat & Sun) and **bus-ticket kiosk** (ul Traktovaya 3). Then it swerves west past the **Altan Mundarga Information Booth** (☎ 97 502; ul Traktovaya 6) and the sprawling Kurort Arshan resort. Keep walking 20 minutes through the forest to find the dinky little **Badkhirkharma datsan** (Buddhist temple) set in an idyllic mountain-backed glade. Or walk up tracks beside the stream to access the mountain footpaths.

SLEEPING

Many log cottages offer very basic homestays from R100 per bed. Look for Дом/Жильё signs.

Priyut Alpinista (☎ 97 697; www.iwf.ru; ul Bratev Domshevikh 8; tw R800-1000, tr R1300) This characterful new climbers' centre has the atmosphere of a Western youth hostel, but rooms have private toilet and better ones have hot showers. Rent bicycles (R65 per hour), buy climbing maps (R25) and watch videos of Arshan's attractions in the comfortable sitting room before adding comments to the 'magic tree'. It's a modest wooden building three minutes' walk along ul Pavlova from the bus stand. The owners also offer pre-erected, supplied tent-places high in the mountains (R350 per person, including food) so that hikers and mountaineers don't need to carry a rucksack.

Hotel Zamok Gornogo Korolya (☎ 97 384; ul Gagarina 18; d R1700-2100) This modern pseudo-castle building has crenellations, green-tipped towers and four comfortable, semismart rooms, with questionable 'artistic' taste in nude derrières.

Kurort Arshan (☎ 97 745; ul Traktovaya 1; dm/s R150/215; reception ⏰ 8am-8pm summer, 9am-1pm & 4-7pm winter) Basic institutional sanatorium with various sized buildings spread through the forest, used mostly by cure-seekers using its mineral springs.

Pansionat Sagaan Dali (☎ 97 468; www.sagaan.ru; ul Deputatskaya 14; s/d/ste R390/780/1170; ℗) Inexpensive but with all the charm of a 1970s council block, rooms are cosmetically upgraded, though still have rather sad old toilets. Suites are bigger but not better. The access footpath from ul Traktovaya skirts the Sayan Sanatorium passing a spluttering sulphurous spring-water faucet marked by prayer flags.

EATING

Sayan Kafe (meals R200-400; ⏰ noon-11pm) Easily missed within the grounds of the Sayan Sanatorium, this small café is Arshan's nicest eatery.

Much cheaper snacks are available from a rustic unmarked **tea house** (ul Traktovaya 1; beers R30), beside Visit grocery shop, and from a bright if unrepentantly Soviet **stolovaya** (canteen; ul Traktovaya 13; meals R35-50; ⏰ 9am-7pm), near the post office.

GETTING THERE & AWAY

Buses run to Kyren (R35, 1¼ hours, 10.30am, noon and 2pm), Slyudyanka (R75, 7.30am and 2pm), Ulan-Ude (R332, 11 hours, 7.30am Tuesday to Sunday) and Irkutsk (R220, 2pm). Buses are sometimes replaced and/or supplemented by *marshrutky*, which cost somewhat more.

Irkutsk to Vladivostok

Just because you've made it to Baikal doesn't mean Russia is over. Almost hugging the Chinese border east of Baikal, the Trans-Siberian clamours along for another 4000km (almost doubling the Moscow–Irkutsk journey), going past untouched taiga and blue mountains and tiny towns of gingerbread houses. This is the heart of Russia's Far East, its own 'wild east' where Cossacks rode hoisting swords and in Soviet times Gulag-bound prisoners packed train carriages rattling towards grim new homes.

Looming near the tracks' end – and the irresistible destination for many – is Vladivostok, a closed-off naval town during the USSR days, with peaks sprinkled along the edge of snaking bays and rattling trams. But on the way are tempting stopoffs, too. Alive with Asian smiles, Ulan-Ude is the launching point for visiting eastern Baikal or for buses to Mongolia. Outside both Ulan-Ude and Chita, Buryat Buddhist monasteries are a major draw. South of the Trans-Siberian on the northern bank of the Amur River, Blagoveshchensk is an alternative exit point from Russia, where daily ferries of commerce-oriented Russians and Chinese cross national lines to the 'new' Chinese town of Heihe, which is quickly outsizing its tsar-era Russian neighbour.

Outside Khabarovsk – itself the most cosmopolitan centre of the Russian Far East, with sushi bars overlooking the wide Amur River – is Birobidzhan and the Jewish Autonomous Region, where Jews relocated during the Soviet days, and a small local population maintains its cultural heritage. In Primorsky Territory (Kray), outside Vladivostok, you can day trip to tiger reserves and see birds on a massive lake that straddles the Chinese border.

HIGHLIGHTS

▪ Boat past naval ships in the picturesque harbour in **Vladivostok** (p230)

▪ Cross the Trans-Siberian's longest bridge over the Amur River at cosmopolitan **Khabarovsk** (p211)

▪ Explore Baikal's lesser-known eastern shore at the rarely visited **Barguzin Valley** (p218)

▪ Sense the resurgence of Buryat Buddhism at **Ivolginsk Datsan** (p217)

▪ Cross into China from the historical border town of **Blagoveshchensk** (p223)

▪ ROUTE DISTANCE: 4104KM   ▪ DURATION: 73 HOURS

IRKUTSK TO VLADIVOSTOK

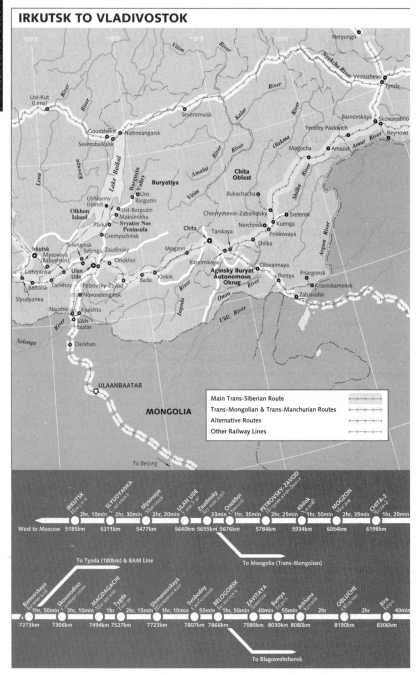

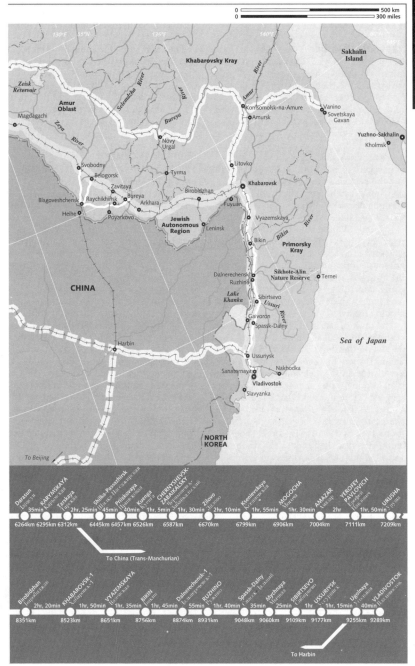

THE ROUTE

Irkutsk to Ulan-Ude

North of the line, at **5228km**, a cheery Vladimir Ilych Lenin waves from the hill side well before the train approaches **Slyudyanka** (5311km; p204). For 200km, the line now runs along the southern shore of **Lake Baikal** (5300km to 5500km), passing through a series of tunnels blasted into the cliffs along the water's edge. Many passengers are glued to the windows gawping at the shore and icy blue waters of the world's deepest lake. In fact the best views are probably in the section immediately after Slyudyanka, before reaching **Baikalsk** (5352km), where the air is soured by a huge, controversial pulp mill.

Around 5390km, the train crosses the river that marks the border of Buryatiya (Buryat Republic), one of Russia's semiautonomous ethnic republics. Closely related to the Mongols, the Buryats have been undergoing something of a Buddhist revival but have largely given up their former nomadic herding lifestyles.

The town of **Tankhoy** (5426km) lies in the centre of the Baikal Nature Reserve. Further along the shore, **Mysovaya** (5477km) is the port where the *Baikal* and *Angara* used to start (or finish) their journeys across the lake, ferrying train carriages and their passengers, before the south-bank railway was completed. The obelisk at Mysovaya *zheleznodorozhny vokzal* (train station) marks the spot where in 1906 tsarist forces shot revolutionary Ivan Babushkin, for whom the surrounding town is now renamed.

Directly below the present line one can clearly make out sections of older tracks. These were half-drowned after the construction of the Angara dam near Irkutsk raised the level of Lake Baikal.

If you are travelling west, keep a lookout for the lake from around **5507km**, when the train suddenly pulls out from between the forested hill sides and reveals a glorious view of Baikal's clear blue waters and the cliffs on the other side.

Just before reaching the train station of **Selenga** (5562km, for the town of Selenginsk) the train line hooks up with the Selenga River, which it will follow into Mongolia if you are on the Trans-Mongolian. Between here and Ulan-Ude, the river

valley provides ample photo opportunities, such as at 5630km, when the train crosses the river.

The train stops for about 15 minutes at **Ulan-Ude** (5640km), the capital of Buryatiya. Sadly, that's not long enough to dash to the centre of this relatively exotic city to see the world's biggest Lenin head. Instead, at the northwestern end of the platform you can admire the old steam locomotive that sits in front of the depot.

Ulan-Ude to Chita

The Trans-Mongolian line (p253) doubles back at **Zaudinsky** (5655km), which is virtually a suburb of Ulan-Ude. The mainline follows the wide Uda Valley. At an unmarked station about half an hour out of Ulan-Ude (before Onokhoi) you'll see a marshalling yard with a graveyard of rusting steam locos. The scenery here is pretty as the wide, flood-prone valleys continue, their rolling meadows backed distantly by trees on the north-facing slopes. Quaint log-cabin settlements are scattered with patches of attractive woodland. Upon entering Chitinskaya region (**5771km**), local time becomes Moscow time plus six hours.

The train stops for about 12 minutes at **Petrovsky-Zavod** (5784km), the station for the town of Petrovsk-Zabaikalsky. The station name (and the old name of the town) means 'Peter's Factory', so-called for the huge ironworks you can still see from the train. Decembrists (see p194) jailed here from 1830 to 1939 are commemorated in a large, photogenic mural at the station.

The railway now heads northeast following the Khilok Valley, with the **Yablonovy Mountains** (between 5800km and 6300km) forming blue shadows in the distance. At the small town of **Bada** (5884km), look for the MiG fighter monument and the cluster of old aircraft on the runway to the north.

Around **5925km**, the train slows as it leaves the valley and moves into the mountains, affording inspiring views of the winding river, and fields filled with wildflowers. It may pause briefly in **Khilok** (5934km), where there is a machine shop for repairing train engines. An old locomotive stands at the eastern end of the platform. There is another 15-minute stop at **Mogzon** (6054km), which is a good place to get some home-made grub from the babushkas on the platform.

The train halts for 20 minutes at **Chita-2** (6198km), the main station of Chita and an interesting point from which to see some intriguing Buddhist sites.

Chita to Mogocha

For the next 250km east, the Trans-Siberian route follows the Ingoda River, which is south of the train. There are good views of the river around **Darasun** (6264km) where the train pauses briefly.

In **Karymskaya** (6295km), the station for the industrial town of Karymskoye, there's a 20-minute stop, shortly before **Tarskaya** (6312km), the Trans-Manchurian junction; for details of this route, see p269.

The main Trans-Siberian route continues northeast through **Shilka-Passazhirsk** (6445km), where there's a five-minute halt. Look south to see piles of train wheels on leaving the station. The hills are pretty as the route follows Shilka River, marred by the derelict factories of Kolbon (there's no stop here).

There's a brief stop at **Priiskovaya** (6457km), where a 10km branch line heads north to the old silver-mining town of **Nerchinsk**. This is where the Treaty of Nerchinsk was signed in 1689, carving up Russian and Chinese spheres of influence in the Far East.

Around **6510km** keep an eye out for the lovely, picturesque church in the Byankino Valley, as well as a few other buildings on the flood plain across the Shilka River, south of the train.

At **Kuenga** (6526km) the Trans-Sib route turns sharply north, while a 52km branch line heads to Sretensk, the eastern terminus of the Trans-Baikal Railway (see p33). Until the Amur Railway was completed in 1916 Trans-Sib passengers used to disembark from the train here and climb aboard steamers to Khabarovsk.

There's an 18-minute stop at **Chernyshevsk-Zabaikalsky** (6587km), giving you some time to stock up from the food and drink sellers. It is named after the 19th-century exile Nikolai Chernyshevsky, whose silver-painted statue is on the platform.

Around **6660km** there are sweeping views to the north of the train across the Siberian plains. The next long stop (15 minutes) is at **Mogocha** (6906km), an ugly place scorched by summer sun and frozen solid during the long winter.

Mogocha to Khabarovsk

For about 700km, starting at around **7000km**, the train line runs only about 50km north of the Amur River, the border with China. At one time, strategic sensitivity meant that carriages containing foreigners had their window blinds fastened down during this stretch – there's still not a whole lot to see with the blinds up!

At **Amazar** (7004km) there's a graveyard of steam locomotives – you'll have 15 minutes here to explore. The terrain now gets so rugged that roads stop and don't resume again until across the border at **7075km** between the Chitinskaya and Amur Regions. This is also where Siberia officially ends and the Russian Far East begins.

Yerofey Pavlovich (7111km) was named in honour of the Siberian explorer Yerofey Pavlovich Khabarov (the remainder of his name went to the big city further down the line). There's a 20-minute halt here and another of 16 minutes at **Urusha** (7209km).

You'll be well into day six of your journey from Moscow by **Skovorodino** (7306km), on the Bolshoi Never River, where there's a five-minute pause. This is where you'll need to change trains to go north along the Baikalo-Amurskaya Magistral (Baikal-Amur Mainline, or BAM); the junction is back at **Bamovskaya** (7273km) – for more details see p239. If you're on the *Rossiya* or any other major eastbound service you'll have to get off at Skovorodino and catch a local train the 33km back to Bamovskaya.

At **Magdagachi** (7494km) there's an 18-minute stop, and then a series of short stops before arriving in **Belogorsk** (7866km). This is the place to change trains if you wish to head southwest to the border town of Blagoveshchensk, the administrative capital of Amur Region.

At **8184km**, the border between the Amur Region and the Yevreyskaya Avtonomnaya Oblast (Jewish Autonomous Region), local time becomes Moscow time plus seven hours. **Birobidzhan** (8351km) is the capital of the Jewish Autonomous Region – note the station name in Hebrew letters during the five-minute stop here. It's easy to make a day trip here from Khabarovsk, too. The Jewish Autonomous Region is also part of the 788,600-sq-km Khabarovsky Territory, rich in timber, minerals and oil, that stretches 2500km north along the Sea of Okhotsk.

Approaching **Khabarovsk** (8523km) from the west, the train crosses a 2.6km bridge over the 2824km-long Amur, the longest span on the whole line and the last stretch of the Trans-Siberian to be completed in 1916. The railway now runs across a new bridge, with a road along the top, completed in the 1990s. There's also a 7km tunnel under the Amur, secretly completed during WWII, and the longest such tunnel on the Trans-Sib route; it's now used only by freight trains.

From Khabarovsk you can take a train to connect with the BAM at Komsomolsk-na-Amure (p250) or go direct to the port at Vanino (p252) for a boat to Sakhalin Island. A statue of Khabarov stands in the square outside the station, which is undergoing a long reconstruction to mirror the fancy design of the old *duma* (parliament) in the city on ul Muravyova-Amurskogo. The *Rossiya* stops here for a luxurious 33 minutes.

THE BURYATS

Numbering over 400,000, this Mongol people is the largest indigenous group in Russia, comprising around 30% of the population of the Buryatiya Republic and 65% of the Agin-Buryat Autonomous District southeast of Chita.

Culturally there are two main Buryat groups. In the 19th century, forest-dwelling Western Buryats retained their shamanic animist beliefs, while Eastern Buryats from the southern steppe-lands mostly converted to Tibetan-style Buddhism while maintaining a thick layer of local superstitions. Although virtually every Buryat *datsan* (Buddhist temple) was systematically wrecked during the Communists' antireligious mania in the 1930s, today Buryat Buddhism is rebounding. Many (mostly small) *datsans* have been rebuilt and seminaries for training Buddhist monks now operate at Ivolginsk (p217) and Aginskoe (p222).

In the Turkic Buryat language, 'hello' is *sainbena/sambaina*, 'thank you (very much)' is *(yikhe) bai yer la*. Buryatiya's trademark snack *pozi* (buuzi) are dangerously juicy lamb balls in ravioli-style pasta. They are widely available from *poznayas* (eateries serving Central Asian food) right across Eastern Siberia and beyond.

Khabarovsk to Vladivostok

This is day seven, and your last 13 hours on the train usually pass in the night. One reason for the cover of darkness is that the line, in places, comes within 10km of the sensitive Chinese border. From Khabarovsk south to Vladivostok the route shadows the Ussuri River, the border with China. At **8597km** you'll cross the Khor River.

At **Vyazemskaya** (8651km) there's a 16-minute stop; there'll be plenty of people selling food, including fresh salmon caviar. From here the forests are dominated by deciduous trees, such as maple and elm, which briefly blaze in a riot of autumn colours during September.

You'll probably be settling down to sleep by the time the train reaches **Bikin** (8756km), where there's a 24-minute halt – the line crosses the Bikin River here and follows it south to the border between Khabarovsky and Primorsky Territories. The southern forests of Primorsky Territory are the world's most northerly monsoon forests and home to black and brown bears, the rare Siberian tiger and the virtually extinct Amur leopard. The territory covers 165,900 sq km, has the Sikhote-Alin Range and runs 2000km from north to south.

There's a 15-minute stop in the dead of night at **Ruzhino** (8931km). Some 40km west of **Sibirtsevo** (9109km) – a 20-minute stop – is Lake Khanka (p237), covering 4000 sq km and famous for its 2m-wide lotus flowers.

At **Ussuriysk** (9177km), you have 10 minutes in which to contemplate changing to the branch line west to Harbin in China; the train goes only twice a week and is monotonously slow. Ussuriysk, formerly named Nikolskoe in honour of the tsarevitch's 1891 visit, was once of greater size and importance than nearby Vladivostok. There's also a line from here south to Pyongyang in North Korea, which may open again for passengers in the future (see p41).

By dawn – and after a week of travel from Moscow – you'll have your first glimpse of the Pacific to the south of the train at around **9245km**. You'll now be travelling along the hilly peninsula that forms the eastern side of Amursky Gulf. Near **Sanatornaya** (9269km) are some of Vladivostok's forlorn beaches and an enclave of hotels.

The city rises in a series of concrete tower blocks on the hill sides; you'll pass older buildings nearer the terminus, **Vladivostok** (9289km). Before leaving take a moment to admire the old locomotive on the platform beside the monument commemorating the completion of the great railroad you've just travelled along.

ULAN-UDE УЛАН-УДЕ

☎ 3012 / pop 380,000 / ⏰ Moscow + 5hr

Ulan means 'Red' in the local Buryat language, yet Ulan-Ude's setting is pleasantly green, cradled attractively in rolling hills. Despite an inevitable concrete suburban sprawl, it remains one of the most likable cities in Eastern Siberia. If you're coming from the west, the distinctively oriental Buryat faces make Ulan-Ude the first strikingly Asiatic city on the Trans-Siberian Railway.

Chartered as Verkhneudinsk in 1775, Ulan-Ude was a trading post on the wealthy tea-caravan route between China and Irkutsk. Soviet industrialisation brought a large locomotive works and secretive aircraft factory. Despite the vastly expanded population, severe Stalinist pressures and the all-seeing eyes of the world's biggest Lenin head, the Buryats clung to their language and faith.

Today the city is the ideal launching point for visits to eastern Baikal while easy quick flits to Ivolginsk allow a fascinating glimpse of the region's resurgent Mongol-Buddhist heritage (see opposite).

Orientation

The city's original axis is tree-lined ul Lenina, which slopes attractively south from central pl Sovetov. An alternative commercial centre is the Elevator area around Hotel Sagaan Morin. Walking into town from the train station requires crossing a long footbridge to ul Borsoeva.

MAPS

Great maps are sold at **Knigi Bookshop** (ul Kuybysheva 28; ⏰ 10am-1pm & 2-7pm Mon-Fri, 10am-5pm Sat).

Information

There are exchange bureaus in the Geser and Buryatiya hotels.

Buryat-Intour (☎ 219 207; tgomboeva@yahoo.com; ul Erbanova 12, Hotel Baikal, Room 209) Well-organised tour agency with its own bus service to Ulaanbaatar. Air tickets sold.

MDM Bank (Sovetskaya ul 32A; ⏰ 9am-1pm & 2-4pm Mon-Fri) Rates for US dollars better than euro.

Naran Tur (☎ 215 097; baikalnarantour@mail.ru; ul Kommunisticheskaya 47A, Hotel Buryatiya, Room 105) Director Sesegma (aka Svetlana) is infectiously passionate about Buryatiya. She organises horse-riding adventures, Ivolginsk tours and much more.

PhotoPlus (ul Kommunisticheskaya 16; ⏰ 9am-7pm Mon-Sat, 10am-5pm Sun) Three-minute passport photos for that Mongolian visa cost R70.

Post office (ul Lenina 61; Internet per hr R35; ⏰ 8am-7pm Mon-Fri, 9am-6pm Sat & Sun)

Telephone office (ul Borsoeva; Internet per hr R30; ⏰ 9am-9pm)

Sights
MERCHANTS' QUARTER

The town's partly pedestrianised, historical main artery is ul Lenina. Here the elegant 19th century architecture is gradually being renovated and boutiques already occupy the smartened-up 1838 **trading arcades**. Especially viewed from near the splendid **Opera House**, ul Lenina is given a photogenic focus by the gold-tipped spires of the attractive whitewashed **Odigitria Cathedral** (ul Lenina 2). Built between 1741 and 1785 the cathedral was rescued from near collapse in the late 1990s and commands an area of appealing if ramshackle old town. The carved wooden cottages extend as far as ul Kirova. The un-aesthetic **Nature Museum** (Muzey Prirody Buryatii; ☎ 214 833; ul Lenina 46; admission R30; ⏰ 10am-6pm Wed-Sun) has big stuffed animals and a scale model of Lake Baikal showing just how deep it is.

PLOSHCHAD SOVETOV

The Stalinist main square, pl Sovetov, is a Soviet marching ground but manageably proportioned and awesomely dominated by the world's largest **Lenin head** – which looks less domineering than comically cross-eyed. The square hides a cute little **Geological Museum** (Geologichesky Muzey; ul Lenina 59; admission free; ⏰ 1-4pm Mon-Fri).

HISTORICAL MUSEUM

Somewhat naughtily, this **museum** (☎ 215 961; Profsoyuznaya ul 29; admission per fl R80; ⏰ 10am-5.30pm Tue-Sun) charges per single-room floor. Floor 3, Buddiyskoye Iskustvo, is by far the most interesting. Its *thangka* (Buddhist iconographic paintings), Buddhas and icons were salvaged from Buryatiya's monasteries

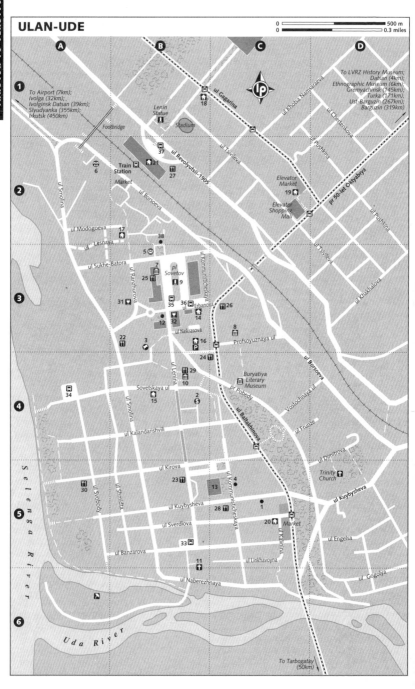

and temples before their Soviet destruction and were originally used for a museum of atheism.

ETHNOGRAPHIC MUSEUM

In a forest clearing 6km from central Ulan-Ude is the excellent **Ethnographic Museum** (Etnografichesky muzey; ☎ 443 210; adult/child/student R60/25/35, photo/video permits R60/120; ☒ 9am-5pm Tue-Sun) is an outdoor collection of local architecture plus some reconstructed burial mounds and the odd stone totem. It features occasional craft demonstrations and has a splendid wooden church and a whole strip of Old Believers' homesteads. *Marshrutka* (fixed-route minibus) 8 from pl Sovetov passes within 1km but on request it will detour to drop you at the door for no extra charge. En route you'll notice Ulan-Ude's attractive new pair of **datsans** (Buddhist temples; Barguzinsky trakt) backed by stupas and forests fluttering with prayer flags.

LVRZ HISTORY MUSEUM

The Locomotive Wagon Repair Factory (Lokomotivo Vagono Remontinii Zavod; LVRZ) has been building and repairing engines since 1932. Unfortunately, it's not possible visit the factory but its **LVRZ History Museum** (☎ 344 340; ul Komsomolskaya 23; admission free; ☒ 9am-5pm Mon-Fri) on pl Slava traces the history of the factory with models of engines that were built and repaired there. To get here, take bus 37.

Festivals & Events

Buryatiya Folk Festival Celebrated at the hippodrome near the ethnographic museum in Ulan-Ude.
Maitreya Buddha Festival Held at Ivolginsk *datsan* (monastery) near Ulan-Ude.

Sleeping

BUDGET

Hotel Zolotoy Kolos (ul Sverdlova 43, top floors; dm R140, s R187-252, tw R304-804) Repainted, simple but sensibly priced, the best singles have private toilets. Showers cost R25 extra. This is a reasonable budget option though the area is slightly dubious late at night and there's an 11pm curfew.

Hotel Barguzin (☎ 215 746; Sovetskaya ul 28; s/tw/tr R600/820/990) Well positioned for the old town, the lacklustre Barguzin has faded corridors and a stuffed bear lurking in the foyer. Just two doubles have their own water heaters.

Hotel Odon (☎ 342 983; ul Gagarina 43; s R330-540, tw R650-890) Uninspiring and usually full of Chinese merchants but only five minutes' walk from the train station, the Odon has a popular if pricey Asian restaurant.

Resting rooms (komnaty otdykha; Ulan-Ude train station; dm R500) Acceptable dorms charge R270 for half-days, R150 for three hours and R60 extra for showers.

MIDRANGE

Hotel Sagaan Morin (White Horse; ☎ /fax 443 647, 444 019; www.morintour.com/tours/acc_uu/index.php; ul

Gagarina 25; s/tw/tr R800/1700/1925). This perfectly appointed new three-star tower is so obviously the best hotel in town that you may need to book (by fax) months ahead for summer.

Hotel Buryatiya (☎ 211 835; ul Kommunisticheskaya 47A; s R725-860, tw R910-1100) A big Soviet tower with decent rooms but no hot water in summer. The English-speaking receptionists are friendly but watch out for the room-cleaners' trick of 'tidying away' items of your luggage into the back corners of wardrobes and drawers.

Hotel Geser (☎ /fax 216 151; hotel_geser@mail .ru; ul Ranzhurova 11; s/tw/ste R1850/2800/6000) Relatively cosy for a Soviet place, this former party hang-out has spacious rooms. Some are decently modernised but others retain clunky old toilets. Check carefully before paying. The semismart restaurant has a menu in English offering sensibly priced Siberian specialities including vegetarian options.

Hotel Baikal (☎ 213 718; ul Erbanova 12; s R650-700, tw R900-1000, tr R1200) Unreconstructed Soviet rooms but with water heaters in most attached bathrooms and a perfect position overlooking pl Sovetov.

Eating

When the weather warms up, *letnii sad* (summer gardens) appear around the Opera House (see p213) and on the banks of the river. They're great if you're after barbecued kebabs.

RESTAURANTS

Stolitsa (☎ 552 836; ul Revolyutsii-1905 31; meals R160-320; ☺ 11am-11pm) Perfectly situated for the train station, this surprisingly elegant upstairs restaurant has red, black and gold décor, modernist Buddhist-influenced art and old Ulan-Ude photos. There's a menu in English and a vastly cheaper zakusochnaya (pub/café; meals R40 to R70) around the side.

Mir Igry (ul Kommunisticheskaya 52; meals R90-220, beers R37-60; ☺ 10am-11pm) This casino complex has three great bar-restaurants each with its own atmosphere. It's popular with young professionals and a great place to strike up conversations over a shot or 10 of vodka. Food menus are appealing but the more intriguing Buryat options have limited availability.

Zolotoy Drakon (☎ 212 109; ul Kirova 8; meals R150-350; ☺ 11am-midnight; 🗷) Redecorated in white-and-scarlet contemporary chinoiserie, Ulan-Ude's best Asian restaurant usefully offers choices of portion sizes plus several European options. One room has an open fire in winter.

Ulger (☎ 218 066; ul Lenina 46; meals R140-350; ☺ 11am-11pm) Middle-class dining at the rear of the Natural History Museum. Pleasantly shaded summer terrace.

Drakon (☎ 215 283; ul Smolina 38; mains R25-50; ☺ 11am-1am) Enormous servings of great Chinese food in a castle-dungeon-effect chamber. Vegetarians might try the delicious *chi-san-tsi* (braised aubergines).

QUICK EATS & SELF-CATERING

King's Burger (ul Lenina 21; burgers R30-38, pizzas R90-110; ☺ 8am-10pm) is a tasteful fast-food emporium. **Poznaya** (ul Lenina 59; pozi R13.50; ☺ 10am-11pm) is ultrabasic, but inexpensive and very central, with R20 bliny.

Stolovaya (ul Kuybysheva 22; meals R25-45, teas R3; ☺ 10am-10pm) Cheaper and less daunting than it looks, Stolovaya is a perversely intriguing blast from the Soviet past.

Sputnik Supermarket (ul Kommunisticheskaya 48; ☺ 24hr) This is a handy central grocery.

Drinking

There are several more café-bars near the Elevator market.

Zeleny Zal (Green Room; pl Sovetov; beers R35-60, coffees R8-24; ☺ 11am-11pm) Stylish green-neon youth hang-out with Fashion TV and views of the main square masked by muslin drapes. To get here, enter via Progress Cinema from ul Lenina, go through the less interesting ground-floor café, and then make your way upstairs.

Zakusochnaya Studencheskaya (ul Ranzhurova 1; beers R25; ☺ 10am-1pm & 2-11pm) Corrugated iron is used to surprising effect, creating a sense of street style in this supercheap student-dive pub.

Getting There & Away

AIR

Siberia Airlines (☎ 220 125; ul Sukhe-Batora 63; ☺ 9am-7pm Mon-Fri, 9am-5pm Sat & Sun) flies to Novosibirsk and Vladivostok and offers deep discounts for early purchase tickets to Moscow (daily, R9980 full price, R3500 two-week advanced purchase). Buryatavia has very scenic flights to Nizhneangarsk near Severobaikalsk (R1860, four per week), with tickets available through **Buryat-Intour** (☎ 219 207; tgomboeva@yahoo.com; ul Erbanova 12, Hotel Baikal, Room 209).

BUS
Buses depart from various points. Use the **main avtovokzal** (bus station; Sovetskaya ul) for Lake Baikal's east coast, and for depart-when-full *marshrutky* to Kyakhta (R150) for the Mongolian border.

Use the Banzarova bus station for Ivolginsk *datsan:* bus 104 departs at 7am, noon or and 4.20pm or use frequent bus 130 to Ivolga and switch to a taxi.

Use the train station forecourt for *marshrutky* to Arshan (R350), Irkutsk or Chita, all overnight.

At 8am on Tuesday, Thursday and Sunday, Buryat-Intour runs buses from outside Hotel Baikal to Bayangol Hotel in Ulaanbaatar (R750, 12 hours) in Mongolia.

TRAIN
The *Rossiya* arrives from Moscow and Vladivostok every second day but there are cheaper alternatives. Beijing-bound trains pass through Ulan-Ude on Tuesday (via Chita) and Saturday (via Mongolia). Fast trains to Ulaanbaatar pass through the city on Sunday and Monday at 1.30am and waste vastly less time at the border than the daily 364 train, which takes 24 hours and costs R1350 *kupe* (*kupeyny*; compartmentalised carriage); there is no *platskart* (*platskartny*; open carriage). It departs at 6am from Ulan-Ude and returns at 6.40pm from Ulaanbaatar. Buy international tickets from the **servis tsentr** (☎ 282 696; ☻ 8am-1pm & 2-6.45pm) upstairs. For Chita, 340 (R535, 10¾ hours) is the handiest overnight train available. Towards Irkutsk (from R280 *platskart,* eight hours) most passengers prefer to take a day train for the Baikal views.

Getting Around
Various *marshrutky* bound for pl Sovetov stop outside the train station but tram 7 from ul Gagarina is usually faster for the market area. From pl Sovetov take *marshrutka* 55 (R10, 20 minutes) for the airport; take 37 for the train-carriage works, *datsans* and (by request) Ethnographic Museum.

AROUND ULAN-UDE
Ivolginsk Datsan Иволгинский Дацан
This **monastery complex** (admission free, guided tour R60), under 40km from Ulan-Ude, was founded in 1946. While not as elaborate as Gandan Khiid in Ulaanbaatar or others around Chita, it is intriguing as the centre of Siberian Buddhism. The local Gelugpa (Yellow Hat) form of Buddhism differs slightly from that in Mongolia and Tibet, for example in allowing lamas to marry. When spinning prayer wheels or just walking around the temple grounds, it's polite to maintain a clockwise direction. Enter any temple building via the left door and don't use the central stairs unless you're a self-realised lama.

Viewed distantly across the grassy fields, morning sunlight glints from the gilded roof-wings of the 1972 **main temple building**. Closer, however, the exterior is less impressive – slapdash paintwork, naïve, tacky tiger guardian-statues and brick patterning painted onto the whitewashed walls. Some of the lovably basic prayer wheels are crafted from old tin cans. The main temple's interior (no photography please) is colourful and very atmospheric despite discordantly chuntering cash registers. Nearby notice the glassed-in **Bodhi Tree**, convolutedly descended from the Bodh Gaya original beneath which the Buddha achieved enlightenment.

Nearing completion within the *datsan* complex is the beautiful, Korean-style wooden **Etigel Khambin Temple** honouring the 12th Khambo Lama whose body was recently exhumed. To general astonishment his flesh had not decomposed seven decades after his death. Some 'experts' have even attested that the corpse's hair is still growing, albeit extraordinarily slowly. The new temple plans to display the worshipful cadaver in a refrigerated display box that looks more suited to soft drinks.

The first direct bus from Ulan-Ude arrives well before the 9am *khural* (prayer service), allowing ample time to wander among the prayer flags of the mosquito-infested surrounding swamp. Returning buses leave at 1.30pm, 5.30pm and 8.30pm. Alternatively, share a taxi to uninteresting Ivolga (Ivolginsk town; R12 per seat, R35 per car), from where *marshrutka* 130 shuttles to Ulan-Ude several times hourly

(R20). Several Ulan-Ude tour agencies (see p213) offer small-group excursions combining visits to Ivolginsk, a local stupa and a hill-top *oova* (shrine) with lovely views and shamanistic overtones. The typical cost is US$30 to US$40 per person.

Novoselenginsk Новоселенгинск

☎ 30145 / pop 9500 / ⌚ Moscow + 5hr

Worth a brief stop en route to Kyakhta, Stockades and wooden houses on broad dust-blown roads give this small, 19th-century town a memorable Wild West feel. Learn something of Novoselenginsk's interesting history at the **Decembrist Museum** (muzey Dekabristov; ☎ 96 716; ul Lenina 53; admission R10; ⌚ 9am-5pm Wed-Sun), in a 200-year-old colonnaded house in the town's centre. Walk 2km east towards the river to see the ruins of the 18th-century **Spassky Church**, isolated on the grassy far bank (no bridge). That's all that remains of Staroselenginsk, the original settlement that was abandoned around 1800 due to frequent flooding. Kyakhta-bound *marshrutky* all pause in Novoselenginsk from Ulan-Ude (R100, 1½ hours, six or seven daily). There's no hotel.

Kyakhta Кяхта

☎ 30142 / pop 18,400 / ⌚ Moscow + 5hr

Right at the Mongolian border, 100km south of Ulan-Ude, the intriguing if somewhat sad town of Kyakhta was formerly called Troitskosavsk. Kyakhta's fortunes boomed with the Chinese tea trade and by the mid-19th century up to 5000 cases of tea were arriving daily on a stream of horse or camel caravans. The caravans returned loaded with exported furs. This all came to an abrupt end with the completion of the Trans-Siberian Railway, after which Kyakhta withered into a remote border garrison town.

The town's centre is around ul Lenina where you'll find the bus terminus next to the 1853 **trading arches** (Ryady Gostinye) and the central park. Kyakhta's smaller Sloboda district, 4km south of the commercial centre (R50 by taxi), is where you'll find the border post.

The impressive shell of the **Trotsky Cathedral** (1817) lies at the heart of the overgrown central park. Northeast is the delightfully eccentric **museum** (ul Lenina 49; admission R40; ⌚ 10am-6pm Tue-Sat), with its imaginative displays of treasures salvaged from Soviet-plundered churches and *datsan*. Running parallel to ul Lenina is ul Krupskaya along which you'll find several attractive wooden buildings, including at No 37, where the first meeting of the Mongolian Revolutionary Party was held in 1921.

In Sloboda a dwarfish Lenin glares condescendingly at the extraordinarily grand but sadly ruined **Voskresenskaya Church** (1838) with its splendid Italianate cupola. Behind Lenin is the big but rather mutilated 1842 **Zdaniye Gostinogo Dvora** (Historic Customs Warehouse) with an appended communist-era spire. Directly behind is the frontier station for crossing into Mongolia.

Beside the Uspensky Church, **Hotel Druzhba** (☎ 91 321; ul Krupskaya 8; dm from R280, ste R560), about 10 minutes' walk south of Kyakhta's main centre, has good-value suites with hot water, sitting room and king-sized bed. Its restaurant-bar is one of the better places to eat in town, too. **Hotel Turist** (☎ 92 431; cnr ul Lenina 21 & ul Sovetskaya; beds R135) has basic rooms with shared cold showers in a wooden house near the market.

Eating options are very limited. **Kafe Viola** (ul Lenina 40, upstairs; meals from R50; ⌚ 10am-3am), near the market, is a reasonably pleasant place with booth seating and a decent menu. For a snack try **Buryatskaya Kukhnya** (ul Menina; pozi each 9R; ⌚ 10am-1am), a small Buryat-style decorated room tucked between the trading arches and Sberbank.

Ulan-Ude–Kyakhta *marshrutky* (R150, 3½ hours) take a pleasantly scenic route with a meal break in Novoselenginsk. If you're heading to Mongolia see p256).

Eastern Lake Baikal

Sparsely scattered beach villages of old-fashioned log cottages dot the pretty East Baikal coast. A usefully practical Pribaikalsky booklet is available for free download from www.tahoebaikal.org. Further north is the dramatic Barguzin Valley, from where Chinggis (Ghenghis) Khaan's mother, Oilun-Ehe, is said to have originated.

Access is across a forested pass from Ulan-Ude via tiny **Baturino** village with its elegantly renovated **Sretenskaya Church**. After about 2½ hours' drive, the road first meets Lake Baikal at pretty little **Gremyachinsk**, which has a wide and sandy but litter-strewn beach some 15 minutes' walk up ul Komsomolskaya.

The main road offers surprisingly few Baikal views until fishing port **Turka**, which has a small house **hotel** (r US$35-60), cheaper homestays and a little museum. Bigger **Gory-achinsk** is centred on a typically institutional hot-springs **kurort** (sanatorium complex; ☎ 55 135; beds from R220) with cheap cottage homestays in the surrounding village. Minibuses run to Ulan-Ude (R140, 3½ hours) at 8am and 4pm. Horse rental is possible on the beach around 3km away.

Picturesque Baikal beaches stretch northwest of quaint little **Maksimikha** fishing hamlet with several huts and *turbazy* (holiday camps) including **Svetlaya Polyana** (tw R1200-1800; ☺ Apr-Oct). Perhaps the most dramatic views are from low-rise **Ust-Barguzin** (☎ 30 131) where main ul Lenina's blue-and-white carved wooden cottages culminate in a river ferry. Across the bay, the high-ridged peaks of the **Svyatoy Nos Peninsula** rise spectacularly sheer.

Experienced tour agent **Alexander Loginov** (☎ 91 591; ul Komsomolskaya 19, Ust Barguzin) speaks passable English, can arrange local homestay accommodation and offers tours of the peninsula and boat trips to see **nerpa seals**. Seals are particularly abundant around the **Ushkanny islands**; typical boat charters start from R3500 plus at least R1000 per person in park fees as the area is a reserve.

Barguzin (☎ 30 131) dates back to 1648 and has a few dilapidated historic buildings along ul Krasnoarmeyskaya and pl Lenina, where there's a run-down **hotel** (☎ 41 229; ul Lenina 25; s R225-335, tw R450). However, the old town is most useful as a base for visiting the timeless Barguzin Valley, which opens out into wide horse-grazed meadows, gloriously edged by a vast Toblerone of mountain peaks. Great views across the meandering river plain from **Uro** village are easily accessible thanks to four daily buses from Barguzin (R12, 35 minutes), though taxis allow much better exploration.

To return to Ulan-Ude (seven hours) there are buses departing 8am and 10.30am, with *marshrutky* leaving when full until around 10am. Book buses ahead.

CHITA ЧИТА

☎ 3022 / pop 370,000 / ☺ Moscow + 6hr

The golden domes of Chita's glorious new cathedral entice train travellers to hop off and explore this historic and patchily attractive city. Despite many architectural gems, each area is a little too diffuse to make a really memorable visual impact, but the friendly, go-ahead atmosphere makes Chita a pleasant place to spend a day or two.

Founded in 1653 Chita developed as a rough-and-tumble silver-mining town. More than 80 Decembrist gentlemen-rebels were exiled nearby, their wives setting up homes on what was known as ul Damskaya (women's street), now lost beneath the southern end of concrete-blighted ul Stolyanova.

As a gateway to the new East Chinese Railway (p253) Chita boomed in the early 20th century and was capital of the short-lived pro-Lenin Far Eastern Republic from 1920 till 1922 – the parliament building still stands at ul Anokhina 63. Although closed to foreigners during the Cold War and still home to a large military presence, today trade with China booms and the city is increasingly internationally minded.

Orientation & Information

The city centre is pl Lenina with a constipated-looking pink Vladimir Ilych in the middle. It's three blocks northeast of the main (Chita II) train station, one stop using any trolleybus. Wide, boulevard-like ul Lenina emerges either side of the square as the city's main thoroughfare.

KiberPocht (ul Butina 35; per hr R25 plus per MB R4; ☺ 8am-9pm) Internet access and stamps.

Lanta (☎ 262 368; ul Leningradskaya 56; ☺ 9am-6pm Mon-Sat)

Magellan Internet (ul Chaykovskogo 24; per hr R50; ☺ 9am-7pm Mon-Fri, 9am-5pm Sat)

Main post office (ul Butina 37; ☺ 8am-7pm Mon-Fri, 8am-6pm Sat & Sun) Quaintly spired wooden building on pl Lenina.

Promstroibank (ul Petrovskaya 41) Changes US dollars, euros and Chinese yuan. Directly east of the train station.

Sights

Ploshchad Lenina has a certain grandeur while Chita's best century-old architecture lies southeast along uls Anokhina, Amurskaya and Lenina. The original historic centre is now mostly trampled by concrete towers, but the lovely 1771 **Archangel Michael log church** (ul Selenginskaya) survives and houses a small but interesting **Decembrist's Museum** (Muzey Dekabristov; ☎ 356 223; admission R20; ☺ 10am-6pm Tue-Sun). Take bus 35 or 77 eastbound on Amurskaya to get close.

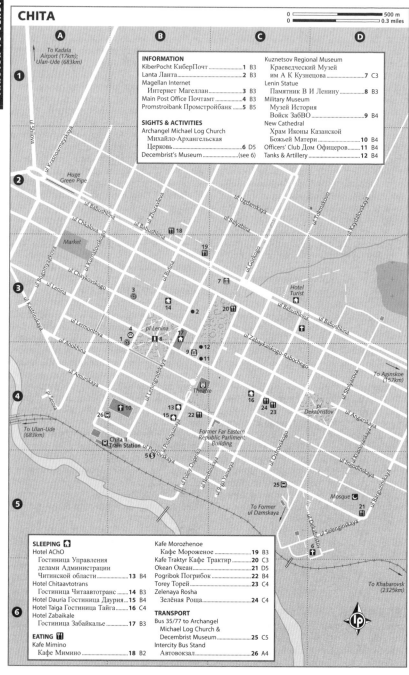

CHITA

0 ————— 500 m
0 ————— 0.3 miles

INFORMATION
KiberPocht КиберПочт 1 B3
Lanta Ланта 2 B3
Magellan Internet
  Интернет Магеллан 3 B3
Main Post Office Почтамт 4 B3
Promstroibank Промстройбанк 5 B5

SIGHTS & ACTIVITIES
Archangel Michael Log Church
  Михайло-Архангельская
  Церковь 6 D5
Decembrist's Museum ....(see 6)

Kuznetsov Regional Museum
  Краеведческий Музей
  им А К Кузнецова 7 C3
Lenin Statue
  Памятник В И Ленину 8 B3
Military Museum
  Музей История
  Войск ЗабВО 9 B4
New Cathedral
  Храм Иконы Казанской
  Божьей Матери 10 B4
Officers' Club Дом Офицеров 11 B4
Tanks & Artillery 12 B4

To Kadala
Airport (17km);
Ulan-Ude (683km)

ul Shilova

ul Krasnoarmeyskaya

Huge
Green Pipe

ul Babushkina

ul Chkalova

ul Babushkina

ul Zhuravleva

18

ul Ugdanskaya

ul Balyabina

ul Takmakovo

ul Kaydalovskaya

Market

ul Kurnatovskogo

ul Chaykovskogo

ul Budina

19

ul Sorbkogo

7

Hotel
Turist

ul Lenina

3

14

20

ul Babushkina

ul Babushkina

ul Lermontova

4

pl Lenina

17

ul Anokhina

1

8

9   12

11

ul Zabaykalskogo-Rabochego

ul Leningradskaya

ul Amurskaya

r Khrva

To Aginskoe
(157km)

Theatre

ul Shilova

To Ulan-Ude
(683km)

26

10

13

15

22

16

24   23

pl
Dekabristov

ul Angarskaya

Chita II
Train Station

5

Former Far Eastern
Republic Parliment
Building

ul Petrovskaya

ul Nerchinsk

ul Oktyabrskaya

ul Ingodinskaya

25

Mosque

21

To Khabarovsk
(2325km)

To Former
ul Damskaya

ul Dekabristov

ul Selenginskaya

6

SLEEPING
Hotel AChO
  Гостиница Управления
  делами Администрации
  Читинской области 13 B4
Hotel Chitaavtotrans
  Гостиница Читавтотранс 14 B3
Hotel Dauria Гостиница Даурия 15 B4
Hotel Taiga Гостиница Тайга 16 C4
Hotel Zabaikale
  Гостиница Забайкалье 17 B3

EATING
Kafe Mimino
  Кафе Мимино 18 B2

Kafe Morozhenoe
  Кафе Мороженое 19 B3
Kafe Traktyr Кафе Трактир 20 C3
Okean Океан 21 D5
Pogribok Погрибок 22 B4
Torey Торей 23 C4
Zelenaya Rosha
  Зелёная Роща 24 C4

TRANSPORT
Bus 35/77 to Archangel
  Michael Log Church &
  Decembrist Museum 25 C5
Intercity Bus Stand
  Автовокзал 26 A4

Beyond a gratuitous stuffed elk, the excellent **Kuznetsov Regional Museum** (Krayevedchesky muzey; ☎ 226 709; ul Babushkina 113; admission R50; ⏰ 10am-6pm Tue-Sun) has interesting exhibits on the city's heritage and architectural renaissance.

The previously interesting **Military Museum** (Muzey istorii voysk ZaBVO; ul Lenina 86) was under reconstruction at the time of research. Its collection of tanks and artillery can still be seen by walking up the passage between the museum and the impressive **Officers' Club**.

Sleeping

Beware that cheap dorms can be uncomfortably male-dominated and off-putting for individual women travellers. The ragged station hotel only accepts those with rail tickets.

BUDGET

Hotel Dauria (☎ 262 350; Profsoyuznaya ul 12; s R600-800, dm/tw/tr R350/1200/1200) Big, unsophisticated old rooms are repainted and airy. Beds in a dormitory triple with attached toilet and bathrooms offer Chita's best backpacker option. It's above Kharbin Chinese Restaurant.

Hotel Taiga (☎ 262 332; ul Lenina 75, 4th fl; dm R190; ✗) Sheets in this survivable crash-pad are clean and guests are usually segregated by gender. You'll have a shared kitchen and shower. The front door is locked at midnight.

Hotel Chitaavtotrans (☎ 355 011; ul Kostyushko-Grigovicha 7; s/tw R550/1000) Cosmetically improved rooms retain wobbly old shower pans. Quiet yet central; one block north of pl Lenina.

MIDRANGE

Hotel AChO (Gostinitsa Upravleniya delami Administratsii Chitinskoi Oblastu; ☎ 351 966; Profsoyuznaya ul 19; tw R1400-2700) Fine 1906 brick mansion has fully rebuilt rooms with polished wooden floors, fridge and closable shower-booths. The wrought-ironwork retains hints of old-world style.

Hotel Zabaikale (☎ 359 819; Hotel-zabaikal@yandex.ru, zabaikalie@yandex.ru; ul Leningradskaya 36; s/tw R1450/2000; 💻) Unbeatably located overlooking pl Lenina with decently upgraded rooms offering Russian MTV. Showers are piping hot if poorly mounted. The 'complimentary' breakfast costs you R100!

Eating

Several dive bars fill basements on ul Amurskaya, two blocks north of the train station. Supercheap beers (R15) mean you'll meet many swaying but friendly local drunks.

Kafe Mimino (☎ 323 338; ul Babushkina 62A; meals R80-240; ⏰ noon-2am, last food 11pm) Genuine if somewhat underspiced Georgian food is easy to choose from helpful picture menus.

Kafe Traktyr (☎ 352 229; ul Chkalova 93; meals R170-400; ⏰ noon-2am) Traditional Russian 'home' cooking served at heavy wooden tables in a rebuilt wooden lace cottage with upmarket Siberian-retro atmosphere.

Kafe Morozhenoe (☎ 266 867; ul Babushkina 50; meals R30-70; ⏰ noon-midnight; ✗) In primary blue and yellow colours this striking ice-cream parlour serves cheap meals, wine by the glass (from R20) and trendy terracotta pots of Chinese green tea.

Pogribok (☎ 265 919; ul Anokhina 67; meals R230-450; ⏰ noon-2am) Despite the mirrored ceiling and sickly green walls, this neat cellar restaurant can be amusing when the local set of *Cheers* characters are perched at its little bar. Food is tasty and good value. Local Chitinskoe Klyuchi beers (R25) come in handsomely tall mugs.

Zelenaya Rosha (☎ 322 417; ul Lenina 53; meals R170-400; ⏰ 10am-2am) Fake trees and a ceiling of plastic foliage form a curious if somewhat tacky forest around a trickling water feature and pavilion bar. When ordering beware that prices are per 100g not per dish.

Torey (ul Lenina 63; pozi R12; ⏰ 10am-10pm) is a cheap *poznaya*, dishing up *pozi* (lamb balls in ravioli-style pasta). **Okean** (ul Amurskaya 2; ⏰ 9am-midnight) is a supermarket.

Getting There & Away

The main train station is Chita II, 6199km from Moscow and 3090km from Vladivostok. The *Rossiya* stops here alternate days but cheaper alternatives include the 349 to Moscow and 8 and 53 to Vladivostok.

For China the *Vostok* (020) runs to Beijing (R2950 *kupe*, 56½ hours) very early Wednesday morning. Trains to Manzhouli (R1100, 25 hours) depart on Thursday and Saturday evenings but it's usually quicker and cheaper to take the nightly service to the border town of Zabaikalsk (R660 to R940 *kupe*, 14 hours) then bus-hop across no-man's land into China.

Other useful destinations might include Ulan-Ude (R540, 9½ hours overnight), Blagoveshchensk (train 250; R1470, 34½ hours, odd days) and Tynda (train 078; R1250, 27 hours). For R72 commission, the helpful **Service Centre** (Chita II station; ⏰ 8am-noon & 1-7.30pm) issues tickets while you relax on comfy settees.

From the intercity bus stand near Chita II train station *marshrutky* run to Aginskoe (R120, three hours) and Duldurga for Alkhanay (R150, three hours). Shared taxis (R200) are faster.

AROUND CHITA

South of Chita are some of Russia's greatest Buddhist sights. The most accessible is Aginskoe, which has the nation's oldest *datsan*, while Alkhanay offers a hike-through-nature alternative to temple-based spirituality.

Aginskoe Агинское

☎ 30289 / pop 15,000

For an intriguing trip from Chita, take a shared taxi (R180, two hours) to the dusty Buryat town of **Aginskoe**, capital of the Agin-Buryat Autonomous Okrug. Scenery en route transforms progressively from patchily forested hills via river valleys into rolling grassy steppe-land. The highlight is a pair of old Buddhist **datsans** 5.5km west of the centre by very rare minibus 14. The 1816 **Aginskoe Datsan** is a white-and-gold, two-storey Tibetan-style structure that is the hub of a Buddhist seminary. Directly to the east, with a big new gate and driveway under construction, is the more photogenic 1883 **Tsakchen Datsan** with grandly impressive upper wooden frontage, partly adorned with colourful Mongolian script motifs. Getting inside is hit and miss.

Return to central Aginskoe's central square where the **Tsybikova Museum** (☎ 34 462; ul Komsomolskaya 11; admission R30; ⏰ 9am-1pm & 2-6pm Mon-Fri) exhibits a shaman's *gabala* cup made from a human skull. Nearby is an attractive church. Take a taxi to have lunch at one of the three great restaurants of the comfortable **Hotel Sapsam** (☎ /fax 34 590; www.megalink.ru/sapsan; tw/d R1200/1500, meals R200-500). **Hotel Dali** (☎ 34 196; ul Komsomolskaya 79, 3rd fl; dm/d R400/600) offers cheaper, simpler accommodation with private bathrooms 2km north of the centre.

Alternatively it's easy enough to get a minibus back to Chita until midafternoon. Hourly minibuses run to Mogoytuy on the Chita–Zabaikalsk line but trains are poorly timed. There's a single daily bus from Aginskoe to Duldurga (90km) for Alkhanay. That road is terribly bumpy.

Alkhanay & Duldurga
Алханай и Дулдурга

☎ 30256 / pop 7000

A Buryat-run national park 130km south of Chita, **Alkhanay** is reckoned by the local Buddhists to be the religion's fifth-most important holy 'mountain'. In fact you'll see forested hills, not mountains, through which a devotional six- to seven-hour return trek takes pilgrims to a small stupa and a window rock. The latter is considered the Gate of Shambala, an entry to spiritual paradise. The beautiful flowers, pious pilgrims and bird-watching opportunities are as interesting as the scenery.

Alkhanay's entrance is 20km (R200 by taxi) from **Duldurga** village where there's a helpful **Alkhanay National Park Office** (☎ 21 458; alkhanai@yandex.ru; ul Gagarina 47) and two simple hotels. There's more accommodation in *turbazy* around the park entrance including a **yurt camp** (beds R500). July to September, Chita-based agency **Lanta** (☎ 3022-262 368; ul Leningradskaya 56; ⏰ 9am-6pm Mon-Sat) runs R1000 weekend tours, departing on Friday and including two nights' accommodation (see p219). No English is spoken. *Marshrutky* from Chita to Duldurga (R150, three hours) run several times daily.

NERCHINSK НЕРЧИНСК

☎ 30242 / pop 15,300 / ⏰ Moscow + 6hr

Once one of Eastern Siberia's foremost towns, forgotten Nerchinsk is quietly intriguing and handily breaks up a long Chita–Blagoveshchensk journey. Venue for the immensely important 1689 border treaty with China, Nerchinsk boomed from the 1860s with discoveries of silver.

Mikhail Butin, the local silver baron, built himself an impressive crenellated palace that he furnished with what were then the world's largest mirrors, carried all the way from Paris. The mirrors form the centrepiece of the recently restored **Butin Palace Museum** (☎ 44 515; lit@rambler.ru; Sovetskaya ul 83; admission R50; ⏰ 9am-1pm & 2-6pm Tue-Sat), in what remains of Butin's mansion. Nearby is the active 1825 **Voskresensky Cathedral** (ul Pogodaeva 85) and the imposing but somewhat dilapidated 1840 **Trading Arches** (Gostiny Dvor) hosting the town's one café.

Trains stop at an unmarked platform facing the pretty wooden-lace **children's music school** (ul Yaroslavskaya 24). The totally unmarked **Hotel PU** (☎ 41 745; ul Dostovalova 3; dm R150) is half a block west of the palace museum; camp beds share a kitchen and sitting room but there's no shower and toilets are outdoor longdrops.

From Chita, a single Nerchinsk-bound *platskart* carriage (R209, 10 hours) is attached conveniently to the overnight Yerofey Pavlovich train 392. To continue east, taxi-hop back to Priiskovaya on the Trans-Siberian mainline, where the 1.20pm train to Blagoveshchensk and 8.55pm to Khabarovsk or the 6.11pm back towards Irkutsk all run on odd days only.

BLAGOVESHCHENSK
БЛАГОВЕЩЕНСК

☎ 4162 / pop 210,000 / ✆ Moscow + 6hr

About 110km south of the Trans-Siberian tracks, where Chinese and Russians rub shoulders, Blagoveshchensk sits across the wide Amur River from the Chinese town of Heihe. Its border position has meant an unsteady history. In 1900, Cossacks slaughtered thousands of Chinese here; during the Cultural Revolution, Chinese propaganda blasted 24/7 from across the river.

Since opening as a free trade zone in 1994, folks of either side swish-swash across the border. Blagoveshchensk (meaning 'good news') is less for tourism than business or gambling, but it's interesting to watch Chinese tourists posing in front of Tsar-era European buildings and statues of Lenin.

Orientation & Information

The train station is 4km north of the river. The main cross-town artery is north–south 50 Let Oktyabrya ul, which meets pl Lenina (and east–west ul Lenina) a block from the river.

Amur Tourist (☎ 53 005; ul Kuzhnechnaya 1; ✆ 8am-noon & 1-5pm) Agency geared mostly for Chinese and Russian daytrippers, but can help with tickets.

Internet Access (☎ 391 276; ul Lenina 142, 2nd fl; per hr R36; ✆ 9am-1pm & 2-8.30pm) About 1km west of pl Lenina.

Sights

Central **pl Lenina** – with Lenin's bronze self, fountains and promenade leading along the river in both directions – is a sort of beer-drinking focal point in good weather.

About 500m west on tree-lined ul Lenina, the large and well laid-out **Amur Regional Museum** (Amursky Oblastnoi Kraevedchesky muzey; ☎ 422 414; ul Lenina 165; admission R80; ✆ 10am-6pm Tue-Sun) is in a smartly kept red building dating from the turn of the 20th century.

Just south, around the WWII-themed **ploshchad Pobody** (a block south of ul Lenina), you can see several prerevolutionary buildings in their faded glory. Look for the **Anton Chekhov bust** on the red building on the square's south side – he stayed here in 1890 on his way to Sakhalin.

Sleeping

Druzhba Hotel (☎ 376 140, 534 789; www.hoteldruzhba .ru; ul Kuznechnaya 1; s R650, d R800-1000) About 600m east of pl Lenina, the riverside Druzhba is a Soviet survivor and the town's best, with friendly service and clean basic rooms.

Zeya Hotel (☎ 539 996; hotel_zeya@amur.ru; ul Lenina 122; r per person from R744) Grey high-rise with clean rooms, just west of pl Pobody.

Eating

Most restaurants – found along ul Lenina – double as casinos. **Russkaya Izba** (☎ 446 661; ul Lenina 48; meals around R250-350; ✆ 11am-11pm) is tiny (four tables) and like a dacha (country cottage), with samovars and engraved wood details. The homey Izba cooks up good Russian meals. It's about 800m east of Druzhba Hotel.

Getting There & Away

Blagoveshchensk is 110km off the Trans-Siberian, on a branch line from Belogorsk (where taxi vans also meet oncoming trains for the two-hour ride; R150).

From the Blagoveshchensk train station, daily trains 185/186 lead to/from Vladivostok, passing through Khabarovsk (R1090, 16 hours). On odd-numbered days, trains 249/250 connect Blagoveshchensk with Moscow, stopping in Irkutsk (R2500, 53 hours); and trains 81/82 go to/from Tynda (R1260, 20 hours).

The **Passazhirskoye Port Amurasso** (☎ 440 703, 555 754; ul Chaikovskovo 1), about 500m east of the Druzhba, sends four daily boats to Heihe,

China (R600, 15 minutes); five boats make the return trip. You'll need a Chinese visa (the nearest consulate is in Khabarovsk; for details see p304) and a multientry Russian one if you plan on coming back. Be sure to fill out a yellow form (for entry) or a blue form (for exit). If you're coming back to Russia, you may have to insist on a migration card. From Heihe, it's possible to connect back with the Trans-Manchurian route on a train through to Harbin (p273).

BIROBIDZHAN БИРОБИДЖАН
☎ 42162 / pop 90,000 / ⏱ Moscow + 7hr

A couple of hours shy of Khabarovsk on the line (heading east), Birobidzhan is actually a more attractive town, with shady streets and a quiet pace. Most visit as a day trip from Khabarovsk. It's interesting mostly for its history, as the big Hebrew letters spelling out the station's name indicate.

Birobidzhan (named for the meeting space of the Bira and Bidzhan Rivers) is capital of the 36,000-sq-km Jewish Autonomous Region. It was opened to settlement in 1927, when the Soviet authorities conceived the idea of a homeland for Jews. Some 43,000 Jews made the trek. In the 1930s growing anti-Semitism led to a ban on the Hebrew language and the synagogue was closed.

Since 1991, diplomatic ties between Russia and Israel have opened an outward flood of Jews. Of the estimated 22,000 who lived here then, only 4800 remain – about 2.4% of the total Jewish population in the region.

For most visitors, an easy DIY day trip from Khabarovsk allows more than enough time. Everywhere is quite walkable. Parallel to the tracks to the south are the main streets ul Lenina, then ul Sholom-Aleykhema. The **Internet centre** (cnr uls Gorkogo & Lenina; per hr R40; ⏱ 8am-10pm) faces pl Pobedy.

Across from the train station, **ploshchad Pobedy** is devoted to WWII. Halfway along the square, west on ul Lenina, are the two main sights in town. **Freid** (☎ 27 708; ul Sholom-Aleykhema 14A), reached from ul Lenina (look for the giant menorah on your left), is Birobidzhan's Jewish culture centre. Ask to see if you can chat with the lively director or buy a souvenir *yarmulke* (skull cap). Next door is a new synagogue you can visit.

About 100m further west, the **Regional Museum** (Kraevedchesky muzey; ☎ 68 321; ul Lenina 25; admission R100; ⏱ 10am-1pm & 2-6pm Tue-Fri) has a smattering of exhibits on local Jewish history, plus boars, bears and a bloody minidiorama of the Volochaevka civil war (below).

Hotel Vostok (☎ 65 330; ul Sholom-Aleykhema 1; s/d R850/1146), Birobidzhan's only hotel, has nice rooms next to a lively market. The hotel's restaurant serves meals, including filling R100 lunch specials.

Most Trans-Siberian trains make a stop in Birobidzhan. The easiest way here is the morning *elektrichka* (suburban train) from Khabarovsk (R120, 2¾ hours). It leaves Khabarovsk at 8am and returns around 6pm. You can also catch buses from the Khabarovsk train station.

KHABAROVSK ХАБАРОВСК
☎ 4212 / pop 620,000 / ⏱ Moscow + 6hr

After dozens of hours of taiga and the isolated Soviet towns of Eastern Siberia, Khabarovsk can put a jolt in the most railweary. A booming river town, 25km from China, Khabarovsk gives off the air of a coastal, almost Mediterranean, resort with tree-lined streets, squares with fountains, 19th-century brick buildings, popular parks overlooking the wide Amur, and real-live Japanese sushi, imported here to serve the frequent Japanese business travellers.

Such business has brought hope and money to locals – and prices show it. One Khabarovsk resident us told us it's brought a 'baby boom', too.

If you stop for just a day, visit the Regional History Museum, the best in the Far East.

History
Khabarovsk was founded in 1858 as a military post by Eastern Siberia's governor general, Count Nikolai Muravyov (later Muravyov-Amursky), during his campaign to take back the Amur from the Manchus. It was named after the man who got the Russians into trouble with the Manchus in the first place, 17th-century Russian explorer Yerofey Khabarov.

The Trans-Siberian arrived from Vladivostok in 1897. During the civil war, it was occupied by Japanese troops for most of 1920. The final Bolshevik victory in the Far East was at Volochaevka, around 45km to the west.

In 1969 Soviet and Chinese soldiers fought a bloody hand-to-hand battle over little Damansky Island in the Ussuri River. Since 1984, tensions have eased. Damansky and several other islands were handed back to the Chinese in 1991.

Khabarovskians are 80% native Russian-speakers. The only indigenous people here in any numbers are the Nanai, whose capital is Troitskoe, three hours north on the Amur.

Orientation

The train station is 3.5km northeast of the Amur waterfront at the head of broad Amursky bul; the airport is 9km east of the centre. Running more or less perpendicular to the river is the busiest street, ul Muravyova-Amurskogo, which becomes ul Karla Marksa east of pl Lenina.

Knizhny Mir (☎ 328 250; ul Karla Marksa 37; 🕑 9am-8pm) stocks a good range of city and regional maps for the entire Russian Far East (city maps are about R50).

Information

For contact details of the Chinese consulate, see p304.

INTERNET ACCESS

Internet Mir (☎ 304 613; ul Muravyova-Amurskogo 28; per hr R40; 🕑 8am-9pm Mon-Fri, 9am-7pm Sat & Sun) Web access, next to the post office.

P@RTY (☎ 308 350; ul Karla Marksa 52; per hr R30; 🕑 10am-8pm) Rather unfestive, actually.

MEDICAL SERVICES

City Hospital No 2 (☎ 306 585, 304 620; ul Muravyova-Amurskogo 54)

MONEY

Exchange offices and ATMs can be found across the city.

Exchange bureau (Amursky bul 2, Hotel Intourist; 🕑 8.45am-11pm) Changes travellers cheques.

Sberbank (Amursky bul 66; 🕑 8am-8pm Mon & Wed-Fri, 9am-8pm Tue, 9am-7pm Sat & Sun) With 24-hour ATM across from the train station.

POST

Main post office (ul Muravyova-Amurskogo 28; 🕑 8am-9pm Mon-Fri, 9am-7pm Sat & Sun) You can also make calls from the centre just below.

TELEPHONE

Main telephone office (ul Pushkina 52; 🕑 8.30am-10pm)

TRAVEL AGENCIES

Any of these can help book rail or plane tickets. Popular city tours feature Russian cuisine classes with dinner (about US$60 per person) or beer-included peeks at the Baltika brewery (US$40 per person).

Dalgeo Tours (☎ 318 829; www.dalgeotours.com; ul Turgeneva 78; 🕑 10am-7pm Mon-Fri) Very helpful English-speaking staff offer a range of local tours.

Intour-Khabarovsk (☎ 312 186; www.intour-khaba rovsk.com; Amursky bul 2, Hotel Intourist; 🕑 10am-6pm Mon-Fri) Friendly staff have plenty of experience with foreigners (mostly prebooked group tours).

Khabarovsk-Tourist (☎ 439 423; ul Sinelvnikova 9, Hotel Turist; 🕑 9am-6pm Mon-Fri) Arranges China visas in a week for R2400, or in a day for R4500.

Sights

ULITSA MURAVYOVA-AMURSKOGO

Khabarovsk is the nicest city in the region to see by foot. Start along ul Muravyova-Amurskogo to admire the graceful **architecture** that survived the civil war. Start at **ploshchad Lenina**, where the pretty fountains are a magnet for locals relaxing in the evening. During January, the square hosts an ice sculpture fest.

The striking old parliament building, the **duma** (ul Muravyova-Amurskogo 17), became the House of Pioneers (Dom Pionerov) in Soviet times. It now houses a souvenir shop (see p229).

A statue of Mercury tops **Tsentralny Gastronom** (ul Muravyova-Amurskogo 9), a glamorous 1895 mint-green Style Moderne building with a decent café (see p228). The **Far Eastern State Research Library** (ul Muravyova-Amurskogo 1), with its intricate red-and-black brick façade, was built from 1900 to 1902.

At Komsomolskaya pl is the newly reconstructed Orthodox church **Khram Uspeniya Bozhei Materi**, a replica of one destroyed during communist times.

THE WATERFRONT

Steps from Komsomolskaya pl lead to the waterfront and a strip of beach that's very popular with sunbathers on hot days. South, there's a string of summertime food stalls and the landing stages for the suburban river boats. Further on, as you climb the steps back up to ul Lenina, you'll encounter Khabarovsk's bombastic **WWII memorial** and the new multidomed **Church of the Transfiguration**.

IRKUTSK TO VLADIVOSTOK (side tab)

KHABAROVSK

0 ——————————— 1 km
0 ——————————— 0.5 miles

INFORMATION
Chinese Consulate
　Китайское Консульство.................**1** A4
City Hospital No 2
　Городская больница номер 2....**2** C5
Dalgeo Tours Далгео Тур **3** A5
Exchange Bureau ....(see 26)
Internet Mir Интернет Мир...........(see 6)
Intour-Khabarovsk
　Интур-Хабаровск ....(see 26)
Japanese Consulate **4** C5
Khabarovsk-Tourist
　Хабаровск-Турист.....................(see 28)
Knizhny Mir Книжный Мир **5** C5
Main Post Office Главпочтамт **6** B5
Main Telephone Office
　Центральный Переговорный
　Пункт **7** C5
P@RTY **8** D4
Sberbank Сбербанк **9** D3

SIGHTS & ACTIVITIES
Archaeology Museum
　Музей Археологии....................**10** A5
Church of Christ's Birth
　Христорождественская
　Церковь **11** D3
Church of the Transfiguration
　Преображенская церковь **12** D3
Count Nikolai
　Maravyov-Amursky Statue ....(see 35)
Duma Дума ....(see 46)
Far Eastern Art Museum
　Дальневосточный
　Художественный Музей..........**13** A5
Far Eastern State Research Library
　Библиотека Дальне-Восточного
　Иследования **14** A5
Khram Uspeniya Bozhei Materi

Храм Успения Божей Матери **15** A5
Military Museum
　Военный Музей **16** A5
Museum of History of the
　Far Eastern Railway
　Музей Истории Дальневосточной
　Железной Дороги **17** D3
Regional History Museum
　Краеведческий Музей..............**18** A5
Tower ....(see 35)
Tsentralny Gastronom
　Центральный Гастроном..........**19** B5
WWII Memorial Памятник Второй
　Мировой Войны **20** A6

SLEEPING
Ali Hotel Гостиница Али................**21** D5
Ekspress Vostok Експресс Восток..**22** A5
Gostinitsa Гостиница **23** A6
Hotel Amethyst
　Гостиница Аметист **24** C4
Hotel Amur Гостиница Амур **25** C6
Hotel Intourist
　Гостиница Интурист **26** A5
Hotel Sapporo
　Гостиница Саппоро **27** A5
Hotel Turist Гостиница Турист **28** D4
Hotel Zarya Гостиница Заря **29** D4
Maly Hotel Restaurant ....(see 30)
Maly Hotel Гостиница Малая **30** B5
Parus Парус **31** A5

EATING
Chocolate Шоколад........................**32** A5
Citi HK Supermarket......................**33** D4
Dalny Vostok Cafe
　Дальний Восток Кафе...............**34** B5
Kafe Utyos Кафе Утёс **35** A5
Metro Метро...................................**36** C5

Overtime..**37** D5
Russky Restaurant
　Русский Ресторан **38** A5
Tsentralny Gastronom
　Центральный Гастроном..........**39** B5
Unikhab ....(see 26)

DRINKING
Open Air Cafés................................**40** A5
Rio **41** C6

ENTERTAINMENT
Drama Theatre Театр Драмы........**42** B5
SovKino СовКино...........................**43** B5
Theatre of Musical Comedy
　Театр Музыкальной Комедии **44** D4

SHOPPING
Market Рынок **45** C4
Taini Remesla Тайны Ремесла......**46** B5

TRANSPORT
Boat Ticket Office **47** A6
Train Ticket Office
　Железнодорожные кассы.......**48** D4
Transport Service Transit................(see 33)

A pleasant **city park** stretches 1.5km downriver (northwards). On the promontory is a cliff-top **tower** in which a troupe of WWI Austro-Hungarian POW musicians was shot dead for refusing to play the Russian Imperial anthem. It now contains a café, Kafe Utyos. Opposite the tower is a statue of **Count Nikolai Muravyov-Amursky**.

MUSEUMS

One of the Far East's best attractions, the **Regional History Museum** (Kraevedchesky muzey; ☎ 312 054; ul Shevchenko 11; admission R140, photo R100; ⏰ 10am-6pm Tue-Sun) earns its roubles with six well laid-out halls in an evocative 1894 red-brick building. Highlights are many, including a far better then average look into native cultures (including eerie bigger-than-life-sized spear-toting wooden figurines); stuffed animals featuring some English captions; a full-on panorama of the snowy 1922 civil war battle at Volochaevka; and a Soviet-fest room complete with medals, photos, stamps and banners.

The nearby **Military Museum** (Voenny muzey; ☎ 326 350; ul Shevchenko 20; admission R84; ⏰ 10am-5pm Tue-Sun) is a four-room frenzy of battle axes, guns, knives, and busts of moustached heroes of past conflicts. In the courtyard is a line of army vehicles including a luxury officers-only rail carriage dating from 1926.

The highlight of the **Archaeology Museum** (Muzey Arkheologii; ☎ 324 177; ul Turgeneva 86; admission R120; ⏰ 10am-5.30pm Tue-Sun) is the reproductions and diagrams of the wide-eyed figures found at the ancient Sikachi-Alyan petroglyphs (p230). Lots of pot parts and spear heads – some dating back 30,000 years.

The **Far Eastern Art Museum** (Dalnevostochny Khudozhestvenny muzey; ☎ 328 338; ul Shevchenko 7; admission US$4; ⏰ 10am-5pm Tue-Sun) has religious icons, Japanese porcelain and 19th-century Russian paintings.

Closed at research time (but apparently reopening) is the small **Museum of History of the Far Eastern Railway** (☎ 383 035; ul Vladivostok-skaya 40; admission free; ⏰ 8.30am-5.30pm Mon-Fri), which has plenty of photos and models.

CHURCH OF CHRIST'S BIRTH

Among the few churches that survived the Soviet years is the cute, red-blue-and-white **Church of Christ's Birth** (Khristorozhdestvenskaya tserkov; ul Leningradskaya 65). Two-hour services are held most days at 7am and 5pm.

Activities

For a short **river trip** along the Amur, various hydrofoils and boats set off from May to October on hour-long beer-soaked trips for R70; 90-minute evening cruises cost R130. There are no set schedules – just watch for one and jump on. Call **Amurrechturist** (☎ 398 269) for more information.

Dinamo Park, behind the Theatre of Musical Comedy, brims with sun- and shade-seekers in good weather; the ponds on the south side are popular swim-and-splash spots.

Sleeping

With advance notice, Dalgeo Tourist arranges homestays (from US$35 including breakfast).

BUDGET

All rooms come with private bathroom, TV and refrigerator. The first two are not far from the train station.

Hotel Zarya (☎ 310 101; hotel_zarya@mail.ru; ul Kim Yu Chena 81/16; s/d with breakfast from R850/1600; 🔀 🖳) A makeover of a drab building gives Zarya a 'boutique hotel' feel. Rooms are small – some have air-con. The staff are great; Internet is available 24 hours.

Hotel Turist (☎ 439 674; postmaster@khabturist.kht.ru; ul Karla Marksa 67; s/d from R1100/1320) Facing the busy street, the eight-storey Turist shows bits of its four decades, but its rooms are well kept up – the cheapies are frequently full.

Hotel Amur (☎ 221 223; fax 217 141; ul Lenina 29; s/d with breakfast from R1500/1600; 🔀) Grand old building with 75 rooms (some with air-con) on the busy residential ul Lenina.

Ekspress Vostok (☎ 384 797; ul Komsomolskaya 67; s/d R1300/1800; 🔀) New hotel geared to Russians – all 29 rooms are clean, with a writing desk and rather cheap vinyl floors.

At last pass, it was possible to bunk on a late-night disco cruise ship at the river-boat landing from June to September; it's simply called **'gostinitsa'** (hotel; ☎ 398 980; s/d R400/800).

MIDRANGE & TOP END

Hotel Intourist (☎ 312 313; www.intour.khv.ru; Amursky bul 2; s/d from R2352/2604; 🖳) This big bolshevik is another monster of the past, but it's quite good. The halls – with dark-wood doors and small, but clean rooms – look over the nearby Amur, and most of the package tourists who come seem to like it. Prices fall in winter.

Hotel Amethyst (☎ 420 766; amethyst@hotel.kht .ru; ul Lva Tolstogo 5A; s/d from R2600/3100; ✹) A boutique-style hotel with just 16 spacious, nicely decorated rooms. The staff is great and there's a sauna. Breakfast is R200.

Maly Hotel (☎ 305 802; fax 305 939; ul Kalinina 83A; s/d US$110/180; ✹) Behind a bank, in a small, quiet brick courtyard, the Maly has just 11 rooms – the doubles are quite bigger than the singles.

Ali Hotel (☎ 217 888; fax 304 403; ul Mukhinu 17; s/d with breakfast US$120/162; ✹ 🖥 🕭) Ali's 20 rooms are Khabarovsk's roomiest – with sparkling bathrooms – though the hotel's a bit stranded (between apartments and garages). Fitness centre with pool and sauna.

Hotel Sapporo (☎ 306 745; sapporo1@gin.ru; ul Kom -somolskaya 79; s/d R2983/3297; ✹ 🖥) Just off the main crawl, the Sapporo's 20 rooms are geared to its many visitors from Japan; small, clean (but not particularly remarkable) rooms in a simple red-brick building. There's a good sauna on-site.

Parus (☎/fax 649 510; guest@parus.vic.ru; ul Shev-chenko 5; s/d with breakfast R3100/4400; ✹ 🖥) Part of a century-old red-and-brick building near the water, the Parus seems more 'business centre' than hotel, though its spacious rooms are comfortable (all but four rooms are in a newer annexe).

Eating

Eating is easy in Khabarovsk: new spots open frequently on and off ul Muravyova-Amurskogo. Also you'll see – weather permitting – tonnes of street vendors selling pizza and the ever-present hot dog (R13).

RESTAURANTS

Russky Restaurant (☎ 306 587; Ussuriysky bul 9; meals R800-1200; ✹ noon-1am) Slightly kitsch and cosy, Russky has four dacha-style cellar rooms decorated with balalaikas and stuffed owls – one room, with live traditional music at 8pm, which fills first. The food is very good. Sizzling sturgeon is the favourite, as is the breaded pork chop covered in dill.

Chocolate (☎ 420 097; ul Turgeneva 74; meals R400-700; ✹ 24hr) Stylish eatery where the cool folk go (and the air-con is cranking in summer) for international snacking (fajitas, burgers) and some superb desserts (the namesake brownie is R180).

Kafe Utyos (☎ 777 050; ul Shevchenko 15; meals R800-1500; ✹ noon-midnight) In the tower in the park overlooking the river, Utyos is one of Khab's swankier restaurants – mostly Russian and Japanese food.

Metro (ul Muravyova-Amurskogo 35; lunches R100-150, meals R400-700; ✹ 11am-5pm & 6pm-2am Mon-Fri, 11am-2am Sat & Sun) Below a university building, the Metro occupies (it's whispered) the spot where medical students once poked at cadavers. Now it's a flashy subterranean drink 'n' eat spot – best for the cheap lunch.

Maly Hotel Restaurant (☎ 305 802; ul Kalinina 83A; meals R600-1000; ✹ 9am-11pm) The hotel's small restaurant is known for the best Japanese in town (all imported) and rather slow service. Worth calling ahead.

Unikhab (☎ 312 315; Amursky bul 2, 11th fl; meals R600-1000; ✹ noon-3pm & 6-11pm) The best of Hotel Intourist's three restaurants, the top-floor Japanese restaurant offers imported-from-Japan sushi with views.

Overtime (☎ 318 547; ul Dikopoltseva 12, Platinum Arena; meals R600-1000; ✹ noon-midnight) If you're here in hockey season, Overtime's primary red, white and blue décor overlooks the rink; photos of local hockey greats adorn walls all year.

CAFÉS & SELF-CATERING

Tsentralny Gastronom (ul Muravyova-Amurskogo 9; meals R150-300; ✹ 10am-10pm) In a 19th-century building, upstairs from a good 24-hour grocery, this cute modern-retro self-service café has a good selection of meals, beer on tap and a refrigerator full of desserts.

Dalny Vostok Cafe (ul Muravyova-Amurskogo 18; meals R150-300; ✹ 9am-midnight) Plump blue booths overlook the street action at this two-line cheapie fast-food pick-and-point stop (go past the doors in the front bar).

Citi HK Supermarket (ul Karl Marksa 76; ✹ 9am-11pm) Best grocery in town.

Drinking

Most drinking occurs at open-air cafés; good ones are along the river, north of the Intourist Hotel. On two levels, **Rio** (☎ 238 420; ul Lenina 49; cover R300; ✹ 9pm-4am or 5am Fri-Sun) is the city's largest club, where photos show what you can expect: topless women engaging in mud conflict.

Entertainment

Drama Theatre (Teatr Dramy; ☎ 310 809; ul Dzerzhin-skogo 44) We bet you a kopeck that Chekhov's on here.

Theatre of Musical Comedy (Teatr Muzikalny komedy; ☎ 211 403; ul Karla Marksa 64; tickets R80-800) Has mostly talking and joking, though heavy-metal legend Dio started his 2005 tour here.

SovKino (☎ 324 065; ul Muravyova-Amurskogo 32) Shows dubbed Hollywood flicks.

Shopping

Taini Remesla (☎ 327 385; ul Muravyova-Amurskogo 17; ⏲ 11am-6pm or 7pm) The best souvenir shop in town, located in the old House of Pioneers building.

Market (cnr Amursky bul & ul Tolstogo; ⏲ 8am-7pm) This main market covers everything from plug adaptors and fishing gear to underwear and fresh produce.

Getting There & Away

AIR

The **airport** (☎ 393 758) offers domestic service to Irkutsk (R5800, three hours, daily), Magadan (R2630 to R3100, 2½ hours, four weekly), Moscow (R11,500, 8½ hours, daily), Nikolaevsk-na-Amure (R4100, 1½ hours, daily), Petropavlovsk-Kamchatsky (R5975, 2½ hours, six weekly), Vladivostok (R2500, 1¾ hours, daily), Yakutsk (R6200, three hours, six weekly) and Yuzhno-Sakhalinsk (R4200, 1½ hours, two daily).

There are international flights to Harbin (US$170) and Guau (US$320) in China, Seoul (from US$300) in Korea, and Niigata (US$340) and (July to September) Aomori (US$340) in Japan. All international flights are subject to a R800 departure tax, usually included in the ticket price.

The foreign airlines all have offices at the airport's international terminal (to the left of the new one). **Intour-Khabarovsk** (☎ 312 186; www.intour.khv.ru; Amursky bul 2, Hotel Intourist; ⏲ 10am-6pm Mon-Fri) books tickets, as does **Transport Service Transit** (☎ 291 692; ul Karl Marksa 76; ⏲ 10am-2pm & 3-8pm), in the HK Citi Mall.

BOAT & BUS

From Khabarovsk's river station, boats sail down the Amur to Fuyuan in northern China (see right). Between May and October hydrofoils run north on the Amur between Khabarovsk and Komsomolsk (R446, six hours) and Nikolaevsk-na-Amure (R2332, 17 hours). You'll save money taking the night bus from here to Komsomolsk-na-Amure (on the BAM line), then catching a

boat up. At research time, boats left here at 7am. The pink *rechnoy vokzal* (river station) houses the **boat ticket office** (☎ 398 654; ⏲ 8am-10pm).

TRAIN

Heading west, apart from 1 *Rossiya*, which departs for Moscow (R8500, 130 hours) and Irkutsk (R5000, 60 hours) on even-numbered dates, there's also daily train 43 to Moscow (R5700) and Irkutsk (R3350) and train 7 to Novosibirsk (R4550, 91 hours). Heading east, Vladivostok is best reached on daily train 6 *Okean* service (R1500, 13 hours).

For details on getting to Birobidzhan, see p224.

Other daily services (all leaving in the evening) include the 226 to Tynda (R1351, 30 hours), and on to Neryungri; the 67 and 953 to Komsomolsk (R860, eight hours), the latter continuing to Sovetskaya Gavan and Port Vanino for the ferry across to Sakhalin; and the 385 to Blagoveshchensk (R1090, 16 hours).

Buy tickets at the station or the quieter (and nearby) **zhelezhodorozhne-avia kassy** (train ticket office; ul Leningradskaya 56V; ⏲ 9.30am-7.20pm), where you'll pay a R60 booking fee.

Getting Around

Trolleybus 1 (R9) runs regularly from the airport to ul Muravyova-Amurskogo, taking around 30 minutes to cover the 5km; minivans also do the journey (R10). A taxi to/from Hotel Intourist should cost no more than R250.

The easiest way to get into the city centre from the train station at the eastern end of Amursky bul is by way of trams 1, 2, 4 or 6 (R10), which cross ul Muravyova-Amurskogo along ul Sheronova. Bus 35 connects the airport and the train station.

Travel agencies can get you a car with driver for US$15 per hour.

AROUND KHABAROVSK
Fuyuan (China)

From mid-May to mid-October, daily hydrofoils leave from Khabarovsk river station for Fuyuan (one-way/return R1400/2000, 1½ hours) at 8am and 10am, returning in the evening (with tonnes of shopping bags) from the small Chinese town on the Amur River. If you're planning to return to Russia, you'll need a Chinese visa and a double-/ multiple-entry Russian visa. There is a Chinese consulate in Khabarovsk (see p304 for details). From Fuyuan you can take a bus to Jiamusi and then on to Harbin.

Sikachi-Alyan Сикачи-Алянь

The main attraction at Sikachi-Alyan, 40km north of Khabarovsk, are the enigmatic riverside stone carvings of strange graphic figures, dating from the 11th century BC. There are a couple of competing museums here – the Ecological Tourist Complex was made by Russians; the local museum by local Nanai.

An eight-hour tour (see Travel Agencies, p225) – with guide, lunch, transport and usually a look at how Nanai locals make crafts out of fish skin – costs about US$130.

VLADIVOSTOK ВЛАДИВОСТОК

☎ 4232 / pop 650,000 / Moscow + 7hr

It has the reputation (everyone around the Far East seems to look up to it) and – once you get here – Vladivostok indeed is pretty good to be in for a couple of days. Some streets are a bit drab, but the setting is remarkable: a series of peaks and peninsulas curl around the Golden Horn Bay (bukhta Zolotoy Rog; named after Istanbul's similar-looking harbour), which is home to huge icebreakers and the Russian Pacific Fleet.

Quite the port-town bustler before communism (back when the Swiss family Brynner brought a bald Yul into the world here in 1920), Vladivostok's cosmopolitan urges have slowly returned after the long Soviet snooze. Vladivostok was firmly off limits to all foreigners (and most Russians) during the USSR days. Today you can (fairly freely) hop on ferries to far-off beaches on former navy-only islands; tour century-old forts or a Soviet sub; and weave past (in summer) battalions of Chinese, Japanese and Korean tourists.

Summer is wet and foggy, and power outages plague winter. September and October, locals swear, is best.

History

Founded in 1860, Vladivostok (meaning 'Lord of the East') became a naval base in 1872. Tsarevitch Nicholas II turned up in 1891 to inaugurate the new Trans-Siberian rail line. By the early 20th century, Vladivostok teemed with merchants, speculators and sailors of every nation in a manner more akin to Shanghai or Hong Kong than to Moscow. Korean and Chinese, many of whom had built the city, accounted for four out of every five of its citizens.

After Port Arthur (Dalian) fell in the Russo-Japanese War of 1904–05, Vladivostok took on an even more crucial strategic role, and when the Bolsheviks seized power in European Russia in 1917, Japanese, Americans, French and English poured ashore here to support the tsarist counterattack. Vladivostok held out until 25 October 1922, when Soviet forces finally marched in and took control.

Josef Stalin deported or shot most of the foreign population of the city. The northern suburb of Vtoraya Rechka became a transit centre for hundreds of thousands of prisoners waiting to be shipped up to the gold fields of Kolyma.

From 1958 to 1992 the city was closed.

Orientation

The heart of central Vladivostok is where Okeansky pr intersects with ul Svetlanskaya, the city's main waterfront axis. Most hotels are west of ul Aleutskaya (a block west of Okeansky pr), which runs past the train station. Ul Admirala Fokina, west of Okeansky pr, is an action-packed pedestrian mall, often called 'Arbat' by locals.

MAPS

City maps are available at stalls bookshops such as **Dom Knigi** (ul Svetlanskaya 43; ☽ 10am-7pm Mon-Sat, 10am-5pm Sun) and **Knigomir** (ul Aleutskaya 23; ☽ 10am-8pm), where you can also get some glossy regional books and postcards.

Information

See p304 for consulate information.

INTERNET ACCESS

Iguana Cafe (☎ 481 367; ul Svetlanskaya 23; per hr R60; ☽ 10am-midnight) Behind the indoor flower market. Beer and coffee handy.

Post office (ul Aleutskaya; per hr R50; ☽ 8am-8pm) Lightning-fast connection.

MEDIA

Vladivostok News (vn.vladnews.ru) An online newspaper in English.

VLADIVOSTOK

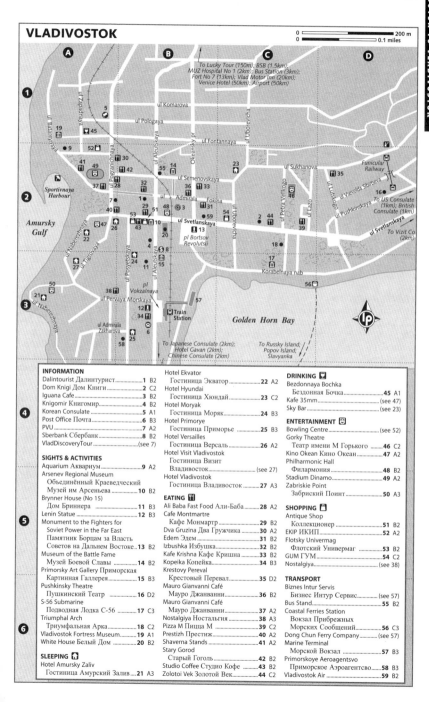

MEDICAL SERVICES

MUZ Hospital No 1 (☎ 258 663; ul Sadovaya 22)
Ambulances take patients here, 2km north of centre.

MONEY

There are currency-exchange desks and
ATMs all over town.

Sberbank (ul Aleutskaya 12; ⏲ 9am-7pm Mon-Sat,
10am-5pm Sun) Accepts travellers cheques.

POST & TELEPHONE

You can make international calls downstairs at the post office.

Post office (ul Aleutskaya; ⏲ 8am-8pm) Opposite the
train station.

TOURIST INFORMATION

PVU (☎ 432 576; ul Pogranichnaya 6) Can help extend
your visa for a day (for a fee, if it isn't for a good reason)
so you can exit Russia. It's best to get help from a travel
agent, though.

TRAVEL AGENCIES

The following agencies can arrange visas to
China from the new consulate (at research
time, it cost about US$125 to receive in
three days or a week – always a week for
Americans), plus set you up with train tickets, homestays and tours.

Dalintourist (☎ 222 949; www.dalintourist.ru; ul
Admirala Fokina 8; ⏲ 10am-5pm Mon-Fri, 10am-2pm
Sat) Best all-round agency, with the cheapest homestays,
most-dependable visa service, good side trips to Vityaz
beach near Slavyanka (see p237) and the Arkhipovka
Lodge (rooms including all meals cost R530), north of
Vladivostok in the Sikhote Alin Mountains.

Lucky Tour (☎ 223 333; www.luckytour.com; ul Moskovskaya 1; ⏲ 10am-6pm Mon-Fri) Helps organise Trans-
Siberian and Kamchatka trips, and has many local trips
on offer. It's on the east side of the park (just northeast of
Okeansky pr).

Vizit Co (☎ 499 799; www.visitfareast.com; ul Svetlanskaya 147; ⏲ 10am-7pm Mon-Fri) A friendly smaller-
scale agency, good for homestays and registration, local
tours and Trans-Siberian tips online.

VladDiscoveryTour (☎ 413 400; www.vdt.ru;
ul Pogranichaya 2; ⏲ 10am-6pm Mon-Sat) New agency
with staff that have experience helping backpackers and
Trans-Siberian travellers.

Sights
WATERFRONT & CITY CENTRE

Vladivostok train station, originally built in
1912 and smartly renovated since, is an
exotic architectural concoction with bold

murals inside. Across the road stands an
unusually animated, finger-pointing **Lenin**.

Ul Aleutskaya is lined with once-grand
buildings. The yellow house at **No 15** was
the home of actor Yul Brynner.

Ploshchad Bortsov Revolutsii has the impressive **Monument to the Fighters for Soviet Power
in the Far East** as its centrepiece. The square,
a focal point for performers and protesters
of all kinds, hosts a market every Friday.
The monolithic slab at the square's western
end is the **White House** (Bely dom), home to
the regional administration.

Heading east from the square, and just
below the reconstruction of a **triumphal arch**
built originally for Tsar Nicholas II in 1902,
you'll see the green-and-grey **S-56 submarine**
(Memornalnoi Gvargeiskoi Podvodnoi Lodke S-56; ☎ 216
757; Korabelnaya nab; adult/child R50/25; ⏲ 10am-8pm).
Lots of original gear inside (plus photos),
but best is just clambering around inside a
WWII sub that sunk 10 enemy ships.

The bulk of local strolls, beer-drinking
and ice cream–eating is back west along
the **Sportivnaya Harbour**, where you'll find
plenty of food stalls, an amusement park
and a rather trashy small beach facing the
Amursky Gulf. Just north is an **aquarium**
(Okeanarium; ul Batareynaya 4; admission R80; ⏲ 10am-
8pm Tue-Sun, 11am-8pm Mon).

ARSENEV REGIONAL MUSEUM

Most intriguing in its unexpectedness, the
Arsenev Regional Museum (Kraevedchesky muzey Ar-
seneva; ☎ 413 977; ul Svetlanskaya 20; adult/child R70/35;
⏲ 10am-7pm Tue-Sun) is named for a late-19th-
century ethnographer. It features two floors
of thematic rooms – some revel in mixing
it up (water fountain and fake plants amid
modern photographs, 'CCCP' sign atop
green-and-red candy cane, the warring em-
brace of a bear and Siberian tiger that looks
a little like ballroom dancing).

MUSEUM OF THE BATTLE FAME

At the **museum** (Muzey boevoy slavy; ☎ 217 904;
ul Semenovskaya 17-19; admission R20; ⏲ 9am-1pm & 2-
6pm Tue-Sat, closed last Fri of month), in a fine old
pillared building, a guy in a navy outfit will
probably help you put shoe covers on for
the carpeted floors of the three-floor exhibit.
The museum is geared chiefly to border pa-
trol history (despite its more marketable
war-oriented name), with imaginative 'boat'
and 'plane' doors to such-themed rooms.

PRIMORSKY ART GALLERY

This **art gallery** (Primorskaya kartinnaya galereya; ☎ 411 195; ul Aleutskaya 12; admission R100; ☺ 10am-1pm & 2-6.30pm Tue-Sat, 11am-5pm Sun) was temporarily closed for renovation at research time. Its collection – a surprising range of 17-century Dutch works and excellent works by Russian artists Ilya Repin and VV Vereshchagin – should be back before you arrive.

FORTS

Vladivostok teems with sprawling subterranean forts built a century ago to repel potential Japanese attacks.

Vladivostok Fortress Museum (Muzey Vladivostokskaya Krepost; ☎ 400 896; ul Batareynaya 4A; admission R70; ☺ 10am-6pm) blasts a giant gun at noon daily (drawing huge crowds of Asian tourists). Inside the renovated fort you can see guns, bombs and fort models. The fort is best accessed from ul Zapadnaya.

Sixteen protective forts encircle Vladivostok. The best (but pricey) is the hill-top **Fort No 7**, 14km north of the centre. It has 1.5km of tunnels, pretty much untouched since its last 400 soldiers left. Visiting on your own is very difficult, as the fort doesn't keep regular hours and it's hard to find. Organise a visit through an agency (about US$30 or US$40 per person including guide, transport and admission).

FUNICULAR

Vladivostokniks' favourite attraction may just be the smoothest-running operation in the Far East: the freshly renovated **funicular railway** (funikulyor; R5; ☺ 7am-8pm), which every few minutes makes a fun 60-second ride up a 100m hill. At the top, go under ul Sukhanova via the slummy underpass to a great (but also slummy) lookout beside the buildings of DVGTU (Far Eastern State Technical University) – the best view of Vladivostok.

Activities

ISLANDS & BOAT TOURS

To catch ferries to the nearby Russky and Popov Islands, part of the archipelago that stretches southwards from Vladivostok towards North Korea, go to the **coastal ferries station** (☎ 220 823), 100m east of the S-56 submarine. Locals will be going with you – bags of cucumbers and *kielbasa* (sausages) in tow – to offshore dachas.

There's still some question as to whether foreigners are technically allowed to visit once-closed Russky Island – at research time, we had no problem, but there's a chance you won't be able to leave the boat. There's no restriction on visiting the smaller Popov, where there is a better beach and guesthouses for an overnighter. Camping's possible on both.

At least three daily boats head to a couple of points on Russky (R40 return, 30 minutes) – around 7am, noon and 6.30pm – staying for 10 minutes, then returning to Vladivostok, making for any easy shoestring bay cruise past the Russian Pacific Fleet and giant icebreakers. If you're planning to tour the island, boats stopping at *podnozhye* (past an island canal) are best. Only one daily boat heads to Popov (R60 return, 1½ hours), leaving at 1pm and returning at 3pm.

A 90-minute bay cruise with a travel agency runs a little high: anywhere from US$100 to US$225 depending on the size of the group.

SWIMMING

The pool at **Hotel Hyundai** (☎ 407 205; ul Semenovskaya 29; pool admission R130) is available for general use.

Sleeping

Vladivostok is poorly served by budget accommodation; if funds are tight it's best to arrange a homestay for around US$20 to US$30, including breakfast, with a travel agency (see opposite). The agency can usually offer registration for a fee of US$25 or so. Cheaper hotels fill first during summer tour–group season. Breakfast isn't included at most hotels.

Note: in winter, Vladivostok routinely experiences energy shortages, which means hot water can be a rarity, and even cold water disappears on occasion. Check what the situation is and keep your bathtub full.

MIDRANGE

Hotel Primorye (☎ 411 422; admin@hbotel.primorye.ru; ul Posetskaya 20; s/d from R1000/1200) A favourite central place on a rather quiet street, this renovated five-floor hotel has half of its quite nice rooms facing the harbour. (Smaller) cheapies go first, so call ahead. The 4th-floor café offers a R180 breakfast.

Hotel Moryak (☎ /fax 499 499; ul Posetskaya 38; s/d from R1000/1100) Cheapest rooms fill with tour groups first, but it's still a good back-up to the Primorye with small (very) but bright rooms – many with a peek at the bay or Vladivostok hills. It's found at the crest of a hilly street, and there is no lift.

Hotel Vladivostok (☎ 412 808; www.vladhotel.vl.ru; ul Naberezhnaya 10; economy s/d R725/1450, standard s/d R1830/2330; 🖳) This one-time flagship of the Soviet era has the best economy single deal in the city, while the standard's slight extra comfort hardly justifies the price hike. Half the rooms have great views over the Amursky Gulf.

Hotel Ekvator (☎ 412 060; www.hotelequator.ru; ul Naberezhnaya 20; s/d from R1300/1800) Rather seedy (fading dark-wood panelling, exposed wiring), but facing the water, the Ekvator is often nevertheless full with groups in summer. Rooms are OK.

Hotel Amursky Zaliv (☎ 225 520; fax 221 430; ul Naberezhnaya 9; s/d from R550/1100; 🐾) An enigmatic rambling place dug into the cliff side right on the water (the top floor is at street level), this hotel is packed with Chinese and Russian tour groups from May to September. There are several price ranges – all were full when we last dropped by.

Hotel Gavan (☎ 495 363; www.gavan.ru; ul Krygina 3; economy s/d R2000/2400, standard s/d with breakfast R3600/4000; 🐾 🖳) About 2km south of the city centre, the Gavan's harbour views are blocked by kept-real apartments, but rooms are nice enough. Economy rooms are nearly identical to standard ones, but don't get free use of the 25m indoor pool. Several buses get here from the centre, including 57 to 62.

TOP END

Hotel Hyundai (☎ 407 205; www.hotelhyundai.ru; ul Semenovskaya 29; s/d with breakfast R6000/6500; 🖳) Probably the city's nicest hotel – with rooms offering excellent views on either side, plus an air ticket agency, casino, sauna, Korean restaurant and top-floor bar on hand.

Hotel Versailles (☎ 264 201; www.versailles.vl.ru; ul Svetlanskaya 10; s/d R4000/5000) Quite a regal place in the centre, with a bring-out-the-tsar dining room and 40 nice rooms that get frequently filled with upmarket tour groups. The buffet breakfast is R280.

Hotel Visit Vladivostok (☎ 413 453; www.vizit .vl.ru; ul Naberezhnaya 10; s/d with breakfast R2650/2950)

Occupying the 4th floor of the Hotel Vladivostok, these refurbished rooms come with maybe a few more comforts than in the main hotel and there is also a small bar handy.

Vlad Motor Inn (☎ 331 351; www.vlad-inn.ru; ul Vosmaya 11, Sanatornaya; r from US$139) For a respite from Russia, this Canadian-Russian joint venture, 20km north of the centre in the leafy coastal suburb of Sanatornaya, is quiet, very comfortable and very Western. Rates include free airport transfers, and the restaurant is superb.

Venice Hotel (☎ 307 600; fax 307 602; ul Portovaya 39; s/d US$76/94) Near the airport, the Venice is a fine place if you arrive late or leave early.

Eating
RESTAURANTS
Russian

Izbushka (☎ 510 269; ul Admirala Fokina 9; meals R250-500; 🕑 11am-11pm) Traditional Russian two-room eatery attracting local couples, most opting for the 'forest' room rather than the front dacha. The food's particularly good (start with a bread-covered bowl of *shchi* – soup of cabbage, potato and beef; R95). Mugs of Russian beer (not the usual costly imports) can be had here.

Kopeika (ul Aleutskaya; meals R100-200; 🕑 8am-midnight) Fast-food, pick-and-point cafeteria with Soviet-era posters and McDonald's-style seating in the modern pyramid across from the train station. The mezzanine café has good espressos for R20.

Nostalgiya (☎ 410 513; ul Pervaya Morskaya 6/25; meals R600-1000; 🕑 8am-11pm) This long-established upscale restaurant and café serves up fine, good-value traditional Russian cuisine, such as the chopped chicken filet stuffed with vegetables (R200). Those diners just off seven days of noodles from train samovars may faint at the tsarist elegance in the small restaurant – for the less-tender few, it's a little too plush.

Stary Gorod (☎ 205 294; ul Semenovskaya 1/10; meals from R600) Good Russian meals in a village-style interior, with stars shining above and waterfalls and fish tanks.

Georgian

Dva Gruzina (Two Georgians; ☎ 268 580; ul Nerchinskaya 10; meals R250-500; 🕑 10am-1am) Wagon-wheel benches and murals of Zapata-moustached men greet mostly local diners. The food is very good – the lone daily soup is especially flavourful – but there's little but pork and beef (and no English menu). Beer is a merciful R50.

Krestovy Pereval (☎ 265 640; ul Lutskogo 12; meals R700-1000; 11am-late) Great two-storey restaurant designed like a rock-garden tree house. Plenty of fish dishes to add to faves like bowl-of-rabbit-and-potatoes (R350) or mutton stew (R360).

Italian

Mauro Gianvanni (☎ 220 782; ul Admirala Fokina 16; meals R400-800; noon-midnight) Slick mirror-windowed Italian restaurant near the water, run by a big Italian guy. The thin-crusted pizza (around R200) is easily the best east of the Urals. The café (Okeansky pr 9) is slightly cheaper (pasta and cocktails only; no pizza).

Pizza M (☎ 268 511; ul Svetlanskaya 51A; meals R350-700; noon-midnight) Classier than its name might suggest, the M (near Gorky Theatre) serves pretty good pizza, and there are several pasta and meat or fish dishes (around R350 to R500).

Japanese

Edem (☎ 261 990; ul Admirala Fokina 22; meals R1200-1800; 11am-midnight Sun-Thu, 11am-2am Fri & Sat) Vladivostok's first and still best sushi bar is in an attractive cellar-like space with nooks in which to sit. Sushi and sashimi combos start at R1200. 'Sushi time' is 11am to 5pm and 6pm to 11pm only.

CAFÉS

Studio Coffee (☎ 552 222; ul Svetlanskaya 18; meals R300-500; 24hr) The cool folk of Vladivostok come to this indoor-outdoor café to enjoy a good range of drinks, excellent hamburgers (R190) and appealing salads (R100 to R250). A big set lunch is R300 (served from noon to 4pm).

Kafe Krishna (Okeansky pr 10/12; meals R100-200; 11am-7pm Mon-Sat) At press time this excellent, cheap lunch turf – with Indian, blissful all-veggie lunches and lots of local hare krishnas supping – was getting muscled out of its prime location. Hopefully it's still here, or at a new location.

Cafe Montmartre (☎ 412 789; ul Svetlanskaya 9/6; meals R300-600; 9am-3am) Down a small alley, the Montmartre offers good desserts, and set lunches for R180.

QUICK EATS

Ali Baba Fast Food (☎ 264 887; ul Pogranichnaya 6/3; 10am-midnight) Cheap Middle Eastern–style pita-bread sandwiches, soup and a Coke cost R70. There's ice cream and salads, too. Caravan-style décor and hangings block the fast-food line from view.

A juicy *shaverma* (kebab) at a stand by Sportivnaya Harbour costs R50.

SELF-CATERING

Prestizh (ul Svetlanskaya 1/2; 24hr) is a supermarket with a good bakery. **Zolotoi Vek** (ul Svetlanskaya 29; 8am-10pm) is another grocery. For fresh fruit and vegetables, there are daily stalls (ul Posetskaya) behind the post office.

Drinking

Cafés can be good for a quiet drink, but best are the outdoor beer gardens by Sportivnaya Harbour – for views and cheaper brews.

Bezdonnaya Bochka (Bottomless Barrel; ☎ 221 383; ul Fontannaya 2; noon-4am Sun-Thu, noon-6am Fri & Sat) This cavern-like bar is Vlad's best beer-binging ground and is a pretty popular place, particularly on weekends, when you should book a table if you want a seat.

Kafe 35mm (ul Naberezhnaya 3; 11am-2am) is a spacious, laid-back bar upstairs at Kino Okean, while **Sky Bar** (ul Semenovskaya 29, Hotel Hyundai, 12th fl; 6pm-2am) has excellent bay views, but just a beer is R180 a pop.

Entertainment

Bowling Centre (☎ 400 728; ul Batareynaya 8; per game R50-100; 10am-2am) Very Soviet eight-laner upstairs in a sports complex (note the old athletic mosaics).

Stadium Dinamo (ul Pogranichnaya) The popular local football team, Luch-Energiya, plays games here from April to November. Many seats have bay views, too.

Kino Okean (☎ 406 406; ul Naberezhnaya 3) Multiplex cinema showing dubbed movies only.

Philharmonic Hall (Filarmoniya; ☎ 260 821; ul Svetlanskaya 15) Come here for classical music performances.

Gorky Theatre (Teatr Gorkogo; ☎ 260 520; ul Svetlanskaya 49) The city's main venue for drama.

BSB (☎ 456 250; Kransogo Znameni pr 67; admission R100-300; 9pm-4am) This is the city's best club/disco, drawing young students. At weekends rock bands hit the stage at midnight.

Zabriskie Point (☎ 215 715; ul Naberezhnaya 9A; cover R300 Mon-Thu, R500 Fri-Sun; ☺ 8pm-4am) Attached to the back of Hotel Amursky Zaliv, Zabriskie is Vladivostok's main rock and jazz club. Live music at 11pm every night but Monday; DVD concerts fill in the gaps.

Shopping

There are plenty of souvenir stands selling *matryoshki* (nesting dolls), lacquered boxes and postcards. Here's the cream of the crop:

Flotsky Univermag (ul Svetlanskaya 11; ☺ 10am-7pm Mon-Fri, 10am-6pm Sat & Sun) Great army and navy supply store with those cute blue-and-white striped navy undershirts (R95) and flap-back shirts (R400), plus army ties, badges and hats.

Antique shop (ul Svetlanskaya 20; ☺ 9.30am-6pm) Small but interesting collection of yesteryear titbits: medals, arts, flags, cameras, coins.

Nostalgiya (ul Pervaya Morskaya 6/25; ☺ 10am-8pm) Has a nice range of traditional handicrafts, plus Vladivostok-themed artwork and Vladimir Putin refrigerator magnets.

GUM (ul Svetlanskaya 35; ☺ 10am-8pm Mon-Sat, 10am-7pm Sun) If you collect GUMs, this is the Far East's most Art Deco–elegant. There are some traditional souvenirs on the ground floor.

EKIP (☎ 400 914; ul Batareynaya 8; ☺ 10am-7pm) Stocks sporting gear including sleeping bags, tents, windsurfing boards and bikes.

Getting There & Away

AIR

Direct flights go to Moscow (R16,700, nine hours, twice daily); flights via Novosibirsk are cheaper (R12,300). Other domestic services include Khabarovsk (R2500, 1¼ hours, daily), Irkutsk (R6000, four hours, six weekly), Magadan (R5000, three hours, two weekly), Petropavlovsk-Kamchatsky (from R7000, four hours, three weekly), Yakutsk (R8500, two weekly) and Yuzhno-Sakhalinsk (R4900 to R6500, 1¾ hours, daily).

Vladivostok Air flies to Harbin, China (R5900, two weekly) and Tianjin (R7300, one weekly). There are less-frequent flights to Dailin. To Japan, Vladivostok Air flies to Niigata (R10,500, two weekly), Toyama (R12,700, two weekly) and once weekly in August to Tokyo (R6900) and twice weekly in summer to Osaka (R15,000). Both Vladi-

vostok Air and Korean Air fly direct six times weekly to Seoul (R11,000) or Pusan (R11,000).

Ticketing agencies:

Primorskoye Aeroagentsvo (☎ 407 707; www.air agency.ru; ul Posyetskaya 17; ☺ 8am-7pm) A reliable chain for tickets, with offices around much of the Russian Far East.

Vladivostok Air (☎ 205 133; ul Svetlanskaya 22; ☺ 9am-7pm) Convenient location for the main carrier serving Vladivostok.

BOAT

The **Biznes Intur Servis** (☎ 497 391; www.bisintour .com; 1 Okeansky pr, Morskoi vokzal, 3rd fl; ☺ 10am-6pm Mon-Fri) sells tickets for the fairly regular ferries (it claims to offer them every Monday and Saturday, but check first) between Vladivostok and the Japanese port of Fushiki from late February to early January. The often rough trip takes 42 hours and the ship is rarely full. Four categories of berths range from US$228 to US$888 one way (meals included) – student discounts are also available.

Dong Chun Ferry Company (☎ 494 060; www.dong chunferry.co.kr; 1 Okeansky pr, Morskoi vokzal, 2nd fl; ☺ 10am-5.30pm Mon-Fri, 7-9am Sat) sells tickets for the weekly ferry service to Sokcho, Korea (US$168 to US$312 one way, 24 hours), generally leaving at 10.30am Saturday. In Sokcho, you can catch a bus to Seoul (W15,000, three hours) every couple of hours.

BUS

The **bus station** (☎ 323 378; ul Russkaya), 3km north of the centre, sends many buses around the Primorsky Territory. You can catch a bus every 30 or 40 minutes to Nakhodka (R180, four hours) or three times daily to Khabarovsk (R665, 15 hours). Some southbound destinations may be off limits to foreigners without a permit.

TRAIN

The 1 *Rossiya* service leaves the **train station** (☎ 491 005) for Moscow (R9100, 6½ days) on even-numbered days, passing through Irkutsk (R6300, 73 hours). A cheaper service, also on even-numbered days, is train 239 – it's R6300 for a Moscow *kupe* ticket. On odd-numbered days train 7 *Sibir* to Novosibirsk (R5150, four days) is a cheaper option for Irkutsk (R4200).

Other trains include the 5 *Okean* overnight to Khabarovsk (R1500, 13 hours, daily) and the 351 via Khabarovsk and Komsomolsk-na-Amure to Vanino (R1700, 41 hours, daily), where you can get ferry service to Sakhalin Island. The 53 service to Kharkiv, Ukraine, via Moscow goes on odd-numbered days.

Leaving (local time) at 2am on Tuesday and Friday, the 185 connects Vladivostok with Harbin, China (R1500, about 30 hours), from where there are daily connections to Beijing (with delays and border checks). The train crosses the border at the Chinese town of Suifenhe and stops at Mudanjiang.

Tickets for long-distance trains are sold in the office beside the main platform. You can also buy tickets at the **Service Centre** (☎ 210 404; ◷ 8am-6.45pm), at the southern end of the building, for a whopping commission of R104, plus R48 if you need information first. Travel agencies (see p232) will also get tickets for you for similar fees.

Getting Around
TO/FROM THE AIRPORT

No direct bus or train links the airport with the centre (50km south). From the centre, take a local train three stops to Vtoraya Rechka (near the bus station), or one of the buses (including bus 23) that goes from the stand at the corner of ul Aleutskaya and ul Semenosvkaya (R7, 30 to 40 minutes).

From the bus station, 150m east of the railway, 'bus' (actually minivan) 101 goes to the airport (R50, one hour) about every hour from 6.30am to 6pm; call ☎ 322 751 for information. Coming from the airport it's the reverse procedure. The whole trip takes about two hours.

A taxi is far easier. A taxi to the airport is about R500 (45 minutes), while the airport taxi gang will try to charge triple (or more) going the other way. Look for minivan taxis heading to the centre.

PUBLIC TRANSPORT

Trolleybuses and trams cost R7 a ride; pay when exiting. From in front of the train station, trams 4 and 5 run north then swing east onto ul Svetlanskaya, to the head of the bay; tram 7 stays on ul Aleutskaya, running north past the market. The many buses are quicker.

For local ferry information, see p233.

AROUND PRIMORSKY TERRITORY

It's hard to explore or raft any of mountainous Primorsky Territory without the help of a travel agent (see p232). Prices vary: tiger trips to Gaivoron, for example, range from US$50 to US$150 per person.

Slavyanka Славянка

Locals enjoy making a day trip by ferry to the port of Slavyanka, 50km south towards the (off-limits) North Korean border. Nearby beaches are good, particularly **Vityaz**, reached by an hour-long 4WD drive south. Dalintourist (p232) in Vladivostok can help make arrangements.

From the coastal ferries station (p233) three daily boats leave for Slavyanka. At the time of research, lone hydrofoil left Vladivostok at noon (R300 return, one hour); a bigger boat left at 8.50am and 6.30pm (R300, 2½ hours).

Buses also go to Slavyanka from Vladivostok, but sometimes foreigners are not permitted to go by land.

Gaivoron & Lake Khanka
Гайворон и Озеро Ханка

About 235km north of Vladivostok, near the 4000-sq-metre Lake Khanka that spans the Chinese border, Gaivoron is the location of the Russian Academy of Sciences biological research reserve, and the chance for a close-up view of a couple of rare Amur tigers (see p275). **Dr Victor Yudin** (☎ 42251-74 249) keeps the duo behind an electrified high-wire fence in a two-hectare compound.

Nearby **Lake Khanka** is home to around 350 different species of birds every summer. The lake's shallow waters – 4m at the deepest – bloom with giant lotus flowers.

It is possible to organise an 11- or 12-hour day trip from Vladivostok to see the tigers (starting at US$200 to US$250 for four people), but it's worth tacking on a couple of hours to see the lake (for about US$30 or US$50 extra, at least). See p232.

Nakhodka Находка

If you want to take the train to the very end, the eastern terminus of the Trans-Siberian is a few hours further east, at the fishing-port town of Nakhodka. The main reason for heading out this way is to inspect the dramatic coastal rock formations near the city; there are several guesthouses in town.

A couple of daily trains leave Vladivostok for Nakhodka (R90, 3½ hours), and there are more-frequent buses (R180, four hours).

Sikhote-Alin Nature Reserve
СИХОТЕ-АЛИНСКИЙ ЗАПОВЕ ДНИК

This 344,000-hectare forested reserve is home to the Russian-American Siberian Tiger project. It's headquartered in the coastal town of Ternei and stretches from the Sikhote-Alin Range past clear salmon streams and a savannahlike oasis to the Pacific coast and rocky beaches. The chances of seeing a tiger are slim, but the reserve is beautiful and worth a visit in its own right.

It is an 11- or 12-hour ride one way. You'll need permission to visit. Contact a Vladivostok agency, who can also sort out transport and accommodation. Dalintourist's five-night 'Tigerland' trip hits several points of the reserve; it costs about R10,000 per person if a group of four goes. You can also travel on your own to its lodge in the south of the reserve for far cheaper access to the area; see p232.

Tayshet to Sovetskaya Gavan via BAM

Don't feel bad if you haven't heard about the remote one-track Baikal-Amur Mainline (Baikalo-Amurskaya Magistral; BAM), an alternate route across almost half of Russia. The BAM departs from the Trans-Siberian at Tayshet, brushes the top of Lake Baikal, cuts past 4300km of taiga and birch, snow-splattered mountains and through 17km tunnels on its way east to Sovetskaya Gavan on the Tatar Strait. Many of the towns built only to serve railroad construction workers – and to justify the project – sport that 1960s and '70s functional communist style. The appeal is more the scenery than the architecture.

Costing (in today's terms) roughly US$500 million – about the cost of the old race-the-USA Soviet space programme – this 'Hero Project of the Century' is a world-class engineering feat, sometimes not immediately visible from the window. Below the surface, permafrost and perpetually thawing/freezing land wreak havoc on any construction project (just check the blackened 'drunken trees', lifelessly leaning due to severed roots from the cruel subterranean forces).

Sixty years in the making, the BAM never had its parade. About the time services first rolled in 1991, Gorbachev was blaming it for the 'stagnation' that sprung during Brezhnev's reign, and which ultimately broke the Soviet back. Many of the old-time workers that can be met in your train carriage often gush with pride over their achievement. One lamented, 'Maybe they're right to criticise it, but it saddens us that no one sees the achievement of BAM. It's not something that could ever have been built these days.'

Other than Lake Baikal's lovely northern lip, adventures on the BAM reach some very rarely seen territory. Locals are likely to be surprised to see your wide-eyed face in places like Bratsk, Tynda or Komsomolsk-na-Amure. For more on the BAM's history, see p40.

HIGHLIGHTS

- Explore Lake Baikal's beautiful north from **Severobaikalsk** (p244)
- Cross **Bratsk dam** (p248), a masterful achievement
- Lounge in hot springs at **Khakusy** (p249)
- Stroll around **Komsomolsk-na-Amure** (p250), a St Petersburg–styled town on the Amur
- Scrub off at the *banya* in **Tynda** (p249), HQ of the BAM construction force

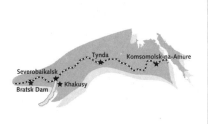

- ROUTE DISTANCE: 4308KM
- DURATION: FOUR DAYS, EIGHT HOURS

TAYSHET TO SOVETSKAYA GAVAN VIA BAM

TAYSHET TO SOVETSKAYA GAVAN VIA BAM

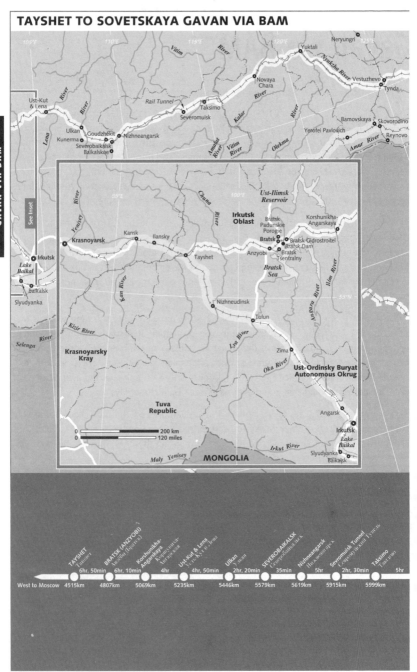

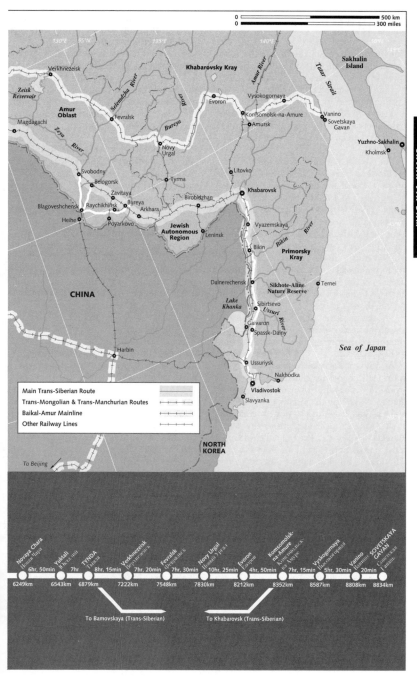

THE ROUTE

The BAM's official start is from **Tayshet** (0km on the BAM and 4515km from Moscow), from where it snakes past Lake Baikal in its long journey towards Sovetskaya Gavan on the Tatar Strait. There's little reason to be stopping off at Tayshet itself, the most convenient connection point for the BAM being Krasnoyarsk (for details of that route, see p184).

The first major stops along the BAM are for **Bratsk**, a sprawling city of 280,000 people on the edge of the Bratsk Sea, an artificial lake created in 1955 by the building of the Bratsk Hydroelectric Station. The railway line actually crosses the top of this gigantic 1km-long dam at the 330km mark presenting wide views on both sides. If you get off you must choose between three Bratsk stations: **Anzyobi** (293km) for the crushingly dreary central (Tsentralny) area, **Padunskiye Porogiye** (326km), or **Gidrostroitel** (339km) for the dam.

The taiga closes in on the line as you travel the next 600km towards the jagged mountains hemming in the northern end of Lake Baikal.

At 552km, **Korshunikha-Angarskaya** is the train station for the claustrophobic 1960s iron-ore processing town of **Zheleznogorsk-Ilimsky**. Walk 2km diagonally uphill to your right as you leave the station to reach the town's one modest attraction, the **Yangel Museum** (🕑 9am-4pm Mon-Fri), celebrating a local astroscientist friend of Yury Gagarin. The town's hotel is halfway, but gets very touchy about visa registrations.

A somewhat more congenial stop is **Lena** (720km), the station for Ust-Kut and for hydrofoil rides up the Lena River to Lensk (and eventually on to Yakutsk, the capital of the Sakha Republic). A few kilometres after Lena the line swings across the Lena River on a single-track bridge with views down on a large timber port to the north. At **Ulkan** halt (931km), a small but eye-catching metallic Lenin relief stands against a bright red 'flag' on the east end of the platform.

The scenery really improves around **Kunerma** (983km), after which the track performs a full 180-degree loop. Hurry for the camera before you disappear into the 6km-long Daban tunnel. Around half an hour before reaching Lake Baikal, there's a very brief stop at picturesque mini-spa **Goudzhekit** (1029km; p247).

Though architecturally rather dreary, **Severobaikalsk** (1064km) makes probably the best stop on this part of the route and the surrounding area is beautiful. The modernist station is one of the most striking along the line, and outside there's a steam train and a statue commemorating the workers who built the BAM.

From Severobaikalsk to the fishing village of **Nizhneangarsk**, 28km north, the line runs along Lake Baikal, though views are often better from the road (unencumbered by tunnels). After **Nizhneangarsk 2** (1104km) station, near the airport, the next 1300km gives you ample time to appreciate the truly massive engineering achievement of the BAM. Many consider this the most interesting section of the line, as it climbs over densely forested, mountainous terrain along switchbacks and through several tunnels. The longest one of 17km at **Severomuysk tunnel** (1400km) was only finished in 2004 after years of severe technical difficulties with the permafrost.

Tynda (2364km), across the Tynda River from the futuristic station, is *the* BAM town, home of the BAM construction company's headquarters and the best BAM museum. It is from here that the Amuro-Yakutskaya Magistral (Amur-Yakutsk Mainline or AYaM) heads north in the direction of Yakutsk, although there's still over 450km of line to be constructed before it eventually – maybe – reaches there. Passenger services only run as far as **Neryungri** and Aldan.

To rejoin the main Trans-Siberian route from here you'll need to head south 180km along the little BAM, the line linking Tynda with **Bamovskaya** (7273km from Moscow). Alternatively you can stay on the BAM, past some 1970s towns that see few visitors. Hilltop **Novy Urgal** (3315km) is a coal-mining town amid mountains and the white waters of the Akisma River, which locals enjoy rafting. The most appealing BAM city is **Komsomolsk-na-Amure** (3837km), with direct links with Khabarovsk on the Trans-Siberian. The BAM terminates further east, just past the ferry town of **Vanino** (4283km), on the Tatar Strait at **Sovetskaya Gavan** (4309km). From Vanino there are ferries to Sakhalin Island.

BRATSK БРАТСК

☎ 3953 / pop 258,000 / ◷ Moscow + 5hr

A stop in Bratsk neatly breaks a Krasnoyarsk to Severobaikalsk trip into two overnight rides, but a day spent here is plenty. Bratsk's raison d'etre is a gigantic 1955 **dam** (GES), which caused the drowning of the original historic town.

New Bratsk is a confusing necklace of disconnected concrete 'subcities', whose high-rise Tsentralny area is spirit-crushingly dull. It does, however, have two English-speaking tour agencies, **Taiga Tours** (☎ 413 951; taigat@bratsk.net.ru; 2nd fl, Hotel Taiga) and **Lovely Tour** (Lavli Tur; ☎ 433 290; baikal@lovelytour.ru; ul Sovetskaya 3, Tsentralny; ◷ 10am-8pm Mon-Fri, 10am-5pm Sat). Either can organise permits and guides to visit the dam's turbine rooms given two days' notice. The dam itself is 30km further north in Energetik and the BAM trains go right across it.

Between Energetik and Tsentralny, the impressive **Angara Village** (☎ 412 834; local/foreigner R12/90; ◷ 10am-5pm Tue-Sun, longer hr in summer) is an open-air ethnographic museum featuring a rare wooden watchtower and buildings rescued from drowned old Bratsk. A series of shaman sites and Tungus/Evenki *chum* (tepee-shaped conical dwellings) lie in the woods behind. The attractive lakeside site is a lonely 3km walk from Sibirsky Traktir, an isolated highway-café on the main *marshrutka* (fixed route minibus) routes 10 or 50. Taking a taxi makes more sense.

Sleeping

Hotel Turist (☎ 378 743; ul Naymushina 28, Energetik; s R350-900, tw R700-1800, ste R2500-3000) Good-value cheaper twins (half-price for single occupancy) are clean if typically Soviet with just-functional bathrooms. 'First class' rooms look better, but new wallpaper and carpet don't justify paying almost triple prices. From here, you can walk to the dam in 15 minutes.

Hotel Lyuks (☎ 363 146; ul Naberezhnaya 62, Padun; s/d/ste R1000/1200/1400) In a quiet, low-rise neighbourhood in woods beside the Bratsk Sea, this six-room wooden mansion was once an exclusive Communist Party retreat. Opt for the large if unstylish suites, with their superb lake views and extensive if somewhat aging bathrooms. Khrushchev, Brezhnev, Yeltsin and even Jacques Chirac have all stayed here. Cheaper rooms are

forgettable and wantonly overpriced. It's an R80 taxi ride from Padunskiye Porogiye train station.

Hotel Taiga (☎ 414 000; ul Mira 35; s/d/tw R1800/1800/2100) Behind a smart new façade, wobbly Soviet-era corridors host very green bedrooms, good singles, but cramped, overly intimate doubles. Some staff speak English, guest visas are registered and rates include breakfast.

Hotel Bratsk (☎ 438 436; ul Deputatskaya 32; s/tw from R350/700; Ⓟ) Upstairs a wide variety of clean but essentially Soviet rooms all have private bathrooms and peeling paint, so unless you want a malfunctioning old TV, take the cheapest available.

Eating

Kalipso (☎ 376 781; ul Naymushina 54; meals R150-400; ◷ noon-7pm & 8pm-3am) The nicest pub-café in Energetik is at bus stop GES. It has a nautical interior, port-hole windows and a beer-garden terrace that almost overlooks the lake. There's another branch in Tsentralny.

Kafe Pitstsa (ul Naymushina 24; meals R90-220; ◷ 9am-8pm & 9pm-2am) Close to Hotel Turist, this mood-lit Russian restaurant offers pizza and various local meals at sensible prices.

Getting There & Around

The three main train stations are an hour's ride apart. Padunskiye Porogiye is closest to Energetik and Padun. Gidrostritel is several kilometres east of the dam. For Tsentralny, get off at Anzyobi and transfer by bus or *elektrichka* (suburban train).

Eastbound there are afternoon and night trains to Severobaikalsk (R760, 15 hours) via Lena/Ust-Kut (R650, eight hours). On odd days a useful 3pm train runs overnight to Krasnoyarsk (16 hours). For Irkutsk train 87 (R970, 18 hours) loops via Tayshet. Alternatively, buses (R500, 11 hours) run from the **Tsentralny bus station** (ul Yuzhnaya), and during summer hydrofoils (13 hours, three weekly) zip down the Angara River from southeast Tsentralny's *rechnoy vokzal* (river station).

Marshrutky 10 and 50 shuttle regularly between Hotel Turist in Energetik and the bus station in Tsentralny (45 minutes). Bus 8 starts at GES beside the Kalipso café and wiggles around Energetik's Mikro-Rayon 7 estate to a no-man's-land bus stop nearly opposite Padunskiye Porogiye train station. For taxis, call ☎ 368 482 or 377 707.

LENA & UST-KUT ЛЕНА И УСТЬ-КУТ

☎ 39565 / pop 70,000 / ◔ Moscow + 5hr

This 15km-long ribbon of town hugs the Lena River's north bank. Though mostly low-rise, its Soviet influences reach a concrete crescendo around Lena, the main BAM station, which stares across an overgrown square towards the river station ('Osetrovo'). Boats along the Lena River to Lensk and Yakutsk (the capital of the Sakha Republic, 2000km downstream) have been Ust-Kut's raison d'etre since it was founded in 1631.

There's not a great deal else to see, but quietly attractive old Ust-Kut, 8km west of Lena station, is worth a stroll if you're stuck here. There are some photogenic wooden cottages dotted about, and the valley has an attractive aspect despite intrusions from derelict Soviet workshops. Towards the sanatorium is the site of one of Siberia's fabled salt mines, which Yerofey Khabarov developed from 1639 to 1650. It was reactivated as a prison camp from the 1860s until WWI.

Near Lena train station, 200m east of the river station, is a **museum** (top fl, ul Rebrova-Denisova 9; ◔ 10am-5pm Tue-Sat), with local artworks, historical artefacts and a hemp-weaving loom. Guests are so rare and staff so enthusiastic that escaping within an hour can be tough. Summer sunsets make the nearby riverside stroll pleasant, as long as you face away from the high-rises.

Sleeping & Eating

Lena Hotel (☎ 51 507; ul Kirova 88; s R550-900, d R1100) Across from Lena train station, this hotel has rooms with shower and toilet.

Sanatorium (☎ 23 292) If the Lena Hotel is full, you could try for a room here. Despite noisy children's groups, the setting is pleasant and peaceful, if not entirely pristine. It's close to the former salt-purifying ponds, 10km west of Lena station; take bus 2.

In summer there are a handful of appealingly positioned if culinarily challenged beer and shashlyk (meat kebab) tents along the river bank beside the river station. Other choices include the **Kafe Ermak** (◔ noon-3pm & 6pm-3am) at the base of the Lena Hotel, plus the minuscule **Bufet Ekspress** (◔ 24hr) on the train station square.

Getting There & Away

Lena (not tiny Ust-Kut halt) is a major BAM station, with useful overnight trains to

Severobaikalsk (7½ hours) via Goudzhekit (seven hours), leaving nightly around midnight. At least two westbound trains stop daily, one continuing to Moscow.

Ust-Kut's small airfield (take infrequent bus 101 from Lena train station) has flights to Irkutsk (six weekly) and weekly flights to Mirny via Lensk. Tickets are sold in the Lena Hotel.

From Osetrovo regular **hydrofoils** (☎ 26394) run to Lensk, normally with one night's stop en route in Peleduy (14 hours).

SEVEROBAIKALSK СЕВЕРОБАЙКАЛЬСК

☎ 30139 / pop 35,000 / ◔ Moscow + 5hr

With friendly, English-speaking help at hand, Severobaikalsk makes a convenient base from which to explore the beautiful yet little-visited North Baikal area. It's a refreshingly uncommercial place and, although the centre is a depressingly typical regiment of prefabricated 1970s apartment blocks, a short walk across the train tracks are some peaceful Baikal viewpoints. Flights from Nizhneangarsk (p248) and (in February and March only) the ice-roads via Ust-Barguzin (p219) make it possible to visit Severobaikalsk instead of Irkutsk (p189) between Krasnoyarsk (p185) and Ulan-Ude (p213).

Information

INTERNET ACCESS

Internet Klub Mega (Leningradsky pr 6; per hr R20 plus per MB R5; ◔ 9am-9pm) Popular with gamers.

Internet Klub Rikom (per Proletarsky 2; per hr R30 plus per MB R10; ◔ 10am-1am) Fast but pricey connection in a basement entered from the rear (forest side).

Post office Internet room (Leningradsky pr 6; per hr R30; ◔ 10am-2pm & 3-7pm Mon-Fri, 10am-2pm & 3-5pm Sat) Located at the post office, entered via separate rear entrance.

INTERNET RESOURCES

North Baikal Tourist Portal (www.sbaikal.ru) A comprehensive website.

MONEY

Sberbank (◔ 8.30am-5.30pm Mon-Thu, 8.30am-1pm Fri) Can change travellers cheques given 20 minutes and 3% commission.

POST

Post office (Leningradsky pr 6; ◔ 10am-2pm & 3-7pm Mon-Fri, 10am-2pm & 3-5pm Sat)

TELEPHONE
Telephone office (per Proletarsky 1; 24hr)

TRAVEL AGENCIES & HELPERS
All of the following agencies and individuals can help you organise accommodation and Baikal boat trips, but check very carefully what is and is not included in any deal you arrange. For another option, see p248.

Baikal Service (/fax 23 912; www.baikaltur.irk.ru) This tour agency is a professional outfit, with its own boat, hotel, permit arrangements and tour programme, but staff don't speak English.

Khozyain (/fax 24 512; irina@myBaikal.ru; Apt 43, Leningradsky pr 5; 8am-6pm Mon-Fri) Coordinates accommodation for Goudzhekit (p247) and sells Khakusy (p249) excursions.

Marysov family (26 491; kolonok2004@yandex.ru; ul Mostovstroitely 12/1) Alyona speaks decent English and her father Yevgeny organises adventure tours through

Tyozhik (20 323; davan2001@mail.ru). Their homestay is 3km out of town in Zarechny.

Rashit Yakhin/BAM Tour (/fax 21 560; www.go baikal.com; ul Oktyabrya 16/2) This experienced full-time travel fixer, guide and ex-BAM worker is quick to reply to emails and always keen to please. He rents a brilliant, central apartment for a negotiable US$15 a night. Since an immobilising stroke he remains disabled and his spoken English can be hard to follow.

Vladimir Yatskovich (20 111; y_v_n@hotmail.com; Apt 112, ul Polygrafistov 5) This proverb-spouting John Cleese lookalike is a local school teacher with great English, and can help organise guides for a range of activities. He offers a family homestay for US$15, including meals.

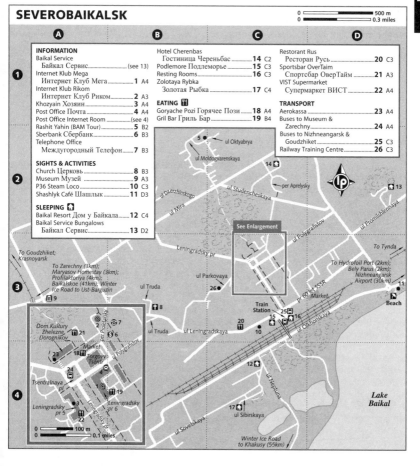

SEVEROBAIKALSK

INFORMATION	
Baikal Service	
Байкал Сервис	(see 13)
Internet Klub Mega	
Интернет Клуб Мега	**1** A4
Internet Klub Rikom	
Интернет Клуб Риком	**2** A3
Khozyain Хозяин	**3** A4
Post Office Почта	**4** A4
Post Office Internet Room	(see 4)
Rashit Yahin (BAM Tour)	**5** B2
Sberbank Сбербанк	**6** B3
Telephone Office	
Междугородный Телефон	**7** B3

SIGHTS & ACTIVITIES	
Church Церковь	**8** B3
Museum Музей	**9** A3
P36 Steam Loco	**10** C3
Shashlyk Café Шашлык	**11** D3

SLEEPING	
Baikal Resort Дом у Байкала	**12** C4
Baikal Service Bungalows	
Байкал Сервис	**13** D2

Hotel Cherenbas	
Гостиница Череньбас	**14** C2
Podlemore Подлеморье	**15** C3
Resting Rooms	**16** C3
Zolotaya Rybka	
Золотая Рыбка	**17** C4

EATING	
Goryache Pozi Горячее Пози	**18** A4
Gril Bar Гриль Бар	**19** B4

Restorant Rus	
Ресторан Русь	**20** C3
Sportsbar OverTaim	
Спортсбар ОверТайм	**21** A3
VIST Supermarket	
Супермаркет ВИСТ	**22** A4

TRANSPORT	
Aerokassa	**23** A4
Buses to Museum &	
Zarechny	**24** A4
Buses to Nizhneangarsk &	
Goudzhiket	**25** C3
Railway Training Centre	**26** C3

Sights & Activities

The friendly little **museum** (☎ 27 644; ul Mira 2; admission R20; 10am-12.30pm & 1.30-5pm Tue-Sun), 1.5km east of the central square, has limited information on BAM railway history, exhibits a few Buryat artefacts and has an associated art gallery. Train buffs might prefer the colourfully painted **P36 steam loco** (pr 60 let SSSR) displayed near the Podlemore, or to peep through the railings at the outdoor signalling paraphernalia of the **Railway Training Centre** (Dorozhnogo Tsentr Uchebniya; ul Parkovaya 11A).

There are lovely lake views from a summer shashlyk café at the eastern end of town (*marshrutka* 3 or 103). A steep path leads down from there onto a scenic pebble beach. In winter you can walk the ice from here to the Neptuna area, where unsophisticated but photogenic dacha-terraces incorporate boat-garages into their lower storeys. In winter a short taxi ride across the white 'desert' of ice is a memorable experience – watch offshore fishermen freezing their hands baiting *omul* (cousin of salmon and trout) through little ice holes. In warmer months Severobaikalsk is a great base for relatively high-endurance hiking adventures and for very pleasant boat rides on Lake Baikal when the unpredictable weather obliges. Severobaikalsk's travel agencies (p245) can assist. If you dare brave the chilly waters, the yacht club **Bely Parus** (☎ 23 950; nordsail@mail.ru; Severobaikalsk port) rents *ails parusniye* (windsurfers), *vodnye lyzhi* (water-skis) and wet suits.

While not historic, the town's blue-and-white plank-clad **church** (ul Truda 21) has a loveably dishevelled appearance. Services are held at 6pm Tuesday and Saturday, and 8.30am Sunday.

Sleeping

Homestays can be organised by Severobaikalsk's many travel agencies and often by staff at Podlemore when its rooms are full. Alternatively, consider staying in Nizhne-angarsk (p248).

Baikal Resort (Dom u Baikala; ☎ 23 950; Baikal-kruiz@Rambler.ru; ul Neptuna 3; tw R700) Unusually comfortable for this price range, the 're-sort' is really just a house, walking distance from Lake Baikal. Rooms each have a new shower and toilet. Outside summer-only hut-units are much more cramped and have no shower. The owner speaks English.

Podlemore (☎ 23 179; pr 60 let SSSR 21A; s/tw/tr R452/904/975) The obvious if unmarked red-and-yellow tower beside the train station is a sanatorium that rents decent-value 7th-floor rooms with attached hot showers. Views of Lake Baikal are across the railway marshalling yard; light sleepers might tire of the ever-disgruntled train dispatcher and her distorting loudspeaker.

Zolotaya Rybka (☎ 22 231; ul Sibirskaya 14; tw R1100-1700) Thoroughly renovated 'cottages' each contain three rooms that share a modern shower, kitchen, tasteful sitting area and two toilets. The pleasant setting between pine trees offers glimpsed views of Lake Baikal and the Neptuna area below.

Baikal Service Bungalows (☎/fax 23 912; www .baikaltur.irk.ru; dm/d/tr incl breakfast €15/50/90) Hidden in a lovely peaceful pine grove at the otherwise unpromising northeast end of town, Baikal Service Bungalows has comfortable chalets with well-appointed doubles and less-appealing upstairs triples (with sitting room). Cheaper options include summer yurts and camping pitches, and dorm beds in the 'student' house sharing a fridge and good hot shower.

Resting Rooms (Komnaty Otdykha; train station; dm per hr R16-30) Offers clean, cheap dorm beds, with a six-hour minimum. Hot shared showers are available.

Hotel Cherenbas (☎ 23 654; dm R150-250) Springy beds are packed together in a tidy but very basic former youth centre. There is a kitchen for self-catering.

Eating & Drinking

Most café-restaurants double as drinking dens and music can be deafening. To avoid ear damage and cover charges (common after 7pm) eat at one of the cheap but unlovely *poznayas* (eatery serving Central Asian food) beside the market, such as **Goryache Pozi** (pr Leningradsky 6; 9am-8pm;), which serves *pozi* (dumplings) for R12.

Gril Bar (pr Leningradsky 6; meals R60-80, cover R30-50; 8pm-2am Mon-Sat) At this small cellar bar-restaurant you can avoid the cover charge by sitting at the bar stools. Perhaps.

Sportsbar OverTaim (meals R80-120, beers R40; 8pm-1am) No sports but no cover charge either. This slightly more upmarket pub-restaurant is popular with youths.

Restoran Rus (☎ 23 914; pr 60 let SSSR 28; mains R40-90, garnish R30, cover R50; 8pm-1am Mon-Sat)

Lively tavern restaurant serving its own full-bodied home-brewed beer (R25) in wood-and-stone alcoves.

VIST supermarket (pr Leningradsky 5; 8.30am-9pm) Sells cheap groceries.

Getting There & Away
AIR
An **aerokassa** (22 746; Tsentralny pl; 9am-noon & 1-4pm Wed-Fri & Sun-Mon) within the Dom Kultury Zheleznodorozhnikov sells air tickets for flights from Nizhneangarsk, 30km northeast. Beware that planes, like Baikal boats, are prone to days of delays in bad weather. Leave plenty of leeway.

BOAT
From late June to late August a hydrofoil service should run the length of Lake Baikal between Nizhneangarsk, Severobaikalsk and Irkutsk (R1400, 12 hours) via Olkhon Island. Unfortunately, the precise timetable is only announced days before the service begins, making advance planning difficult.

Boat trips are fun and reveal the lake's vastness. Baikal's mountainous backdrop looks most spectacular from about 3km offshore, so going all the way across doesn't add a lot scenically and you'll need permits to land on the almost uninhabited east coast (see p249). It's possible to negotiate cheap charters with fishermen at Severobaikalsk, Nizhneangarsk or Baikalskoe, but think carefully before taking a boat that's small, slow or seems unreliable if you're going far: storms can come from nowhere and getting help in the middle of icy-cold Baikal is virtually impossible. To rent better, long-distance boats usually costs R1000 to R1800 per hour. For a reliable charter, contact the charming Viktor Kuznetsov (see p248).

BUS
From outside the train station, *marshrutky* run to Baikalskoe (six weekly), Goudzhekit (four daily) and half-hourly to Nizhneangarsk airport (No 103, R29, 25 minutes). The latter passes Severobaikalsk hydrofoil port (2km) and follows Lake Baikal's shore.

CAR
In February and March it's possible to hitch a (paid) ride across Lake Baikal to Ust-Barguzin. Ask locals to help you locate a driver.

TRAIN
Westbound trains run daily to Moscow, attaching a carriage to Tomsk (42½ hours) on alternate days. On odd-numbered days train 71 loops round to Irkutsk (33 hours). On even-numbered days train 347 runs to Krasnoyarsk (33 hours). Any of these stop at Lena/Ust-Kut (seven hours) and Bratsk (14 to 16 hours). Goudzhekit (R130, 35 minutes) is vastly cheaper by *elektrichka* (R20, one hour, twice daily). Eastbound trains 76 (odd-numbered days) and 98 (Tuesday and Saturday) go all the way to Tynda.

Getting Around
Marshrutka route 3 connects the new, low-rise Zarechny suburb to Tsentralnaya pl (Tsentralnaya sq) via the museum, then continues to the train station, looping right around to the far side of the tracks, passing the Baikal Resort one way. *Marshrutka* 1 passes the access road for Baikal Service en route to the train station, Tsentralnaya pl and the museum.

AROUND SEVEROBAIKALSK
Baikalskoe Байкальское
The timeless fishing village of Baikalskoe, 45km south of Severobaikalsk, has an old bridge and a picturesque lakeside location. From the fishing port, walk past the **wooden church** and continue for 20 minutes up the cliff-side path towards the radio mast for particularly superb **views**. Head to the bay beyond for camping opportunities. With a knowledgeable guide you might even find Baikalskoe's shamanic **petroglyphs** as pictured in the Severobaikalsk museum.

Minibuses leave Severobaikalsk at 8am and 5pm on Tuesday, Friday and Sunday, returning an hour or so later. A taxi for the 45-minute drive costs from R250 each way plus waiting time.

You'll need to charter a boat to reach **Cape Kotelnikovsky**, from where a difficult trek on overgrown, ill-defined trails leads to lovely **Gitara Lake**, several waterfalls around **Tazik Lake** and eventually to the glaciers that descend from **Mt Cherskogo**, the region's highest peak.

Goudzhekit Гоуджекит
Goudzhekit's lonely BAM station is beautifully situated between bald, high peaks that stay snow-dusted until early June.

Five minutes' walk to the right, the only habitation is a low-rise spa and **hotel** (dm R200-350, d R800-1000), where the best bungalows have private toilets and showers. Tour agency Khozyain (p245) in Severobaikalsk handles bookings.

With suitable guides, a 12-day trekking expedition can take you through the lovely if mosquito-plagued mountains behind Goudzhekit into the impressive, very isolated **Tyya Valley**.

Nizhneangarsk Нижнеангарск

Although Nizhneangarsk has its own BAM station, it's generally easier to access by *marshrutka* from Severobaikalsk. Nizhneangarsk forms a quietly attractive low-rise ribbon stretching 5km along the lakeside from the port to the airport. The centre is marked by a red, triangular monument. Opposite, the **tourist office** (room 1, ul Pobedy 55; ☺ 10am-5pm Mon-Fri) helps with permits for visiting northeast Baikal. A small **museum** in the high school traces the town's history back to the 17th century. For boat rentals or expeditions, track down super-enthusiastic **Viktor Kuznetsov** (☎ 47 005; frolicha@mail.ru or baikal .nordtour@mail.ru; ul Pobedy 9/7, Nizhneangarsk), who

also has an *aerosani* (propeller-powered sledge), several horses and reindeer to act as pack animals when trekking.

SLEEPING
Gostiny Dom Portal (☎ 47 280; ul Rabochaya 10; tw/ste R720/960) This very appealing, new wooden house-hotel has well-appointed en suite standard rooms, and two suites with big double beds and great views across the mudflats towards Lake Baikal. There's no café.

The town's **hospital** (☎ 47 719) maintains two ultra-basic, saggy-bedded hostels in clinics at **ul Lenina 123** (dm R220) and **ul Lenina 133** (dm R176; ☺ Jun-Sep). There's a communal kitchen and toilet but no showers.

GETTING THERE & AWAY
Scenic low-altitude flights cross Lake Baikal to Ulan-Ude (R1810, four weekly) and Irkutsk (R2250, two weekly) when weather allows.

Marshrutka 103 from Severobaikalsk travels every 30 minutes along the coast to the airport via the tourist office, returning via uls Kozlova and Lenina. The last service is at 8pm, or 6pm at weekends.

BAM-MATES *Robert Reid*

On the BAM, wheels seem to rattle a bit louder and jaws of (most) carriage-mates fall a bit lower. It's great getting off the tracks and seeing how life is lived in such remote areas, but often the highlights are the people you bunk with for a dozen or more hours.

Between Tayshet and Severobaikalsk, a woman looking like Joe Pesci tugged me out of the carriage to see the 1km-long Bratsk dam go by. 'Look at how beautiful this is,' she said. Our other roommate was a former gymnast, who swung onto the top bunk, hands on opposite bunks, as if on parallel bars. He complained about recent Olympians, 'You must have heart to succeed at the bars. They have none.'

East from Severobaikalsk to Tynda, my mates were exactly those I had hoped to avoid all trip: crew-cut drunks with tattooed knuckles. They ignored any offer of 'hello', 'good night' or 'good morning' for 35 quiet hours. One, at last, nodded when they departed shortly before Tynda. I took it as a personal victory.

But on the Tynda–Neryungri overnighter, a respectable elderly couple leapt to their feet when I knocked on the door. The tiny husband lifted the lower bunk and stored my bag underneath, while his wife readied the sheets for my bed ('this is for women to do'). Soon bags and slices of cucumbers and sausages appeared – along with bottles of vodka that those old-timers could knock back. Managed about 1½ hours of sleep before Neryungri came with dawn.

On the next ride, leaving the BAM, I joined two hilariously wild truck drivers heading for a rig in Vladivostok. One hadn't been on a train since he was 11 – I pointed out where to store bags. Both drained vodka and beer till 3am – with occasional eruptions of good-natured finger-pointing laughter (at me), and immediate apologies. They were up at 7am to finish half-drunk bottles. 'You speak Russian badly – like a Slovenian,' the reddest-faced driver said when I left them. My best compliment of the trip.

Akokan Gulag

Some 25km north of Nizhneangarsk, 3km north of the Kholodnaya turning, a forest hike leads to remnants of the small mica-mining **Akokan Gulag** (1931–33). You'll need a good guide, such as Nikolai Sorokin, a hearty taxi driver at Severobaikalsk train station (he only speaks Russian), to find the 'officers' huts', collapsed watchtower and mini-railway, whose tiny bucket wagons lie beside a magical pile of mica remnants near the collapsed mine entrance. Reckon on paying around R800, including transport. Don't forget good tick-protection.

Khakusy & Northeast Baikal

If you want to cross Lake Baikal, you'll need permits (available in Nizhneangarsk) before landing on lovely, shaman-haunted **Ayaya Bay** or trudging a mud-soaked 7km beyond to biologically unique **Lake Frolikha**. An easier trip is to Khakusy, an idyllically isolated hot-spring **turbaza** (holiday camp; dm/tw/tr R400/1100/1450; ☺ mid-Jun–early-Sep). Khakusy also requires permits in summer, but these are waived in February and March when it takes about an hour to drive across the ice from Severobaikalsk (around R1200 return taxi). Bathing (per person R40) is fun in the snow and frozen steam creates curious ice patterns on the otherwise unremarkable wooden spa buildings. Occasionally the resort's summer ferry will take nonguests across for R800 return (or R914, if you book through Khozyain in Severobaikalsk; see p245).

In spring and autumn when the ice is half-melted or half-formed, all these places are totally cut off.

TYNDA ТЫНДА

☎ 41656 / pop 39,000 / ☺ Moscow + 6hr

If BAM gets you giddy, Tynda's your town. Flanked by low-lying, pine-covered hills, modern Tynda is the BAM HQ and a hub for trains between Severobaikalsk (p244) and Komsomolsk-na-Amure (p250); the 'Little BAM' connects to Blagoveshchensk to the south; the AYaM (Amuro-Yakutskaya Magistral) heads north, getting as far as Neryungri (p250) – plans to reach Yakutsk remain on hold.

Tynda flares its Soviet roots: it was a shack village before BAM centralised its efforts here in 1974.

Orientation

The train station – the city's most striking landmark – is across the Tynda River. A pedestrian bridge leads 1km north to the central ul Krasnaya Presnaya.

Information

At the time of writing the only ATM (good for Cirrus and Eurocards) was at the train station.

Alexei Podprugin (☎ 29 126; bamland@mail.ru) Contact for kayaking, hiking and cross-country skiing trips.

Nadezhda Nizova (☎ 29 655; td_nadejda@amur.ru; ul Festivalnaya 1; ☺ 9am-1pm & 2-6pm Mon-Sat) This travel agent may be able to help with tours of the area.

Post office (ul Krasnaya Presnaya 53; per hr R40; ☺ 8am-noon & 1-7pm Mon-Fri, 8am-2pm Sat & Sun) Has a good Internet connection; at the street's east end.

Service Centre (per hr R65; ☺ 8am-7pm) At the train station; provides Internet access.

Sights & Activities

The **BAM Museum** (☎ 41 690; ul Sportivnaya 22; admission R60; ☺ 10am-1pm & 2-6pm Mon-Fri, 10am-7pm Sat), a couple of blocks southwest of the red-brick Orthodox cathedral (Svetoi Troitsi Sabor), covers native Evenki culture, local art, WWII artefacts and regional wildlife, but is known for its four rooms of BAM relics and photos (no English labels). Two cover the railroad's early years – and the Gulag prisoners who built it. Look for sci-fi author Ivan Evremev's photo, who secretly wrote while in the Gulag.

Zarya is a native Evenki village nearby. Bus 105 from the train station goes eight times daily (30 minutes).

Clean and well patronised, Tynda's public **banya** (hot bath; ☎ 40 030; ul Amurskaya; admission R60, lyux from R300; ☺ women 2-8.30pm Thu, 10am-8.30pm Sat, men 2-8.30pm Fri, 10am-8.30pm Sun) is the real McCoy when it comes to a hellishly hot steam room and chilly dunks in a pool. Freshly cut birch branches are available. The *lyux banya* is open 9am to 9pm Tuesday to Sunday. It's in a red-brick building 50m south of a dramatic sledge-hammer-wielding **statue** at the eastern end of ul Krasnaya Presnaya.

Sleeping

Hotel Nadezhda (☎ 27 021; 4th fl, ul Festivalnaya 1; r with shared bathroom per person R290-450) With rooms that date from days when the nation still mourned Brezhnev, the Nadezhda is nevertheless clean and central, and there's a kitchen. The 15 rooms sometimes fill with construction workers. You pay per bed; two or three beds per room. It's in the enigmatic Torgovi Dom Nadezhda, a long white-brick building behind Hotel Yunost.

Komnaty Otdykha (☎ 73 297; train station; beds per 6/12/24hr R150/240/420, lyux beds R198/335/610) Surprisingly comfy and clean 'rest' rooms. Showers cost R55.

Vagon Gostinitsa (beds per 6/12/24hr R101/161/261) A parked *kupe* (*kupeyny;* compartmentalised) carriage on platform one.

Hotel Yunost (☎ 23 534; ul Krasnaya Presnaya 49; r from R500) This crumbling hotel has overpriced rooms, with cold water only.

Eating & Drinking

Tynda is low-key meal-wise.

Midina (ul Krasnaya Presnaya 49; dishes R120-170; ⏰ 11am-2am Mon-Sat) Behind Hotel Yunost and above a casino, this is a rather splashy restaurant that serves big, shareable portions of Chinese (and some Russian) dishes. Karaoke at 8pm.

50/50 (ul Krasnaya Presnaya 43; dishes from R30) About 150m west, 50/50 is a beer-snack bar, with surprisingly tasty Russian meals served on its outside porch.

Getting There & Around

Train 75/76 links Tynda with Moscow on odd-numbered days, and 77/78 with Novosibirsk via the western BAM, also on odd-numbered days. These stop in Severobaikalsk (R1335, 26 hours). Train 963/964 connects Tynda with Komsomolsk (R1351, 37 hours, daily), 81/82 with Blagoveshchensk (R1260, 16 hours, daily) and 325/326 with Khabarovsk (R1351, 30 hours, daily). Many of these trains go on to Neryungri (R411, five hours), as do Tynda–Neryungri link trains 958 and 957.

Buy regional air tickets at **Vesta Service Centre** (ul Krasnaya Presnaya 39; ⏰ 9am-noon & 1-6pm).

Bus 5 outside the train station goes every 20 or 30 minutes along ul Krasnaya Presnaya (R10). A taxi to the centre is R60.

NERYUNGRI НЕРЮНГРИ

☎ 8247 / pop 70,000 / ⏰ Moscow + 6hr

Set on a flat-top hill about 220km north of Tynda, modern Neryungri (*nare*-yoon-gri) loses most views due to its three-decade old housing blocks. It's worth a visit only for the land link with Yakutsk, 800km north. The banks have no ATMs.

One of the world's largest open-cut **coal mines** *(roz rezo)* is just outside town – where adventurers can fairly freely wander the facilities and see mammoth trucks that transport chunks of coal. Take bus 3 (R7, 25 minutes).

Sleeping & Eating

Hotel Arigus (☎ 30 173; arigus@rambler.ru; pr Druzhni Narobov 27; s/d R850/1100) Book ahead for one of its four clean rooms.

Hotel PLINZ (☎ 44 234; ul Yuzhno-Yakutskaya 18/5; bed per person R180-400) Scrappy back-up.

Pizzeria (ul Karla Marksa 23; meals R200-300; ⏰ noon-2am) Cosy central spot that focuses more on its Russian dishes.

Getting There & Away

See left for information about train links to Neryungri. Taxi vans leave from the train station, 3km east of the town centre, a couple of times daily to Yakutsk (R1800, 20 to 24 hours), usually following morning train arrivals from Tynda. The trip can be gruelling, but actually a little smoother in winter when hardened ice covers the bumpy road. See Lonely Planet's *Russia & Belarus* for coverage of Yakutsk.

KOMSOMOLSK-NA-AMURE
КОМСОМОЛЬСК-НА-АМУРЕ

☎ 4217 / pop 305,000 / ⏰ Moscow + 7hr

By far the eastern BAM's most appealing town, Komsomolsk-na-Amure (City of Youth; located a whopping 1500km east of Tynda) sports a carefully planned treelined, brick-paved centre with long prospects, European-style buildings and rattling trams.

Built in a hey-ho fervour in 1932, Komsomolsk was a Soviet-dream transformation of a swamp into a planned city for the Komsomol (Young Communist League) to help populate the east (and strengthen area defences, with steelworks, an aircraft factory and shipbuilding yards on the Amur River). Activity here has slowed since the glory days.

It's a convenient hub between Tynda, Khabarovsk 290km south, Vanino's ferry service to Sakhalin Island and Nikolaevskna-Amure up the river.

Information

Far Eastern Mutual Bank (pr Mira 26; ☑ 9am-7pm Mon-Fri, 9am-6pm Sat & Sun) Has a 24-hour ATM.

Gladiator (2nd fl, Dom Kulturi Stroiltini, pl Lenina; per hr from R25; ☑ 10am-10pm) In pillared building behind Lenin's statue, with King Arthur theme inside.

Nata Tour (☎ 530 332; www.amurnet.ru/natatour/index .html; room 104, Hotel Voskhod, pr Pervostroiteley 31; ☑ 10am-2pm & 3-6pm Mon-Fri) Experienced travel service that books rafting, birding, fishing, skiing, Gulag, windsurfing and other trips in the region. Ask about overnight stays in the Nanai village of Nizhni Khlabni (about US$20).

Post office (pr Mira 27; ☑ 8am-7pm Mon-Fri, 8am-6pm Sat, 8am-3pm Sun)

Telephone office (pr Mira 31; ☑ 8am-11pm)

Sights

Just northwest of the river station, Komsomolsk's landmark sight is the **WWII memorial**, which features stoic faces chipped from stone, with pillars marking the years of WWII nearby.

Worth it even if you can't read Russian, the **Regional Museum** (☎ 592 640; pr Mira 8; admission R25; ☑ 10am-1pm & 2-6pm Tue-Fri, 11am-6pm Sat & Sun) features several rooms filled with old, but well-cared for, exhibits (we like the BAM construction hats best) showing how Komsomolsk came to be.

The **Fine Art Museum** (☎ 590 822; pr Mira 16; admission R100; ☑ 10am-5.45pm Tue-Sun) has a couple of floors of changing exhibits.

Look around for **Soviet mosaics** on back streets aside housing blocks. There's a simple **Japanese POW memorial** off pr Mira. If things seem quiet on a sunny day, half of the town's probably at the **beach**, just east of the river station.

It's a long shot, but you could ask Nata Tour about (rare) visits to the **Yury Gagarin Aircraft Factory** east of the town centre.

Sleeping

There are three good options here. All come with TV and private bath.

Hotel Voskhod (☎ 535 131; pr Pervostroiteley 31; s/d from R560/800) This eight-storey grey hotel has boxy rooms – some renovated, all quite clean. The top-floor café serves good food, and there's bowling and a disco next door.

Dacha Krushcheva (☎ 540 659; ul Khabarovska 47; r R1500-2500) Built for Nikita Khrushchev – and where Gorbachev and Brezhnev have slept – the Dacha is a step back. Nikita's

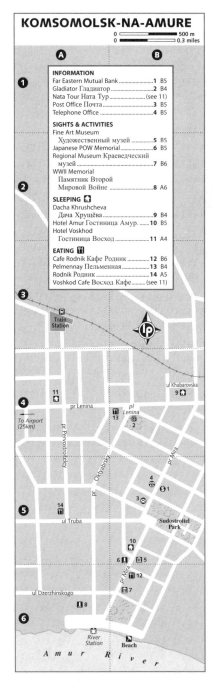

KOMSOMOLSK-NA-AMURE

0   500 m
0   0.3 miles

INFORMATION
Far Eastern Mutual Bank 1 B5
Gladiator Гладиатор 2 B4
Nata Tour Ната Тур ....(see 11)
Post Office Почта 3 B5
Telephone Office 4 B5

SIGHTS & ACTIVITIES
Fine Art Museum
  Художественный музей 5 B5
Japanese POW Memorial 6 B5
Regional Museum Краеведческий
  музей 7 B6
WWII Memorial
  Памятник Второй
  Мировой Войне 8 A6

SLEEPING 🏠
Dacha Khrushcheva
  Дача Хрущёва 9 B4
Hotel Amur Гостиница Амур. 10 B5
Hotel Voskhod
  Гостиница Восход 11 A4

EATING 🍴
Cafe Rodnik Кафе Родник 12 B6
Pelmennay Пельменная 13 B4
Rodnik Родник 14 A5
Voshkod Cafe Восход Кафе ....(see 11)

room is a massive suite with private balcony; gun-toting goons likely took the
cheaper rooms downstairs. It's behind a
green plank fence.

Hotel Amur (☎ 590 984; ruma@kmscom.ru; pr Mira
15; r R925-1425) The Hotel Amur has 15 renovated rooms in a bright, lovely 1930s-era
building.

Eating

Komsomolsk isn't Russian for 'spirited dining scene'.

Rodnik (☎ 531 396; pr Pervostroiteley 15; meals
R500-1000; ☺ noon-3pm) Slightly formal two-
floor restaurant/bar with private banquet
rooms and nightly music – plus its own
beer Flora on tap (R50 for a frosted mug;
it's a little sweet).

Cafe Rodnik (pr Mira 12; ☺ 8am-11pm) Rodnik's
more relaxed and cheaper option.

Voskhod Cafe (pr Pervostroiteley 31; meals R150-300)
Hotel Voskhod's 8th-floor café offers good
Russian meals in a simple setting.

Pelmennay (pr Lenina 21; meals R150-250; ☺ 10am-
8pm Mon-Fri, 11am-7pm Sat) Offers old-school,
pick-and-point eating.

Getting There & Around

From the pink **train station** (pr Pervostroiteley),
train 67/68 runs daily overnight to/from
Khabarovsk (R860, 9½ hours). Heading east,
trains 954 and 352 go to Vanino (R660, 18
hours), for ferries to Sakhalin Island. Train
964 runs to Tynda (R1351, 37 hours).

Within the city, tram 2 runs from the
train station (R7), past all hotels to the river
station.

Bus 102 leads from the infrequently used
airport (25km west of town) to the river
station; a taxi there costs R250.

Few do it, but the 12-hour boat ride north
along the Amur River to rather grim Nikolaevsk-na-Amure is a relaxing trip that gets
you a few clicks into a more remote part of
the Far East. Hydrofoils leave daily between
June and August from Komsomolsk's **river
station** (☎ 592 935). See Lonely Planet's *Russia
& Belarus* for more coverage.

Buses bound for Khabarovsk (R300, six
hours) leave from the river station (including after the boat from Nikolaevsk arrives)
and pl Lenina.

VANINO ВАНИНО

☎ 42137 / ☺ Moscow + 7hr

The reason for heading 500km east of Komsomolsk is if you plan to take the (supposedly daily in summer) ferry from Vanino
to Kholmsk, on Sakhalin Island (around
R780, 16 hours). Weather plagues the sailing schedule at times. If you have to wait,
the **Hotel Vanino** (☎ 7473, 512-28; ul Chekova 1; s/d
incl breakfast R680/900) is located above the train
station (where boat tickets often attract
hordes). Call ahead to prebook a seat from
the **ferry station** (☎ 57 708). (See Lonely Planet's *Russia & Belarus* for more information
on Sakhalin Island.)

Daily trains en route to/from Sovetskaya
Gavan (the next, and last, stop east) connect Vanino with Komsomolsk (R660, 18
hours). Train 351/352 connects Vanino
with Vladivostok (R1700, 41 hours) via
Khabarovsk and Komsomolsk.

Ulan-Ude to Beijing via Mongolia

Branching off the Trans-Siberian just after Ulan-Ude, the Trans-Mongolian route follows the well-trodden path of the tea caravans between Beijing and Moscow in the 18th and 19th centuries. In those days, travellers and traders made the journey in no less than 40 days. Since the 7865km-long Trans-Mongolian railroad began operating in the mid-1950s, the journey has taken a week nonstop. However, with scenically beautiful and culturally fascinating Mongolia en route, you'd be crazy not to schedule a stop at its lively, friendly capital of Ulaanbaatar (aka 'UB').

This book can only give you a taster of what's on offer in Mongolia, a country that is a byword for all that is remotely exotic and adventurous. Many travellers spend around a month seeing the country's highlights ranging from Khövsgöl Nuur – a beautiful lake close to the Russian border – to the dusty dunes of the Gobi Desert. Even with only a few days at your disposal, it's possible to break out into the vast open spaces of the magnificent countryside. And then there's Mongolia's yearly highlight of Naadam, a spectacular sporting and cultural festival that drags in thousands of visitors, turning UB's streets into an international melting pot akin to Bangkok's Koh San Rd.

Before heading for Mongolia, pause to explore Ulan-Ude, where you could leave the train briefly for a minibus ride to the border, taking in the historic towns of Novoselenginsk and Kyakhta. Of course, the delights of Beijing, at the start or end of your journey, demand as much time as you can manage.

ULAN-UDE TO BEIJING VIA MONGOLIA

HIGHLIGHTS

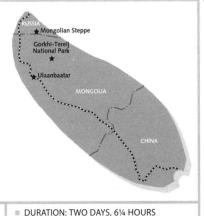

- Gaze from the train as the **Siberian taiga** south of Ulan-Ude transforms itself into the beguiling **Mongolian steppe**
- Witness a mystical ceremony at the country's largest and liveliest monastery, Ulaanbaatar's **Gandantegchinlen Khiid** (p260)
- Marvel at the dinosaur skeletons at Ulaanbaatar's **Museum of Natural History** (p261)
- Grab a seat for the sports and nomadic culture of the **Naadam Festival** (p262)
- Hike to the meditation retreat of Aryapala in **Gorkhi-Terelj National Park** (p268)

| ROUTE DISTANCE: 2217KM | DURATION: TWO DAYS, 6¼ HOURS |

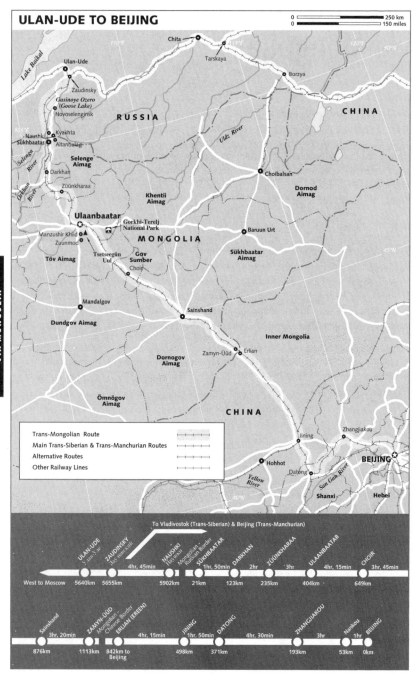

ULAN-UDE TO BEIJING

ULAN-UDE TO BEIJING
VIA MONGOLIA

THE ROUTE

The Trans-Mongolian line branches off from the main Trans-Siberian route at Zaudinsky, about 13km east of Ulan-Ude. Mongolia and China each have their own kilometre markers. In Mongolia, the markers measure the distance to the Russian–Mongolian border, so 0km is the border town of Naushki. Once into China, the markers measure the distance to Beijing.

For more on Mongolia, grab a copy of Lonely Planet's *Mongolia* guidebook.

Zaudinsky to Naushki

At **Zaudinsky** (5655km) the branch line turns south and continues to follow the Selenga River, crossing at around 5701km. The scenery here is characterised by herds of cattle grazing across low green hills and beside a wide, lazy river, and by villages of wooden houses with brightly painted window shutters and flourishing gardens that explode with fruits and flowers in summer.

After you pass the town of **Zagustay** (5769km) the train follows the shores of Gusinoye Ozero (Goose Lake), surrounded by thick woods of pine and birch that are usually prevalent further north. The train crosses the Selenga again at 5885km before stopping at **Naushki** (5902/0km), a small, uneventful town that serves as the Russian border post.

Sükhbaatar to Zamyn-Üüd

Sükhbaatar (21km) is Mongolia's chief border town. Set at the junction of the Selenga and Orkhon Rivers, Sükhbaatar (population 20,0300), the capital of the Selenge *aimag* (province), is a quiet place founded in the 1940s and named after the revolutionary hero Damdin Sükhbaatar (see p261).

Entering Mongolia brings a change of scenery; the forests thin out into the lush green pastures of the fertile Selenge Gol (Selenga River) basin. When you cross the river at 63km you may spot cranes, heron and other waterfowl in·the marshy areas on the west side of the train.

Darkhan (123km) is Mongolia's third-largest city with a population of 73,400, built only in 1961 to take pressure off a rapidly expanding Ulaanbaatar. A bleak and industrial place (its name means 'blacksmith'), its most interesting sight is Kharaagiin Khiid, an active monastery housed in a pretty log cabin. The train stops for about 15 minutes, so you can get out and admire the sheep heads and other local specialities being sold on the platform.

The scenery south of Darkhan is lovely, especially on the western side of the train. As the landscape becomes less verdant, *gers* (traditional felt tents) dot the wide grassy expanses, giving a glimpse of the grasslands to come further south. Birch and pine trees cluster on the hills in the distance. You spend 10 minutes in **Züünkharaa** (231km), where trains loaded with tree trunks and processed wood stop en route from Siberia and northern Mongolia.

North of Ulaanbaatar the rolling hills are covered come summer with wildflowers and grazing animals, making for exquisite scenery. However, around 384km you will be able to catch views of the smokestacks and urban sprawl of **Ulaanbaatar** (404km) as the train descends into the valley. The train stops in the Mongolian capital for 30 minutes, just enough time for you to sprint out to see a collection of steam engines, about 1km east of the station, where the tracks cross under the highway.

South of Ulaanbaatar, the line winds through the gently swelling hills of the **Bogdkhan Uul** mountain range. Trees eventually disappear and the landscape becomes a 180-degree panorama of steppe, the only interruptions being grazing horses and the occasional *ger*.

There's a 15-minute stop at **Choir** (649km). A statue of the first Mongolian cosmonaut stands in front of the station. Prior to 1992 this grim town of 12,200 was home to Mongolia's biggest Soviet military air base. After the Russians left, many of the buildings sat empty and were vandalised. Despite having declared itself a Free Trade Zone, Choir continues to languish.

The train continues south entering the flat, arid and sparsely populated Gobi Desert. In a good year, the desert sprouts short grass, which sustains a limited number of sheep, goats and camels for their ethnic Khalkh owners. In a bad year, the wells go dry, the grass turns brown and the animals die. From the train, the view of this desolate landscape is impressive. Any small bodies of water (such as at 729km on the western side

BORDER CROSSINGS

Russia–Mongolia: Nauski–Sükhbaatar

Russia and Mongolia both use the same rail gauge, so no bogie-changing on trains is required. However, the time saved is eaten up in drawn-out customs procedures and general hanging around – anything up to 11 hours!

In Naushki travellers must fill out customs forms in duplicate, and Russian border guards collect passports. Mongolian traders get the most attention from the customs officers. When you get back your passport, you can get off the train. You can change money here and there's a farmers market just outside the train station (walk to the southern end of the platform and cross the street). If you arrive in Naushki from Kyakhta (p218) it's possible to buy a ticket for the Naushki Sükhbaatar train for R230 *kupe* (*kupeyny;* compartmentalised carriage), often just a single carriage. When officially 'full', a suitably tipped *provodnitsa* (carriage attendant) may still be prepared to get you aboard for the one-hour hop across no-man's-land. Naushki to Ulan-Ude, for R210 *platskart* (*platskartny;* open carriage), is an attractive but excruciatingly slow ride; it may well be faster taking the more frequent *marshrutky* (fixed-route minibuses) from Kyakhta.

The customs and immigration process is repeated by Mongolian officials in Sükhbaatar where, if you need it, there should be no problem buying a ticket for the nightly train to Ulaanbaatar that departs around 9.20pm. The trip takes nine hours and costs T3300 *obshchy* (4th class) or T8400 *kupe*. Travellers on through trains from Irkutsk to Ulaanbaatar will have to wait for their carriages to be hitched to this service before they can continue on their way. There are some cafés near Sükhbaatar station, and moneychangers hang out around the station itself.

Russia–Mongolia: Kyakhta–Altanbulag

You can avoid the extreme tedium of the direct train crossing by taking this alternative road route into or out of Mongolia. There's a through bus to Ulaanbaatar organised three times weekly by Buryat-Intour in Ulan-Ude (see p213). More interesting, though, is to make minibus hops to the Mongolian border via Novoselenginsk (p218) and the once-opulent tea-route town of Kyakhta (p218). It's quite possible to briefly see both towns during the day, cross the border and still catch the nightly train to Ulaanbaatar.

The **border** (🕓 9am–noon & 2-6pm) is open to bicycles and vehicles, and some officials speak English. You can't walk across, so pedestrians need to negotiate passage with private drivers. Start as close as possible to the front of the chaotic queue: processing takes about an hour with only a handful of vehicles allowed through at any one time. The going rate is R150 per passenger across no-man's-land; if you're heading into Mongolia it's well worth negotiating a ride all the way to Sükhbaatar train station (around R100 extra) rather than becoming prey to rip-off taxi drivers in Altanbulag, the dreary Mongolian border village.

Mongolia–China

This border crossing takes about five hours no matter which direction you are travelling. Some trains cross the border at night, which guarantees that you won't get much sleep. In Zamyn-Üüd, Mongolian customs officials and border guards do their thing. Officials reserve most of their energy for Chinese and Mongolian traders. This process can take up to two hours.

In Erlian, Chinese customs and passport officials repeat the process (or start it, if you are travelling west). You must fill out customs forms and departure/arrival cards. The Erlian station is usually quite lively, even at night. Once your passport is returned, catch some fresh air and explore the station and surroundings where you can change money or get something to eat. If you do get off, you will not have a chance to get back on the train for about two hours while the bogies are changed.

As in Russia, Mongolia's trains run on a 5ft (1.5m) gauge, which is slightly wider than the standard gauge used in the rest of the world. Before the train can continue its journey, it must make a stop at the bogie-changing shed, where the carriages are raised and the bogies are replaced with the appropriate size. If you wish to watch the bogie-changing operations, stay on the train until it leaves the platform and gets to the shed. You may be able to watch and take photos. You can then walk or take a rickshaw back to the station.

of the tracks) attract wildlife, and you will probably spot horses, sheep and goats.

The train stops for around 15 minutes at **Sainshand** (876km), which means, ironically, 'Good Pond'. As the capital of the local province, Sainshand sports a couple of museums, a modern monastery and several hotels and *ger* camps, should you feel the urge to jump the train and get closer to the Gobi.

Back on the Trans-Mongolian route the bleak dusty landscape continues to the border town of **Zamyn-Üüd** (1113km), famed for being the hottest place in Mongolia!

Erlian to Beijing

As the train approaches **Erlian** (842km) from the no-man's-land between Mongolia and China you won't fail to notice the giant rainbow arch at the road border post, proof of China's determination to build big and bold, even in the most inhospitable of environments. From here it takes about 13 hours to get to Beijing by direct train.

For the first several hours the train continues through the Gobi, now in the so-called autonomous region of Inner Mongolia. Mongolians make up only about 15% of the total population here and since 1949 the Chinese have done their best to assimilate them, eradicating their nomadic lifestyle even though they have been permitted to keep their written and spoken language.

Further south, green hills, valleys and more prosperous looking towns appear. There may be a stop at the main rail junction of **Jining** (498km) – this is the best place to change trains if you're not on a direct Ulaanbaatar to Beijing service (see p267).

You'll get your first glimpse of the Great Wall as the line passes through it at about 385km. This is now Shanxi province, one of the earliest centres of Chinese civilisation. The ancient capital of this region was **Datong** (371km), now an industrial metropolis of 2.7 million people. The train halts here for 10 minutes, but there are a couple of reasons for lingering longer: the awesome Yungang Caves, 16km west of the city, containing some 50,000 Buddhist statues carved between AD 460 and 494; and train fanatics will thrill to the Datong Locomotive Factory, the last in China to produce the 'iron rooster' steam engines until 1989. Inquire at the local **China Inter-**

national Travel Service (CITS; ☎ 0352-712 4882) at the station about tours to the caves and the factory. Note that onward tickets for trains not originating in Datong can be hard to secure; you might end up only being able to get a standing room only ticket on an already crowded train.

From Datong, the line turns east, entering Hebei province, primarily a coal-mining region, at around 300km. Hebei is characterised by its mountainous tableland where the Great Wall runs. There are good views of the wall on the eastern side of the tracks between 295km and 275km.

The train stops for about 15 minutes in the industrial city of **Zhangjiakou** (193km). Formerly known as Khaalga, which means 'door' or 'gate' in Mongolian, this town was the place where the ancient tea caravans crossed the Great Wall. From here the terrain becomes increasingly mountainous and the scenery is quite dramatic. At 99km the train crosses the San Gan River. At 95km, the mountains provide a spectacular backdrop to the vibrant blue waterway. Farms and orchards surrounded by mountains make for a visually stimulating ride.

Because of the steep ascent, the train requires a banking engine; the train stops briefly at **Kanzuang** (82km) to attach/detach it (depending on which direction you are travelling). Between 80km and 50km, the train goes through a series of thrilling tunnels that cut through the mountains. Each time the train emerges into daylight there's a fabulous view of the Great Wall and the surrounding mountains. The first is at **Badaling** (73km), immediately after the long 2km tunnel. The train then makes another, longer stop at **Qinglongqiao** (70km), where you can take photos from the platform.

The final stop is at **Nankou** (53km), where the rear engine is attached/detached. About an hour later, the train pulls into **Beijing**.

ULAANBAATAR УЛААНБААТАР

☎ 011 / pop 800,000 / Moscow + 5hr

By no stretch of the imagination could Ulaanbaatar be called pretty. In fact the preponderance of jerry-built Soviet apartment blocks, polluting factories and general urban sprawl make it an ugly scar on an otherwise lovely country. However, there is much to recommend Mongolia's bustling capital, not least its friendly, switched-on people and the fact that if you want to get out into the countryside this is the best place from which to arrange your trip.

On top of this, UB, as it's known to ex-pats (but certainly not locals!), has enough worthwhile sights to comfortably fill several days and has far and away the best dining scene this side of Beijing. Built along the Tuul Gol and in the valleys of the Four Holy Peaks, UB is surrounded by some wonderful opportunities for outdoor enthusiasts. Hiking, biking, golf and horse riding are all possible within an hour of the capital – see p260, for outfits that organise these activities.

History

The first recorded capital city of the Mongolian empire, Örgöö, was established in 1639 at the Da Khuree monastery, about 420km from Ulaanbaatar. The monastery was the residence of the five-year-old Zanabazar, who had been proclaimed the head of Buddhism in Mongolia. In keeping with the nomadic lifestyle, the capital was moved frequently to various locations along the Orkhon, Selenge and Tuul Rivers (with a name change accompanying each move).

The capital was finally established in its present location in 1778 and grew quickly as a religious, commercial and administrative centre. Its architecture remained predominantly *gers*, earning the capital the name 'City of Felt'. Further name changes accompanied invasions by the Russians and the Chinese. In 1924 the city was renamed Ulaanbaatar (Red Hero) in honour of the communist triumph, and declared the official capital of an 'independent' Mongolia (independent from China, not the Soviet Union).

In 1933 Ulaanbaatar gained autonomy and separated from the surrounding Töv aimag.

From the 1930s the Soviets built the city in typical Russian style: lots of ugly apartment blocks, large brightly coloured theatres and cavernous government buildings. Tragically, the Soviets also destroyed almost all of the monasteries and temples.

Orientation

The station is in the city's southwestern corner around 1km from the centre. Most of the city spreads east–west along the main road,

Enkh Taivny Örgön Chölöö, also known as Peace Ave. The centre is Sükhbaatar Sq – at the time of research there was a chance that it might be renamed Chinggis Khaan Sq after Mongolia's most famous leader.

MAPS

The 1:10,000 *Ulaanbaatar City Map* is updated yearly – buy it at the **Map Shop** (Ikh Toiruu; ☺ 9am-1pm & 2-6pm Mon-Fri, 10am-4pm Sat), near the Elba Electronics shop.

Information
BOOKSHOPS

Xanadu Books & Fine Wines (☎ 319 748; www
.xanadu.mn; Marco Polo Bldg; ☺ 10am-7pm Mon-Sat)
Mongolia's only real English-language bookstore stocks some Lonely Planet titles.

EMERGENCY

It may take a few minutes to get an English-speaker on these numbers.
Emergency aid & ambulance (☎ 103)
Fire (☎ 101)
Police emergency (☎ 102)

INTERNET ACCESS

There are scores of Internet cafés, all charging around T800 per hour; expect to pay double that for hotel business centres. Connections are generally good. You can scan photos in many places for around T200.
icafé (☎ 313 316; fax 320 616; Baga Toiruu west; per
hr T600; ☺ 9am-10pm Mon-Fri, 11am-10pm Sat & Sun)
Located at the southern door of the National Information Technology Park, here you can also send and receive faxes.
Internet Centre (☎ 312 512; Tserendorjiin Gudamj 65;
per hr Mon-Fri T700, Sat & Sun T600; ☺ 9am-1.30am)
Za Internet (☎ 320 801; Peace Ave 62; per hr T700;
☺ 24hr) Located 100m west of the State Department Store.

MEDIA

Pick up the English-language weekly newspapers the **Mongol Messenger** (www.mongolmessenger.mn) and the **UB Post** (http://ubpost.mongolnews.mn), each T500 per issue, for local news and entertainment information.

MEDICAL SERVICES

If your situation is not an emergency, consider travelling to Beijing, where the range and quality of service is much better.
Yonsei Friendship Hospital (☎ 310 945; Peace Ave;
☺ 9am-4.30pm Mon-Fri) This South Korean–sponsored clinic provides the best medical service.

ULAANBAATAR

0 —————— 300 m
0 —————— 0.2 miles

INFORMATION
Air Market.....................................**1** C5
Blue Bandana Expeditions & Seven
  Summits Camping Shop............**2** C5
Central Post Office......................**3** C5
Chinese Embassy.........................**4** D4
French Embassy............................**5** C4
German Embassy...........................**6** C4
icafe..**7** C4
Internet Centre............................**8** B5
Japanese Embassy........................**9** C4
Juulchin...................................(see 30)
Karakorum Expeditions...............**10** B5
Legend Tour................................**11** C5
Map Shop....................................**12** B5
Masterfoods Supermarket............**13** C4
Ministry of External Relations.....**14** C4
Nomadic Expeditions...................**15** B5
Russian Embassy..........................**16** C4
Tourist Information Visitor Centre..(see 3)
Trade & Development Bank..........**17** C4
UK Embassy.................................**18** D4
US Embassy..................................**19** D4
Xanadu Books & Fine Wines.........**20** C5
Yonsei Friendship Hospital..........**21** D5
Za Internet..................................**22** B5

SIGHTS & ACTIVITIES
Gandantegchinlen (Gandan) Khiid.**23** B4
Golden Dedenpovaran Süm.......(see 23)
Government (Parliament) House..**24** C4
Migjid Janraisig Süm..................(see 23)
Monastery-Museum of Choijin
  Lama......................................**25** C5
Mongolian National Modern Art
  Gallery..................................(see 63)
Museum of Natural History.........**26** C4
National Museum of Mongolian
  History...................................**27** C4

Ochirdary Süm.........................(see 23)
Winter Palace of the
  Bogd Khaan..........................**28** C6
Zanabazar Museum
  of Fine Arts...........................**29** C4

SLEEPING
Bayangol Hotel............................**30** C5
Bolod's Guesthouse.....................**31** C5
Gana's Guest House.....................**32** B5
Genex Hotel................................**33** B5
Hostel Sandwich.........................**34** C6
Idre's Guest House.......................**35** C5
Khongor Guesthouse....................**36** B5
Natural Hotel..............................**37** C5
Tuushin Hotel.............................**38** C4
UB Guesthouse............................**39** C5
Ulaanbaatar Hotel......................**40** C5
Zaluuchuud Hotel.......................**41** C4
Zaya Backpacker Hostel...............**42** B5

EATING
Abtai Sain Khaani Örgöö.............**43** D4
California....................................**44** B5
Chez Bernard..............................**45** C5
Chin Van Khandorjiin Örgöö.......**46** C5
Chinggis Restaurant....................**47** C4
Dalai Eej & Merkuri Markets.......**48** B5
Khaan Buuz.................................**49** B5
Le Bistro Français........................**50** C4
Marco Polo..................................**51** B5
Sacher's Café...............................**52** C4
Silk Road Bar & Grill....................**53** C5
Stupa Café..................................**54** C5
Taj Mahal................................(see 30)
UB Deli.......................................**55** C5
Zochin Buuz................................**56** C5

DRINKING
Brau Haus...................................**57** B5
Chinggis Club..............................**58** C4
Dave's Place................................**59** C5
Ikh Mongol.................................**60** C5
Khan Brau...................................**61** C5
Millie's Expresso......................(see 20)
Millie's Expresso......................(see 40)

ENTERTAINMENT
National Academic Drama
  Theatre..................................**62** C5
Palace of Culture........................**63** C4
River Sounds...............................**64** C5
State Circus.................................**65** B5
State Opera & Ballet Theatre.......**66** C5
Tengis...**67** B4
Tumen Ekh Song & Dance
  Ensemble...............................**68** C5

SHOPPING
Egshiglen Magnai National Musical
  Instrument Shop.....................**69** C4
Moda Mongolia...........................**70** B5
Mongolian Wool Craft.................**71** B5
State Department Store................**72** B5

TRANSPORT
Aeroflot......................................**73** B5
Air China.....................................**74** D4
Buses to Terelj.............................**75** B5
International Railway Ticketing
  Office....................................**76** A5
Korean Air...................................**77** D4
MIAT...**78** C4
Taxi Stand...................................**79** C4
Taxi Stand...................................**80** B5

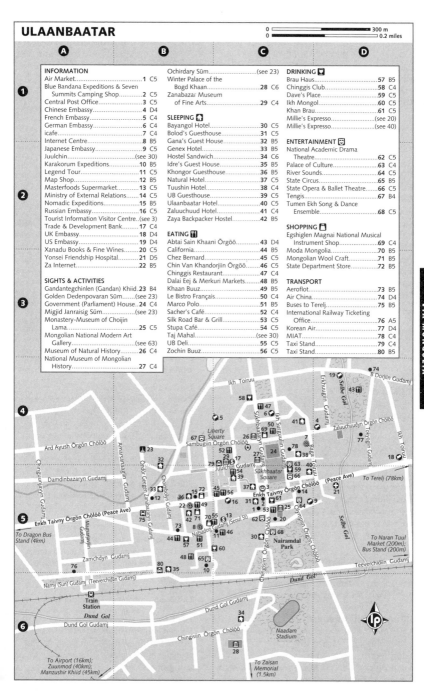

ULAN-UDE TO BEIJING VIA MONGOLIA

MONEY

ATMs (accepting Visa cards only) are popping up across the city; find them in the lobbies of the major hotels and in many banks. **Masterfoods supermarket** (Seoul St; ☽ 24hr) Has an ATM.

State Department Store (Peace Ave 44) You can change money in the lobby.

Trade & Development Bank (☎ 327 020; cnr Juulchin Gudamj & Baga Toiruu; ☽ 9am-4pm Mon-Fri) Cash advances in US dollars are available here, and travellers cheques can also be cashed for tögrög or US dollars.

POST

Central post office (☎ 313 421; cnr Peace Ave & Sükhbaataryn Gudamj; ☽ 7.30am-9pm Mon-Fri, 9am-8pm Sat & Sun)

TOURIST INFORMATION

Tourist Information Visitor Centre (☎ 311 423; www.mongoliatourism.gov.mn) The useful main office is in the central post office, on the corner of Peace Ave and Sükhbaataryn Gudamj. There are also booths at the train station and the airport.

TRAVEL AGENCIES

Ulaanbaatar has no shortage of tour operators who can help organise excursions or obtain train tickets. Most guesthouses offer their own range of tours, too.

Air Market (☎ 305 050; www.air-market.net; Urguu Plaza) South of the corner of Peace Ave and Chingisiin Örgön Chölöö. Good for flight tickets.

Blue Bandana Expeditions (☎ 329 456; www.active mongolia.com; btwn Peace & Seoul Aves; ☽ 10am-6pm) In the Seven Summits camping supplies shop.

Juulchin (☎ 328 428; www.juulchin.com; Chingisiin Örgön Chölöö 5B, Bayangol Hotel) Former state-owned company, now privatised and quite competent.

Karakorum Expeditions (☎ /fax 315 655; www .gomongolia.com; Gangaryn Gurav Bldg) Behind the State Circus. Rents mountain bikes (per day US$25).

Legend Tour (☎ 315 158; www.legendtour.ru; Seoul St, Sant Asar Trading Centre, 2nd fl) Not great service but about the only place that may be able to secure you a Russian visa if you need it (for a price).

Nomadic Expeditions (☎ 313 396; www.nomadicex peditions.com; 76 Peace Ave) Organises Gobi Desert tours.

Dangers & Annoyances

Ulaanbaatar is a reasonably carefree and easy-going city. However, pickpockets and late-night muggings are a recent and growing problem. Theft is seldom violent against foreigners, just opportunistic.

Sights

GANDANTEGCHINLEN (GANDAN) KHIID

Mongolia's largest and most important **monastery** (☎ 360 164; www.gandan.mn; Öndör Geegen Zanabazaryn Gudamj; admission free; ☽ 9am-9pm) is a lively place that you shouldn't miss. The name translates roughly as 'the great place of complete joy'. Built in the mid-19th century, the monastery survived the communist purges of the 1930s. Today there are over 150 monks in residence and in its main building, the **Migjid Janraisig Süm** (admission T2500; ☽ 9am-6pm) you can view the 26.5m-tall gilded statue of Buddha, a replacement for one moved to St Petersburg in 1937.

The courtyard on the right of the main entrance contains two temples, the **Ochirdary Süm** and the smaller **Golden Dedenpovaran Süm**. If you come in the morning you can witness the fascinating ceremonies that take place here.

WINTER PALACE OF THE BOGD KHAAN

Mongolia's eighth living Buddha and last king, Jebtzun Damba Hutagt VIII, lived for 20 years in this **palace** (☎ 342 195; Chingisiin Örgön

---

ULAANBAATAR IN...

One Day

Catch a morning ceremony at the **Gandantegchinlen Khiid** (above). Walk back to town for lunch at **Stupa Café** (p265) before an afternoon exploring the **Natural History Museum** (opposite) and **National Museum of Mongolian History** (opposite), both close to Sükhbaatar Sq. Dinner at the **Silk Road Bar & Grill** (see p265) is a must, topped off by a pint at **Khan Brau** (p266).

Two Days

On your second day, visit the **Winter Palace of the Bogd Khaan** (above) before huffing it up to the **Zaisan Memorial** (opposite). In the afternoon, visit the rather atmospheric **Monastery-Museum of Choijin-Lama** (opposite), then be entertained by the **Tumen Ekh Song and Dance Ensemble** (p266).

Four Days

Get out into the countryside with a visit to **Manzushir Khiid** (p267) or **Terelj** (p268), spending the night in a *ger* (traditional felt tent) camp.

SÜKHBAATAR, AXE HERO

Despite an impoverished background, Damdin Sükh (meaning 'axe') learned to read and write and excelled at horsemanship as a child. In 1911 he was conscripted into the army, where he developed nationalist convictions and gathered a loyal following of like-minded soldiers. His courageous performance combating the Chinese earned him the title *baatar* (hero).

When his unit was disbanded by the Chinese in 1919, Sükhbaatar used his network to form a nationalist army. He eventually joined forces with the revolutionary Khorloogiin Choibalsan, who had close contact with the communist movement in Russia. With the assistance of the Soviet Red Army, they succeeded in defeating both the Chinese and the White Russians. On 11 July 1921, Sükhbaatar declared the People's Government of Mongolia.

Sükhbaatar was known as the 'people's warrior', and was also considered to be a true Mongol. At the 1922 Naadam Festival, which celebrated the first anniversary of the revolution, the new governor is said to have delighted the crowds when, riding down the field at full gallop, he leaned from his saddle to pick up silver coins from the ground. The following year – at the age of 30 – Sükhbaatar died of undetermined causes. Still visible astride his horse at the centre of Ulaanbaatar, he lives on in Mongolian history as an unrivalled national hero.

Chölöö; admission T2000; ☺ 9am-5.30pm daily May-Sep, 9am-5.30pm Fri-Tue Oct-Apr). The grounds house six ornate temples; the white building on the right is the Palace itself. It contains an eclectic collection of gifts received from foreign dignitaries and an extraordinary array of stuffed animals. Take bus 7 or 19.

MONASTERY-MUSEUM OF CHOIJIN LAMA

This beautiful **museum** (☎ 324 788; admission T2400; ☺ 9am-5pm Jun-Oct, 10am-5pm Nov-May) is also known as the Museum of Religion and hasn't operated as a monastery since 1938. There are five temples within the tranquil grounds and a concrete *ger* with a good selection of souvenirs and books about Buddhism and Mongolia.

MUSEUM OF NATURAL HISTORY

The best reason for visiting this old and rambling **museum** (☎ 321 716; cnr Sükhbaataryn Gudamj & Sambugiin Örgön Chölöö; adult/student T2000/1000; ☺ 10am-5.30pm daily May-Sep, 10am-5.30pm Wed-Sun Oct-Apr) is to see the massive dinosaur fossils and skeletons dug up from the Gobi. The museum houses two impressive complete skeletons of a *Tarbosaurus* and a *Saurolophus*, as well as petrified dinosaur eggs and fossils.

AROUND SÜKHBAATAR SQUARE

Big changes are slated for UB's central Sükhbaatar Sq. The statue of the revolutionary hero Damdin Sükhbaatar (see above) is to be moved to Liberty Sq, while his remains, once in the mausoleum in front of

Government House at the northern end of the square, have been removed to the Altan Olgii burial ground on the city's edge. The restructured south face of Government House will become the Chinggis Khaan Memorial Complex, and a statue of the Mongolian legend will stand on the plinth vacated by Sükhbaatar.

No changes are planned for the Palace of Culture (p266), which contains the **Mongolian National Modern Art Gallery** (☎ 313 191; admission T2000; ☺ 10am-6pm), on the northeast side of square, nor to the **National Museum of Mongolian History** (☎ 325 656; cnr Juulchin Gudamj & Sükhbaataryn Gudamj; admission T2500; ☺ 10am-4.30pm Tue-Sat) opposite the northwest corner. This museum contains exhibits (with English captions) on ancient burial sites, folk art and culture, Buddhist ceremonial objects and the Mongol horde, and is worth a visit.

ZANABAZAR MUSEUM OF FINE ARTS

This **art museum** (☎ 326 060; Juulchin Gudamj; adult/student T2500/400; ☺ 9am-5pm May-Sep, 10am-5pm Oct-Apr) has an excellent collection of paintings, carvings and sculptures, including many by the revered sculptor and artist Zanabazar. It also contains other rare religious exhibits such as *thangka* (scroll paintings) and Buddhist statues, representing the best display of its kind in Mongolia.

ZAISAN MEMORIAL

This memorial is the tall, thin landmark on top of the hill south of the city. Built by the Russians to commemorate 'unknown soldiers and heroes' from various wars, this masterpiece of socialist realism offers sweeping views of the city and surrounding hills, as well as a work-out on the climb up. Bus 7 from Bayangol Hotel will get you here.

Festivals & Events

Ikh Duichin On 18 May, Buddha's birthday is marked by dancing in Gandantegchinlen Khiid in Ulaanbaatar and by special services in most other monasteries.

Naadam Mongolia's No 1 festival draws the multitudes to Ulaanbaatar on 11 and 12 July. There are also many smaller Naadams around the country at the same time.

Sleeping

New guesthouses are opening up all the time in Ulaanbaatar. Touts meet all international trains arriving at the station – some may offer good options, but be sure to check the location before you commit. All room rates include breakfast, although at the budget places this may just be tea, coffee and some bread and jam.

BUDGET

The private rooms at guesthouses offer far greater value than those at the midrange hotels, plus you get the added benefit of clued-up hosts who can arrange tours and the company of fellow travellers. Many guesthouses are in apartment buildings and can be difficult to find; however, most will send someone to meet your train if you call or email ahead.

THE NAADAM FESTIVAL

The highpoint of the Mongolian year is the Naadam Festival, held on 11 and 12 July. Part family reunion, part fair and part nomad Olympics, Naadam (meaning 'holiday' or 'festival') has its roots in the nomad assemblies and hunting extravaganzas of the Mongol armies.

Smaller Naadams are held throughout the country and are well worth attending if you want to get close to the action, witness genuine traditions, and even make up the numbers during a wrestling tournament! That said, UB's Naadam is the biggie, with parades, cheesy carnival events and souvenir salesmen outside the Nadaam Stadium (located around 1km south of Sükhbaatar Sq). The colourful and lively opening ceremony is well worth catching even if you're not interested in the three traditional 'manly' sports of wrestling, archery and horse racing, as well as the quirky anklebone shooting.

Get yourself to Sükhbaatar Sq just before 9am on day one to see a fantastic ceremony outside State Parliament House, complete with mounted cavalry and full military band. You can then follow the cavalry on its stately clop towards the stadium where the opening ceremony kicks off around 11am, lasting about 1½ hours.

Wrestling

The wrestling starts at the stadium immediately after the opening ceremony. The final rounds on day two, just before the closing ceremony, are the most exciting matches. Mongolian wrestling has no time limits; a match ends only when a wrestler falls (or any body part other than feet or hands touches the ground). It also has no weight divisions, so the biggest wrestlers (and they are big!) are often the best.

The 'eagle dance' is performed beforehand by contestants to pay respect to the judges, and again afterwards by the winner. The loser must walk under the right arm of the winner, symbolising peace between the wrestlers. Another special feature of wrestling is the uniform, complete with heavy boots, tiny tight briefs and open midriff-baring vests.

Archery

Archery is held in an open stadium next to the main stadium. The sport of archery originated in the 11th century and modern-day competitors still don traditional garb to compete. Archers use a bent composite bow made of layered horn, bark and wood. Arrows are usually made from willow branches and vulture feathers.

The target is a line of up to 20 or 30 colourful rings on the ground. Male contestants stand 75m from the target while female contestants stand 60m from it. After each shot, the judges emit a shout and raise their arms to indicate the quality of the shot. The winner who hits the targets the most times is declared the best *mergen* (archer).

UB Guesthouse (☎ 311 037, 9119 9859; www.ub guest.com; cnr Baga Toiruu & Juulchin Gudamj; dm/d US$4/12; 🖳) Expect a friendly welcome and some of the cleanest dorms and bathrooms you've ever seen at this long-running guesthouse. Located above Golomt Bank on Baga Toiruu west; the entrance is around the back.

Khongor Guesthouse (☎ 316 415, 9925 2599; http://get.to/khongor; Peace Ave 15, Apt 6; dm/s/d US$4/10/12; 🖳) Knowledgeable English-speaking Toroo offers reasonably well-appointed accommodation in three separate buildings, each convenient and central. The entrance of the main guesthouse is around the back of the third building west of the State Department Store.

Bolod's Guesthouse (☎ 9919 2407; www.bolodtours .com; Peace Ave 61, Room 22, Door 20; dm US$5; 🖳) More spacious than most other apartment guesthouses, Bolod's is a good-value option with a cosy atmosphere and a great location between the central post office and National Academic Drama Theatre. Bolod is a gracious host and provides good tours and visa support if you're stuck. Enter through the white and grey gate opposite the post office.

Hostel Sandwich (☎ 342 512, 343 185; www .newhostel.mn; Chingisiin Örgön Chölöö 10; dm US$15; 🖳) Overpriced but extremely well appointed is this purpose-built new place bang opposite Naadam Stadium and not far from the Winter Palace. It's hardly Mongolian

Horse Racing

Horse racing is held about 28km west of the city on an open plain called Hui Doloon Khutag. The only way to get out here is by taxi (about T14,000 return). Your hotel or guesthouse can probably arrange a vehicle, or ask at Chez Bernard restaurant.

Horse racing, which takes place not on a track but on the open steppe, has six categories, based on the age of the horse and distance of the race (either 15km or 30km). Before the race the jockeys – children aged five to 13 – parade their horses in front of the judges to show respect, and the audience often sings traditional songs.

The races are gruelling and dangerous – sadly, every year horses and jockeys die. Around the finish line, spectators wait breathlessly as contestants speed across the hill side in a cloud of dust. The winning horses and riders are then the subject of laudatory poems and songs performed by the crowds. The five winning riders must drink some special *airag* (fermented mare's milk), which is then sprinkled on the riders' heads and horses' backs.

Anklebone Shooting

Held in a large tent next to the archery stadium, this entails flicking a sheep's anklebone at a small target (also made from anklebones) about 3m away. Apart from providing some shade, the tent has an electric atmosphere as competitors are spurred on by the yodelling of spectators.

Tickets

Admission to the stadium (except for the opening and closing ceremonies), archery and horse racing are free, but you'll definitely need a ticket for the opening ceremony and possibly the last round or two of the wrestling and closing ceremony. Ticket costs vary per section; the north side of the stadium (which is protected from the sun and rain by an overhang and has the best view of the opening event) is more expensive with tickets going for T30,000 (valid for both the opening and closing ceremonies). These tickets are distributed via the tour operators and hotels.

Alternatively you can get a ticket for as low as T2000 from scalpers who hang around the stadium or even from the police at the gates. The original price will be printed on the ticket; you can expect to pay twice this for the service charge. Guesthouse owners normally help their guests to buy tickets. A cheap ticket will get you through a designated gate, but these sections are grossly oversold and there is no guarantee you'll get a seat. If you are a lucky seat holder you may soon find a granny or kid on your lap.

To find out what is going on during the festival, look for the events program in the two English-language newspapers; there are often sports matches and other events in the lead-up to the main two days.

in atmosphere, but it's clean, and will fit the bill if you're looking for somewhere that's quiet.

Also recommended:

Idre's Guest House (☎ 316 749, 9911 2575; www.idre tour.com; Teeverchidiin Gudamj; dm/d US$3.50/9; 🖵) Walk behind the old long-distance bus station, turn right and look for the nine-storey apartment block. It is building 23, entrance 2, door 44 on the 3rd floor.

Zaya Backpacker Hostel (☎ 316 696, 9918 5013; www.magicnet.mn/~backpackza; Peace Ave 63; dm/s/d US$4/10/16; 🖵) Located inside a courtyard off Peace Ave, next to Za Internet.

MIDRANGE

These hotels offer guaranteed privacy and, usually, your own shower.

Natural Hotel (☎ 324 090; Baga Toiruu; s/d without bathroom US$20/25, d with bathroom US$30). About the best value for what it offers, which are simply furnished small rooms with TV and showers. The location, behind Art Kino Cinema, is central and it also has a sauna, snooker table and karaoke.

Zaluuchuud Hotel (☎ 325 544; www.zh.mn; Baga Toiruu 43; s/d/ste US$35/65/90) The spiffy rooms here have been renovated to a modern, simple design and are equipped with TV, fridge and kettle. It's popular with Chinese and Russian businessmen.

Genex Hotel (☎ 326 763; www.generalimpex.mn; Choimbolyn Gudamj 10; s/d from US$35/50, half-luxury US$48/80; 🖵) Near the Elba Electronics shop on Ikh Toiruu, this clean, modern hotel has appealing rooms in the half-luxe category. Standard rooms include a washbasin and toilet only.

THE AUTHOR'S CHOICE

Gana's Guest House (☎ /fax 367 343; www .ganasger.mn; Gandan Khiid ger district, house No 22; dm in r/ger US$3/5, s/d without bathroom US$12/15, d with bathroom US$20; 🖵) This may be Ulaanbaatar's oldest travellers' hangout, offering dorm beds in *gers* (traditional felt tents) as well as one large regular dorm, but it has stayed ahead of the pack by upgrading double rooms with ensuite showers and cosy decoration. Friendly service, an outdoor terrace and an airy perch overlooking downtown UB are also pluses, as is its proximity to atmospheric Gandantegchinlen Khiid.

TOP END

Expect 15% Value-Added Tax (VAT) to be tacked onto your bill.

Bayangol Hotel (☎ 312 255; www.bayangolhotel.mn; Chingisiin Örgön Chölöö 5; s/d from US$76/97; 🖵) Popular with upmarket organised tours, the Bayangol comes closest to offering a true upmarket hotel experience. Bathrooms are small but otherwise rooms have contemporary furnishings. The location is spot-on and there's a great range of bars and restaurants on-site.

Ulaanbaatar Hotel (☎ 320 620; www.ubhotel.mn; Sükhbaatar Sq 14; s/d from US$60/90; 🖵) One of the very few hotels that was built and flourished during the communist era, the Ulaanbaatar harks back to that time but still has decent rooms. Excellent facilities include a sauna, billiard room, business centre, travel agency, coffee shop, two restaurants and even a practice golf range on the 6th floor.

Tuushin Hotel (☎ 323 162; www.ulaanbaatar.net; Amaryn 2; s/d from US$66/88; 🖵) With a great location directly north of the Palace of Culture, the Tuushin offers pleasant service and spacious rooms with 1970s furnishings. There's a good gift shop in the lobby.

Eating

Ulaanbaatar's restaurants offer a surprisingly decent variety of cuisines and atmospheres. Enjoy the choice and quality because out in the countryside it's another matter entirely!

RESTAURANTS

Taj Mahal (☎ 311 009; Chingisiin Örgön Chölöö 5, Bayangol Hotel, Tower A, 3rd fl; meal with drink T10,000; ⏰ noon-midnight) Excellent Indian cuisine, including a great-value *thali* (set menu) meal for T6500, is served in this restaurant that's decorated with a papier-mâché elephant and reconstruction of the Taj Mahal's façade. Amiable owner Babu is sure to check you're having a good time.

Le Bistro Français (☎ 320 022; Ikh Surguuliin Gudamj 2; meal with wine T15,000; ⏰ 8am-11pm) The choice of businessmen and diplomats, this relaxed bistro with an open frontage in summer serves fine but pricey French-style cuisine, all of which can be washed down with good wine.

California (☎ 319 031; Seoul St; meal with drink T9000; ⏰ 8am-midnight Mon-Sat, 9am-midnight Sun) One of UB's most popular restaurants, this place

ULAN-UDE TO BEIJING VIA MONGOLIA

stands out for its American-style breakfasts, burgers, steaks, salads and a few things you can't get anywhere else, like a properly made iced tea.

UB Deli (☎ 325 240; Seoul St 48; main dishes T3500-5000; ☻ 9am-midnight) This challenger for the title of top American-style restaurant is an un-deli-like place. Expats and clued-up locals scarf chicken Caesar salad, grilled sandwiches and burgers washed down with its signature iced strawberry tea.

Chinggis Restaurant (☎ 321 257; Baga Toiruu; buffet T10,000; ☻ 11am-midnight) Although the food is Korean the interior is decidedly Mongolian, plus there's singing and dancing performances in the evenings. The house speciality is *kalbitan* (beef-rib soup) while the buffet includes a healthy salad bar.

Marco Polo (☎ 318 433; Seoul St 27; pizzas T3500; ☻ noon-midnight) This place gets our vote for the best pizza in town. Its outdoor terrace is popular in summer, while the strip show upstairs pulls in the punters year-round.

More for atmosphere than fine dining are a couple of restaurants set in giant *gers* and geared towards tour groups. A set meal at either of the following places will cost around T12,000 and you must make a booking:

Abtai Sain Khaani Örgöö (☎ 9988 8090; B Dorjiin Gudamj; ☻ 10am-10pm) Near the US embassy, it's decked out with snow leopard pelts and bear skins.

Chin Van Khandorjiin Örgöö (☎ 320 763; Seoul St; ☻ 10am-10pm) Classy and central, it's tacked onto an authentic 19th-century aristocrat's home.

CAFÉS & QUICK EATS

For fast Mongolian fare, cheap, tasty *buuz* (steamed meat dumplings) or *khuushuur* (fried mutton pancakes) are sold at kiosks and modern canteens around town; try Zochin Buuz, which has least 10 outlets across the city, including on Peace Ave near Chez Bernard, or Khaan Buuz opposite the State Department Store. Both are open 24 hours, ideal for when that late-night *buuz* craving strikes!

Chez Bernard (☎ 324 622; www.happycamel.com; Peace Ave 27; breakfast T6000; ☻ 7am-2am) *Le tout* UB meets and greets at this long-running Belgian-owned café that dishes up excellent European-style breakfast platters, along with a good selection of bakery items. The owners organise trips and there's a travellers noticeboard.

Millie's Expresso (☎ 330 338; Marco Polo Bldg; snack & drink T3500; ☻ 9am-7pm Mon-Sat) Tops with consultants, aid workers and journalists sipping excellent shakes and freshly squeezed orange juice. Also excellent are the steak sandwiches, lasagne and lemon pie. It also has a small branch serving coffee and cakes in Ulaanbaatar Hotel.

Sacher's Café (☎ 324 734; Baga Toiruu west; breakfast T2000; ☻ 8am-10pm) Indulge yourself with the excellent Austrian-style cakes, pretzels and breads, including Chinggis Beer bread. It also offers filtered coffee, German magazines and indoor and outdoor seating.

Stupa Café (☎ 9911 9765; Juulchin Gudamj; Builder's Sq; snack & drink T2000; ☻ 9am-8pm Sun-Fri) Attached to a Buddhist cultural centre, this very appealing café is ideal for a quiet pit stop and has some great handmade souvenirs as well as newspapers and a free English library.

SELF-CATERING

Stock up for your train ride or a trip to the countryside by visiting the ground floor of the State Department Store or the neighbouring **Dalai Eej Market** (☻ 10am-8pm) and **Merkuri Market** (☻ 10am-8pm), which are both off Seoulyn Gudamj not far from the State Circus.

Drinking

Locally brewed beers have taken off in UB. Most bars are open 11am to midnight daily and all serve food of the meat-and-potatoes variety.

Ikh Mongol (☎ 320 450; Tserendorjiin Gudamj; ☻ closed Tue) Opposite the State Circus, this new brewhouse serves up very decent dark and hops and malt beers from T1200 a glass. On warm nights the crowds gather on the large outdoor deck while live music entertains those inside.

Dave's Place (☎ 316 798; Sükhbaatar Sq) Located on the patio of the Cultural Palace and run by an Englishman named Dave, this is a great place to observe the comings and goings of central UB. Head here for Thursday's 'Quiz Night', starting at 9.30pm (tip: read up on the local news first) and on Friday for live music. In cool weather the whole operation retreats to the basement bar.

Brau Haus (☎ 313 172; Seoul St) This flash and spacious bar and restaurant combo is part of the Khan Brau family. There's live music on Wednesday, Friday and Saturday.

Khan Brau (☎ 324 064; Chingisiin Örgön Chölöö) At some point you'll most likely wash up at this lively central bar with outdoor seating and live music most nights. Note the dark beer is way better than the *shar* (light).

Chinggis Club (☎ 325 820; Sükhbaataryn Gudamj 10) The beer is recommended at this German-run microbrewery, with a lively atmosphere and good German-inspired grub.

Entertainment

Check the English-language weeklies for events (see p258). The **Arts Council of Mongolia** (☎ 319 015; www.artscouncil.mn) produces a monthly cultural events calendar that covers most theatres, galleries and museums.

State Circus (☎ 320 795, 9918 1134, 9525 8788; admission T5000) Come to the circus, formed in 1940, to see the impressive acrobatics, juggling and extraordinary contortionists. Performances are sporadic so check the local media or Arts Council. The circus is closed during August.

TRADITIONAL MUSIC & DANCE

A performance of traditional music and dance will be one of the highlights of your visit to Mongolia and should not be missed. The State Folk Song and Dance Ensemble performs throughout the summer in the **National Academic Drama Theatre** (☎ 310 466; cnr Seoul St & Chingisiin Örgön Chölöö; admission T6000; ☿ 6pm May-Sep). Shows are less frequently staged at the **Palace of Culture** (☎ 321 444) on the northeast corner of Sükhbaatar Sq.

Tumen Ekh Song and Dance Ensemble (☎ 327 916; State Youth & Children's Theatre, Nairamdal Park, admission T6000; ☿ 6pm) This nightly performance is the most popular cultural show in Ulaanbaatar.

State Opera & Ballet Theatre (☎ 322 854; Sükhbaatar Sq; admission T5500; ☿ Sep-Jul) Stages productions in Mongolian of many of the classics, as well as works by Mongolia's most famous poet and playwright Natsagdorj.

NIGHTCLUBS

River Sounds (☎ 320 497; Olympiin Örgön Chölöö; admission T3000-5000; ☿ 8pm-3am) UB's only dedicated live-music venue usually hosts jazz and occasionally rock bands.

CINEMA

Tengis (☎ 313 105; www.tengis.mn; Liberty Sq; regular show T2500, matinee T1500) Mongolia's first multiplex cinema screens local movies and Hollywood blockbusters (shown in English with Mongolian subtitles) in its three comfy air-conditioned halls.

Shopping

UB abounds with shops selling tacky tourist souvenirs as well as locally produced cashmere clothing and blankets. A few of the better places for that special Mongolian keepsake:

Egshiglen Magnai National Musical Instrument Shop (☎ 312 732; Sükhbaataryn Gudamj; ☿ 9am-6pm Mon-Sat) This is the place to get your *morin khuur* (horse-head fiddle).

Moda Mongolia (☎ 232 925; Tserendorjiin Gudamj; ☿ 9am-8pm) Offers slightly more stylish cashmere clothes than elsewhere, although it's far from cheap.

Mongolian Wool Craft (☎ 318 591; Tserendorjiin Gudamj; ☿ 10am-7pm Mon-Sat) Colourful and inventive products made from felt, including slippers and hats.

State Department Store (☎ 324 311; Peace Ave 44; ☿ 9am-8pm Mon-Sat, 10am-6pm Sun) The 'big shop', as it is commonly called, has a decent collection of souvenirs and cashmere products.

Getting There & Away

AIR

The Mongolian airline **MIAT** (☎ 322 686; www .miat.com) has flights to Beijing, Berlin, Irkutsk, Moscow, Osaka, Seoul and Tokyo. Its office, close to the east side of Sükhbaatar Sq, may move in 2006 but the phone number will remain the same. **Aero Mongolia** (☎ 9191 2903; www.aeromongolia.mn) operates the very infrequent domestic flights.

Other international flights are available:

Aeroflot (☎ 320 720; Seoul St 15) To Moscow, Irkutsk and Ulan-Ude.

Air China (☎ 328 838; Ikh Toiruu, Bldg 47)

Korean Air (☎ 326 643; Tokyogiin Gudamj, Chinggis Khaan Hotel, 2nd fl) to Seoul.

BUS

Minivans heading for destinations in the north and west (but not east) leave from the Dragon Bus Stand on Peace Ave 7km west of Sükhbaatar Sq. Minivans for all destinations use the Naran Tuul Market. For the Gobi Desert, the Mandalgov-bound minivans use the Dragon Bus Stand while vans for Ömnögov usually use Naran Tuul.

Both stations are essentially a bunch of vans sitting in a lot with their destinations posted in the dashboard (in Cyrillic). Buses are becoming infrequent with the surge in minivans. Tell the drivers where you want to go and you'll be directed to the correct van. Some vehicles may be ready to go, others may not be leaving for another day. Buy your ticket on the bus.

TRAIN

For details of the international train services to and from UB, including the Trans-Mongolian, see p324.

International train tickets are available at the **International Railway Ticketing Office** (☎ 944 868; Zamchydn Gudamj) at the foreigners' booking office in Room 212 (☉ 8am to 8pm Monday to Friday); at weekends you use the downstairs booking desk. Tickets for international trains can be booked up to one month in advance but those for the Moscow–Beijing trains don't go on sale until the day before departure.

If you run into problems most guesthouses and hotels should be able to assist.

Getting Around

From the train station to the city centre is about 20 minutes' walk (about 1km). Alternatively, metered taxis charge a standard T250 per kilometre (check the current rate as this increases regularly); most taxi drivers are honest and will use their meters. Expect to pay around T800 from the station to Sükhbaatar Sq, while a taxi from Buyant-Ukhaa International Airport, 18km southwest of the city, should be around T6000. Bus 11 also runs from the airport to the Bayangol Hotel (T200).

AROUND ULAANBAATAR

Mongolia's real attraction lies in the untouched beauty of the countryside, its exhilarating wide open spaces and rich nomadic culture. Fortunately, these aspects are within reach on day trips or overnights from Ulaanbaatar.

Manzushir Khiid Манзширийн хийд

Just over 50km south of Ulaanbaatar, Manzushir Khiid was a monastery – established in 1733 – that once contained more than 20 temples and housed 350 monks. Destroyed during the 1930s, the main temple has been restored and now functions as a museum, but the other temples remain in ruins.

The monastery itself is not as impressive as Gandan Khiid in Ulaanbaatar, but the setting is exquisite. Hidden away in the **Bogdkhan Uul Strictly Protected Area** (admission T3000), the monastery overlooks a beautiful valley of pine, birch and cedar trees, dotted with granite boulders. Behind the main temple, climb up the rocks to discover some **Buddhist rock paintings**.

You can catch a taxi straight to Manzushir Khiid from Ulaanbaatar. Alternatively, take one of the hourly minibuses to

---

ALTERNATIVE ROUTES TO BEIJING

Immediately after Naadam, with thousands of visitors heading out of Ulaanbaatar, it's practically impossible to score last-minute reservations on the direct trains and flights to Beijing. If you haven't booked well in advance, all is not lost as there are alternatives.

Train tickets are often available on the Ulaanbaatar to Hohhot services; buy a ticket as far as the main junction at Jining (T41,670 kupe) where you can connect with a nightly train to Beijing (Y130 hard sleeper). To be sure of getting a ticket for this connection there's an agency on the ground floor of UB's International Railway Ticketing Office (see above) who can make the arrangements. It charges the tögrög equivalent of Y250 for the same hard-sleeper ticket from Jining to Beijing; you'll be met at Jining by its local agent, who will have your ticket.

An even cheaper option is to get the train as far as Erlian (T25,000) just across the Mongolian border. From here comfortable sleeper buses to Beijing (Y120, 14 hours) wait outside the station to meet each train.

the nearby town of Zuunmod (T700, one hour) and then walk the 5km to the monastery through the Bogdkhan Uul Strictly Protected Area. Laid-back Zuunmod (population 17,000) is also a conveniently close place to UB to catch a local Naadam festival (see p262).

Tsetseegun Uul Цэцээ Гүн Уул

Of the Four Holy Peaks that surround Ulaanbaatar, the most magnificent is Tsetseegun Uul (2256m). The Siberian larch forest and abundance of bird and animal life make this a great place to escape the city.

The easiest way to explore Tsetseegun Uul is to hike from Manzushir Khiid (p267). Even if you do not enter the monastery/museum, you will have to pay the T3000 admission fee for Bogdkhan Uul Strictly Protected Area. The trail is reasonably marked, but you should also use a compass. A hike from Manzushir Khiid to the Zaisan Memorial (p261) in Ulaanbaatar takes about 10 hours, so be prepared to camp and bring all the food and water you will need for at least two days.

From the monastery, follow the stream east until it nearly disappears, then turn north. About three hours' walking should bring you out over a ridge into a broad boggy meadow, which you will have to cross. If you walked due north, the twin rocky outcrops of the summit should be right in front of you. When you start to see Ulaanbaatar in the distance, you are on the highest ridge and close to the two large *ovoo* (sacred pyramid-shaped collection of stones) on the summit.

From the *ovoo* you can return to Manzushir Khiid or descend to Ulaanbaatar. Finding the most direct route to Ulaanbaatar is difficult, since you must estimate your location by your visual reference to the city. The quickest way is to head due north of UB's Observatory, and down to the valley where you'll cross the train tracks. The road is close by and you can catch a taxi to UB for around T3000. The longer route takes you to the Zaisan Memorial. Be careful not to drop down too soon otherwise you'll end up beside the

Presidential Palace in the Ikh Tenger Valley. The guards here can be uptight about perceived 'trespassers'.

Terelj Тэрэлж

Although it's fast becoming developed, Terelj, about 80km northeast of UB and part of the **Gorkhi-Terelj National Park** (admission T3000), is still a beautiful and relaxing place to head to. At 1600m, this area is cool and the alpine scenery spectacular. There are many opportunities for hiking, rock-climbing, swimming (in icy water), rafting and horse-riding (around T12,000 per day).

One potential destination for hiking or horse-riding is the appropriately named **Turtle Rock**, easily spotted along the main road through the park. From here it's less than an hour's hike up to the picturesque Buddhist meditation retreat of Aryapala from where you can look back on a stunning landscape straight out of *Lord of the Rings*.

Another place worth heading to is **Gunjiin Sün**, a Manchurian-influenced temple surrounded by forests. From the main *ger* camp area, Gunjiin Sün is about 30km as the crow flies, but it is easier to find if you take the longer route along the Baruun Bayan Gol. Other picturesque routes are along the Terelj and Tuul Rivers towards Khentii Nuruu. Horses can be hired at any *ger* camp for about US$5 per hour or US$15 to US$20 per day.

Terelj is a great place to go camping, or guesthouses can arrange accommodation in the park – sometimes staying in local *gers* with local families. Most of the tourist *ger* camps in Terelj offer similar facilities and prices – about US$30 per person, including three hearty meals, or US$15 without food. Among the better ones are **Buuveit** (☎ 322 870; www.tsolmontravel.com), which has a beautifully secluded location, and the friendly **Miraj** (☎ 325 188), 14km along the main road from the park entrance.

A bus for Turtle Rock in Terelj leaves at 4.30pm from the corner of Peace Ave and Öndör Geegen Zanabazaryn Gudamj. The same bus returns directly to Ulaanbaatar. If this doesn't pan out hire a taxi for about T30,000 one way.

Chita to Beijing via Harbin

Once a week, the 19/20 *Vostok* train chugs in each direction over the Trans-Manchurian route, taking just over a week to travel between Moscow and Beijing. The train branches off the main Trans-Siberian line shortly after Chita, crossing the border at Zabaikalsk/Manzhouli and passing through several major cities en route to the Chinese capital. The most interesting of these is Harbin, whose history is inextricably bound up with the development of the Trans-Siberian Railway – indeed it was once on the direct line to Vladivostok. For die-hard rail fanatics, it's still possible to travel this route on a twice-weekly and excruciatingly slow international train connection.

Another nonstandard Trans-Manchurian route is to hop across the Amur River from the Russian city of Blagoveshchensk to Heihe, which also has regular rail connections with Harbin. Whichever way you get there, Harbin is a fascinating place where elements of precommunist Russia still poke through the surface of a thoroughly modern Chinese city. The prime time to visit is midwinter when Harbin hosts the spectacular Ice Lantern Festival. Nature lovers will also want to make time to see the many Siberian tigers at Harbin's Siberian Tiger Park or the thousands of birds, including rare cranes, at Zhalong Nature Reserve.

Other possible stops en route include Shenyang, which hides some well-preserved relics of the Manchu era amid its traffic-clogged heart, and the major coastal city of Tianjin, which like Harbin harbours great examples of concession-era architecture: for full details of both these cities refer to Lonely Planet's *China*. In Russia you could also use Chita as a base for visiting some lesser-known Buddhist temples in the beautiful Siberian countryside.

HIGHLIGHTS

- Chill out at Harbin's spectacular **Ice Lantern Festival** (p276)
- Discover remnants of the Russian past in Harbin's evocative **Daoliqu district** (p275)
- Eyeball majestic felines at the **Siberian Tiger Park** (p275)
- Go bird-watching in the peaceful wetlands of **Zhalong Nature Reserve** (p278)
- Gaze out at the verdant grasslands of Inner Mongolia in **Manzhouli** (p271)

CHITA TO BEIJING VIA HARBIN

- ROUTE DISTANCE: 2790KM
- DURATION: TWO DAYS, EIGHT HOURS

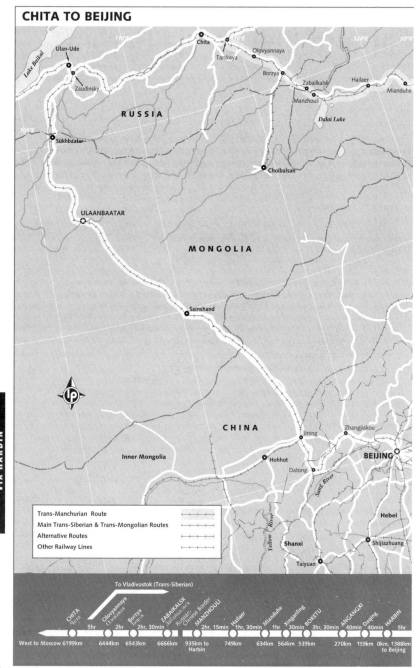

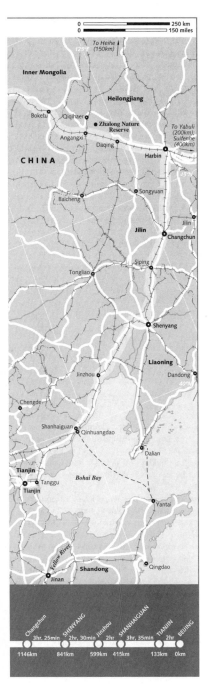

THE ROUTE

In Russia, the kilometre markers show the distance to Moscow. Once in China, they show the distance to Harbin; south of Harbin, they show the distance to Beijing.

Chita to Zabaikalsk

After **Chita** (6199km) the next major stop is **Karymskaya** (6293km), from where it's 12km down the line to Tarskaya, the official start of the Trans-Manchurian route; here the train crosses the Ingoda River and heads southeast.

There is a short stop at 6444km in **Olovyannaya**, then the train crosses the Onon River, a tributary of the Ingoda. This area is said to be the birthplace of Chinggis (Genghis) Khaan (p54).

The train makes another 10-minute stop at **Borzya** (6543km). There's little to see in this sparsely populated area, and even the Russian border town of **Zabaikalsk** (6666km) is a sleepy and run-down place. Zabaikalsk is where the bogies are changed before the train continues across the border into China. The station was under reconstruction when we passed through and promises to be by far the smartest place in town when finished. Passably edible meals are available in the bar of the nearby Rossiya Hotel.

Manzhouli to Harbin

The Chinese border town **Manzhouli** (935km to Harbin), established in 1901 as a stop for the train, is booming thanks to cross-border trade. The Russians have played a major role throughout Manzhouli's history, including developing the open-pit coal mine at nearby **Zalainuo'er**; the train passes this mine as it heads out of town, but steam-train fans will want to come out here in person to see the nearby steam locomotive storage and repair yards – steam engines are still used to haul the coal.

Vast grasslands, typical of the Mongolian steppe, surround Manzhouli; if you stop over, **China International Travel Service** (CITS; ☎ 0470-622 4241; 2nd fl, International Hotel, 35 Erdao Jie) can arrange excursions here including a stay in a yurt with a Mongolian family. Also consider visiting **Dalai Hu** (Dalai Lake), Inner Mongolia's largest lake, 39km southeast of Manzhouli.

CHITA TO BEIJING VIA HARBIN

The northernmost major town in Inner Mongolia and another base for visiting the grasslands is **Hailaer** (749km), where the train stops for about 10 minutes. Around 650km, the train enters the Greater Hinggan mountains. It may make stops at towns such as **Mianduhe** (634km), **Yilick Ede** (574km) and **Xinganling** (564km). From here the train descends on the eastern side of the range.

Shortly after the 15-minute halt at **Boketu** (539km), the train leaves Inner Mongolia and enters the province of Heilongjiang, meaning Black Dragon River. Known in Russian as the Amur River, Heilongjiang's namesake river marks the border with Russia in northeastern China.

The train makes another 15-minute stop at **Angangxi** (270km), then heads eastward through an area of wetlands, part of which has been designated as the Zhalong Nature Reserve (p278). The train makes a brief stop in **Daqing** (159km) at the centre of a large oilfield; look out for the rigs pumping crude oil out of the ground.

Harbin (1388km from Beijing), the capital of Heilongjiang province, is a 15-minute stop; see opposite for more about the city. If you're not stopping, the view of the skyline on the eastern side of the tracks as you leave Harbin gives a sense of the city's size.

Harbin to Beijing

South of Harbin, the train enters Jilin province, also part of the historic territory of the Manchus. The Japanese industrialised this region when they shaped it into the puppet state of Manchukuo (1931–45). The capital of Manchukuo, and today's provincial capital, is **Changchun** (1146km), where the train stops for 10 minutes. Home to China's first car-manufacturing plant (as well as 2.3 million people), it's also where the Japanese installed the last emperor Henry Puyi: his former palace is the city's attraction.

From here, the train heads southward towards **Shenyang** (841km). This industrial city of 3.5 million people was a Mongol trading centre from the 11th century, becoming the capital of the Manchu empire in the 17th century. The founder of the Qing dynasty, Huang Taiji, is buried here in an impressive tomb. The train stops here for 15 minutes.

After a brief stop in **Jinzhou** (599km), the line roughly follows the coast. You'll get a view of the Great Wall as the train passes through the wall just north of **Shanhaiguan** (415km). About 4km from Shanhaiguan's centre, the Great Wall meets the sea.

The last stop before Beijing is **Tianjin** (133km), a sprawling metropolis of 9.6 million people. During the 19th century this

CROSSING THE RUSSIA–CHINA BORDER

Expect to spend at least half a day crossing from Zabaikalsk to Manzhouli and vice versa, with time eaten up by thorough customs procedures on the Russian side, and the need to change the bogies on the train to match the narrower gauge used in China.

If you're not on the *Vostok* or the Manzhouli–Chita train (Friday and Saturday from Manzhouli, Thursday and Saturday from Chita), crossing this border involves taking one of the regular bus services that connect Manzhouli and Zabaikalsk.

There are daily overnight trains connecting Zabaikalsk and Chita (*kupe* R750, 12 hours); if these are full you can also take a train to Borzya and connect with a slower train to Zabaikalsk from there. Harbin and Manzhouli are also connected by a good overnight train (Y216 hard sleeper, 17 hours).

Regular buses for the border leave throughout the day from outside Zabaikalsk station (R150) or from the Manzhouli bus station (Y50), a Y10 taxi ride from the train station. If you're heading into Russia from China, there are also Russian buses leaving from behind the **Friendship Hotel** (Youyi Binguan; ☎ 0470-622 3977; 26 Yidao Jie); this tends to be faster getting through customs because mainly Russians take these buses and they proceed more quickly through Russian customs.

At the Chinese border post you'll have to pay Y10 departure tax: do this at the door left of the entrance and then give the receipt to the immigration officials as they stamp you out of the country. Luggage and passport inspection by Russian customs and immigration is rigorous but you'll see that for the Chinese, who flood daily into Russia as illegal workers and traders, they're much worse. There's an exchange office in the Russian customs hall where your immigration card will be registered.

port city attracted the interest of almost every European nation with a ship to put to sea. The evidence is that Tianjin is a living museum of early-20th-century European architecture. You will have 10 minutes to stroll around its modern train station.

Ninety minutes later, the train pulls into **Beijing** (0km); for further information see p279.

HARBIN 哈尔滨

☎ 0451 / pop 3.37 million / Moscow + 5hr

There's a relaxed, vacation feel to Harbin's tree-lined streets and riverfront promenade. One of the largest cities in northeastern China, Harbin is influenced by its relationship with nearby Russia; it's dotted with architectural gems handed down from the Russian era. Plenty of first-rate snack shops and restaurants will sustain you as you explore sights ranging from a Russian Orthodox church to a Siberian tiger sanctuary and the grim remains of a WWII germ-warfare base. Glitzy modern buildings are muscling out Harbin's historic neighbourhoods, threatening the city's unique allure. Enjoy its charm while it lasts.

History

At the end of the 19th century, Harbin was a quiet village on the Songhua River. However, when the Russians negotiated the contract to construct the East Chinese Railway line through Manchuria, Harbin's role was changed forever. Although the Japanese gained control of the new railway because of the Russian defeat in the Russo-Japanese War, Russian refugees flocked to Harbin in 1917, fleeing the Bolsheviks. The Russians would continue to influence the town's development until the end of WWII, when the region was finally handed over to the Kuomintang (China's Nationalist Party).

Orientation

The main train station is in the centre of Harbin, surrounded by a cluster of hotels. The Daoliqu area, which also contains a few hotels and many of the city's attractions, is about 2km northwest of the train station. At the northern end of Daoliqu's main thoroughfare, Zhongyang Dajie, Stalin Park is on the shores of the wide Songhua River. Across the river lies Sun Island Park and the Siberian Tiger Park.

TRANS-MANCHURIAN CHEMICAL SPILL

In late November 2005, the authorities in Harbin were forced to cut off the water supply to the city's population for several days following a chemical plant explosion that killed five people and dumped 100 tons of highly toxic benzene into the Songhua River. Those who could afford it raided supermarkets for bottled water, but Harbin's poor were forced to take their chances with the polluted water flowing in the river. By mid-December, when the benzine slick had entered the Amur River, the people of Khabarovsk were facing a similar situation, compounded by the fact that pure water was also needed to keep the city's central heating system ticking over smoothly. Environmentalists were also concerned about the affect the pollution would have on the region's wildlife, including the rare Siberian tiger, which could become sick and die through eating fish poisioned by the chemical spill.

Information

Most large hotels will change US dollars. There are also many banks and ATMs along Zhongyang Dajie in the Daoliqu district. There's also a telephone office and a convenient Internet bar (Y3 per hr) on the 2nd floor of the main train station.

China Telecom (Guogeli Dajie) Northwest of the main post office.

CITS Modern Hotel (☎ 8469 2168); Tielu Jie (☎ 5366 1159; fax 5362 1088; 11th fl, Hushi Bldg) The extremely helpful international department of the Tielu Jie branch (across the street from the train station) assists with train and airline tickets. The branch on the 2nd floor of the Modern Hotel can also arrange all sorts of tours and activities.

Post office Daoliqu (111 Zhongyang Dajie; ◷ 8.30am-7pm); Dongdazhi Jie (328 Dongdazhi Jie; ◷ 8am-7pm Mon-Fri, 8am-6.30pm Sat); train station (Tielu Jie; ◷ 8.30am-5.30pm Mon-Fri, to 5pm Sat) The main post office is on Dongdazhi Jie, a shopping district in the city centre. The Daoliqu branch is between Xi Wu Jie and Xi Liu Jie. The train station branch is to the right as you exit the station.

Sights

CHURCH OF ST SOPHIA 索菲亚教堂

Most of Harbin's Orthodox churches were ransacked during the Cultural Revolution and have since fallen into disrepair. But,

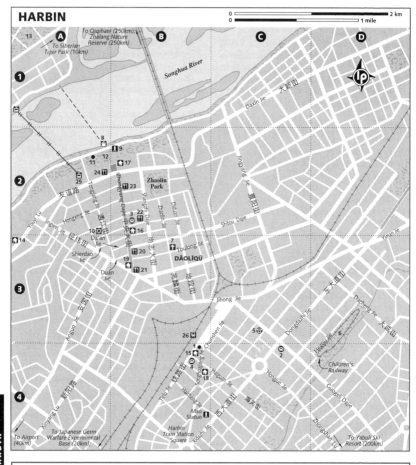

HARBIN

the majestic **Church of St Sophia** (Shèng Sùfēiyà Jiàotáng; cnr Zhaolin Jie & Toulong Jie; adult/student Y25/15; ☼ 9.30am-5.30pm), built by the Russians in 1907 in the Daoliqu district, has been beautifully restored. The church sits on a delightful open square, fronted by a fountain. It now houses the **Harbin Architecture Arts Centre**, which displays black-and-white photographs of the city from the early 1900s as well as some icons from the Russian era. The entrance ticket also includes a visit to the subterranean exhibition hall (enter from the eastern end of the square behind the church), displaying an impressive scale model of modern Harbin.

DAOLIQU 道里区

Don't miss strolling the atmospheric Daoliqu area, along cobblestone-lined, pedestrianised Zhongyang Dajie and the surrounding side streets. The architecture here shows a strong imperial-Russian influence, with spires, cupolas and scalloped turrets. Thirteen preserved buildings have plaques outlining their histories including the Modern Hotel (p277) and a former synagogue on Tongjiang Jie.

SIBERIAN TIGER PARK 东北虎林园

The mission of the **Siberian Tiger Park** (Dōngběi Hǔ Línyuán; ☎ 8808 0098; www.dongbeihu.net.cn in Chinese; 88 Songbei Jie; adult/child Y50/25; ☼ 8am-4.30pm, last tour at 4pm) is to study, breed, release and ultimately save the Manchurian (aka Siberian) tiger from extinction (see below).

The park houses some 400 of these magnificent animals, as well as a pride of African lions, a leopard, a panther and a pair of rare white tigers. While you definitely get an up-close look at the cats as you drive safarilike through the fenced-off fields, those who are not keen on zoos might want to give this supposed sanctuary a miss. The minibus drivers encourage passengers to buy chunks of meat to throw to the tigers, which makes you wonder exactly how the park is preparing these animals for the wild.

The park is located roughly 15km north of the city. From the corner of Youyi Lu and Zhongyang Dajie in Daoliqu, take bus 65 westbound to its terminus, then walk one block east to pick up bus 85, heading north on Hayao Lu. Bus 85 doesn't go all the way to the park. The bus stop is a 15- to 20-minute walk or a Y10 to Y15 (return) pedicab ride away from the park entrance. Alternatively, to take a taxi from the city centre, figure around Y100 (return), but expect to bargain.

You can combine the trip with a visit to Sun Island Park (see p276). Bus 85 stops at the western end of Sun Island Park en route from the city to the Siberian Tiger Park.

SPECIES UNDER THREAT

The Manchurian tiger is one of the rarest of all tigers. Long resident in China, these big cats, also known as the Amur, Siberian and Northeastern China tiger, today make their home in eastern Russia, North Korea and northeastern China.

The average male can grow up to 4m long, with a healthy weight of 300kg. But have no fear – it's extremely unlikely that you'll run into one of these beasts in the wild. Estimates put the number of remaining Manchurian tigers somewhere between 360 and 400, with only 30 to 35 of those roaming freely in China.

Though given protection by the Chinese government and recognised as one of the world's most endangered species, the Manchurian tiger's situation remains perilous, due to urban encroachment on the tigers' territory and a lucrative poaching business. Tiger bones are prized in traditional Chinese medicine, while tiger skins also fetch a hefty price on the black market. One tiger can earn up to 10 years' income for a Chinese poacher.

In response to the tigers' plight, the Chinese government set up a number of breeding centres, including the Siberian Tiger Park (above) outside Harbin. The purpose of these centres is ostensibly to restore the natural tiger population by breeding them and reintroducing them into the wild. However, conservationists stress the need for the tigers to have minimal human contact, and for the centres to emulate as much as possible the life that the tigers will face once released. China's centres, which see busloads of tourists snapping photos of big cats munching on cows and chickens, may instead produce tigers with a taste for livestock who will associate people with feeding time.

OTHER PARKS

Stalin Park (Sīdàlín Gōngyuán) is a pleasant tree-lined promenade, dotted with statues, playgrounds and a café in a brightly painted historic **Russian wooden chalet**, strung along the 42km embankment built to curb unruly Songhua River. At the end of Zhongyang Dajie, the **Flood Control Monument**, built in 1958, commemorates the thousands who died in the floods up to that time.

A resort feel holds sway in summer, with ice-cream stands, photo booths and boating trips (Y30) along the river and across to **Sun Island Park** (Tàiyángdǎo Gōngyuán), which features landscaped gardens, forested areas and water parks. Buy ferry tickets for Y5 from the dock directly north of the Flood Control Monument. You can also take a cable car (one-way/return Y20/30) from the foot of Tongjiang Jie, one block west.

Just southeast of the centre, the **Children's Park** (Értóng Gōngyuán; cnr Guogeli Dajie & Hegou Jie; adult/child Y2/1; ☽ 4.30am-10pm May-Sep, 6.30am-8pm Oct-Apr) has the very cute **Children's Railway** (Y5). Its 2km of track are plied by a miniature diesel pulling seven cars. Engineers, ticket collectors and rail guards are all kids. Take bus 8 from the southern end of Zhongyang Dajie or bus 109 from the train station.

GERM WARFARE BASE

侵华日军第731部队遗址

The extreme horrors of war are on display at the **Japanese Germ Warfare Experimental Base – 731 Division** (Qīnhuá Rìjūn Dì 731 Bùduì Yízhǐ; ☎ 8680 1556; Xinjiang Dajie; admission Y20; ☽ 9am-5pm, last entry at 4pm), 20km south of the city.

During 1939 the Japanese army set up this top-secret research centre, where Japanese medical experts experimented on prisoners of war. More than 4000 people were infected with bubonic plague, injected with syphilis or roasted alive in furnaces. When the Soviets took Harbin in 1945, the Japanese blew the place up, but a tenacious Japanese journalist dug up the story in the 1980s. The exhibition consists of only two small rooms plus a nearby vestige of the original base. The display captions are in Chinese only. The base is a 45-minute trip on bus 343 from the train station.

Activities

The Songhua River comes alive in winter with ice-skating, ice hockey, tobogganing and even ice-sailing (where vessels sail on the ice surface, assisted by wind power, and reach speeds of 30km/h). Equipment for each of these sports can be hired from vendors who set up shop along the river bank. Slightly madder folk astound onlookers by swimming in gaps in the ice. To round out the winter-sports fest, head 200km southeast of Harbin to China's premier ski resort, Yabuli on Daguokui Mountain, with 11 runs and nine lifts. **Windmill Village** (☎ 5345 5088; www.yabuliski.com; d Y380-780), the resort village, hosted the 1996 Asian Winter Games. Weather permitting, the ski season lasts from late November until early April. CITS (p273) offers packages that include transport, ski passes, equipment hire and accommodation. One-day trips start at around Y380.

Festivals & Events

Harbin's peak tourist season is during the **Ice Lantern Festival** (Bīngdēng Jié; ☎ 8625 0068; ☽ 8am-10pm), held in Zhaolin Park and along the Songhua River, where fanciful and elaborate ice sculptures sparkle in the frigid air. Past sculptures have included a miniature Great Wall of China and a scaled-down Forbidden City. At night the sculptures are illuminated from the inside with coloured lights, turning the area into a fantasy world. Figure-skating shows, hockey tournaments and other winter events round out the calendar. Officially, the festival runs from 5 January to 15 February, although it frequently starts a week earlier and glistens into March.

Sleeping

During the Ice Lantern Festival, prices are at least 20% higher than those listed here.

BUDGET

Follow the train station touts if you're looking for a cheap dive.

Zhōngdà Dàjiǔdiàn (☎ 8463 8888; fax 8465 2888; 32-40 Zhongyang Dajie; d Y200; ☒) Good value in pricey Daoliqu, this decent, if slightly run-down place has spacious rooms, some overlooking Zhongyang Dajie.

Tiānzhú Bīnguǎn (☎ 8647 2109; fax 5364 3720; 6 Songhuajiang Jie; s Y238, d Y238-298, tr Y290) This tower is about two blocks south of the train station; bear right as you exit. Rooms are decent and clean, if old.

MIDRANGE & TOP END

Kunlun Hotel (☎ 5361 6688; www.hljkunlun.com in Chinese; 8 Tielu Jie; s/d from Y338/640; ❄ ☐ ☎) To your right as you exit the station, this first-class hotel is an oasis of calm with an indoor pool, sauna and six restaurants. Expect a 15% service charge added to all rates.

Modern Hotel (☎ 8488 4000; www.modern.com.cn in Chinese; 89 Zhongyang Dajie; r from Y300; ❄ ☐ ☎) This hotel defies its name, as it is housed in a historic Daoliqu building dating from 1906. Rooms are comfortable, rates include a buffet breakfast and the location is un-beatable. There's also a decent-sized pool in the adjacent building (Y38).

Songhuajiang Gloria Inn (☎ 8463 8855; www.gi harbin.com; 257 Zhongyang Dajie; r from Y300; ❄) Half a block from Stalin Park, this inn offers plush rooms in a prime location.

Harbin Shangri-La Hotel (☎ 8485 8888; www .shangri-la.com; 555 Youyi Lu; r US$175/195 plus 15% service charge; ❌ ❄ ☎) Not the most convenient location, but with great views of the Ice Lan-tern Festival, this is Harbin's most luxurious choice.

Eating

The lanterns hanging above restaurant entrances in Harbin are actually a rating system – the more lanterns, the higher the standard and price. Red mean Chinese food, while blue denote pork-free cuisine from the Muslim Hui minority (mainly lamb dishes).

Harbin's culinary trademark is sausage, lengths of which hang in shop windows up and down Zhongyang Dajie. The street is also lined with bakeries, cafés and kiosks. For a cheap meal try the food court on the top floor of the department store **Cerialia** (87 Zhongyang Dajie; ☯ 9.30am-8.30pm).

Russia Tea House (☎ 8456 3207; 57 Xi Toudao Jie; mains from Y20; ☯ 11am-10pm) Housed in a historic building dating from 1914, this quaint restaurant serves faux-Russian food and drink.

Dōngfāng Jiǎozi Wáng (Kingdom of Eastern Dump-lings; ☎ 8465 3920; 39 Zhongyang Dajie; dumplings Y4-8; ☯ 11am-10pm) Serves royal helpings of *jiǎozi* (dumplings) with a large choice of fillings; try the pork with coriander or the veggie with egg. Look for the large walking dump-ling out front.

Portman (☎ 8468 6888; 63 Xi 6 Dao Jie; mains from Y30; ☯ 11am-2am) This restaurant has a com-fortable, pub atmosphere and serves tasty Western food.

Wal Mart Supercentre (187 Youyi Lu; ☯ 7am-10pm) This giant supermarket on several floors is the place to stock up on supplies for the train.

Getting There & Away

If you have problems getting train tickets try the international department of CITS (p273).

The *Vostok* passes once a week, on Thursday heading to Beijing and on Sunday to Moscow. The best connection with Bei-jing is the very comfortable Z15/16 sleeper service (soft/1st-class Y411/800).

If you want to go to Vladivostok (p230), take the train to Suifenhe, cross the border and then take a bus – it's much faster than the train. For Blagoveshchensk (p223) take a Heihe-bound train.

The following table presents the costs for trains out of Harbin:

Destination	Frequency (daily)	Cost hard/soft sleeper (Y)	Duration (hr)
Beijing	3	289/429	12
Heihe	1	153/ -	12
Manzhouli	1	216/325	14½
Suifenhe	2	173/215	9

CHITA TO BEIJING VIA HARBIN

Getting Around

The easiest way to get around Harbin is by taxi. The minimum fare is Y8. Buses 101 and 103 (Y1) regularly travel between Stalin Park and the train station.

NORTH TO HEIHE

An alternative route into Russia is to take a train to Heihe on the banks of the Amur River across from Blagoveshchensk (p223). Along the way you could pause at Qiqihaer, 250km northwest of Harbin and three to four hours (Y50) by train, to visit the Zhalong Nature Reserve.

Zhalong Nature Reserve 自然保护区

Twitchers will be thrilled by this **nature reserve** (Zhālóng Zìrán Bǎohùqū; admission Y20; ⏱ 7am-5pm), 210,000 hectares of wetlands that are home to some 260 species of bird, including the rare red-crowned crane (see p277).

Thousands of birds arrive from April to May, rear their young from June to August and depart from September to October. Even if you're not a bird fan, a trip into this peaceful countryside is bliss. During the summer, you can hire a boat to explore the freshwater marshes. Be warned: in summer giant mosquitoes are out in force – take repellent!

The reserve is 30km from Qiqihaer. **CITS** (☎ 0452-240 7538) offers day tours of the reserve (approximately Y100 per person, plus Y150 to Y200 for transportation), though it's easy enough to explore on your own on a half-day trip. Either take one of the erratic buses from Qiqihaer or a taxi (around Y150).

Beijing 北京

Capital of a land that has fired the global imagination, Beijing is the striking metropolitan core of a country with one of the world's oldest civilisations. It is also the start or finish of a trip along the Trans-Mongolian or the Trans-Manchurian lines, the Yin to Moscow's Yang.

Like its Russian counterpart, Beijing is a city of awesome – even frightening – scale. It's fascinating to compare Tiananmen Sq with Red Square, each complete with Mao's and Lenin's mausoleums, and match up the Forbidden City with the Kremlin. But pretty soon the similarities end and you're left with a dynamic modern city that stumps first-time visitors who arrive expecting to witness the last gasp of communist China. Beijing is intent on reinventing itself for the 2008 Olympics and the coming decades, evolving from an ancient city of low-rise, warrenlike neighbourhoods to a 21st-century icon, packed with skyscrapers, Prada-toting fashionistas and avant-garde artists.

Still, in this headlong rush into the future, history – an increasingly precious commodity – has not been totally condemned. Even with just a few days to spare before or after your train journey you'll discover that Beijing's environs harbour some of China's most stunning sights: the Forbidden City, the Summer Palace, Temple of Heaven Park, the Lama Temple and the Great Wall, to name just a few. Yes, the crowds can be oppressive (as can the climate), but there are also lovely parks and appealing lakeside areas in which to relax. It's also a fantastic place to sample China's glorious food and an ideal launching pad for exploring the most populous nation on earth; grab a copy of Lonely Planet's *China* and get planning!

HIGHLIGHTS

- Brave the crowds at the **Forbidden City** (p281), China's centre of power for over 500 years
- Rove through the ragged **hutong** (p286), Beijing's traditional alleyways
- Survey the spectacular achievement of the **Great Wall** (p292) outside town
- Admire the cosmic harmonies of the **Temple of Heaven** (p285)
- Feast on **Peking duck** (p288) and China's myriad other speciality foods

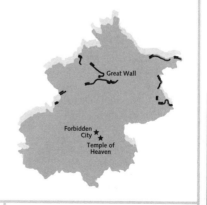

■ AREA CODE: 010 ■ POPULATION: 13.8 MILLION

BEIJING

HISTORY

Beijing – affectionately called Peking by diplomats, nostalgic journalists and wistful academics – seems to have ruled over China since time immemorial. In fact, Beijing (Northern Capital) emerged as the preeminent cultural and political force only with the 13th-century Mongol occupation of China, when Chinggis (Genghis) Khaan descended on the city. His grandson, Kublai Khaan (c 1216–94), renamed the city Khanbalik (Khan's town). From here, Kublai Khaan ruled the largest empire in world history.

Although the capital was moved for a brief period, Emperor Yongle (of the Ming dynasty) re-established Beijing as the capital in the 1400s and spent millions of taels of silver to refurbish the city. Yongle is known as the architect of modern Beijing, building the Forbidden City and the Temple of Heaven, as well as developing the bustling commercial streets outside the inner city. The Qing dynasty expanded the construction of temples, palaces and pagodas.

In January 1949, the People's Liberation Army (PLA) entered the city. On 1 October of that year Mao Zedong proclaimed a 'People's Republic' to an audience of some 500,000 citizens in Tiananmen Sq.

Like the emperors before them, the communists significantly altered the face of Beijing to suit their own image. Whole city blocks were reduced to rubble to widen major boulevards. From 1950 to 1952, the city's magnificent outer walls were levelled in the interests of traffic circulation. Before the Sino-Soviet split of the 1960s, Russian experts and technicians poured in, leaving their own Stalinesque touches.

The capitalist-style reforms of the past quarter of a century have transformed Beijing into a modern city, with skyscrapers, slick shopping malls and heaving flyovers. The once flat skyline is now spiked with vast apartment blocks and office buildings. Recent years have also seen a convincing beautification of Beijing: from a toneless and unkempt city to a greener, cleaner and more pleasant place, ready to host the world at the 2008 Olympics.

ORIENTATION

With a total area of 16,800 sq km, Beijing municipality is roughly the size of Belgium. Don't panic, though, as it's also a city of very orderly design, built on one giant grid, with the Forbidden City at its centre.

Beijing Train Station, one block south of Jianguomenwai Dajie, is 3km southeast of the Forbidden City, and is accessible by the metro circle line. Jianguomenwai Dajie, the most important east–west avenue, running just south of the Forbidden City, has many hotels and facilities. The east–west line of the metro follows this major road.

Five ring roads circle the city centre in concentric rings. Beijing's Capital Airport is 27km from the city centre; see p291 for information on getting to and from the airport.

Maps

English-language maps of Beijing can be bought at the airport, train station newspaper kiosks, and the Foreign Languages Bookstore. They can also be picked up for free at most big hotels and, for Y8, branches of the Beijing Tourist Information Center.

WHEN TO GO

Autumn (September to early November) is the optimal season to visit Beijing as the weather is gorgeous – clear skies and breezy days – and fewer tourists are in town. In winter, tourists are also scarce and many hotels offer substantial discounts – but it's glacial outside (dipping as low as -20°C) and the northern winds cut like a knife through bean curd. Arid spring is OK, apart from the (worsening) sand clouds that sweep in from Inner Mongolia and the static electricity that discharges everywhere. From May onwards the mercury can surge well over 30°C, reaching over 40°C at the height of summer, which also sees heavy rainstorms late in the season. Maybe surprisingly, this is also considered the peak season, when hotels typically raise their rates and the Great Wall nearly collapses under the weight of marching tourists. Note that air pollution can be very harsh in both summer and winter (although Beijing is obliged to clean up its act for the 2008 Olympics).

INFORMATION

Bookshops

Foreign Languages Bookstore (Wàiwén Shūdiàn; ☎ 6512 6911; 235 Wangfujing Dajie; Ⓜ Wangfujing) Has a reasonable selection of English-language novels, as well as travel books, including Lonely Planet titles, all on the 3rd floor.

Xidan Bookshop (Xīdàn Túshū Dàsha; ☎ 6607 8477; 17 Xichang'an Jie; Ⓜ Xidan) This vast bookshop has an extensive range of English-language titles.

Emergency

Ambulance (☎ 120)
Fire (☎ 119)
Police (☎ 110)

Internet Access

Internet cafés have become harder to find in Beijing over the past few years. Many cheaper hotels and youth hostels provide Internet access at around Y10 per hour.

Moko Coffee Bar (Mòkè Wǎngbā; ☎ 6525 3712; 57 Dongsi Nandajie; per hr incl coffee upstairs/downstairs Y4/12; Ⓜ Jianguomennei Dajie) No English sign, but it's next to a chemist.

Qian Yi Internet Café (☎ 6705 1722; 3rd fl, Old Station Bldg; per hr Y20; ☷ 9am-midnight; Ⓜ Qianmen) Expensive, but well located.

Yongning Internet Café (Yǒngníng Wǎngbā; 71 Chaoyangmen Nanxiaojie; per hr Y2; Ⓜ Chaoyangmen) There are no English signs here; look for the Chinese characters 网 吧.

Media

Pick up the free monthly listings magazines **That's Beijing** (www.thatsbj.com) and *Time Out Beijing* from expat bars and restaurants in the Sanlitun and Qianhai Lake areas.

Medical Services

Beijing has some of the best medical facilities and services in China. Note that it is much cheaper just to ask what medicines you need and then buy them at a pharmacy on the street rather than purchasing them on-site at an international clinic.

Beijing International Medical Center (☎ 6465 1561/2/3, emergencies ☎ 6465 1560; Suite 106-7, 1st fl, Lufthansa Center Youyi Shopping City, 50 Liangmaqiao Lu; ☷ 24hr; Ⓜ Dongzhimen) Medical, pharmacy, dental and counselling services; English-speaking staff.

Beijing Union Medical Hospital (Běijīng Xiéhé Yīyuàn; ☎ 6529 6114, emergencies ☎ 6529 5284; 53 Dongdan Beidajie; ☷ 24hr; Ⓜ Jianguomennei Dajie) Foreigners' and VIP wing in the back building.

Money

Foreign currency and travellers cheques can be changed at large branches of the Bank of China, CITIC Industrial Bank, the airport and hotel moneychanging counters, and at several department stores (including the Friendship Store), as long as you have your passport.

There's a Bank of China ATM in the Capital Airport arrivals hall, and several others across the city.

Bank of China Lufthansa Center Youyi Shopping City (1st fl, Lufthansa Center Youyi Shopping City; Ⓜ Dongzhimen); Oriental Plaza (Oriental Plaza, cnr Wangfujing Dajie & Dongchang'an Jie; Ⓜ Wangfujing); Sundongan Plaza (Ⓜ Wangfujing); The ATM at Sundongan Plaza is next to the main plaza entrance on Wangfujing Dajie.

Post

There are convenient post offices in the CITIC building next to the Friendship Store and in the basement of the China World Trade Center. Large post offices are generally open 9am to 5pm daily.

International Post Office (Guójì Yóudiànjú; Jianguomen Beidajie; ☷ 8am-7pm Mon-Sat; Ⓜ Jianguomen)

Tourist Information

Beijing Tourism Hotline (☎ 6513 0828; ☷ 24hr) English-speaking operators available to answer questions and hear complaints.

Beijing Tourist Information Center (Běijīng Lǚyóu Zīxún Fúwù Zhōngxīn; ☷ 8.30am-6pm) airport (☎ 6459 8148); Beijingzhan (☎ 6528 8448; www.bjta.gov.cn; 16 Beijingzhan Jie; Ⓜ Beijingzhan); Chaoyang (☎ 6417 6627; 27 Sanlitun Beilu; Ⓜ Dongsishitiao) Beijingzhan is a one minute walk north of Beijing Train Station; Chaoyang is west of the Sanlitun Yashou Clothing Market.

SIGHTS

Forbidden City

The largest and best-preserved cluster of ancient buildings in China is the **Forbidden City** (Zǐjìn Chéng; ☎ 6513 2255; admission Y60; ☷ 8.30am-4pm May-Sep, 8.30am-3.30pm Oct-Apr; Ⓜ Tiananmen Xi or Tiananmen Dong). It was home to two dynasties of emperors, the Ming and the Qing, who rarely strayed from this pleasure dome, although it was off limits to everyone else (thus, the name).

Renting the cassette for the self-guided tour (available in several languages) is worth the extra Y40; the English version is narrated by one-time 007 Roger Moore. Tickets and cassette rental are available at

BEIJING

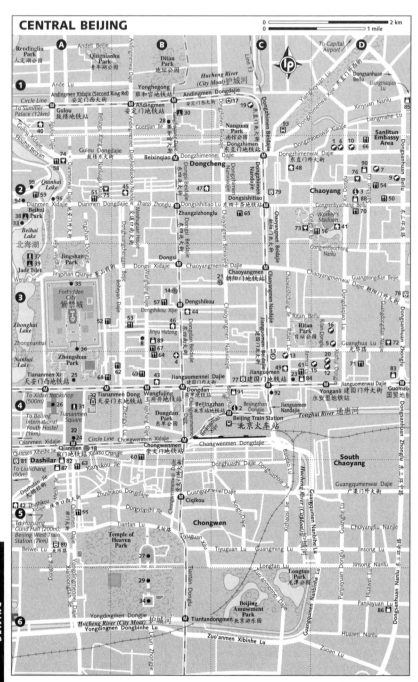

CENTRAL BEIJING

the Forbidden City's south gate, not to be confused with the Gate of Heavenly Peace (Tiananmen) facing onto the square of the same name. Continue through Tiananmen and go northward until you can't proceed without paying. (The booth in the centre of the first plaza sells tickets to climb Tiananmen, *not* to the Forbidden City.)

The palace is huge (800 buildings, 9000 rooms) and under constant renovation. The main **ceremonial buildings** lie along the north–south axis in the centre. Despite its vast scale this area is frequently crowded; you may prefer to explore the **courtyards** and **pavilions** (and mini-museums within them) on either side of the main drag.

Tiananmen Square & Around

The world's largest public square, **Tiananmen Sq** (Ⓜ Tiananmen Xi, Tiananmen Dong or Qianmen) is a vast slab of paving stones at the heart of Beijing and a poignant epitaph to China's hapless democracy movement. It may be a grandiose, Maoist tourist trap, but there's more than enough space to stretch your legs and the view can be breathtaking, especially on a clear day and at nightfall.

Although the square is the symbolic centre of the Chinese universe, what you see today is a modern reconception by Mao to project the enormity of the Communist Party. His giant portrait still hangs over the **Gate of Heavenly Peace** (Tiānānmén; ☎ 6309 9386; admission Y15, bag storage Y2; ☀ 8.30am-4.30pm) at the northern end of the square, flanked by the slogans 'Long Live the People's Republic of China' (left) and 'Long Live the Unity of the Peoples of the World' (right).

BEIJING IN...

One Day
You'll need at least a morning to cover the **Forbidden City** (p281) and some of the nearby sights of **Tiananmen Sq** (above). Grab lunch at **Quanjude Roast Duck Restaurant** (p289) or **Wangfujing Snack St** (p289), then jump in a taxi to the **Temple of Heaven** (opposite) or spend the afternoon exploring the *hutong* (narrow alleyways) close to mellow **Qianhai Lake**.

Two Days
Rise early the next day for a trip to the **Great Wall** (p292), and spend the evening enjoying a performance of **Chinese acrobatics** (p290) before rounding off the day wining and dining in Sanlitun.

Three Days
Follow the two-day itinerary above, and on your third day make an early morning visit to the **Lama Temple** (right) before browsing among the stalls and bric-a-brac shops of **Liulichang** (p291). In the afternoon, make an expedition to the **Summer Palace** (opposite). In the evening, dine at the **Courtyard** (p289), snack at **Donghuamen Night Market** (p289) or spend the evening enjoying **Beijing opera** (p290) at one of the city's numerous theatres.

At the square's southern end, **Front Gate** (Qián Mén; ☎ 6525 3176; admission Y10; ☀ 8.30am-4pm; Ⓜ Qianmen) is a remnant of the wall that guarded the ancient Inner City as early as the 15th century. It actually consists of two gates: the Arrow Tower to the south and the Main Gate to the north.

On the site of the old Outer Palace Gate, the **Monument to the People's Heroes** is a 36m obelisk that bears bas-relief depictions of key revolutionary events. Just behind this monument is **Chairman Mao's Mausoleum** (Máo Zhǔxí Jìniàntáng; ☎ 6513 2277; admission free, bag storage Y10; ☀ 8.30-11.30am Mon-Sat, 2-4pm Mon, Wed & Fri). Most Chinese continue to respect and revere this leader, who died in 1976, despite the atrocities carried out during his rule; expect long queues and only the briefest glimpse of the body. The official Party line is that Mao was 70% right and 30% wrong in his ruling. Appropriately, a visit to the 'Maosoleum' is about 70% solemnity and 30% absurdity, especially considering the well-stocked gift shop, which does a brisk trade in Chairman Mao thermometers and alarm clocks.

The National People's Congress, China's rubber-stamp legislature, sits on the western side of the square in the monolithic and intimidating **Great Hall of the People** (Rénmín Dàhuìtáng; ☎ 6309 6668; admission Y20, bag storage Y2; ☀ 9am-3pm, closed when Congress is in session). Many of the lifeless halls are named after provinces and regions of China and decorated appropriately.

On the eastern side of the square, the **Museum of Chinese History** (Zhōngguó Lìshǐ Bówùguǎn; ☎ 6512 8986; admission Y30; ☀ 8.30am-4.30pm Tue-Sat) and the **Museum of the Chinese Revolution** (Zhōngguó Gémìng Lìshǐ Bówùguǎn; ☎ 6512 8986; admission Y30; ☀ 8.30am-4.30pm Tue-Sat) are clumped together in a sombre building, but served by individual ticket offices. From 1966 to 1978 the museums were closed so that history could be revised in the light of recent events, and the tradition continues today with frequent closures. Several halls of the Museum of Chinese History stage temporary art and culture exhibitions.

North of the Forbidden City

LAMA TEMPLE

This exquisite **temple** (Yōnghé Gōng; ☎ 6404 4499, ext 252; 28 Yonghegong Dajie; admission Y25, English audio guide Y20; ☀ 9am-4pm; Ⓜ Yonghegong) is vast and riotously colourful. The five main halls and

10 exhibition rooms contain countless serene and smiling Buddhas, the most notable of which is the 18m-high statue of the **Maitreya Buddha** sculpted from a single piece of sandalwood.

The Lama Temple was once the official residence of Count Yin Zhen, who later became emperor and moved to the Forbidden City. In 1744 the buildings were converted into a lamasery. The temple somehow miraculously survived the Cultural Revolution and was 'restocked' with novice monks from Inner Mongolia in the 1980s. Today it is the most important Tibetan Buddhist temple in China (outside of Tibet itself).

CONFUCIAN TEMPLE & IMPERIAL COLLEGE

Just a short distance down the *hutong* opposite the entrance to the Lama Temple is the **Confucian Temple and Imperial College** (Kǒng Miào & Guózǐjiàn; ☎ 8401 1977; 13 Guozijian Jie; admission Y10; ❧ 8.30am-5pm; Ⓜ Yonghegong). The unkempt grounds and undisturbed peace are a pleasant contrast to just about every other sight in Beijing. The **steles** in the temple courtyard record the names of those successful in the civil service examinations (possibly the world's first) of the imperial court. The Imperial College was where the emperor annually expounded the Confucian classics to an audience of thousands of kneeling students and professors.

BEIHAI PARK

A relaxing place for a stroll is **Beihai Park** (Běihǎi Gōngyuán; ☎ 6407 1415; admission Y5, Jade Islet Y10; ❧ 6.30am-8pm, buildings open till 4pm; Ⓜ Tiananmen Xi, then bus 5), northwest of the Forbidden City. There are four gates to the park, which is formed around Beihai Lake.

The site is associated with Kublai Khaan's palace, the navel of Beijing before the creation of the Forbidden City. Dominating **Jade Islet** on the lake, the 36m-high **White Dagoba** was originally built in 1651 for a visit by the Dalai Lama, and was rebuilt in 1741. You can reach the dagoba through the **Yongan Temple**, with its halls decorated with statues of Buddhist figures and past lamas, as well as a bamboo grove. The pretty **Xitian Fanjing** (Western Paradise) temple and the **Nine Dragon Screen**, a 5m-high and 27m-long wall of coloured glazed tiles, are also worth searching out within the park.

JINGSHAN PARK

This **park** (Jǐngshān Gōngyuán; ☎ 6403 3225; admission Y2; ❧ 6am-9.30pm; Ⓜ Tiananmen Xi, then bus 5) is worth visiting for its priceless views over the Forbidden City immediately to its south. Its central hill, shaped from the earth excavated to create the palace moat, supposedly protects the palace from the evil spirits – or dust storms – from the north (the billowing dust clouds in the spring have to be seen to be believed). Clamber to the top of this regal pleasure garden for a magnificent panorama of the capital.

Summer Palace

The immense park of the **Summer Palace** (Yíhé Yuán; ☎ 6288 1144; 19 Xinjian Gongmen; admission Y40-Y50, audio guides Y30; ❧ 8.30am-5pm) requires at least half a day of your time. Nowadays teeming with tour groups, this complex, dominated by **Kunming Lake**, was once a playground for the imperial court. Royalty came here to elude the summer heat that roasted the Forbidden City. Empress Dowager Cixi rebuilt the park in 1888 with money supposedly intended for the creation of a modern navy. (At least the empress restored the still-immobile marble boat for lakeside dining.)

The palace's main building is the **Hall of Benevolence and Longevity**, near the lake towards the eastern gate, which is where the emperor handled state affairs and received visitors. The 700m **Long Corridor** along the northern shore is decorated with mythical scenes. Visitors can also see exhibitions specific to the Empress Dowager Cixi, including her furniture and memorabilia. The park also contains several **temples** with elaborate artwork and good views of the lake, on which you can row a boat in summer and skate in winter.

The park is about 12km northwest of the city centre of Beijing; get there by taking the subway to Xizhimen station, then a minibus or bus 375.

Temple of Heaven Park

China's finest example of Ming architecture is the **Temple of Heaven** (Tiāntán Gōngyuán; ☎ 6702 8866; Tiantan Donglu; admission low season Y10-30, high season Y15-35; ❧ park 6am-9pm, sights 8am-6pm; Ⓜ Chongwenmen or Qianmen). This complex, set in a 267-hectare park, functioned as a stage for the solemn rites performed by the Son of Heaven, who came here to pray for good harvests, seek divine clearance and atone for the sins of the people.

The design and position of the park, as well as the shape and colour of structures within, have symbolic significance for the ancient interplay between heaven and earth. The **Round Altar**, for example, possesses an obsessive symmetry revolving around the heavenly number nine (nine rings of stone, each ring composed of multiples of nine stones etc). The altar's most mystifying fea-ture is its ability to amplify voices emanat-ing from the centre of the upper terrace.

Just north of the Round Altar is the **Imperial Vault of Heaven**, which is surrounded by the **Echo Wall**. Sixty-five metres in diameter, the wall allows a whisper to travel clearly from one end to the other.

The crown of the whole complex is the **Hall of Prayer for Good Harvests**. Amazingly, this temple's wooden pillars support the ceiling without nails or cement!

BEIJING'S HUTONG

Beijing's homely interior lies waiting to be discovered in the city's *hutong* (narrow alleyways). Crisscrossing east–west across the city, these alleyways link to create a huge, enchanting warren of one-storey, ramshackle dwellings and historic courtyard homes.

After Chinggis Khaan's army reduced Beijing to rubble, the city was redesigned with *hutong*. By the Qing dynasty there were over 2000 such passageways riddling the city, leaping to around 6000 by the 1950s; now the figure has dwindled again to around 2000, home to around a quarter of Beijing's residents. Marked with white plaques, historic homes are protected, but for many others a way of life is being ruthlessly bulldozed, at a rate of over 10,000 dwellings a year.

Hutong land is a hodgepodge of the old and the new, with Qing dynasty courtyards rid-dled with modern brick outhouses and socialist-era conversions, and cruelly overlooked by grim apartment blocks.

Layout

Old walled *siheyuan* (courtyard homes) are the building blocks of this delightful world. Many are still lived in and hum with activity. From spring to autumn, men collect outside their gates, drinking beer, playing chess, smoking and chewing the fat. Inside, trees soar aloft, providing shade and a nesting ground for birds.

More venerable courtyards are fronted by large, thick, red doors, outside of which perch either a pair of Chinese lions or *bavoguvshi* (drum stones; two circular stones resembling drums, each on a small plinth and occasionally topped by a miniature lion or a small dragon head).

Foreigners have cottoned on to the charm of courtyards and have breached this very con-servative bastion; however, many have been repelled by poor heating, no hot water, no cable TV, dodgy sanitation and no place to park the 4WD. Many *hutong* homes still lack toilets, explaining the multitude of malodorous public loos strung out along the alleyways. Other homes have been thoroughly modernised and sport varnished wood floors, fully fitted kitchens, a Jacuzzi and air-con.

Hutong nearly all run east–west to ensure that the main gate faces south, satisfying the re-quirements of feng shui. This south-facing aspect guarantees a lot of sunshine and protection from more negative forces from the north. This positioning also mirrors the layout of all Chinese temples, nourishing the Yang (the male and light aspect), while checking the Yin (the female and dark aspect). Little connecting alleyways that run north–south link the main alleys.

Hutong Tour

The best way to see *hutong* is just to wander or cycle around the centre of Beijing, as the al-leyways riddle the town within the Second Ring Rd. Otherwise, limit yourself to historic areas, such as around the Lusongyuan Hotel. Or you could do the pedicab tourist trip with the **Beijing Hutong Tour Co Ltd** (☎ 6615 9097; 🕒 8.50am & 1.50pm Nov-Apr, 8.50am, 1.50pm & 6.50pm May-Oct), departing from a point 200m to the west of the north entrance of Beihai Park (p285). Any number of other pedicab tours infest the roads around Qianhai Lake – they will circle you like hyenas, baying '*hutong, hutong*'.

SLEEPING

Beijing has a reasonably wide range of places to stay, from hostels to five-star luxury. The most atmospheric hotels are those built in the courtyards of the *hutong* neighbourhoods. All hotels are subject to a 10% to 15% service charge (on top of the prices quoted here), but many cheaper hotels don't bother to charge it.

Budget

Far East International Youth Hostel (Yuǎndōng Guójì Qīngnián Lǚshè; ☎ 6301 8811, ext 3118; courtyard@elong .com; 113 Tieshuxie Jie; dm from Y45; Ⓜ Qianmen; ☒ 🖵) Based in a courtyard with loads of character, this pleasant hostel offers bike rental (per day Y20), a kitchen, a laundry, a fine café-bar, a table tennis room, and a shop (selling Internet phonecards). Rooms come without TV, phone or shower. To get here head south on Nanxinhua Jie. About 200m after you pass Liulichang you'll see a sign (in English) on the right-hand side of the street saying 'Far East Hotel'. Follow the *hutong* for about 50m.

Beijing Gongti International Youth Hostel (Běijīng Gōngtǐ Qīngnián Lǚshè; ☎ 6552 4800; bih-yh@ sohu.com; East Gate, Worker's Stadium; 2-/4-bed dm Y70/ 50, s Y100; Ⓜ Dongsishitiao; 🖵) This clean and appealing hostel offers both excellent value and position. The dorm rooms (Y10 extra for nonmembers) are bright, clean and spacious, and come equipped with phone (incoming only), TV and radiator. Inquire about camping outside during the summer months. The hostel also has a bar, Chinese restaurant and a useful travellers' notice board.

You Yi Youth Hostel (Yǒuyì Qīngnián Jiǔdiàn; ☎ 6417 2632; fax 6415 6866; 43 Beisanlitun Lu; dm/tw incl breakfast Y70/180; Ⓜ Dongsishitiao; ☒ 🖵) Smack in the middle of the Sanlitun bar district, this is a good choice if you wish to party (although a sign says 'Gambling, prostitution and drunkenness are strictly forbidden'). Twins (with phone, TV, radiator and air-con) are bright and spacious with large beds. The free laundry service is a nice touch.

Eastern Morning Sun Youth Hostel (Běijīng Dōngfāng Chénguāng Qīngnián Lǚguǎn; ☎ 6528 4347; fl B4, Oriental Plaza, 8-16 Dongdansantiao; s/d/tr Y80/120/180; Ⓜ Wangfujing; 🖵) The central location makes up for its position four floors below ground level (memorise where the fire escape is!). Despite the sign outside, this is not a bona fide Hostelling International member. Single rooms are simple and small; the better doubles have TV (no phone).

Beijing Feiying International Youth Hostel (Běijīng Fēiyīng Qīngnián Lǚshè; ☎ 6315 1165; iyhfy@ yahoo.com.cn; No 10 Bldg, Changchun Jie Hou Jie, Xuan-wumen Xidajie; 10-/5-bed dm Y30/50, d 180; Ⓜ Chang-chunjie; ☒ 🖵) All rooms have showers and air-con at this hostel near Changchunjie subway (take exit C from the station and head east past the McDonald's for around 150m). At hand are bicycles for hire, a washing machine, kitchen and tourist info.

Midrange

Haoyuan Guesthouse (Hǎoyuán Bīnguǎn; ☎ 6512 5557; www.haoyuanhotel.com; 53 Shijia Hutong; d Y468-572; Ⓜ Dongdan; ☒ 🖵) This delightful Qing courtyard hotel has pleasant staff and a handful of tastefully finished rooms. Laid out with trees, the courtyard at the rear is gorgeous. There is a restaurant as well as bike rental and rates include breakfast.

Red Capital Residence (Xīnhóngzī Kèzhàn; ☎ 6402 7150; www.redcapitalclub.com.cn; 9 Dongsi Liutiao; d from US$148; Ⓜ Dongsishitiao) An unusual guesthouse heady with the nostalgia of a vanished age. The five rooms are decked out with stuff that wouldn't look out of place in a museum. For real class take a swing through town in the Red Flag limo, once the property of Mao's inner circle.

Bamboo Garden Hotel (Zhúyuán Bīnguǎn; ☎ 6403 2229; fax 6401 2633; 24 Xiaoshiqiao Hutong; s/d/ste Y380/530/680; Ⓜ Gulou; ☒) This cosy, intimate and tranquil courtyard hotel is in buildings dating back to the late Qing dynasty, while the gardens belonged to a eunuch from Empress Cixi's entourage. Rooms are tastefully decorated with reproduction Ming furniture and the abundant foliage is pleasant. Reception is through the gates on your left.

Novotel Peace Hotel (Běijīng Nuòfùtè Hépíng Bīnguǎn; ☎ 6512 8833; fax 6512 6863; 3 Jinyu Hutong; d US$80-110, ste US$100-130; Ⓜ Jianguomennei Dajie; ☒) This efficient and inviting refurbished hotel has a fresh and cosmopolitan touch and a fantastic central location. The cheaper rooms – not huge but perfectly serviceable – are in the older and more scuffed West Wing. Ask for promotional rates.

Red House Hotel (Ruìxiù Bīnguǎn; ☎ 6416 7500; www.redhouse.com.cn; 10 Chunxiu Lu; s/d Y300/400; Ⓜ Dongzhimen; ☒ 🖵) Handy for Sanlitun, the

---

THE AUTHOR'S CHOICE

Lusongyuan Hotel (Lǔsōngyuán Bīnguǎn; ☎ 6404 0436; 1syhotel@263.net; 22 Banchang Hutong; dm/s/d/ste US$10/35/60/110; Ⓜ Andingmen; 🔀 💻) Built by a Mongolian general during the Qing dynasty, this courtyard hotel's location makes it an excellent base for exploring the city. For a double bedroom, book ahead as the hotel only has two (the other rooms all have two single beds). Pocket-sized singles come with pea-sized baths (albeit quite cute); dorms have three beds (with TV) and there is one suite. All rooms facing onto the courtyard are slightly more expensive. Bicycle rental (per day Y30) is available.

---

refurbished rooms here have cable TV. There are lockers, laundry facilities and breakfast is included. Also in the building are the Monkey Business office and the popular sports bar Club Football Center.

Top End

St Regis (Běijīng Guójì Jùlèbù Fàndiàn; ☎ 6460 6688; www.stregis.com/beijing; 21 Jianguomenwai Dajie; d from US$340, ste US$500-5300; Ⓜ Jianguomen; 🔀 💻 🏊) Top-notch elegance complemented by professionalism and a superb location make the St Regis a marvellous choice. The splendid foyer and an enticing complement of restaurants compound this hotel's undeniable allure.

Grand Hyatt Beijing (Běijīng Dōngfāng Jūnyuè Dàjiǔdiàn; ☎ 8518 1234; www.hyatt.com; 1 Dongchang'an Jie; d from US$320; Ⓜ Wangfujing; 🔀 💻 🏊) Bang in the midst of the Wangfujing shopping district this contemporary-designed and opulent hotel offers a great location and sizable rooms.

China World Hotel (Zhōngguó Dàfàndiàn; ☎ 6505 2266; www.shangri-la.com; 1 Jianguomenwai Dajie; d US$300-410; Ⓜ Guomao; 🔀 💻) Acres of marble greet guests at this five-star performer. Plus all your shopping and dining needs met at the China Word Trade Center. Full tariff rate includes airport transfer, laundry, dry-cleaning, breakfast and local phone calls.

EATING

Some of your best memories of Beijing are likely to be those involving eating. The best areas to look for restaurants, cafés and bars

include Sanlitun and around Qianhai and Houhai Lakes. Unless stated otherwise in the review, restaurants and cafés are open from 11am to 11pm.

For upmarket dining, Beijing offers some exceptional restaurants that serve Chinese-influenced food with a modern twist. Reservations are necessary. Both Courtyard and Green T House also have small galleries where you can view some of Beijing's striking contemporary art.

Some of the best and cheapest places to sample local cuisine are the food stalls and local markets.

Restaurants

Gongdelin Vegetarian Restaurant (Gōngdélín Sùcàiguǎn; ☎ 6511 2542; 158 Qianmen Dajie; meals Y25-40; Ⓜ Qianmen) Restore your karma with dishes of mock meat that taste better than the real thing. Service is pedestrian and the décor strictly no-frills.

Niúgē Jiǎozi (☎ 6525 7472; 85 Dong'anmen Nanjie; meals Y15; Ⓜ Tiananmen Dong) Dumpling fans should hasten to this pocket-sized restaurant which dishes up dozens of yummy varieties – there's no English menu, though, and no English sign either, but it's opposite the building with the sign on the roof saying 'Hualong Street'.

Xiao Wang's Home Restaurant (Xiǎowáng Fǔ; meals Y70) Guanghua Dongli (☎ 6594 3602; 2 Guanghua Dongli; Ⓜ Yonganli); Sanlitun (☎ 6594 3602, 6591 3255; 4 Gongrentiyuchang Beilu; Ⓜ Dongsishitiao) Treat yourself to home-style Beijing cuisine from this excellent restaurant with outdoor seating. Try one of the specials: fried hot and spicy Xinjiang-style chicken wings or deep-fried spareribs with pepper salt. The branch in the Sanlitun area is the classier of the two.

Tiāndì Yījiā (☎ 8511 5556; tiandicanyin@163.com; 140 Nanchizi Dajie; meals around Y300; Ⓜ Tiananmen Dong) This refined Chinese courtyard-style restaurant is decked out with traditional furniture, water features and side rooms for snug hotpot dinners. Graze on Cantonese dim sum (served from 11am to 2pm and 5pm to 9.30pm).

Bǎguó Bùyī (☎ 6400 8888; 89-3 Dianmen Dongdajie; dishes from Y8; Ⓜ Zhangzizhonglu) Spicy Sichuan cuisine is served in a marvellous Chinese inn–style restaurant setting. There's a range of good-value dishes for Y8, including Chongqing hot pepper chicken and chilli fish slices.

Green Tianshi Vegetarian Restaurant (Lǜsè Tiānshí Sùcàiguǎn; ☎ 6524 2349; 57 Dengshikou Dajie; meals from Y50; Ⓜ Dengshikou) This venerable vegetarian restaurant cooks up simulated meat dishes, presented in a relaxed and attractive environment. A handy picture menu helps with the ordering.

Liqun Roast Duck Restaurant (Lìqún Kǎoyādiàn; ☎ 6702 5681; 11 Beixiangfeng Hutong; roast duck Y68; Ⓜ Qianmen) Book a table before arriving at this tiny, busy Peking duck restaurant buried away in a maze of *hutong* in east Qianmen. No medals for service but the duck is excellent.

Kaorouji (☎ 6404 2554; 14 Qianhai Dongyuan; meals Y55; Ⓜ Gulou) An old standby overlooking lovely Qianhai Lake and serving delicious coriander-laced roast mutton (Y45) as well as a good range of other Muslim Uighur dishes.

Courtyard (Sìhéyuàn; ☎ 6526 8883; 95 Donghuamen Dajie; meals from Y200; Ⓢ 6-10pm Mon-Sat, noon-10pm Sunday; Ⓜ Tiananmen Dong) The view across to the Forbidden City is only surpassed by the cooking which is delicious. Sunday lunch is an affordable option at Y150 per person.

Green T House (☎ 6552 8310; 6 Gongti Xilu; meals from Y400; Ⓢ 6-10pm; Ⓜ Dongsishitiao) A dining wonderland of fabulous furniture and inventive, beautifully presented dishes with poetic names.

Red Capital Club (☎ 6402 7150 weekdays, ☎ 8401 8886 evenings & weekends; 66 Dongsi Jiu Tiao; meals from Y200; Ⓜ Dongsishitiao) This meticulously restored courtyard restaurant serves flavoursome dishes that each come with their own elaborate myth. Look for the red doors with no sign.

THE AUTHOR'S CHOICE

Quanjude Roast Duck Restaurant (Quànjùdé Kǎoyādiàn; ☎ 6525 3310; 9 Shuaifuyuan Hutong; half/whole duck Y84/168; Ⓜ Wangfujing) You've not really visited Beijing unless you've scoffed the city's signature dish. Quanjude has an impeccable pedigree (Mao ate here) and is a fine place to sample the Peking duck as well as more specialist dishes such as duck feet with mustard sauce, salted duck's liver or deep-fried duck heart. There's also a more famous and touristy branch at **Qianmen** (☎ 6511 2418; 32 Qianmen Dajie; Ⓜ Qianmen).

Makye Ame (Mǎjí Āmǐ; ☎ 6506 9616; 2nd fl, A11 Xiushui Nanjie; dishes from Y20; Ⓜ Jianguomen) Behind the Friendship Store, this is one of Beijing's few Tibetan restaurants, where you can sample boiled yak with chilli and *tsampa* (roasted barley meal). There's a comfy upper room decorated with a generous crop of Tibetan ornaments.

Serve the People (Wèi Rénmín Fúwù; ☎ 8454 4580; 1 Sanlitun Xiwujie; meals Y50; Ⓜ Dongzhimen) This is Beijing's trendiest Thai restaurant; its warm décor, *tom yam* (spicy, lemongrass-flavoured soup) and other Thai dishes are deservedly popular.

Taj Pavilion (Tàijī Lóu Yìndù Cāntīng; ☎ 6505 5866; 1st fl, West Wing, China World Trade Center; meals from Y100; Ⓜ Guomao) Hankering for an Indian meal? The food and service here consistently get top marks.

1001 Nights (Yìqiānlíngyī Yè; ☎ 6532 4050; Gongti Beilu; meals Y100; Ⓢ 11am-2am; Ⓜ Dongsishitiao) Widely acknowledged as the best Middle Eastern restaurant in Beijing, this lively place also offers belly-dancing shows and late-night dining. Opposite Zhaolong Hotel.

Cafés & Quick Eats

Kosmo (☎ 6657 0007; 5 Lotus Lane, Qianhai Xiyan; sandwich & drink Y30; Ⓜ Gulou) Facing Qianhai Lake, this stylish contemporary café, serving organic and healthy food, is a standout among the trendy offerings of Lotus Lane – and not just because it donates some of its profits to Unicef.

Downtown Café (☎ 6415 2100; 26 Sanlitun Lu; meals Y70; Ⓜ Dongsishitiao) This popular Western café hogs the lion's share of hungry expats on Sanlitun Lu. The menu delivers dependable European fair.

Donghuamen Night Market (Dōnghuámén Yèshì; Dong'anman Dajie; Ⓢ 3-10pm, closed Chinese New Year; Ⓜ Dengshikou) A sight in itself is this bustling night market near Wangfujing Dajie. It's for tourists, so expect to pay around Y5 for a lamb kebab (much more than you would from a *hutong* vendor).

Wangfujing Snack St (Wángfǔjīng Xiǎochījiē; west off Wangfujing Dajie; kebabs from Y3, dishes from Y5; Ⓜ Wangfujing) Fronted by an ornate archway, here you'll find a good selection of small restaurants and stalls overhung with colourful banners and bursting with character and flavour. Try Xinjiang or Muslim Uighur cuisine such as lamb kebabs and flat bread.

Food Court (basement, Oriental Plaza, 1 Dongchang'an Jie; dishes from Y10; **M** Wangfujing) If the outdoor stalls leave you nonplussed try this spacious, hygienic food court offering a world of Chinese cuisine, plus other Asian dishes. You can eat very well for around Y20. Buy a card (Y5 deposit; cards come in denominations of Y30, Y50, Y100, Y200, Y500 and Y1000 units) at the kiosk at the entrance; credits are deducted with each dish ordered so you can pick and mix your plates from different outlets.

Self-Catering

At Beijing's supermarkets you'll find everything you need for long train journeys. Some options:

Lufthansa Center Youyi Shopping City (Yānshā Yǒuyì Shāngchǎng; 50 Liangmaqiao Lu; ☺ 10am-8pm; **M** Dongzhimen)

Super 24 (Sanlitun Lu; ☺ 24hr; **M** Dongzhimen)

Yansha Supermarket (Yānshā Chāoshì; basement, Henderson Center, Jianguomennei Dajie; ☺ 10am-8pm; **M** Jianguomen)

DRINKING

The hubs for expat drinking are Sanlitun and, increasingly, the streets around Qianhai and Houhai Lakes. Yandai Xijie – a small street just east of Silver Ingot Bridge – and Lotus Lane on the west side of Qianhai Lake are worth checking out. Most bars and clubs are open daily from about noon until the last customer leaves, unless otherwise specified.

Pass By Bar (Guòkè; ☎ 8403 8004; 108 Nanluogu Xiang; **M** Zhangzizhonglu) In a courtyard house, this traveller-friendly bar has a great atmosphere as well as a book exchange and decent food.

Guangfuguan Greenhouse (Guǎngfúguàn de Wènshì; ☎ 6400 3234; 36 Yandai Xijie; **M** Gulou) Sink those beers in a former Taoist temple with the religious statuary still gazing on.

Tree (Yǐnbǐ de Shù; ☎ 6415 1954; www.treebeijing .com; 43 Bei Sanlitun Nan; **M** Dongsishitiao) Recently uprooted to a new location, the Tree has a cellar packed with Belgian brews. The beer garden opens from late spring, the menu's Mediterranean (pizzas around Y70) and the interior's candlelit.

Poachers Inn (☎ 6417 2632, ext 8506; 43 Bei Sanlitun Lu; **M** Dongsishitiao) Party central at weekends, this long-running bar remains one of the most popular expat watering holes, with inflated prices and occasional live acts.

Club Football Center (☎ 6417 0497; Red House Hotel, 10b Chunxiu Jie; **M** Dongzhimen) A genuine British pub with wall-to-wall football trophies and memorabilia, live English premiership action and a big sports screen. The food's OK, too.

Destination (☎ 6551 5138; www.bjdestination.com; 7 Gongti Xilu; cover incl 1 drink Y20; **M** Dongsishitiao) Beijing's premier gay dance bar is a stylish, lively place with a mixed crowd. It hosts the occasional lesbian night.

A couple of upmarket hotel bars with soothing ambience and music are **Centro** (Xuànkù; ☎ 6561 8833, ext 6388; Kerry Center Hotel, 1 Guanghua Lu; ☺ 24hr; **M** Guomao) and **Red Moon Bar** (Dōngfāng Liàng; ☎ 8518 1234, ext 6366; Grand Hyatt Beijing, 1 Dongchang'an Jie; **M** Wangfujing).

ENTERTAINMENT
Opera

Beijing opera (p52) is the most famous of the many forms of performance art on offer in the city. You can catch performances at the following theatres:

Chang'an Grand Theatre (Chángān Dàjùchǎng; ☎ 6510 1309; Chang'an Bldg, 7 Jianguomennei Dajie; tickets Y40-150; ☺ performances 7.15pm; **M** Jianguomen)

Huguang Guild Hall (Húguǎng Huìguǎn; ☎ 6351 8284; 3 Hufang Lu; tickets Y100-380; ☺ performances 7.15-9pm; **M** Hepingmen) Decorated in a similar fashion to the Zhengyici Theatre, with balconies surrounding the canopied stage, this theatre dates back to 1807.

Zhengyici Theatre (Zhèngyīcí Jùchǎng; ☎ 6303 3104; 220 Xiheyan Dajie; tickets from Y50; ☺ performances 7.30-9pm; **M** Qianmen) Oldest wooden theatre in the country and the best place in the city to experience Beijing opera.

Acrobatics

Chaoyang Theatre (Cháoyáng Jùchǎng; ☎ 6507 2421; 36 Dongsanhuan Beilu; tickets Y80; ☺ performances 7.30pm; **M** Chaoyangmen) The Chaoyang Theatre is the venue for visiting acrobatic troupes, who fill the stage with plate-spinning and hoop-jumping.

Universal Theatre (Heaven & Earth Theatre; Tiāndì Jùchǎng; ☎ 6416 0757/9893; 10 Dongzhimen Nandajie; tickets Y60-200; ☺ performances 7.15pm; **M** Dongsishitiao) Around 100m north of Poly Plaza; come here to see young performers from the China Acrobatic Circus and the China National Acrobatic Troupe.

Wan Sheng Theatre (Wànshèng Jùchǎng; ☎ 6303 7449; Tianqiao; tickets Y100-150; ☺ performances 7.15pm;

M Qianmen) West of the Temple of Heaven, this theatre offers one of Beijing's best acrobatic displays, performed by the Beijing Acrobatics Troupe.

SHOPPING

'Let the People Shop' might as well be the new Party mantra. Whatever you want, from antiques to Versace, chances are you'll find it in Beijing. Get lucky and some pieces might even be genuine rather than fake! The best bargains include silk, cashmere and brand-name clothing (often fake). Pirated CDs and DVDs abound. While prices are fixed in the department stores, bargaining is expected – even encouraged – everywhere else.

Wangfujing Dajie is a lively shop-lined pedestrianised street, two blocks east of the Forbidden City. Its name, meaning 'Well of Princely Palaces', dates to the 15th century, when this area was the site of several royal palaces, long since destroyed to make way for the palaces of the people. The mammoth **Oriental Plaza** (Dōngfāng Guǎngchǎng; 1 Dongchang'an Jie; M Wangfujing) shopping mall anchors the southern end of the street, while elsewhere along it you'll find tea emporium **Ten Fu's Tea** (Tiānfú Míngchá; ☎ 6527 4613; www.tenfu.com; 88 Wangfujing Dajie; M Wangfujing).

Dashilar (M Qianmen), a colourful *hutong* off Qianmen Dajie, is a jumble of silk shops, tea and herbal medicine shops, theatres and restaurants. Also known as 'Silk Street', it is a hangover from when specialised products were sold in particular areas. Good places to buy silk near Dashilar are **Ruifuxiang** (☎ 6303 2808; 5 Dazhalan Jie) and the **Beijing Silk Store** (☎ 6301 6658; 5 Zhubaoshi, Qianmen Dajie).

Beijing's premier antique street is tree-lined **Liulichang** (M Hepingmen), west of Dashilar. Designed to look like an ancient Chinese village, it's a nice place to stroll even if you don't want to buy Chinese paintings, calligraphy materials, art books or ceramics.

Pānjiāyuán (☉ dawn–around 3pm Sat & Sun; M Guomao) Hands-down the best place to shop for arts, crafts and antiques – everything from Cultural Revolution memorabilia to Buddha heads – is the 'Dirt Market'. Come early and bargain hard. Located off Dongsanhuan Nanlu.

Sanlitun Yashou Clothing Market (Sānlǐtún Yǎxiù Fúzhuāng Shìchǎng; 58 Gongrentiyuchang Beilu; M Dongsishitiao) Offering five floors of all the clothing you may need.

GETTING THERE & AWAY
Air

Beijing's **Capital Airport** (☎ 6459 9567 for international flights, 1689 6969 for domestic flights) has direct air connections to most major cities in the world and every major city in China. For more information about international flights to Beijing, see p319.

Train

Moscow, Ulaanbaatar and Harbin trains depart from and arrive at **Beijing Train Station** (Běijīng Huǒchēzhàn; ☎ 6563 3262/3242; M Beijingzhan), southeast of the Forbidden City. **Beijing West Train Station** (Běijīng Xīzhàn; ☎ 6321 6253; M Junshibowuguan), near Lianhuachi Park, has trains for Hong Kong and Vietnam.

Avoid buying tickets in the main ticket hall at Beijing Train Station, as the crowds can be overwhelming. There's a **ticketing office for foreigners** (☉ 5.30-7.30am, 8am-6.30pm & 7-11pm) in the northwestern corner of the 1st floor, accessed through the soft seat waiting room. This is an excellent place to sit down and take a breather in the comfy armchairs provided. There's also a foreigners ticketing office on the 2nd floor of Beijing West Train Station (open 24 hours).

If you're having trouble getting a train ticket go to **BTG Travel & Tours** (☎ 6800 5588; A9 Fuwai Dajie; ☉ 8am-8pm; M Jianguomen) between the New Otani and Gloria Plaza Hotels; it has a desk dedicated to booking Trans-Mongolian/Trans-Manchurian trains, and can also (for a Y100 fee) book Harbin to Manzhouli trains via the CITS office in Harbin.

GETTING AROUND
To/From the Airport

The airport is 27km from the city centre. A service desk inside the airport terminal sells tickets for buses (Y16) into town. Buses leave every half-hour between 5.30am and 7pm, and include routes to Beijing Train Station, Xidan metro and the China Art Gallery north of Wangfujing Dajie. A taxi should cost only about Y85 from the airport to the centre (including the Y15 road toll).

A light-rail link from Capital Airport to Beijing is under construction, but is not due for completion until 2007.

Bicycle

To get around the city in true Beijing style, consider riding a bicycle, which can be rented from many hotels, especially those in the budget range. **Universal Bicycle Rental Outlet** (Qianhai Lake; single/tandem bike per hr Y10/20, deposit Y500; Ⓜ Gulou) has two outlets in the vicinity of Qianhai Lake.

Public Transport

Given frequently appalling traffic the subway is a hassle-free way to get around the centre of Beijing, even though its current three lines limit its overall usefulness. It operates from 5am to 11pm and the fare is a flat Y3. Signs are in English and easy to understand. Stations are marked by a blue sign with the capital 'D'. Beijing Train Station is a stop on the circle subway line (Beijingzhan). The new Line 5 is due for completion in 2007.

Taxi

Taxis are cheap and plentiful: the standard per-kilometre charge ranges from Y1.20 to Y2, with a Y10 minimum. Make sure your driver turns on the meter, especially coming from the airport or the train station. Most taxi drivers do not speak English (although some are learning in preparation for the 2008 Olympics!); it's best to have somebody write down your destination so you can show it to the driver.

AROUND BEIJING

GREAT WALL OF CHINA 长城

Stretching 7200km from the Bo Sea in the east to the Gobi Desert in the west, the Great Wall of China is truly a wonder, due to both its breathtaking beauty and its ancient architectural achievement. Several sections of the Great Wall, particularly at Badaling, have been recently revamped for the benefit of tourists. Also renovated but less touristed are the sections at Simatai and Jinshanling.

History

The 'original' construction of the Great Wall is credited to Emperor Qin Shihuang (221–207 BC), China's first sovereign emperor. He accomplished this feat by reconstructing and linking the ruins of older walls, which had been built by the vassal states under the Zhou dynasty in the 7th century BC. The result was a magnificent 4800km stretch of wall, which was meant to keep out the marauding nomads in the north. The effort required hundreds of thousands of workers, many of them political prisoners. Over the course of 10 years, an estimated one million people died; legend has it that the bodies of deceased workers were among the building materials used.

By the collapse of the Qin, the Great Wall had already started to crumble due to years of neglect. Emperor Han Wu-Di once again undertook the task of rebuilding the existing wall, and extending it 480km further west into the Gobi Desert. During this period, the wall served mainly as an elevated highway, along which men and equipment could be transported across mountainous terrain. Furthermore, the Hans established a system of smoke signals, by which they could warn each other of enemy attacks. Thus, the wall protected traders and explorers who were travelling the ancient caravan routes between China and Europe.

The wall that you see today is largely a product of the Ming dynasty (1368–1644). The Ming wall was taller, longer and more ornate than any earlier incarnations. It was also stronger, due in part to the advanced brick technology the Ming workers used.

Badaling 八达岭

Most visitors see the Great Wall at **Badaling** (Bādálíng Chángchéng; ☎ 6912 1338/1423/1520; admission Y45; ☺ 6am-10pm summer, 7am-6pm winter), 70km northwest of Beijing, at an elevation of 1000m. The section of masonry at Badaling was first built during the Ming dynasty, and was heavily restored in the 1950s and the 1980s. Punctuated with watchtowers, the 6m-wide wall is clad in brick, typical of the stonework employed by the Ming when they restored and expanded the fortification.

The surrounding scenery is raw and impressive and this is the place to come to see the wall snaking off over the undulating hills. Also come here for guard rails, souvenir stalls, a fairground feel and the companionship of squads of tourists surging over the ramparts. If you time your visit to coincide with a summer weekend, you won't be able to move against the wall of humanity on the battlements. Come during the week instead, and if possible, during the colder months when it's covered in snow.

Cable cars exist for the weary (round trip Y50), but don't take the slide (Y30) as it's a colossal waste of money.

Apart from the pristine battlements, you can be conveyed back into history via 15-minute films about the Great Wall at the **Great Wall Circle Vision Theatre** (admission Y25; ☼ 9am-9.45pm), a 360-degree amphitheatre. The admission fee also gets you into the **China Great Wall Museum** (☼ 9am-4pm).

GETTING THERE & AWAY

The cheapest and easiest way to get to Badaling is to take bus 919 from just north of the old gate of Deshengmen, about 500m east of the Jishuitan subway stop. Buses leave regularly from 5.30am. Ordinary buses take two hours and cost Y5, while the faster, nonstop luxury air-con buses take one hour and cost Y10. The last bus leaves Badaling for Beijing at 6.30pm.

CITS (☎ 6515 8566), the Beijing Tourist Information Center, **Panda Tours** (☎ 6525 8372; www.pandatourchina.com), big hotels and everyone else in the tourist business does a tour to Badaling. Watch out for high-price hotel tours (up to Y300 per person).

A taxi to the wall and back will cost a minimum of Y400 for an eight-hour hire with a maximum of four passengers.

Mutianyu 慕田峪

The 2250m-long granite section of wall at **Mutianyu** (Mùtiányù; ☎ 6162 6873; admission Y35; ☼ 6.30am-5.30pm), 90km northeast of Beijing, was developed as a decoy alternative to Badaling and is, on the whole, a less commercial experience. Despite some motivated hawking and tourist clutter, the stretch of wall is notable for its numerous Ming dynasty guard towers and stirring views. The wall is also equipped with a **cable car** (round trip Y50; ☼ 8.30am-4.30pm). October is the best month to visit, for the autumn colours of the trees that envelop the surrounding countryside.

GETTING THERE & AWAY

From **Dongzhimen long-distance bus station** (Dōngzhímén Chángtú Qìchēzhàn; ☎ 6467 4995) you can take either bus 916 (Y8, one hour) or 936 (Y5) to Huairou then change for a minibus to Mutianyu (Y25). Alternatively, the less frequent 916 branch line goes all the way from Dongzhimen to Mutianyu (Y15).

Tour bus 6 (☎ 6601 8285) runs to Mutianyu (Y50) from outside the South Cathedral at Xuanwumen, operating between 6.30am and 8.30am on Saturday, Sunday and public holidays from April to October.

Juyongguan 居庸关

Originally constructed in the 5th century and rebuilt by the Ming, **Juyongguan** (Juyong Pass; ☎ 6977 1665; admission Y40; ☼ 6am-4pm) was considered one of the most strategically important sections of the Great Wall, only 50km northwest of Beijing. However, this section has been thoroughly renovated to the point where you don't feel as if you're walking on a part of history. Still, if you're in a hurry, it's the closest section of the wall to the city and is usually quiet. You can do the steep and somewhat strenuous circuit in under two hours.

Juyongguan is on the road to Badaling, so any of the buses for Badaling listed earlier will get you there (but tell the bus driver you want to be dropped off at Juyongguan Changcheng).

Simatai 司马台

The stirring remains at **Simatai** (Sīmǎtái; ☎ 6903 5025/5030; admission Y30; ☼ 8am-5pm), 110km northeast of Beijing, make for a more exhilarating Great Wall experience. Built during the reign of Ming dynasty emperor Hongwu, the 19km stretch is marked by watchtowers, steep plunges and scrambling ascents.

Not for the faint-hearted, this rough section of the wall is very steep. A few slopes have a 70-degree incline and you need both hands free, so bring a day-pack to hold your camera and other essentials. The **cable car** (round trip Y50) could be an alternative to a sprained ankle. Take strong shoes with a good grip.

Simatai has some unusual features, such as 'obstacle-walls' – walls-within-walls used for defending against enemies who had already scaled the Great Wall. There's also a **toboggan ride** (Y30), and unfazed by the dizzying terrain, hawkers make an unavoidable appearance.

GETTING THERE & AWAY

Direct minibuses depart from **Dongzhimen long-distance bus station** (☎ 6467 4995) from 6am (Y20). Otherwise take a minibus from

Dongzhimen to Miyun (Y8, 1¼ hours) and change to a minibus to Simatai, or a taxi (round trip Y120).

Weekend tour bus 12 (☎ 6601 8285) leaves from outside the South Cathedral at Xuanwumen for Simatai (Y50) between 6.30am and 8.30am Saturday, Sunday and public holidays. Backpacker hotels often run morning trips by **minibus** (not incl admission ticket Y60; ⏱ 8.30am). A taxi from Beijing for the day costs about Y400.

Jinshanling 金山岭

Though not as steep (and therefore not as impressive) as Simatai, the Great Wall at **Jinshanling** (Jīnshānlíng Chángchéng; admission Y40), near the town of Gubeikou, has 24 watchtowers and is considerably less developed (and therefore much quieter) than any of the sites previously mentioned, despite undergoing some restoration work.

Perhaps the most interesting thing about Jinshanling is that it's the starting point for a 10km hike to Simatai. It takes nearly four hours because the trail is steep and stony. Parts of the wall along the route are in a state of ruin, but it can be traversed without too much difficulty. Upon arrival at Simatai, however, you may have to buy another ticket.

You can do the walk in the opposite direction, but getting a ride back to Beijing from Simatai is easier than from Jinshanling. Of course, getting a ride should be no problem if you've made arrangements with your driver to pick you up (and didn't pay in advance).

To get to Jinshanling from **Dongzhimen long-distance bus station** (☎ 6467 4995), take a minibus to Miyun (Y8, 1¼ hours), then change to a minibus to Gubeikou, and get off at Bakeshiying (Y7).

Directory

ACCOMMODATION

For several, if not all, nights of your Trans-Siberian journey your bed will be on the train (for the options, see p331). But at either end of your journey and most likely at points along it you'll be looking for more traditional accommodation.

Russia

Russia's range of accommodation is constantly improving, with everything from camp sites and cosy homestays to five-star luxury hotels on offer. You'll occasionally come across hotels (Novosibirsk is infamous) that refuse to let you stay because you're a foreigner, or will only allow you to stay in the most expensive rooms. Other-

wise you can generally stay where you like, though beware that cheaper hotels will rarely be able to register your visa.

It's a good idea to book a few nights in advance for Moscow and St Petersburg, elsewhere it's usually not necessary. Make bookings by email or fax rather than telephone, and note that many hotels charge a *bron* (booking surcharge) up to 50% of the first night's accommodation rate.

If you're looking for cheaper places to stay, head for the smaller towns or consider a homestay; many travel agencies can arrange these. Moscow, Irkutsk and St Petersburg each have one or more youth or backpacker hostels, most able to offer visa support. Camping in the wild is generally allowed – check with locals if you're in doubt. *Kempingi* (organised camp sites) are rare and, usually, only open from June to September. Unlike Western camp sites, small wooden cabins often take up much of the space, leaving little room for tents. Some *kempingi* are in quite attractive woodland settings but communal toilets and washrooms are often in poor condition and other facilities few.

Komnaty otdykha (resting rooms) are found at all major train stations along the Trans-Siberian route and are very cheap (from R10 per hour, R120 per half-day), which is why they are often booked up. Rooms are usually shared and there are often no bathrooms. At the bigger stations, such as Novosibirsk, the *komnaty otdykha* are excellent and the private luxe rooms are well worth the extra expense. At many other stations the rooms are very basic.

In hotels *potselenye* (twin rooms) are occasionally cheaper than singles. It's often possible to pay half again when only one person is staying, especially in small towns – though in twin rooms you may end up sharing with a stranger. A *lyux* room equates to a suite with a sitting room in addition to the bedroom and bathroom. A *polu-lyux* room is somewhat less spacious. Note that size doesn't always equate to better quality.

Often each hotel floor has a *dezhurnaya* (floor lady) to keep an eye on it and to supply guests with snacks, bottled drinks or boiled water. They might even do your laundry.

DIRECTORY

Check-out time is usually noon, but it's unlikely that anyone will mind if you stay an extra hour or two. It's usually no problem storing your luggage.

Hotels with significant numbers of foreign guests also attract prostitutes; you'll usually be left alone if you make it clear you're not interested.

For a hostel dorm bed in Moscow and St Petersburg you can expect to pay around R600, while a double room with bathroom in a budget hotel in these cities will cost anything up to R2500. Elsewhere budget hotels can be as cheap as R300 a night with shared facilities, although R600 is a more realistic minimum for many cities.

You'll pay R600 to R1500 for a midrange twin (except in Moscow and St Petersburg, where it's R2500 to R5000). Luxury hotels in the major cities charge US$200 for singles, US$400 for doubles. In provincial cities, expect to pay upwards from R2000, although you may get better prices through a travel agent. Prices in top-end places will usually be quoted in dollars, sometimes euros, on top of which you'll typically pay 20% Value Added Tax (VAT) and 5% local tax (not included in prices quoted in this book).

China

Overall, accommodation in China is quite humdrum. Be warned that the star rating

---

PRACTICALITIES

■ Electrical power in Russia, China and Mongolia is 220V, 50Hz. Sockets in Russia and Mongolia are designed to accommodate two round prongs in the European style. Chinese plugs come in at least four designs: three-pronged angled pins as used in Australia; three-pronged round pins as in Hong Kong; two-pronged flat pins as in the USA; or two narrow round pins as in Europe. For more information, check www.kropla.com.

■ Russia and Mongolia both follow the international metric system. Although China also officially subscribes to the metric system, ancient Chinese weights and measures persist. Fruit and vegetables are sold by the *jin*, which is 0.5kg (1.32lb). Tea and herbal medicines are usually sold by the *liang*, which is 37.5g (1.32oz).

■ In Moscow the best source of English-language news is the daily *Moscow Times*, available free across the city; in St Petersburg, the *St Petersburg Times* is an excellent free biweekly read. Top-end hotels in these cities usually have copies of the *International Herald-Tribune*, the *Financial Times* and occasionally some of the British broadsheets, as well as weekly magazines such as *The Economist* and *Time*. Elsewhere in Russia the pickings of English media are very slim, and most likely nonexistent. China's main English-language newspaper is the *China Daily*. Imported English-language newspapers and magazines can be bought from five-star hotel bookshops. Look out for free expat-focused English-language listings magazines, including *That's Beijing* and *Time Out Beijing*. In Ulaanbaatar there are two English-language weekly newspapers, *The Mongol Messenger* and *The UB Post*, both good for local news and entertainment information. On the train you'll sometimes come across the free glossy monthly magazine *Ekspress* (in Russian). It's also common for deaf-and-dumb hawkers to sell newspapers, magazines and books along the carriages – a pile will be left in your compartment to leaf through.

■ Radio in Russia is broken into three bands: AM, UKV (66MHz to 77MHz) and FM (100MHz to 107MHz). A Western-made FM radio usually won't go lower than 85MHz. The BBC's World Service's short-wave (SW) frequencies in the morning, late evening and night are near 9410kHz, 12,095kHz (the best) and 15,070kHz, though the exact setting varies with locations. In China listen to the **BBC World Service** (www.bbc.co.uk/worldservice/tuning/) or **Voice of America** (www.voa.gov) – check the websites for frequencies. China Radio International (CRI) is China's overseas radio service and broadcasts in about 40 foreign languages. In Mongolia BBC World Service has a nonstop service at 103.1FM. Local stations worth trying include Jag (107FM), Blue Sky (100.9FM) and Radio Ulaanbaatar (102.5FM). Voice of America news is occasionally broadcast on 106.6FM.

at China's hotels can be very misleading. Hotels are often awarded four or five stars, when they are patently a star lower in ranking. Take time to wander round and make a quick inspection of the overall quality or stick to chain hotels with recognisable names.

Camping is not really feasible in China, especially within sight of a town or village. Wilderness camping is more appealing, but most areas require special permits, which are difficult to obtain. The good news, however, is that other cheap accommodation options are available. University dormitories sometimes rent rooms to tourists, and there is a good range of hostels in Beijing.

The price and quality of hotels in China vary considerably, especially in Beijing. A typical hotel room is a 'twin' – two single beds in one room. A 'single room' (one bed per room) is a rarity, although they do exist. The Western concept of a 'double room' (a room with one double bed shared by two people) is also rare in China. In most cases, your choice will be between a twin room or a suite. However, two people are usually allowed to occupy a twin room for the same price as one person, so sharing is a good way to cut expenses.

A dorm bed in the centre of Beijing goes for about US$7. Twin hotel rooms there start at around US$25.

Mongolia

Mongolia is perhaps the most perfect camping destination in the world. Excellent camping sites are everywhere, even near Ulaanbaatar in places such as Terelj. If you are travelling in the countryside, camping is an even better option, considering the lack of hotels and the expense of *ger* (yurt) camps. Be sure to carry enough supplies and water for the duration of your stay, since they may be hard to come by, depending on where you are.

A tourist *ger* camp is a 'camping ground' with traditional *gers,* a separate building for toilets and showers, and a restaurant-bar. The *gers* are furnished with two or three beds. Toilets and bathrooms, which are separate and shared, are usually clean. Most *ger* camps in Terelj are open from June to September. In the Gobi Desert, they are open from May to October.

Ulaanbaatar has an abundant range of guesthouses targeting foreign backpackers.

Most guesthouses are in apartment blocks and have dorm beds as well as private rooms. Many guesthouses also offer laundry services, Internet connection and travel services. Some of the guesthouses can also arrange for long-term guests (staying one week or more) to rent a private apartment. At around US$20 per day, an apartment is much better value than Ulaanbaatar's hotels, which are decent but overpriced. Comfortable and clean, guesthouse and apartment rooms usually have hot water and satellite TV, and maybe even English-speaking staff members.

Dorm beds at Ulaanbaatar guesthouses start as low as US$3, private rooms around US$10. You will be hard-pressed to find a double at a midrange hotel for less than US$40.

Ger camps typically charge US$30 to US$40 per person per night, including three hearty meals, but prices are negotiable, and they may drop considerably if you bring your own food.

ACTIVITIES

The countryside traversed by the Trans-Siberian rail routes is a veritable playground for outdoor (and some indoor) activities. Some of the options, from steaming in *banai* (hot baths) to diving and ice fishing in Lake Baikal, are covered below.

Banai

A combination of dry sauna, steam bath, massage and plunges into ice-cold water, the *banya* is a weekly event that is a regular part of Russian life (see p44). All Russian cities will have *banai,* and they're generally worth visiting.

Beaches

There are some good beaches at the Vladivostok end of the Trans-Siberian, especially if you head out to the more remote areas of Primorsky Kray. In St Petersburg, the locals are partial to a spot of sunbaking beside the Peter & Paul Fortress. Perhaps more surprising are the opportunities to strip off and lounge on the sand within Russia. Moscow, Kazan and Khabarovsk all have riverside beach areas where the locals flock on steamy days. On the artificial Ob Sea at Novosibirsk (p165) there's even a nudist beach.

DIRECTORY

Cycling

Poor roads and manic drivers are two of the main hazards to cyclists in Russia. Otherwise you will find rural Russians quite fascinated and friendly towards long-distance riders. Just make certain you have a bike designed for the harshest of conditions and that you carry plenty of spare parts.

Cycling is a practical means of transportation, as well as an entertaining way to explore Beijing. The neighbourhoods and *hutong* (narrow alleyways) seem to have been built with bicycles in mind, as they are the only vehicles that can fit down some of them.

In Ulaanbaatar, cycling is more enjoyable (and safer) outside the city.

There are a number of agencies offering organised bike tours:

Ekaterinburg Guide Center (☎ 343-268 1604; www
.ekaterinburg-guide.com; ul Krasnoarmeyskaya 1, side entrance, Yekaterinburg)
Team Gorky (☎ 8312-651 999; www.teamgorky.ru; ul 40 let Oktyabrya 1a, Nizhny Novgorod)
Ural Expeditions & Tours (☎ 343-376 2800; http://
welcome-ural.ru; 23 Posadskaya ul, Yekaterinburg)

Diving

Fancy diving in Lake Baikal? Such specialist trips can be arranged through **Diveworldwide** (☎ 0845 130 6980; www.diveworldwide.com) in the UK, or **MGU** (☎ 095-105 7799; www.dive.ru/English) in Moscow.

Fishing

Siberia and the Russian Far East are an angler's paradise with rivers swollen with grayling and various species of salmon. Organised fishing trips, however, can be heart-stoppingly expensive. While it is possible to go it alone and just head off with rod and tackle, most regions have severe restrictions on fishing. Travel agencies in Irkutsk (p191), Ulan-Ude (p213), Khabarovsk (p225) and Vladivostok (p232) can arrange fishing trips in their regions.

Hiking & Mountaineering

The best place for trekking along the Trans-Siberian route is around Lake Baikal, with the most adventurous options being at the northern end of the lake. There's even a project to create a hiking trail around the entire circumference of the lake: see www
.earthisland.org (select 'Baikal Watch' from the Earth Island Projects drop-down menu) for details.

Many of the towns that lie along the Baikal-Amur Mainline (Baikalo-Amurskaya Magistral, or BAM) are good bases for heading out into the wilds and further afield. Krasnoyarsk's Stolby Nature Reserve (p187) is a striking landscape in which you can easily organise a day's hike. The hills and islands around Vladivostok also provide a full range of trekking options.

HIKING SAFETY

Before embarking on a hike, consider the following:

- Be sure you're healthy and feel comfortable about hiking for a sustained period. The nearest village in Russia can be vastly further away than in other countries.

- Get the best information you can about the physical and environmental conditions along your intended route. Russian 'trails' are generally nominal ideas rather than marked footpaths so employing a guide is very wise.

- Walk only in regions, and on trails, within your realm of experience.

- Be prepared for severe and sudden changes in the weather and terrain; always take wet-weather gear.

- Pack essential survival gear including emergency food rations and a leak-proof water bottle.

- If you can, find a hiking companion. At the very least tell someone where you're going and refer to your compass frequently so you can find your way back.

- Unless you're planning a camping trip, start early so you can make it home before dark.

- Allow more time than you anticipate.

- Consider renting, or even buying (then later reselling), a pack horse, especially in southern Siberia where this is fairly inexpensive.

Possibilities for more serious mountain-climbing exist in the Sayan Mountains (on the Russian-Mongolian border; p184) and in the Baikalsky Range on the western shore of Lake Baikal.

Both China and Mongolia offer excellent opportunities for hiking within day trips of the capitals. The most popular (and deservedly so) locales for hikes near Beijing are along the Great Wall (p292), with a wide variety in terms of levels of challenge and degree of remoteness. Hiking destinations near Ulaanbaatar include Manzushir Khiid (p267), the Gorkhi-Terelj National Park (p268) and Tsetseegun Uul (p268).

Horse Riding
A visit to Mongolia is not complete without a ride on a horse. *Ger* camps at Terelj (p268) rent horses and can direct riders to trails with some spectacular scenery. Most travel agencies in Ulaanbaatar also organise more extensive treks.

River Trips & Rafting
River trips are offered across Russia from May to October, with cruises along the Volga being particularly popular. It's possible to sail between St Petersburg and Kazan, with stops at Moscow and Nizhny Novgorod en route; see p120 for details of agents offering tickets on such cruises. Other river trips include excursions along the Irtysh between Omsk and Tobolsk (p165), along the Yenisey from Krasnoyarsk (p189) and on the Amur from Khabarovsk (p229). And, of course, there are also the sailings down the Angara River from Irkutsk to Lake Baikal (p197).

For those looking for a bit more adventure on the water, rafting trips can be organised out of Nizhny Novgorod, Yekaterinburg, Novosibirsk (in the Altai region of southern Siberia), and Vladivostok.

Winter Sports
With all that snow could you really pass up the chance to indulge in some winter sports while crossing Siberia? Possibilities include cross-country skiing, skating, troika rides – even dog sledding! Lake Baikal is a particularly spectacular place to visit in winter: at Baikalsk there's a ski resort and you can even drive across the frozen lake and go ice fishing.

BUSINESS HOURS
Russia
In Russia government offices open from 9am or 10am to 5pm or 6pm weekdays. Banks usually open from 9am to 6pm Monday to Friday, and some open 9am to 5pm Saturday. Currency-exchange booths open long hours, and on Saturday and sometimes Sunday too. Museum hours change often, as do their weekly days off. Most stop selling tickets 30 minutes to an hour before closing.

Most Russian shops are open Monday to Saturday, although increasingly you will find seven-day and even some 24-hour operations. Food shops tend to open from 8am to 8pm except for a *pereryv* (break) between 1pm and 2pm or 2pm and 3pm; some close later, and some open Sunday until 5pm. It's rare not to be able to find kiosks selling food and drink around the clock. Restaurants typically open from noon to midnight except for a break between afternoon and evening meals.

China & Mongolia
Government offices and businesses in China and Mongolia operate on a five-day work week, generally from 9am to 5pm, often closing for lunch between noon and 2pm. Shops and museums are usually open on weekends, and may be closed instead for one or two days midweek. Some branches of the Bank of China may be open on the weekend.

In Ulaanbaatar, however, the banks usually open from 9am to 7pm weekdays, and there are several offering 24-hour banking. Many museums and tourist attractions have shorter hours and more days off in winter.

CHILDREN
Travelling in Russia, China or Mongolia with children can be a ball as long as you come well prepared with the right attitudes, equipment and patience.

Practicalities
Baby-changing rooms are not common in any of the three countries and you wouldn't want to use many public toilets yourself, let alone change your baby's nappy in them. Nappies, powdered milk and baby food are widely available except in very rural areas.

Finding English-language kids' publications will be a challenge, although there's no shortage of toy shops.

Lonely Planet's *Travel with Children* contains useful advice on how to cope with kids on the road and what to bring to make things go more smoothly.

Sights & Activities

In Moscow and St Petersburg there are the old stand-bys of the zoo, various parks and the circus, but elsewhere, diversions are more problematic. On trains, children are likely to find playmates of their own age, but as many distractions such as toys and books as you can manage would be wise. Consider using the trip as an opportunity to teach children about the region's history and geography.

One thing to inquire about in the summer months are the children's railway parks dotted all across Russia. They have actual working trains which are accurate small-scale replicas of the bigger ones. Children take part in all of the activities from ticket sales to engineers; it's all in Russian, but it could also be interesting to watch and you could arrange for a guide to assist you with translations. The website **Children's Railways** (http://railways.id.ru/english/index.html) gives details of the parks. There's also one in Harbin (p276).

Beijing's historical and architectural masterpieces will probably bore the children to pieces. That is, only until they spot the toboggans at the Great Wall at Mutianyu (p293) and the flying saucer boats at Beihai Park (p285). Other favourite spots for children in Beijing include **Ritan Park** (☎ 010-8563 5038; Ritan Lu; adult Y1; ☯ 6am-9pm; Ⓜ Chaoyangmen) and the **Beijing Zoo & Beijing Aquarium** (☎ 010-6831 4411; 137 Xizhimenwai Dajie; adult Y10, pandas Y5 extra; ☯ 7.30am-5.30pm; Ⓜ Xizhimen). Harbin also has the Siberian Tiger Park (p275).

Unfortunately Ulaanbaatar does not cater so much to visiting children, although the dinosaur exhibit at the Museum of Natural History (p261) should certainly capture their imaginations.

CLIMATE CHARTS

See p13 and p280 for advice on the best times to visit the regions covered by the Trans-Siberian Railway.

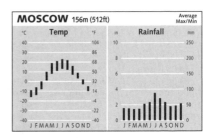

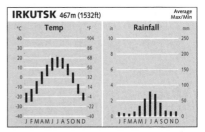

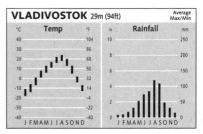

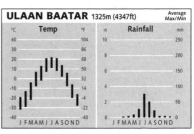

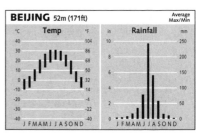

CUSTOMS
Russia

Customs controls are relatively relaxed these days, although if you leave Russia by a land border, they can be lengthy. Apart from the usual restrictions, bringing in and out large amounts of cash is limited, although the amount at which you have to go through the red channel changes frequently. At the time of writing visitors were allowed to bring in US$10,000 (or equivalent) in currency and take out US$3000 without making a customs declaration.

On entering Russia you might be given a *deklaratsiya* (customs declaration), on which you should list any currency you are carrying and any items of worth. List mobile phones, cameras and laptops to avoid any potential problems on leaving Russia. It's best if you can get your declaration stamped on entry (to do so go through the red lane at bigger airports) and then simply show the same declaration on exiting Russia. However, sometimes customs points are totally unstaffed, so it's not always possible. The system seems to be in total flux, with officials usually very happy for you to fill out declarations on leaving the country if necessary.

If you plan to export anything vaguely 'arty' – manuscripts, instruments, coins, jewellery, antiques, antiquarian books – it must be assessed by the **Committee for Culture** (Moscow ☎ 095-921 3258; ul Neglinnaya 8/10, room 298; St Petersburg ☎ 812-311 5196; Malaya Morskaya ul 17). The bureaucrats will issue a receipt for tax paid (usually 100% of the purchase price; bring your sales docket), presented to customs on your way out. If you buy something large, a photograph is usually fine for assessment purposes.

China

Chinese customs generally pay tourists little attention. There are no restrictions on foreign currency, but you should declare any cash exceeding US$5000 (or its equivalent in another currency).

Objects considered to be antiques require a certificate and red seal to clear customs. To get the proper certificate and red seal, your antiques must be inspected by the **Relics Bureau** (Wénwù Jiàndìng; ☎ 010-6401 4608, no English spoken). Basically anything made before 1949 is considered an antique and needs a certificate, and if it was made

before 1795 it cannot legally be taken out of the country.

Mongolia

Again, customs procedures are fairly straightforward and the main issue for the foreign traveller is the export of antiques. For any antiques you must have a receipt and customs certificate from the place you bought them; most reliable shops in Ulaanbaatar can provide this. If you don't get one of these you'll need to get one from the **Centre of Cultural Heritage** (☎ 011-312 735, 323 747) in the Palace of Culture in Ulaanbaatar. You'll need to fill in a form giving your passport number, details of where the antique was purchased and two photos of the antique itself. If you have anything that even *looks* old, it is a good idea to get a document to indicate that it is not an antique. That goes for Buddha images and statues as well.

DANGERS & ANNOYANCES

Russia, China and Mongolia are generally safe countries and crime against foreigners is rare. Pickpocketing is probably the biggest threat for the traveller, especially in crowded places such as public transport, markets and tourist attractions. The risk is greatly reduced if you keep valuables in money belts or under a layer of clothes. Hotels are generally quite safe, but leaving valuables lying around your room would be tempting providence. Always take precautions at youth hostels and guesthouses, where other travellers may be trying to subsidise their journeys.

You needn't be too concerned about the so-called 'Mafia'. Russia's organised crime problem is far more complex, and far less of a threat to visitors, than one might guess from reading an issue of *Newsweek*. In general, Moscow's and St Petersburg's streets are about as safe, or as dangerous, as those of New York or London and, with the possible exception of Irkutsk (where some muggings have been reported), you're highly unlikely to suffer any problems in Siberia or the Russian Far East.

The key is to be neither paranoid nor insouciant. Use common sense and be aware that it's pretty obvious you're a Westerner. Anything you can do to try to fit in is a good idea, so scrap the day-pack and carry your goods in a plastic bag.

On the whole the trains are reasonably safe, but it always pays to take simple precautions with your luggage. If you've got the compartment to yourself, ask the *provodnitsa* (carriage attendant) to lock it when you leave for the restaurant car or get out at the station platforms.

Queuing is basically nonexistent in China and Mongolia and there are very specific rules for it in Russia. In most cases, neither being polite nor getting angry will help. If you have the head for it, sharpen your elbows, learn a few scowling phrases in the appropriate languages, and plough head-first through the throng. Good luck.

Spitting in China is only slightly less popular than badminton. Although it is technically illegal in Beijing, everyone does it everywhere, loudly and flamboyantly.

Mosquitoes are the bane of summer throughout the region. Mostly, they're an annoyance, but in rural areas of Siberia they can be a grave health threat. For some precautions to take against them, see p340.

Although the situation is constantly improving, plumbing is at best erratic and at worst atrocious in all three countries.

Scams

In Russia, be very wary of officials, such as police (or people posing as police), asking to see your papers or tickets at train stations – there's a fair chance they are on the lookout for a bribe and will try to find anything wrong with your documents, or basically hold them for a ransom. The only course of action is to remain calm, polite and stand your ground. Try to enlist the help of a passerby to translate for you (or at least witness what is going on).

Another scam involves the use of devices in ATMs that read credit card and PIN details when you withdraw money from the machines, enabling accounts to be accessed and additional funds withdrawn. In general, it is safest to use ATMs in carefully guarded public places such as major hotels and restaurants.

It's possible on the Trans-Siberian and Trans-Mongolian railway routes to encounter official-looking men or women requesting that you buy insurance for around US$10 – there is no need to do this. We've had reports, too, that the carriage attendants on the Mongolian trains are asking for a small

fee for use of hot water from the samovar: there's no obligation to pay this.

In Russia, there have been reports of employees of currency-exchange offices putting glue or chewing gum on the tray where they put the money, so one note sticks to it – it's usually a R1000 or R500 note. The simple way to avoid this situation is to count your money immediately.

DISABLED TRAVELLERS

Russia, China and Mongolia can be difficult places for disabled travellers. Most buildings, buses and trains are not wheelchair accessible. In China and Russia, crossing busy streets often requires using underground walkways with many steps. Uneven pavements in the cities and rough roads in the countryside make for uncomfortable and potentially dangerous travel.

Travelling on Trans-Siberian trains, while not impossible for the disabled, will certainly be a challenge. People in wheelchairs will have to be carried on and off the train and into their compartments, not to mention to the utterly disabled-unfriendly toilets.

Before setting off get in touch with your national support organisation (preferably with the travel officer, if there is one). The website www.everybody.co.uk has an airline directory that provides information on the disability-friendly facilities offered by various airlines. There are a number of organisations that offer general travel advice:

Accessible Journeys (☎ 800-846 4537; www.disability travel.com; USA)

Holiday Care Service (☎ 0845-124 9974; www.holiday care.org.uk; 7th fl, Sunley House, 4 Bedford Park, Croydon, Surrey CR0 2AP, UK)

Mobility International USA (☎ 541-343 1284; www .miusa.org; PO Box 10767, Eugene, Oregon 974400, USA)

Nican (☎ 02-6285 3713; www.nican.com.au; PO Box 407, Curtin, ACT 2605, Australia)

DISCOUNT CARDS

Full-time students and people aged under 26 can sometimes (but not always) get a substantial discount on admissions – always flash your student card or International Student Identity Card (ISIC) before paying. If you're not a student but are under 26, ask a student agency at home for an ISIC Youth Card.

Senior citizens also *might* get a discount, but no promises: carry your pension card or passport anyway.

EMBASSIES & CONSULATES
Embassies & Consulates Abroad
RUSSIA

Check out www.russianembassy.net for a full list of overseas Russian embassies and consulates.

Australia Canberra (☎ 02-6295 9033; rusemb@dynamite.com.au; 78 Canberra Ave, Griffith, ACT 2603); Sydney consulate (☎ 02-9326 1188; russcon@ozemail.com.au)

Canada Ottawa (☎ 613-235 4341; rusemb@intranet.ca; 285 Charlotte St, Ottawa, Canada K1N 8J5); Montreal consulate (☎ 514-843 5901; consulat@dsuper.net); Toronto consulate (☎ 416-962 9911; rusconsul@bellnet.ca)

France Paris (☎ 01 45 04 05 50; rusembfr@club-internet.fr; 40-50 Blvd Lannes, 75116 Paris); Marseilles consulate (☎ 04 91 77 15 15; consrus@aix.pacwan.net); Strasbourg consulate (☎ 03 88 36 73 15; representationpermde russie@wanadoo.fr)

Germany Berlin (☎ 030-220 2821; russembassyg@trionet.de; Unter den Linden 63-65, 10117 Berlin); Bonn consulate (☎ 228-619 6076; bonn@russische-botschaft.de); Hamburg consulate (☎ 40-227 3424; general.konsulat-hamburg@metronet.de); Leipzig consulate (☎ 341-585 1876; rusgenkon_leipzig@t-online.de); Munich consulate (☎ 89-592 503; ruskonsmchn@t-online.de); Rostock consulate (☎ 381-492 2742)

Ireland (☎ 1-492 3525; russiane@indigo.ie; 184-186 Orwell Rd, Rathgar, Dublin 14)

Japan Tokyo (☎ 03-3583 4224; rosconsl@ma.kcom.ne.jp; 2-1-1 Azabudai, Minato-ku, Tokyo 106-0041); Niigata consulate (☎ 25-244 6015; niruscon@fsinet.or.jp); Osaka consulate (☎ 66-848 3452; ruscons@mb.kcom.ne.jp); Sapporo consulate (☎ 11-0561 3171; Caa09680@smtp01.odn.ne.jp)

Netherlands (☎ 70-345 1300; ambrusnl@euronet.nl; Andries Bickerweg 2, 2517 JP Den Haag)

New Zealand (☎ 04-476 6113; eor@netlink.co.nz; 57 Messines Rd, Karori, Wellington)

UK London (☎ 020-7229 3628; www.rusemblon.org; 5 Kensington Palace Gardens, London W8 4QX); Edinburgh consulate (☎ 131-225 7098; visa@edconsul.co.uk)

USA Washington (☎ 202-298 5700; 2650 Wisconsin Ave NW, Washington, DC 20007); New York consulate (☎ 212-348 0926; mail@ruscon.org); San Francisco consulate (☎ 415-928 6878; consulsf@sbcglobal.net); Seattle consulate (☎ 206-728 1910; consul@seanet.com)

CHINA

For a full list of diplomatic representation abroad, go to www.fmprc.gov.cn/eng/and click on Missions Overseas.

Australia Canberra (☎ 02-6273 4780, 6273 4781; www.chinaembassy.org.au; 15 Coronation Dr, Yarralumla, ACT 2600); Sydney consulate (☎ 02-9699 2216; http://sydney.chineseconsulate.org/eng); Melbourne consulate (☎ 03-9822 0604); Perth consulate (☎ 08-9321 8193)

Canada Ottawa (☎ 613-789 3434; www.chinaembassycanada.org; 515 St Patrick St, Ottawa, Ontario K1N 5H3); Toronto consulate (☎ 416-964 7260); Vancouver consulate (☎ 604-736 3910); Calgary consulate (☎ 403-264 3322)

France Paris (☎ 01 47 36 02 58; www.amb-chine.fr; 9 Ave V Cresson, 92130 Issy les Moulineaux, Paris)

Ireland (☎ 1-269 1707; www.chinaembassy.ie; 40 Ailesbury Rd, Dublin 4)

Japan Tokyo (☎ 03-3403 3389, 3403 3065; 3-4-33 Moto-Azabu, Minato-ku, Tokyo); Fukuoka consulate (☎ 92-713 1121; chinaconsul_fuk_jp@mfa.gov.cn); Osaka consulate (☎ 06-6445 9483; chinaconsul_osa_jp@mfa.gov.cn); Sapporo consulate (☎ 11-563 5563; chinaconsul_sap_jp@mfa.gov.cn)

New Zealand Wellington (☎ 04-472 1382; www.chinaembassy.org.nz; 2-6 Glenmore St, Wellington); Auckland consulate (☎ 9-525 1587)

UK London (☎ 020-7636 8845, 24hr visa information ☎ 0891 880 808; www.chinese-embassy.org.uk; 31 Portland Place, London); Manchester consulate (☎ 0161-224 7480); Edinburgh consulate (☎ 0131-316 4789)

USA Washington (☎ 202-338 6688; www.china-embassy.org; room 110, 2201 Wisconsin Ave NW, Washington, DC); Chicago consulate (☎ 312-803 0098); Houston consulate (☎ 713-524 4311); Los Angeles consulate (☎ 213-380 2508); New York consulate (☎ 212-330 7410); San Francisco consulate (☎ 415-563 9232)

MONGOLIA

Canada (☎ 613-569-3830; www.mongolembassy.org; 151 Slater St, Suite 503, Ottawa, ON K1P 5H3)

China Beijing (☎ 010-6532 6216; www.mongolianembchina.org.cn; 2 Xiushui Beilu, Jianguomenwai Dajie, Beijing); Hohhot consulate (☎ 0471-430 3254; fax 0471-430 3250; Xincheng Gu Wulanxiagu, Bldg No 5, Hohhot)

France (☎ 01 46 05 23 18; info@ambassademongolie.fr; 5 Ave Robert Schumann, 92100 Boulogne-Billancourt, Paris)

Germany (☎ 030-447 35122; mongolbot@aol.com; Dietzgen-Str 31, 13156, Berlin)

Japan (☎ 033-469 2088; embmong@gol.com; 21-4 Kumiyama-cho, Shibuya-ku, Tokyo 150-0047)

Kazakhstan (☎ 3272-200 865; monkazel@kazmail.asdc.kz; Ul Aubakerova 1/1, Almaty)

Russia Moscow (☎ 095-290 6792; bayar@msk.tsi.ru; Borisoglebsky per 11, Moscow); Irkutsk consulate (☎ 3952-342 145; irconsul@angara.ru; ul Lapina 11, Irkutsk); Ulan-Ude consulate (☎ 3012-220 499; mnc@burnet.ru; Hotel Baikal, ul Erbanova-12, Ulan-Ude) The embassy is close to Smolenskaya metro station. Visas are obtained from the consular section (☎ 095-244 7867; Spasopeskovsky per 7, Moscow) from 9am to 1pm Monday to Friday.

UK (☎ 020-7937 0150; www.embassyofmongolia.co.uk; 7-8 Kensington Ct, London W8 5DL)

USA Washington (☎ 202-333-7117; www.mongolian embassy.us; 2833 M St NW, Washington, DC 20007); New York consulate (☎ 212-472 6517; fax 212-861 9464; 6 East 77th St, New York, NY 10021)

Foreign Embassies & Consulates Along the Route

Generally speaking, embassies won't be much help if you are in some kind of trouble and are at fault. Remember: you are bound by local law and embassies will not be sympathetic if you end up in jail after committing a crime locally, even if such actions are legal in your own country.

In genuine emergencies you might get some assistance, but only if other channels have been exhausted. For example, if you have all your money and documents stolen, the embassy might assist with getting a new passport, but a loan for onward travel is out of the question.

If you will be travelling in these countries for a long period of time (say a month or over) and particularly if you're heading to remote locations, it's wise to register with your embassy. This can be done over the telephone or by email.

RUSSIA
Irkutsk
Mongolia (☎ 3952-342 145; irconsul@angara.ru; ul Lapina 11; ☼ 9.30am-noon & 2.30-5pm Mon, Tue, Thu & Fri) One-month/three-day visas cost US$30/20 processed in nine days, US$43/28 in three to six days, US$55/45 in two days or US$105/85 in 24 hours. Visas for longer stays require invitation letters.

Khabarovsk
China (☎ 4212-302 519; fax 4212-328 390; Lenin Stadium 1) Visa applications taken 10.30am to 1pm Monday, Wednesday and Friday. A visa can be arranged in a day for about R4200 or in a week for R2400.
Japan (☎ 4212-326 907; fax 4212-327 212; ul Pushkina 38a)

Moscow
For a full list of embassies check www.the moscowtimes.ru/travel/facts/embassies .html.
Australia (☎ 095-956 6070; www.australianembassy.ru; Podkolokny per 10A/2)
Canada (☎ 095-105 6000; fax 095-105 6025; Starokony-ushenny per 23)
France (☎ 095-937 1500; www.ambafrance.ru; ul Bolshaya Yakimanka 45)

Germany (☎ 095-937 9500; www.germany.org.ru; Mosfilmovskaya ul 56)
Ireland (☎ 095-937 5911; fax 095-975 2066; Grokholsky per 5)
Netherlands (☎ 095-797 2900; fax 095-797 2904; Kalashny per 6)
UK (☎ 095-956 7200; www.britemb.msk.ru; Smolenskaya nab 10)
USA (☎ 095-728 5000; www.usembassy.state.gov /moscow; Bol Devyatinsky per 8)

Novosibirsk
Germany (☎ 383-223 1411; www.nowosibirsk.diplo.de; Krasny Pr 28)

St Petersburg
Belarus (☎ 812-273 0078; Office 66, nab Robespiera 8/64)
Canada (☎ 812-325 8448; fax 812-325 8364; Malodetskoselsky pr 32B)
France (☎ 812-312 1130; fax 812-311 7283; nab reki Moyki 15)
Germany (☎ 812-327 2400; fax 812-327 3117; Furshtatskaya ul F39)
UK (☎ 812-320 3200; fax 812-325 3111; pl Proletarskoy Diktatury 5)
USA (☎ 812-275 1701; fax 812-110 7022; ul Furshtatskaya 15)

Ulan-Ude
Mongolia (☎ 3012-211 078; ul Profsoyuznaya 6; ☼ Mon, Wed & Fri) Apply for visas from 10am to 12.30pm; collect them at 5pm. One-month tourist visas cost US$30 issued in nine days, US$35 in a week, US$45 in two days, US$55 same day. Transit visas cost US$20 to US$35.

Vladivostok
China (☎ 4232-495 037; Hotel Gavan, ul Krygina 3) Visa applications accepted 9am to 12.30pm Monday, Wednesday and Friday. A visa costs about US$125 and takes three to seven days.
Japan (☎ 4232-267 513; ul Verkhne-Portovaya 46)
Korea (☎ 4232-402 222; ul Pologa 19)
USA (☎ 4232-300 070; ul Pushkinskaya 32)

Yekaterinburg
Germany (☎ 343-359 6399; gk_jeka@yahoo.de; ul Kuybysheva 44)
UK (☎ 343-379 4931; britcon@sky.ru; ul Gogolya 15)
USA (☎ 343-379 4691; www.uscgyekat.ur.ru; ul Gogolya 15)

CHINA
Beijing
There are two main embassy compounds in Beijing – Jianguomenwai and Sanlitun.

Embassies are open from 9am to noon and 1.30pm to 4pm Monday to Friday, but visa departments are usually only open in the morning.

The following embassies are in the Jian-guomenwai area:

Ireland (☎ 010-6532 2691; fax 010-6532 2168; 3 Ritan Donglu)
Japan (☎ 010-6532 2361; fax 010-6532 4625; 7 Ritan Lu)
Mongolia (☎ 010-6532 1203; fax 010-6532 5045; 2 Xiushui Beijie)
New Zealand (☎ 010-6532 2731; fax 010-6532 4317; 1 Ritan Dong Erjie)
UK (☎ 010-6532 1961; fax 010-6532 1937; 11 Guanghua Lu)
USA (☎ 010-6532 3831; fax 010-6532 6057; 3 Xiushui Beijie)

The Sanlitun compound is home to the following embassies:
Australia (☎ 010-6532 2331; fax 010-6532 6957; 21 Dongzhimenwai Dajie)
Canada (☎ 010-6532 3536; fax 010-6532 4072; 19 Dongzhimenwai Dajie)
France (☎ 010-6532 1331; fax 010-6532 4841; 3 Dongsan Jie)
Germany (☎ 010-6532 2161; fax 010-6532 5336; 17 Dongzhimenwai Dajie)
Russia (☎ 010-6532 1381; fax 010-6532 4853; 4 Dongzhimen Beizhongjie) West of the Sanlitun compound in a separate compound.

MONGOLIA
Ulaanbaatar
Canada (☎ 011-328 285; canada@mongolnet.mn; Bodicom Tower, 7th fl, Sükhbaataryn Gudamj)
China (☎ 011-320 955; fax 011-311 943; 5 Zaluuchuudyn Örgön Chölöö) The consular section is to the left of the embassy's front gate.
France (☎ 011-324 519; www.ambafrance-mn.org in French; Apt 48, Diplomatic Services Corps Bldg 95)
Germany (☎ 011-323 325; fax 011-312 118; Negdsen Undestnii Gudamj 7)
Japan (☎ 011-320 777, 313 332; Olympiin Gudamj 6)
Russia (☎ 011-326 836; fax 011-327 018; Peace Ave A6)
UK (☎ 011-458 133; britemb@magicnet.mn; Peace Ave 30)
USA (☎ 011-329 095; www.us-mongolia.com; Ikh Toiruu 59/1)

FESTIVALS & EVENTS
For our selection of the top 10 festivals to attend while travelling along the Trans-Siberian routes, see p15.

January
Russian Orthodox Christmas (Rozhdestvo) On 7 January; begins with midnight church services.

February, March & April
Chinese New Year/Spring Festival Be warned: this is China's biggest holiday and all transport and hotels are booked solid. Although the demand for accommodation skyrockets, many hotels close down at this time and prices rise steeply. If you can't avoid being in China at this time, then book your room in advance and sit tight until the chaos is over. The Chinese New Year will fall on the following dates: 18 February 2007, 7 February 2008 and 26 January 2009.
Easter (Paskha) The main festival of the Orthodox Church year, in March or April. Easter Day begins with celebratory midnight services. Afterwards, people eat *kulichy* (dome-shaped cakes) and *paskha* (curd cakes), and may exchange painted wooden Easter eggs. The devout deny themselves meat, milk, alcohol and sex during Lent's 40-day pre-Easter fasting period.
Guanyin's Birthday The birthday of Guanyin, the Goddess of Mercy, is a fine time to visit China's Buddhist temples, many of which have halls dedicated to the divinity. Guanyin's birthday is the 19th day of the second moon and will fall on the following dates: 6 April 2007 and 26 March 2008.
Ice Festival Held at Khövsgöl Lake, Mongolia, near the border with Russia on 19 to 20 February. This is another chance (besides the Ice Lantern Festival in Harbin) to enter a winter wonderland of ice sculptures.
Lantern Festival This festival in China is not a public holiday, but it is very colourful. People make (or buy) paper lanterns and walk around the streets in the evening holding them. It falls on the 15th day of the first moon, and will be celebrated on the following dates: 5 March 2007, 22 February 2008 and 9 February 2009.
Pancake Week (Maslenitsa) Folk shows and games in Russia celebrate the end of winter, with lots of pancake-eating before Lent (pancakes were a pagan symbol of the sun). Held late February and/or early March.
Tibetan Buddhist New Year (Tsagaalgan) A moveable feast lasting 16 days, Tsagaalgan celebrates the lunar new year and hence advances by about 10 days annually. It's mainly celebrated at family level in Buryatiya (p213).
Winteriada: International Baikal Nordic Games Festival (www.winteriada.ru) Winter games festival held near Irkutsk from February to March.

May
Graduates Day A day for those finishing school in Russia, who parade about their hometowns in traditional student garb; traditionally held on 25 May.

June
Roaring Hoofs International Live Music Festival (www.roaringhoofs.de) Lively music and performing arts

festival. Has been held in June and July in Ulaanbaatar in the past, but check the website for up-to-date information.

September & October

Birthday of Confucius The great sage has his birthday on 28 September. This is an interesting time to visit Beijing's Confucian Temple (p285).

Mid-Autumn Festival Also known as the Moon Festival; this is the time to gaze at the moon and eat tasty *yuè bǐng* (moon cakes); it's also a traditional holiday for lovers. The festival takes place on the 15th day of the eighth moon, and will be celebrated on 6 October 2006, 25 September 2007, 14 September 2008 and 3 October 2009.

November

National Reconciliation Day The old Great October Socialist Revolution Anniversary in Russia – still a big day for Communist Party marches. Otherwise, monarchists mourn and others drink while closing down their dachas for winter. Held on 7 November.

December

Sylvester and New Year The main winter and gift-giving festival in Russia, when gifts are put under the *yolka* (traditional fir tree). See out the old year with vodka and welcome in the new one with champagne while listening to the Kremlin chimes on TV. Held on 31 December and 1 January.

Russian Winter Festival Features tourist-oriented troika rides and folklore performances at Irkutsk through into January.

FOOD

Dining options across Russia have improved immeasurably in recent years and you should have little problem in most parts of the country finding somewhere or something decent to eat. In general for a budget meal you'll be looking at R100 or less, a midrange place will cost around R500 and top-end places over R1000.

There's a fantastic array of food available in China, and particularly so in Beijing. Even in the capital it's still possible to dine at budget eateries for under Y30; midrange dining options will cost between Y30 and Y80, and top-end choices over Y80.

Mongolia isn't going to get many awards for its culinary offerings, although Ulaanbaatar has some surprisingly good places to eat. Expect main dishes to cost T800 to T1500 in budget joints, T2000 to T3000 in midrange places and T4000 to T8000 in most top-end restaurants.

For more on food and drink in all three countries, see p66.

GAY & LESBIAN TRAVELLERS

Russia

While girls holding hands and drunken men showing affection towards each other are common sights throughout Russia, open displays of same-sex love are not condoned. In general, however, the idea of homosexuality is tolerated (particularly by the urban younger generation), although overt gay behaviour is frowned upon.

There is an active gay and lesbian scene in Moscow and St Petersburg, and newspapers such as the *Moscow Times* and *St Petersburg Times* feature articles and listings on gay and lesbian issues, clubs and bars and events (but don't expect anything near as organised as you might find in other major world centres). Away from the two major cities, the gay scene is much less open.

For a good overview, visit www.gay.ru/english, with up-to-date information, good links and a resource to put you in touch with personal guides for Moscow and St Petersburg. St Petersburg's **Krilija** (Wings; ☎ 812-312 3180; www.krilija.sp.ru) is Russia's oldest officially registered gay and lesbian community organisation.

China & Mongolia

In China, greater tolerance of homosexuality exists in the big cities than in the more conservative countryside. Still, even in urban China it's not recommended that gays and lesbians be too open about their sexual orientation in public, even though you will see Chinese same-sex friends holding hands or putting their arms around each other. The situation is slowly improving, but the police periodically crack down on gay meeting places.

Mongolia is not a gay-friendly place, nor one to test local attitudes towards homosexuality. Ulaanbaatar has a small gay community that will occasionally convene at a tolerant restaurant or bar, but it moves around every few months, so you'll need to quietly tap into the scene and ask.

For up-to-date information on the latest gay and lesbian hot spots in Beijing and Ulaanbaatar look at the website www.utopia-asia.com/tipschin.htm.

HOLIDAYS

Russia

New Year's Day 1 January
Russian Orthodox Christmas Day 7 January

Defenders of the Motherland Day 23 February
Easter Monday
International Women's Day 8 March
International Labour Day (Spring Festival) 1 and 2 May
Victory Day 9 May
Russian Independence Day 12 June; celebrates the day the Russian republic inside the USSR proclaimed its sovereignty in June 1991
Unity Day 4 November

Many businesses are closed from 1 January to 5 January.

China
New Year's Day 1 January
Chinese New Year (Spring Festival) Usually February
International Women's Day 8 March
International Labour Day 1 May
Youth Day 4 May
International Children's Day 1 June
Birthday of the Chinese Communist Party 1 July
Anniversary of the Founding of the People's Liberation Army 1 August
National Day 1 October

International Labour Day is a week-long holiday, as is National Day. Chinese New Year is also a week-long holiday for many. It's not a great idea to arrive in China or go travelling during these holidays as things tend to grind to a halt. Hotel prices all over China rapidly shoot up during the May and October holiday periods.

Mongolia
Shin Jil (New Year's Day) 1 January
Constitution Day 13 January; the adoption of the 1992 constitution
Tsagaan Sar (Lunar New Year) January/February; a three-day holiday celebrating the Mongolian New Year
Women's Day 8 March
Mother & Children's Day 1 June; a great time to visit parks
National Day Celebrations (Naadam Festival) 11 to 12 July
Mongolian Republic Day 26 November

Constitution Day, Women's Day and Mongolian Republic Day are generally normal working days.

INSURANCE
It's wise to take out travel insurance to cover theft, loss and medical problems. There are many policies available, so check the small print for things like ambulance cover or an emergency flight home. Note: some policies specifically exclude 'dangerous activities', which can apply to scuba diving, motorcycling and trekking.

You may prefer the policy to pay doctors or hospitals directly, rather than you paying on the spot and claiming later (if you have to claim later make sure you keep all documentation). Some policies ask you to phone back (reverse charge) to a call centre in your home country, where an immediate assessment of your problem is made.

INTERNET ACCESS
For recommended websites, see p19.

Russia
Internet cafés are common across Russia – all but the smallest towns have connections. The best place to start is the main post office or telephone office, as they often have the cheapest rates, typically around R28.80 an hour.

Wi-fi is becoming more common, particularly in Moscow and St Petersburg where several bars and regular cafés have it, as well as many top-end hotels. Go to www.intel.com /products/services/emea/rus/mobiletechnology/unwire/hotspots.htm (in Russian) for a listing of wi-fi hotspots in the major cities.

China
Chinese may be the world's largest online language by 2007, but the authorities have closed scores of wǎngbā (Internet cafés) after a fire in a Beijing Internet café in 2002 killed 25 people. Cafés that are allowed to operate have to use filters to strain out 'irregular' content. Rates at China's Internet cafés should be around Y2 to Y3 per hour for a standard, no-frills outlet, but comfier and smarter options naturally charge more (up to Y20 per hour). You may have to endure agonisingly slow connections in China's Internet cafés, especially on congested sites such as Hotmail.

To access the Internet using a laptop from your hotel room (if it has no broadband Internet connection), you can use free dial-up access by hooking up through the phone line and using the local dial-up number (usually 163 or 169, but ask your hotel what the local number is). Use the same number for the account name and password, and you can get online.

RUSSIAN STREET NAMES

We use the Russian names of all streets and squares in this book to help you when deciphering Cyrillic signs and asking locals the way. To save space the following abbreviations are used:

- bul – bulvar бульвар – boulevard
- nab – naberezhnaya набережная – embankment
- per – pereulok переулок – side street
- pl – ploshchad площадь – square
- pr – prospekt проспект – avenue
- ul – ulitsa улица – street
- sh – shosse шоссе – road

Mongolia

You'll find Internet cafés on nearly every street in downtown Ulaanbaatar; the standard charge is T800 per hour. Some hotel business centres and guesthouses have Internet access for guests, but prices are more expensive. If you have your own laptop it's easier to get an Internet card (sold at the exchange kiosks in the State Department Store, Peace Ave 44, Ulaanbaatar). A 10-hour Internet card costs just T5000.

LAUNDRY

While self-service laundries are almost unheard of in Russia, you can get laundry done in most hotels: ask the floor attendant. It usually takes at least a day and costs around R200 a load, but if you plan on doing it yourself, bring along a universal sink plug. There are several laundries scattered around Ulaanbaatar, where a load will cost around T4000.

LEGAL MATTERS

In Russia, and to a lesser extent in Mongolia, it's generally best to avoid contact with the police. Some are known to bolster their puny incomes by robbing foreigners – either outright or through sham 'fines'. If you do need police assistance (ie you've been the victim of a robbery or an assault) it's best to go to a station with a local for both language and moral support. You will have to be persistent and patient, too.

If you are arrested, the police in all three countries are obliged to inform your embassy or consulate immediately and allow you to communicate with it without delay. Although you can insist on seeing an embassy or consular official straight away, you can't count on the rules being followed, so

be polite and respectful towards officials and hopefully things will go far more smoothly for you. In Russian, the phrase 'I'd like to call my embassy' is *'Pozhaluysta, ya khotel by pozvonit v posolstvo moyey strany'*.

MAPS

Maps of all the major cities covered in this guide are on sale in each city, although in general you'll be best off buying regional city and area maps of Russia in Moscow or St Petersburg before you start.

Good overseas sources for maps:

Librairie Ulysse (☎ 01 43 25 17 35; www.ulysse.fr; 26 rue Saint Louis en L'Isle, Paris, France)

Mapland (☎ 03-9670 4383; www.mapland.com.au; 372 Little Bourke St, Melbourne, Victoria, Australia)

Map Link (☎ 800-962-1394; www.maplink.com; Unit 5, 30 S La Patera Lane, Santa Barbara, CA, USA)

Stanfords Map Centre (☎ 020-7836 0189; www.stanfords.co.uk; 12-14 Long Acre, London, UK)

Travel Bookshop (☎ 02-9261 8200; www.travelbooks.com.au; Shop 3, 175 Liverpool St, Sydney, NSW, Australia)

MONEY

Consult the inside front cover for a table of exchange rates. For information on costs, see p17.

The Russian currency is the rouble (*ru*-bl), which is written as 'рубль' or abbreviated as 'py' or 'p' and is made up of 100 kopecks. These come in coin denominations of one (rarely seen), five, 10 and 50. Also issued in coins, roubles come in amounts of one, two and five, with banknotes in values of 10, 50, 100, 500 and 1000 roubles.

In Russia, it's illegal to make purchases in any currency other than roubles. Prices are often quoted in dollars (or the pseudonym 'units', often written as 'ye' – the abbreviation for *uslovnye yedenitsy*, conventional units), since dollars have a more stable exchange rate, but you will still be presented with a final bill in roubles. In this guide we list whichever currency is quoted on the ground.

The Chinese currency is the Renminbi (RMB), or 'People's Money'. Formally the basic unit of RMB is the *yuán*, which is divided into 10 *jiǎo,* which is again divided into 10 *fēn.* Colloquially, the *yuán* is referred to as *kuài* and *jiǎo* as *máo.* The *fēn* has so little value these days that it is rarely used.

The Bank of China issues RMB bills in denominations of one, two, five, 10, 20, 50 and 100 *yuán.* Coins come in denominations of one *yuán,* five *jiǎo,* one *jiǎo* and five *fēn.* Paper versions of the coins remain in circulation.

The Mongolian unit of currency is the tögrög (T), which comes in notes of T5, T10, T20, T50, T100, T500, T1000, T5000 and T10,000 (T1 notes are basically souvenirs). There are also T50 and T100 coins. The highest-value note is worth around US$9 so when changing a lot of cash you'll be given a stack of machine-collated bills.

ATMs

Plastic is the way to go with ATMs, linked to international networks such as Amex, Cirrus, MasterCard and Visa, common right across Russia – look for signs that say *bankomat* (БАНКОМАТ). As well as roubles, some ATMs dispense US dollars, too.

It's also pretty easy to find ATMs accepting overseas cards in Beijing and Harbin, although in Ulaanbaatar the ATMs currently only accept Visa cards.

If you are going to rely on ATMs, make certain you have a few days' supply of cash at hand in case you can't find a machine to accept your card.

Cash

There are no official facilities for exchanging money on the train itself (it's possible some of the *provodnitsas* or the restaurant staff will accept foreign cash but at very poor exchange rates – don't count on this), so you'll need to stock up at your major stops. There are usually exchange places at border-town train stations.

You'll usually get the best exchange rates for US dollars though euros are increasingly widely accepted and in rare cases get even better rates in bigger cities where there's a specialist bank. British pounds are sometimes accepted in big cities, but the exchange rates are not so good; other currencies incur abysmal rates and are often virtually unchangeable.

Any currency you bring should be in pristine condition: banks and exchange bureaus do not accept old, tatty bills with rips or tears. For US dollars make certain they are the new design, with the large offset portrait, and that they look and smell newly minted.

Credit Cards

Across Russia and China credit cards are becoming more accepted, but don't rely on them outside of the major cities. Most sizable cities have banks or exchange bureaus that will give you a cash advance on your credit card, but be prepared for paperwork in the local language.

In Mongolia credit cards are often accepted at top-end hotels, the expensive souvenir shops, airline offices and travel agencies. The Trade & Development Bank in Ulaanbaatar can arrange a US dollar cash advance on your Visa, MasterCard and American Express. Plastic is not accepted outside the capital.

Moneychangers

There's no advantage to using moneychangers in either Russia or China, but in Mongolia they sometimes offer good rates for US dollars and are usually safe. However, the risks are obvious. Remember to change all your tögrög when leaving the country as it's worthless elsewhere.

Tipping

In Russia, tipping is standard in the better restaurants – count on leaving 10% – whereas elsewhere 5% to 10% of the total is fine. Tipping your guide, if you have one, is an accepted practice. Generally about US$5 to US$10 is OK.

Tipping is neither required nor expected in China, except in the case of porters in upmarket hotels. In Mongolia, tipping is optional; if you round up the bill, then your server will be satisfied.

Travellers Cheques

These are worth taking with you if you are only going to be getting off the train in large cities. The exchange rates might be more favourable than the rate for cash. However, you should always check whether there are any exchange fees incurred.

PHOTOGRAPHY

All major towns and cities will have several photographic shops to download digital snaps to CDs, buy memory cards and major brands of print film. Slide film is not widely sold so bring plenty of rolls with you. The same rare specialist shops that sell slide film will also have a smattering of camera gear by leading brands such as Nikon and Canon.

Camera batteries get sluggish in the cold, so carry your camera inside your coat and keep spare batteries warm in your pocket. For more professional tips on taking decent photos, read Lonely Planet's *Travel Photography*, by Richard I'Anson.

Photographing People

As anywhere, use good judgement and discretion when taking photos of people. It's always better to ask first and if the person doesn't want to be photographed, respect their privacy; a lifetime living with the KGB may make older people uneasy about being photographed, although a genuine offer to send on a copy can loosen your subject up. Remember that many people will be touchy if you photograph 'embarrassments' such as drunks, run-down housing and other signs of social decay.

In Russian, 'May I take a photograph of you?' is *'Mozhno vas sfotografirovat?'*, and in Mongolian it is *'Bi tany zurgiig avch bolokh uu?'*

Restrictions

In all three countries (but especially in Russia), you should be particularly careful about taking photographs of stations, official-looking buildings and any type of military/security structure – if in doubt, don't snap! Travellers, including an author of this book, have been arrested for such innocent behaviour.

Some museums and galleries forbid flash pictures, some ban all photos and most will charge you extra to snap away. Some caretakers in historical buildings and churches charge mercilessly for the privilege of using a still or video camera.

POST

If there is a mail car attached to the train, there will be a slot in the side into which you can drop letters. However, there's no guarantee that your mail will reach its destination, so it's best to post things from cities along the way or in post boxes at the stations.

The major Russian cities, plus Beijing and Ulaanbaatar, have international private courier firms such as **FedEx** (www.fedex.com) and **UPS** (www.ups.com).

Russia

Russia's main post offices are open 8am to 8pm or 9pm, with shorter hours on Saturday and Sunday; in big cities one office will possibly stay open 24 hours a day. Outward post is slow but fairly reliable. Airmail letters take two to three weeks from Moscow and St Petersburg to the UK, longer from other Russian cities, and three to four weeks to the USA or Australasia. To send a postcard/letter to anywhere in the world costs R10/14.

Incoming mail is unreliable and anything addressed to poste restante should be considered lost before it's sent. Should you decide to send mail to Russia or to receive it, note that addresses should be written in reverse order: Russia, postal code (if known), city, street address, name.

China

The Chinese postal system is efficient: airmail to Europe and North America takes about one week. It is possible to post your letters from most hotels, as well as at the post office. Packages, however, should be sent from the **International Post Office** (Guójì Yóudiànjú; Jianguomen Beidajie; ☯ 8am-7pm Mon-Sat) in Beijing. Officials there do inspect all parcels, so don't wrap and seal them until after inspection.

Large post offices are generally open 9am to 5pm daily. Postcards to overseas destinations cost Y4.20. Airmail letters up to 20g cost Y5.40 to Y6.40 to all countries except Hong Kong, Macau and Taiwan (Y2.50). Domestic letters cost Y0.80 and postcards Y0.30.

Mongolia

The postal service is reliable but can often be *very* slow. Allow *at least* a couple of weeks for letters and postcards to arrive home from Mongolia. Foreign residents of Ulaanbaatar find it much faster to give letters (and cash to buy stamps) to other foreigners who are departing.

In most cases, you will have to post your letters from the post office. Postal rates are often relatively expensive, especially for parcels, for which there is only an 'airmail' rate – yet they often arrive months later (probably by sea). Normal-sized letters cost T640 and postcards cost T460 to all countries.

SHOPPING

See the destination sections of the route chapters earlier in this guide for details on where to shop.

Apart from in tourist-orientated souvenir markets bargaining is not the done thing in Russia. Even when it is expected, it will not be a protracted process as in parts of Asia. In China and Mongolia, in large shops and department stores where prices are clearly marked, there is usually no latitude for bargaining (but if you ask, the staff sometimes might be able to give you a small discount). Elsewhere bargaining is expected.

In all three countries the one important rule to follow is: be polite. Your goal should be to pay the local price, as opposed to the foreigners' price – if you can do that, you've done well.

Russia

The classic Russian souvenir is a *matryoshka* (set of wooden dolls stacked within dolls). Although often kitsch, they're a true folk art, and there are all manner of intricate painted designs. A small, mass-produced set should cost just a couple of dollars, but the best examples may set you back US$100. For this price you can also take along a family photo to Izmaylovsky Park in Moscow and come back the following week to collect your very own personalised *matryoshka* set.

Other items to look out for:

- *Palekh* – enamelled wooden boxes, each with an intricate scene painted in its lid
- *Khokhloma* ware – the gold, red and black wooden bowls, mugs and spoons from near Nizhny Novgorod (p134)
- *Gzhel* – blue-and-white ornamental china
- *Platok Pavlovo Posad* – the floral-designed 'Babushka scarf'
- *Yantar* – amber from the Baltic coast, though beware of fake stuff in some St Petersburg and Moscow outlets

---

MORE THAN MEETS THE EYE...

Once upon a time in China you got what you paid for. If the sales clerk said it was top-quality jade, then it was top-quality jade. Times have changed, and cheap forgeries and imitations of everything from Qing coins to the latest movie DVDs now flood the market.

Despite all the government's bluster and periodic CCTV footage of steamrollers grinding fake Rolexes and CDs, the pirating industry is in fine fettle. Fake goods just reappear in force after hitting the deck for a while. Wherever you voyage in China, you'll be cursing the number of forgeries, then snapping them up when you glance at the price tag. Just make sure your change doesn't include a counterfeit note. And if you are after genuine antiques, try to get an official certificate of verification – and make sure the ink is dry.

Russian records and cassettes – rock, jazz, classical – are cheap. For the same price you can get all manner of pirated CDs, video cassettes and software – just don't expect any of them to be of decent quality. Other ideas include paintings from the street; *plakat* (posters), both old Socialist exhortation and modern social commentary, from bookshops or specialist poster shops; and little Lenin busts at street stands and in tourist markets.

China

Although tourists are unlikely to find true antiques at bargain prices, China is still a great place to buy handmade arts and crafts and furniture. Even if the seller claims it is old, it is more likely a reproduction, but that does not mean that it is not a good buy. Most Chinese markets are chock-full of exquisite traditional furniture, iron teapots, bronze figures and Tibetan carpets, most of which are sold at prices considerably lower than in the West. Shoppers can get fantastic bargains on jewellery, especially pearls. Silk is high-quality and priced low compared to material you can buy in the West. China also offers an impressive selection of fake brand-name clothing and pirated CDs and DVDs for very cheap prices.

Mongolia

Mongolian crafts are made almost exclusively for tourist consumption, and they are expensive. Some potentially good buys are traditional Mongolian clothing and boots, landscape paintings and Mongolian games such as *khorol* (checkers) and *shagai* (dice). Cashmere sweaters are an important export item, but they are usually overpriced, especially for the limited selection. Traditional musical instruments can be a beautiful and unique memento of a trip.

TELEPHONE & FAX

City codes are listed in this book under the relevant section headings. In all three countries faxes can be sent from most post offices and the better hotels.

Russia

The country code for Russia is ☎ 7.

Local calls from homes and most hotels are free. To make a long-distance call from most phones first dial ☎ 8, wait for a second dial tone, then dial the city code etc. To make an international call dial ☎ 8, wait for a second dial tone, then dial 10, then the country code etc. See below for details of future changes to this system, though. Some phones are for local calls only and won't give you that second dial tone.

From mobile phones, just dial + followed by the country code to place an international call.

MOBILE PHONES

Russia has several large cross-country networks, including Beeline, Megafon, MTS and Skylink, most of which operate on the pay-as-you-go system. However, beware that depending on the SIM card that you opt for, you might only be able to call from local parts of the network. Reception is increasingly spreading to more rural areas and is already available right along the Trans-Siberian Railway. MTS probably had the widest network at the time of research.

To call a mobile phone from a landline, the line must be enabled to make paid (ie nonlocal) calls. SIM and phone call credit top-up cards, available at any mobile phone shop and costing as little as US$15, can be slotted into your home handset during your stay. Call prices are very low within local networks, but charges for roaming larger regions can mount up, and cost-conscious locals switch SIM cards when crossing regional boundaries.

PAY PHONES

Taksofon (pay phones, ТАКСОФОН) are located throughout most cities, and are usually in working order. Most take prepaid phonecards. There are several types of cardphones, and not all cards are interchangeable. Cardphones can be used for local and domestic or international long-distance calls.

PHONECARDS & CALL CENTRES

Local *telefonnaya karta* (phonecards), in a variety of units, are available from shops, kiosks and metro stations in Moscow and St Petersburg, and can be used to make local, national and international calls.

Sometimes better value for international calls is a call centre, where you give the clerk the number you want to call, pay a deposit and then go to the booth you are assigned to make the call. Afterwards you either pay the difference or collect your change. Such call centres are common in Russian cities and towns – ask for *mezhdunarodny telefon*.

China

The country code for China is ☎ 86.

If calling internationally from China, drop the first zero of the area or city code after dialling the international access code, and then dial the number you wish to call. Local calls from hotel-room phones are generally cheap (and sometimes free), although international phone calls are expensive; it's best to use a phonecard.

CHANGING TELEPHONE NUMBERS

Russian authorities have an annoying habit of frequently changing telephone numbers, particularly in cities. We've tried to list the correct telephone number at the time of research but it's likely that some will change during the lifetime of this book. There are plans to change city codes that start with 0, generally substituting 4 for the initial 0. This is because in 2007/2008 intercity and international connection codes will be changed to 0 and 00 respectively (from the current 8 and 8 + 10).

MOBILE PHONES

Shŏujīdiàn (mobile-phone shops) can sell you a SIM card which will cost around Y200; you then buy credits on the following denominations of cards: Y50, Y100, Y300 and Y500 (each valid for a limited period). It's possible to do all this before even leaving Beijing airport!

Local and long-distance calls are pretty cheap. Overseas calls can be made for Y4.80 per minute plus the local charge per minute by dialling ☎ 17951, followed by 00, the country code then the number you want to call. Otherwise you will be charged the IDD call charge plus six *jiăo* per minute.

PAY PHONES

Public telephones are plentiful, although finding one that works can be a hassle. The majority of public telephones take IC cards (see below) and only a few take coins. If making a domestic call, look out for public phones at newspaper stands and hole-in-the-wall shops; you make your call and then pay the owner (local calls are typically around four *jiăo*). Domestic and international long-distance phone calls can also be made from main telecommunications offices.

PHONECARDS

There are two main types of prepaid phonecards: Integrated Circuit (IC) cards, best used for local and long-distance calls, and Internet Phone (IP) cards, best for international calls. Both are sold at kiosks, shops, Internet cafés and China Telecom offices and come in a variety of denominations from Y20 to Y200. Note some cards can only be used in Beijing (or locally, depending on where the card is purchased), while other cards can be used throughout China.

Purchasing the correct card can be confusing, as the instructions for use on the reverse of the card are usually only in Chinese.

With an IP card, you dial a local number, then punch in your account number, followed by a pin number and finally the number you wish to call. English-language service is usually available.

Mongolia

The country code for Mongolia is ☎ 976.

If you are calling out of Mongolia, and are using an IDD phone, just dial ☎ 00 and then your international country code. On non-IDD phones you can make direct long-distance calls by dialling the international operator (☎ 106), who may know enough English to make the right connection (but don't count on it).

The other options are making a call from a private international phone office (Olon Ulsiin Yariin), which are becoming common in Ulaanbaatar but not in other cities. These charge reasonable rates to call abroad. To make the call, you need to pay a deposit in advance (a minimum equivalent of three minutes). The most expensive, but often the most hassle-free, option is to call from the business centres or reception desks at top-end hotels.

MOBILE PHONES

Sotovye telefony (mobile phones) are now ubiquitous in the capital, as Muscovites bypassed the antiquated landline system. The two main companies are Mobicom and Skytel. The mobile-phone network is GSM. If you bring a GSM phone you can get a new SIM card installed in Mongolia. The process is simple – just go to a mobile-phone office (a Mobicom office is conveniently located on the 3rd floor of the State Department Store, Peace Ave 44, Ulaanbaatar), sign up for basic service (around T15,000), and buy units as needed. Cards come in units of 10 (T2500), 30 (T6600), 50 (T10,250) and 100 (T19,000). It is free to receive calls and text messaging charges are almost negligible.

If you are abroad, and calling a mobile-phone number in Mongolia, just dial the country code (☎ 976) without the area code. Note that you drop the '0' off the area code if dialling an Ulaanbaatar number *from* a mobile phone but you retain the '0' if using other area codes.

PHONECARDS

International phonecards are sold in various outlets including the post office, the State Department Store or mobile-phone shops. The Personal Identification Number (PIN) for these cards is the last four digits of the code on the card. There are a variety of phonecards available, and you usually get what you pay for – the cheaper ones (such as Bodicom) have terrible sound quality and echo, but cost less than US$0.10 per minute.

DIRECTORY

TIME

No one on the train knew what time it was. Some people said the train travelled on Moscow time but operated on local time, if you can figure that out. But half the people were on Beijing time and one diplomat said he was on Tokyo time, which was the same for some reason as Ulaanbaatar time. Our Chinese porter changed his watch 15 minutes every few hours or so but this was a system of his own devising.

Mary Morris, Wall to Wall

One of the most disorienting aspects of a Trans-Siberian trip is working out what time it is. The important thing to remember is that all long-distance trains run on Moscow time – so check carefully when you buy a ticket exactly what time *locally* you should be at the station. Once inside the station and on the train all clocks are set to Moscow time.

In the guide we list how far major cities and towns are ahead of Moscow time, eg 'Moscow + 5hr' means five hours ahead.

From the early hours of the last Sunday in September to the early hours of the last Sunday in March, Moscow and St Petersburg time is GMT/UTC plus three hours. From the last Sunday in March to the last Sunday in September, 'summer time' is in force and it's GMT/UTC plus four hours.

Most of European Russia is in the same time zone as Moscow and St Petersburg. The exception along the Trans-Siberian route is Perm, which is two hours ahead of Moscow. East of the Ural Mountains, Yekaterinburg is on Moscow time plus two hours, Irkutsk on Moscow time plus five hours and Vladivostok on Moscow time plus seven hours.

All of China is on Beijing's clock, which is eight hours ahead of GMT. Daylight-savings time was abandoned in 1992, so the time difference with Europe and the USA is reduced by one hour during the summer months.

Mongolia is divided into two time zones. Most of the country, including Ulaanbaatar, is GMT plus eight hours, so it is the same time zone as Beijing except during the summer when it's one hour ahead.

TOILETS

It's rare that paper will actually be available in the stalls of public toilets, so always bring a supply of toilet paper or tissue with you. Plumbing systems in all three countries often have problems digesting toilet paper. If there is a rubbish basket next to the toilet, this is where the paper should go.

Russia

Pay toilets are identified by the words платный туалет *(platny tualet).* In any toilet Ж *(zhensky)* stands for women's, while M *(muzhskoy)* stands for men's.

In cities, you'll now find clusters of temporary plastic toilets in popular public places, although other public toilets are rare and often dingy and uninviting. A much better option are the loos in major hotels or in modern food outlets. In all public toilets, the attendant who you pay your R5 to R10 to can provide miserly rations of toilet paper.

China & Mongolia

Public toilets in hotels, *ger* camps and restaurants are usually European-style, moderately clean facilities. On the other hand, public facilities in parks, stores and train stations usually require that you squat over a smelly hole. In China you'll also come across toilets without doors and separated only by a low partition, making it easy to strike up a conversation with the person squatting next to you.

Along the Route

Toilets on Russian and Mongolian trains are the Western variety, although you'll notice when you lift the seat that the bowl rim is also designed for those who would prefer to squat rather than sit. The *provodnitsas* generally do a good job of keeping the toilets reasonably clean, particularly on the more prestigious class of trains.

It is also important to remember that shortly before and after any major stops, and along any densely populated stretches of the line, the toilets will be locked; a timetable for this is usually posted on the toilet door.

On Chinese trains toilets are often of the squat variety.

TOURIST INFORMATION
Russia

Tourist offices like you may be used to elsewhere are few and far between in Russia. Along the Trans-Siberian routes the only places we've found them are St Petersburg (p84), Irkutsk (p191) and Olkhon (p203).

HOW TO HAVE A TRANS-SIBERIAN SHOWER *Steve Noble*

Travellers often moan about not being able to shower on trains. But what is your definition of a shower? If it's high pressure hot/cold water in an elegantly tiled bathroom, you will not find this. However, if you are resourceful, adaptable and imaginative, you can shower as much as you like in the toilet/washroom at the end of each *kupe* (*kupeyny;* compartmentalised) carriage. Some people are happy for just an APC (armpits and crotch) wash, others prefer to splash water a little more liberally. Here are some proven methods I have tried:

- Stab lots of small holes in the bottom of a plastic (0.5L or 1L) bottle, just like your shower head at home. Fill it with water and either hold it with one hand and wash or tie some rope around the bottle neck and hook it on the back of the door. Use one bottle to wet yourself and one bottle to rinse off.
- Any size cup or bottle can be filled with water and thrown liberally over yourself.
- Use a collapsible plastic shower bag with showerhead and tap, for sale in any good camping store.
- Attach a small length of rubber hose to the tap.
- Use a sponge or quick-dry towels to have a sponge bath.

If you want hot water, get some from the samovar before you enter the toilet. Check the floor drain is unplugged before you start to shower and remember to wipe the walls down after you're done. You don't want to leave a mess and upset the *provodnitsa*!

Elsewhere you're mainly dependent for information on the moods of hotel receptionists and administrators, service bureaus and travel firms. The latter two exist primarily to sell accommodation, excursions and transport – if you don't look like you want to book something, staff may or may not answer questions.

Russia has no overseas tourist offices and most of its consulates and embassies have little practical information. Travel agencies specialising in Russian travel (p325) can be useful.

China

While Beijing's tourist information structure is improving, on the whole tourist information facilities in China are largely rudimentary and of little use for travellers. In the absence of a national tourism board, individual provinces, cities, towns and regions promote tourism independently. The fallback position is the China International Travel Service (CITS) with branches in all major towns and cities. There is usually a member of staff who can speak English who may be able to answer questions and offer some travel advice, but the main purpose of CITS is to get you onto an expensive tour.

Mongolia

Ulaanbaatar has a reasonably good tourist information centre; see p260. Juulchin, once Mongolia's sole tourist agency, has been privatised. It's still the biggest operator, though.

VISAS

It's highly advisable to obtain all visas in your home country before setting out. Some tour companies can arrange your visas as part of their package. Remember if you're also travelling through Belarus, Ukraine, the Baltic countries or Central Asia, you may need visas for those countries, too.

Russia

Everyone needs a visa to visit Russia and it's likely to be your biggest single headache if you run into complications, so allow yourself at least a month before you travel to secure one. There are several types of visa, but for most Trans-Siberian travellers a tourist visa, valid for 30 days from the date of entry, will be sufficient. If you plan to stay longer, it's best to apply for a business visa. The good news is that these days getting a visa is, usually (but not always), a straightforward process. The process has three stages – invitation, application and registration.

INVITATION

To obtain a visa, you first need an invitation. Hotels and hostels will usually issue an invitation (or 'visa support') to anyone staying with them for free or for a small fee (typically around US$30). If you are not staying in a hotel or hostel, you will need to buy an invitation. This can be done through most travel agents and online through websites such as www.waytorussia.com and www.expresstorussia.com, which can both also help arrange invitation letters for business visas (see right).

APPLICATION

Invitation in hand you can then apply for a visa at any Russian embassy. Costs vary – anything from US$20 to US$200 – depending on the type of visa applied for and how quickly you need it. Russian embassies are practically laws unto themselves, each with different fees and slightly different application rules; to avoid potential hassles, check well in advance what these might be. It's also best to apply for your visa in your home country rather than on the road; Trans-Mongolian and Trans-Manchurian travellers should note that getting visas for Russia in both Beijing and Ulaanbaatar can be a frustrating, costly and ultimately fruitless exercise.

REGISTRATION

On arrival in Russia, you will need to fill out an immigration card – a long white form issued at passport control throughout the country. You surrender one half of the form immediately to passport control, while the other you keep for the duration of your stay and give up only on exiting Russia. Take good care of this as you'll need it for registration and could face problems while travelling in Russia, and certainly will upon leaving, if you cannot produce it.

You must register your visa within three working days of arrival. Registration essentially means a stamp on the immigration card by your hotel or hostel. Note that the very cheapest places sometimes can't oblige. If staying in nonhotel accommodation, you'll need to pay a travel agency (about US$30) to register it for you (most will do this through a hotel). Every time you move city or town and stay for more than three days it's necessary to get another stamp on the immigration card. There's no need to be overly paranoid about this but the more stamps you have on the card the safer. Keep all train tickets (especially if you spend nights sleeping on trains) to prove to any overzealous policemen exactly when you arrived in a new place.

Registrations are regularly checked in Moscow by the fine-hungry cops who lurk around train stations and other places hoping to catch tourists too hurried or disorganised to be able to keep their registration up to date.

TYPES OF VISAS

Apart from the tourist visa, there are other types of visa that could be useful to travellers.

Business Visa

This is far more flexible and desirable for the independent traveller. These can be issued for three months, six months or two years, and are available as single-entry, double-entry or multiple-entry visas. To obtain a business visa you must have a letter of invitation from a registered Russian company guaranteeing to provide accommodation during the entire length of your stay, and a covering letter from your company (or you) stating the purpose of your trip. **Way to Russia** (www.waytorussia.net) and **Express to Russia** (www.expresstorussia.com) can arrange this for you.

Transit Visa

If you're taking a nonstop Trans-Siberian journey this visa is valid for 10 days, giving westbound passengers a few days in Moscow; those heading east, however, are not allowed to linger in Moscow.

VISA EXTENSIONS & CHANGES

The Interior Ministry's passport and visa agency is called the *passportno-vizovoye upravleniy* (PVU), although you'll still often hear the old acronym OVIR used. It's to this agency that you must apply if you wish to extend or change your visa.

Visa extensions are time-consuming, if not downright difficult; tourist visas can't be extended at all. Try to avoid the need for an extension by asking for a longer visa than you think you might need. Note that many trains out of St Petersburg and Mos-

VISA AGENCIES

If you're really pressed for time, or badly affected by impersonal bureaucracies, there are agencies that specialise in getting visas. In the USA, try **Zierer Visa Service** (☎ 866-788-1100; www.zvs.com) which has offices in Chicago, Houston, New York, San Francisco and Washington DC, as well as the UK, France, Germany and Australia.

Also in the UK, **Thames Consular Services** (☎ 020-7494 4957; www.visapassport.com; 3rd fl, 35 Piccadilly, London) charges from £50, plus value added tax (VAT), on top of the Russian visa fees.

cow to Eastern Europe cross the border after midnight, so make sure your visa is valid up to and including this day. Don't give border guards any excuses for making trouble.

China

All foreigners need to get a visa to visit the People's Republic of China (PRC). Your passport should have at least six months' validity and one empty page. Submit your passport, a covering letter, an application, one passport photo and a money order for the appropriate fee. Processing should take four working days for a walk-in application; by mail requires more time and usually a higher fee.

Be aware that you must submit these documents to the consulate whose jurisdiction includes the state or city where you reside. Exact requirements and fees vary depending on where you apply, so be sure to check the details with your nearest Chinese consulate.

A standard visa is valid for one entry and a 30-day stay in China. A double entry is fairly straightforward. You can also get a transit visa, which is good for seven days. Requirements are more stringent for multiple entries or for longer stays in China.

Visa extensions, which are relatively easy to get, are the domain of the Public Security Bureau's (PSB) Foreign Affairs Branch. In Beijing, **PSB** (☎ 010-8402 0101; 2 Andingmen Dongdajie; ◷ 8.30am-4.30pm Mon-Sat) is located 300m east of the Lama Temple. Note that he penalty for overstaying your visa is Y500 per day!

Mongolia

Most nationalities require a visa to enter Mongolia, with the following exceptions: US citizens, for stays up to 90 days; Israeli and Malaysian citizens, for up to 30 days; and Hong Kong and Singaporean citizens, for up to 14 days. To obtain a Mongolian visa, your passport must have at least six months' validity.

Standard tourist visas are valid for 30 days and cost US$25. Processing the application usually takes three to five days. For longer than 30 days, you must obtain an invitation from a travel agency or 'sponsoring organisation'. If you are not leaving the train in Ulaanbaatar, or you are getting off only for a very short stay, you may obtain a transit visa in advance – good for 72 hours from the date of entry and costing US$15.

For visa extensions, go to the **Ministry of External Relations** (cnr Peace Ave & Olympiin Gudamj; ◷ 9.30am-noon Mon-Fri). Enter from the back of the building. The extension is US$15 for seven days and requires a passport photo. Some guesthouses will handle visa extensions for a small fee. Transit visas cannot be extended.

If you intend to stay in Mongolia for more than 30 days, you must register with the **Office of Immigration, Naturalization & Foreign Citizens** (INFC; ☎ 011-315 323; ◷ 9am-1pm & 2-5pm Mon-Fri), on the west side of Ulaanbaatar's Peace Bridge, opposite the NIC petrol station.

WOMEN TRAVELLERS

Bring sanitary towels or tampons only if there is a brand you absolutely must use. Otherwise you can find locally produced products.

You need to be wary; a woman alone should certainly avoid private taxis at night. Never get in any taxi with more than one person – the driver – already in it. In Russia, any young or youngish woman alone in or near flashy bars frequented by foreigners risks being mistaken for a prostitute.

You're unlikely to experience sexual harassment on the streets in most parts of Russia, though sexual stereotyping remains strong. In more remote areas, the idea that women are somehow less capable than men may persist. In rural areas, revealing clothing will probably attract unwanted attention (whereas on hot days in Moscow women wear as little as possible).

Russian women relish the chance to talk alone with a foreign woman, and the first thing they'll tell you is how hopeless their menfolk are. When journeying by train, women might consider buying a *platskart* (*platskartny;* open carriage) rather than a *kupe* (*kupeyny;* compartmentalised carriage) ticket, to avoid the risk of getting stuck in a closed compartment with three shady characters. If you do decide to travel *kupe* and don't like your cabin mates, tell the conductor who will more than likely find you a new place.

China is probably among the safest places in the world for foreign women to travel alone. Women are generally treated respectfully, because principles of decorum are ingrained deeply in the culture.

Mongolia doesn't present too many problems for foreign women travelling independently. The majority of Mongolian men behave in a friendly and respectful manner, without ulterior motives. However, you may come across an annoying drunk or the occasional macho idiot. There are occasional incidents of solo female travellers reporting being harassed by their male guide. If your guide is male, it is best to keep in touch with your tour agency in Ulaanbaatar, perhaps making contingency plans with them if things go awry. Better yet, take a female guide whenever possible.

Transport

GETTING THERE & AWAY

Most travellers will start their Trans-Siberian or Trans-Mongolian trip in either Moscow or Beijing; this section of the chapter covers details for getting to or from either city. It's also possible to fly into or out of other major gateways, such as St Petersburg (p93), Vladivostok (p236) or Ulaanbaatar (p266). In addition, there are many options for overland approaches from Europe or Asia – mainly by rail but also by road – as well as arriving in or departing from the Far East by sea.

ENTERING THE COUNTRY

There are no particular difficulties for travellers entering Russia, China or Mongolia. The main requirements are a valid pass-port (valid for travel for six months after the expiry date of your visa) and a visa (see p315). Visas are not available at the borders.

AIR
Airports & Airlines

Moscow's **Sheremetyevo-2** (airport code SVO; ☎ 095-956 4666; www.sheremetyevo-airport.ru) and the more modern **Domodedovo** (airport code DME; ☎ 095-933 6666; www.domodedovo.ru) airports host the bulk of Russia's international flights. There are also many daily international services to St Petersburg's **Pulkovo-2** (airport code LED; ☎ 812-704 3444; eng.pulkovo.ru).

You don't necessarily have to fly into either Moscow or St Petersburg – plenty of other cities along the Trans-Siberian route have direct international connections, including Kazan (p145), Khabarovsk (p229), Krasnoyarsk (p189), Irkutsk (p197), Nizhny Novgorod (p139), Novosibirsk (p177), Perm (p141), Vladivostok (p236) and Yekaterinburg (p155).

Beijing's **Capital Airport** (airport code PEK; ☎ 010-6459 9567 for international, 010-1689 6969 for domestic) is served by both international and domestic connections, as is Ulaanbaatar's **Buyant Ukhaa Airport** (airport code PEK; ☎ 198, 011-983 005).

Airlines flying into all these airports include the following:

Aeroflot Russian International Airlines (airline code SU; ☎ 495-753 5555; www.aeroflot.com/eng; hub Sheremetyevo Airport, Moscow)

Air China (airline code CA; ☎ 495-292 3387, 292 5440; www.china-airlines.com/en/index.htm; hub Beijing Capital Airport, Beijing)

Air France (airline code AF; ☎ 495-937 3839; www.airfrance.com; hub Charles de Gaulle Airport, Paris)

Alitalia (airline code AZ; ☎ 495-258 3601; www.alitalia.it; hub Malpensa Airport, Milan)

American Airlines (airline code AA; www.aa.com; hub Fort Worth, Texas)

Austrian Airlines (airline code OS; ☎ 495-995 0995; www.aua.com; hub Vienna International Airport, Vienna)

Bashkir Airlines (BAL; airline code V9; ☎ 3472-733 656 in Ufa; www.bal.ufanet.ru, in Russian; hub Ufa)

British Airways (airline code BA; ☎ 495-363 2525; www.britishairways.com; hub London Heathrow, London)

ČSA (Czech Airlines; airline code OK; ☎ 495-973 1847, 978 1745; www.csa.cz/en/; hub Prague)

THINGS CHANGE...

The information in this chapter is particularly vulnerable to change. Check directly with the airline or a travel agent to make sure you understand how a fare (and ticket you may buy) works and be aware of the security requirements for international travel. Shop carefully. The details given in this chapter should be regarded as pointers and are not a substitute for your own careful, up-to-date research.

Delta Air Lines (airline code DL; ☎ 495-937 9090; www.delta.com; hub Hartsfield Atlanta International Airport, Atlanta)

Dragonair (airline code KA; www.dragonair.com; hub Hong Kong)

El Al Israel Airlines (airline code LY; ☎ 495-232 1017; www.elal.co.il; hub Ben Gurion Airport, Tel Aviv)

Finnair (airline code AY; ☎ 495-933 0056; www.finnair .com; hub Helsinki-Vantaa Airport, Helsinki)

Japan Airlines (airline code JL; ☎ 495-921 6448, 921 6648; www.jal.co.jp/en; hub Narita Airport, Tokyo)

KLM (airline code KL; ☎ 495-258 3600; www.klm.com; hub Amsterdam Schiphol Airport, Amsterdam)

Kogalymavia (airline code 7K; www.kolavia.narod.ru /index.htm)

Korean Air (airline code KE; ☎ 495-725 2727; www .koreanair.com; hub Incheon International Airport, Seoul)

Krasair (airline code 7B; ☎ 3912-555 999 in Krasnoyarsk; www.krasair.ru in Russian; hub Krasnoyarsk)

LOT Polish Airlines (airline code LO; ☎ 495-229 5771; www.lot.com; hub Fredrick Chopin Airport, Warsaw)

Lufthansa (airline code LH; ☎ 495-737 6400; www.luft hansa.com; hub Frankfurt International Airport, Frankfurt)

Magadan Airlines (airline code H5; ☎ 41322-97610 in Magadan; http://mavial.magtrk.ru in Russian; hub Magadan)

MIAT Mongolian Airlines (airline code OM; ☎ 495-241 0754 in Moscow, 976-11-379935 in Ulaanbaatar; www.miat.com; hub Ulaanbaatar)

Pulkovo (airline code FV; ☎ 495-925 4747; http://eng .pulkovo.ru; hub Pulkovo International Airport, St Petersburg)

Qantas (airline code QF; www.qantas.com.au; hub Kingsford Smith Airport, Sydney)

SAS (airline code SK; ☎ 495-925 4747; www.scandinavian .net; hub Copenhagen Airport, Copenhagen)

Siberia Airlines (airline code S7; ☎ 495-777 9999 in Moscow, ☎ 383-359 9090 in Novosibirsk; www.s7.ru; hub Novosibirsk)

Singapore Airlines (airline code SQ; www.singaporeair .com; hub Changi Airport, Singapore)

Swissair (airline code LX; ☎ 495-937 7799; www.swiss air.com; hub Zurich Airport, Zurich)

Transaero Airlines (airline code UN; ☎ 495-241 4800, 241 7676; www.transaero.com/noframes/eng/home.htm; hub Sheremetyevo-2 Airport, Moscow)

Turkish Airlines (airline code TK; ☎ 495-292 1667; www.turkishairlines.com; hub Istanbul Ataturk International Airport, Istanbul)

Ural Airlines (airline code U6; ☎ 343-264 3600 in Yekaterinburg; www.uralairlines.ru; hub Yekaterinburg)

Vladivostok Air (airline code XF; ☎ 4232-426 296 in Vladivostok; www.vladavia.ru; hub Vladivostok)

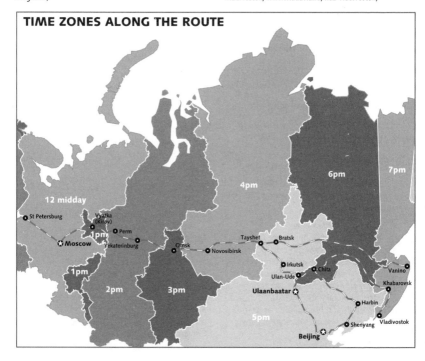

Tickets

Good deals on tickets can be found both online and through discount agencies. Use the fares quoted in this book as a guide only. They are approximate and based on the rates advertised by travel agencies and online at the time of research. Quoted airfares do not necessarily constitute a recommendation for the carrier.

There are many websites specifically aimed at selling flights; sometimes these fares are cheap, often they're no cheaper than those sold at a standard travel agency, and occasionally they're way too expensive – but it's certainly a convenient way of researching flights from the comfort of your own home or office. Many large travel agencies also have websites, but not all of them allow you to look up fares and schedules. See p325 for a list of agencies that specialise in tours along the Trans-Siberian routes; some of these will offer discount fares, too.

Websites worth checking include the following:

www.cheapflights.co.uk Really does post some of the cheapest flights (out of the UK only), but book early to get the bargains.

www.dialaflight.com Offers worldwide flights out of Europe and the UK.

www.expedia.com A good site for checking worldwide flight prices.

www.lastminute.com This site deals mainly in European flights, but does have worldwide flights, mostly package returns. There's also a link to an Australian version.

www.statravel.com STA Travel's US website. There are also UK (www.statravel.co.uk) and Australian (www.statravel.com.au) sites.

www.travel.com.au A good site for Australians to find cheap flights. A New Zealand site (www.travel.co.nz) also exists.

To bid for last-minute tickets online try **Sky-auction** (www.skyauction.com). **Priceline** (www.priceline.com) aims to match the ticket price to your budget. Another cheap option is air courier tickets but they do carry restrictions; for more information check out organisations such as **Courier Association** (☎ 1800-461 9497; www.aircourier.org) or the **International Association of Air Travel Couriers** (IAATC; www.courier.org).

Australia

Two well-known agencies for cheap fares, with offices throughout Australia, are **Flight Centre** (☎ 133 133; www.flightcentre.com.au) and **STA Travel** (☎ 1300 733 035; www.statravel.com.au).

The cheapest flight you're going to get would be something like Sydney to Seoul and then Seoul to Moscow; a Korean Air

---

RUSSIA THROUGH THE BACK DOOR

There are plenty of options to reach Moscow or St Petersburg using budget flights out of European cities. Germany is particularly well served with **Germania Express** (airline code ST; ☎ 49-01805-737 100 in Germany; www.gexx.de; hubs Berlin, Düsseldorf and Munich) connecting Berlin, Düsseldorf and Munich with Moscow's Domodedovo, and **German Wings** (airline code 4U; ☎ 49-01805-955 855 in Germany; www27.germanwings.com; hubs Hamburg, Cologne/Bonn, Stuttgart and Dresden) flying Berlin, Bonn and Cologne to Moscow's Vnukovo airport. SAS's budget airline **Snowflake** (www.flysnowflake.com; ☎ 46-8-797 4000 in Stockholm; hubs Stockholm and Copenhagen) has services from Copenhagen and Stockholm to both Moscow's Sheremetyevo-2 and St Petersburg. From the Baltic countries, you can fly Tallinn to Sheremetyevo on **Estonian Air** (airline code OV; ☎ 372-640 1160 in Tallinn; www.estonian-air.ee; hub Tallinn) and Rīga to Moscow and St Petersburg with **Air Baltic** (airline code BT; ☎ 371-720 7473 in Rīga; www.airbaltic.com; hub Rīga).

Finland is also a popular back-door way into Russia with both Helsinki and Tampere being connected by various budget airlines to other parts of Europe. From either city you can take a bus or trains to St Petersburg. Also check out www.waytorussia.net/transport/international/budget.html for some ideas of how to get cheaply to Moscow or St Petersburg from London or Germany via the Baltic countries. One more option is to get yourself through Poland to Kaliningrad and then take an internal Russian flight from there.

There are also (particularly during the summer season) charter flights to and from Russia, mainly to resort towns in Turkey, Greece, Egypt and other countries. These flights, which never show up on regular schedules, may be cheap, but sometimes the planes being used leave a lot to be desired in terms of comfort and, more worryingly, safety. Buyer beware!

deal starts at return A$1400. Seoul is also the most convenient transfer point for flights on to Vladivostok or Khabarovsk.

To Beijing the low-season return fares from Sydney start at around A$1000.

Canada

Canadian discount agencies, also known as consolidators, advertise their flight specials in major newspapers such as the *Toronto Star* and the *Vancouver Sun*. The national student travel agency is **Travel CUTS** (☎ 800-667-2887; www.travelcuts.com).

In general, fares from Canada to Russia or China cost 10% more than from the USA. From Vancouver to Moscow return low-season fares start from C$1145; from Montreal C$1400. From Vancouver to Beijing you'll pay from around C$1200, from Montreal around C$1460.

China

There are daily flights offered by China Airlines and Aeroflot Russian International Airlines to Moscow from Beijing (return Y8700). There are five flights a week between Shanghai and Moscow (return Y8700). There are also flights from Beijing to Novosibirsk (one-way US$505); Guangzhou to Khabarovsk (one-way US$320); Harbin to Khabarovsk (one-way US$170) and Vladivostok (one-way R5900); Shenyang to Irkutsk (one-way from US$170); and Ürümqi to Novosibirsk (one-way US$184). Tianjin and Dalian also have infrequent connections with Vladivostok.

Transaero Airlines flies occasionally from Moscow to Hong Kong. Three carriers fly the Beijing–Hong Kong route: China Airlines, China Southern and Dragonair. Fixed return tickets between Beijing and Hong Kong start at HK$1600.

Continental Europe

Generally there is not much variation in air-fare prices from the main European cities. All the major airlines, as well as travel agencies, are usually offering some sort of deal, so shop around.

Return fares to Moscow from major Western European cities start at around €250, to Beijing €870.

FRANCE

French travel agencies with branches around the country specialising in youth and stu-

dent fares include **OTU Voyages** (www.otu.fr) and **Nouvelles Frontières** (☎ 0825 000 747; www.nouvelles-frontieres.fr). Also try **Anyway** (☎ 0892 893 892; www.anyway.fr) and **Lastminute** (☎ 0892 705 000; www.fr.lastminute.com).

GERMANY

Germany is an excellent jumping-off point for Russia, with not only plenty of connections to a range of Russian cities with Lufthansa, but also connections through budget airlines such as Germania Express and German Wings (see p321). The following airlines also fly direct between Germany and the Caucasus: **Kuban Air** (www.alk.ru/eng/alk), **Don Aeroflot** (www.aeroflot-don.ru) and **KMV Avia** (www.kmvavia.ru/engl). Krasair and Siberia Airlines all have direct connections to Krasnoyarsk and Novosibirsk respectively.

Recommended agencies in Germany include **Just Travel** (☎ 089-747 3330; www.justtravel.de), **STA Travel** (☎ 01805-456 422; www.statravel.de) and **Travel Overland** (☎ 01805-276 370; www.travel-overland.de). **J&S ONG** (☎ 02361-904 7981; jsohg@gmx.de; Hernerstr 26, 45657 Recklinghausen) is useful for booking tickets on regional Russian airlines.

ITALY

CTS Viaggi (☎ 06 462 0431; www.cts.it) specialises in student and youth travel fares.

NETHERLANDS

A recommended agency is **Airfair** (☎ 020-620 5121; www.airfair.nl).

SPAIN

Try **Barcelo Viajes** (☎ 902 116 226; www.barceloviajes.com).

Japan

Reliable discount agencies in Japan include **No 1 Travel** (☎ 03-3200 8871; www.no1-travel.com) and **Across Travellers Bureau** (☎ 03-3373 9040; www.across-travel.com) as well as **STA Travel** (☎ 03-5485 8380; www.statravel.co.jp), which has branches in both Tokyo and Osaka.

Return flights from Tokyo to Moscow are around ¥220,000, although at certain times of the year 60-day excursion fares on Aeroflot can go as low as ¥60,000. Air China and Japan Airlines have several flights per week from Tokyo and Osaka to Beijing. Return fares start from ¥30,000.

Other useful connections are from Vladivostok to Niigata (one-way/return from

¥41,000/48,000), Osaka (¥46,000/42,000) and Toyama (¥47,000/58,000). In August there are also weekly direct flights between Tokyo and Vladivostok (R6900). From Khabarovsk there are weekly flights to Niigata, and from July to September, a service to Aomori (both one-way/return ¥42,000/60,000).

Mongolia & Central Asia

Ulaanbaatar is connected by plane with Moscow (one-way/return from US$330/580) and Irkutsk (one-way/return US$210/400), though the latter can be discounted to under one-way/return US$70/140 in winter.

There are dozens of connections to Central Asia. From Moscow there are many direct flights. Also from Novosibirsk you can reach Almaty (US$160) in Kazakhstan; Andizhan (US$125) and Tashkent (US$135) in Uzbekistan; Dushanbe (US$145) and Khujand/Khodzhent (US$140) in Tajikistan; and Bishkek (US$170) in Kyrgyzstan. Tyumen, Omsk and Krasnoyarsk have a slightly smaller range of similar destinations.

New Zealand

The *New Zealand Herald* has a travel section in which travel agencies advertise fares. **Flight Centre** (☎ 0800 243 544; www.flightcentre.co.nz) and **STA Travel** (☎ 0508 782 872; www.statravel.co.nz) have branches in Auckland and elsewhere in the country; check the websites for complete listings.

Airfares from New Zealand to Russia are similar to those from Australia; for details see p321.

Singapore

In Singapore, **STA Travel** (☎ 737 7188; www.statravel.com.sg; 33A Cuppage Rd, Cuppage Tce) offers competitive discount fares for Asian destinations and beyond. Singapore, like Bangkok, has hundreds of travel agents, so you can compare prices on flights.

South Korea

Seoul in South Korea is a possible international travel hub for Siberia and the Russian Far East, with weekly flights to Khabarovsk (from US$300 one-way) and Novosibirsk (one-way/return US$490/670) and services to Vladivostok (R11,000) at least twice per week. There are also flights connecting Pusan to/from Vladivostok.

Thailand

Although most Asian countries are now offering fairly competitive deals, Bangkok is still one of the best places to shop around for discount tickets. Khao San Rd in Bangkok is the budget travellers' headquarters. Bangkok has a number of excellent travel agencies but there are also some suspect ones; ask the advice of other travellers before handing over your cash. **STA Travel** (☎ 02-236 0262; www.statravel.co.th; room 1406, 14th fl, Wall St Tower, 33/70 Surawong Rd) is a reliable place to start. Aeroflot has direct flights to Moscow from Bangkok. Siberia Airlines flies to Novosibirsk (US$303) and several other Russian airlines offer seasonal charters.

UK & Ireland

Newspapers and magazines such as *Time Out* and *TNT Magazine* in London regularly advertise low fares to Moscow. Start your research with the major student or backpacker-oriented travel agencies such as STA and Trailfinders. Through these reliable agents you can get an idea of what's available and how much you're going to pay – although a bit of ringing around to the smaller agencies afterwards will often turn up cheaper fares.

Reputable agencies in London include the following:

Bridge the World (☎ 0870-814 4400; www.b-t-w.co.uk)
Flightbookers (☎ 0870-010 7000; www.ebookers.co.uk)
Flight Centre (☎ 0870-499 0040; www.flightcentre.co.uk)
STA Travel (☎ 0870-160 0599; www.statravel.co.uk)
Trailfinders (☎ 020-7938 3939; www.trailfinders.co.uk)

Shop around and you might get a low-season one-way/return fare to Moscow for UK£150/200. Flights to St Petersburg are a bit more expensive at around UK£200/250. Aeroflot generally offers the cheapest deals. Return fares from London to Beijing start at UK£470.

USA

Discount travel agencies in the USA are called consolidators (although you won't see a sign on the door saying 'Consolidator'), and they can be found in the travel sections of major daily newspapers such as the *New York Times, Chicago Tribune* and *Los Angeles Times,* as well as in alternative weeklies. Good deals can generally be found at agencies in San Francisco, Los Angeles, New York and other gateway cities.

TRANSPORT

Try **STA Travel** (☎ 1-800 781 4040; www.statravel .com), which has a wide network of offices. A specialist agency is **Interactive Russia** (☎ 866-680-1373; travel.in-russia.com).

Economy-class airfares from New York to Moscow or Beijing can go as low as return US$700. From Los Angeles you're looking at return fares to Moscow of around US$880, to Beijing of US$600.

LAND

Both Russia and China each share borders with 14 countries, so if you're planning on travelling overland to join or leave the Trans-Siberian routes there is no shortage of options.

More often than not it will be by train that you cross into or leave this region, but there are also several useful bus services; we list some here. You should also check well in advance whether or not you will need a visa for any of the countries you will be passing through en route to Russia or China.

If you are really up for an epic train journey – 17,852km across 12 countries – the Trans-Mongolian route is the lynchpin of the longest possible trip entirely by rail from Vila Real de Santo Antonio in Portugal to Ho Chi Minh City (Saigon) in Vietnam.

Border Crossings

See p256 for details of the border crossing between Russia and Mongolia, p256 for between Mongolia and China, and p272 for the Russia/China crossing. For overland routes into China, see Lonely Planet's *China* guidebook for full details.

Belarus

Belarus' capital Minsk is well connected by train with Moscow (BR66,000 to BR104,000, 11 hours, 20 daily); there's also a daily service to St Petersburg (BR113,000, 16 hours). There are two weekly buses to Moscow (BR34,000, 14½ hours) and a weekly service to St Petersburg (BR50,000, 19 hours).

Estonia

The nearest border crossing from Tallinn is at Narva. There's a daily train between Moscow and Tallinn (R1560, 16 hours) and seven express buses daily from St Petersburg (R550 to R650, 7½ hours).

Finland

There are two daily trains between St Petersburg and Helsinki; see p95 for details. There's also the daily 31/34 'Leo Tolstoy' service between Moscow and Helsinki (13½ hours). There are many daily buses between Helsinki and St Petersburg. For more details, see p93.

Kazakhstan

Trains to/from Kazakhstan run every two days between Moscow and Almaty (R4100, 78 hours). There is also a service between Novosibirsk–Almaty, and some of the services between Yekaterinburg and Omsk also cut through Kazakhstan, stopping at the city of Petropavlovsk.

Latvia

Handy overnight trains run daily between Rīga and Moscow (R1404 *platskart,* 15 hours) and St Petersburg (R1812, 13 hours). There are two daily buses from Rīga to St Petersburg (R500, 11 hours); see p93. There are also two to three buses daily to Moscow (14 to 16 hours). See http://ecolines.lv for more bus information.

Lithuania

From Vilnius trains leave for Moscow (R1588, 15 hours) three times a week and for St Petersburg (R1387 to R1499, 15¼ hours) every other day. The St Petersburg trains cross Latvia, and the Moscow ones cross Belarus; you'll need a transit visa.

Mongolia

Apart from the Trans-Mongolian train connecting Moscow and Beijing, there's a direct train twice a week from Ulaanbaatar to Moscow (R3800, 101 hours) as well as a daily service to and from Irkutsk (R1600, 25 to 35 hours). There's also a bus service connecting Ulan-Ude and Ulaanbaatar (p217).

Poland

There are daily services linking Warsaw with Moscow (R2200, 20 hours) and St Petersburg (R2240, 29 hours). The Moscow trains enter Belarus near Brest. The St Petersburg trains leave Poland at Kuznica, which is near Hrodna (Grodno in Russian) in Belarus. Changing the wheels to/from Russia's wider gauge adds three hours to the journey.

UK & Europe

Travelling overland by train from the UK or Western Europe takes a minimum of two days and nights. It is, however, a great way of easing yourself into the rhythm of the Trans-Siberian Railway.

There are no direct trains from the UK to Russia. The most straightforward route is on the **Eurostar** (www.eurostar.com) to Brussels, and then a two-night direct train to Moscow via Warsaw and Minsk (Belarus). The total cost can be as low as £217 one-way. See www.seat61.com/russia.htm#moscow for details of this and other train services to Moscow.

To avoid the hassle of getting a Belarus transit visa consider taking the train to St Petersburg from Vilnius (opposite), which runs several times a week via Latvia. There are daily connections between Vilnius and Warsaw.

From Moscow and St Petersburg there are also regular international services to European cities including Berlin, Budapest, Prague, Vienna and Warsaw; see p120 and p94 for details.

For European rail timetables check www.railfaneurope.net, which provides a central link to all of Europe's national railways.

Ukraine

Most major Ukrainian cities have daily services to Moscow, with two border crossings: one used by trains heading to Kyiv (Kiev), the other by trains passing through Kharkiv.

Between Kyiv and Moscow (R1033, nine hours, nine services daily) the best trains to take (numbers are southbound/northbound) are the *Metropolitan Express*, the 1/2 (the *Ukraïna*) or 3/4 (the *Kyiv*). The best train between Moscow and Lviv (Lvov in Russian; 28 hours, daily via Kyiv) is 73/74. Between Moscow and Odesa (28 hours, daily via Kyiv) there's the *Odesa* (23/24). There are also daily trains to/from St Petersburg to Lviv (31 hours via Vilnius) and Kyiv (26 hours).

From Kharkiv to Moscow (13 hours, about 14 daily via Kursk) the best service is the *Kharkiv* (19/20). Other services connecting with Moscow include Simferopol (26 hours, daily via Kharkiv), Donetsk (22 hours, three daily), Dnipropetrovsk (20 hours, twice daily), Zaporizhzhya (Zaporozhye in Russian; 19 hours, twice daily) and Sevastopol (29½ hours, daily).

There are also daily international trains passing through Ukraine to/from Moscow's Kyivsky vokzal. These include the 15/16 Kyiv–Lviv–Chop–Budapest–Belgrade, with a carriage to Zagreb three times a week.

RIVER & SEA

The Amur River, which forms part of the border between Russia and China, can be crossed by ferries from Khabarovsk to Fuyuan (p229) and from Blagoveshchensk to Heihe (p223).

Russia

St Petersburg is regularly connected by **Silja Line** (www.silja.fi) cruises with Helsinki in Finland (from €120, 15 hours) and less frequently by ferry with Tallinn in Estonia (€20, 14½ hours) and Rostock in Germany (€90, 42 hours). **Baltfinn** (www.baltfinn.ru) offers weekly ferry service on the ship *George Ots,* travelling between Baltisk (the port near the Russian enclave of Kaliningrad) and St Petersburg. **Baltic Line** (www.baltics.ru/bl/eng/) and **Trans Russia Express** (www.tre.de) both run weekly ferries to Lubeck in Germany which also go via Baltisk; check their websites for current details. For details of ferries from Vladivostok to Japan and South Korea, see p236.

China

Beijing's nearest seaport is Tianjin Municipality's port district of Tanggu. Ships travel between Tianjin and Kobe, Japan, once a week (from Y1875, 48 hours) and Incheon, South Korea, twice a week (from Y1000, 28 hours). In China buy tickets at the Tanggu **passenger ferry terminal** (☎ 022-2570 6728) or Tianjin's **CITS** (☎ 022-2835 8309; 22 Youyi Lu, Tianjin; ☽ 8.30am-5pm Mon-Fri).

TOURS

If you have time, and a certain degree of determination, organising your own trip to Russia is easily done; see p14. But for many travellers, opting for the assistance of an agency in drawing up an itinerary, booking train tickets and accommodation, not to mention helping with the visa paperwork, will be preferable.

The following agencies and tour companies provide a range of travel services. Numerous more locally based agencies can provide tours once you're in Russia; see the destination chapters for details. Many work in conjunction with overseas agencies so if you go to them directly you'll usually pay less.

Australia

Eastern Europe/Russian Travel Centre (☎ 02-9262 1144; www.eetbtravel.com; Level 5, 75 King St, Sydney, NSW 2000)

Passport Travel (☎ 03-9867 3888; www.travelcentre .com.au; Suite 11A, 401 St Kilda Rd, Melbourne, Vic 3004)

Russian Gateway Tours (☎ 02-9745 3333; www .russian-gateway.com.au; 48 The Boulevarde, Strathfield, NSW 2135)

Sundowners (☎ 03-9672 5300; www.sundowners travel.com; Suite 15, 600 Lonsdale St, Melbourne, Vic 3000) Specialises in Trans-Siberian packages and tours.

Travel Directors (☎ 08-9242 4200; www.travel directors.com.au; 177 Oxford St, Leederville, WA 6007) Upmarket Trans-Siberian tour operator.

Canada

Trek Escapes (☎ 866-338-TREK; www.trekescapes.com /index.cfm; 223 Carlton St, Toronto, Ontario M5A 2L2) Canada's top adventure tour agency offers Trans-Siberian packages with Sundowners and Imaginative Traveller. Also has branches in Calgary, Edmonton and Vancouver.

China

Beijing Tourism Group (BTG; ☎ 010-6515 8562; Beijing Tourist Bldg, 28 Jianguomen Wai Dajie, Beijing) Formerly known as the China International Travel Service (CITS).

Monkey Business (☎ 010-6591 6519; www.monkey shrine.com; room 35, Red House Hotel, 10 Chu Xiu Lu, Dongzhimenwai, Beijing) Offers tours on the Trans-Siberian, Trans-Manchurian and Trans-Mongolian trains.

Moonsky Star Ltd (☎ 852-2723 1376; Chung King Mansion, E-4-6, Nathan Rd 36-44, Kowloon, Hong Kong) Monkey Business' Hong Kong partner.

Germany

Lernidee Reisen (☎ 030-786 0000; www.lernidee -reisen.de; Eisenacher Strasse, D-10777 Berlin)

Japan

MO Tourist CIS Russian Centre (☎ 03-5296 5783; www.motcis.com, in Japanese; 2F Kandatsukasa-cho Bldg, 2-2-12 Kandatsukasa-cho, Chiyoda-ku, Tokyo 101 0048) Can help arrange ferries and flights to Russia.

UK

GW Travel Ltd (☎ 0161-928 9410; www.gwtravel.co.uk; Denzell House, Denzell Gardens, Dunham Rd, Altrincham, Cheshire WA14 4QF) Offers luxury Trans-Siberian tours on private Pullman-style carriages with restaurants, showers and lectures.

Imaginative Traveller (☎ 0800-316 2717; www .imaginative-traveller.com; 1 Betts Ave, Martlesham Heath, Suffolk IP5 7RH)

Intourist Travel (☎ 020-7538 8600; www.intourist.co.uk; 219 Marsh Wall, London E14 9PD)

Regent Holidays (☎ 0117-921 1711; www.regent -holidays.co.uk; 15 John St, Bristol BS1 2HR)

Russia Experience (☎ 020-8566 8846; www.trans -siberian.co.uk; Research House, Fraser Rd, Perivale, Middlesex UB6 7AQ) Also runs the Beetroot Bus (www.beetroot .org), a backpacker-style tour between St Petersburg and Moscow, as well as adventurous programmes in the Altai and Tuva.

Russian Gateway (☎ 08704-46 1690; www.russian gateway.co.uk) Web-based agency.

Steppes East (☎ 01285-880 980; www.steppeseast.co .uk; The Travel House, 51 Castle St, Cirencester, Gloucestershire GL7 1QD) Specialises in catering to off-beat requirements.

Travel for the Arts (☎ 020-8799 8350; www.travel forthearts.co.uk; 12-15 Hangar Green, London W5 3EL) Specialist in luxury culture-based tours to Russia for people with a specific interest in opera and ballet.

Voyages Jules Verne (☎ 020-7616 1000; www.vjv.co .uk; 21 Dorset Sq, London NW1 6QG) Offers a variety of upmarket tours in Russia.

USA

Cruise Marketing International (☎ 800-578-7742; www.cruiserussia.com; Suite 3, 3401 Investment Rd, Hayward, CA 94545) Books tours on cruises along Russian waterways such as the Volga River.

Far East Development (☎ 206-282-0824; www .traveleastrussia.com; 1321 W Emerson 6, Seattle, WA 98119) Eco-adventure tour company specialising in Far East Russia.

Mir Corporation (☎ 206-624-7289; www.mircorp.com; Suite 210, 85 S Washington St, Seattle, WA 98104) Options include private train tours along the Trans-Siberian route in Pullman-style carriages.

Red Star Travel (☎ 206-522-5995; www.travel2 russia.com; Suite 102, 123 Queen Anne Ave N, Seattle, WA 98109)

Russiatours (☎ 800-633-1008; www.russia tours.com; Suite 102, 13312 N 56th St, Tampa, FL 33617) Specialises in luxury tours to Moscow and St Petersburg.

Sokol Tours (☎ /fax 724-935-5373; www.sokoltours .com; 27 Meeting House Lane, Bradford Woods, PA 15015-1310) Tour options include train trips, Tuva and Kamchatka.

White Nights (☎ /fax 916-979-9381; www.wnights .com; 610 La Sierra Dr, Sacramento, CA 95864) This company also has offices in Germany, the Netherlands, Russia and Switzerland.

GETTING AROUND

For most, if not all, of your Trans-Siberian journey you're going to be getting around on the train, but sometimes you might need to take an internal flight or a bus. The following details apply mainly for getting around Russia, with significant differences mentioned for China and Mongolia. There's also some information for those thinking of driving or cycling through Russia (see p329).

AIR
Russia

It's no problem buying a ticket, with *avia kassy* (ticket offices) all over most large towns and cities. Generally speaking, you'll do better booking internal flights once you arrive in Russia. Fares are generally 30% cheaper (60% on major Moscow routings) for advance bookings or evening departures. Finding out fares before you arrive can be tricky; try the airline websites listed on p319, or contact **Primorskoye Aeroagentsvo** (☎ 4232-407 707; www.airagency.ru), a Vladivostok-based agency with branches in Moscow and St Petersburg as well as across the Russian Far East, which will quote fares and have English-speaking agents.

Tickets can also be purchased at the airport right up to the departure of the flight and sometimes even if the city centre office says that the plane is full. Return fares are usually double the cost of one-way fares.

Make sure you reconfirm your flight at least 24 hours before takeoff: Russian airlines have a nasty habit of cancelling unconfirmed tickets. Airlines may also bump you if you don't check in at least 90 minutes before departure. Unlike the train, the idea of schedules being stuck to remains in the realms of fantasy: delays and cancellations are common.

The mechanical safety of the planes is an issue, as are the safety procedures (or lack of) for protecting against terrorist attacks. Generally, **Aeroflot Russian Airlines** (www.aeroflot .com), **Transaero** (www.transaero.ru/english) and **Krasair** (www.krasair.ru) are the airlines with a consistent safety record.

To minimise the danger of loss or theft, try not to check in any baggage: many planes have special stowage areas for large carry-on pieces. Russian airlines can be very strict about charging for bags that are overweight, which generally means anything over 20kg.

China

The Civil Aviation Administration of China (CAAC; Zhōngguó Mínháng) is the civil aviation authority for numerous airlines, including **Air China** (www.airchina.com.cn), **China Eastern Airlines** (www.ce-air.com) and **China Southern Airlines** (www.cs-air.com).

CAAC publishes timetables in both English and Chinese in April and November each year, available at airports and CAAC offices in China. Tickets are easy to purchase from branches of CAAC nationwide, other airline offices and travel agents or from the travel desk of your hotel; at most times there is an oversupply of airline seats (except during major festivals and holidays). Ask around for discounts. Return tickets cost twice the single fare.

On domestic and international flights the free baggage allowance for an adult passenger is 20kg in economy class and 30kg in 1st class. You are also allowed 5kg of hand luggage, though this is rarely weighed.

Mongolia

Although Mongolia has 81 airports and airstrips, only 31 can be used permanently and only eight of these are paved. Almost all of the destinations are served directly from Ulaanbaatar. The domestic fleet of **Mongolian Airlines** (www.miat.com) has been retired due to age and the cash-strapped government has been reluctant to buy or lease new planes, knowing full well that the domestic market is virtually unprofitable. Possible alternatives are **Aero Mongolia** (☎ 011-330 373; www.aeromongolia.mn) and **Blue Sky Aviation** (☎ 011-312 085; www.bsamongolia .com), which has a nine-seat Cessna that can be chartered for any part of the country.

CAR & MOTORCYCLE
Russia

Russian main roads are a really mixed bag – sometimes they are smooth, straight dual carriageways, sometimes rough, narrow, winding and choked with the diesel fumes of the slow, heavy vehicles that make up a high proportion of Russian traffic. Driving much more than 300km in the course of a day is pretty tiring.

Russian drivers use indicators far less than they should, and like to overtake everything on the road – on the inside. Priority rules at roundabouts seem to vary from area to area: all you can do is follow local practice. Russian drivers rarely switch on anything more than sidelights – and often not even those – until it's pitch black at night. Some say this is to avoid dazzling others, as for some reason dipping headlights is not a common practice.

FUEL
Western-style gas stations are common. Petrol comes in four main grades: 76, 93, 95 and 98 octane. And prices are cheap by European standards: R8 a litre for 76 octane and R10 a litre for 98 octane. Unleaded gas is available in major cities; BP gas stations usually always sell it. *Dizel* (diesel) is also available (around R13 a litre). In the countryside, petrol stations are usually not more than 100km apart, but you shouldn't rely on this.

ROAD RULES
Russians drive on the right-hand side of the road and traffic coming from the right has the right of way. Speed limits are generally 60km/h in towns and between 80km/h and 110km/h on highways. There may be a 90km/h zone, enforced by speed traps,

---

THE GAI

Not to put too fine a point on it, many officers of the State Automobile Inspectorate, GAI (*gah-yee*, short for Gosudarstvennaya Avtomobilnaya Inspektsia), are nothing short of highway bandits. GAI officers are authorised to stop you (they do this by pointing their striped, sometimes lighted, stick at you and waving you towards the side of the road), issue on-the-spot fines and shoot at you if you don't pull over.

Watch for speed traps on major roads into Moscow and St Petersburg. There are permanent GAI checkpoints at the boundary of many Russian cities and towns, while in cities, the GAI is everywhere, stopping cars for no reason and collecting 'fines'. For serious infractions, the GAI can confiscate your licence, which you'll have to retrieve from the main station. Get receipts for any fine you pay and if you think you've been ripped off, head for the nearest GAI office and complain. Get the shield number of the arresting officer.

---

as you leave a city. Children under 12 may not travel in the front seat, and safety-belt use is mandatory. Motorcycle riders (and passengers) must wear crash helmets.

Technically the maximum legal blood-alcohol content is 0.04%, but in practice it is illegal to drive after consuming *any* alcohol at all. This is a rule that is strictly enforced. The normal way of establishing alcohol in the blood is by a blood test, but apparently you can be deemed under the influence even without any test.

Traffic lights that flicker green are about to change to yellow, then red.

You'll need to be 18 years old and have an International Driving Permit with a Russian translation of your licence, or a certified Russian translation of your full licence (you can certify translations at a Russian embassy or consulate).

Don't forget your vehicle's registration papers, proof of insurance (be sure it covers you in Russia) and a customs declaration promising that you will take your vehicle with you when you leave. To get the exact details on all this it's best to contact your automobile association (eg the AA or RAC in the UK) at least three months before your trip.

China
The authorities remain anxious about foreigners driving at whim around China, so don't plan on hiring a car and driving wherever you want. Cars can be hired in Beijing for local use only. Road conditions in China should abolish any remaining desire to get behind the wheel. Bilingual road signs are making a slow appearance along some highways, but much remains to confuse would-be drivers from abroad.

DRIVING LICENCE
To hire a car, you will need to come armed with an International Driving Permit. Foreigners can drive motorcycles if they are residents in China and have a Chinese motorcycle licence.

HIRE
Although tourists are permitted to rent vehicles in Beijing and a handful of other major cities it's not worth the hassle and inconvenience. You will be restricted to driving around within the perimeters of each city. Although expat residents report little

TRANS-SIBERIAN DRIVING & CYCLING

In 2004 the final missing link in a Trans-Russian highway was filled when a section of road opened between Chita and Khabarovsk. It's now possible to drive or cycle the 10,000-plus kilometres from St Petersburg to Vladivostok, although only about one-quarter of the eastern section of the highway is paved. The rest is gravel-topped, but there are plans to have the entire highway paved in the coming years.

A few intrepid souls have been known to rise to the challenge of driving, even cycling, across the country. Recently Ewan McGregor and Charley Boorman wrote about their Russian adventures in *Long Way Round* (www.longwayround.com/lwr.htm); their round-the-world route took them from Volgograd all the way to Yakutsk and Magadan via Kazakhstan and Mongolia. The celebrity bikers had a camera crew and support team following them. For tales of how to cross part of Russia the hard way check out www.roundtheworldbybike.com, the website of Alistair Humphreys who cycled from Magadan to Vanino in the depths of winter!

Before following in these footsteps, bear in mind the often numbing monotony of the landscape, the sometimes dire quality of the roads, the lack of adequate signposting, the keen-eyed highway police on the lookout for a bribe, and the difficulty of obtaining spare parts. Should you still feel inspired, the crucial information is outlined on p327.

problem driving into provinces neighbouring the above locations, we cannot advise attempting to drive beyond these few cities as hire cars carry easily identifiable licence plates. Rates for hire cars start at around Y300 per day, with monthly rates from around Y5000; on most occasions, using taxis all day will work out much cheaper.

If you want to use a car, it's easy enough to book a car with a driver. Basically, this is just a standard long-distance taxi. Travel agencies like CITS or even hotel booking desks can make the arrangements. They generally ask excessive fees – the name of the game is to negotiate. If you can communicate in Chinese or find someone to translate, it's not particularly difficult to find a private taxi driver to take you wherever you like for less than half the CITS rates.

Mongolia

Travelling around Mongolia with your own car or motorcycle – without a driver – is not recommended. What look like main roads on the map are often little more than tyre tracks in the dirt, sand or mud. All maps are inadequate, and there is hardly a signpost in the whole country. In Mongolia, roads connect nomads, most of whom by their nature keep moving so even the roads are seminomadic, shifting like restless rivers. Remote tracks quickly turn into eight-lane dirt highways devoid of any traffic making navigation tricky – some drivers follow the telephone lines when there are any, or else

ask for directions at *gers* (felt tents) along the way. Towns with food and water are few and far between, and very few people in the countryside will speak anything but Mongolian or, if you are lucky, Russian.

If all this hasn't put you off, keep in mind that foreigners have been jailed for being involved in traffic accidents, even if they were not at fault. We've heard horror stories of Mongolians purposely causing accidents with foreigners simply to make them pay for damages (police tend to side with the home team). Contact your embassy immediately if you get in trouble. Another way to avoid jail is to claim an injury, in which case you'll be taken to a hospital.

HIRE

There is nowhere official in Mongolia to rent a car or motorcycle. If you want to buy one, you will have to ask around, or check out the 'car market' *(Tsaiz zakh)* in the northeastern part of Ulaanbaatar.

HITCHING

Hitching is never entirely safe in any country in the world, and Lonely Planet doesn't recommend it. Travellers who hitch should understand that they are taking a small but potentially serious risk.

Russia

Hitching in Russia is a very common method of getting around. In cities, hitching rides is called hailing a taxi, no matter what type of vehicle stops (see opposite for more information). In the countryside, especially in remote areas not well served by public transport, hitching is a major mode of transport.

China

Passengers are expected to offer at least a tip when hitching in China. Some drivers might even ask for an unreasonable amount of money, so try to establish a figure early to avoid problems later. Even when a price is agreed upon, don't be surprised if the driver raises it when you arrive at your destination and creates a big scene (with a big crowd) if you don't cough up the extra cash. Indeed, they may even pull this scam halfway through the trip, and if you don't pay up you get kicked out in the middle of nowhere.

In other words, don't think of hitching as a means to save money – it will rarely be any cheaper than the bus. The main reason to do it is to get to isolated outposts where public transport is poor. There is, of course, some joy in meeting the locals this way, but communicating is certain to be a problem if you don't speak Chinese.

Mongolia

Because the country is so vast, public transport so limited and the people so poor, hitching (usually on trucks) is a recognised – and, often, the only – form of transport in the countryside. Hitching is seldom free and often no different from just waiting for public transport to turn up. It is *always* slow – after stopping at *gers* to drink, fixing flat tyres, breaking down, running out of petrol and getting stuck in mud and rivers, a truck can take 48 hours to cover 200km.

Hitching is not generally dangerous personally, but it is still hazardous and often extremely uncomfortable. Don't expect much traffic in remote rural areas; you might see one or two vehicles a day on many roads, and sometimes nobody at all for several days. The best place to wait is the petrol station on the outskirts of town, where most vehicles stop before any journey.

LOCAL TRANSPORT

For details of local trains see opposite. Also see the Getting Around sections of the city and route guide chapters for details of local bus, metro, tram and boat services.

Boat
RUSSIA

In summer it's possible to travel long distances across Russia on passenger boats. You can do this either by taking a cruise, which you can book through agencies in the West or in Russia, or by using scheduled river passenger services. The season runs from late May through to mid-October, but is shorter on some routes.

There are numerous boats plying the routes between Moscow and St Petersburg, many stopping at some of the Golden Ring cities on the way; and along the Volga River from Moscow to other Trans-Siberian cities such as Nizhny Novgorod and Kazan. In Siberia and the Russian Far East there are services along the Ob and Irtysh Rivers (between Omsk and Tobolsk), the Yenisey from Krasnoyarsk, the Lena from Ust-Kut via Lensk to Yakutsk, the Amur from Khabarovsk to Komsomolsk, as well as across Lake Baikal from Irkutsk to Nizhneangarsk.

Beware that boat schedules can change radically from year to year (especially on Lake Baikal) and are only published infuriatingly close to the first sailing of each season.

Bus

Long-distance buses complement rather than compete with the rail network. They generally serve areas with no railway or routes on which trains are slow, infrequent or overloaded.

RUSSIA

Most cities have a main intercity автовокзал (*avtovokzal,* bus station). Like long-distance bus stations everywhere they are often scoundrel magnets, and are rarely pleasant places to visit after dark. Tickets are sold at the station or on the bus. Fares are normally listed on the timetable and posted on a wall. As often as not you'll get a ticket with a seat assignment, scribbled almost illegibly on a till receipt. Prices are comparable to 2nd-class train fares; journey times depend on road conditions. A sometimes hefty fee is charged for larger bags.

Marshrutky (a diminutive form of *marshrutnoye taksi,* meaning a fixed-route taxi) are minibuses that are quicker than the rusty old buses and rarely cost much more. Where roads are good and villages frequent, *marshrutky* can be twice as fast as buses, and well worth the double fare.

CHINA

Chángtú gōnggōngqìchē (long-distance buses) are one of the best means of getting around China. Services are extensive, main roads are improving and with the increasing number of intercity highways, bus journeys are getting quicker (often quicker than train travel). It's also easier to secure bus tickets than train tickets and they are often cheaper. Buses also stop in small towns and villages, so you get to see parts of the countryside you wouldn't see if you travelled by train, although breakdowns can be a problem.

On the down side, some rural roads and provincial routes are in shocking condition, dangerously traversed by nerve-shattering hulks. Long-distance bus journeys can be cramped and noisy, with Hong Kong films on overhead TVs and three-dimensional sound. Drivers lean on the horn at the slightest detection of a vehicle in front.

Routes between large cities sport larger, cleaner and more comfortable fleets of private buses, such as comfy Volvos; shorter and more far-flung routes still rely on rattling minibuses into which the driver crams as many fares as is possible.

On popular long-haul routes, *wòpù qìchē* (sleeper buses) may cost around double the price of a normal bus service, but many travellers swear by them. Some have comfortable reclining seats, while others have two-tier bunks. Watch out for your belongings on them, however.

Taxi
RUSSIA

There are two main types of taxis in Russia: the official ones, metered taxis you order by phone or the rarer four-door sedans with a chequerboard strip down the side and a green light in the front window that cruise the streets of Moscow; and 'private' taxis (any other vehicle on the road).

Hail rides by standing at the side of the road and flagging passing vehicles with a low, up-and-down wave (not an extended thumb). State your destination and negotiate the fare before getting in. You are expected to pitch in for petrol; paying what would be the normal bus fare for a long-haul ride is considered appropriate. If the driver's game,

they'll ask you to *sadites* (get in), but always act on the cautious side before doing this. Check with locals to determine the average taxi fare in that city at the time; taxi prices around the country vary widely. The better your Russian, generally the lower the fare. If possible, let a Russian negotiate for you: they'll do better than you will.

As a precaution have the taxi stop at the corner nearest your destination, not the exact address, if you're staying at a private residence. Trust your instincts. If a driver looks creepy, take the next car, and don't get in a car with more than one person inside.

TRAIN

For more detailed information about train travel in Mongolia and China, see Lonely Planet's *Mongolia* and *China* guides.

Russia

Russian trains have a remarkable record for punctuality, with most departing each station on their route to the minute allotted on the timetable. However, there are underlying reasons for this punctuality: managers have a large portion of their pay determined by the timeliness of their trains. This not only inspires promptness, but it results in the creation of generous schedules. You'll sometimes find your train stationary for hours in the middle of nowhere only to start up and roll into the next station on time.

Timetables are posted in stations and are revised twice a year. The Russian rail network mostly runs on Moscow time, so timetables and station clocks from St Petersburg to Vladivostok will be written in and set to Moscow time. The only exception is suburban services, which are listed in local time.

Most stations have an information window; expect the attendant to speak only Russian and to give a bare minimum of information. Sometimes you may have to pay a small fee (around R10) for information. See p332 for ways to crack the timetable code on your own.

CLASSES

The regular long-distance service is a *skory poezd* (fast train), which rarely gets up enough speed to merit being called 'fast', but is indeed much quicker than the frequently stopping *passazhirsky poezd* (passenger trains) found mainly on routes of

1000km or less. A *prigorodny poezd* (suburban train), nicknamed an *elektrichka*, is a local service linking a city and its suburbs or nearby towns, or groups of adjacent towns.

The premium trains are *firmennye poezdy* and often have proper names (eg *Rossiya*). These generally have cleaner and more upper-class carriages, polite attendants, more convenient arrival and departure times and a reasonable (or at least functioning) restaurant car. Sometimes the ticket prices will also include your linen and breakfast.

Russians make themselves very much at home on trains. This often means they'll be travelling with plenty of luggage. It also means some juggling of the available space will become inevitable.

In all but local trains there's a luggage bin underneath each of the lower berths that will hold a medium-sized backpack or small suitcase. There's also enough space beside the bin to squeeze in another medium-sized

bag. Above the doorway (in 1st and 2nd class) or over the upper bunks (in 3rd class) there's room for a couple more rucksacks.

In classes with sleeping accommodation you'll be asked if you want *pastil*. If you accept (recommended) you'll be given two sheets, a washcloth, a pillowcase and a blanket; you'll usually have to pay extra (R40 to R60) for this to the *provodnitsa* (carriage attendant). In 1st class the bed is often made up already and with some types of fare the cost of bedding is included.

All compartments are air-conditioned in summer and heated in winter – that's why the windows are locked shut (though sometimes you'll be able to open them). There a speaker above the window through which the *provodnitsa* can inflict her music on you – you can switch this off with the knob.

Note that no account is taken of sex when allocating a cabin, so a single woman might find herself sharing with three men. If you

READING A RUSSIAN TRAIN TIMETABLE

Russian train timetables generally list a destination, train number, category of train, frequency of service and time of departure and arrival, in Moscow time unless otherwise noted.

Trains in smaller city stations generally begin somewhere else, so you'll see a starting point and a destination on the timetable. For example, when catching a train from Yekaterinburg to Irkutsk, the timetable may list Moscow as an origination point and Irkutsk as the destination. The following are a few key points to look out for.

Number

The higher the номер (*nomer*, number) of a train, the slower it is; anything over 900 is likely to be a mail train. The number also indicates train standard: the lower the number, the higher the standard and the higher the price; if you want the best trains look for numbers under 100. Odd-numbered trains head towards Moscow; even-numbered ones head east away from the capital.

Category

Скорый (*Skory*, fast), Пассажирский (*Passazhirsky*, passenger), Почтово-багажный (*Pochtovo-bagazhny*, post-cargo) and Пригородный (*Prigorodny*, suburban) – and various abbreviations thereof – are the categories you will encounter. There may also be the name of the train, eg 'Россия' ('*Rossiya'*).

Frequency

Frequency is shown as Ежедневно (*yezhednevno*, daily), чётные (*chyotnye*, even-numbered dates), нечётные (*nechyotnye*, odd-numbered dates) or отменён (*otmenyon*, cancelled). All of these, as well, can appear in various abbreviations, notably еж, ч, не and отмен. Days of the week are listed usually as numbers (where one is Monday and seven Sunday) or as abbreviations of the name of the day (Пон, Вт, Ср, Чт, Пт, С and Вск are, respectively, Monday to Sunday). Remember that time zone differences can affect these days. So in Chita (Moscow time plus six hours), a train timetabled at 23.20 on Tuesday actually leaves 5.20am on Wednesday.

In months with an odd number of days two odd days follow one another (eg 31 May, 1 June). This throws out trains working on an alternate-day cycle so if travelling near month's end pay special attention to the hard-to-decipher footnotes on a timetable (eg '27/V – 3/VI Ч means that from 27 May to 3 June the train runs on even dates).

don't feel comfortable, ask the *provodnitsa* if you can swap – it's often possible.

If you want true luxury, you'll need to shell out for the trips offered by companies such as **Mir Corporation** (☎ 206-624-7289; www .mircorp.com; Suite 210, 85 S Washington St, Seattle, WA 98104) in the US and **GW Travel Ltd** (☎ 0161-928 9410; www.gwtravel.co.uk; Denzell House, Denzell Gardens, Dunham Rd, Altrincham, Cheshire WA14 4QF) in the UK, which use private rail cars that are complete with plush compartments and showers.

Deluxe 1st class

These are only available on the 3/4 Trans-Mongolian train. These two-berth compartments are roomy, have wood-panelling, are carpeted and have a sofa. A shower cubicle is shared with the adjacent compartment.

1st Class – SV

Most often called SV (short for *spalny vagon*, or sleeping wagon), 1st-class compartments are also called *myagky* (soft class) or *lyux*. They are the same size as 2nd class but have only two berths, so there's more room and privacy for double the cost. Some 1st-class compartments have TVs on which you can watch videos/DVDs supplied by the *provodnitsa* for a small fee (or bring your own). You can unplug the TV and plug in your computer or other electrical equipment. These carriages also have the edge in that there are only half as many people queuing to use the toilet every morning. So far, on only a couple of services (Moscow to St Petersburg and Moscow to Kazan) will you find luxury SV compartments each with their own shower and toilet.

2nd Class – Kupeyny

The compartments in a *kupeyny* (2nd class, also called 'compartmentalised') carriage (often shortened to *kupe*) are the standard accommodation on long-distance trains. These

---

On some trains, frequency depends on the time of year, in which case details are usually given in similar abbreviated small print.

Arrival & Departure Times

Most train times are given in a 24-hour time format, and almost always in Moscow time (Московское время, *Moskovskoye vremya*). But suburban trains are usually marked in local time (местное время, *mestnoe vremya*). From here on it gets tricky (as though the rest wasn't), so don't confuse the following:

■ время отправления (*vremya otpravleniya*, time of departure)

■ время отправления с начального пункта (*vremya otpravleniya s nachalnogo punkta*, time of departure from the train's starting point)

■ время прибытия (*vremya pribytiya*, time of arrival at the station you're in)

■ время прибытия на конечный пункт (*vremya pribytiya v konechny punkt*, time of arrival at the destination)

■ время в пути (*vremya v puti*, duration of the journey)

Corresponding trains running in opposite directions on the same route may appear on the same line of the timetable. In this case you may find route entries like время отправления с конечного пункта (*vremya otpravleniya s konechnogo punkta*), or the time the return train leaves its station of origin.

Distance

You may sometimes see the расстояние (*rastoyaniye*, distance in kilometres from the point of departure) on the timetable as well. These are rarely accurate and usually refer to the kilometre distance used to calculate the fare.

Note that if you want to calculate where you are while on a journey, keep a close look out for the small black-and-white kilometre posts generally on the southern side of the track. These mark the distance to and from Moscow. In between each kilometre marker are smaller posts counting down roughly every 100m. The distances on train timetables don't always correspond to these marker posts (usually because the timetable distances are ones used to calculate fares).

carriages are divided into nine compartments, each with four reasonably comfortable berths, a fold-down table and enough room between bunks to turn around.

In every carriage there's also one half-sized compartment with just two berths. This is usually occupied by the *provodnitsa,* or reserved for railway employees, but there is a slim chance that you may end up in it, particularly if you do a deal directly with a *provodnitsa* for a train ticket.

3rd Class – Platskartny

A reserved-place *platskartny* carriage, sometimes also called *zhyostky* ('hard class', or 3rd class) and usually abbreviated to *platskart,* is

---

HOW TO READ YOUR TICKET

When buying a ticket in Russia you'll always be asked for your passport so that its number and your name can be printed on your ticket. The ticket and passport will be matched up by the *provodnitsa* (carriage attendant) before you're allowed on the train – so make sure the ticket-seller gets these details correct.

Most tickets are printed by computer and come with a duplicate. Shortly after you've boarded the train the *provodnitsa* will come around and collect the tickets; sometimes they will take both copies and give you one back just before your final destination, sometimes they will leave you with the copy. It's a good idea to hang onto this ticket, especially if you're hopping on and off trains, since it provides evidence of how long you've been in a particular place if you're stopped by police.

Sometimes tickets are also sold with separate chits for insurance in the event of a fatal accident (this is a small payment, usually less than R30); for linen; and for some or all meals. The following is a guide for deciphering the rest of what your Russian train ticket is about:

1 Train number

2 Train type

3 Departure date – shows day and month

4 Departure time – always Moscow time for long-distance trains

5 Carriage number and class: Л = two-bed SV; М = four-bed SV; К = *kupeyny*; П = *platskartny*; О = *obshchy*

6 Supplement for class of ticket above *platskartny*

7 Cost for *platskartny* ticket

8 Number of people travelling on ticket

9 Type of passenger: полный (*polny,* adult); детский (*detsky,* child); студенческий (*studenchesky,* student)

10 From/to

11 Bed number

12 Passport number and name

13 Total cost of ticket

14 Tax and service fee

15 Arrival date

16 Arrival time – always Moscow time for long-distance trains

essentially a dorm carriage sleeping 54. The bunks are uncompartmentalised and are arranged in blocks of four down one side of the corridor and in twos on the other, with the lower bunk on this side converting to a table and chairs during the day.

Platskart is ideal for single-night journeys. However, on multiday journeys the scene often resembles a refugee camp, with clothing strung between bunks, a swapping of bread, fish and tea and babies sitting on potties while their snot-nosed siblings tear up and down the corridor. That said, many travellers (women in particular) find this a better option than being cooped up with three Russian men. It's also a great way to meet ordinary Russians. *Platskart* tickets cost half to two-thirds the price of a 2nd-class berth.

If you do travel *platskart*, it's worth requesting specific numbered seats when booking your ticket. The ones to avoid are 1 to 4, 33 to 38, 53 and 54, found at each end of the carriage, close to the samovar and toilets, where there is lots of activity. Note 39 to 52 are the doubles with the bunk that converts to a table – you may want to avoid these ones too, especially if you're tall.

4th Class – Obshchy

Also called 4th class, *obshchy* (general) is unreserved. On long-distance trains the *obshchy* carriage looks the same as a *platskart* one, but when full, eight people are squeezed into each unenclosed compartment so there's no room to lie down. Suburban trains normally have only *obshchy* class, which in this case means bench-type seating. On a few daytime-only intercity trains there are higher-grade *obshchy* carriages with more comfortable, reserved chairs.

LEFT LUGGAGE

Many train stations have either a secure камера хранения (*kamera khraneniya,* left-luggage room) or автоматические камеры хранения (*avtomaticheskiye kamery khraneniya,* left-luggage lockers). Make sure you note down the room's opening and closing hours and, if in doubt, establish how long you can leave your stuff for. Typical costs are R40 to R80 per bag per day (depending on size) or R72 per locker.

Here is how to work the left-luggage lockers (they're generally the same everywhere). Be suspicious of people who offer

---

SHE WHO MUST BE OBEYED

On any long-distance Russian train you'll soon learn who's in charge: the *provodnitsa* (carriage attendant). Although they are sometimes male *(provodniks)*, these attendants are usually women, with some of the most distinctive hairdos you'll come across this side of a drag-queen convention.

Apart from checking your ticket before boarding the train, doling out linen and shaking you awake in the middle of the night when your train arrives, the *provodnitsa's* job is to keep her carriage tidy (some are more diligent at this than others) and to make sure the samovar is always fired up with hot water. They will have cups, plates and cutlery to borrow, if you need them, and can provide drinks and snacks for a small price; some have even been known to cook up meals and offer them around.

On long journeys *provodnitsas* work in teams of two; one will work while the other rests. Butter them up the right way and your journey will be all the more pleasant.

---

to help you work them, above all when it comes to selecting your combination.

- Buy two *zhetony* (tokens) from the attendant.
- Put your stuff in an empty locker.
- Decide on a combination of one Russian letter and three numbers and write it down.
- Set the combination on the inside of the locker door.
- Put one token in the slot.
- Close the locker.

To open the locker, set your combination on the outside of your locker door. Even though it seems as if the knobs on the outside of the door should correspond directly with those on the inside, the letter is always the leftmost knob, followed by three numbers, on both the inside and the outside. After you've set your combination, put a token in the slot, wait a second for the electrical humming sound and then pull it open.

RESERVATIONS

At any station you'll be confronted by several ticket windows. Some are special windows reserved exclusively for the use of the elderly or infirm, heroes of the Great Patriotic War or members of the armed forces. All will have different operating hours and generally unhelpful staff.

The sensible option, especially if there are horrendous queues, is to avail yourself of the *servis tsentr* (service centre) found at most major stations. At these air-conditioned centres – a godsend in summer – you will generally encounter helpful, and sometimes English-speaking staff who, for a small fee (typically around R100), can book your ticket. In big cities and towns it's also usually possible to buy tickets at special offices and some travel agencies away from the station; again, individual chapters provide details.

Whoever you end up buying your ticket from, it's a good idea to have the following written down, in Cyrillic, to hand over to the sales assistant:

- your destination
- the train number
- date and time of departure
- class of ticket required
- number of tickets
- your name (though they'll check on your visa anyway)

When writing dates, use ordinary (Arabic) numerals for the day of the month and Roman numerals for the month. See p332 for more information.

Even if the ticket-sellers tell you a particular service is sold out, it still might be possible to get on the train by speaking with the chief *provodnitsa*. Tell her your destination, offer the face ticket price first, and move slowly upwards from there. You can usually come to some sort of agreement.

Tickets for suburban trains – which are very cheap – are often sold at separate windows or from *avtomaticheskiye kassy* (ticket machines). A table beside the ticket machine tells you which price zone your destination is in.

STOPS

Every carriage has a timetable (in Cyrillic) posted in the corridor, which notes how long the train will stop at each station. These timetables, however, are not set in stone, so always ask the *provodnitsa* when getting off the train how long you're going to be at a station. Usually, stops last from two to five minutes, but at least twice a day the train stops for 15 or 20 minutes, allowing time to get off, stretch your legs and stock up on food from sellers on the platform.

China

China has some 52,000km of domestic train lines, and this is in fact the most comfortable and reliable way to travel around the country. The network covers every province except Tibet.

Your degree of comfort on the train depends on your class of travel. The 'hard-seat' actually – technically – has padded seats. But this class is still hard on one's sanity, as it is generally dirty, noisy and smoky. You may or may not have a seat reservation. Some shorter journeys have *ruǎnxi/ruǎnzuò* (soft-seat) carriages, where overcrowding and smoking are not permitted. The *yìngxi/yìngzuò* (hard-sleeper) carriage consists of doorless compartments with half a dozen bunks in three tiers; this is the most common way for long-distance travel and quite acceptable for a night. 'Soft-sleeper' carriages have four comfortable bunks in a closed compartment; on Z class trains (the best) you'll also have your own TV. Z class trains also have luxury two-berth compartments with their own shower and toilet facilities.

Once you are on the train, the conductor may be able to upgrade your ticket if space is available in other carriages. The cost of the upgraded ticket is prorated to the distance travelled in the higher class. For more about trains in China, see www .seat61.com/china.htm.

Mongolia

Mongolia's rail network is primarily made up of the Trans-Mongolian Railway, with both the domestic and international trains using this same line. It was built during the Soviet era so there are lots of similarities between the Mongolian and Russian train systems. Note that you can't use the Trans-Mongolian Railway for domestic transport.

If you're travelling from Ulaanbaatar, it is important to book a soft seat well in advance – this can be done up to 10 days before departure. There may be a small booking fee. In general, booking ahead is a good idea for any class, though there will always be hard-seat tickets available.

Health

CONTENTS

Although on the whole Russians are far from a healthy people, the dangers to visitors are quite minimal. The same goes for China. As for Mongolia, its cold, dry climate and sparse human habitation mean there are few of the infectious diseases that plague tropical Asian countries. However, there are a few health issues to be aware of. This chapter offers very basic advice; for more details check the Internet resources provided and pick up Lonely Planet's *Healthy Travel – Asia & India*.

BEFORE YOU GO

Prevention is the key to staying healthy while away. A little planning before departure, particularly for pre-existing illnesses, will save trouble later. See your dentist before a long trip, carry a spare pair of contact lenses and glasses, and take your optical prescription with you. Bring medications in their original, clearly labelled, containers. A signed and dated letter from your physician describing your medical conditions and medications, including generic names, is also a good idea. If carrying syringes or needles, be sure to have a physician's letter documenting their medical necessity.

INSURANCE

Good emergency medical treatment is not cheap in this region, so seriously consider taking out a policy that covers you for the worst possible scenario, such as an accident requiring an emergency flight home. Find out in advance if your insurance plan will make payments directly to providers (the preferable option) or reimburse you later for overseas health expenditures.

RECOMMENDED VACCINATIONS
Diphtheria & Tetanus
Recommended for everyone, vaccinations for these two diseases are usually combined.

Hepatitis A
Vaccines including Avaxim, Havrix 1440 and VAQTA provide long-term immunity after an initial injection, then a booster at six to 12 months. Alternatively, an injection of gamma globulin can provide short-term immediate protection; it's reasonably effective, unlike the vaccine, but because it is a blood product, there are current concerns about its long-term safety. Hepatitis A vaccine is also available as Twinrix, combined with hepatitis B vaccine. Three injections over a six-month period are required, the first two providing substantial protection against hepatitis A.

Hepatitis B
This vaccination, involving three injections with a booster at 12 months, is recommended for Russia. Rapid courses are available.

Japanese B Encephalitis
Consider vaccination if spending a month or longer in parts of the Russian Far East and Siberia, or if making repeated trips to at-risk areas. It involves three injections over 30 days.

Polio
You should keep up to date with this vaccination, normally given in childhood – a booster every 10 years ensures immunity.

Rabies
Consider vaccination if you're spending a month or longer travelling, especially if cycling, handling animals, caving or travelling to remote areas; children should also

HEALTH

have it. Pretravel vaccination involves three injections over 21 to 28 days. If someone who has been vaccinated is bitten or scratched by an animal, they'll need two booster injections; those not vaccinated require more.

Tuberculosis
If you'll be living among local people in high-risk areas for three months or more, consider being vaccinated for TB.

Typhoid
Available as an injection or oral capsules. A combined hepatitis A/typhoid vaccine was launched recently but availability is limited; check with your doctor.

INTERNET RESOURCES
The World Health Organisation's (WHO) publication *International Travel and Health* is revised annually and is available online at www.who.int/ith/. Other useful websites:

- www.ageconcern.org.uk – advice on travel for the elderly
- www.fitfortravel.scot.nhs.uk – general travel advice for the layperson
- www.mariestopes.org.uk – information on women's health and contraception
- www.mdtravelhealth.com – travel health recommendations for every country; updated daily

IN RUSSIA, CHINA & MONGOLIA

AVAILABILITY & COST OF HEALTH CARE
Medical care is readily available across Russia but the quality can vary enormously. The biggest cities and towns have the widest choice of places, with both Moscow and St Petersburg well served by sparkling international-style clinics that charge handsomely for their admittedly generally excellent and professional service; except to pay around US$50 for an initial consultation.

Some foreigners (eg British) are theoretically entitled to free treatment in state-run noncommercial clinics, according to bilateral agreements from Soviet times. In practice this means that in Moscow they might be treated for free in cases of major injury. In remote areas doctors won't usually

---

SARS

The Severe Acute Respiratory Syndrome (SARS) health crisis continues to plague China and, in 2005, Russia. For the latest travel advisories, check the following websites (which are also good for general travel advice):

Australia (www.dfat.gov.au/travel)
Canada (www.voyage.gc.ca)
New Zealand (www.mft.govt.nz)
UK (www.fco.gov.uk/travel)
US (www.travel.state.gov/travel/warnings.html)

---

charge you either, but it's recommended to give them gifts – like a bottle of Armenian cognac, chocolate or money.

In some cases, medical supplies required in hospital may need to be bought from a pharmacy and nursing care may be limited. Note that there can be an increased risk of hepatitis B and HIV transmission via poorly sterilised equipment.

Beijing and Harbin and other metropolitan areas of China have good medical facilities well up to international standards. Mongolia however suffers from a serious lack of medical facilities. In short, an ill person is better off in Ulaanbaatar than in the countryside, and better off in Beijing than in Ulaanbaatar. If you must obtain medical assistance in Mongolia, seek out a hospital or private clinic that caters to foreigners and be sure to bring a translator. In China and Mongolia expect to pay anything up to US$100 for an initial consultation at a private clinic.

Apart from the chief *provodnitsa* (carriage attendant) probably having a first-aid box, there is no medical assistance available on the train itself.

INFECTIOUS DISEASES
Influenza
This will be your main health concern across Russia and China, particularly in winter. Symptoms include muscle ache, high fever, runny nose, cough and sore throat. Vaccination is particularly recommended for those aged 65 and over.

Rabies
Spread through bites or licks on broken skin from an infected animal. It is always

fatal unless treated promptly. Animal handlers should be vaccinated, as should those travelling to remote areas where a reliable source of postbite vaccine is not available within 24 hours; see p337.

Tickborne Encephalitis
Spread by tick bites, this is a serious infection of the brain and vaccination is advised for those in risk areas who are unable to avoid tick bites (such as campers, forestry workers and walkers). Two doses of vaccine will give a year's protection, three doses up to three years'. For more information see www .masta.org/tickalert.

Typhoid & Hepatitis A
Spread through contaminated food (particularly shellfish) and water, typhoid can cause septicaemia (blood poisoning); hepatitis A causes liver inflammation and jaundice. Neither is usually fatal but recovery can be prolonged; see opposite and p337.

TRAVELLER'S DIARRHOEA
To prevent diarrhoea, avoid tap water unless it has been boiled, filtered or chemically disinfected (with iodine tablets) and steer clear of ice. Only eat fresh fruits or vegetables if cooked or peeled; be wary of dairy products that might contain unpasteurised milk. Eat food that is hot through and avoid buffet-style meals. If a restaurant is full of locals the food is probably safe.

DRINKING WATER

- Never drink tap water.
- Check the seal on bottled water is intact on purchase.
- Avoid ice and fresh juices if you suspect they have been watered down.
- Boiling water is the most efficient method of purifying it. Trains have a samovar (hot-water heater) in every carriage.
- The best chemical purifier is iodine. It should not be used by pregnant women or those with thyroid problems.
- Water filters should also filter out viruses. Ensure your filter has a chemical barrier such as iodine and a small pore size, eg less than four microns.

If you develop diarrhoea, be sure to drink plenty of fluids, preferably an oral rehydration solution (eg Dioralyte). A few loose stools don't require treatment, but if you start having more than four or five stools a day, you should start taking an antibiotic (usually a quinolone drug) and an antidiarrhoeal agent (such as Loperamide). If diarrhoea is bloody, persists for more than 72 hours or is accompanied by fever, shaking, chills or severe abdominal pain you should seek medical attention.

ENVIRONMENTAL HAZARDS
The temperatures on the trains are generally kept at a comfortable level, but once out in the wide open spaces of Russia, Mongolia and China the main environmental hazards to be careful of are heat exhaustion in summer and frostbite in the winter.

Heat Exhaustion & Heat Stroke
Best avoided by drinking water on a constant basis, heat exhaustion occurs following excessive fluid loss with inadequate replacement of fluids and salt. Symptoms include headache, dizziness and tiredness. Dehydration is already happening by the time you feel thirsty. To treat heat exhaustion, replace lost fluids by drinking water and/or fruit juice, and cool the body with cold water and fans. Treat salt loss with salty fluids such as soup or Bovril, or add a little more table salt to foods than usual.

Heat stroke is much more serious, resulting in irrational and hyperactive behaviour and eventually loss of consciousness and death. Rapid cooling by spraying the body with water and fanning is ideal. Emergency fluid and electrolyte replacement by intravenous drip is recommended.

Hypothermia & Frostbite
Proper preparation will reduce the risks of getting hypothermia. Even on a hot day in the mountains the weather can change rapidly; carry waterproof garments and warm layers, and inform others of your route.

Acute hypothermia follows a sudden drop of temperature over a short time. Chronic hypothermia is caused by a gradual loss of temperature over hours.

Hypothermia starts with shivering, loss of judgment and clumsiness. Unless rewarming occurs, the sufferer deteriorates

HEALTH

AVIAN INFLUENZA *Dr Trish Batchelor*

Avian influenza, or 'bird flu', presents only a very remote risk to travelers at this time. In 2004 and 2005 the avian H5N1 virus caused illness in domestic birds around the world. This virus is passed from healthy migratory birds to domestic birds such as chickens and ducks, which then may sicken and die. Transmission has occurred from domestic birds to humans; however, it is rare, and requires close contact with an infected bird or its droppings. By early December 2005 there were a total of 133 human cases confirmed by the World Health Organization (WHO), and 68 people had died. These human cases occurred in Indonesia, Thailand, Vietnam, Cambodia and China. At the time of writing, China had reported three human cases and two deaths.

The WHO recommends the following precautions for travellers to affected countries: avoid live poultry markets; avoid eating raw or undercooked poultry or eggs; wash hands frequently; and seek medical attention if you develop a fever and respiratory symptoms (cough, shortness of breath etc).

You can keep up to date on the current situation by visiting the World Health Organization website (www.who.int/en).

into apathy, confusion and coma. Prevent further heat loss by seeking shelter, warm dry clothing, hot sweet drinks and shared bodily warmth.

Frostbite is caused by freezing and subsequent damage to bodily extremities. As it develops the skin blisters and then becomes black. Adequate clothing, staying dry, keeping well hydrated and ensuring adequate calorie intake best prevent frostbite. Treatment involves rapid rewarming. Avoid refreezing and rubbing the affected areas.

Insect Bites & Stings

LEECHES
You'll often find leeches in damp forest conditions; they attach themselves to your skin to suck your blood. Trekkers often get them on their legs or in their boots. Salt or a lighted cigarette end will make them fall off. Do not pull them off, as the bite is then more likely to become infected. Clean and apply pressure if the point of attachment is bleeding. An insect repellent may keep them away.

LYME DISEASE
This is a tick-transmitted infection that may be acquired throughout the region. The illness usually begins with a spreading rash at the site of the tick bite, accompanied by fever, headache, extreme fatigue, aching joints and muscles and mild neck stiffness. If untreated, these symptoms usually resolve over several weeks, but over subsequent months disorders of the nervous system, heart and joints may develop. There

is no vaccination against the disease. Treatment should be sought as soon as possible for best results.

MOSQUITOES
A problem in summer all across Russia, mosquitoes here may not carry malaria but can cause irritation and infected bites. Use some form of insect repellent and keep covered up.

From May to September in the rural areas bordering Mongolia, China and North Korea, take extra special care as mosquito bites can cause Japanese encephalitis. If visiting rural areas you should consider the immunisation.

TICKS
From May to July, tick-borne encephalitis is a risk anywhere in rural Russia. Always check all over your body if you have been walking through a potentially tick-infested area as ticks can cause skin infections and other more serious diseases. If you find a tick attached, press down around its head with tweezers, grab the head and gently pull upwards. Avoid pulling the rear of the body as this may squeeze the tick's gut contents through the attached mouth parts into the skin, increasing the risk of infection. Smearing chemicals on the tick will not make it let go and is not recommended.

Snake Bites
Avoid getting bitten – do not walk barefoot or stick your hand into holes or cracks. Half of those bitten by venomous snakes are not

actually injected with poison (envenomed). If bitten by a snake, do not panic. Immobilise the bitten limb with a splint (eg a stick) and apply a bandage over the site firmly, similar to a bandage over a sprain. Do not apply a tourniquet, or cut or suck the bite. Get the victim medical help as soon as possible so that antivenin can be given if necessary.

TRAVELLING WITH CHILDREN
All travellers with children should know how to treat minor ailments and when to seek medical treatment. Make sure the children are up to date with routine vaccinations, and discuss possible travel vaccines well before departure as some vaccines are not suitable for children under a year.

If your child is vomiting or has diarrhoea, lost fluid and salts must be replaced. It may be helpful to take rehydration powders for reconstituting with boiled water.

Children should be encouraged to avoid and mistrust any dogs or other mammals because of the risk of rabies and other diseases. Any bite, scratch or lick from a warm-blooded, furry animal should immediately be thoroughly cleaned. If there is any possibility that the animal is infected with rabies, immediate medical assistance should be sought.

WOMEN'S HEALTH
Emotional stress, exhaustion and travelling through different time zones can all contribute to an upset in the menstrual cycle. If using oral contraceptives, remember some antibiotics, diarrhoea and vomiting can stop the pill from working and lead to the risk of pregnancy – remember to take condoms with you just in case. Time zones, gastrointestinal upsets and antibiotics do not affect injectable contraception.

Travelling during pregnancy is usually possible but always consult your doctor before planning your trip. The most risky times for travel are during the first 12 weeks of pregnancy and after 30 weeks.

SEXUAL HEALTH
Condoms are available across Russia, China and in Ulaanbaatar from pharmacies and certainly should be used. The **International Planned Parent Federation** (www.ippf.org) can advise about the availability of contraception in different countries.

When buying condoms, look for a European CE mark, which means they have been rigorously tested, and then keep them in a cool dry place or they may crack and perish.

HIV & AIDS
Infection with human immunodeficiency virus (HIV) may lead to acquired immune deficiency syndrome (AIDS), which is a fatal disease. Russia is experiencing one of the fastest rises of reported HIV and AIDS cases in the world. China is also said to be on the brink of a major epidemic.

Any exposure to blood, blood products or body fluids may put the individual at risk. The disease is often transmitted through sexual contact or dirty needles – vaccinations, acupuncture, tattooing and body piercing can be potentially as dangerous as intravenous drug use. HIV/AIDS can also be spread through infected blood transfusions. If you do need an injection, ask to see the syringe unwrapped in front of you, or take a needle and syringe pack with you.

Sexually Transmitted Diseases
HIV/AIDS and hepatitis B can be transmitted through sexual contact; see the relevant sections earlier for more details. Other STDs include gonorrhoea, herpes and syphilis; sores, blisters or rashes around the genitals and discharges or pain when urinating are common symptoms. In some STDs, such as wart virus or chlamydia, symptoms may be less marked or not observed at all, especially in women. Chlamydia infection can cause infertility in men and women before any symptoms have been noticed. Syphilis symptoms eventually disappear completely but the disease continues and can cause severe problems in later years. While abstinence from sexual contact is the only 100% effective prevention, using condoms is also effective. The treatment of gonorrhoea and syphilis is with antibiotics. Different STDs each require specific antibiotics.

HEALTH

Language

CHINESE

The Chinese spoken in Manchuria is the dialect spoken in Beijing. It is the official language of the People's Republic of China (PRC) and is usually referred to in the west as 'Mandarin' – the Chinese call it *pǔtōnghuà* (common speech).

For a more detailed guide to the language, get a copy of Lonely Planet's *Mandarin Phrasebook*.

PRONUNCIATION

Chinese is a tone language. This means that variations in pitch within syllables are used to determine word meaning. For example, in Mandarin the word *ma* can have several different meanings, depending on which tone is used:

High tone: *mā*, 'mother'.
Rising tone: *má*, 'hemp' or 'numb'.
Falling-rising tone: *mǎ*, 'horse'.
Falling tone: *mà*, 'scold' or 'swear'.

In pinyin, apostrophes are sometimes used to separate syllables, eg *ping'an* prevents the word being pronounced as *pin'gan*. The English 'v' sound doesn't occur in Chinese. For beginners, the trickiest sounds are **c**, **q** and **x** because their pronunciation isn't remotely similar to English.

c	as the 'ts' in 'bits'
ch	as in 'church', but with the tongue curled back
h	guttural, a bit like the 'ch' of 'loch'
q	as the 'ch' in 'chicken'
r	as the 's' in 'pleasure'
sh	as in 'ship', but with the tongue curled back
x	as the 'sh' in 'ship'
z	as the 'ds' in 'suds'
zh	as the 'j' in 'judge' but with the tongue curled back

USEFUL WORDS & PHRASES

Hello.
Nǐ hǎo. 你好
Goodbye.
Zàijiàn. 再见
Thank you.
Xièxie. 谢谢
You're welcome.
Búkèqi. 不客气
I'm sorry.
Duìbùqǐ. 对不起
May I ask your name?
Nín guìxìng? 您贵姓?
My (sur)name is ...
Wǒ xìng ... 我姓 ...
Where are you from?
Nǐ shì cōng nǎr láide? 你是从 ... 哪儿来的?
I'm from ...
Wǒ shì cōng ... láide. 我是从 ... 来的
No. (don't have)
Méi yǒu. 没有
No. (not so)
Búshì. 不是
No, I don't want it.
Búyào. 不要
I don't understand.
Wǒ tīngbudǒng. 我听不懂
Could you speak more slowly, please?
Qǐng nǐ shuō màn yīdiǎn, hǎo ma? 请你说慢一点，好吗?

IN TOWN

How much is it?
Duōshǎo qián? 多少钱?
That's too expensive.
Tài guìle. 太贵了
Bank of China
Zhōngguó Yínháng 中国银行
change money
huàn qián 换钱
telephone
diànhuà 电话
Where is the ...?
... zài nǎlǐ? ... 在哪里?
hotel
lǚguǎn 旅馆

EMERGENCIES – CHINESE

I'm sick.
Wǒ shēng bìng. 我生病

Help!
Jiùmìng a! 救命啊

Thief!
Xiǎo tōu! 小偷

emergency
jǐnjí qíngkuàng 紧急情况

hospital
yīyuàn 医院

police
jǐngchá 警察

foreign affairs police
wàishì jǐngchá 外事警察

---

tourist hotel
bīnguǎn/fàdiàn/ 宾馆/饭店/
jiǔdiàn 酒店

Is there a room vacant?
Yǒu méiyǒu kōng 有没有空房间?
fángjiān?

Yes, there is/No, there isn't.
Yǒu/Méiyǒu. 有/没有

single room
dānrénfáng 单人房

twin room
shuāngrénfáng 双人房

toilet (restroom)
cèsuǒ 厕所

men/women
nan/nün 男/女

toilet paper
wèishēng zhǐ 卫生纸

bathroom (washroom)
xǐshǒu jiān 洗手间

TRAIN TALK

train station
huǒchē zhàn 火车站

ticket office
shòupiào chù 售票处

I want to go to ...
Wǒ yào qù ... 我要去 ...

buy a ticket
mǎi piào 买票

one ticket
yìzhāng piào 一张票

two tickets
liǎngzhāng piào 两张票

hard-seat
yìngxí/yìngzuò 硬席/硬座

soft-seat
ruǎnxí/ruǎnzuò 软席/软座

hard-sleeper
yìngwò 硬卧

soft-sleeper
ruǎnwò 软卧

NUMBERS

0	líng	零
1	yī/yāoo	一/幺
2	èr/liǎng	二/两
3	sān	三
4	sì	四
5	wǔ	五
6	liù	六
7	qī	七
8	bā	八
9	jiǔ	九
10	shí	十
11	shíyī	十一
12	shí'èr	十二
20	èrshí	二十
21	èrshíyī	二十一
100	yìbǎii	一百
200	liǎngbǎi	两百
1000	yìqiān	一千

MONGOLIAN

The official national language of Mongolia is Mongolian. Since 1944, the Russian Cyrillic alphabet has been used to write Mongolian (see p345). The only difference between Mongolian and Russian Cyrillic is that the Mongolian version has two additional characters (ө and ү), for a total of 35. Double vowels indicate that the vowel is stressed.

For a more detailed look at the language, pick up a copy of Lonely Planet's *Mongolian Phrasebook*.

USEFUL WORDS & PHRASES

Hello.
sain bai·na uu Сайн байна уу?
(literally: How are you?)

Fine. How are you?
sain ta sain bai·na uu Сайн. Та сайн байна уу?

What's new?
so·nin sai·khan Сонин сайхан
yu bai·na юу байна?

Nothing really.
tai·van sai·khan Тайван сайхан.
(literally: It's peaceful.)

Goodbye.
ba·yar·tai Баяртай.

EMERGENCIES – MONGOLIAN

Help!
tus-*laa*-rai
Туслаарай!
Call a doctor!
emch duu-*daa*-rai!
Эмч дуудаарай!
I'm ill.
mi-*nii* bi-ye *öv*-döj bai-na
Миний бие өвдөж байна.

What's your name?
ta-*ny* ne-riig khen   Таны нэрийг хэн
ge-deg *ve*   гэдэг вэ?
My name is ...
mi-*nii* ne-riig ... ge-deg   Миний нэрийг ... гэдэг.
Yes.
tiim   Тийм.
No.
ü-*güi*   Үгүй.
Thanks.
ba-yar-la-*laa*   Баярлалаа.
Excuse me.
uuch-*laa*-rai   Уучлаарай.
What country are you from?
ta a-li ul-*saas* ir-sen *be* Та аль улсаас ирсэн бэ?
I'm from ...
bi ... ul-saas *ir*-sen   Би ... улсаас ирсэн.
Do you speak English?
ta an-*gliar* yair-dag *uu*   Та англиар ярьдаг уу?
I don't understand.
bi *oil*-gokh-güi bai-na   Би ойлгохгүй байна.

Do you have a (town) map?
ta-*naid* (kho-*tyn*) zu-rag bai-na *uu*
Танайд (хотын) зураг байна уу?
Where's the train station?
galt te-re-ge-*nii buud*-al *khaa*-na bai-dag *ve*
галт тэрэгний буудал хаана байдаг вэ?
hotel
zo-chid *buu*-dal
зочид буудал
Do you have any rooms available?
ta-*naid* sul ö-*röö* bai-na *uu*
Танайд сул өрөө байна уу?
I'd like a single room.
bi neg khü-*nii* ö-*röö* av-*maar* bai-na
Би нэг хүний өрөө авмаар байна.
I'd like a double room.
bi kho-*yor* khü-*nii* ö-*röö* av-*maar* bai-na
Би хоёр хүний өрөө авмаар байна.
What's the price per night/week?
ene ö-*röö kho*-nogt/do-*loo kho*-nogt *ya*-mar ün-*tei* ve
Энэ өрөө хоногт/долоо хоногт ямар үнэтэй вэ?

RUSSIAN

Russian is written in variants of the Cyrillic alphabet (see p345). It's easy to find English speakers in the big cities but not so easy in the smaller towns (sometimes not even in tourist hotels).

For a more detailed guide to the language, get a copy of Lonely Planet's *Russian Phrasebook*.

PRONUNCIATION

The 'voiced' consonants (ie when the vocal cords vibrate) **б**, **в**, **г**, **д**, **ж**, and **з** are not voiced at the end of words (eg хлеб, 'bread', is pronounced *khlyep*) or before voiceless consonants.

Two letters have no sound but are used to modify the pronunciation other letters. A consonant followed by the 'soft sign' **ь** is spoken with the tongue flat against the palate, as if followed by a faint 'y'. The 'hard sign' **ъ** is rarely seen; it occurs after consonants and indicates a slight pause before the next vowel.

USEFUL WORDS & PHRASES

Two words you're sure to use are the universal 'hello', здравствуйте (*zdrast*-vuy-te), and пожалуйста (pa-*zhal*-sta), the word for 'please' (commonly included in all polite requests), 'you're welcome', 'pardon me', 'after you' and more.

Hello.
zdrast-vuy-te   Здравствуйте.
Hi.
pri-*vyet*   Привет.
Good morning.
do-*bra*-e u-tra   Доброе утро.
Good afternoon.
do-bri dyen'   Добрый день.
Good evening.
dob-ri vye-cher   Добрый вечер.
Goodbye.
da svi-*da*-ni-ya   До свидания.
Bye.
pa-*ka*   Пока.
How are you?
kak de-*la*   Как дела?
What's your name?
kak vas za-*vut*   Как вас зовут?
My name is ...
me-*nya* za-vut ...   Меня зовут ...

THE RUSSIAN CYRILLIC ALPHABET

Cyrillic	Roman	Pronunciation
А, а	a	as the 'a' in 'father' (in stressed syllable); as the 'a' in 'ago' (in unstressed syllable)
Б, б	b	as the 'b' in 'but'
В, в	v	as the 'v' in 'van'
Г, г	g	as the 'g' in 'god'
Д, д	d	as the 'd' in 'dog'
Е, е	ye/e	as the 'ye' in 'yet' (in stressed syllable and at the beginning of a word); as the 'e' in 'ten' (in unstressed syllable)
Ё, ё *	yo	as the 'yo' in 'yore'
Ж, ж	zh	as the 's' in 'measure'
З, з	z	as the 'z' in 'zoo'
И, и	i	as the 'ee' in 'meet'
Й, й	y	as the 'y' in 'boy' (not transliterated after ы or и)
К, к	k	as the 'k' in 'kind'
Л, л	l	as the 'l' in 'lamp'
М, м	m	as the 'm' in 'mad'
Н, н	n	as the 'n' in 'not'
О, о	o/a	as the 'o' in 'more' (in stressed syllable); as the 'a' in 'hard' (in unstressed syllable)
П, п	p	as the 'p' in 'pig'
Р, р	r	as the 'r' in 'rub' (rolled)
С, с	s	as the 's' in 'sing'
Т, т	t	as the 't' in 'ten'
У, у	u	as the 'oo' in 'fool'
Ф, ф	f	as the 'f' in 'fan'
Х, х	kh	as the 'ch' in 'Bach'
Ц, ц	ts	as the 'ts' in 'bits'
Ч, ч	ch	as the 'ch' in 'chin'
Ш, ш	sh	as the 'sh' in 'shop'
Щ, щ	shch	as 'sh-ch' in 'fresh chips'
Ъ, ъ	-	'hard sign' (see p344)
Ы, ы	i	as the 'i' in 'ill'
Ь, ь	'	'soft sign'; (see p344)
Э, э	e	as the 'e' in 'end'
Ю, ю	yu	as the 'u' in 'use'
Я, я	ya/ye	as the 'ya' in 'yard' (in stressed syllable); as the 'ye' in 'yearn' (in unstressed syllable)

* Ё, ё are often printed without dots

Where are you from?
at-*ku*-da vi   Откуда вы?
I'm from ...
ya iz ...   Я из ...
Yes.
da   Да.

No.
nyet   Нет.
Please.
pa-*zhal*-sta   Пожалуйста.
Thank you (very much).
(bal'-*sho*-e) spa-*si*-ba   (Большое) спасибо.
Excuse me.
pras-*ti*-te   Простите.
I'm sorry.
iz-vi-*ni*-te   Извините.
No problem/Never mind.
ni-che-*vo*   Ничего.

Do you speak English?
vi ga-va-*ri*-te pa an-*gli*-ski
Вы говорите по-английски?
I don't understand.
ya pye pa-ni-*ma*-yu
Я не понимаю.
Could you write it down, please?
za-pi-*shi*-te pa-*zhal*-sta
Запишите, пожалуйста?
Can you help me, please?
pa-ma-*gi*-te pa-*zhal*-sta
Помогите, пожалуйста.

IN TOWN

I need ...
mnye *nuzh*-na ...   Мне нужно ...
Do you have ...?
u vas yest' ...   У вас есть ...?
How much is it?
skol-ka *sto*-it   Сколько стоит?
Where is ...?
gdye ...   Где ...?
hotel
gas-*ti*-ni-tsa   гостиница
room
no-mer   номер
telephone
te-le-*fon*   телефон
Toilet
tu-a-*let*   Туалет
Men
muzh-*skoy*   Мужской (М)
Women
zhen-*ski*   Женский (Ж)

Do you have a ... room?
u vas yest' ...
У вас есть ...?
    single
    ad-na-*myest*-ni *no*-mer
    одноместный номер
    double
    no-mer z dvu-*spal*-ney kra-*va*-t'yu
    номер с двуспальней кроватью

EMERGENCIES – RUSSIAN

I'm ill.

| ya *bo*·len (m) | Я болен. |
| ya bal'·*na* (f) | Я больна. |

I need a doctor.

| mnye *nuzh*·na vra·*ch* | Мне нужно врач. |

hospital

| bal'·*ni*·tsa | больница |

the police

| mi·*li*·tsi·yu | милицию |

Help!

| pa·ma·*gi*·te | Помогите! |

Thief!

| vor | Вор! |

Where is the toilet?

gdye zdyes' tu·al·*yet* Где здесь туалет?

How much is a room?

skol'·ka *sto*·it *no*·mer Сколько стоит номер?

Do you have a cheaper room?

u vas yest' de·*shyev*·le У вас есть дешевле номер?
no·mer

TRAIN TALK

I want to go to ...

ya kha·*chu* ye·*khat'* v ...
Я хочу ехать в ...

When is the next train?

kag·*da* slye·du·yu·shchi *po*·est
Когда следующий поезд?

When does it leave?

kag·*da* at·prav·*lya*·e·tsya
Когда отправляется?

Are there SV/kupe/platskartny tickets on train number ... to ...?

yest' bi·*lye*·ti dlya es ve/dlya ku·*pe*/f plats·*kar*·te na *po*·est *no*·mer ... na ...
Есть билеты для СВ/для купе/в плацкарте на поезд номер ... до ...?

I'd like to buy an SV/kupe/platstkartny ticket for train number ... to ...

ya kha·*tyel* (m)/kha·*tye*·la (f) bi ku·*pit'* bi·*lyet* dlya es ve/dlya ku·*pe*/f plats·*kar*·te na *po*·est *no*·mer ... na ...
Я хотел/хотела бы купить билет для СВ/для купе/в плацкарте на поезд номер ... на ...

Which platform does the train leave from?

s ka·*koy* plat·*for*·mi at·*kho*·dit *po*·est
С какой платформы отходит поезд?

Please tell me why I can't buy a ticket.

ska·*zhi*·te pa·*zhal*·sta pa·che·*mu* ya nye ma·*gu* ku·*pit'* bi·*lye*·ta
Скажите¨ пожалуйста¨ почему я не могу купить билета!

There's no train today.

se·*vod*·nya nye *bu*·det pa·ez·*da*
Сегодня не будет поезда.

The train is full.

fsye bi·*lye*·ti na *et*·at *po*·est *pro*·da·ni
Все билеты на этот поезд проданы. (literally: all tickets are sold)

There are no SV/kupe/platskartny tickets left for the train.

bi·*lye*·ti dlya es ve/dlya ku·*pe*/f plats·*kar*·te u·*zhye* vsye ras·pra·*da*·lis'
Билеты для СВ/для купе/в плацкарте уже все распродались.

Tickets for that service aren't on sale until ...

bi·*lye*·ti na *e*·tat *go*·rat *bu*·dut na pra·*da*·zhe s ...
Билеты на этот город будут на продаже с ...

You're at the wrong ticket window. Please go to window ...

vi sta·*i*·te nye f tom *myes*·te a·bra·*shchay*·tes' k a·*kosh*·ku ...
Вы стоите не в том месте. Обращайтесь к окошку ...!

map	
kar·ta	карта
platform	
plat·*for*·ma	платформа
train station	
zhe·lez·na·da·*rozh*·ni	железнодорожный (ж. д.)
vag·*zal*	вокзал
ticket, tickets	
bi·*lyet*, bi·*lye*·ti	билет, билеты
ticket office	
bi·*lyet*·na·ya *ka*·sa	билетная касса
timetable	
ras·pi·*sa*·ni·e	расписание
one-way	
v a·*din* kan·*yets*	в один конец
e·*di*·ni	единый
return, round trip	
tu·*da* i a·*brat*·na	туда и обратно
baggage	
ba·*gazh*	багаж
arrival	
pri·*bi*·ti·e	прибытие
departure	
at·prav·*lye*·ni·e	отправление

TIME, DAYS & NUMBERS

When?	
kag·*da*	Когда?
At what time?	
f ka·*to*·ram cha·*su*	В котором часу?
today	
se·*vod*·nya	сегодня
tomorrow	
zaft·ra	завтра

LANGUAGE

day after tomorrow
  pos·le·*zaf*·tra   послезавтра
yesterday
  vche·*ra*   вчера

Dates are given day-month-year, with the month usually in Roman numerals. Days of the week are often represented by numbers in timetables (Monday is 1).

Monday	pa·ne·*dyel'*·nik	понедельник
Tuesday	*ftor*·nik	вторник
Wednesday	sre·*da*	среда
Thursday	chet·*vyerk*	четверг
Friday	*pyat*·ni·tsa	пятница
Saturday	su·*bo*·ta	суббота
Sunday	vas·kre·*syen'*·e	воскресенье

January	yan·*var'*	январь
February	fev·*ral'*	февраль
March	mart	март
April	ap·*ryel'*	апрель
May	may	май
June	i·*yun'*	июнь
July	i·*yul'*	июль
August	*av*·gust	август
September	sen·*tyabr'*	сентябрь
October	ok·*tyabr'*	октябрь
November	na·*yabr'*	ноябрь
December	de·*kabr'*	декабрь

How much/many?
  skol'·ka   Сколько?

1	a·*din*	один
2	dva	два
3	tri	три
4	che·*ti*·re	четыре
5	pyat'	пять
6	shyest'	шесть
7	syem'	семь
8	*vo*·sem'	восемь
9	*dye*·vyat'	девять
10	*dye*·syat'	десять
11	a·*di*·na·tsat'	одиннадцать
12	dve·*na*·tsat'	двенадцать
13	tri·*na*·tsat'	тринадцать
14	che·*tir*·na·tsat'	четырнадцать
15	pyat·*na*·tsat'	пятнадцать
16	shest·*na*·tsat'	шестнадцать
17	sem·*na*·tsat'	семнадцать
18	va·sem·*na*·tsat'	восемнадцать
19	de·vyat·*na*·tsat'	девятнадцать
20	*dva*·tsat'	двадцать
21	*dva*·tsat' a·*din*	двадцать один
22	*dva*·tsat' dva	двадцать два
30	*tri*·tsat'	тридцать
40	*so*·rak	сорок
50	pyat'·*des*·yat	пятьдесят
60	shes·des·*yat*	шестдесят
70	syem'·des·*yat*	семьдесят
80	*vo*·sem'·de·syat	восемьдесят
90	de·vya·*no*·sta	девяносто
100	sto	сто
1000	*ti*·sya·cha	тысяча
1,000,000	(a·*din*) mi·li·*on*	(один) миллион

Glossary

This glossary is a list of Russian (R), Chinese (C) and Mongolian (M) terms you may come across during your Trans-Siberian journey. See p73 for words that will help you while dining.

aimag (M) – province or state within Mongolia
airag (M) – fermented mare's milk
apteka (R) – pharmacy
arkhi (M) – the common word to describe homemade vodka
avtostantsiya (R) – bus stop
avtovokzal (R) – bus terminal

babushka (R) – grandmother
BAM (R) – Baikalo-Amurskaya Magistral (Baikal-Amur Mainline)
bankomat (R) – ATM
banya (R) – bathhouse
bashnya (R) – tower
bei (C) – north
benzin (R) – petrol
biblioteka (R) – library
binguan (C) – tourist hotel
biznesmen, biznesmenka (R) – literally, businessman/woman, but often used to mean a small-time operator on the fringe of the law
Bogd Gegen (M) – hereditary line of reincarnated Buddhist leaders of Mongolia, the third highest in the Buddhist hierarchy, which started with Zanabazar
Bogd Khaan (M) – Holy King; title given to the eighth Bogd Gegen (1869–1924)
bolnitsa (R) – hospital
bulvar (R) – boulevard

CAAC (C) – Civil Aviation Administration of China, which controls most of China's domestic and foreign airlines
CCP (C) – Chinese Communist Party
CIS (R) – Commonwealth of Independent States; an alliance of independent states comprising the former USSR republics, with the exception of the three Baltic countries
CITS (C) – China International Travel Service
CTS (C) – China Travel Service

dacha (R) – country cottage, summer house
dajie (C) – avenue
datsan (R) – Buddhist monastery
detsky (R) – child's, children's
dezhurnaya (R) – woman looking after a particular floor of a hotel

dom (R) – house
dong (C) – east
duma (R) – parliament
dvorets (R) – palace
elektrichka (R) – suburban train

fen (C) – one-tenth of a jiao, in Chinese currency

GAI (R) – Gosudarstvennaya Avtomobilnaya Inspektsia; State Automobile Inspectorate (traffic police)
gavan (R) – harbour
gazeta (R) – newspaper
ger (M) – traditional, circular felt yurt
gol (M) – river
gorod (R) – city, town
gostinitsa (R) – hotel
gostiny dvor (R) – trading arcade
gudamj (M) – street
Gulag (R) – Glavnoe Upravlenie Lagerey (Main Administration for Camps); the Soviet network of concentration camps
GUM (R) – Gosudarstvenny Univermag; State Department Store

hu (C) – lake
hutong (C) – narrow alleyway

Inner Mongolia (M) – a separate province within China
Intourist (R) – the old Soviet State Committee for Tourism, now hived off, split up and in competition with hundreds of other travel agencies
izba (R & M) – traditional single-storey wooden house

Jebtzun Damba (M) – also known as Bogd Gegen; a hereditary line of reincarnated spiritual leaders of Mongolia
jiao (C) – one-tenth of a yuan, in Chinese currency
jie (C) – street

kamera khraneniya (R) – left-luggage room
karta (R) – map, or multiride metro pass cards
kassa (R) – ticket office, cashier's desk
Kazakh (M) – Turkic ethnic group from Central Asia, also found in the west of Mongolia; people from Kazakhstan
KGB (R) – Komitet Gosudarstvennoy Bezopasnosti; Committee of State Security
khaan (M) – a king or chief
Khalkh (M) – the major ethnic group living in Mongolia
khiid (M) – Buddhist monastery
khorol (M) – traditional Mongolian game similar to checkers
khram (R) – church

kino (R) – cinema
kladbishche (R) – cemetery
kniga (knigi) (R) – book (books)
komnaty otdykha (R) – literally 'resting rooms';
cheap lodgings in Siberian train stations
Komsomol (R) – Communist Youth League
kopek (R) – kopeck; the smallest, worthless unit of
Russian currency
kray (R) – territory
kreml (R) – kremlin, a town's fortified stronghold
Kuomintang (C) – Chiang Kaishek's Nationalist Party,
the dominant political force after the fall of the Qing
dynasty; now Taiwan's major political party
kupeyny (R) – kupe; compartmentalised carriage

lama (M) – Tibetan Buddhist monk or priest
lavra (R) – senior monastery
Living Buddha (M) – common term for reincarnations of
Buddhas; Buddhist spiritual leader in Mongolia
lu (C) – road
lyux (R) – a lyux room in a hotel is a kind of suite, with a
sitting room in addition to the bedroom and bathroom

Mafia (R) – anyone who has anything to do with crime,
from genuine gangsters to victims of their protection
rackets; also applied to anyone who's successful at
anything
magazin (R) – shop
Manchus (C) – non-Chinese ethnic group from Manchuria
(present-day northeast China) which took over China and
established the Qing dynasty
manezh (R) – riding school
marshrutky (R) – minibus that runs along a fixed route
matryoshka (R) – set of painted wooden dolls stacked
within dolls
mestnoe vremya (R) – local time
militsia (R) – police
more (R) – sea
morin khuur (M) – horsehead fiddle
most (R) – bridge
MPRP (M) – Mongolian People's Revolutionary Party
muzey (R) – museum; also some palaces, art galleries
and nonworking churches
muzhskoy (R) – men's (toilet)

Naadam (M) – game; the Naadam Festival
naberezhnaya (R) – embankment
nan (C) – south
novy (R) – new
nuruu (M) – mountain range

oblast (R) – region
obshchy (R) – 4th-class train compartment
okrug (R) – district
örgön chölöö (M) – avenue

ovoo (M) – shamanistic collection of stones, wood
or other offerings to the gods, usually placed in high
places
ozero (R) – lake

Paskha (R) – Easter
pereryv (R) – break (when shops, ticket offices, restaurants
etc close for an hour or two during the day)
pereulok (R) – lane
peshchera (R) – cave
Pinyin (C) – the system of writing the Chinese language
in the roman alphabet adopted by the Communist Party
in 1958
PLA (C) – People's Liberation Army
platskartny (R) – platskart; open carriage on a
train
ploshchad (R) – square
poezd (R) – train
posolstvo (R) – embassy
PRC (C) – People's Republic of China
prichal (R) – landing, pier
prigorodny poezd (R) – suburban train
prospekt (R) – avenue
provodnik, provodnitsa (R) – carriage attendant on
a train
PSB (C) – Public Security Bureau; the arm of the police
force that deals with foreigners

rayon (R) – district
rechnoy vokzal (R) – river terminal
remont, na remont (R) – closed for repairs
Renminbi (C) – literally 'people's money', the formal name
for the currency of China; shortened to RMB
Rozhdestvo (R) – Christmas
rubl (R) – rouble

sad (R) – garden
samovar (R) – urn with an inner tube filled with hot
charcoal used for heating water for tea
selo (R) – village
shagai (M) – traditional Mongolian dice game
shosse (R) – highway
siheyuan (C) – traditional courtyard house
sobor (R) – cathedral
soviet (R) – council
stupa (M) – Buddhist religious monument composed
of a solid hemisphere topped by a spire, containing relics
of the Buddha; also known as a pagoda, or suburgan in
Mongolian
süm (M) – Buddhist temple

taiga (R) – northern pine, fir, spruce and larch forest
teatr (R) – theatre
tögrög (M) – unit of currency in Mongolia
traktir (R) – tavern

troika (R) – vehicle drawn by three horses
Tsagaan Sar (M) – 'white moon' or 'white month'; a festival to celebrate the start of the lunar year
tserkov (R) – church
tualet (R) – toilet

ulitsa (R) – street
univermag, **universalnyy magazin** (R) – department store
urtyn-duu (M) – traditional singing style
uul (M) – mountain

vokzal (R) – station
vostok (R) – east

xi (C) – west

yezhednevno (R) – daily
yuan (C) – the Chinese unit of currency, also referred to as RMB

zal (R) – hall, room
zapovednik (R) – nature reserve
zhenskiy (R) – women's (toilet)

Behind the Scenes

THIS BOOK

This second edition of *Trans-Siberian Railway* was updated by Simon Richmond, Mark Elliott, Robert Reid and Mara Vorhees. The first edition was written by Simon Richmond and Mara Vorhees. This guidebook was commissioned in Lonely Planet's London office, and produced in the Melbourne office.

THANKS from the Authors

Simon Richmond I was fortunate to have a great commissioning editor in Fiona Buchan and a splendid team of co-authors in Mark, Mara and Robert. In St Petersburg a huge *spasibo* goes to Peter Kozyrev, Chris Hamilton and Yegor and his helpful colleagues at Wild Russia for arranging my visa and accommodation. Cheers to Yulia at the tourist office for persevering with me through the whole police report business. In Moscow, Leonid kept me factually on track and went into bat against the old Soviet machine of Russian Railways. In Siberia, thanks to Jack for helping me get to Olkhon. In Beijing, a futon at Thomas' was very much appreciated as was his general company. In Ulaanbaatar, many thanks to my tireless host Toro; Peter and Sylvia for expert advice and insight; colleague Michael Kohn; Zanjan Fromer for helping me get out to the great Mongolian countryside; Andre Tolme for a memorable round of golf; and Lee Linehan and Steve Noble for sharing their perspectives on the train trip. I very much enjoyed the company and feedback I received from the many travellers I met along the way including Alexandra Stark, Ruby and Ron,

Monica and Magda, Rebecca, Eric and Katrina, Eddie and Yvonne and Jane and Kirsty: may all your memories of your various Trans-Sib journeys be happy ones. Finally, Tonny whom I can never thank enough for providing me with a home and the emotional support during the long process of crafting this book.

Mark Elliott Thanks to the hundreds of people who helped with tips, directions, emails and suggestions as well as for continual guidance, kindness and hospitality right across Siberia. Particular thanks to Igor in Omsk, the ever inspiring Minsalim in Tobolsk, Petr in Severobaikalsk, Jack in Irkutsk, Rada, Vera, Aylana and Aldar in Tuva, Alatoliy and family in Krasnoyarsk, Valentina in Aktash and the team at LP. As ever my work is dedicated to my beloved wife and parents whose love and support allow me to live with happily opening eyes.

Robert Reid Thanks to Fiona Buchan of Lonely Planet for offering this superb opportunity, and to Simon Richmond for flapping wings of coordinating-authorship with greater intensity than I've seen before. Many, many, many people offered great advice and kindness on the road, including Leonid Ragozin of Moscow, the customs police who gave me a free ride in Vladivostok, and a Kenny G lookalike who presented me with the pencil drawing outside Khabarovsk. Also travel agencies helped out with info, including Anastasia in Khabarovsk, Julia of Vladivostok and everyone at Vizit in Vladivostok. Thanks to Mai for putting up with such a long road trip.

THE LONELY PLANET STORY

The story begins with a classic travel adventure: Tony and Maureen Wheeler's 1972 journey across Europe and Asia to Australia. There was no useful information about the overland trail then, so Tony and Maureen published the first Lonely Planet guidebook to meet a growing need.

From a kitchen table, Lonely Planet has grown to become the largest independent travel publisher in the world, with offices in Melbourne (Australia), Oakland (USA) and London (UK). Today Lonely Planet guidebooks cover the globe. There is an ever-growing list of books and information in a variety of media. Some things haven't changed. The main aim is still to make it possible for adventurous travellers to get out there – to explore and better understand the world.

At Lonely Planet we believe travellers can make a positive contribution to the countries they visit – if they respect their host communities and spend their money wisely. Every year 5% of company profit is donated to charities around the world.

Mara Vorhees Of all the places to stay in Moscow, none is so comfortable, convenient and completely welcoming as Tommo and Julia's flat, where accommodation comes with guaranteed good company, not to mention a friendly, fat cat. Thanks to Jimmy and Belen (et al.), who showed me first-hand what to do with kids in Moscow. Kathleen Pullman, Dmitry Menshikov and Anna Lebedeva were all fonts of information about the capital. I appreciated meeting Viktor Aleksandrovich and Igor Nikolaevich at Perm-36; and Konstantin Bryliakov and Oleg Demiyanenko in Yekaterinburg. Returning to Yekaterinburg is always a highlight, especially when I can hang out with Tim O'Brien and Nadia Altukhova and take advantage of their wealth of knowledge about my favourite Russian city. Somehow 'Nasha Pasha' Yesin still manages to help me out every time I go to Russia, even though he lives in Prague. Back at LP, I am grateful to Fiona Buchan, Simon Richmond, Mark Elliott and Robert Reid. And thank you Jerz: you are my creative inspiration, even when you're thousands of miles away.

SEND US YOUR FEEDBACK

We love to hear from travellers – your comments keep us on our toes and help make our books better. Our well-travelled team reads every word on what you loved or loathed about this book. Although we cannot reply individually to postal submissions, we always guarantee that your feedback goes straight to the appropriate authors, in time for the next edition. Each person who sends us information is thanked in the next edition – and the most useful submissions are rewarded with a free book.

To send us your updates – and find out about Lonely Planet events, newsletters and travel news – visit our award-winning website: **www.lonelyplanet.com/feedback**.

Note: We may edit, reproduce and incorporate your comments in Lonely Planet products such as guidebooks, websites and digital products, so let us know if you don't want your comments reproduced or your name acknowledged. For a copy of our privacy policy visit www.lonelyplanet.com/privacy.

CREDITS

Commissioning Editor Fiona Buchan
Coordinating Editor Brooke Lyons
Coordinating Cartographer Csanad Csutoros, Jolyon Philcox
Coordinating Layout Designer Indra Kilfoyle
Managing Cartographer Mark Griffiths
Assisting Editors Liz Heynes, Nancy Ianni, Jeannette Kimmel, Anne Mulvaney, Joanne Newell, Kristin Odijk
Assisting Cartographers Joshua Geoghegan, Valentina Kremenchutskaya, Kusnandar, Malisa Plesa, Amanda Sierp, Simon Tillema
Assisting Layout Designers Wibowo Rusli, Jacqui Saunders
Cover Designer Sonya Brooke
Project Manager Ray Thomson
Language Content Coordinator Quentin Frayne, with assistance from Branislava Vladisavljevic

Thanks to Adriana Mammarella, Celia Wood, Imogen Bannister, Mark Germanchis, Melanie Dankel, Sally Darmody, Sam Benson, Suzannah Shwer

THANKS from Lonely Planet

Many thanks to the travellers who used the last edition and wrote to us with helpful hints, useful advice and interesting anecdotes:

A Mirko Addis, Pauliina Ahti **B** Dorothy Black, John Black, Hervé Borrion, Robert Braun, Michael Brayshaw **C** Martin Caminada, Peter Carr, Jemetha Clark, Robert Cosgrove **D** Chételat Dany, Bosz de Kler, Annette Dellevoet, Wendy DeWild, Andy Diamond **F** Colin Francis **G** Michael Gershowitz, Les Goedbloed, Sarah Goldschagg, Sam Golledge, Justin Grace, Mathias Greger **H** Chris Hartill, Jim Hendrickson, Jenny Hogg, Wim Hooghe, Eric Huntington **J** Aysha Johnson **K** Ruth Kennedy, David Kerkhoff, Sam Kimmins **L** Kimberly Lang, Corey Langenbach, Philip Livingstone, Johanna Lofvenius, Thomas Lohr, Johann Lundström **M** Yuji Maruyama, Michael and Beatrix Mathew, Trevor Mazzuchelli, Shana McCombs, Elizabeth McZeo, Andrew Mearns, Martin Mitchell, Dayan Muntz **N** Terry Nakazono **O** Rob O'Brien, Viktoria Olausson **P** Frans Jaap Pannekoek, Richard Partridge, Christina Paul, Julia Pearce, Oyvind Pedersen, Hannele Pietilä **R** Ken Reed, Mary Richards **S** Fred Sargent, Julie Schatzkine, Jack Sheremetoff, Iwan Snels, Mara Soplantila, Linda Svanberg **T** Allan Tighe **V** Leander van Delden, Simon van den Boom **W** E Weidenkopf, Sharon Weiner **Y** Artour Yatchenko, Andrew Young, DC Young

ACKNOWLEDGMENTS

Many thanks to the following for the use of their content: Globe on back cover; map data contained in colour highlights map – Mountain High Maps® © 1993 Digital Wisdom, Inc.

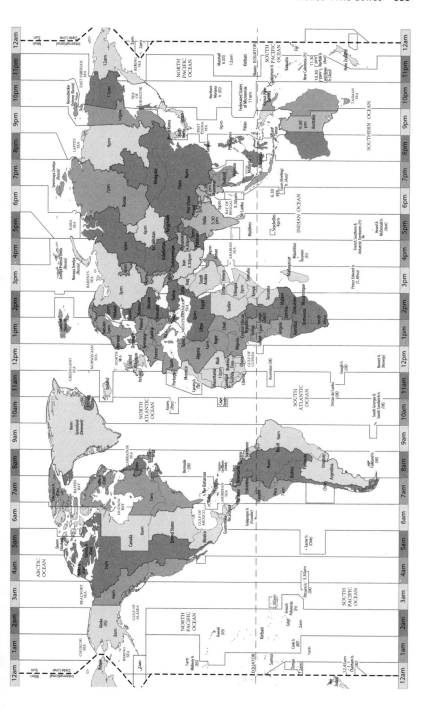

Index

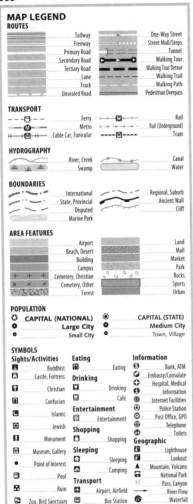

MAP LEGEND

LONELY PLANET OFFICES

Australia
Head Office
Locked Bag 1, Footscray, Victoria 3011
☎ 03 8379 8000, fax 03 8379 8111
talk2us@lonelyplanet.com.au

USA
150 Linden St, Oakland, CA 94607
☎ 510 893 8555, toll free 800 275 8555
fax 510 893 8572
info@lonelyplanet.com

UK
72-82 Rosebery Ave,
Clerkenwell, London EC1R 4RW
☎ 020 7841 9000, fax 020 7841 9001
go@lonelyplanet.co.uk

Published by Lonely Planet Publications Pty Ltd
ABN 36 005 607 983

© Lonely Planet Publications Pty Ltd 2006

© photographers as indicated 2006

Cover photographs: man in front of Center of Asia Monument, Kyzyl, Russia, Jerry Kobalenko/Getty Images (front); provodnitsa (carriage attendant) in front of 9/10 Baikal train, Simon Richmond/Lonely Planet Images (back). Many of the images in this guide are available for licensing from Lonely Planet Images: www.lonelyplanet images.com.